Local Government in Rural America

POLITICAL SCIENCE SERIES

Edited by R. Taylor Cole

VERNON VAN DYKE, *International Politics*

ARTHUR W. BROMAGE, *Introduction to Municipal Government and Administration,* 2d ed.

CLYDE F. SNIDER, *Local Government in Rural America*

ELTON ATWATER, WILLIAM BUTZ, KENT FORSTER, and NEAL RIEMER, *Problems of Interndtional Understanding and World Affairs,* in preparation

CLYDE F. SNIDER
University of Illinois

Local Government in Rural America

GREENWOOD PRESS, PUBLISHERS
WESTPORT, CONNECTICUT

Library of Congress Cataloging in Publication Data

Snider, Clyde Frank, 1904-
Local government in rural America.

Reprint of the ed. published by Appleton-Century-Crofts, New York, in series: ACC political science series.
Bibliography: p.
1. Local government--United States. I. Title.
[JS408.S6 1974] 352.073 74-10652
ISBN 0-8371-7648-4

Originally published in 1957 by Appleton-Century-Crofts, New York

Reprinted with the permission of Prentice-Hall, Inc.

Reprinted in 1974 by Greenwood Press, a division of Williamhouse-Regency Inc.

Library of Congress Catalog Card Number 74-10652

ISBN 0-8371-7648-4

Printed in the United States of America

To

Betty Snider Needham

Preface

THIS BOOK is concerned with counties, townships, towns of the New England variety, and special districts—the principal types of local government prevailing in rural areas in the United States. Units of all of these types operate in urban communities as well as rural, and it has not seemed practicable to attempt to segregate and give exclusive attention to the governments of these categories which are wholly rural in nature. Indeed, rural and urban areas merge into each other so gradually that it is not always possible to distinguish clearly between the two save by arbitrary definition. Furthermore, complete exclusion of urban units from the present survey would not appear desirable, even if it were practicable, since experience of urban governments may be valuable to governments of the same legal nature operating in rural areas. For these reasons, much of the book's subject matter relates to counties, townships, towns, and special districts generally, although a genuine effort has been made throughout to emphasize the problems and needs of local government in rural communities. Villages and other small municipalities, though operating in many instances in areas classified by the Census Bureau as rural, are accorded no specific consideration here, inasmuch as such units are usually treated in books dealing with city government; and attention is given to municipalities generally only where this has appeared necessary in order to portray an accurate picture of local government in over-all perspective.

For assistance and advice in the course of the book's preparation my obligations are many. My debt is especially heavy to the late Professor John A. Fairlie, my teacher and former colleague at the University of Illinois, and to Professor Charles M. Kneier, my present colleague. Professor Fairlie, a pioneer scholar in the field of local government, did much to stimulate and guide my interest therein, and Professor Kneier has been most generous in his availability for consultation throughout the preparation of this work. In addition, permission has been graciously extended me to draw freely from *County Government and Administration* (New York, D. Appleton-Century Company, Inc., 1930), a book of their co-authorship which has now been out of print for several years. Chapter 1 of the present book is for the most part an abridgement of the historical chapters of the "Fairlie and Kneier," and at other points the older book has been helpful.

The present volume was originally projected under the editorship of the late Professor Frederic A. Ogg of the University of Wisconsin, whose wise counsel was available at the planning stage. For reading portions of the manuscript and offering helpful suggestions or in some other manner making distinct contributions to the task of preparation, I am indebted to Professors William J. Block of The Citadel, John C. Bollens of the University of California at Los Angeles, R. Taylor Cole of Duke University, Neil F. Garvey of the University of Illinois, and Andrew E. Nuquist of the University of Vermont; to Dr. Jack F. Isakoff, Director of Research of the Illinois Legislative Council; and to my wife, Lois Riley Snider. To authors and compilers of the books, monographs, articles, and official reports which have served as sources of information and guidance my obligation is heavy, as I have sought to indicate in the reference lists and footnotes. Publications of the Governments Division of the Census Bureau have been particularly helpful in providing factual information and illustrative materials. Appreciation is extended to the *National Municipal Review* for permission to use in substantially their original form excerpts from articles of my authorship in that journal. Numerous state and local officials have been most helpful in answering inquiries, supplying public documents, and affording ready access to their records. Special acknowledgment for assistance of this nature is due the many New England town officers who gave so generously of their time and knowledge in a series of interviews with the author during the summer of 1955. Sincere gratitude is extended also to Miss Nelle Signor, History and Political Science Librarian at the University of Illinois, for aid in securing reference materials, and to Miss Eula Clanton for her diligence and proficiency in typing the manuscript.

C.F.S.

Contents

PART FOUR

Functions

PART FIVE

Fiscal Policy and Administration

PART SIX

Reorganization

List of Tables

List of Figures

PART ONE

Historical and Legal Foundations

CHAPTER I

Historical Development of Local Government

IN ENGLAND

LOCAL GOVERNMENT IN the United States has developed from institutions established in the English colonies in America, which institutions were in many respects similar to those existing in contemporary England.[1] The origin and early history of these English institutions are difficult to trace. In some features the later Anglo-Saxon system bears analogies to the Germanic system in the first century A.D., as described by the Roman historian Tacitus, and it seems probable that the one developed from the other. But in the historical records there is a long gap which makes it impossible to describe the process of evolution. There are also questions as to the extent of early Roman influence on the development of institutions in England during the first centuries of the Anglo-Saxon period. It will be sufficient for our purpose here to sketch briefly the growth of English local institutions from the time when they can be clearly understood, that is, from the latter part of the Anglo-Saxon period, describing at somewhat greater length the system of local government existing at the time of the first settlements in America.

Anglo-Saxon Institutions. When in the ninth century the various Anglo-Saxon kingdoms had been united in the kingdom of England, the country

[1] On the matter of English origins and background, see Dudley J. Medley, *A Student's Manual of English Constitutional History,* 6th ed. (New York, Macmillan, 1925); William Stubbs, *The Constitutional History of England* (London, Oxford University Press, 1891-1898), 3 vols.; Frederick W. Hackwood, *The Story of the Shire* (London, Heath Cranton, n.d.); Charles A. Beard, *The Office of Justice of the Peace in England* (New York, Columbia University Press, 1904); M. M. Knappen, *Constitutional and Legal History of England* (New York, Harcourt, Brace, 1942), especially chaps. 7, 8.

was divided for purposes of local government into shires, these into districts known as hundreds, and these in turn into townships. The township, whether a development from the so-called Teutonic mark or from the Roman villa, was a social and economic, rather than a political, district. It was a small rural community composed mainly of peasants. Local affairs were managed by an assembly of the inhabitants, who elected a president, known as the town reeve, a tithing man, a constable, and four men who with the reeve and priest represented the township in the courts of the hundred and the shire. After the organization of the church, parishes had also been established, usually coterminous with townships; and ecclesiastical affairs were managed by a similar assembly of inhabitants under the name of the vestry.

The hundred was a district of varying size, consisting of several townships. Here the management of affairs was in the hands of a monthly court composed of all landlords within the district and representatives as noted above from the various townships. As executive officials there were a deputy of the shire reeve, an elected hundred-ealdor, and (at any rate toward the close of Anglo-Saxon times) a standing committee of 12 senior thegns. The main functions of the hundred court were judicial in character, including both civil and criminal jurisdiction. In theory justice was administered by the whole body of lawful attendants or suitors at the court; but in practice the responsibility fell largely to the committee of 12, whose further duty it was to present in the shire court persons accused of more serious crimes. Twice a year the sheriff held a "tourn" of the hundred courts.

Above the hundreds were the shires. These were, in the south and extreme north, the districts of older kingdoms or distinct bodies of the Teutonic peoples which retained certain features of self-government after their absorption into the larger kingdom. In the Midlands the shires were artificial districts created for convenience of administration. Whatever its origin, each shire was provided with a semiannual court, composed of the representatives from each township and the individual landowners, though later the place of the latter may have been taken by the 12 senior thegns from each hundred. The principal function of this court, as in the case of the hundred tribunal, was the administration of justice in civil and criminal matters.

The initiative and active control of business rested in three officials: the ealdorman or earl, the shire reeve or sheriff, and the bishop. The ealdorman represented the extinct royalty of the earlier kingdoms, and although later nominated by the king, he retained much of the dignity suggested by the origin of the office. Several shires were grouped under each ealdorman, who was pre-eminently the leader of the military forces. The sheriff originally had been the steward of the royal estates and chief representative of the crown, but became also the president and chief executive of the shire court. In ecclesiastical cases, however, the bishop presided over the court.

After the Norman Conquest. After the Norman Conquest the earls retired from the active administration of shire business, and the position became merely a title of nobility and dignity. At the same time the separation of civil and ecclesiastical jurisdiction led to the disappearance of the bishop from the shire court. These changes paved the way for the supremacy of the sheriff in the county, as the shire came to be called. This official became the king's representative in military affairs; as a police officer he was responsible for maintaining the peace and supervising the elaborate system of securities for good behavior; as steward of the royal estates he was given greater financial powers; and for a time his judicial functions gained in importance with the development of the shire court and the decline of the hundred tribunal. The jurisdiction of the shire court was extended, and its sessions became more frequent until they were held as often as once a month. This led to a falling off in attendance of the local representatives, with a corresponding increase in the influence of the sheriff. Criminal courts in each hundred were also held by the sheriff twice a year. In fact the sheriff became the chief agent in a strongly centralized administration.

Another result of the Norman Conquest was the development of feudal manorial courts, at the expense of the hundred courts. Even in Saxon times many thegns had judicial jurisdiction within their estates, covering one or more townships; and these were exempt from the hundred court. This system was now extended with other features of the feudal regime. In each manor, courts or assemblies for the inhabitants were held, different sessions being known as the court customary, the court baron, and the court leet. Here, as in the hundred and shire courts, the judgments were rendered by the whole body of attendants, but under the supervision of the lord's steward, who occupied in a smaller way a position similar to that of the sheriff in the shire court.

Arbitrary exercise of his enormous powers made the sheriff an unpopular official, and at the same time the tendency for the office to become hereditary in powerful local families caused it to be distrusted by the crown. As a consequence, the sheriff's authority was gradually reduced by the development, on the one hand, of the itinerant royal courts and, on the other, of the justices of the peace to be mentioned presently, until he became simply a ministerial officer of the courts, a conservator of the peace, keeper of public prisoners, and returning officer in elections.

Special royal commissioners had occasionally been sent throughout the kingdom from the time of Alfred. A regular system of circuit judges was established under Henry I; and under Henry II this developed into the common-law courts, which took over the most important judicial business from the sheriffs and the shire courts.

During the thirteenth century peace officers of a new type, known as justices of the peace, were appointed from time to time. Vested with executive police authority somewhat broader than that of the old constables, the justices were landowners who served without salary. In the reign of Edward III judicial powers were given to these magistrates; in the next century many of the functions of the sheriff were transferred to the justices; and in other respects they replaced the manorial courts. Most of the remaining jurisdiction of the shire court was transferred to the quarter sessions of the justices, and the former remained in existence mainly for the election of coroners and members of Parliament. The hundred as an administrative district almost disappeared. The old local officials—sheriffs, coroners, constables, and manorial bailiffs—became the servants of the justices and often their nominees. The justices at their quarter sessions also constituted the fiscal board of the shire, which levied taxes, managed the expenditure of county funds, and maintained county roads and bridges, prisons, and public buildings.

The Tudor Period. The fifteenth century was a period of notable constitutional development but increasing administrative disorder. It was the task of the Tudors in the following century to establish order, and in this process important changes were made in the system of local government. There was a further development in the powers of the justices of the peace, with other changes in county government; and at the same time the establishment of new organs of local government in the parishes made the township of greater relative importance than before.

Additions to the authority of the justices may be noted in three directions: (1) they became charged with the duty of preliminary investigations in criminal cases of all kinds; (2) they were given control over the administration of a vast mass of statutory police legislation, both old and new, including laws against vagabonds and beggars, the regulation of wages, apprenticeship and prices, the licensing of beerhouses and other trades, and, after the Reformation, ecclesiastical laws against papists and nonconformists; and (3) they were given important powers of supervision over the newly established parish system in reference to police matters, poor relief, highways, and local taxation. These, together with the former powers of the office, gave the justice of the peace a position well described as "the state's man-of-all-work."

Other changes in county government affected the militia system, the local administration of which was placed in the hands of a new official, known as the lord lieutenant. Most of the important judicial business was now in the hands of the royal judges, although the sheriff's county court and, in some places, the manorial courts lingered on as decaying institutions.

Although in earlier times the township had never been an important unit of civil administration, on its ecclesiastical side the parish had an active and continuous existence. With the separation from Rome, the priest was replaced by the rector as the ecclesiastical head of the parish, assisted in financial matters by two churchwardens chosen by the parish vestry, which had the power to levy a local tax or church rate for the maintenance of church property.

This ecclesiastical organization was now made the basis of a distinctly civil administration. Under Mary, the parish vestry was authorized to elect a surveyor of highways and to levy a highway rate; but local roads continued to be maintained for the most part by a labor tax. Poor relief had always been considered an ecclesiastical affair, administered through the parish or in later times largely by the monasteries. But the dissolution of the monasteries and economic changes made necessary a new system; and a long line of parliamentary statutes, beginning in the reign of Henry VIII and culminating in the Poor Law of 1601, definitely established a system of parish taxation for the care of the poor, to be administered by the churchwardens and a new class of officials known as overseers of the poor. It may also be noted that whatever was done in the way of popular education was also done through the parish officials, but this as yet was considered a purely ecclesiastical matter.

As has been seen, the parish officials in the exercise of these new functions were placed under the active supervision of the justices of the peace. The justices, in turn, along with other executive officers, were controlled in all their functions by statutes of Parliament enforced by the royal judges. An active administrative control was exercised by the Privy Council; and, as a further means of central control, sheriffs, justices, and local executive officers down to village constables were subject to dismissal from office by the central authorities.

The Seventeenth Century. Few changes of importance were made in English local government under the first two Stuarts, and those made can best be noted in a description of the whole system as it existed in the early part of the seventeenth century, at the time when the first permanent English settlements were being made in America.

At the head of the county or shire during this period were two officials, the sheriff and the lord lieutenant. The sheriff was the more important and was still an official of considerable power and dignity, although the requirement of constant residence in the county and the expenditures made necessary by law and social custom were heavy burdens. Sheriffs in most cases were chosen by the crown, each from a list of three selected by the Privy Council, and by law the same man could not be appointed for two successive years. Of even greater dignity was the position of lord lieutenant, which in some degree revived that of the Anglo-Saxon earl. This post was usually given to the highest nobleman with estates in the county, and incumbents were not frequently changed. The main duty of the lord lieutenant was supervision of the local militia, which was called into service to suppress riots and the like.

Much less dignified and less powerful than either of these was the ancient office of coroner, filled by election in the county court. The functions of this office were now mainly confined to the duty of investigating sudden deaths. As a survival of his former importance, the coroner under some circumstances took the place of the sheriff.

But the real work of county administration was now performed by the justices of the peace. There were from 20 to 60 of these in each county, chosen by the lord chancellor from the rural gentry. They were usually men of good family and property and of some ability, who discharged their duties practically without pay, but were recompensed by the social dignity and sense of authority conferred by the office.

The powers and duties of the justices of the peace were so multifarious as to defy classification or simplicity of statement. A writer of the time names 293 statutes passed before 1603 in which justices are mentioned and given some jurisdiction and duties; and 36 more were added in the reign of James I. Legal textbooks on the subject required 500 to 600 pages to enumerate the list. Some of their functions were performed by individual justices, others by two or more acting jointly, and the most important by the justices in each county in their regular quarter sessions, held four times a year.

At the quarter sessions all of the justices in the county were presumed to attend, but in practice attendance was irregular and incomplete. At least one justice present had to be from those known as the "quorum," presumably those learned in law. There had also to be present the *custos rotulorum,* or keeper of the rolls, who was apt to be the lord lieutenant, though that official might be, and usually was, represented by a deputy. Others present included the sheriff or his deputy, the jailer with his prisoners, the high constable and bailiffs, the coroner, jurors, and all persons committed for trial. The quarter session was primarily a court of criminal jurisdiction for the trial of all but the most petty and the most serious crimes. However, it was also the administrative board for the county, charged with the care of roads and bridges and county property and with the levy of county taxes.

In petty sessions of two or more, the justices also performed both judicial and administrative functions. They had summary jurisdiction in petty cases, and single justices committed accused persons to trial before the higher courts. They granted licenses to alehouses, regulated wages and apprenticeship, and punished ecclesiastical recusants. They were frequently called on to give special relief or to take other action in emergencies; in addition, they were constantly subject to the instructions of the Privy Council, whose communications became more frequent and more drastic from the end of the sixteenth century.

Some important functions which later came within the sphere of civil administration in America were under the control of the ecclesiastical courts, held in each diocese by the bishop or a judge ordinary appointed by him. These included substantially all matters connected with marriage and divorce, the proof of wills, the granting of letters of administration and guardianship, and the administration of personal estates.

The hundred had come to be the least important of the administrative subdivisions. However, the sheriff continued to hold a desultory semi-annual tourn in each hundred, and the district was also used for purposes of taxation, military organization, and maintenance of peace. The high constables, chosen annually at the quarter sessions, were the only officers of the hundred.

For the smallest administrative district the use of terms was confusing and often indiscriminate. Town or township was the most general term, applying to either manor or parish. Manors, with their special privileges and duties, were becoming obsolete; but courts leet and courts baron continued irregularly in a few places. Parish was now the most common name for the smallest unit of local government; and the development of its functions, already described, made it a district of some importance.

The most active officer of the parish was the constable, chosen in some places by the steward or lord of the manor and elsewhere by the court leet, the vestry, or the justices of the peace. Although charged with a long list of duties as peace officer on his own initiative, for all practical purposes the constable was now simply the agent or instrument of the justices for making arrests, executing warrants and judicial sentences, collecting taxes, and carrying out similar duties. Other parish officials of importance were the churchwardens, who were chosen at a vestry meeting of the parishioners in Easter week of each year and often served ex officio as overseers of the poor. A vestry clerk existed in some parishes, the prototype of the American town clerk, and there were other petty officers. The duties of the parish officials in rural communities were relatively simple and required little time; and, except for constables and a few others paid by fees, no provision was made for their compensation.

It remains to describe the vestry meeting, or general assembly of the parish. All inhabitants were ordinarily entitled to attend these meetings, as well as persons who held land in the parish but lived elsewhere. However, there is little evidence of actual practice, and existing records do not suggest an active assembly. Attendance seems to have been confined ordinarily to the more substantial members of the community and the officers who had to present reports. The name vestry, taken from the small room where the meetings were held, indicates that only a few persons were actually present. Early in the seventeenth century it was customary to appoint in the open vestry a select committee to advise the parish officers, which suggests the selectmen of the New England towns. In England, however, in many parishes the committee came to fill vacancies in its own membership, and this *select vestry* became practically a close corporation, whose powers were later recognized as legal by prescription.

Urban communities, and even small villages, were organized as boroughs, or in a few cases as cities, operating under royal charters, many of which dated from the Middle Ages. In most cases the borough government was controlled by a small number of persons. Frequently the council of mayor and aldermen was a close corporation, filling vacancies in its own membership. In some places aldermen were chosen by a limited class of freemen, and in some places by the local taxpayers.

The entire system of local administration was under the control of an energetic national government. The bulk of active administration was performed by county officials drawn from the propertied classes but acting largely under instructions from above; and at the bottom was the parish with indefinite but largely unutilized powers of self-government. The system differed from the decentralization of the Anglo-Saxon period, from the feudal disorganization of the Plantagenet era, and also from the extreme centralization under the Norman kings. In form, it was highly centralized, with sheriffs and justices appointed by the central government and under the active supervision of the Privy Council. But the hierarchy of control was not systematically organized, as it might have been had the former authority of the sheriff been revived. Moreover, the local officers, instead of being trained and salaried, were usually unpaid, and the most important of them were drawn from the rural gentry, with the traditions of the offices going back to a time of broad local autonomy.

Such were the local institutions with which the English colonists in America were familiar; and, as was natural, most of them were introduced into the new colonies. But different conditions led to many important changes. The central government of England could not exercise direct control over minor officials at such a distance, and indirect control through the colonial governors was ineffective. Some of the most important functions of local government in England, such as poor relief, were of little importance in the colonies; others, such as education, soon became important. The class of rural gentry did not appear in many colonies, and even with similar laws a different class of officials appeared. As time went on additional changes were introduced from various causes. But the development of American local government is a continuous process from the English institutions of the early seventeenth century.

IN THE AMERICAN COLONIES

In the European settlements established within the limits of the 13 colonies, there was at first no distinction between the local and central governments of each colony. But as population increased and spread over a larger area, special local institutions became necessary, and those established were naturally similar to those of the mother country. There were, however, important modifications of the English institutions almost from the beginning, and other changes developed during the colonial period.

Virginia and Maryland. The first subdivisions of colonial Virginia were styled plantations and hundreds, but there was no revival of the organization of the old English hundred. These early districts soon became de facto parishes; and before long the latter name became the more common, and new parishes were established from time to time. Each parish, as in England, was both an ecclesiastical and a civil district, with a vestry, minister, and churchwardens for the management of local affairs. The vestry consisted usually of 12 "selected men," chosen at first by the parishioners, though later the practice of co-optation became established, as in the select vestry of England.

On the large scattered plantations which physical conditions made the economic unit in Virginia, many local matters were attended to by the owners. There was little opportunity for political activity, and before long the parish was overshadowed by the county as a district for local administration. In 1634 the colony was divided into eight shires, and new shires or counties were gradually organized. The county became the unit of representation in the colonial assembly and, also, the unit of military, judicial, highway, and fiscal administration. The usual officers were the county lieutenant, the sheriff (who acted as tax collector and treasurer), justices of the peace, and coroners. All were appointed by the governor of the colony on the recommendation of the justices, and the latter thus became a self-perpetuating body of aristocratic planters controlling the whole county administration. The justices appointed the clerk of the monthly county court, who acted also as recorder of deeds; and each county had a land surveyor appointed by the surveyor general of the colony.

Maryland was originally organized for purposes of local government, like the county palatine of Durham in England, with hundreds and manors as the subdivisions. In 1650, however, three counties were established, and additional counties were organized from time to time. The hundred was continued as a subdivision of the county, and new districts of this name were organized for election, fiscal, and military purposes. The erection of manors also continued until toward the close of the seventeenth century. Soon after the colony became a royal province, however, the counties were subdivided into parishes, and during the eighteenth century a number of towns were created by special acts.[2] Thus, although the organization of hundreds and manors delayed the development of counties and parishes in Maryland, toward the end of the colonial period the local institutions tended to become more nearly like those in Virginia.

[2] Newton D. Mereness, *Maryland as a Proprietary Province* (New York, Macmillan, 1901), chap. 6.

New England Colonies. In New England the primary unit of local government was the town, although the county was also organized as in England. The notable development of the New England town was due to various causes. It has been described as a revival of early Germanic and Anglo-Saxon institutions, and analogies can be drawn in many features. But the historical connection is through the later English parish and manor, and there is no evidence of conscious imitation of older institutions. The recurrence of primitive conditions explains the reappearance of some similarities, but a more important factor was the system of settlement in compact communities (partly as a means of protection against Indian attacks) by groups of landed proprietors, each of which formed at the same time a church congregation; and an underlying cause was the social philosophy of the Puritans, which affected alike their economic, ecclesiastical, and political organization.

The New England town has been described as a manor without a lord. Its activities, however, included those of the English manor, the civil functions of the parish, and many others. In addition to maintaining highways and caring for the poor, it supported public schools and regulated private business in minute fashion. It was the unit for assessment and collection of taxes, for militia organization, for representation in the colonial assemblies, and, in some instances, for land records and judicial purposes. In most of the New England colonies some of the towns were older than the central government; and in Connecticut and Rhode Island the latter was considered more a federation of towns than a superior sovereign authority. At the same time, the general court of each colony exercised control over the institutional development of the towns, and to this is due much of the uniformity of system which prevailed. Town bylaws were subject to approval by the county justices, and towns could be fined or otherwise punished for failure to perform duties assigned by law.[3]

Control of town affairs was in the hands of the town meeting, held annually and at such other times as deemed necessary. Each town meeting organized itself by the election of a moderator. At the annual meeting various town officers were elected. These officers, however, were limited by the appropriations made, taxes levied, and bylaws passed by the town meeting, which thus retained an active supervision over every branch of local administration. The meeting resembled the assembly of freeholders and tenants in the manorial courts, without the presence of the lord's steward. It was clearly more democratic than the close vestry, and probably was more democratic in practice than the open vestry.[4]

[3] Anne Bush MacLear, *Early New England Towns* (New York, Columbia University, 1908); John F. Sly, *Town Government in Massachusetts* (Cambridge, Mass., Harvard University Press, 1930), chaps. 1-4.

[4] Town meetings were of two kinds: those open to all town inhabitants and those confined to freemen with full political power.

Most important of the town officers were the selectmen or townsmen, a committee of three to 13 members elected annually at the town meeting. This feature of town government seems to have been a development from the committee or "selected men" which formed a stage in the evolution of the select vestry in England and Virginia. But the New England selectmen were an executive body for the town meeting and never became a close corporation taking the place of the open meeting of all the inhabitants. Even where the same persons continued to fill the office from year to year, they were regularly elected at the town meeting, which issued instructions and formed an active center for discussion of their actions. In Rhode Island the body corresponding to the selectmen was known as the town council.

For the most part the functions of the selectmen were regulated by the town meeting; and on this account their duties were so varied that exact statement is impossible. Nearly everything that could be done by the town meeting was performed at times by the selectmen. In general they were "to manage the prudential affairs of the town." More specifically, they conducted the financial administration, acted as legal agents of the town, had charge of the common lands, summoned the town meeting, and acted as election officers. At times the selectmen appointed minor town officers and even assessed taxes and enacted bylaws under authority from the town meeting. To some extent duties were imposed by the general court or assembly of the colony; and they were in this way made direct agents of the central government and in a slight degree of the English crown. Thus in Connecticut and Plymouth they were given judicial powers; and in Connecticut and Rhode Island they had probate jurisdiction.

A constable was a necessary officer in every town; but in New England he was pre-eminently the agent of the town meeting and freed from the active tutelage of the justices of the peace. Of more importance and higher social rank was the town clerk, who far surpassed his prototype, the English vestry clerk. He was not only secretary to the town meeting and the selectmen but a register of deeds and a recorder of vital statistics. Other officers of some importance were the treasurer, assessors, collectors, surveyors of highways, fence viewers, and clerks of the markets. Besides these, various petty functionaries were chosen, such as hog reeves, field drivers, poundkeepers, overseers of the poor, tithing men, and town criers. Not all of these were chosen by every town; but the list in each case was numerous enough to give a public position to a good proportion of the inhabitants.

In emphasizing the development of the town, many writers have neglected or ignored the county as an area of local government in New England. But in Massachusetts the county was established early and influenced the development of the county system throughout the country.

In the neighboring colonies, also, counties were organized, at least for judicial purposes.[5]

The first steps in the development of the Massachusetts county were taken in 1636, when the colony was divided into four judicial districts, in each of which a quarterly court was provided. At the same time three militia districts were created. In 1643 four shires or counties were definitely organized, as both judicial and militia districts; and additional counties were afterward established. Local magistrates for the county courts and town commissioners for trying petty cases were appointed at first by the general court; but after 1650 they were nominated by local election, subject to approval by the higher authorities.

Fiscal administration was also of some importance. Although the town was the primary unit for the assessment of taxes, there was established before 1650 a system of representative commissioners from each town, who met at the shire town to equalize the apportionment of taxes between the various towns—a plan which foreshadows the boards of supervisors that later developed more fully in New York. Since as yet there was no sheriff, the elective office of county treasurer was created in 1654 to look after fiscal affairs.

Other county functions and officials soon were added to these. The county was a militia district; but in place of an appointed lieutenant, the chief militia officer in each district was made elective. The county further became the district for the system of registering land titles, which originally had been established as a duty of town officers. In 1642 it was enacted that the clerk of every shire town should record deeds; and later the county clerk was given the additional title of county recorder. In the absence of the ecclesiastical courts of the Anglican church, probate duties became a function of county administration. This jurisdiction was at first vested in the governor and council; but in 1652 the clerks of the county courts were made registers of wills, and in 1685 the county courts were authorized to act as probate courts.

Minor changes were made in this county system from time to time; and under the provincial charter of 1691 there was a general reorganization more along the lines of the English system. Sheriffs, justices, and militia officers henceforth were appointed by the governor or the general court; and, as in England, the justices exercised administrative as well as judicial functions.

In three of the other New England colonies the development of the county was largely influenced by Massachusetts. New Hampshire was under the jurisdiction of that colony from 1641 to 1679, and Maine after 1652; and the county system was applied to these areas. Plymouth in

[5] George E. Howard, *An Introduction to the Local Constitutional History of the United States* (Baltimore, The Johns Hopkins University, 1889), Vol. I, chap. 7.

1685 was divided into three counties, and in a few years these became part of Massachusetts.

Connecticut first established county courts, with judicial and probate authority, in 1666, soon after the charter uniting New Haven and Hartford. Each court was held by one of the assistants and two commissioners appointed by the general court, but the term *justices of the peace* was introduced in place of commissioners by Governor Andros and continued in use thereafter. In connection with these county courts there developed an important change in methods of criminal prosecution, which eventually was to be extended to other jurisdictions. In England there had been no system of local prosecuting officers; but in Connecticut there was authorized, in 1704, an attorney for each county to prosecute all criminal offenders and to do all other things necessary to suppress vice and immorality.[6] From this there has developed the important American office of prosecuting attorney, which now exists under various titles in practically all of the states. In Connecticut the county was used in militia as well as judicial administration; but as a whole it was of less importance than in Massachusetts.

Not until 1703 were counties organized in Rhode Island, and in this colony they served only as judicial districts.

The Middle Colonies. In the middle colonies, the early Dutch settlements established by patroons were manors similar to the feudal institutions of continental Europe. A little later, however, there grew up along the Hudson and on Long Island a number of self-governing village communities. After the English conquest of New Netherlands in 1664, a system of local government was prescribed by the "Duke of Yorke's Laws" which combined features of the English and New England systems with some novel developments. Existing institutions and customs were recognized by making the town the basis of local government. Here authority was vested in a constable and several overseers elected by the freeholders and empowered to adopt bylaws, levy taxes, and act as executive and judicial officers. Two overseers were to act as churchwardens. There was a town meeting, but its functions seem to have consisted simply in the election of officers. At the same time, rudimentary counties were established. The name Yorkshire was given to Long Island, which was divided into three ridings, as was the English county of that name. In each riding there was a court of sessions held several time a year by justices of the peace; and a high sheriff was provided for the entire area.

From Long Island, where they were first applied, these provisions were extended with some modification to other parts of New York and to New

[6] William Hamersley, "Connecticut—The Origin of Her Courts and Laws," in William T. Davis, ed., *The New England States* (Boston, D. H. Hurd & Co., 1897), Vol. I, pp. 472-498, at 489.

Jersey and Pennsylvania. Courts of sessions were established in 1676 for the settlements on the Delaware, these agencies exercising fiscal and administrative as well as judicial functions. Towns were organized in New Jersey, but as yet were of little importance, and in many regions the parish was the smallest unit of local government.[7]

A few years later the English county system was more definitely introduced. In 1682 new counties were established or old counties reorganized in New Jersey, Pennsylvania, and Delaware. A year later New York was divided into ten counties. For these were established the usual appointed sheriffs and justices, the latter having both judicial and administrative functions; and probate or orphans' courts were also provided in each county.

In 1691, following the establishment of an elective legislative assembly in New York, came a most important change in the local government of that province. This was the creation of elective county boards of town supervisors, which were to become the principal feature in the local institutions of some of the leading states. This action at that time was the more striking in contrast to the contemporaneous legislation in Massachusetts, limiting somewhat the sphere of local elections. The new body established for New York counties consisted of a freeholder elected from each town to supervise, levy, and assess the local taxes for county purposes. This did not do away with the justices of the peace or even take away at once all of their administrative functions; but, during the next half century, the latter powers were gradually transferred from the justices to the supervisors. Thus the justices were left with only judicial authority, and this in turn was limited by the development of other courts.[8]

New Jersey developed a system similar to that of New York. In 1693 provision was made for the election of town assessors to assist the justices in each county in the assessment of taxes; and from these were developed the county boards of chosen freeholders. In Pennsylvania a special county administrative authority also developed, but the absence of strong town governments led to a different organization—one which was to spread through a large part of the United States. Assessors to assist the justices in tax matters were provided, as in New Jersey, at first chosen by the local members of the assembly but after 1696 elected from the county at large. Later, the place of the justices in tax assessment was taken by three elected commissioners in each county, and these commissioners became the chief county administrative authority corresponding to the New York board of supervisors. Meanwhile, as early as 1705, the office of sheriff had, for the first time, been made elective; and in 1715 there had been established the

[7] Herbert L. Osgood, *The American Colonies in the Seventeenth Century* (New York, Macmillan, 1904-1907), Vol. II, p. 285.

[8] John A. Fairlie, *The Centralization of Administration in New York State* (New York, Columbia University, 1898), pp. 114, 151.

new county office of recorder of deeds, filled by appointment by the governor.

Even without these changes the county in the middle colonies would have been a more important administrative area than in New England. With the development of these elective officers, however, the county, which was also the district for electing members of the colonial assemblies, became the center of political activity. In New York and New Jersey the towns had important powers of local government and were recognized in the county organization. In Pennsylvania, on the other hand, the towns were of little importance, and the machinery and functions of town government were vague and indefinite.

The Carolinas and Georgia. Active settlement in the colonies south of Virginia did not set in until the eighteenth century, and the development of an organized system of local government could come only after this had begun. Locke's Fundamental Constitutions for Carolina had provided an elaborate scheme; but this was never carried out, and the institutions established were for the most part similar to those of England.

In North Carolina justices of the peace and county courts with judicial, probate, and administrative powers had been established before the colony became a royal province.[9] In 1746 the system was reorganized, and the county courts more fully developed. Quarterly sessions were to be held, and the system of public prosecutions, previously established in Connecticut, was introduced, with a deputy attorney general for this purpose being appointed in each county by the attorney general of the province.[10] Counties rapidly increased in number, there being 32 in the province by 1765.

South Carolina was divided into three counties as early as 1682; but although county courts were ordered to be established, there are no records of them, all important cases having been tried at Charleston. Justices of the peace for the arrest of offenders and the trial of minor cases, however, were in existence by the end of the seventeenth century. In 1706 the province was divided into parishes for ecclesiastical purposes, each with a rector, seven vestrymen, and two churchwardens. A few years later the care of the poor was given to the parish officers, and the parishes were made election precincts for members of the assembly.[11] However, no strong local government developed under this system.

In 1721, soon after the transfer of the province from the proprietors to the crown, another act was passed providing for county courts; but

[9] The records of a precinct court for 1688 have been preserved. Paul W. Wager, *County Government and Administration in North Carolina* (Chapel Hill, University of North Carolina Press, 1928), p. 4.

[10] Charles Lee Raper, *North Carolina: A Study in English Colonial Government* (New York, Macmillan, 1904), chap. 7.

[11] Edward McCrady, *The History of South Carolina under the Proprietary Government* (New York, Macmillan, 1897), pp. 193, 447, 559, 693.

as their jurisdiction was limited and the judges were not trained in the law, the tendency continued for the central court at Charleston to absorb all business. Dissatisfaction with this situation became more pressing as the back districts became settled, but it was not until 1769 that an act providing circuit courts became law and not until four years later that the courts were opened.[12]

Local government experienced less development in Georgia during the colonial period than in any of the other colonies. The only court of general jurisdiction was held at Savannah, although justices for petty cases were provided after the transfer to the crown in 1754. Parishes were erected in 1758 for ecclesiastical purposes, the care of the poor, and the election of members of the assembly. However, the large element of dissenters in the population prevented the Anglican parish from becoming an active center of local political life.[13] Counties were not organized in Georgia until after the Revolution.

UNDER STATE AND TERRITORIAL GOVERNMENTS

After the Revolution. With the organization of state governments following the Declaration of Independence some changes in American local institutions were effected, but for the most part the main features of the old systems continued in the various states. Towns in New England and the middle states, and parishes in the South, remained unaltered and, in fact, were rarely mentioned in the constitutions of the Revolutionary period. The New Jersey constitution was exceptional in specifying that constables should be elected in townships "at their annual town meetings for electing other officers," to this extent giving the township a constitutional basis.

More frequently the Revolutionary constitutions contained provisions concerning county government, and there were some important departures from colonial practices. In Virginia no change was made. As theretofore, Virginia county officers were to be commissioned by the governor on nomination of the county justices, but this self-renewing system was now established in the constitution. In Massachusetts, New Hampshire, and Maryland, the governor and council continued to appoint most of the county officers, though the justices were now given a short, definite term. County treasurers and registers of deeds in those states were elective as before. New York entrusted the selection of county officers,

[12] Edward McCrady, *The History of South Carolina under the Royal Government* (New York, Macmillan, 1899), pp. 43-45, 642-643.

[13] Charles C. Jones, *The History of Georgia* (Boston, Houghton Mifflin, 1883), Vol. I, pp. 465, 524; William Bacon Stevens, *A History of Georgia* (New York, Appleton, 1847), Vol. I, pp. 391, 444.

formerly appointed by the governor, to a council of appointment consisting of the governor and four members of the state senate chosen by the assembly; the supervisors, however, continued to be elected in the towns.

Somewhat more striking changes were made in other states. Justices of the peace were to be chosen by the legislature in New Jersey, South Carolina, and Georgia,[14] and appointed on the nomination or recommendation of the legislature in Delaware and North Carolina. Sheriffs and coroners in New Jersey, and sheriffs in Maryland, were made elective; and in Pennsylvania two nominees for each of these offices were to be chosen by popular vote, one of whom would be commissioned by the governor.[15] The Georgia constitution established counties and county courts and provided that all civil officers not otherwise provided for should be elected.

In summary it may be said that there was a tendency in most states toward decentralization, with an increase of local influence in the choosing of county officials. However, local influence was exercised mainly through members of the legislature, with direct election of the old appointive officials being established in only a few cases. As the tide of settlement moved westward, the local institutions of the older states were introduced in the new communities, roughly following parallel lines of latitude. In Kentucky, for example, the Virginia county system had been introduced before the separation of the new state; and, although the first constitution provided for elective sheriffs and constables, the second in 1799 practically restored an older method by providing that county officers should be appointed by the governor from double lists of nominations submitted by the county courts of justices.

The Northwest Territory. In the Northwest Territory and the states carved therefrom [16] the development of local government was influenced largely by institutions of older states. Indeed, the Ordinance of 1787 enacted by the Confederation Congress for the government of the territory provided that prior to establishment of an elective general assembly, the territorial governor and judges, serving in a legislative capacity, should adopt for the territory such laws of the original states as they deemed necessary and suited to local conditions. County officers in the territory were appointed by the territorial governor; and, in fact, the earlier of the territorial counties were themselves laid out by guberna-

[14] Also chosen by the legislature were court clerks in New Jersey and registers of probate in Georgia. By the Georgia constitution of 1798, justices of the peace were to be nominated by the county courts under an arrangement for self-renewal similar to that in Virginia.

[15] After 1792 sheriffs and coroners in Delaware were chosen by the popular nomination of two candidates, as in Pennsylvania.

[16] Five states ultimately were formed from the territorial area: Ohio, Indiana, Illinois, Michigan, and Wisconsin.

torial proclamation. In 1790, when the first county was established, appointments were made to the offices of sheriff, coroner, treasurer, recorder of deeds, probate judge, and justices. Legislation adopted in the same year made provision for establishment of rudimentary townships, for each of which a clerk, constables, and overseers of the poor were to be appointed by the county court of quarter sessions. At first the latter body constituted the county fiscal and administrative board, as in the southern states. Before the end of the century, however, county boards of three appointed commissioners had been created for the levy and assessment of taxes and the audit of claims.

Town meetings were instituted in 1802, but only for election purposes, popular election of township officers thus replacing appointment by the court of quarter sessions. Each township was to elect a board of three or more trustees, a clerk, overseers of the poor, fence viewers, assessors, constables, and road supervisors.[17] The geographical townships marked out by the rectangular land surveys of the national government commonly provided the areas for new civil townships (except in eastern Ohio); and the artificial nature of these areas has been an important factor in preventing the township in these regions from attaining the social unity and political importance of the New England town. Moreover, settlement was largely on isolated farmsteads rather than in compact communities; and this again hindered the development of strong township government.

When Ohio, in 1803, became the first state formed from the Northwest Territory, various changes were made in the county system within the new state. The local courts were reorganized; sheriffs, coroners, and justices of the peace were made elective; and in 1804 boards of elective county commissioners were established with the fiscal and administrative powers of the former quarter sessions. These changes, together with the township system inaugurated earlier, formed the main outlines of the "county-township" system, similar to that of Pennsylvania, which was to predominate in the Midwest.

Indiana followed Ohio closely in the development of local institutions. Through territorial years appointment continued as the method of selecting county and township officials, though near the end of the period a demand for their popular election began to be discernible.[18] The first state constitution (1816) provided for the election of sheriffs, coroners, clerks of courts, recorders, and justices; and before long an elective board of three county commissioners was established by statute for each county.

The county system established in Illinois was similar to that of Ohio and Indiana. The first Illinois constitution (1818) provided for the elec-

[17] Howard, *op. cit.*, p. 144.

[18] Clyde F. Snider, "Indiana Counties and Townships," *Indiana Magazine of History*, Vol. XXXIII, pp. 119-152 (June, 1937).

tion in each county of three commissioners "for the purpose of transacting all county business," a sheriff, and a coroner. Before many years statutory provision was made for the popular election of county clerks, treasurers, and surveyors, and for the election of constables and justices of the peace from districts within the county. The earliest settlers of Illinois came largely from the South, where there was no organized township government, and, as a result, county government was permitted to absorb the township. A series of statutes enacted in the 1820's effected the gradual elimination of the civil township as a subdivision of the county; though subsequently the township system was re-established on a county-option basis.[19]

Mississippi and Alabama. Mississippi and Alabama, which became states in 1817 and 1819, respectively, did not follow closely the local government of the states immediately to the north, but were largely influenced by the more democratic institutions of Georgia. In that state the elective principle had already been extended to clerks of courts and justices of the peace. Both of the new southern states provided for elective sheriffs, Alabama for elective court clerks, and Mississippi for elective coroners. In both, justices of the peace were to be appointed as provided by law.[20]

It is noteworthy that in all of the states admitted after 1800, the tendency was strongly in the direction of extending the practice of local elections, particularly for the old offices of sheriff and coroner. South of the Ohio River justices of the peace continued to be administrative as well as judicial officers, but to the north the Pennsylvania plan of a special county board was rather generally adopted.

Changes in the Older States. Most of the older states had thus far shown few signs of changing their local government from the arrangements made at the end of the eighteenth century. The Connecticut constitution of 1818 continued the choice of sheriffs by the legislature; and the Maine constitution of 1820 carried on the plan of the former Massachusetts government.

But the second constitution of New York, adopted in 1821, made important changes in the local government of that state. The council of appointment was abolished. District attorneys were to be appointed by the courts, and sheriffs and county clerks were made elective. During the decade which followed there was also a significant transfer of poor-relief administration from the towns to the counties, altering the balance of power between these two local districts and affecting later developments in other states.

[19] Clyde F. Snider, *County Government in Illinois* (Springfield, Illinois Tax Commission, 1943), chap. 1.

[20] Concerning Mississippi, see Gordon K. Bryan, "The Mississippi County: An Historical Sketch," *Social Science Bulletin*, publication of Mississippi State College, Vol. V, No. 2, pp. 1-9, 33 (December, 1951).

Several New England states, in the same decade, established elective county administrative authorities. In 1828 elective county commissioners were provided in Massachusetts to exercise the administrative powers formerly vested in the courts of sessions. About the same time (1827), New Hampshire established direct local control over county taxation by giving this power to county conventions composed of the representatives in the legislature from the towns in each county. In 1831 Maine provided an elective board of commissioners for each county.

During the 1830's certain other states instituted broader application of the elective system. Delaware made sheriffs and coroners elective. Mississippi made justices of the peace and constables elective and provided for a probate judge and board of police (both elective) in each county. Tennessee provided for election of court clerks, sheriffs, county trustees, registers, justices, and constables; but coroners were to be appointed by the justices. Pennsylvania applied the elective principle to coroners, court clerks, registers of wills, registers of probate, and justices of the peace.

With these changes the elective system was well established in the Middle Atlantic states, the new states to the westward, and the most southerly states. New England had its well-developed town government, but important county officers were still appointive. From Maryland to South Carolina and westward in Kentucky the only effective local government, that of the county, was still administered by appointive officials.

In the states thus far noted, where an elective county board was established apart from the justices, it was organized on the Pennsylvania model. But, beginning with Michigan, the New York method was introduced in several states. The county system of the Northwest Territory had been extended to the Michigan settlements; and when Michigan was organized as a separate territory, similar county government was continued. In 1825 townships were established with town meetings and elective officers. Two years later, boards of elective town supervisors were established for the various counties in place of small boards of county commissioners—a change doubtless due to the immigration from New York which had begun after the opening of the Erie Canal. When Michigan became a state in 1837 the elective system was definitely established for all township and county officers.

When Wisconsin Territory was organized the small board of county commissioners was provided, and a bit later townships were organized for judicial, police, and road administration. In 1841, an optional system was inaugurated whereby each county was permitted to choose between the small board of commissioners and the larger board of town supervisors. But with admission to statehood in 1848 the constitution required the legislature to establish a uniform county system; and the New York and Michigan plan was then made general. Township and other county officers were made elective as a matter of course.

Meanwhile, immigration from the northern states into Illinois had led to a demand for township government in that state. Accordingly, the second state constitution (1848) authorized an optional system, and where the township plan was adopted, the county board was composed of town supervisors, as in Michigan and Wisconsin. The northern and central Illinois counties rapidly adopted the township system, but several of those in the southern portion of the state adhered to the older form of county government.

West of the Mississippi. In the region west of the Mississippi, periods of territorial government and early statehood witnessed experimentation with various forms of local institutions; in most instances, however, the statehood period was not far advanced until local government had become in large measure stabilized along the lines of some one of the patterns developed in the earlier states. Thus both county and township governments were established in Iowa, Minnesota, and Kansas, but with a small county board, as in Ohio and Indiana, rather than the large board of town representatives, as in Michigan and Wisconsin.

Arkansas, in its first constitution (1836), made the older county offices—those of sheriff, coroner, treasurer, and surveyor—elective. Provision was made also for the election by "townships" of justices of the peace and constables and for the establishment in each county of a county court of the justices as the fiscal authority, the presiding judge having probate functions also. This arrangement, although it preserved the terminology of the older southern system, organized the county board along lines similar to the boards of supervisors in New York and other northern states. Arkansas townships, however, were little more than election and judicial districts.

Texas and California. When Texas became an independent republic in 1836, the American county system was substituted for the earlier Mexican local government. Those controlling the government, however, did not introduce the decentralized system of local elections that had already become established throughout the United States. Sheriffs, coroners, justices of the peace, and constables were appointed; and when Texas was admitted as a state in 1845, the same system was continued.

California, like Texas, was first organized as a part of Mexico. Under a Mexican law of 1836 the entire department of California, including the lower peninsula, was divided into three districts, and these into subdistricts (*partidos*), with a centralized hierarchy of officials similar to the French administrative system. Over each district was a prefect, nominated by the governor of the department and confirmed by the central government of Mexico for a term of four years. In each subdistrict was a subprefect, nominated by the prefect and approved by the governor. The urban communities were organized as *ayuntamientos,* and in the rural regions there were petty justices proposed by the subprefects, nominated by the prefects, and confirmed by the governor.[21]

With the organization of state government in 1850, the Mexican system was discontinued, and 27 counties were organized. Each county was provided with a full quota of officials—sheriff, district attorney, treasurer, assessor, recorder, clerk, surveyor, and constables—all elective. Justices of the peace and county courts also were established.[22] However, in the mining camps which appeared rapidly after the discovery of gold, local government apparently was carried on for some years with little reference to the statutory system, each camp forming its own local institutions.[23]

Constitutional Revision and Amendment. During the years from 1844 to 1856 most of the older states made important changes in their systems of local government, either in connection with general revisions of their constitutions or by specific constitutional amendments. One very definite purpose ran through all of these constitutional changes in local government—the more extended application of the formula of popular election. Old appointive offices were made elective, and new elective offices were established. In Virginia and Kentucky there was a complete revolution, from the appointive system controlled by self-renewing justices to the election of all county officers and justices of the peace. At the same time, the county court in these states was reduced to a small body of judges specially elected for that purpose; and in Virginia provision was made for elective commissioners of revenue in each county. In the New England states, sheriffs, probate officers, and, sometimes, other officers became elective.[24] Justices of the peace were made elective in Connecticut and Vermont, though remaining appointive in Massachusetts, Maine, and New Hampshire. In the last-named state elective boards of county commissioners were established in 1855. In states where the elective method had previously been widely introduced, its application was now extended to still other offices: in New Jersey to county clerks, surrogates, and justices; in New York to county judges and district attorneys; in Ohio to court clerks and probate judges; in Indiana to the new office of county auditor; and in Illinois to county judges and justices.

Thus, by the time of the Civil War the main features in the development of local institutions had been established. Throughout the country the states were divided into counties, each with a considerable number of elective offices but with important differences in the organization of the fiscal authority. Everywhere, too, the county was subdivided into

[21] H. H. Bancroft, *History of California,* in *The Works of Hubert Howe Bancroft* (San Francisco, 1882-1890), Vol. XX, p. 585, Vol. XXI, p. 533; Theodore H. Hittell, *History of California* (San Francisco, Pacific Press, 1885), Vol. II, p. 258.

[22] Bancroft, *op. cit.,* Vol. XXIII, p. 317; Hittell, *op. cit.,* pp. 792-797.

[23] H. H. Bancroft, *Popular Tribunals,* in *The Works of Hubert Howe Bancroft,* Vols. XXXVI-XXXVII; Josiah Royce, *California* (Boston, Houghton Mifflin, 1886), chap. 4.

[24] Except in New Hampshire, where appointment continued until 1879.

smaller districts, but these varied in importance from the New England town, through the township of the Midwest, to the election and judicial precincts of the South.

After the Civil War. After 1860 there were further changes in local institutions. Some features of the northern systems were introduced into the southern states; and the development of local government in the newest states of the Far West has some points of significance.

One matter of interest was the attempt to transplant the northern township to the southern states. When West Virginia was formed into a separate state in 1863, its constitution provided for dividing the counties into townships with a number of elective officers; and the county board was to be composed of the township supervisors.[25] In 1864 a new Maryland constitution required the general assembly to provide for township government. The Reconstruction constitutions of North Carolina and Alabama provided for townships for the election of justices and constables, and in 1870 a new Virginia constitution established an elaborate township system similar to that of West Virginia. But the permanent influence of these measures was slight. In three years Maryland again revised its constitution, and in the new document the provision for township government disappeared. In 1872 West Virginia abolished boards of supervisors and townships, and revived the county court of justices elected by districts. Two years later Virginia replaced townships by magisterial districts for the election of justices, supervisors, constables, and overseers of the poor. In a number of states the name *township* has replaced the former *precinct,* but no fully organized township system has developed as in the northern states.

Some other changes were made in the Reconstruction constitutions. In the Carolinas and Texas the elective system was finally instituted for the traditional county officers, and elective boards of county commissioners were established. Georgia provided for a probate judge under the old ecclesiastical title of *ordinary,* and gave to this single official the administrative powers of the county court over roads and finances. Mississippi changed the title of the county boards of police to boards of supervisors, but they remained small boards of five members elected by districts.

The Far West. In the most recently established states of the West a striking feature of local government is the prominence of the county and the nonexistence or distinctly minor position of the township. The organization of counties by the territorial governments proceeded in the western regions as rapidly as population advanced. Counties were established before 1850 in New Mexico, Utah, and Oregon; by 1860 in Washington; and by 1870 in Colorado, Dakota, Montana, Idaho, Wyoming, Nevada,

[25] Richard Ellsworth Fast, "A Southern Experiment in Township Government," *Sewanee Review,* Vol. X, pp. 134-142 (April, 1902).

and Arizona. By the latter date practically the entire area within the United States, except Indian Territory and Indian reservations elsewhere, had been formed into counties; and, since then, new counties have been formed by subdividing and rearranging the boundaries of the older ones.

Township government, it is true, has also been established to some extent in several of the western states. Note has already been taken of the provision for township government west of the Mississippi in the states of Iowa, Minnesota, and Kansas; and the township system was subsequently established in South Dakota and Oklahoma. Optional plans of township government, patterned in their general features on the Illinois system, were introduced in the 1870's in Missouri and Nebraska and adopted later by North Dakota and Washington. But in the states west of the Dakotas, although counties were commonly divided into judicial, election, and school districts, township government made little headway.

Incorporation of Urban Communities. Local government in the United States has been profoundly affected by the development of urban communities and their separate organization as cities, boroughs, villages, and incorporated towns. Throughout the country these municipal corporations, large and small, now number more than 16,000. In the New England states the separate organization of small municipalities within the towns is not common, but in all the other states they are to be found in abundance. This separate incorporation of small villages has been one of the most important factors in determining the relative importance of the town and county in different parts of the country. It is due in considerable part to them that the township of the Midwest is of so much less importance than the New England town; and in much the same measure these corporations have enabled the states of the South and Far West to do without township organization.

RECENT DEVELOPMENTS

As previously noted, local government organization in the United States had achieved a considerable degree of stability well before the end of the nineteenth century. During the present century the general outline of local institutions has remained much the same, but significant developments have occurred within the established framework. A few of the more important of these developments may be mentioned briefly at this point, notwithstanding that they are considered at some length in subsequent chapters.[26]

One of the most significant developments in the structure of local government has been the rise of the special-purpose district as a major type of local unit. Except for school districts, the number of which has

[26] Cf. Clyde F. Snider, "American County Government: A Mid-century Review," *American Political Science Review,* Vol. XLVI, pp. 66-80 (March, 1952).

recently been drastically reduced through consolidation programs, there has been a distinct tendency to increase the number and broaden the variety of special districts for providing services which, it is believed, can be administered and financed more satisfactorily through such units than through the governments of the counties, townships, and municipalities. Sanitary districts, water-supply districts, health districts, park districts, and fire-protection districts are but a few examples of the types of local governments in this category that have appeared in abundance. Another significant development has been the steady decline in importance of the midwestern township as a unit of local government. State after state has transferred to county jurisdiction one or more of the major functions traditionally performed by township government, with a consequent weakening of the township as a political institution; and in some instances this transfer has proceeded to the point where the township has been virtually or completely eliminated.

As the township has waned, county government has gained in relative importance. It is true that counties in some instances have lost functions through their transfer to the state or to special districts, but this loss has been more than offset by the transfer of township functions to the counties and the assignment to counties of functions newly undertaken as governmental services. The increase in importance of county government has heightened the need for additional county revenue and for efficient county administration. In an attempt to meet these needs, county tax revenues have been supplemented by various forms of state aid, and steps have been taken in some instances toward administrative improvement. Some counties, for example, have been provided with central executive officers, elective or appointive. The county executive in a few cases is an appointive manager, with powers and duties similar to those of the managers found in many municipalities. In New England, where the town has retained its pre-eminence among local government units, a considerable number of towns have adopted the manager plan. Some states, to facilitate the provision of a county executive and the introduction of other organizational improvements, have adopted constitutional provisions for county home rule or enacted optional-charter laws for counties.

Finally may be noted the multiplication of contacts on the part of local governmental units with each other and with the state and national governments. The day is past when an individual unit could conduct its affairs with little reference to the needs and programs of other units. Numerous local governments now compete for public funds and popular favor. In an effort to provide more adequate public service at reasonable cost, functions once the sole province of individual units now are performed in numerous instances by two or more units co-operatively. Supervision of local government by state administrative agencies has developed on a widespread basis, ranging all the way from the mere advising of local officials to the direct state administration of local services. And, through federal advisory services and financial assistance to local units, the national government has substantially intensified its impact upon local affairs. Altogether, the operation of modern local government has come to involve multifarious interrelationships, on the one hand, among the local units themselves and, on the other, between those units and the governments of state and nation.

REFERENCES

Books and Special Studies

AURNER, Clarence Ray, *History of Township Government in Iowa* (Iowa City, privately printed, 1914).

BEARD, Charles A., *The Office of Justice of the Peace in England* (New York, Columbia University Press, 1904).

BEMIS, Edward W., *Local Government in Michigan and the Northwest* (Baltimore, The Johns Hopkins University, 1883).

———, and others, *Local Government in the South and Southwest* (Baltimore, The Johns Hopkins University, 1893).

CHANNING, Edward, *A History of the United States* (New York, Macmillan, 1905), Vol. I, chap. 15.

———, *Town and County Government in the English Colonies of North America* (Baltimore, The Johns Hopkins University, 1884).

HACKWOOD, Frederick W., *The Story of the Shire: Being the Lore, History, and Evolution of English County Institutions* (London, Heath Cranton, n.d.).

HOWARD, George E., *An Introduction to the Local Constitutional History of the United States* (Baltimore, The Johns Hopkins University, 1889), Vol. I.

KNAPPEN, M. M., *Constitutional and Legal History of England* (New York, Harcourt, Brace, 1942).

MACLEAR, Anne Bush, *Early New England Towns: A Comparative Study of Their Development* (New York, Columbia University, 1908).

MEDLEY, Dudley J., *A Student's Manual of English Constitutional History,* 6th ed. (New York, Macmillan, 1925).

OSGOOD, Herbert L., *The American Colonies in the Seventeenth Century* (New York, Macmillan, 1904-1907), 3 vols.

———, *The American Colonies in the Eighteenth Century* (New York, Columbia University Press, 1924), 4 vols.

PORTER, Albert O., *County Government in Virginia: A Legislative History, 1607-1904* (New York: Columbia University Press, 1947).

STUBBS, William, *The Constitutional History of England* (London, Oxford University Press, 1891-1898), 3 vols.

Articles

ALDERFER, Harold F., "Historical Foundations of the American County," *The County Officer,* Vol. XX, pp. 246-248, 250-251 (December, 1955).

BRYAN, Gordon K., "The Mississippi County: An Historical Sketch," *Social Science Bulletin,* publication of Mississippi State College, Vol. V, No. 2, pp. 1-9, 33 (December, 1951).

FAST, Richard Ellsworth, "A Southern Experiment in Township Government," *Sewanee Review,* Vol. X, pp. 134-142 (April, 1902).

GOODMAN, A. Bristol, "Westward Movement of Local Government," *Journal of Land and Public Utility Economics,* Vol. XX, pp. 20-34 (February, 1944).

POLLOCK, Ivan L., "Historical Background of the County in Iowa," *Iowa Journal of History and Politics,* Vol. XXIII, pp. 3-57 (January, 1925).

SNIDER, Clyde F., "Indiana Counties and Townships," *Indiana Magazine of History,* Vol. XXXIII, pp. 119-152 (June, 1937).

WILGUS, James A., "Evolution of Township Government in Ohio," *Annual Report of the American Historical Association* (1894), pp. 403-412.

CHAPTER 2

Present-day Local Units

HAVING TRACED BRIEFLY the historical development of American local government, we are now prepared to make a summary survey of the governmental units currently in existence in this country. Though our primary interest is in units which are predominantly rural in character, both here and in subsequent chapters some attention will be accorded those of an urban nature in an effort to present a realistic picture of the over-all pattern of local government and the position of rural units in the general setting.

NUMBER OF UNITS

No one can know the exact number of local governmental units existing in the United States at any given time. Neither in Washington nor in any state capital is provision made for a comprehensive recording of the creation and abolition of local units; and the local records of such transactions are by no means always complete and clear. Moreover, any attempt to take a "census" or enumeration of governmental units meets with serious obstacles. Since organization and dissolution of units are going on continually, any enumeration is likely to be somewhat out of date before it is finished. This difficulty, however, can be at least partially overcome by making the enumeration as of a designated past date. But the result of an enumeration will depend also upon the definition of governmental unit which the enumerator adopts. Different definitions will include different geographic areas as units of government; and, in the application of a single definition, the question will frequently arise as to whether a given area, in view of its organization and powers, is entitled to be classed as a governmental unit.[1] Under some definitions certain

[1] Some of the subdivisional *areas* of the various states which, though used for governmental purposes, have no governmental organization of their own and hence are not entitled to be classed as *units* of government include voting precincts, wards for elect-

public agencies, such as toll-road and bridge authorities, are considered units of local government, though not confined in their operations to an explicit geographic area.

Notwithstanding these difficulties, certain persons and organizations during recent decades have provided us with nation-wide data concerning local governmental units which are as accurate as can reasonably be expected. The pioneer in the work of enumerating local units was Professor William Anderson of the University of Minnesota, whose first enumeration was made during the early 1930's. His original data were subsequently revised as of January, 1941; and, during the early 1940's, the Governments Division of the United States Bureau of the Census, aided by Professor Anderson's files, made an enumeration as of 1942.[2] The most recent general enumeration is that made by the Census Bureau as of 1952.[3]

In conducting its 1952 survey, the Census Bureau counted as a unit of government any "organized entity having governmental attributes and sufficient discretion in the management of its own affairs to distinguish it as separate from the administrative structure of any other governmental unit."[4] Applying this definition the bureau found, in addition to the

---

ing members of city councils, tax-assessment districts, districts for the election of state legislators, congressional districts, districts for the election of judges, and commissioner districts for election of members of the county board.

[2] William Anderson, *The Units of Government in the United States*, new ed. (Chicago, Public Administration Service, 1942); United States Bureau of the Census, *Governmental Units in the United States: 1942* (Washington, Government Printing Office, 1944).

[3] United States Bureau of the Census, *Governments in the United States in 1952* (Washington, Government Printing Office, 1953). For school districts as of 1954, see United States Bureau of the Census, *School Districts in the United States in 1954* (Washington, 1955). Most of the statistical data presented in this chapter are from the 1952 census, although the Anderson study cited above has also been a source of much helpfulness. An advance release of the 1957 enumeration of governmental units made as a part of the 1957 census of governments was issued while this book was in press: United States Bureau of the Census, *Governments in the United States in 1957* (Washington, 1957).

[4] *Governments in the United States in 1952*, p. 6. "To be regarded as a government, any entity must possess all three of the attributes reflected in this definition: existence as an organized entity; governmental character; and substantial autonomy." In enumerating some of the characteristics which serve as evidence of these attributes, the bureau suggests that evidence of existence as an organized entity "is provided by the presence of some form of organization and the possession of some corporate powers, such as perpetual succession, the right to sue and be sued, have a name, make contracts, acquire and dispose of property, and the like." Governmental character "is indicated where officers of the entity are popularly elected or are appointed by public officials. A high degree of responsibility to the public, demonstrated by requirements for public reporting or for accessibility of records to public inspection, is also taken as critical evidence of governmental character." The requirement of substantial autonomy "is met where, subject to statutory limitations and any supervision of local governments by the state, an entity has considerable fiscal and administrative independence." Fiscal independence generally relates to discretion in the raising and spending of public moneys. An agency is considered as having substantial administrative independence if its govern-

TABLE 1

Units of Local Government in the United States: 1952 *

State	*All local units*	*Counties*	*Munici-palities*	*Towns and town-ships*	*School districts*	*Special districts*
Alabama	547	67	302	....	108	70
Arizona	366	14	48	....	270	34
Arkansas	1,088	75	360	....	422	231
California	3,763	57	306	....	2,010	1,390
Colorado	1,952	62	241	....	1,352	297
Connecticut	362	8	33	152	3	166
Delaware	107	3	49	....	15	40
District of Columbia	2	...	1	....	....	1
Florida	616	67	294	....	67	188
Georgia	975	159	475	....	187	154
Idaho	937	44	193	....	305	395
Illinois	7,722	102	1,157	1,433	3,484	1,546
Indiana	3,049	92	540	1,009	1,115	293
Iowa	5,856	99	934	....	4,653	170
Kansas	6,932	105	605	1,514	3,984	724
Kentucky	795	120	313	....	232	130
Louisiana	488	62	215	....	67	144
Maine	663	16	42	473	4	128
Maryland	327	23	146	....	....	158
Massachusetts	583	12	39	312	....	220
Michigan	6,765	83	489	1,264	4,845	84
Minnesota	9,025	87	796	1,844	6,227	71
Mississippi	692	82	263	....	93	254
Missouri	7,001	114	781	329	4,891	886
Montana	1,597	56	121	....	1,287	133
Nebraska	7,980	93	533	477	6,392	485
Nevada	242	17	15	....	166	44
New Hampshire	550	10	12	222	228	78
New Jersey	1,150	21	334	233	481	81
New Mexico	288	32	72	....	106	78
New York	5,482	57	610	932	2,915	968
North Carolina	607	100	401	....	....	106
North Dakota	3,967	53	348	1,393	2,079	94
Ohio	3,935	88	904	1,338	1,465	140
Oklahoma	2,770	77	499	....	2,100	94
Oregon	1,722	36	208	....	1,071	407
Pennsylvania	5,155	66	990	1,564	2,506	29
Rhode Island	88	...	7	32	....	49
South Carolina	412	46	237	2	49	78
South Dakota	4,916	64	307	1,090	3,399	56
Tennessee	434	95	241	....	13	85
Texas	3,962	254	738	....	2,479	491
Utah	384	29	209	....	40	106
Vermont	413	14	71	238	20	70
Virginia	365	100	223	....	....	42
Washington	1,538	39	240	70	545	644
West Viriginia	349	55	216	....	55	23
Wisconsin	7,257	71	534	1,281	5,298	73
Wyoming	518	23	86	....	318	91
United States Total	116,694	3,049	16,778	17,202	67,346	12,319

* Adapted from United States Bureau of the Census, *Governments in the United States in 1952* (Washington, Government Printing Office, 1953), p. 11.

national government and the governments of the 48 states, *local* governments in the United States numbering 116,694. The total number in each state and the number belonging to each of the major types or categories of units are indicated in Table 1.

It will be noted that among the individual states, the total number of local units ranged from 88 in Rhode Island to 9,025 in Minnesota. For the entire country the average number per state was 2,431, although 25 states had less than 1,000 units each. In general, local governmental units tend to be least numerous in the South, with most of the southern states

FIG. I

Average Number of Governmental Units per County by State: 1952

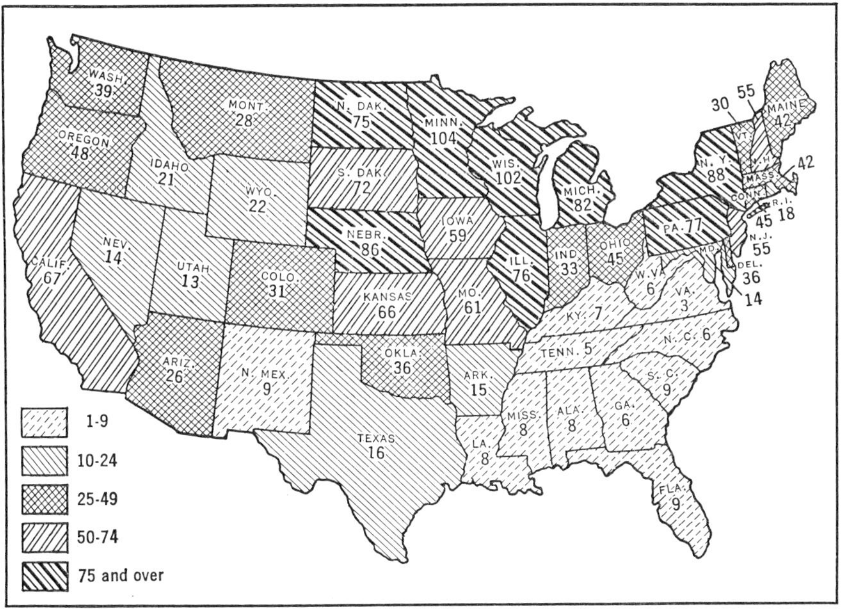

SOURCE: United States Bureau of the Census, *Governments in the United States in 1952* (Washington, Government Printing Office, 1953), p. 6.

having, on the average, fewer than ten units per county. On the other hand, the highest concentration of units, as of 1952, was found in New York and Pennsylvania and the north central states of Illinois, Michigan, Minnesota, Nebraska, North Dakota, and Wisconsin. In each of these eight states the average number of units per county exceeded 75, reaching a maximum of 104 in Minnesota. The average number of governmental units per county in each of the 48 states, as of 1952, is shown in Fig. I.

ing body is popularly elected; consists of representatives of two or more state or local governments; or, if appointed, "performs functions that are essentially different from those of, and are not subject to specification by, its creating government"—*ibid.*, pp. 6-7.

Taking the country at large, the average number of units per county was approximately 38.

TRENDS IN NUMBERS

Recent years have witnessed a marked reduction in the total number of local governmental units in the United States. According to the Census Bureau's data, this number decreased from 155,067 in 1942 to 116,694 in 1952—a reduction of more than 38,000, or approximately 25 per cent. For the most part the curtailment has been the result of widespread consolidation of school districts. Indeed, during the decade under consideration more than 41,000 school districts—some 38 per cent of the total number reported for the earlier year—were eliminated, though in the over-all net picture this reduction was offset in some measure by the modest increases in the numbers of units of certain other types. Except for school districts, the principal trend toward reduction is found in the case of townships, although here it is much less pronounced. The number of townships reported was about 10 per cent less in 1952 than in 1942; but this is explained mainly by the fact that Iowa's townships, counted in the 1942 census, were considered in 1952 to have reached a state of such negligible importance that they no longer deserved inclusion in an enumeration of separate governmental units. The most striking increase is in the special-district type of local governments, those units increasing in number between 1942 and 1952 by almost 50 per cent. Municipalities showed a net gain in number for the decade of about 3 per cent. Of all local units, counties remain the most nearly constant in number. Between 1942 and 1952 one new county was organized, and two counties included in the 1942 count were excluded from that of 1952 on the ground that one had merged its government with that of an overlying city and the other with that of an overlying town. As a result, the number of counties reported was one less for 1952 than for the earlier year. Fig. II, showing the number of units of each principal type as of 1942 and 1952, affords a graphic portrayal of the increase or decrease of each during the ten-year period.

Since the 1952 census of local governments, some new units have been created, of course, and some of those then in existence have been dissolved, but the general trends indicated by that enumeration apparently have continued. The number of organized counties has been reduced by two as a result of one Virginia county becoming a part of an independent city and another converting itself into such a city. Municipalities probably have increased in number and townships declined, though in neither case is it likely that the change has been substantial from a percentage standpoint. Special districts for nonschool purposes have probably continued to grow in number. The most significant change, by far, has been a further reduction in the number of school districts resulting from the continuance of active consolidation programs in several states. Apart from this reduction and the corresponding decrease in the total number of local units, the 1952 data presented in Table 1 serve still to give a substantially accurate over-all picture.

FIG. II

Number of Local Governments in the United States, by Type: 1942 and 1952

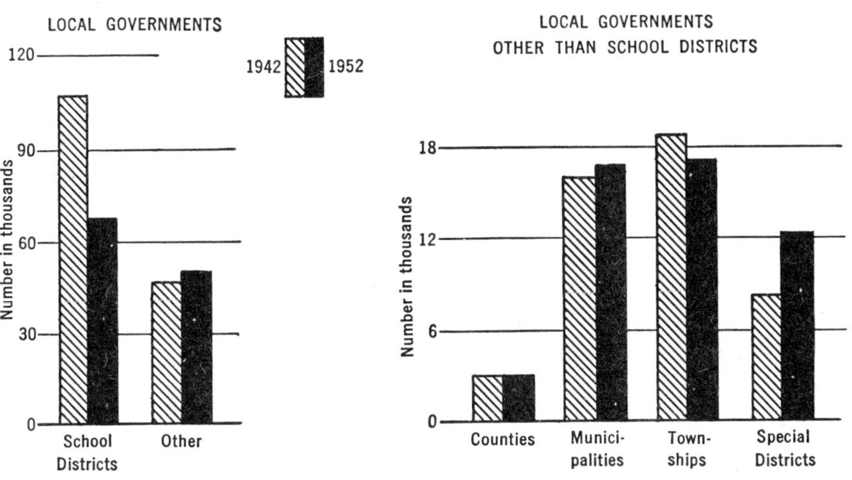

SOURCE: United States Bureau of the Census, *Governments in the United States in 1952* (Washington, Government Printing Office, 1953), p. 1.

CLASSES OF UNITS

Units of local government show many variations, both among different states and within a single state, with respect to such matters as legal nature, form of governmental organization, and functions. However, if we ignore countless differences in terminology and organizational detail, it is possible to group local units into a relatively small number of classes on any of several bases. On the basis of their legal nature, for example, units may be divided into two groups or classes, namely, municipal corporations and quasi-municipal corporations. The distinction between these two kinds of public corporation is considered at some length in the following chapter.[5] Again, depending upon whether they are empowered to perform numerous governmental services or a single function, local units may be classified as being either *general-purpose* governments or *special-purpose* districts. The former class would include counties, cities, villages, towns, and townships; the latter would embrace school

[5] See below, chap. 3, "Legal Nature of Local Governments."

districts, irrigation districts, fire-protection districts, and any variety of district established for the performance of a single service.[6] Convenience in our present discussion will best be served, however, by dividing all units of local government into four principal classes: (1) counties, (2) municipalities, (3) towns and townships, and (4) special districts.[7] The units of these respective classes, their relative prevalence and importance, and their relations with the state and federal governments and with each other will constitute the subject matter of the remaining sections of this chapter.[8]

COUNTIES

The county is the most nearly universal of all units of local government. Counties are found in every state (see Fig. III), and almost every point in the continental United States is situated within some county.[9] There are, however, a few counties which do not maintain independently organized county governments, and there are some areas—principally those within certain cities—which are not legally within any county. In all, 54 areas were reported in the Census Bureau's 1952 enumeration as lacking distinct county governments. Included in the list of such areas were the following 21 "geographic" counties:

1. Rhode Island's counties—five in number—which, though serving as judicial districts, do not have county governing bodies for performing the usual county functions.
2. Four "unorganized" counties in western South Dakota, which do not have their own governmental organization but are attached to adjoining counties for judicial and administrative purposes.
3. The five counties within New York City, the Louisiana parishes of Orleans (city of New Orleans) and East Baton Rouge (city of Baton Rouge), the Massachusetts counties of Suffolk (city of Boston) and Nantucket (town of

[6] Occasionally, a district created to provide a single service is subsequently empowered to provide one or more additional services. In such a case, however, the unit would continue to be classed as a special district unless given governmental powers of a broad and general nature, such as those possessed by counties, cities, and townships.

[7] Cf. Anderson, *op. cit.*, pp. 15-16.

[8] Representative studies of governmental units in individual states are Frank M. Landers, *Units of Government in Michigan* (Ann Arbor, University of Michigan Bureau of Government, 1941); University of Texas Bureau of Municipal Research, *Units of Local Government in Texas* (Austin, University of Texas Press, 1941); Joseph W. Reid, Jr., *The Units of Government in Alabama* (University, University of Alabama Bureau of Public Administration, 1946); Robert B. Highsaw and Carl D. Mullican, Jr., *The Units of Government in Mississippi* (University, University of Mississippi Bureau of Public Administration, 1949); Max R. White, *Units of Local Government in Connecticut* (Storrs, University of Connecticut Institute of Public Service, 1953). For a study of Illinois local governments authorized to impose property taxes, see Clyde F. Snider, Gilbert Y. Steiner, and Lois Langdon, *Local Taxing Units: The Illinois Experience* (Urbana, University of Illinois Institute of Government and Public Affairs, 1954).

[9] The parishes of Louisiana occupy a legal and political position comparable to that of counties in other states and are considered as counties throughout this book.

Nantucket), and Philadelphia county (city of Philadelphia) in Pennsylvania—all of which retain certain county offices but have become so completely merged with their central municipalities that they may be considered to have lost, for all practical purposes, their separate corporate existence.

4. The city and county of Denver and the city and county of San Francisco, which have consolidated city-county governments but operate primarily as cities.

The remaining 33 areas also lacking county government, in this instance because they are not located within any county, were as follows:

1. St. Louis, Mo.; Baltimore, Md.; and 27 "independent" Virginia cities. Each of these municipalities has been legally separated from county territory, and county functions are performed within its boundaries by the city government.

2. The District of Columbia.

3. Yellowstone Park areas within the states of Idaho, Montana, and Wyoming, respectively.[10]

Excluding the nonfunctioning counties and the areas outside counties enumerated in the preceding paragraph, the Census Bureau found 3,049 counties operating with organized county governments in 1952. The number of counties per state ranged from three in Delaware to 254 in Texas. In area, organized counties vary from 20,131 square miles in the case of San Bernardino County, Cal., to 25 square miles in the case of Arlington County, Va. As Fig. III indicates, the larger counties, from the standpoint of area, are found for the most part in the western states. The population of individual counties varied, according to the 1950 census, from more than 4,000,000 in Cook County (Chicago), Ill., and Los Angeles County, Cal., to less than 1,000 in a dozen or so of the most sparsely populated western counties.

Counties are primarily units for rural government. However, with the exceptions previously noted, incorporated municipalities remain parts of the respective counties in which they are situated, and property within their limits is taxable for county purposes. Population shifts of recent years have served to intensify the governmental problems of many counties. The farm population of the country is declining while the nonfarm population in unincorporated areas is increasing rapidly. During the 1940's, notwithstanding an over-all increase of more than 19,000,000 in the national population, half of the nation's counties actually suffered population losses.[11] For the most part, people leaving rural areas move

[10] *Governments in the United States in 1952,* p. 8. Cf. Anderson, *op. cit.,* pp. 19-25. Concerning the independent cities of Virginia, see Raymond B. Pinchbeck, "City-county Separation in Virginia," *National Municipal Review,* Vol. XXIX, pp. 467-472 (July, 1940). Subsequent to the 1952 census, an additional independent city was established in Virginia, and one of South Dakota's four unorganized counties was annexed to an adjacent organized county.

[11] Roy V. Peel, "Political Implications of the 1950 Census of Population," *Western Political Quarterly,* Vol. III, pp. 615-619 (December, 1950).

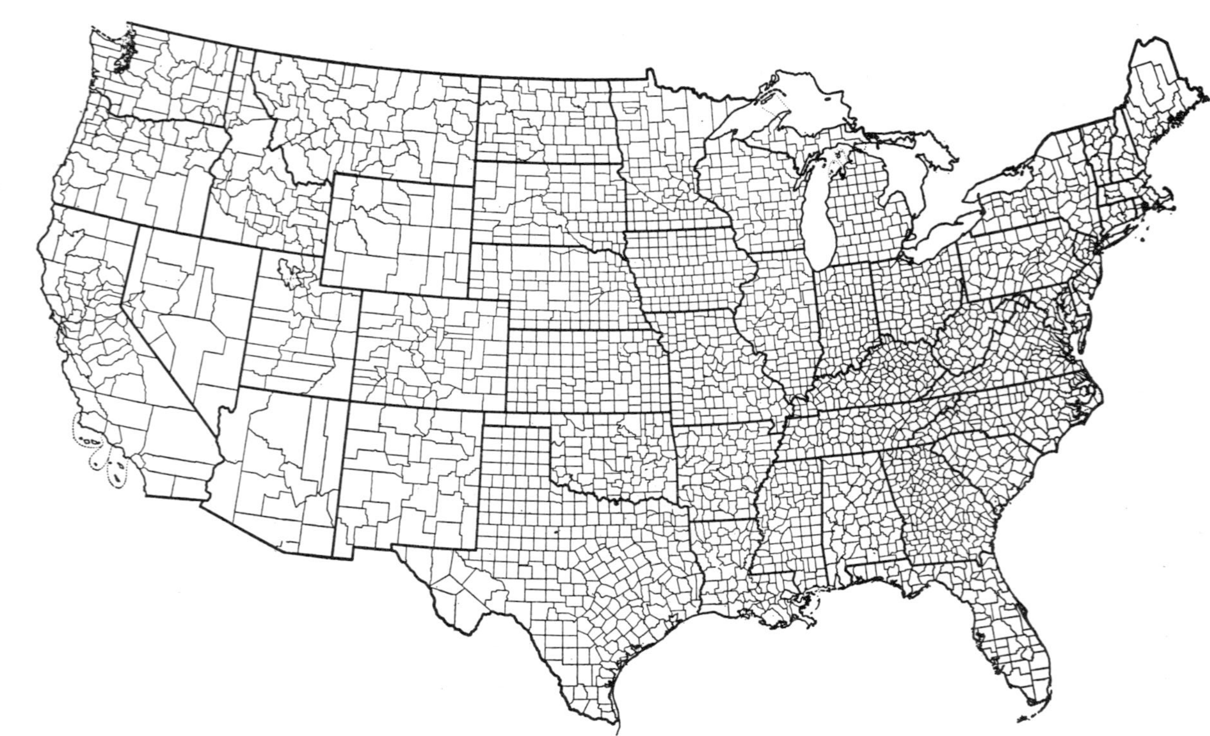

SOURCE: United States Department of Agriculture, Agricultural Marketing Service.

FIG. III

County Boundaries in the United States: 1940

to the cities and their suburbs, and any substantial shift of population from rural to urban communities is likely to have serious implications for both the counties gaining population and those losing. Counties in the former group, and particularly those with rapidly growing suburban populations, find themselves faced with the problem of providing for the residents of unincorporated areas more and more services, such as water supply, sewerage, and police and fire protection, which are ordinarily considered to be properly the functions of municipal governments. On the other hand, the sparsely populated rural counties are confronted with the problem of supporting normal county services with even fewer people and more limited resources than before.[12]

The traditional functions of county government are law enforcement, judicial administration, construction and maintenance of roads and bridges, recording of legal documents, relief of the poor, and, in some states, school administration. These basic functions, in some instances greatly enlarged and expanded, have maintained first-rate importance to the present day, and during recent decades many new functions have been added. Among the newer fields of activity opened to counties by the legislatures of various states are hospitals and health protection, agricultural aid, conservation of natural resources, weed control, predatory animal control, fire protection, libraries, parks and forests, planning and zoning, utility services, airports, civilian defense, and the regulation of liquor establishments and amusements in unincorporated areas.[13] In addition to being assigned responsibility for various newly inaugurated governmental services, counties have had transferred to them some functions previously performed by townships or other minor subdivisions of the county. Several states, for example, have transferred to the counties from townships or road districts the duty of maintaining farm-to-market roads; and there is a growing disposition to make property assessment a function of the county rather than the township.

On the other hand, as a part of the shifting of functions from smaller to larger units which has characterized American government in recent decades there has been some transfer of functions from counties to the states.[14] Thus some states have assumed responsibility for maintaining county highways; and under the federal Social Security Act, the categorical-assistance programs have been taken over largely by the state and federal governments, though in some instances the counties are

[12] Cf. Allen D. Manvel, "Recent Population Changes and County Government," *The County Officer,* Vol. XV, No. 6, pp. 14-15, 31-32 (September, 1950).

[13] Charles M. Kneier, "Development of Newer County Functions," *American Political Science Review*, Vol. XXIV, pp. 134-140 (February, 1930); M. H. Satterfield, "The Growth of County Functions since 1930," *Journal of Politics,* Vol. III, pp. 76-88 (February, 1941); Clyde F. Snider, "American County Government: A Mid-century Review," *American Political Science Review,* Vol. XLVI, pp. 66-80 (March, 1952).

[14] See below, chap. 20, "Transfer of Functions."

permitted to participate in their administration.[15] It is therefore apparent that counties have been acquiring some new functions and, at the same time, losing others previously performed. On balance, however, it seems clear that the counties have scored a net gain. The list of present-day county functions and the record of their growth present an imposing picture. The Citizen's Governmental Research Bureau of Milwaukee, Wis., has recently reported that the Milwaukee County board of supervisors, which a century ago handled only 36 different services, is today responsible for more than 200; and in Los Angeles County, Cal., functions are reported to have increased in number from 22 in 1852 to approximately 784 in the mid-1930's.[16] Though, as would be expected, the list of current functions reaches its greatest length in highly urbanized counties, especially in metropolitan counties such as Milwaukee and Los Angeles, even the sparsely settled rural counties today provide services more numerous and varied than in former years. Functionally, the American county is of greater importance today than a generation ago, and the expansion of the services provided by its government appears likely to continue.[17]

County boundaries may be changed by the state legislature subject to any restrictions that may be imposed upon the legislative power by the state constitution.[18] Typical of such restrictions are those requiring approval of changes by the voters of the counties or territory concerned, and those which provide that the legislature shall exercise its power through general law and not by special act. Many states now have general laws providing that county boundaries may be changed by local action, which usually involves petition followed by popular vote. In practice, however, county boundary changes seldom occur. The map of county boundaries shown in Fig. III was prepared some years ago, but subsequent changes have been so few that they would be of negligible importance for illustrative purposes.

MUNICIPALITIES

Whereas counties are principally units for rural government, municipalities exist primarily to serve the special needs of urban communities. When a particular area ceases to be strictly rural in nature through the settlement of families in proximity to each other, this more densely populated region has a need for various governmental services, such as fire protection and sewage disposal, which is lacking, or at least not acute, under purely rural conditions. When this situation arises, it is

[15] See below, chap. 16, "The Categorical Programs."

[16] Citizens' Governmental Research Bureau, *Citizens at Work* (Milwaukee, Wis., 1950); Los Angeles County Bureau of Efficiency, *Growth of County Functions, Los Angeles County, California: 1852 to 1934* (Los Angeles, 1936).

[17] Cf. Snider, "American County Government: A Mid-century Review," *loc. cit.*

[18] See below, chap. 3, "Legislative Powers and Limitations."

usually found that the governments already existing within the territory—county, township, or both—are without legal authority to provide the services required by the urban or semiurban area, or, if the necessary authority does exist, that the rural dwellers are unwilling to be taxed to provide these additional services for their urban neighbors.[19] It then becomes desirable to create an additional governmental unit, in the form of a municipal corporation, through which the urban inhabitants may provide for themselves those services which their circumstances require.

In every state the most populous municipalities are legally designated *cities,* and this designation is used in some states for all municipalities, regardless of size. Many states, however, apply a different designation to their smaller municipalities. Most commonly employed in this connection are the designations *village* and *town,*[20] though *borough* is used in a few states. In states employing such designations, it is usual for a municipality to incorporate first as a village, town, or borough, as the case may be, and, later, when it has acquired the requisite population, to change to city organization. Mere increase in population, however, ordinarily does not operate to change automatically the legal status of a municipality; usually a popular vote is required. It is therefore not unusual to find communities in a given state still operating as villages, towns, or boroughs, notwithstanding that they have more than enough inhabitants for city status. Conversely, a city may lose population until it has less than that required for initial incorporation as a city without reverting to village status. Apart from the matter of population, the principal differences between cities, on the one hand, and villages, towns, and boroughs, on the other, lie in the fact that the "lesser" municipalities are usually provided with somewhat simpler governmental organization and endowed with less extensive powers than are cities.

Incorporated municipalities range in area from Los Angeles, whose 450.3 square miles (as of 1940) give it by far the greatest extent of any city in the United States and probably in the world, down to tiny incorporated places of less than one square mile. In population, New York City, of course, takes first place among American municipalities, with more than 7,800,000 inhabitants as of 1950. The smallest municipality, from the standpoint of population, which actually carries on a government is not known, but it appears that there are many with less than 25 inhabitants.[21]

The functions performed by municipalities, though overlapping in some

[19] Cf. Lane W. Lancaster, *Government in Rural America,* 2d ed. (New York, Van Nostrand, 1952), pp. 25-27.

[20] These small municipalities are not to be confused with the subdivision of the county called towns in New England and a few other states. See below, "Towns and Townships."

[21] Anderson, *op. cit.,* pp. 28-29; Earl Hanson and Paul Beckett, *Los Angeles: Its People and Its Homes* (Los Angeles, Haynes Foundation, 1944), p. 4.

measure those of counties and townships, are for the most part new or expanded ones made necessary by urbanization. Among the most essential are police and fire protection, sewage and garbage disposal, water supply, health service, and park and recreation facilities. In general, the more populous the municipality, the more numerous and varied will be the services that it is called upon to provide for its inhabitants.

TOWNS AND TOWNSHIPS

Governmental subdivisions of the county, known as towns or townships, exist in 22 states. Save for certain "wildland" tracts in Maine, New Hampshire, and Vermont, and a relatively small number of incorporated cities, all of the territory of the six New England States is divided into towns,[22] and these constitute the principal units of local government in that region. Though some New England villages are incorporated separately and carry on their own governments, most so-called villages are merely the more populous portions of the respective towns within which they are situated and are under the jurisdiction of the town government.[23] New England towns are usually of irregular shape and contain from 20 to 40 square miles. The typical town includes considerable rural territory but also one or more village settlements or trading centers. However, some towns are completely rural, and others are more thoroughly urbanized. Town functions vary with the type of town. In purely rural areas, they are confined for the most part to supplying those basic governmental services, such as highways, education, and public assistance, that are essential even in sparsely settled communities. Towns with semiurban settlements are likely to provide various additional services, such as fire protection, sewers, lights, water, parks, and libraries.[24] And the most highly urbanized towns may supply practically all governmental services which elsewhere are provided by cities. New England towns are created, their boundaries are established, and they are, on occasion, deorganized by their respective state legislatures, usually by special acts. In 1952, New England towns totaled 1,429, the number in individual states ranging from 32 in Rhode Island to 473 in Maine.[25]

[22] *Governmental Units in the United States: 1942,* p. 3; Lancaster, *op. cit.,* p. 34. The unorganized or wildland tracts in Vermont and New Hampshire are small, but in Maine they comprise some 40 per cent of the state's total area. Cf. John W. Fleming, "Maine's Unorganized Territory Creates Few Problems," *National Municipal Review,* Vol. XXVIII, pp. 228-233, 237 (March, 1939); cf. below, chap. 20, "Deorganization."

[23] The separate incorporation of villages has made most headway in Vermont. See Frank G. Bates, "Village Government in New England," *American Political Science Review,* Vol. VI, pp. 367-385 (August, 1912). Concerning an interesting development in another New England state, see below, chap. 10, "New Hampshire's Village Districts."

[24] Cf. Bates, *loc. cit.*

[25] The Maine figure includes some units known officially as plantations. See below, chap. 8, "Maine Plantations."

Outside New England there are 16 states, principally in the northeast and north central regions, in which civil townships are employed for governmental purposes.[26] In about half of the township states, township organization covers the entire state area. Illinois, Missouri, Nebraska, and Washington, however, make township government optional with the respective counties, and, as a result, there are townships in some counties only. A few other states, notably Minnesota and the Dakotas, contain some sparsely settled areas in which township government does not exist; and South Carolina is reported as having only two organized townships.

In 1952 there were 15,773 townships in the 16 township states. Apart from South Carolina, the number in individual states ranged from 70 in Washington, where townships exist in only one county and part of another, to 1,844 in Minnesota. Townships vary widely in shape and size. However, except in New York, New Jersey, Pennsylvania, and eastern Ohio, there is a fairly general tendency, resulting from the influence of the *congressional*-township system, to lay out the civil township in the form of a square, 6 miles to the side, thus embracing an area of 36 square miles.[27] With respect to inclusion of municipally incorporated areas within townships, practice differs considerably among the states. In some states all municipal territory is excluded from township jurisdiction; in others all such territory is included within the townships; and in a third group of states the more populous cities are excluded, whereas villages or other less populous municipalities are included.

Except where urbanized townships have been empowered to perform certain services usually provided by municipalities, township functions are distinctly rural in nature. The most prevalent major functions are those of maintaining country roads and providing outdoor assistance to the needy. In a few states the township is a unit for school administration. Local law enforcement in rural areas is carried on in part by constables and justices of the peace elected in the respective townships. Other township functions in various states include the assessment of property for taxation, issuance of public-health regulations, maintenance of ceme-

[26] These "township" states are Illinois, Indiana, Kansas, Michigan, Minnesota, Missouri, Nebraska, New Jersey, New York, North Dakota, Ohio, Pennsylvania, South Carolina, South Dakota, Washington, and Wisconsin. In New York and Wisconsin, following New England terminology, the subdivisions here under discussion are officially designated *towns,* but because in nature and functions they are more similar to townships outside New England they are considered here as townships. In the statutes of some other township states the term *town* is used interchangeably with that of *township.* The civil township, here under consideration, is to be distinguished from the congressional or survey township. See next paragraph and n. 27.

[27] Kansas townships, for example, range in size from 1.5 to 430.5 square miles but have an average area of 36.6 square miles. See John L. Eberhardt, "Township Government in Kansas," *Your Government,* bulletin of the University of Kansas Governmental Research Center, Vol. IX, No. 2 (October 15, 1953). Regarding congressional townships, see below, chap. 9, "The Congressional Township: Its Influence on Local Government."

teries and drains, control of noxious weeds, and provision of parks and libraries. By and large, township functions during recent years have steadily declined in importance, and the trend toward curtailment of township activities gives promise of continuing without abatement.[28] Note has already been taken of the current disposition to transfer certain township functions to the county. In some jurisdictions, indeed, the transfer of powers and duties to the larger units has been so complete that township government has been entirely eliminated.[29]

Township boundaries are usually established and may be changed by the county governing board. However, the discretion of the board in exercising this power frequently is limited by statutory stipulations that boundary changes may be made only upon petition by the local residents concerned or with their approval at a referendum election.

SPECIAL DISTRICTS

The fourth class of local governments consists of special districts, sometimes referred to by the title, perhaps more accurately descriptive, of *special-purpose* districts. Each unit in this category is established for the performance of a single governmental function or, in occasional instances, of a few related functions. Of the various types of district, the best known and by far the most numerous is, of course, the school district. In 1952, 67,346 school districts were reported in existence in 43 states.[30] In the five states having no districts, all local schools were operated by general-purpose governments—principally by towns in Rhode Island and Massachusetts and by counties in Maryland, North Carolina, and Virginia. Several states in which the towns, townships, or counties administer most schools nevertheless have some districts; and nearly half of the states employ the district system as the predominant form of local school organization.[31]

More than 12,000 special districts for nonschool purposes were in existence in 1952, with every state reporting some such units and the number in individual states ranging from 23 in West Virginia to 1,546 in Illinois. These districts are extremely varied in nature. To mention but a few types, there are park districts, sanitary districts, health districts, road districts, fire-protection districts, flood-prevention districts, soil-conservation districts, drainage districts, utility districts, water-supply dis-

[28] Cf. Clyde F. Snider, "The Twilight of the Township," *National Municipal Review*, Vol. XLI, pp. 390-396 (September, 1952); James W. Drury, "Townships Lose Ground," *ibid.*, Vol. XLIV, pp. 10-13 (January, 1955); see also below, chap. 9, "Declining Importance of the Township."

[29] See below, chap. 20, "Township Abolition," "Local Deorganization."

[30] By 1954 the number of districts had been reduced to 59,631. See *School Districts in the United States in 1954*.

[31] See below, chap. 17.

tricts, and even mosquito-abatement districts. As previously indicated, the present tendency is toward a decrease in the number of school districts and an increase in the number of special districts for other purposes.[32]

URBAN UNITS V. RURAL

In classifying the inhabitants of the country as urban and rural, the Census Bureau in the course of its history has employed various definitions of urban population. According to the definitions used for purposes of the 1950 census, the urban population comprises all persons living in (a) incorporated municipalities of 2,500 or more inhabitants, (b) densely settled urban fringe areas, whether incorporated or not, around cities of 50,000 or more inhabitants, and (c) unincorporated places of 2,500 or more inhabitants outside any urban fringe. The population outside these various areas is considered as rural. Applying this classification, the urban population of the United States in 1950 numbered 96,467,686 persons, or 64 per cent of the total population of the nation, and rural inhabitants numbered 54,229,675.[33] Within rural areas, persons living on farms and ranches are further classified as *rural farm* population, and other inhabitants as *rural nonfarm.*

From the standpoint of census classification, many of our less populous municipalities operate within territory considered rural,[34] while many counties, townships, and special districts include highly urbanized areas. Municipalities, nevertheless, are organized primarily to serve needs arising from urban life, whereas basic services for the open-country population are normally provided, as far as local government is concerned, by units of the other types. It is significant, furthermore, that the great majority of counties, townships, and special districts are largely or wholly rural in the sense of having relatively small and scattered populations. Though the average population of American counties in 1950 was 43,770, no fewer than 1,933 of the 3,049 counties had populations of less than 25,000, of which number 762 had fewer than 10,000 inhabitants and 254 fewer than 5,000.[35] Of the 17,202 towns and townships reported as of 1952, 10,981 had 1950 populations of less than 1,000,[36] many of these having only a few hundred inhabitants and some less than 100.[37] Population data are not

[32] See above, "Trends in Numbers."

[33] United States Bureau of the Census, *Census of Population, 1950: Number of Inhabitants* (Washington, Government Printing Office, 1952), Vol. I, pp. xv, xvii.

[34] About three fourths of all incorporated municipalities have a population of less than 2,500.

[35] *Governments in the United States in 1952,* p. 2.

[36] *Ibid.,* p. 3.

[37] More than one fifth of all Kansas townships were reported, as of 1951, to have populations of less than 200, with one having as few as 23 inhabitants. James W. Drury, *Township Government in Kansas* (Lawrence, University of Kansas Governmental Research Center, 1954), pp. 13-16.

readily available for most special districts, but large numbers of districts are partly or wholly rural. Among school districts, which comprise the great majority of all special-purpose units, the predominance of rural character is indicated in some measure by the fact that notwithstanding many recent consolidations, two thirds of the total number in 1952 still had enrollments of fewer than 50 pupils.[38]

In the strictest sense, a treatment of rural local government would include consideration of small municipalities operating in rural areas and might perhaps exclude discussion of units of other classes that serve areas which are largely or wholly urban. However, such an organization of the subject matter of local government offers difficulties of presentation and does not accord with the usual breakdown of the field for purposes of college and university courses. Municipalities, large and small, are the subject of discussion in several standard treatises, of textbook nature and otherwise, and are considered in this book only incidentally as their interrelations with other units seem to require. Our principal concern is with counties, townships (including New England towns), and special districts. These are the three types of units charged with primary responsibility for local public services in unincorporated areas, whether rural, urban, or semiurban in character; and in many instances, their governments operate, at least for some purposes, within the boundaries of incorporated municipalities. Much that is said in the course of our discussion will, of necessity, relate to counties, townships, and special districts generally, regardless of whether their territory is rural or urban. An effort will be made, however, to emphasize the problems of these governmental units as they relate to *rural* communities, and especially those problems which are of particular concern to the rural *farm* population.

RELATIVE IMPORTANCE OF VARIOUS CLASSES OF UNITS

Within municipalities, and particularly in the larger cities, municipal government tends to overshadow the governments of other local units, except perhaps those of school districts. Nevertheless, as previously noted, county government operates within most municipalities, as does township government also within many. School-district government is of major importance wherever the district system prevails for educational purposes; and, for reasons indicated in a subsequent chapter,[39] special districts for various nonschool purposes are growing in number in both urban and rural areas and are constantly assuming a greater significance in the overall governmental picture. In unincorporated areas, however, counties and

[38] *Governments in the United States in 1952*, p. 4.
[39] See below, chap. 10.

townships have always been, and remain today, the principal local units of a general-purpose nature for providing rural services.

From the standpoint of relative importance of the county and township, respectively, the states may be divided roughly into three groups.[40] In the six New England states the township, known there as the town, has been from earliest times the primary unit of local government, with counties relegated to a distinctly inferior role. In one New England state—Rhode Island—counties, though existing as geographic subdivisions, are not organized for local government purposes; and in the remaining five states, though county organization exists, the functions of county government are extremely meager. So minor, indeed, is the present-day significance of New England county government that some responsible New Englanders favor its complete abolition and the transfer of the few functions the counties now perform to state and town agencies.[41]

In 26 states, principally in the South and the Far West, but including Iowa in the midwestern region, township government is nonexistent or virtually so, and the county is therefore the paramount unit of local government in rural areas. Though county subdivisions called townships are found in some of these states, they serve merely as administrative areas for such purposes as elections, tax assessment, and judicial administration; or, as in the case of Iowa, have suffered such diminution in functional importance that they no longer deserve consideration as distinct governmental units.[42]

Comprising the third group are the 16 "township" states, for the most part in the northeastern and north central portions of the country.[43] In these states both county and township continue to perform services of some consequence, though the county is distinctly the more important unit of the two. Several of the states, as noted earlier, have large areas without township organization, and the governments of some organized townships are largely or wholly inactive. Where both county and township actually operate within the same territory, the township occupies the junior position, and its relative importance is further declining.[44]

[40] This analysis follows in some measure that by Kirk H. Porter, *County and Township Government in the United States* (New York, Macmillan, 1922), chap. 4.

[41] See James M. Langley, *The End of an Era: County Government Has Become Obsolete in New Hampshire* (Concord, N. H., Concord Monitor, 1947); James M. Langley, "Citizens Would End Counties," *National Municipal Review*, Vol. XXXVII, pp. 541-545 (November, 1948); "Maine Paper Recommends Abolition of County," *ibid.*, Vol. XLI, p. 155 (March, 1952); "Governor Urges Elimination of Connecticut Counties," *ibid.*, Vol. XLIV, p. 99 (February, 1955).

[42] Though now omitted by the Census Bureau from its count of local units, Iowa townships continue to function in certain minor capacities. See Richard C. Spencer, "Iowa Townships Still Here?" *National Municipal Review*, Vol. XLI, pp. 397-399 (September, 1952).

[43] See above, "Towns and Townships."

[44] Cf. below, chap. 9, "Declining Importance of the Township."

THE STATE-LOCAL RELATIONSHIP

In the matter of intergovernmental relations, the closest association of local units, whatever their nature, is with their respective states. So vital, indeed, is the relationship of the states to their local governments that it forms the subject matter of much that follows in subsequent chapters, and only the basic legal relationship between the two levels of government will be mentioned briefly at this point. The outstanding characteristic of this relationship, in its usual form, is its *unitary* nature. Under the federal form of relationship prevailing between the nation and the states, governmental powers are divided between the general and subdivisional governments by constitutional provisions which can be changed only by concurrent action of political agencies at both levels. The unitary relationship, on the other hand, involves the conferring of powers upon subdivisional governments by the legislative body of the general government. Thus state constitutions establish the state governments and confer broad powers upon them, and state legislatures, in turn, create units of local government and delegate powers thereto. Counties, it is true, are established in a few states by constitutional provision, but even in such instances county powers are derived for the most part from legislative delegation. Since their powers have their source in state legislative action, local units are accorded no protection of these powers against the state legislatures comparable to that enjoyed by the several states, under the United States Constitution, against congressional action.

To the general rule that the state-local relationship is strictly unitary in character there is one major exception. In approximately 20 states some or all municipalities, and in a half-dozen states some or all counties, are granted certain powers of local government by constitutional provision. Such "home-rule" provisions involve a limited application of the federal principle in the relation between the states and their subdivisions. An element of federalism is found also in those states wherein constitutional provisions establishing certain county offices known to the common law have been interpreted to vest those offices by implication with all common-law powers and duties, with the result that the state legislature, though free to confer additional functions upon the offices concerned, is powerless to deprive them of their common-law authority. Notwithstanding such exceptions, however, the state-local relationship is predominantly unitary. Particular aspects of state-local relations, such as the creation of local units, the scope of legislative authority with respect to those units, forms of state control, and the law and practice of county home rule, will be considered at some length in Chapters 3 and 4.

FEDERAL-LOCAL RELATIONS

The United States Constitution makes no mention of local government, and, consequently, the power to establish and control local governmental units is reserved to the several states by the Tenth Amendment. Congress provides for governing the District of Columbia and for establishing local governments in federal territories, but the creation and regulation of political subdivisions within the states is a state function. Over the years, nevertheless, numerous contacts between the national and local governments have developed.

Older Federal Services. Prior to the depression of the 1930's, federal-local relations were relatively informal in nature, consisting for the most part of advice, information, and services offered to the local units by various agencies of the national government. A few examples will indicate the general character of the federal services provided during this earlier period. The United States Bureau of Standards made federal specifications available to local purchasing officers and published informational pamphlets on local planning and zoning; the Office of Education issued numerous publications of interest to local school officers and teachers, conducted local school surveys upon request, and provided a consultative and advisory service for local boards of education; the Public Health Service made health surveys for local governments upon request and assisted in the organization of local health departments; the Bureau of Public Roads assisted local highway officers on problems of road construction and maintenance; and the United States Civil Service Commission made its examinations available for use by local personnel agencies.[45]

More Recent Developments. During more recent years, these earlier federal services have been continued and expanded and, in addition, many new contacts, some involving a direct contractual relationship, have developed between the nation and the local governmental units. The immediate occasion for this development was the economic maladjustment and widespread unemployment of the depression period. Confronted with an urgent need for vastly increased relief expenditures and, at the same time, with dwindling tax revenues, the local governments appealed to the states and nation for financial assistance. But the expenditures required were of such magnitude that they could not practicably be financed from current revenues, and most of the state governments, like the local units, operate under legal debt limitations. Since the borrowing power of Con-

[45] The predepression services offered by the national government to cities are catalogued and discussed in Paul V. Betters, *Federal Services to Municipal Governments* (New York, Municipal Administration Service, 1931). No comparable listing is available of early services to local governments in rural areas, but developments in this field during a period of a dozen years, beginning in the mid-1930's, are discussed briefly in annual articles on county and township government in the *American Political Science Review*.

gress is legally unlimited, it was almost inevitable that the problem of supplying a large part of the needed funds should ultimately be passed on to the federal government. Recognizing that the depression was a calamity of nation-wide extent, Congress embarked upon a national borrowing program to raise funds for the assistance of the hard-pressed states and their local governments.

Public Works. For a brief period during the early years of the depression, federal funds were made available to local governmental units, through state channels, for direct relief purposes.[46] Of more lasting importance, however, were the various federal work-relief programs—especially federal loans and grants to the state and local governments for public-works purposes.

The best-known of the federal agencies operating in this field was the Public Works Administration (PWA), established in 1933 for a two-year period but extended by subsequent legislation. The PWA made loans and grants to states and local governments for a great variety of projects, including school buildings, county courthouses and jails, city halls, hospitals, streets and highways, sewerage systems, and electric and water utilities.[47] Originally the administration was authorized to make grants of 30 per cent of the cost of approved projects and loans for the remaining 70 per cent; but in 1935 the statutory provisions were liberalized to permit grants of 45 per cent and loans of 55 per cent. As is usual in the case of financial assistance given by one government to another, federal loans and grants to local units under these provisions were not made unconditionally. When an allotment of federal funds was made, a formal contract was entered into between the PWA and the local government concerned, setting forth the terms and conditions under which the contemplated project was to be constructed. The conditions thus imposed upon the local units were numerous. The administration reserved the right to inspect the construction to see that all terms of the loan and grant were complied with; all construction work was usually required to be done under contracts let on the basis of open competitive bidding; in selecting labor, designated classes of applicants, including ex-servicemen and their dependents, were to be given preference; certain stipulations were made concerning wages and hours of labor, and proper safety appliances for the protection of laborers were required; the use of materials produced by convict labor was prohibited; and funds for the payment of construction costs were

[46] See Edward A. Williams, *Federal Aid for Relief* (New York, Columbia University Press, 1939); Henry J. Bittermann, *State and Federal Grants-in-aid* (Chicago, Mentzer, Bush & Co., 1938), chap. 11.

[47] Jack F. Isakoff, *The Public Works Administration* (Urbana, University of Illinois Press, 1938); J. Kerwin Williams, *Grants-in-aid under the Public Works Administration* (New York, Columbia University Press, 1939). The PWA was consolidated in 1939 into the new Federal Works Agency, which, in turn, was abolished in 1949 and had its functions transferred to the General Services Administration.

required to be deposited in a banking institution protected by the Federal Deposit Insurance Corporation.[48] A special phase of the federal works program was the subsidy for low-cost housing provided by the United States Housing Act of 1937 and amendments thereto. Under this legislation, which is considered in a subsequent chapter,[49] many city and county housing authorities organized under state law have received federal loans and grants for the construction and operation of low-rent housing projects.

Local Debt Adjustment. A unique type of national-local relationship growing out of the depression results from federal legislation concerning the composition of local indebtedness, commonly referred to as municipal bankruptcy or municipal debt-adjustment laws. Some states, as is pointed out in a subsequent chapter,[50] provide administrative receiverships or their equivalent for defaulting local governments. Since, however, the United States Constitution forbids the states to pass laws impairing the obligation of contracts,[51] the authority of state legislatures to provide for the composition of local indebtedness is subject to serious restriction, and effective provision for debt-adjustment plans of a compulsory nature can be made only by the federal government in pursuance of its power over bankruptcy.[52] Faced with mounting local defaults, Congress in 1934 enacted the first Municipal Debt-Adjustment Act. This initial statute was declared unconstitutional by the United States Supreme Court, on the ground that it constituted an attempt to use the bankruptcy power for the unlawful purpose of interfering with the reserved power of the states to control their local governments; but subsequent legislation was sustained as making adequate provision for safeguarding state sovereignty.[53] Under the present law, dating in most of its features from 1946, a defaulting county, municipality, or other local unit may propose a plan for the composition or adjustment of its indebtedness.[54] If this plan is approved (1) by creditors of the defaulting unit holding two thirds in amount of the claims affected by the plan and (2) by a federal court

[48] Cf. Isakoff, *op. cit.*, pp. 111-127.

[49] Below chap. 15, "Local Housing Authorities," "Farm Housing Programs."

[50] See below, chap. 4, "Substitute Administration."

[51] Art. I, sec. 10.

[52] In Faitoute Iron & Steel Co. *v.* City of Asbury Park, 316 U.S. 502 (1942), the United States Supreme Court held that notwithstanding the contract clause, a state composition law could, within appropriate limits, provide for debt adjustments which would be compulsory upon minority creditors. The Municipal Bankruptcy Act of 1946, however, stipulates that no composition effected under state law shall be binding upon any creditor who does not consent to it, so that in practice, minority creditors can now be forced into line only by recourse to the federal legislation. See Jefferson B. Fordham, *Local Government Law* (Brooklyn, N. Y., Foundation Press, 1949), pp. 693-694.

[53] Ashton *v.* Cameron County Water Improvement District, 298 U.S. 513 (1936); United States *v.* Bekins, 304 U.S. 27 (1938).

[54] See *U. S. Code* (Washington, Government Printing Office, 1946), Title 11, secs. 401-403.

having bankruptcy jurisdiction, it becomes binding upon all creditors. The local units which have actually taken advantage of the federal law have not been numerous and have consisted for the most part of irrigation, drainage, and other special districts.[55] However, the mere existence of the law has doubtless been a factor in stimulating the unanimous agreement of creditors to voluntary compositions.

Other Relationships. Certain additional federal-local relationships, some recently inaugurated and others of longer standing, may be mentioned for purposes of further illustration. From federal aid received by the states for highway purposes, substantial sums have been allocated during recent years for expenditure on county and township roads and city streets. Federal funds have been made available to local governmental units for aid in airport construction. The Tennessee Valley Authority (TVA) sells electric power to a number of cities and counties in the valley area and, by contract with the local governments, fixes resale rates to consumers.[56] Capital loans for establishing rural electric co-operatives are provided by the federal Rural Electrification Administration; and many of the local co-operatives purchase power for resale from the TVA or other federal projects. Federal grants are made to local health departments to aid in the support of qualified, full-time personnel, this assistance being especially important to county and district departments in rural areas. Counties and municipalities share in federal grants made available under the Hill-Burton Act for hospital construction. In some states counties administer categorical-assistance programs which are financed in part from federal funds. Many school districts receive federal aid for vocational-education and school-lunch programs. Under the George-Deen Act, federal vocational education funds are made available to the states for public-service training; and several states, with this assistance, have organized programs of in-service training for local government officials.

County agricultural extension programs are financed in part from federal funds, and the Soil Conservation Service of the United States Department of Agriculture assists in the work of local soil-conservation districts. Approved county jails are used by the United States Department of Justice for temporary detention of federal prisoners; and the federal Bureau of Prisons seeks in various ways to encourage improvement in local jail administration. Bureau activities directed to this objective include the preparation and distribution of a manual of jail management, the opening of officers' training classes in federal penal institutions to selected jail

[55] Wylie Kilpatrick, *State Supervision of Local Finance* (Chicago, Public Administration Service, 1941), p. 41.

[56] For discussion of numerous other contacts of the authority with local governments, see Lawrence L. Durisch, "Local Government and the T.V.A. Program," *Public Administration Review*, Vol. I, pp. 326-334 (Summer, 1941); M. H. Satterfield, "TVA-state-local Relationships," *American Political Science Review*, Vol. XL, pp. 935-949 (October, 1946).

personnel, and the holding of institutes for jailers, at which sheriffs, jailers, and police officers may receive practical training in the various aspects of jail management.[57] Finally may be mentioned the work of the Governments Division of the Census Bureau, which compiles and publishes data on the finances of local units, issues periodic reports on employees and payrolls of state and local governments, and makes special studies in the local government field.

In considering the present status of federal-local relations it is significant to note that the federal government, in several of its grant-in-aid programs, has found it more convenient to deal with counties than with municipalities. After pointing out this fact, the Commission on Intergovernmental Relations observes in its recent report: [58]

> The county seat is commonly the headquarters for officials administering certain Federal programs, and the county government is often the only available local unit with which the National Government may co-operate. In three fields where Federal grants-in-aid directly affect large numbers of people—welfare, health, and agriculture—the county is involved in varying degrees. Welfare is administered at the county level, sometimes by the State and sometimes by a county welfare board that is a substantially independent agency. In public health, it is the National policy to encourage local administration by county or intercounty health units. The National agricultural programs, except for soil-conservation technical assistance, are based on the county, either as an administrative area or as a unit of government, and as a matter of fact about 80 per cent of the soil conservation districts are coterminous with the county. Counties, of course, participate in the highway program and are sometimes involved in other national programs.

Present Outlook. As even a cursory analysis suggests, contacts between the national and local governments are growing both in number and in importance, and this growth gives every promise of continuing. One major problem arising from expansion of national-local relationships concerns inherent potentialities for federal control over the local units. Where the national government merely provides advice or information, no element of national control is involved. Federal grants of money, on the other hand, almost invariably carry with them some measure of control, the receiving units being required to comply with federally prescribed standards with respect to the service or project concerned and to submit, in some instances, to varying degrees of federal supervision.

Noting the continued, though as yet modest, growth of federal aid to local governments, some students of the problem fear that an insidious extension of national authority into local affairs may undermine the states and ultimately result in a breakdown of the federal system. Developments

[57] United States Bureau of Prisons, *Federal Prisons: 1950,* Annual Report of the Director of the Bureau of Prisons (Washington, 1950), p. 34.

[58] *Report of the Commission on Intergovernmental Relations* (Washington, Government Printing Office, 1955), pp. 53-54.

to date, however, scarcely justify so dire a foreboding. It is significant to note in this connection that local governments must, perhaps without exception, have state consent before entering into relationships with the national government involving any direct contractual obligation or any possible impingement of state authority. Thus, local governments in a particular state, by the terms of the federal laws concerned, can enter into contracts for federal aid for public works or housing or take advantage of the Municipal Debt-Adjustment Act, only if there is state legislation empowering them to do so. But although state sovereignty is legally safeguarded, state legislatures in actual practice are not so free as they appear to be to give or withhold consent to local participation in federal-aid programs. When aid from federal tax funds is offered in support of a local function, the legislature of a given state may well feel that it has little choice but to authorize its local units, whose taxpaying citizens in any event will be bearing a share of the federal cost, to accept the proffered assistance, notwithstanding that acceptance involves submission to federal control. Under these circumstances it can hardly be denied that with the adoption of any new federal-aid program or the enlargement of existing programs, federal influence in local affairs will be further enhanced.

INTERLOCAL RELATIONS

Local governmental units, even within a single state, are for the most part quite independent of each other. Each unit normally has its own officials and revenue-raising power and conducts its affairs with little regard for neighboring or overlapping governments. To this general rule, however, there are exceptions, including some instances of duplication or overlap in official personnel. In certain cases, as in that of Illinois township supervisors, designated officers of the township serve also as members of the county governing body, thus, in a sense, gearing the two units together. Tax levies for township roads sometimes require approval by county authorities. Occasionally, the governing body of one local unit serves ex officio in the same capacity for another. Also deserving of note is the fact that officers of one local unit are sometimes appointed by those of another unit. This situation is found most frequently in the case of special districts, the governing authorities of which are appointed in numerous instances by the court or governing body of the overlying county.

Notwithstanding the high degree of autonomy usually enjoyed by individual units, it has been inevitable that numerous interrelationships, both legal and extralegal, should develop at the local level. This has been particularly true in view of the large number of local units and the fact that within a given area several units ordinarily operate concurrently. Some of the relationships thus evolved are of a competitive nature. This is often the case, for example, in revenue matters, with each of the various units or classes of units seeking to secure as large a portion as possible of the public moneys. Thus, municipalities may contend with counties before the legislature for grants of taxing power or shares of state-distributed funds; and in states imposing over-all limits on property-tax rates, it is commonly necessary, because of intergovernmental competition, to establish at either the state or the county level an administrative agency to apportion the total rate among the different units within a given area.[59]

More and more, however, relationships among local units are assuming a co-operative rather than a competitive character. Through state-wide organizations, some of which are associated in national federations, local government officials work together in seeking solutions to common problems and in sponsoring programs of state and national legislative action.[60] Although intergovernmental aid of a monetary nature usually flows from the national government to the states or their local units, or from state to local governments, instances are not wanting of financial assistance by one local government to another. In Minnesota, for example, counties frequently make grants from their road and bridge funds to townships for emergency construction purposes, and some counties distribute to their townships a portion of their state-derived gasoline-tax revenues.[61] A type of co-operation which is constantly growing in significance is that wherein two or more units of local government, of the same or different classes, collaborate in the performance of some common function. Aptly referred to as functional consolidation, co-operation of this kind may take the form of joint performance of the function by the units involved or may consist of one unit providing the service for the other, or others, under contractual agreement. Co-operative performance of local functions by means such as these is considered in the final chapter of this book.[62]

REFERENCES

Books and Special Studies

ANDERSON, William, *The Units of Government in the United States*, new ed. (Chicago, Public Administration Service, 1942). This bulletin was reprinted with a brief appendix in 1945, and again with an additional appendix in 1949.

HIGHSAW, Robert B., and MULLICAN, Carl D., Jr., *The Units of Government in Mississippi* (University, University of Mississippi Bureau of Public Administration, 1949).

[59] Cf. Clyde F. Snider, "Fiscal Control at the County Level," *National Municipal Review*, Vol. XXX, pp. 579-586 (October, 1941).

[60] Cf. below, chap. 6, "Organizations of County Officers."

[61] R. A. Gomez, *Intergovernmental Relations in Highways* (Minneapolis, University of Minnesota Press, 1950), p. 98.

[62] See below, chap. 20, "Functional Consolidation."

Illinois Tax Commission, *Atlas of Taxing Units [in Illinois]*, Survey of Local Finance in Illinois (Springfield and Chicago, 1939), Vol. I, published in co-operation with the Works Progress Administration.

LANDERS, Frank M., *Units of Government in Michigan* (Ann Arbor, University of Michigan Bureau of Government, 1941).

REID, Joseph W., Jr., *The Units of Government in Alabama* (University, University of Alabama Bureau of Public Administration, 1946).

SNIDER, Clyde F., STEINER, Gilbert Y., and LANGDON, Lois, *Local Taxing Units: The Illinois Experience* (Urbana, University of Illinois Institute of Government and Public Affairs, 1954).

SWANSON, K. T. W., *Governmental Units in Spokane County* (Spokane, Wash., Spokane County Planning Commission, 1955).

United States Bureau of the Census, *Governmental Units in the United States: 1942* (Washington, Government Printing Office, 1944).

———, *Governments in the United States in 1952* (Washington, Government Printing Office, 1953).

———, *Local Government Structure in the United States* (Washington, Government Printing Office, 1954).

University of Texas Bureau of Municipal Research, *Units of Local Government in Texas* (Austin, University of Texas Press, 1941).

WHITE, Max R., *Units of Local Government in Connecticut* (Storrs, University of Connecticut Institute of Public Service, 1953).

Articles

DURISCH, Lawrence L., "Local Government and the T.V.A. Program," *Public Administration Review*, Vol. I, pp. 326-334 (Summer, 1941).

EGGER, Rowland, "County-state Relations in Virginia," *Social Forces*, Vol. XI, pp. 102-109 (October, 1932).

HIGHSAW, Robert B., "Government Units in Mississippi Decline," *Public Administration Survey*, publication of the University of Mississippi Bureau of Public Administration, Vol. II, No. 2 (November, 1954).

LANGLEY, James M., "Citizens Would End Counties," *National Municipal Review*, Vol. XXXVII, pp. 541-545 (November, 1948).

MANVEL, Allen D., "Local Government in the United States," *The County Officer*, Vol. XVII, pp. 192-193, 219 (July, 1952).

SATTERFIELD, M. H., "TVA-state-local Relationships," *American Political Science Review*, Vol. XL, pp. 935-949 (October, 1946).

CHAPTER 3

Local Government Law

LEGAL NATURE OF LOCAL GOVERNMENTS

IN LAW, local governmental units are usually accorded the status of public corporations. To comprehend their nature, therefore, it is necessary to understand something of the character of corporate organization generally and of public corporations in particular. In the celebrated Dartmouth College Case the United States Supreme Court many years ago defined a corporation as "an artificial being, invisible, intangible, and existing only in contemplation of law." [1] In simple terms, a corporation is a legal person separate and distinct from the natural persons who comprise it. It is a device whereby numerous natural persons may, as a single legal entity, enjoy perpetual succession; acquire, hold, and dispose of property; sue and be sued in the courts; and engage in other activities within the powers conferred by the charter creating the corporation or by other law. Existing only by virtue of the law, a corporation has, of course, only those powers which have been given it by law, either in express terms or by reasonable implication. Though corporations of certain special kinds are created by the national government, most corporations in this country are established by the respective states.

American corporations fall into two general classes—private and public. Though some private corporations are established for educational, charitable, or other nonprofit purposes, the great majority of corporations in this category are organized for the primary purpose of making a profit for their stockholders. Prominent in this group are the business corporations which carry on so large a part of the country's industry and trade. A public corporation, on the other hand, has been defined by eminent authority as "a corporation created by the state for public purposes only,

[1] Trustees of Dartmouth College *v.* Woodward, 4 Wheat. 518, 636 (1819).

as an instrumentality to increase the efficiency of government, supply the public wants, and promote the public welfare." [2] It will thus be seen that a public corporation has as its primary purpose, not the making of profit but the supplying of services to the inhabitants within its boundaries; and this is one of the principal respects in which the public corporation differs from the private. In addition to this difference as to purpose, however, private and public corporations differ from each other in their respective constitutional relationships to the state. Both private and public corporations, it is true, are created under state authority. Ever since the Dartmouth College decision, however, a charter creating a private corporation has been regarded in American law as a contract between the corporation and the granting state within the provision of the United States Constitution which declares that no state shall pass any law impairing the obligation of contracts.[3] As a result, when a charter has once been granted to a private corporation, it may not subsequently be changed by the state without the corporation's consent unless (as is now commonly the case) the original grant is made with the right reserved to the state to make subsequent modifications. Charters to public corporations, on the other hand, are not considered as having the status of contracts and, consequently, as far as the "impairment" provision is concerned, are subject at any time to revocation or alteration at the hands of the state.

With corporations classified as private or public, the courts have distinguished further between two types or grades of public corporation, commonly referred to as municipal and quasi-municipal.[4] According to this distinction, municipal corporations are created at the request of the local inhabitants, or with their consent, and primarily for local benefit or advantage, whereas quasi-municipal corporations are established without reference to local wishes and for the benefit of the inhabitants of the state at large. Municipal corporations are established primarily to carry on activities and provide services which are local in nature, such as the provision of public utilities and the enactment and enforcement of regulatory ordinances. Quasi-municipal corporations, on the other hand, are created primarily as administrative subdivisions of the state for the better carrying on of governmental activities of statewide interest and importance, such as the assessment and collection of taxes, provision of educational facilities and health services, and the enforcement of state

[2] Roger W. Cooley, *Handbook of the Law of Municipal Corporations* (St. Paul, Minn., West, 1914), p. 10.

[3] Art. I, sec. 10.

[4] Governmental units failing to meet the standards required for classification as municipal corporations are sometimes characterized as quasi corporations rather than quasi-municipal corporations. The present writer, however, believes the latter term to be more accurately descriptive and therefore preferable, since it appears that the units concerned are properly to be regarded as genuine public corporations, though lacking certain of the qualities of the true municipal corporation.

law. At times the courts have insisted that quasi-municipal corporations exist *solely* as state agencies; and where, as is more commonly the case, they recognize that certain functions carried on by these units are essentially local in character, they seldom fail to emphasize that such activities are merely secondary and incidental to the primary function of serving the state in an administrative capacity.

Cities, together with lesser municipalities variously designated as villages, towns, and boroughs, are classified as municipal corporations, but in most states all other local units are considered as falling within the quasi-municipal category. Nearly a century ago, in a case which has since been widely cited with approval, the Ohio supreme court distinguished counties from true municipal corporations in the following words: [5]

> Municipal corporations proper are called into existence, either at the direct solicitation or by the free consent of the people who compose them.
>
> Counties are local subdivisions of a state, created by the sovereign power of the state, of its own sovereign will, without the particular solicitation, consent, or concurrent action of the people who inhabit them. The former organization is asked for, or at least assented to by the people it embraces; the latter is superimposed by a sovereign and paramount authority.
>
> A municipal corporation proper is created mainly for the interest, advantage, and convenience of the locality and its people; a county organization is created almost exclusively with a view to the policy of the state at large, for purposes of political organization and civil administration, in matters of finance, of education, of provision for the poor, of military organization, of the means of travel and transport, and especially for the general administration of justice. With scarcely an exception, all the powers and functions of the county organization have a direct and exclusive reference to the general policy of the state, and are, in fact, but a branch of the general administration of that policy.

Many years later the nature of the county as a quasi-municipal corporation was described in somewhat similar terms by the supreme court of Illinois: [6]

> Municipal corporations are those called into existence either at the direct request or by consent of the persons composing them. *Quasi*-municipal corporations, such as counties and townships, are at most but local organizations, which are created by general law, without the consent of the inhabitants thereof, for the purpose of the civil and political administration of government, and they are invested with but few characteristics of corporate existence. They are, in other words, local subdivisions of the State created by the sovereign power of the State of its own will, without regard to the wishes of the people inhabiting them. A municipal corporation is created principally for the advantage and convenience of the people of the locality. County and township organizations are created in this State with a view to aid in carrying out the policy of the State at large for the administration of matters of political government, finance, education, taxing, care of the poor, military organizations, means of travel and the administration of justice. The powers and functions of county and township

[5] Commissioners of Hamilton County *v.* Mighels, 7 Ohio St. 109, 118-119 (1857).

[6] County of Cook *v.* City of Chicago, 311 Ill. 234, 239-240 (1924).

organizations, therefore, as distinguished from municipal corporations, have a direct and exclusive bearing on and reference to the general, rather than local, policy of government of the State.

And still more recently the supreme court of Alabama has declared: [7]

It is well settled in this jurisdiction that while a county has corporate characteristics, it is not, strictly speaking, a municipal corporation as is a city or town. A county is an involuntary political or civil subdivision of the state, created to aid in the administration of the government. It is an arm of the state, through which the state operates for convenience in the performance of its governmental function.

As suggested in the above statement by the Illinois supreme court, townships of the midwestern variety are usually classified along with counties as quasi-municipal corporations. New England towns, though in many respects resembling true municipal corporations, are ordinarily accorded the same legal status as counties and townships. Also generally classified as quasi-municipal corporations are school districts, park districts, sanitary districts, and the varied array of districts formed for other special purposes.[8]

In a few states, contrary to the more common practice, counties and townships are considered as municipal corporations proper, and a like status is occasionally accorded to units of the other types ordinarily classed as quasi-municipal. With appropriate allowance made for such deviations from the general rule, public corporations may be classified in the following manner:

1. Municipal corporations:
   a. Cities
   b. Villages
   c. Towns (as equivalent of villages)
   d. Boroughs
2. Quasi-municipal corporations:
   a. Counties
   b. Townships
   c. Towns (New England variety)
   d. Special districts

Thus it appears that all governmental units of a strictly rural character—those with which this book is primarily concerned—are treated in most states as belonging to the quasi-municipal category.

Though the distinction between municipal corporations proper and quasi-municipal corporations is firmly embedded in American law and unlikely soon to be discarded, its practical significance is steadily declining. Actually, many counties and townships have been established at the

[7] Moore *v.* Walker County, 236 Ala. 688, 690 (1938).
[8] Cf. Cooley, *op. cit.*, pp. 493-496.

instigation of local inhabitants; and the will of the local electorate is today quite commonly taken into account in the establishment of special districts. No longer can it be said, if indeed it ever could be said realistically, that quasi-municipal corporations serve *exclusively* as state agencies. Both municipal and quasi-municipal corporations ordinarily serve at the same time as state administrative areas *and* as organs of local self-government. The difference between the two is at most one of degree only: the quasi-municipal corporation is *primarily* an administrative subdivision of the state, and the true municipal corporation is *primarily* an instrumentality of local government. As counties and townships, during recent decades, have increasingly been authorized to exercise powers and perform services similar to those of cities and villages, their differentiation from genuine municipal corporations has become progressively less distinct. Even in the matter of tort liability, where the traditional distinction is still applied with much of its original vigor,[9] its importance is gradually waning as quasi-municipal corporations are increasingly held liable in connection with functions which would be considered as "corporate" in nature and therefore involving liability if performed by municipal corporations. All in all, though retaining some of its traditional significance in local government law, the distinction between municipal and quasi-municipal corporations is today of diminishing usefulness to students of government.[10]

CREATION AND DISSOLUTION

In a few states, counties are established and their boundaries defined by constitutional provision.[11] Elsewhere these major subdivisions, as is true of other types of local units in all states, are established under legislative authority, either directly by legislative enactment or by local action pursuant to power conferred by statute. Except as limited by constitutional provision, the power of a state legislature to create local governmental units of whatever character is complete and plenary. Though some state constitutions expressly authorize the creation of counties and other political subdivisions, it appears that the legislature possesses power to take

[9] See below, "Liability of Local Units."

[10] Cf. Jefferson B. Fordham, *Local Government Law* (Brooklyn, N. Y., Foundation Press, 1949), pp. 15-17.

[11] The power of a constitutional convention to create counties was questioned before the Oklahoma supreme court in 1907. In considering this power on the part of a convention the court said: "In the absence of any express prohibition upon the convention, it had full and complete power to establish and define all the counties in the proposed state, as a necessary incident to the formation of a state government. The power to form a state government clearly implies the power to create and define every county within the limits of the new state . . ."—Frantz *v.* Autry, 18 Okla. 561, 618 (1907). One limitation in this respect, relative to the Osage Indian Reservation, had been imposed upon the convention by the congressional enabling act.

such action without express grant. Although, for example, the Mississippi constitution of 1868 authorized the legislature to provide for the organization of new counties and for altering the boundaries of existing counties, the supreme court of that state declared that "without an express grant of power in the constitution it would have been entirely competent for the legislature to form new counties and alter the boundaries of others at its pleasure." [12]

Most counties have been created directly by statutory enactment, as have also the towns of New England; and this was once the generally accepted method of establishing municipalities. Today, however, new counties are seldom organized,[13] and other local units, except in the dozen or so states where special legislation is still permitted,[14] are ordinarily created by local action under statutory authority. In the township states of the Midwest statutory provision is commonly made for the laying out of townships and subsequent alteration of their boundaries by action of the governing bodies of the respective counties.[15] As in the case of counties, most present-day townships have been in existence for a considerable time, and even changes in their boundaries are now relatively infrequent. Municipalities and special-purpose districts are sometimes created by special legislative act but, in a majority of the states, are now more commonly established by local petition and vote under authority of state enabling legislation, which, in form at least, is of general application. However established, whether by constitutional provision, by legislative enactment, or by local action under legislative authority, local-government units of all kinds, as public corporations, are mere creatures of the state, existing at its will and subject to its absolute control.

From the principle that local governments can be created only by virtue of state action and, once established, are subject to complete state control flows the corollary that their corporate existence may be terminated only by state authority. As the state breathes the breath of life into these subdivisions, so it, and it alone, is competent to bring their legal existence to an end. The rule of law is well established that a governmental corporation cannot, in the absence of authorization from the parent state, cease to exist of its own volition; nor does the mere failure to exercise corporate powers or to elect officers operate to dissolve the legal entity. Though a corporation may become dormant or have its functions suspended for

[12] Portwood *v.* Board of Supervisors of Montgomery County, 52 Miss. 523, 528 (1876).

[13] The first new county to be created in many years was established in 1949 in the area embracing the federal government's atomic energy installation in New Mexico. Created by special act of the New Mexico legislature, the new county of Los Alamos, with its county seat at Los Alamos, was formed from portions of the counties of Sandoval and Sante Fe—*Laws of New Mexico* (1949), chap. 134.

[14] See below, "Special Legislation."

[15] In some instances petition by local voters is made prerequisite to county board action.

want of population or of officers, it can be dissolved only as the result of state authorization or consent.[16]

In dissolving or deorganizing local governmental units, as in the matter of their creation, state legislatures possess plenary power, except as their authority may be limited by constitutional provision.[17] General statutes authorizing the establishment of units by local petition and vote commonly provide for their deorganization in a similar manner. On the other hand, in states where special legislation still prevails, deorganization is usually effected or assented to in each individual case by specific legislative enactment. When deorganization occurs, services formerly provided by the unit abolished are usually supplied in the unorganized territory by a designated neighboring or overlying unit. At times, the deorganizing unit becomes merged with, and a part of, a neighboring unit of like nature, in which event the process is properly characterized as consolidation.

County deorganization, notwithstanding the existence of a considerable body of enabling legislation, in practice, has been of rare occurrence. Deorganization of townships and towns, though not common, has taken place somewhat more frequently. During the depression years of the 1930's, for instance, a number of Minnesota townships were deorganized by local action pursuant to statute; and various Maine towns have vacated their charters and reverted to unorganized status under the terms of special legislative acts granting the necessary permission.[18] Municipalities and special districts are dissolved from time to time, though apparently on numerous occasions such corporations, upon becoming dormant through population loss or otherwise, have remained in that state indefinitely without going through the process of formal deorganization.

FORMS OF BASIC LAW

Every government rests on a body of basic law which prescribes its organization and determines its powers. In the case of the nation and the respective states, this fundamental law is called a constitution. At the local level use is frequently made of the term *charter.* If the term is defined broadly enough to include all the legal rules determining the organization and powers of a local governmental unit, regardless of their form or where they are found, then every unit possesses a charter. Often, however, the term is employed with a more restricted meaning to designate only those charters which have been framed and adopted by local action under authority conferred by direct constitutional grant or to include, at most, in

[16] Cf. Beale *v.* Pankey, 107 Va. 215 (1907).

[17] The terms *dissolution* and *deorganization* tend to be used interchangeably to designate the process whereby local units are abolished, and they are so employed here. Cf. William S. Carpenter, *Problems in Service Levels* (Princeton, Princeton University Press, 1940), p. 95.

[18] See below, chap. 20, "Deorganization."

addition to such home-rule charters, those granted to particular units by special acts of the state legislature or selected by local units from alternative plans of government offered through optional legislation. In this narrower sense of the term, only a minority of all municipalities and a mere sprinkling of other local units have basic laws that would be characterized as charters. The basic laws of other local governments, including most rural units as well as a majority of all municipalities, consist of provisions, sometimes widely scattered, in state constitutions and statutes.

Though constitutional provisions are important, and in the case of counties are rather extensive, by far the major portion of legal provisions concerning the organization and powers of local governments is to be found in statutes enacted by the state legislatures. Some of these statutes apply to all units of a given category (counties, for example, or townships); some are special acts applying only to individual units; others classify units of a particular kind according to population or on some other basis and make different provision for those of each class; and still others are of optional nature, offering provisions which individual units may adopt or not, as they see fit. In over-all view, then, the basic legal provisions determining the organization and powers of local governmental units may be said to consist of:

1. State constitutional provisions
2. State statutes
    a. Special acts
    b. General laws
    c. Classification statutes
    d. Optional laws
3. Home-rule charters

Constitutional provisions apart, it should be noted that a particular state, in providing for the organization and functioning of local governments, does not ordinarily use a single form of basic law to the exclusion of all others. Most states employ *primarily* either special legislation, general laws, or classification statutes; but many provide, as alternatives, either optional-charter laws or the privilege of framing home-rule charters, or both.

CONSTITUTIONAL PROVISIONS

Though systems of local government in the respective states are, for the most part, the product of legislative action, state constitutions contain various provisions on the subject, and these, to some degree, determine the framework within which the legislatures must act. Counties in a number of states, and townships in a few, are given specific constitutional recognition as legal subdivisions of the state and therefore could not be entirely eliminated, even if it were thought desirable to do so, without constitutional amendment.[19] In other instances these units are firmly embedded in the governmental system by provisions such as those requiring that members of the state legislature be elected from counties and justices of the peace from townships. Many constitutions contain restrictive provisions applicable to local governments generally, among the most common being those which prohibit state legislatures from enacting special legislation in the local government field and limit the debt-incurring power of local units.

It is with respect to counties and their government, however, that constitutional provisions are most numerous. In a majority of the states the constitution prescribes the circumstances under which new counties may be established and the procedure to be followed in their establishment; and in a number of instances the method of making boundary changes is also stipulated. Most important of all, perhaps, are the provisions establishing county offices and also prescribing, in many cases, the terms of their incumbents. Scarcely a constitution fails to provide for one or more county officers, and in a majority of the states the list of officials so provided is a lengthy one. Though sometimes the method of choosing county officers is left to legislative determination, it is more common to require by constitutional provision that they be popularly elected.[20] The restrictive effect of such provisions upon legislative authority over local government is considered in the following section.

LEGISLATIVE POWERS AND LIMITATIONS

As previously noted, the power of state legislatures to organize and control local governments within their borders is full and complete, except for the limitations imposed by the respective state constitutions, either in express terms or by necessary implication. Within such limitations, the legislative power extends to the creation of governmental units, the determination of their form of organization and their powers and liabilities, the alteration of their boundaries, and their dissolution. In the absence of constitutional prohibition, the legislature may even levy local taxes within a governmental unit and determine the use of the proceeds therefrom. Thus it was recently held by the Alabama supreme court that the legislature of that state was free to levy a sales tax for a designated county

[19] Cf. Howard P. Jones, "Constitutional Barriers to Improvement in County Government," Committee on County Government of the National Municipal League Report No. 1, *National Municipal Review*, suppl., Vol. XXI, pp. 525-542 (August, 1932).

[20] For analyses of constitutional provisions relating to county government in the various states, see William L. Bradshaw, *County Government Manual for the Missouri Constitutional Convention of 1943* (Columbia, Mo., Statewide Committee for the Revision of the Missouri Constitution, 1943); John Paul Duncan, *County Government: Constitutional Data* (Oklahoma City, Oklahoma State Legislative Council, 1948).

without submitting the matter for approval by the voters of that county and even over their protest.[21]

Some of the constitutional restrictions imposed upon legislative authority with respect to local government apply to all or several types of governmental units; others, however, apply to units of but a single type. More than 30 state constitutions carry prohibitions of special legislation in local government, and these generally apply to units of most or all kinds. Also, frequently of general application are the limitations on bonded indebtedness imposed upon local units in a majority of the states. To the extent that debt limits for local governments are prescribed by constitutional provision, legislative authority to confer local borrowing power is correspondingly restricted.[22] In addition to such restrictions of fairly general application, many states contain provisions relating to units of a particular class or category. Most of these provisions relate to counties and concern such matters as the creation of new counties, the alteration of county boundaries, and the organizational framework of county government. Subject to the requirement, in states where special legislation is prohibited, that they act through statutes which the courts will accept as being general or at least nonspecial in nature, state legislatures are relatively free to provide as they will for the creation and government of municipalities and special-purpose districts. Save for the fact that a few states make provision in their constitutions for township officers, the same is true in somewhat lesser degree of the legislative power with respect to townships and their government. In dealing with counties and county government, on the other hand, the legislative power in most states is seriously circumscribed by constitutional limitations.

In the few instances in which division of the state into counties is made in the constitution itself, new counties may be created or county boundaries altered only by constitutional amendment unless authority to take such action is expressly conferred upon the legislature by constitutional provision.[23] Where, as is much more commonly the case, establishment of counties and the regulation of their boundaries is left to legislative action, the legislature's power is usually limited in various respects by constitutional restrictions. Many constitutions provide that a new county must have a specified minimum area; some fix a minimum population; and a few set a minimum assessed valuation. In a third or more of the states there is a requirement that the establishment of a new county or the effecting of any boundary change be approved by the local voters in a referendum election. Another fairly common provision is that territory

[21] Bonds *v.* State Department of Revenue, 254 Ala. 553 (1950).

[22] The limit is usually expressed as a percentage of the assessed valuation of taxable property.

[23] The Oklahoma constitution divides the state into counties but then stipulates that the legislature shall provide by general laws for creation of new counties and for altering county lines.

taken from a given county, either to form a new county or to be added to another, shall be liable for its proportionate share of any pre-existing indebtedness of the county from which taken. A majority of the constitutions provide that a county seat may be removed from one location to another only with the approval of the county voters.

Of more present-day importance than requirements relating to the creation of new counties and the changing of county boundaries and county seats are constitutional provisions concerning county officers. In many states the form of county governing body is prescribed in the constitution, and in some instances its exact composition is decreed. Most constitutions require the election in every county of an enumerated list of administrative and judicial officers. Though the length of this list varies from state to state, the number is rarely less than four or five and in some instances reaches ten or more. Offices thus established in the constitution cannot be abolished or consolidated by the legislature unless the necessary authority is specifically conferred by constitutional provision. Furthermore, where the constitution prescribes popular election, the legislature is powerless to make an office appointive; and thus the evils of the long ballot are accorded a fortified position against legislative attack.[24] Some constitutions, by declaring that the legislature shall provide for the *election* of such county officers as may be necessary, make it impossible to provide for filling by appointment even those offices which are established by statute. A provision of this nature in Nebraska, for example, caused the state supreme court to declare unconstitutional an optional statute permitting counties to adopt the manager form of government with the manager, as is usual under that type of organization, appointed by the county board.[25]

In establishing county offices constitutions ordinarily do not prescribe their powers and duties, and in these matters, therefore, the legislatures usually enjoy broad discretion. This discretion, however, has been considerably curtailed in some states by judicial interpretation. In these states the courts take the view that when an office known to the common law is provided for in a state constitution, it is vested by implication with all of its common-law powers and duties and, therefore, that although the legislature is free to confer additional powers and duties, it may not deprive the office of its common-law functions and devolve them upon an agency established by legislative authority. At times it has even been held that offices unknown to the common law may not, if given constitutional status, be deprived of their "usual" powers.

In Illinois, doctrines of the kind referred to in the preceding paragraph have been applied to the offices of sheriff, county clerk, and county treasurer. Among the common-law powers and duties of the sheriff of which

[24] See below, chap. 11, "The Task of the Local Voter."

[25] State *v.* Tusa, 130 Neb. 528 (1936).

he may not be deprived by statute are the care and custody of the courthouse and jail and the service of court process.[26] Thus, in interpreting an Illinois statute which authorized the county judge to issue a venire and deliver the same to the sheriff or coroner, the state supreme court held that the act must be construed as authorizing delivery to the coroner only if the sheriff is disqualified within the terms of the statutory provision that the coroner shall act as sheriff in case of the latter's disqualification. In the opinion of the court the alternative interpretation, namely, that the act conferred discretion upon the judge to deliver the venire to either the sheriff or the coroner at his option, would have rendered the statute invalid as an unconstitutional attempt to abridge the common-law powers vested in the sheriff by constitutional implication.[27] By similar reasoning, the Illinois courts have concluded that the county clerk may not be deprived by statute of the duty of serving as custodian of documents and records relating to business of the county board; [28] nor may the county treasurer be interfered with in his control over public funds entrusted to his care. In accordance with this view it has been held, for instance, that the treasurer cannot be compelled by law to deposit county funds in a bank or banks designated by a board of county officials, even though the treasurer is himself a member of the board.[29]

Several constitutions, not content with a mere prohibition of special legislation, require that the form of county government provided by the legislature be uniform throughout the state or that it be "as nearly uniform as practicable." Idaho, for example, has a provision that the legislature shall establish "a system of county governments which shall be uniform throughout the state." Wisconsin's constitution declares that "the legislature shall establish but one system of town and county government, which shall be as nearly uniform as practicable." In view of this provision the Wisconsin supreme court, in 1934, declared unconstitutional a statute which would have permitted any county (other than Milwaukee) so choosing to be governed by a board of commissioners with members elected from commissioner districts instead of the usual board of supervisors composed of representatives from townships and municipalities. In the opinion of the court the commission plan constituted an additional *system* of government contrary to the constitutional requirement that there be but a single system; but, said the court, even if the view were

[26] County of McDonough *v.* Thomas, 84 Ill. App. 408 (1899); County of Edgar *v.* Middleton, 86 Ill. App. 502 (1899); People *v.* Board of Commissioners of Cook County, 397 Ill. 293 (1947).

[27] People *v.* Clampitt, 362 Ill. 534 (1936).

[28] Moffett *v.* Hicks, 229 Ill. App. 296 (1923).

[29] People *v.* West Englewood Trust and Savings Bank, 353 Ill. 451 (1933). On the other hand, see Schultz *v.* Milwaukee County, 245 Wis. 111 (1944), sustaining the power of the Wisconsin legislature to transfer the holding of inquests in Milwaukee county from the constitutionally provided elective coroner to a medical examiner appointed by the county board of supervisors.

taken that the legislation merely modified the existing system rather than establishing a new one, in offering an optional form of government so different from the form already provided it would still have been invalid as violating the requirement that the single system be as nearly uniform as practicable.[30] The effectiveness of uniformity requirements as limitations on legislative action depends in the last analysis, as does the effectiveness of constitutional provisions generally, upon their interpretation by the courts. Though in general such requirements operate to restrict the legislature more severely than do prohibitions of special legislation, instances are not wanting in which some differential treatment of counties has been sustained even in states with uniformity provisions.[31]

Still other restrictions on legislative authority are found in the constitutions of various states. A dozen or so constitutions, for example, impose limitations on county tax rates; some prescribe the fee system as the basis for compensating county officers; and a few set limitations on county salaries.[32] Finally, it should be noted that provisions, found in a half-dozen states, conferring charter-making authority on some or all counties, operate as a limitation on legislative action. To the extent that these home-rule provisions vest in the local electorate authority to determine the forms of county government, the power of the state legislature in such matters is correspondingly reduced.[33]

In the light of these general considerations concerning legislative powers and limitations, attention will now be given to the various forms of statutory enactment employed by state legislatures in exercising their authority in local government.

SPECIAL LEGISLATION

During the early years of our national history, state legislatures commonly created political subdivisions and provided for their government by means of special statutes, each directed to a specifically named county, municipality, or other unit. This practice of dealing with local governments through special laws had the obvious merit of affording flexibility, since it was possible to provide for each locality in accordance with its peculiar needs. Offsetting this advantage, however, was the fact that the system opened the door to favoritism and discrimination and, what was perhaps even more serious, imposed a very heavy burden upon the legislative body. A great deal of the legislature's time, which should have been devoted to matters of state-wide concern, was spent in granting and amending local charters and legislating on local affairs in their manifold

[30] State ex rel. Adams *v.* Radcliffe, 216 Wis. 356 (1934).
[31] See below, "Classification Statutes."
[32] The fee system and its attendant evils are considered below, chap. 6.
[33] See below, chap. 4, "Constitutional Home Rule."

aspects. When it is remembered that special legislation during this period was not limited to matters of local government but was widely used also for such private purposes as changing the names of persons and granting divorces, it will be realized that a large proportion of legislative time was frittered away on matters that were, from the standpoint of the state at large, relatively trivial.

In view of these evils, it is not surprising that the system of special legislation gradually fell into disfavor and that demand arose that the power of state legislatures to enact special and private laws be curtailed by constitutional provision. This demand for constitutional restrictions reached its height in the middle decades of the last century. New constitutions adopted during this period usually contained prohibitions of special legislation, and some states that did not frame new constitutions adopted restrictive amendments. As would be expected, these constitutional provisions show considerable variation in their nature, their phraseology, and the subjects to which they apply. Among the most common provisions, so far as local government is concerned, are those prohibiting special or local laws incorporating municipalities, regulating county or township affairs, or changing county seats. One of the more comprehensive prohibitions, in its application to local government, is that contained in Minnesota's constitution of 1857. The Minnesota constitution declares:[34]

> The legislature shall pass no local or special law regulating the affairs of, or incorporating, erecting or changing the lines of, any county, city, village, township, ward or school district, or creating the offices, or prescribing the powers and duties of the officers of, or fixing or relating to the compensation, salary or fees of the same, or the mode of election or appointment thereto . . . regulating the powers, duties and practice of justices of the peace, magistrates and constables . . . locating or changing county seats; regulating the management of public schools, the building or repairing of schoolhouses, and the raising of money for such purposes . . .

Although some of the prohibitory provisions are considerably narrower in scope than that of Minnesota, about three fourths of the state constitutions today restrict in some measure the power of the legislature to enact special laws relating to local government.

It must not be concluded, however, that constitutional restrictions have completely eliminated special legislation concerning local affairs. Indeed, special laws continue to constitute a considerable portion of the basic legislation in this field. The constitutions of ten or a dozen states in the East and South still contain no provision limiting in any substantial measure the power of the legislature to enact special laws. In one of these states, Maryland, 70 per cent of the bills passed at the 1951 legislative session were local in nature, applying to only one, or at most a few, of the

[34] *Constitution of Minnesota* (1857), Art. IV, sec. 33.

state's counties, cities, and towns.[35] In Georgia, out of 551 laws enacted in 1949, 355 were local in nature.[36] In 1949, Tennessee, another special-law state, enacted more than 1,000 private laws, applicable in almost every instance to but a single city or county.[37] A county in each of the three states just mentioned—Anne Arundel in Maryland, Fulton in Georgia, and McMinn in Tennessee—has recently been granted a manager charter by special legislative act.[38] And throughout the group of special-law states, though general legislation is by no means nonexistent, special statutes are still considered a normal means of dealing with local political units and their governments.[39] Finally, it is to be noted that even in states having restrictive provisions in their constitutions, much legislation that in reality is special in character is enacted under the guise of classification. This method of circumventing constitutional prohibitions is considered in a subsequent section of this chapter.[40]

GENERAL LAWS

General laws for the establishment and organization of local governments, each applying uniformly to all units of a given type, were the most obvious answer to constitutional prohibitions of special legislation. In fact, some constitutions, in addition to prohibiting special legislation, specifically declared that the legislature shall provide by general law for the organization and government of counties and other political subdivisions. Most states today have general statutes relating to the establishment and government of counties, municipalities, and school districts; several have such statutes relating to townships; and many have laws of a general nature covering the creation and government of special districts for various nonschool purposes. These statutes commonly provide that any community, upon meeting stipulated requirements concerning such matters as area and population, may be organized as a county, municipality,

[35] *Local Legislation in Maryland,* Commission on Administrative Organization of the State Report No. 2 (Baltimore, 1952), p. 1.

[36] Cullen B. Gosnell and Lynwood M. Holland, *State and Local Government in the United States* (Englewood Cliffs, N. J., Prentice-Hall, 1951), p. 282. Georgia's constitution of 1945 (Art. III, sec. 7, par. 15), requires that introduction of local or special bills be preceded by published notice in the locality affected.

[37] Thomas G. Roady, Jr., "Special Legislative Acts and Municipalities under the Tennessee Constitution," *Tennessee Law Review,* Vol. XXI, pp. 621-629, n. 1 (February, 1951).

[38] The Georgia statute was couched in general terms to apply to all counties having a population of 200,000 or more—a classification, however, which includes only Fulton.

[39] In addition to Maryland, Tennessee, and Georgia, the states most commonly considered special-law states are Maine, New Hampshire, Vermont, Connecticut, Rhode Island, Delaware, and Florida. See Norman N. Gill and Mary S. Benson, "Classes and Forms of Municipal Government," *The Municipal Year Book* (Chicago, International City Managers' Association, 1945), pp. 90-96.

[40] See below, "Classification Statutes."

township, or special district in accordance with procedures laid down in the legislative enactment. Required procedures most commonly involve local petition, followed by a favorable referendum vote or, particularly in the case of townships and some special-purpose districts, by action of the county governing body. Having provided procedures for the creation of local units, the statutes then proceed to prescribe in some detail what officers they shall have, how those officers shall be chosen, what powers shall be possessed by the units and their governing agencies, and the manner in which these powers shall be exercised. The general laws relating to each major type of local governmental unit commonly constitute a separate chapter or section in the state's revised or compiled statutes.

By dealing with all units of a given type through a single set of statutory provisions, legislatures are relieved of much of the time-consuming burden imposed upon them under the special-law system. General legislation also, by providing uniform treatment for the units of each category, avoids the favoritism and discrimination which inevitably characterize the special-law plan. But in the very fact that it *does* treat all units alike lies the principal weakness of general legislation of universal application, namely, its inflexibility. Whereas special legislation often results in excessive variation in treatment, general laws may not permit enough. Counties differ among themselves, as do units of other types, in such matters as area, population, and property valuation; and these differences are reflected in differing needs with respect to services. General laws tend to force all units of each type into a common mold by providing them with the same governmental machinery and powers. Offices and powers serving small units satisfactorily may be quite inadequate to meet the needs of larger units; and organization and authority designed for the latter may be top-heavy if applied to smaller communities. Variations in the needs of local units with respect to organizational forms and governmental powers should be met by commensurate variations in treatment. It may be fully as undesirable to treat all units alike as to provide individual treatment for each.

CLASSIFICATION STATUTES

The classification system of dealing with local governments represents a compromise between special legislation and uniform laws, permitting more variation of treatment than the latter but less than the former. Under the classification plan, units of a given type are divided into classes or groups, according to population or on some other basis, and different statutory provisions are enacted for governing the units of each class. In some states, the constitutions themselves set up classifications, or specifically empower the legislature to do so, and authorize the enactment of different legislation for the units of each class. Quite commonly, however, classification is effected through legislative enactment without express authorization by the constitution.

Courts take the view that a legislative enactment relating to local government, in order to meet constitutional requirement that it be general, or at least nonspecial, need not be of universal application to *all* units of a given category. Notwithstanding prohibitions of special legislation, the legislature is free to classify counties, municipalities, or other units and to make different provision for different classes as long as the classification is reasonable in nature and all units within each class are treated alike. The question of reasonableness is one for judicial determination, and in deciding how far legislative classification may go without violating constitutional prohibitions the courts have shown varying degrees of lenience. The basis of classification most commonly used, and the one most widely approved by the courts, is that of population. In many states counties and municipalities are divided into classes, usually numbering from three to five, on a population basis. Other states, though establishing no classification for general legislative purposes, enact from time to time laws applying to counties, cities, or townships falling within specified population limits. Though ordinarily each class will embrace several units, the mere fact that a class contains but a single unit does not necessarily render it invalid. In Illinois, for example, many statutes have been enacted for counties of 500,000 or more inhabitants, a classification that includes only Cook County (Chicago). Since, however, Cook County has 20 times as many inhabitants as the next most populous county of the state, its problems clearly are sufficiently unique to justify its being placed in a class by itself.

In passing upon the validity of population classifications, courts have shown a preference for classifications set up in such a manner that as units gain or lose in population, they may move accordingly from one class to another. Thus it is safer, from a constitutional standpoint, to legislate for counties having a population of not less than 40,000 nor more than 50,000 "according to the last preceding United States census" than for counties falling within those population limits according to a specified census of a date prior to the legislative enactment. The former leaves the classification "open," so that counties having less than 40,000 inhabitants at the time of the enactment may, by reaching that population at some future time, grow into the designated class; the latter, however, "closes" the class to all counties but those with the required population as of the specified census date and lends color to a charge that the legislature sought in reality to legislate for specific counties, or perhaps even for a single county, without violating constitutional prohibitions of special legislation. Courts are inclined to look askance also at classifications based upon geographic or other factors which because of their permanence or rigidity tend to exclude perpetually any and all units other than those originally included. This sort of classification is illustrated by an act of the Pennsylvania legislature, passed in 1878, applying to "all counties . . . where there is a population of more than 60,000 inhabitants, and in which there shall be any city incorporated at the time of the passage of this act with a population exceeding 8,000 inhabitants, situate at a distance from the county seat of more than 27 miles by the usually traveled public road." In finding the statute invalid as a violation of the constitutional prohibition of special legislation regulating county affairs, the Pennsylvania supreme court declared: [41]

> This is classification run mad. Why not say all counties named Crawford, with a population exceeding 60,000, that contain a city called Titusville, with a population of over 8,000, and situated 27 miles from the county seat? . . . The moment we resort to geographical distinctions we enter the domain of special legislation, for the reason that such classification operates upon certain cities or counties to the perpetual exclusion of all others. . . . That is not classification which merely designates one county in the commonwealth, and contains no provision by which any other county may, by reason of its increase of population in the future, come within the class.

But although legislative classifications have, on occasion, been declared unconstitutional as special legislation in disguise, the courts in general are loath to overturn such enactments. Notwithstanding Minnesota's elaborate prohibition of special legislation,[42] a law of that state refers to "counties now or hereafter having twenty-four organized townships and a population of not less than 23,500 and not more than 24,000, and a land area of not less than 795 and not more than 805 square miles."[43] And in California, despite constitutional prohibition of local or special laws "regulating county and township business," the legislature has found it possible to place each of the state's 58 counties in a separate class for the purpose of salary schedules.[44] Thus, although classification is advantageous in permitting flexibility in the state's dealings with local governments, the power of the legislature to classify is readily subject to abuse unless the courts are more willing to intervene than they have been in most states. Especially where the legislature is free to classify and subclassify virtually at will, placing a county or other unit in different classes for different purposes, the result all too frequently has been special legislation in the guise of classification statutes. When classification reaches a point where, as in the California example just mentioned, each county is in a class by itself, the legislature is able to legislate for a particular county by refer-

[41] Commonwealth *v.* Patton, 88 Pa. St. 258, 260 (1879).

[42] See above, "Special Legislation."

[43] Quoted in William Anderson and Edward W. Weidner, *State and Local Government in the United States* (New York, Holt, 1951), p. 131.

[44] John C. Bollens and Stanley Scott, *Local Government in California* (Berkeley, University of California Press, 1951), p. 71.

ring to its class or population limits just as effectively as though it called the county by name.[45]

OPTIONAL-CHARTER LAWS

Under the optional-charter system local units are permitted to make a selection, by popular vote, from among two or more forms of government provided by statute. The plan is advantageous in that it combines flexibility in governmental structure with a degree of local self-determination. Optional statutes permitting cities to choose from among the mayor-council, commission, and manager plans of government have existed in a number of states for a quarter century or more; and the optional-law principle has not been unknown to counties. In Illinois, Nebraska, Missouri, and Washington, for example, optional statutes have long been provided, under constitutional requirement or authorization, whereby any county may establish township organization; and some counties in each state have adopted the township system.[46] But it is only in recent decades, and particularly since 1925, that laws providing optional forms of county government organization have gained substantially in popularity. During this period several states, usually pursuant to constitutional amendments relaxing requirements of uniformity, have offered their counties one or more new forms of government as alternatives to the traditional pattern of organization. Noteworthy among the states offering more than a single alternative are Virginia, North Dakota, and New York.

In 1932 the Virginia legislature enacted an optional statute permitting any county other than Arlington, which had already adopted a manager charter provided by special law, to adopt either of two new forms of government. Known respectively as the county-manager form and the county-executive form, each of the plans provides for a principal county executive officer appointed by the county governing board. The two plans differ principally in the fact that under the manager plan department heads are appointed by the manager solely on his own authority and responsibility, whereas under the county-executive form their appoint-

[45] Some states in which there is no constitutional bar to legislating for a specifically named unit nevertheless make considerable use of the classification device as a means of effecting special legislation. In Tennessee, for example, of the 1,000 or so acts of 1949 applicable to a single city or county, more than 300 used population classifications. Roady, *loc. cit.*, nn. 1, 2. Also, see above, n. 38.

[46] See above, chap. 2, "Townships." For the Missouri constitutional provision, see *Constitution of Missouri* (1875), Art. IX, secs. 8, 9. The state's present constitution declares that "the existing organization of counties shall continue until further provisions applicable thereto shall be provided, as authorized in this Constitution;" that "provision shall be made by general laws for the organization and classification of counties except as provided in this Constitution;" and that "alternative forms of county government for the counties of any particular class . . . may be provided by law"—*ibid.* (1945), Art. VI, secs. 2, 8, 9.

ment is by the county board on recommendation of the chief executive.[47] In 1950 a third option, known as the county-board form, was provided. Under this plan, as under the earlier options, the county board appoints an executive officer (called, in this instance, the executive secretary), but most county elective officers are retained, and the executive's authority is much less extensive than under the manager and county-executive plans.[48]

North Dakota's optional legislation, enacted in 1941, permits any county of the state to retain its existing form of organization or to adopt any of three new forms.[49] The options thus offered are known respectively as the consolidated-office form, the county-manager form, and the "short form of county manager." Under the consolidated-office form, the county board is the sole elective agency of the county; and the duties of several of the traditional officers are consolidated in the appointive office of auditor, the incumbent of which is designated as "chief administrative officer." The county-manager option provides for an appointive manager, who, in turn, appoints the heads of administrative departments and exercises general supervision over county activities. Departments of finance, public works, and public welfare are established by statutory provision; and additional departments may be created by the county board on recommendation of the manager. Under the short form of county managership, designed especially to meet the simple administrative needs of small rural counties, the departmental setup is omitted, and the manager himself placed in direct charge of financial administration, public works, and welfare activities.[50]

It is in New York, however, that the greatest amount of optional legislation has been enacted. Beginning with the so-called Buckley law of 1935, which offered the manager plan and a "county president" plan with an elective executive, the New York legislature provided at one time more than a dozen major alternatives in the matter of county organization.[51] These included, among other features, appointive and elective executives with varying degrees of administrative authority and a choice between the usual board of supervisors and a smaller county board. Not content with this generous offering, the legislature further provided that a county might select at will and combine in various ways individual features from two or more of the major options. When all possible com-

[47] *Acts of Virginia* (1932), chap. 368. The International City Managers' Association recognizes both as manager plans.

[48] *Ibid.* (1950), chap. 388. Cf. "Virginia Counties Get Third Option," *National Municipal Review*, Vol. XXXIX, p. 408 (September, 1950).

[49] *Laws of North Dakota* (1941), chaps. 130, 131, 132.

[50] Cf. Clyde F. Snider, "County and Township Government in 1941," *American Political Science Review*, Vol. XXXVI, pp. 1109-1127 (December, 1942).

[51] *Laws of New York* (1935), chap. 948; *ibid.* (1936), reg. sess., chap. 828; *ibid.* (1937), chaps. 862, 863.

binations are considered, it appears that the total number of "plans" offered by the New York statutes in the late 1930's reached several hundred.[52] Notwithstanding this wide variety of statutory alternatives, virtually no action was taken thereunder save for adoption of the manager plan by Monroe County, and in 1952 the optional legislation was revised and simplified. Under the new law, the numerous previous alternatives were replaced by four basic options: (1) a county-president form with an elected executive; (2) a county-manager form; (3) a county-director form—a modified manager plan under which the executive is appointed for a definite term and removable only for specified causes; and (4) a county-administrator form providing for appointment of a nominal administrative officer with limited authority. Some additional flexibility is provided by permitting the county executive and the board of supervisors to make certain further adaptations within the framework of the statute, but the degree of choice is substantially less than under the former legislation.[53]

In addition to states, such as those just mentioned, which offer their counties two or more alternatives to the traditional form of organization, there are several, such as North Carolina, Oregon, and Montana, that have enacted optional manager laws. Though the number of counties adopting newer forms of organization under the manager and other optional statutes has been modest, it appears, in general, that those counties that have used this means of "streamlining" their governmental machinery have been well pleased with the results.

HOME-RULE CHARTERS

Concluding the list of basic laws determining local organization and powers are the home-rule charters framed and adopted by local units under direct constitutional authorization.[54] Such charters have now been adopted by several hundred cities and a few counties, and the number of home-rule governments seems certain to increase in the future. A home-rule charter is framed by a charter commission, sometimes called a board of freeholders, which in all but name is a miniature constitutional convention. The commission varies in size, roughly from five to 25 members, with a membership of around 15 fairly common. Members are ordinarily elected by popular vote, but in a few instances are appointed by the courts or chosen in some other manner. An election for the choice of a charter commission is usually called either by the governing body of

[52] Cf. Elwyn A. Mauck, "Home Rule for Counties Continues Its Progress," *National Municipal Review*, Vol. XXVIII, pp. 89-95, 179 (February, 1939).

[53] *Laws of New York* (1952), chap. 834. Richard A. Atkins, "New County Plans Offered," *National Municipal Review*, Vol. XLI, pp. 288-293 (June, 1952). Provision was made for repeal of the old optional statutes as of 1954.

[54] See below, chap. 4, "Constitutional Home Rule."

the local unit concerned (city council or county board) or by initiative petition, with the requirement in some instances that there first be a referendum election on the question of whether a commission shall be chosen. Home-rule charters in every instance must be referred to the local voters and receive their approval, by a prescribed majority, before becoming effective. Charter amendments in most states may be proposed either by the local governing body or by popular initiative. However proposed, amendments, like the charters themselves, must be ratified by the voters before taking effect.[55] Home-rule charters are ordinarily published in pamphlet form, and a copy of any such charter may usually be secured from the clerk of the city or county concerned.

LOCAL POWERS

Local governments in the United States have strictly limited powers. As the various local units are created by the state, so they derive from the state, either by express grant or by necessary implication, all the powers they possess. They have no inherent powers whatsoever, and even their delegated powers are strictly construed by the courts.

The principle of delegation and strict construction of powers, with respect to municipal corporations proper, has been given its classic statement by Judge John F. Dillon in the following form, frequently referred to as Dillon's Rule: [56]

> It is a general and undisputed proposition of law that *a municipal corporation possesses and can exercise the following powers, and no others*: First, those granted in *express words;* second, those *necessarily or fairly implied* in or *incident* to the powers expressly granted; third, those *essential* to the accomplishment of the declared objects and purposes of the corporation,—not simply convenient, but indispensable. Any fair, reasonable, substantial doubt concerning the existence of power is resolved by the courts against the corporation, and the power is denied.

Substantially the same rule applies to quasi-municipal corporations, which the courts have held again and again to possess only those powers delegated to them in express words or by reasonable implication.[57] Except for the home-rule powers conferred upon certain municipalities and

[55] Cf. Anderson and Weidner, *op. cit.*, pp. 140-141; Austin F. Macdonald, *American City Government and Administration,* 5th ed. (New York, Crowell, 1951), pp. 87-89. In a few states home-rule charters, after popular approval thereof, must be approved by a designated state authority (legislature or governor). In practice, however, such state approval, where required, appears to be granted as a matter of course.

[56] John F. Dillon, *Commentaries on the Law of Municipal Corporations,* 5th ed. (Boston, Little, Brown, 1911), Vol. I, sec. 237.

[57] See, for example, Barbor *v.* County Court of Mercer County, 85 W. Va. 359 (1920); King *v.* Maries County, 297 Mo. 488 (1923); Dodge County *v.* Kaiser, 243 Wis. 551 (1943).

counties by constitutional provision in some states,[58] all powers possessed by the various units of local government are conferred by the state legislature through statutory enactment and may be modified or revoked in like manner.[59]

LIABILITY OF LOCAL UNITS

A final problem of local government law concerns the legal liability of local units for personal or property damage sustained by individuals or private corporations as the result of negligence or other wrongful acts on the part of local officers and employees. The question of liability resolves itself into two principal aspects: that of tort liability and that of contractual liability.[60]

In the tort field, questions frequently arise as to whether damages may be recovered from the governmental unit concerned for injuries sustained from such causes as a defective county bridge, a defective stairstep in a county courthouse, the negligent operation of a city fire truck, or negligence in connection with a municipally operated utility.[61] In the exercise of their broad powers of control over local governments, state legislatures are free to impose tort liability upon local units if they see fit to do so. Some such legislation of a piecemeal nature has been enacted, providing for liability in connection with particular functions, but apparently nothing approximating a comprehensive regulation of tort liability by statute has been attempted in any state. Hence our inquiry becomes limited, for the most part, to the common-law rules of liability, which the courts will enforce in the absence of regulatory legislation.

In the case of municipal corporations proper, the courts emphasize the fact that their governments act in a dual role: as agencies of the state, and acting in a *governmental* capacity, they perform on behalf of the state at large various public services of state-wide interest; and, at the same time, as agencies of the local inhabitants, and acting in a *corporate* capacity, they perform other services of a more strictly local nature and carry on activities similar to business enterprises conducted by private corporations. Projecting this distinction into the field of tort liability,

[58] See below, chap. 4, "Constitutional Home Rule."

[59] New Jersey's constitution of 1947 contains an unusual declaration to the effect that constitutional and statutory provisions concerning local governments shall be liberally construed in their favor; see *Constitution of New Jersey* (1947), Art IV, sec. 7, par. 11.

[60] *Tort* is a legal term used to denote a civil wrong (as distinguished from a crime) arising otherwise than from breach of contract.

[61] On the subject of governmental tort liability in general, see Dillon, *op. cit.*, Vol. IV, chap. 32; Eugene McQuillin, *The Law of Municipal Corporations,* 3d ed. (Chicago, Callaghan, 1951), Vol. XVIII, chap. 53; Fordham, *op. cit.*, chap. 11; Edwin M. Borchard, "Government Liability in Tort," *Yale Law Journal,* Vol. XXXIV, pp. 1-45, 129-143, 229-258 (November, December, 1924; January, 1925).

the courts hold that a municipality, when acting in a governmental capacity, partakes of the state's immunity and is therefore not liable for its torts unless made so by statute. When, on the other hand, the municipal corporation acts in its corporate capacity, it assumes the same degree of liability that would attach to a private corporation under similar circumstances.

Though this distinction between governmental and corporate functions is easily stated, its application in practice involves some difficulty. With respect to certain municipal functions, the courts of the various states are in substantial agreement concerning the category to which they belong; but other functions are considered as governmental in some states and corporate in others. Police and fire protection, education, and health activities, for instance, are almost universally held to be of a governmental nature, and hence municipalities are not liable for injuries arising from the performance of these functions. On the other hand, municipally owned utilities and markets are quite generally held to be corporate. But there is yet a third, or borderline, group of functions, including, for example, parks, street maintenance, sewers, and swimming pools, with respect to which the courts are in disagreement as to their classification, and the matter of liability depends, therefore, upon the state in which the alleged wrongful act is committed.[62]

With respect to most quasi-municipal corporations, the rule has long been established that since these units are exclusively, or at least primarily, mere subdivisions of the state for the performance of governmental functions, they share in the state's immunity and hence are not liable for torts in connection with any of their activities unless made so by statutory provision. Counties, civil townships, and school districts, in the words of the South Dakota supreme court, "are merely instrumentalities of the state for the purpose of carrying into effect the functions of government, and, as such, are not liable for damages caused by neglectful performance of such duties, unless cause of action is expressly given by statute."[63] A county, the Iowa court has said, "is a political body or subdivision, and comes into being as a quasi corporation by statutory enactment. It may sue and be suable because, and only because, of statutory permission."[64] And in similar vein the Mississippi court has declared: "counties are political subdivisions of the state, created for the purpose of discharging public duties, and . . . no suit can be maintained against a county for the

[62] Cf. Charles M. Kneier, *City Government in the United States,* rev. ed. (New York, Harper, 1947); chap. 10.

[63] Jensen *v.* Juul, 66 S.D. 1, 5 (1938).

[64] Brown *v.* Davis County, 196 Ia. 1341, 1349 (1924). Means Johnston, "Legal Principles Governing County Boards of Supervisors [in Mississippi]," *Mississippi Law Journal,* Vol. XXI, pp. 340-359, 353 (May, 1950), states: "At common law a county could neither sue nor be sued, and it is only by virtue of express or implied statutory authority that any action may be maintained either in its behalf or against it."

negligence of its officers unless such liability is created by some statute, expressly or by necessary implication." [65]

The broad immunity from tort liability enjoyed by counties and most other quasi-municipal corporations, however, is not extended in its fullness to the towns of New England. Though usually classified as quasi-municipal corporations, New England towns, as previously noted, bear a closer resemblance to true municipal corporations than do counties and townships; and courts have frequently taken the view that, like municipal corporations proper, towns act in both a governmental and a corporate capacity and are liable for torts committed in performing functions of a corporate nature.[66] The distinction between their corporate and governmental capacities has been stated by the supreme court of Maine as follows: [67]

> The several towns in this state sustain the twofold character of corporations and political divisions. So far as they may own and manage property, make contracts, sue and be sued, they are corporations; but, in matters pertaining to the preservation of the public health and peace, the making and repairing of highways and bridges, the support of the poor, and the assessment and collection of taxes, they are political divisions, established and designed the better to enable the inhabitants to exercise and enjoy portions of the political power of the state.

In line with this distinction, no action lies against a Maine town for what is done by it in its governmental capacity; but "in its corporate capacity as the owner of property held for its profit and advantage, the rights and liabilities of the town are measured strictly by the laws which determine all private rights and liabilities, and under the same conditions as a private corporation." [68]

In the case of Massachusetts towns the rule of nonliability for neglect of duty has been held to apply [69]

> only to the neglect or omission of a town to perform those duties which are imposed on all towns, without their corporate assent, and exclusively for public purposes; and not to the neglect of those obligations which a town incurs, when a special duty is imposed on it, with its consent, express or implied, or a special authority is conferred on it, at its request. In the latter cases, a town is subject to the same liabilities, for the neglect of those special duties, to which private corporations would be, if the same duties were imposed or the same authority were conferred on them—including their liability for the wrongful neglect as well as the wrongful acts of their officers and agents.

And in New Hampshire "it has also been determined that towns possess a private corporate capacity in accordance with which they perform cer-

[65] Pidgeon Thomas Iron Co. *v.* Leflore County, 135 Miss. 155, 166 (1924).
[66] See above, "Legal Nature of Local Governments."
[67] Small *v.* Inhabitants of Danville, 51 Me. 359, 361 (1864).
[68] Stanley *v.* Inhabitants of Town of Sangerville, 119 Me. 26, 28 (1920).
[69] Bigelow *v.* Inhabitants of Randolph, 14 Gray (Mass.) 541, 543 (1860).

tain acts as a private corporation might, and in consequence of which their liability for damages to others is tested by the principles applied to private persons."[70]

Save in some circumstances for New England towns, nonliability for torts continues to be the general rule with respect to quasi-municipal corporations, but there has been some disposition during recent years to depart from the rule on occasion in jurisdictions outside New England when such corporations are engaged in functions similar to those which, when performed by municipalities, are regarded as corporate in character.[71] Furthermore, some state legislatures, in pursuance of their power to enlarge or curtail the legal liability of local governments, have imposed tort liability upon quasi-municipal corporations in certain cases by statutory enactment. Several states, for example, make counties liable for personal injuries or property damage resulting from mob violence.[72] South Carolina provides that "in all cases of lynching when death ensues the county in which such lynching takes place shall, without regard to the conduct of the officers, be liable in exemplary damages of not less than two thousand dollars, to be recovered by action instituted in any court of competent jurisdiction by the legal representatives of the person lynched."[73] Ohio counties are made liable for injuries inflicted upon livestock or poultry by dogs. And in the same state it is provided that "a person bitten or injured by an animal afflicted with rabies, if such injury has caused him to employ medical or surgical treatment or required the expenditure of money," may recover from the county the amount of expenses incurred up to a maximum of $200.00 for each injury.[74]

In the matter of contractual liability, municipal and quasi-municipal corporations are accorded much the same status. In most states both are held fully responsible for the performance of contracts into which they have lawfully entered and must respond in damages for breach of such contracts.[75] The distinction between governmental and corporate func-

[70] Gates *v.* Milan, 76 N.H. 135, 136 (1911).

[71] Cf. Charles M. Kneier, "The Legal Nature and Status of the American County," *Minnesota Law Review,* Vol. XIV, pp. 141-156 (January, 1930). Our concern here is only with the liability of local governmental units themselves as distinguished from the individual liability of their officers and employees. In the absence of statutory provision to the contrary, public officers and employees are ordinarily personally liable for their wrongful acts, whether or not there is liability on the part of the governmental unit concerned.

[72] *Page's Ohio Revised Code Annotated* (1953), secs. 3761.01–3761.05; *Illinois Revised Statutes* (1955), chap. 38, secs. 512-524; *Wisconsin Statutes* (1953), sec. 66.091.

[73] *Code of Laws of South Carolina* (1952), sec. 10-1961. Cf. *West Virginia Code* (1955), sec. 6038.

[74] *Page's Ohio Revised Code Annotated* (1953), secs. 955.29–955.42. Cf. Robert M. Hunter and Ralph E. Boyer, "Tort Liability of Local Governments in Ohio," *Ohio State Law Journal,* Vol. IX, pp. 377-411 (1948).

[75] Dillon, *op cit.,* Vol. IV, sec. 1610; Kneier, "The Legal Nature and Status of the American County," *loc. cit.*

tions has no application in the determining of contractual liability; nor does the state's immunity from suit extend in this field even to quasi-municipal corporations. When a county or other quasi-municipal corporation has entered into a contract pursuant to statutory authority and all statutory requirements of a procedural nature have been complied with, the governmental unit is as fully liable and subject to suit thereon as would be the case if it were a private corporation.

REFERENCES

Books

COOLEY, Roger W., *Handbook of the Law of Municipal Corporations* (St. Paul, Minn., West, 1914).

DILLON, John F., *Commentaries on the Law of Municipal Corporations*, 5th ed. (Boston, Little, Brown, 1911), 5 vols.

FORDHAM, Jefferson B., *Local Government Law* (Brooklyn, N. Y., Foundation Press, 1949).

MCQUILLIN, Eugene, *The Law of Municipal Corporations*, 3d ed. (Chicago, Callaghan, 1949-1951), 20 vols. with cumulative supplement.

Articles

ATKINS, Richard A., "New County Plans Offered [in New York]," *National Municipal Review*, Vol. XLI, pp. 288-293 (June, 1952).

BLAIR, George S., "The Changing Legal Status of Counties," *The County Officer*, Vol. XXI, pp. 92-94 (May, 1956).

BORCHARD, Edwin M., "Government Liability in Tort," *Yale Law Journal*, Vol. XXXIV, pp. 1-45, 129-143, 229-258 (November, December, 1924; January, 1925).

HUNTER, Robert M., and BOYER, Ralph E., "Tort Liability of Local Governments in Ohio," *Ohio State Law Journal*, Vol. IX, pp. 377-411 (1948).

JOHNSTON, Means, "Legal Principles Governing County Boards of Supervisors [in Mississippi]," *Mississippi Law Journal*, Vol. XXI, pp. 340-359 (May, 1950).

JONES, Howard P., "Constitutional Barriers to Improvement in County Government," Committee on County Government of the National Municipal League Report No. 1, *National Municipal Review*, suppl., Vol. XXI, pp. 525-542 (August, 1932).

KNEIER, Charles M., "The Legal Nature and Status of the American County," *Minnesota Law Review*, Vol. XIV, pp. 141-156 (January, 1930).

"Liability of County for Damages Resulting to an Individual from Nuisances," *Tennessee Law Review*, Vol. XX, pp. 619-620 (February, 1949).

ROADY, Thomas G., Jr., "Special Legislative Acts and Municipalities under the Tennessee Constitution," *Tennessee Law Review*, Vol. XXI, pp. 621-629 (February, 1951).

SATTERFIELD, M. H., "Counties in a Straitjacket," *National Municipal Review*, Vol. XXXVII, pp. 81-85, 124 (February, 1948).

WEIDNER, Edward W., "County Reform Run-around," *National Municipal Review*, Vol. XXXIV, pp. 386-392, 400 (September, 1945).

CHAPTER 4

State Control and Home Rule

THE PRECEDING CHAPTER emphasized the plenary power of the states over the creation of local governmental units and the regulation of their affairs. Correlative to this position of supreme legal authority is the duty on the part of the states to provide their local governments with adequate organization and powers and with necessary guidance and supervision in the exercise of their functions. Local organization and powers constitute the major subject matter of succeeding portions of the book. It is the purpose of this chapter to examine some of the legal techniques through which state supervision and control over local government are administered, and to consider the home-rule form of state-local relationship.

FORMS OF STATE CONTROL

All measures of state control over local government have their ultimate basis either in constitutional provisions or in enactments of the state legislature. Depending upon the primary means by which these measures are executed or carried out, it is helpful to distinguish two broad forms of control, namely, judicial and administrative.[1] In judicial control, constitutional and statutory provisions relating to local government are enforced directly by the courts, either in ordinary civil or criminal suits or in special proceedings. Since the so-called local courts are actually units in the state judicial system, judicial control over local government, whether exercised by courts at the state or the local level, is properly considered as state control. As contrasted with judicial control, administrative control involves the primary enforcement of pertinent constitu-

[1] What is here designated as judicial control is called legislative control by some writers. However, since administrative control also has its basis in legislation, the term *judicial control* seems preferable.

tional and statutory provisions by agencies of the executive or administrative branch of the state government—by the governor, lesser executive officers, or boards or commissions of an administrative nature. Action taken by administrative agencies in such matters, however, frequently is subject to ultimate appeal to the courts for judicial determination.

JUDICIAL CONTROL

Questions relating to the legal powers and duties of local governmental units and their officers may be brought before the courts by civil proceedings begun by the units concerned or their officers or by suits against them. If a court finds that an act of a local officer is beyond his legal competence, it will be declared invalid. As previously noted, local governments are usually held responsible for the performance of their contractual obligations and, in some instances, are held liable for the torts of their officers and employees. In other cases, local officers are held personally responsible for illegal action. If local officers commit acts of a criminal nature, they are subject to prosecution in the criminal courts in the same manner as private individuals.

Judicial control over local government is exercised in some instances through the power of the courts to appoint or remove local officers. In Illinois, the governing boards of fire-protection districts, tuberculosis sanitarium districts, mosquito-abatement districts, and most sanitary districts are appointed by the county court. Prosecuting attorneys in Connecticut are court appointed, as are public defenders in the same state, in a number of Illinois counties, and in several communities elsewhere. Scattered examples of court appointment of county officers are found in various other states. In general, however, judicial appointment of local officers is not widespread.

Much more common than court appointment is provision for judicial removal of local officers. Some state constitutions disqualify from holding public office persons convicted of felonies or other infamous crimes, specific provision being made in certain instances with regard to such offenses as bribery, perjury, election offenses, malfeasance or corruption in office, and misuse of public funds. Under provisions of this nature, conviction of a local officer on any of the specified charges operates to effect his removal.

Many states have constitutional or statutory provisions expressly authorizing the removal of county and other local officers by judicial proceedings. There is a good deal of variety in the grounds for removal, but corruption, incompetence, and neglect of duty are among the more common. County officers in Nebraska, for example, are subject to trial and removal from office for any of eight specified causes: (1) habitual or willful neglect of duty, (2) gross partiality, (3) oppression, (4) extortion,

(5) corruption, (6) willful maladministration in office, (7) conviction of a felony, and (8) habitual drunkenness. Any person may prefer the charge, and the district court has exclusive original jurisdiction. Questions of fact are tried as in other actions and, if the accused officer is found guilty, judgment is entered by the court removing him from office.[2] On accusation by the county board or the grand jury, county officers in Oklahoma may be removed for causes which parallel in many respects those in Nebraska.[3] In Nevada county officers may be removed, on accusation presented by the grand jury, for willful or corrupt misconduct in office.[4] County officers in Kentucky are subject to fine and removal for misfeasance or malfeasance in office or willful neglect in the discharge of official duties.[5]

County and township officers in Indiana may be removed by the circuit or criminal court by a proceeding which is known locally as impeachment but which consists of accusation by grand jury and trial by petit jury. Such officers may also be removed by the circuit court for charging illegal fees, for refusing or neglecting to perform official duties, or for intoxication during office hours or habitual intoxication. Local judges and prosecuting attorneys who have been convicted of "corruption or other high crime" may be removed by the Indiana supreme court upon information filed in the name of the state.[6] In Illinois any elective office, state or local, becomes vacant on conviction of the incumbent of an infamous crime or any offense involving a violation of the official oath.[7]

One of the most effective means of judicial control over local government and local officers is through the issuance of certain special or "extraordinary" writs designed to meet situations which cannot adequately be met by ordinary civil or criminal suits.[8] Of particular importance are the writs of mandamus, injunction, certiorari, quo warranto, and habeas corpus. Of these, the most commonly used are the mandamus and the injunction.

MANDAMUS AND INJUNCTION

A writ of mandamus is a court order directing a public officer to perform some duty imposed upon him by law, and an injunction is an order

[2] *Nebraska Revised Statutes* (1943), secs. 23-2001–23-2009.

[3] *Oklahoma Statutes* (1941), Title 22, chap. 23.

[4] *Nevada Compiled Laws* (1929), secs. 10691–10704.

[5] *Kentucky Revised Statutes* (1953), sec. 61.170.

[6] *Constitution of Indiana* (1851), Art. VII, sec. 12; *Burns Annotated Indiana Statutes* (1951 replacement), secs. 49-821–49-837. Cf. Clyde F. Snider, "State Control over Counties and Townships in Indiana," *John Marshall Law Quarterly,* Vol. III, pp. 556-569 (June, 1938).

[7] *Illinois Revised Statutes* (1955), chap. 46, sec. 25-2.

[8] Cf. Lane W. Lancaster, *Government in Rural America,* 2d ed. (New York, Van Nostrand, 1952), pp. 83 ff.

prohibiting the commitment of an illegal act.[9] If a local officer fails or refuses to perform a ministerial duty required of him by the constitution or statutes, the courts may issue a writ of mandamus to compel performance of the duty; when unlawful action by local officials is proposed or threatened, such action may be prevented by injunctions issued by the courts under their equity jurisdiction. Suits for mandamus or injunction are usually instituted by local taxpayers, because of their financial interest, or by other private persons or public officers who have some direct and substantial interest in the matter concerned. Violation of a writ of mandamus or injunction constitutes contempt of court, for which the offender may ordinarily be punished summarily by fine or imprisonment, or both.

The specific circumstances under which writs of mandamus or injunction have been, or may be, used by the courts to command or restrain action by local government officers and agencies are extremely varied. Mandamus has been used, for example, to compel county governing boards to call local tax elections on proper petition, to publish a statement of claims audited, to repair a bridge, to provide a suitable courthouse and jail, and to keep the jail in a condition that will not endanger the lives or health of prisoners. As applied to county treasurers, the writ has been employed, among other things, to compel the treasurer to repay taxes illegally collected and to turn over to road commissioners the proceeds of bonds belonging to them.

Injunctions to restrain local officers appear to be somewhat more frequent than mandamus proceedings to compel action. It has been held in many cases that a taxpayer may sue a local government unit in equity proceedings to enjoin the illegal creation of a debt to be paid by taxation or the wrongful and illegal appropriation, expenditure, or disbursement of public funds. With respect to counties, injunctions have been issued against the creation of a debt in excess of a constitutional or statutory debt limit, the award of a contract in an illegal manner, the entering into or performance of an illegal contract, the allowance of a claim not legally chargeable to the county, the negotiation or issuance of unauthorized bonds, the holding of a bond-issue election without the preliminary proceedings required by statute, the levy or collection of an illegal tax, the retention by the treasurer of commissions not authorized by law, the issuance of unauthorized or illegal warrants, and unauthorized payment of money on warrants or otherwise.[10]

It should be emphasized that mandamus will ordinarily issue only to compel the performance of a clear, ministerial duty imposed by law upon

[9] Occasionally, though not typically, the injunction has as its purpose the positive compelling of action rather than negative restraint of action.

[10] 20 *Corpus Juris Secundum*, "Counties," sec. 296, and cases there cited.

the official or officials concerned. Likewise, injunction can normally be invoked only to prevent the perpetration of an unlawful act for which, if committed, the law affords no adequate remedy. Judicial review of the *discretionary* powers and acts of local officers, as distinguished from those that are clearly ministerial in character, is very limited in scope. With respect to county boards, for example, it has generally been held that "when authority to act appears, a wide discretion in acting should be accorded to county commissioners, where no question of fraud is presented. The courts will not control the discretionary acts of county commissioners done within their statutory powers where fraud or abuse of discretion is not clearly shown." [11] There must be either complete disregard of a positive duty as prescribed by statute or clear abuse of discretion before the courts will interfere. The presumption is that the officers exercised their discretion fairly and reasonably, and so long as the action is "within the express or implied terms of the act granting the power to them and there is an absence of 'fraud, corruption, or unfair dealing,' their acts will not be controlled by any judicial tribunal." [12] As pointed out by the supreme court of Nebraska, with respect to the exercise of discretionary authority by a board of county commissioners, "infallibility of judgment is never expected or required. The most that can be required is that it act in good faith, and not in an unwarranted and arbitrary manner and without regard to the evidence before it." [13]

In upholding the validity of a lease of county property the Nebraska court has held that in the absence of fraud or collusion, a contract made in good faith by a board of county commissioners on behalf of the county and within their powers will not be interfered with by the courts merely because they may be of the opinion that the county might have made a better bargain. "The board may have erred in judgment in looking at the matter and may have made a bad bargain, but there is no fraud or collusion shown; nor has there been a gross abuse of discretion established. The direction of county affairs is entrusted by law to the county board, and not to the courts." [14] According to the Texas court of civil appeals, in denying an injunction to restrain the relocation of a road, the courts are not justified in interfering with the action of a county board solely because they might reach a different conclusion, if the board acted within the scope of its authority. Since the people of the county select the county board to act for them, unless a gross abuse of discretion is shown, the courts are "not in position to disturb the honest discretion so exercised, for, to do so would be assuming to act as commissioners in lieu of the

[11] Bowden *v.* Ricker, 70 Fla. 154, 160-161 (1915).

[12] Bice *v.* Foshee, 97 So. 764, 765 (Alabama Court of Appeals, 1923).

[13] Getzschmann *v.* Board of Commissioners of Douglas County, 76 Neb. 648, 651 (1906).

[14] Lancaster County *v.* Lincoln Auditorium Association, 87 Neb. 87, 93 (1910).

duly qualified and elected officers selected by the voters to represent them in that capacity."[15]

The general rule, therefore, is that the courts will not interfere with local officers in the exercise of discretionary authority vested in them by law unless such officers abuse their powers by acting capriciously or arbitrarily.[16] In its application to counties, this rule has been well summarized by the supreme court of Washington as follows:[17]

> The general rule, of course, is that the discretionary power of the board of county commissioners is not subject to review by the court. But this is not a universal rule. If the action of the board of county commissioners is arbitrary or capricious, or if its action is prompted by wrong motives, there is not only an abuse of discretion but, in contemplation of law, there has been no exercise of the discretionary power. If an honest discretion, as demanded by the law, has not been exercised, the result is to substitute arbitrary action for such discretion. If a tribunal such as the board of county commissioners acts arbitrarily, or refuses to exercise its discretion, the law will by mandamus require it to exercise its discretionary power.

In short, therefore, although mandamus will lie to compel a local public agency to exercise discretion conferred upon it by law, the writ will not be used to control the manner in which that discretion is, in good faith, exercised or the decision flowing therefrom. "Mandamus may not compel the exercise of . . . discretion in any particular manner. It may only direct that the officer act, and must leave the matter as to what action he will take to his determination."[18]

OTHER SPECIAL WRITS

Less frequently used than mandamus and injunction, yet significant in the judicial control of local government, are the writs of certiorari, quo warranto, and habeas corpus. Certiorari is a court order addressed to a lower court that has decided a case, or to an administrative agency that has made a judicial or quasi-judicial determination, directing that the record of proceedings in the case or controversy be certified to the issuing court for review. The writ is a means whereby judicial review is sometimes obtained of certain acts of county governing boards and other local agencies charged with quasi-judicial functions, when those agencies have overstepped their jurisdictional limits or have proceeded illegally or improperly and no other method of review is available. The leading doctrine is that certiorari will not issue to review proceedings of administrative agencies that are ministerial, administrative, or legislative in na-

[15] Wright *v.* Allen, 257 S.W. 980, 986 (Texas Court of Civil Appeals, 1923).

[16] Jeffries *v.* Police Jury of Rapides Parish, 53 So. 2d 157 (La. Court of Appeal, 1951).

[17] State *v.* Maschke, 90 Wash. 249, 253 (1916).

[18] Patten *v.* San Diego County, 235 P. 2d 217, 219 (California District Court of Appeal, 1951).

ture, but only those of a judicial or quasi-judicial character. Within this general doctrine, however, the courts of the various states are by no means in agreement as to the kinds of determinations that meet the judicial test. Some have interpreted the doctrine so broadly as to permit review of practically any determination involving the exercise of judgment; others, however, have followed a much narrower construction. In various jurisdictions the writ has been issued, for example, to review the legality of removals from office, the action of a county board in designating an official newspaper, the action of county commissioners in granting salary increases to county employees, and the action of school trustees in uniting or dividing school districts. On the other hand, it has been held that the writ would not issue to review county-board action in rejecting the bill of a jail physician, fixing the boundary of a drainage district, or designating a state highway, or action of a local board of health in ordering the cleaning of a pond or cellar.[19]

Quo warranto proceedings may be used to determine the validity of local elections or to test the legal right of a person in possession of a local office to hold the same. Thus a person legally elected to an office may invoke the writ to obtain possession thereof and oust an incumbent who continues to hold the office illegally. With respect to officers who serve until their successors are elected and qualify, it has been held that an incumbent official may maintain an action to determine the validity of the election at which his successor is chosen. It is to be noted, however, that although quo warranto is the normal means of testing title to public *office,* it is not available to determine the right to positions, such as those of courthouse custodian and jail physician, which are in the nature of employments rather than offices. In addition to its use in testing title to office, quo warranto may be employed to determine whether a community acting as a public corporation has been lawfully organized. Quo warranto suits are sometimes filed by private individuals having an interest in the matter at stake, but more commonly they are instituted in the name of the state by the prosecuting attorney, either on his own authority or at the request of interested parties.

Judicial review of the acts of sheriffs, jailers, and other local authorities is sometimes obtained through the writ of habeas corpus. This writ has as its object the speedy release by judicial decree of persons illegally restrained of their liberty or illegally detained from the custody of those entitled to have custody of them. It may be used where the restraint or detention is by commitment under public authority or by private parties. The writ affords a means of raising in court questions concerning such matters as lawfulness of arrest, admission to bail, denial of speedy trial by failure to indict, and defectiveness or insufficiency of the indictment.

[19] Cf. John Dickinson, "Certiorari," *Encyclopaedia of the Social Sciences* (New York, Macmillan, 1937), Vol. III, pp. 317-319.

Addressed "to the person who is alleged wrongfully to detain a prisoner," the writ of habeas corpus commands him "to produce the body of the prisoner before a court or a judge thereof at a designated time and place and to show the cause of the detention." [20] Habeas corpus proceedings are commonly used by, or on behalf of, persons held in jail or otherwise restrained of their liberty by law-enforcement officers to secure judicial determination of the legality of their detention.

ADMINISTRATIVE CONTROL

Judicial control over local officers serves as a means of securing obedience to, and preventing or penalizing violations of, clearly defined legal duties. Court procedure, however, is tedious and highly technical, and judges, for the most part, can exercise their powers of control only in cases of flagrant abuse. Thus judicial control, though helping to keep local officers within the law, is largely ineffective as a means of securing competent and intelligent action. Judges, moreover, lack the specialized knowledge of particular fields of public administration needed for the exercise of adequate supervision. Largely because of these shortcomings of judicial control, there has been a marked tendency, particularly during recent decades, to place more and more supervisory authority over local officers and affairs in the hands of state administrative agencies. Administrative control over local government has long been common in England and on the continent of Europe and has now become firmly established in the United States. Though scarcely any field of local activity in this country is today completely free from it, control by administrative agencies has been most widely developed in the fields of finance, education, highways, health, and welfare. Since the spread of administrative control has been dependent, for the most part, upon action by the legislatures of the respective states, it has inevitably made more progress in some states than in others. By and large, however, the tendency today, as has been the case for some years past, is toward a continual broadening of control programs.

State administrative supervision over local government assumes a wide variety of forms. Ranging from mere advisory services through control mechanisms involving varying degrees of compulsion, these include, among others: (1) reports, advice, and assistance; (2) inspection; (3) regulations; (4) appointment and removal of local officers; (5) approval and review of local action; (6) grants-in-aid and tax sharing; and (7) substitute administration.[21] In the discussion which follows, each of these devices will be considered briefly, with mention of typical examples.

[20] Pendleton Howard, "Habeas Corpus," *ibid.*, Vol. VII, pp. 233-236, 233.

[21] Cf. Schuyler C. Wallace, *State Administrative Supervision over Cities in the United States* (New York, Columbia University Press, 1928), chap. 2.

REPORTS, ADVICE, AND ASSISTANCE

Prerequisite to any system of supervision is the collection of information concerning local conditions. This may be secured by reports from local officials, by inspections, and by special investigations. Of these, the requirement of reports is most general and is found in many fields of local administration. Most states require reports on the assessment of property for taxation, and many call for more complete reports on local finances. By the beginning of the 1940's, for example, 23 states required all local units to submit annual reports of their taxes, revenues, expenditures, and indebtedness; and 11 others collected similar data from counties. Some of these, though all too few, published comparative financial data for local governments, compiled from the reports.[22] All states require reports on school affairs; and in practically every state reports are required of vital statistics and information concerning local health conditions. A number of states require reports on county jails and almshouses.

Of major importance, notwithstanding that the element of compulsion is wanting, is the rendering to local governments by state administrative agencies of advice, information, and service. Many state departments and boards give advice and assistance to local agencies, either voluntarily or by statutory requirement. In several states the state tax commission or an equivalent agency holds annual "schools," or short courses, for local assessors, at which the latter are instructed in the duties of their office and the proper procedures to be followed in the performance of those duties. Short courses similar in purpose are sometimes provided by other state agencies, such as departments of health, welfare, and highways, for the benefit of local personnel in their respective fields. Closely related to the short courses are the manuals prepared by some state agencies for the guidance of local officials in the performance of their duties. Some states permit local governmental units to purchase materials and supplies through the state purchasing office and thus to benefit from scientific purchasing procedures and the lower prices that result from large-scale buying. State police frequently give assistance to sheriffs and other local law-enforcement officers in the apprehension of criminals.

INSPECTION

Inspection of local government facilities and activities by state agencies is a widely used form of administrative control. School "visitors" from a state department of education inspect local schools in many states with respect to both physical plant and instruction. State health departments study community health and sanitary conditions to determine whether

[22] Wylie Kilpatrick, *State Supervision of Local Finance* (Chicago, Public Administration Service, 1941), pp. 18-19.

local health officers are performing their duties in a satisfactory manner. Local jails, almshouses, and institutions for children are often subject to inspection by the welfare department or some other state agency.

One of the most important of state inspectional activities is the state audit of local accounts. As long ago as 1940, according to Wylie Kilpatrick, all but three of the states provided some form of auditing service for local governments, on either a compulsory or an optional basis, through state auditors or state-supervised private accountants. Some states extend auditing service only to designated classes of local units, with county audits most common, whereas others extend the service to all local governments. In some instances provision is made for regular annual audits, but in others examinations are made only biennially or at irregular intervals. About half of the states make the cost of the audit chargeable to the local unit concerned, but in others the state itself bears a part or all of the cost.[23] The local auditing function in some states is assigned to the office of the elective state auditor, and in others it is vested in a special state agency. A good example of the specialized type of agency is found in Indiana in the office of state examiner. Assisted by two deputy examiners, chosen from different political parties, and working through a staff of field examiners, recruited through competitive examination but with the provision that not more than half of the force shall be members of any one party, the state examiner makes regular audits of all state and local offices which receive and disburse public funds.[24]

When, as a result of state inspection in any field, practices on the part of local officers are discovered which are inefficient, irregular, or illegal, it is ordinarily the duty of the inspecting agency to take whatever steps are necessary to correct the situation. This can usually be accomplished through administrative suggestions or orders, but if necessary resort may be had to the courts. For example, if a shortage in the accounts of a local officer is revealed by a state audit and is not made good voluntarily, a civil suit may be instituted against the officer or his bondsman to recover the amount of the deficit; and, if evidence is found of criminal intent, the matter may be referred to the regular law-enforcement authorities for prosecution. In practice the recoveries, as the result of state audits, of money illegally or irregularly expended have frequently amounted to substantial sums. It seems clear, however, that, though such recoveries are important, the principal virtue of competent state auditing lies in its deterrent effect upon illegal and irregular practices.[25]

[23] *Ibid.*, pp. 13-17, 60.

[24] The state examiner and the two deputies constitute a state board of accounts, which, with the approval of the governor and the state auditor, prescribes forms of accounts and reports for state and local offices.

[25] Cf. H. K. Allen, *Control of Expenditures in the Local Governmental Units of Illinois* (Urbana, University of Illinois Bureau of Business Research, 1940), p. 14; Snider, *loc. cit.*

REGULATIONS

Another method of control is by means of regulations prescribed by state agencies, under statutory authority, for governing local officers and affairs. A major form of control in this category is the prescribing of accounting and budgeting forms for use by local governmental units. In many states administrative agencies prepare accounting forms for some or all classes of local governments, and frequently the use of the state-prepared forms is mandatory upon the local units concerned. About three fourths of the states provide state-prepared budget forms for some or all local units, in most cases making their use mandatory.[26] Health, welfare, and other state departments frequently prescribe record and reporting forms to be used by, and procedures to be followed in carrying on the work of, local administrative departments in corresponding fields. Public school curricula are rather generally prescribed by state educational authorities.

APPOINTMENT AND REMOVAL

Though local selection and removal of local officers is the usual practice in this country, provisions for state appointment or removal of certain local officers are not wanting and, where they exist, constitute an effective means of state control. State appointment is provided in occasional instances for a considerable variety of local officials in different fields of administration. The appointing power in such cases rests in some instances with the governor, usually subject to confirmation by the senate or executive council; in others with an administrative department or board functioning in the same field as the appointed officer; and in a few instances with the legislature.

Trial-court judges, who though technically state officers are in many respects local functionaries, are appointed by the governor in six states and by the legislature in four.[27] Other law-enforcement or judicial officers chosen by gubernatorial appointment in a few states include prosecuting attorneys, coroners, medical examiners, and justices of the peace. In Rhode Island, where counties are not organized for governmental purposes, local sheriffs are appointed by the governor. Local health officers are appointed in occasional instances by state health authorities, local assessors by state tax agencies, and certain local school officials by state boards of education.

In some cases where the power of appointment is not vested solely in state agencies, state authorities nevertheless share in the exercise of the

[26] Kilpatrick, *State Supervision of Local Finance*, pp. 8-12, 23-24, 55, 62-63.

[27] Council of State Governments, *Trial Courts of General Jurisdiction in the Forty-eight States* (Chicago, 1951), p. 29. Gubernatorial appointment is found in Delaware, Maine, Massachusetts, New Hampshire, New Jersey, and Rhode Island; legislative appointment in Connecticut, South Carolina, Vermont, and Virginia.

power through approval of nominations made by local agencies or the making of nominations for local approval. Appointments in local health, welfare, and assessment agencies, for example, sometimes require approval by the state department operating in the pertinent field; and in other instances the state department certifies a list of eligibles from which the local appointment must be made. Similar provisions are sometimes found in the highway field. Thus county highway engineers in Kansas are appointed by the board of county commissioners with the approval of the state highway commission. In Illinois, county highway superintendents are appointed by the county governing board from a list of eligibles established by the state highway division on the basis of a competitive examination that is administered by the division to candidates originally nominated by the local board.

Provisions for state removal of local officers are more common than those for state appointment. Where the removal power is granted, it is most frequently vested in the governor, but in some instances it rests with other state agencies. In a few cases the power extends to local officers generally, but more often it is restricted to specified classes of officers. Where so restricted, it applies most commonly to law-enforcement officers, but it is sometimes applicable to officials engaged in financial, health, educational, and other activities.

The governor of Minnesota may remove a county officer or justice of the peace when it appears to him, by competent evidence and after opportunity for hearing, that such person has been guilty of malfeasance or nonfeasance in the performance of his official duties.[28] In North Dakota the governor, on competent evidence and after a hearing, may remove county officers for misconduct, malfeasance, crime in office, neglect of duty, habitual drunkenness, or gross incompetency.[29]

In several states sheriffs and prosecuting attorneys are removable by the governor, usually after a public hearing, for such causes as nonfeasance, malfeasance, incompetency, and official misconduct. Another group of states confers the removal power upon the governor but provides that it shall be exercised only with the consent, or at the request, of the legislature, senate, or executive council. In some jurisdictions the removal power applies not only to sheriffs and prosecuting attorneys but to various other law-enforcement officers, such as coroners and constables.[30] A number of states provide that for neglect of duty, local school officials may be

[28] *Minnesota Statutes* (1953), sec. 351.03.

[29] *North Dakota Revised Code* (1943), sec. 44-1101.

[30] John A. Fairlie and Donald F. Simpson, "Law Departments and Law Officers in the States," *State Government,* Vol. XIV, pp. 237-238, 251-254 (October, 1941); John A. Fairlie and Donald Simpson, "Law Officers in Illinois," *John Marshall Law Quarterly,* Vol. VIII, pp. 65-79 (September, 1942); M. H. Satterfield, "State Appointment and Removal of Local Law Enforcement Officers," *Southwestern Social Science Quarterly,* Vol. XII, pp. 277-295 (March, 1932).

removed by the state department of education and local health officers by the state department of health. In some states, as, for example, in Kansas, county highway engineers are removable by state highway authorities for incompetency.

State removal of local officers, by its very nature, is negative in effect, designed merely to check or prevent dishonesty and maladministration. By way of contrast, selection of local officials by state authorities, or state participation in their selection, has as its positive objectives (1) the choice of honest and competent officers and (2) through such choice, the promotion of efficiency in local administration. Because it runs counter to the long-established practice of local selection, direct appointment of local officers by state agencies is unlikely to spread substantially, though it might be justified as applied to some officials who function primarily as agents of the state government. On the other hand, the according to the state of *some part* in the selection process, such as approval of local nominations or examination and certification of eligible candidates, is gaining favor and contributing significantly to improving the standards of local personnel. State participation in the selection of local officials is already fairly common in health, welfare, education, highways, and assessment administration, and it seems destined to be accorded even broader application in the future in these and other fields.

APPROVAL AND REVIEW

Making state approval prerequisite to local action or, as an alternative, providing for state review of local action on appeal, is employed rather extensively as a means of supervision. Provisions for approval or review of local financial activities are quite common, particularly as they apply to local budgets and borrowings. Several states require that all local budgets be submitted to a state administrative board or department for approval.[31] In some instances, as in New Jersey, the supervisory authority of the state agency extends merely to matters of form and legality; but in others, as in New Mexico, the agency also is authorized to pass upon the purpose and amount of proposed expenditures. Some states require state administrative approval of local bond issues. As in the case of budgets, the authority of the state agency is limited in some states to questions of legality but extends in others to matters of policy as well. One of the states where supervision of local borrowing has been most fully developed is North Carolina. There, every proposal to issue local bonds or tax-anticipation notes must be submitted to the state local government commission for its approval. In deciding whether or not it will approve the

[31] For a comprehensive discussion, see Wylie Kilpatrick, *State Supervision of Local Budgeting* (New York, National Municipal League, 1939).

issue, the commission is required to consider such matters as the necessity or expediency of the issue, the reasonableness of the amount, the probable burden of the tax that would have to be levied for repayment of the issue, the adequacy of sinking funds, and the record of the issuing unit with respect to defaults.[32] Though action of the state commission in disapproving a proposed bond issue may be overridden by the local voters in a special election called for the purpose, in practice this has rarely been done.

Instead of requiring state approval of local budgets and borrowings as a matter of course, some states provide for their review on appeal by local taxpayers. One of the older and better known programs of this nature is that of Indiana. On appeal by ten taxpayers of the local governmental unit concerned, the Indiana state board of tax commissioners will review any proposed local budget and tax levy, or any proposal of local fiscal authorities to issue bonds in an amount exceeding $5,000. After a public hearing in the locality concerned on any proposal appealed from, the state board may approve the proposal in its original form, reduce it in amount and approve it as thus reduced, or disapprove it entirely.[33] During the first 11 years of the plan's operation, proposed tax levies exceeding 1,200 in number and proposed bond issues exceeding $73,000,000 in aggregate amount were appealed to the state board for review. Of the levies appealed, more than half were reduced by the state board, with a consequent reduction in taxes of more than $21,000,000; of the bond proposals appealed, a total of over $30,000,000 was disapproved.[34] Iowa provides for the review of local budgets and tax levies by a state appeal board along lines similar to the Indiana system.

With respect to matters less strictly financial in character, provisions for approval or review of local action are by no means unusual. Plans and specifications for the construction of local roads and bridges sometimes require the approval of the state highway department. A number of states

[32] Cf. Emmett Asseff, R. B. Highsaw, and C. E. Looper, *State Supervision of Local Finance in Louisiana* (Baton Rouge, Louisiana State University Bureau of Government Research, 1951), p. 12.

[33] This so-called Indiana plan of state control over local finance has been widely publicized. An excellent account is Frank G. Bates, "State Control of Local Finance in Indiana," in Charles G. Haines and Marshall E. Dimock, eds., *Essays on the Law and Practice of Governmental Administration: A Volume in Honor of Frank Johnson Goodnow* (Baltimore, The Johns Hopkins Press, 1935), pp. 229-268. See also, Carl R. Dortch, "The 'Indiana Plan' in Action," *National Municipal Review,* Vol. XXVII, pp. 525-529 (November, 1938); Edwin E. Warner, "A Study of the Indiana Plan of Budgetary Review," *Legal Notes on Local Government,* Vol. IV, pp. 279-295 (March, 1939). Adopted in 1921, the plan's operation with respect to local tax rates was somewhat modified by the enactment, in the 1930's, of statutory over-all rate limits administered in each county by a county board of tax adjustment.

[34] Philip Zoercher, *The Indiana Plan of Controlling Expenditures* (Indianapolis, 1931), pp. 7, 18. Cf. Snider, *loc. cit.,* p. 566.

provide that local health ordinances must have the approval of the state department of health. It is not uncommon to require state approval of plans for the construction of various local public buildings, such as jails, almshouses, and school buildings. States in which local welfare departments administer federal funds for public-assistance programs provide that decisions of the local departments denying applications for assistance, or approving such applications only in reduced amounts, may be appealed to a state supervisory agency.

GRANTS-IN-AID AND TAX SHARING

The offering of financial assistance subject to specified conditions is a well-known means of federal control over the states and is widely used also in state-local relations. State aid to local governments takes two principal forms: (1) grants of funds to local units from the general state treasury, and (2) the sharing with local governments, according to stipulated formulas, of the proceeds from designated state tax levies.[35] Though state grants and tax sharings are occasionally made available to local units for the support of their governmental functions generally, they are more often provided for the support of designated local services. The grant-in-aid is employed most extensively in the fields of education, health, welfare, and highways; and the most common form of tax sharing is the allocation of state gasoline-tax funds to local governments for highway purposes. State aid is occasionally extended with no conditions attached, but this is distinctly the exception to the general rule. As the price of state financial assistance, the receiving units are usually required to meet standards of service prescribed by state administrative agencies, to submit to state inspection with respect to the activity concerned, and to make a specified contribution to the support of the service from local funds.

In view of the unitary character of the state-local relationship, the states in reality are not obliged to purchase local compliance with their standards by financial subsidies, since they are legally competent to impose directly upon local governmental units whatever requirements they may see fit.[36] However, local officers and citizens are likely to accept state supervision with less complaint when it is accompanied by a cash consideration than when it is imposed in the form of an outright mandate. In practice, the threat of withholding state aid for noncompliance with state-prescribed standards and regulations has proved to be both effective and feasible as a control device.

[35] For comprehensive discussions of state grants-in-aid, see Russell J. Hinckley, *State Grants-in-aid,* Special Report of the New York State Tax Commission (Albany, 1935); Henry J. Bittermann, *State and Federal Grants-in-aid* (Chicago, Mentzer, Bush & Co., 1938). Concerning the respective merits of state grants and shared taxes, and their fiscal significance, see below, chap. 19, "State Aid."

[36] See above, chap. 2, "The State-local Relationship."

SUBSTITUTE ADMINISTRATION

The most drastic form of administrative control is that in which some local service, the performance of which by local officials has proved for some reason to be unsatisfactory, is actually taken over by a state agency and administered directly by its own personnel, but usually at the expense of the local taxpayers. This device sometimes is called "direct state administration" and sometimes, since it involves a substitution of state for local personnel in conducting the service concerned, "substitute administration." This type of state control is intended only as a temporary expedient, and provision is ordinarily made for returning the function's administration to local officials when the situation which occasioned state assumption of control has been corrected.

Substitute administration is most widely used in the public-health field, some 40 states providing that local health activities may be taken over by the state in the event that local health officers fail to perform their duties satisfactorily.[37] The Indiana statute on this subject, which is fairly typical, provides as follows:[38]

> When, in the opinion of the state board of health, any local health authority shall fail or refuse to enforce the laws and regulations necessary to prevent and control the spread of communicable or infectious disease declared to be dangerous to the public health, or when, in the opinion of the state board of health, a public health emergency exists, the state board of health may enforce the rules and regulations of the state board within the territorial jurisdiction of such local health authorities, and for that purpose shall have and may exercise all the powers given by law to local health authorities. All expenses so incurred shall be a charge against the respective counties or cities . . .

In various circumstances, state law-enforcement officials may supersede local officers. Thus, if local officers prove incapable of dealing with emergency situations arising from fire, flood, or other disaster, the state militia, by order of the governor, may assume control. Substitute administration is sometimes used in financial matters. For example, several states, including Maine, New Jersey, and Alabama, have statutes which provide what is virtually a state administrative receivership for local governmental units unable to meet their financial obligations.[39] These laws vary greatly in detail, but the general import of their provisions is everywhere the same. If a local unit defaults on the payment of principal or interest on its obligations, the state supervisory agency may assume control of the collection

[37] Cf. W. Brooke Graves, *American State Government*, 4th ed. (Boston, Heath, 1953), p. 821.

[38] *Burns Annotated Indiana Statutes* (1949 replacement), sec. 35-216.

[39] Some laws of this nature apply to any local unit within the state which is in default, but others are applicable only to units of one or more designated classes, such as cities or counties.

and disbursement of some or all of the unit's revenues and continue its supervision until the default has been removed. In some instances, unsound financial conditions short of actual default provide occasion for the state's assumption of control.

MERITS OF ADMINISTRATIVE CONTROL

The rapid spread of administrative control during recent decades is to be attributed in large measure to certain advantages of this form of supervision over the older judicial form. In the first place, administrative control, or at least the possibility of its application, is continuous. Legislative requirements and restraints enforceable only by the courts through the regular judicial process are applied only intermittently as interested officers or citizens institute suits for their enforcement. In contrast, a state administrative agency charged with enforcing statutory controls is on duty at all times and may usually go into action on its own initiative as well as at the request of interested parties. Again, administrative action is likely to operate more expeditiously. Judicial procedure is slow and complicated, and court dockets are frequently so crowded as to entail long delays. Administrative agencies are ordinarily free to follow simpler procedures, and if properly staffed, should be able to handle their business promptly. In the third place, administrative control is more flexible than judicial. Regulatory statutes are usually enacted in general terms, and courts, in interpreting statutory provisions, lean heavily upon precedent. Furthermore, local needs vary as between different governmental units and with differences in time. Administrative agencies, if granted adequate discretion, are in a position to deal with individual problems of supervision as they arise, treating each according to its own merits. Finally, the administrative branch is the only department of government having trained, professional personnel in those activities that involve state control. Legislators are elected from the general public to represent the voters in the formation of policy; and the principal qualities to be desired in judges are judicial temperament and knowledge of the law. Administrators, on the other hand, are or should be chosen because of their competence, gained through training or experience, or both, in the fields in which they are to work. Local governmental problems, such as those of health and education, are largely technical in nature. The legislature, of course, is the proper agency for determining general policies of control; but of the three branches of state government, only the administrative is equipped to provide the element of "expertness" desired in the day-by-day supervision of local affairs.

Notwithstanding the various advantages just indicated, the success of administrative control over local government depends largely, in the final analysis, upon the personnel of the state agencies in which control powers are vested. If the supervising agencies are headed by politicians and staffed under the spoils system, the theoretical benefits of administrative control are unlikely to be realized in practice. On the other hand, agencies headed by competent administrators and staffed by personnel recruited on a merit basis will go far toward assuring a control system gratifying alike to the local governmental units and to the state as a whole.

COMPULSION V. PERSUASION

As suggested at an earlier point, the mechanisms of administrative supervision and control range from the mere offering of assistance or advice, through devices involving varying degrees of coercion, to the complete superseding of local authorities in the case of substitute administration. In this connection the question arises as to what relationship exists, if any, between the degree of compulsion involved in a particular mechanism and its effectiveness as a control device. Offhand, it might be assumed that the degree of effectiveness would vary directly with the degree of compulsion. Actually, however, it appears that in many instances this is by no means the case. To be sure, such "strong" methods of control as appointment of local officers and review of local action place in the hands of the supervising agency legal authority to substitute its judgment or will for that of the local electorate or officers. But state control programs are administered by officials who, if only for political reasons, are usually not anxious to antagonize local communities by harsh action, even though such action may be clearly within their power. On the other hand, where the element of compulsion is largely lacking, local officers are generally willing, and often eager, to accept instruction, suggestions, and assistance from supervisory agencies. Though they and their constituents may resent state dictation, most local officers are anxious to administer their offices with reasonable efficiency, not only from a sincere desire to be of genuine service but because good administration may be good politics in the sense of facilitating reappointment or re-election.

All in all, it appears difficult to draw any general conclusion concerning the relative effectiveness of different control devices, beyond the statement that authorization of compulsion does not always reflect effectiveness in practice. As Professor Edward Weidner, in considering state supervision in Minnesota, has pointed out, there may be substantial variation between law and practice in control programs.[40] Not only may state legislatures be reluctant to confer the more drastic powers upon supervisory agencies, but where those powers are conferred they may not be fully

[40] Edward W. Weidner, "State Supervision of Local Government in Minnesota," *Public Administration Review*, Vol. IV, pp. 226-233 (Summer, 1944).

exercised. Furthermore, if the ultimate objective of state supervision is to preserve and strengthen local government, rather than to displace it, the milder control devices have much to be said in their favor. As suggested by Professor James Fesler, a preference for the less stringent devices has been implicit in the work of North Carolina's local government commission. Writing after the first decade of the agency's operation, he points out that although the commission's director is empowered to appoint an administrator of finance to take over the fiscal affairs of a unit in default of its obligations, it had never done so. He states: [41]

> The commission's neglect of this power fits in with the basic philosophy motivating all of its work. This philosophy stresses the view that the commission exists to advise, help, and counsel local governments, to provide such central services as those for the refunding and marketing of bonds, and to discourage unwarranted increase of local government debts. These essential services would be undermined if the commission boldly went into defaulting units of government, took the handling of financial affairs out of the hands of local officials, and sent in an agent of the state to collect taxes from an enraged citizenry. The technique of persuasion, rather than that of coercion, is the only method that will work in the long run, thinks the commission.

Such a preference for persuasion does not mean, of course, that coercion is to be denied an appropriate place in control programs. In some circumstances compulsion is certainly justifiable, particularly in connection with local functions in which the state has a paramount interest; and the mere existence of compulsory authority on the part of a supervisory agency doubtless encourages local officers to accept its advice and suggestions. But substantial improvement in local government has been achieved through use of the persuasive devices, and they appear to be gaining steadily in favor. Except where coercion appears clearly essential, persuasion is preferable as a long-term policy.

A STATE DEPARTMENT OF LOCAL GOVERNMENT?

As the preceding discussion has indicated, administrative relations between the states and their local units are now carried on, for the most part, between local authorities and state agencies operating in the same respective fields. For example, the state auditor or tax commission may supervise local finance, the department of health local health activities, and the department of highways local roads and streets. Thus it results that state administrative work relating to local government is widely scattered among numerous state agencies. In large measure this is unobjec-

[41] James W. Fesler, "North Carolina's Local Government Commission," *National Municipal Review*, Vol. XXX, pp. 327-334, 333 (June, 1941). Cf., Asseff, Highsaw, and Looper, *op. cit.*, pp. 14-15.

tionable, since often the state agency best fitted to deal with a particular local matter is the regular department operating at the state level in the field concerned.

But the increasing extent and importance of state-local contacts has led some students of the problem to believe that there is needed at the state level a special "department of local government" to deal with local units in many or most of their contacts with the state. Several states, indeed, have now established special agencies to administer one or more state programs relating to local government, particularly in the field of finance. Maine's emergency municipal finance board, for example, administers temporarily the affairs of cities, towns, or plantations which, while receiving state aid for poor relief, default on their indebtedness or are in arrears on employee salaries or tax payments due the state. North Carolina's local government commission approves local bond issues and exercises other types of supervisory authority with respect to local finance. In Alabama a division of local finance in the state department of finance is charged with a number of duties, for the most part advisory in nature, concerning local purchasing, indebtedness, budgeting, and accounting.[42] Perhaps the state supervisory agency with broadest authority is New Jersey's division of local government in the state department of the treasury. In addition to exercising extensive powers over local governments in fiscal matters, this division is authorized to study all local governmental problems and make reports thereon to the governor and legislature.[43]

Though a single state administrative agency for the supervision of local government seems scarcely feasible, a good deal may be said for a central research and service agency charged with collecting information on state-local problems in all their ramifications and making recommendations concerning state-local programs. The case for an agency of this character has been ably stated by the Committee on State-Local Relations of the Council of State Governments in the following words: [44]

> States might well designate or establish a professionally-staffed office concerned with (a) making continuous studies of state-local relations; (b) publishing relevant facts concerning them; and (c) making recommendations to appro-

[42] John W. Fleming and Roy H. Owsley, "Maine's Emergency Municipal Finance Board," *National Municipal Review*, Vol. XXVII, pp. 143-147, 184 (March, 1938); Fesler, *loc. cit.*; Weldon Cooper, "Alabama Plans Supervision of Local Government Finance," *National Municipal Review*, Vol. XXVIII, pp. 476-477 (June, 1939).

[43] Council of State Governments, *State-local Relations* (Chicago, 1946), pp. 37-38, 48-49. See also, Samuel D. Hoffman, "A State Department of Local Government," *National Municipal Review*, Vol. XXVIII, pp. 348-354 (May, 1939); Asseff, Highsaw, and Looper, *op. cit.*, pp. 17-22. The New Jersey agency, originally established as a department, was given the status of a division in the department of the treasury in 1948.

[44] *State-local Relations*, p. 50.

priate state officers. Such an office could be advantageously attached either to the governor's staff or to the legislative reference service. It needs no statutory authority except the right to collect information. It could perform many services: from encouraging the codification of laws to studying proper methods of distributing state aid; from issuing studies of comparative local costs to devising recommendations with respect to the distribution of functional responsibilities.

Above all, such an agency would serve as a source of information for both state and local officers and would be a valuable tool for supplementing the present segmented approaches to state-local problems. It would supply the needed continuous scrutiny of the entire field. Policy and administration both profit from this type of integrating agency.

CONSTITUTIONAL HOME RULE

Up to this point the present chapter has been concerned with the exercise of state control and supervision over local-government officers and services, and attention has been called to the marked expansion of state supervision, particularly that of an administrative variety, during recent years. Accompanying this expansion of control over local activities, however, has been a tendency to confer upon local governmental units a greater degree of freedom in the selection of their forms of organization. To some extent, as indicated in the preceding chapter, this has been accomplished by statutes permitting local units to make a selection from various optional forms.[45] Some states have gone further, however, and provided still greater freedom of choice through constitutional home rule.

Constitutional home rule is a form of state-local relationship in which local governmental units are granted, by state constitutional provision, authority to exercise certain local powers free from control by the state legislature. Foremost among these is the power of the local units concerned to frame and adopt their own charters and thereby to determine the form and organization of their local government. Provisions pertaining to municipalities usually confer, in addition, rather broad authority to determine and regulate all matters which are primarily of local concern as distinguished from those of general state-wide interest. County home-rule provisions, in contrast, are confined almost exclusively to matters of charter-making and organizational forms and do not carry any broad grant of substantive authority over local affairs generally. The scope of county activities, in home-rule counties as in others, is regulated for the most part by general state law. Even the power of home-rule counties to determine the structure of their government is limited in some instances by constitutional requirement that certain specified county officers be provided for in every home-rule charter. Thus, the California pro-

[45] See above, chap. 3, "Optional-charter Laws."

vision requires that in addition to an elective board of supervisors of not less than three members, each county charter shall provide a sheriff, clerk, treasurer, recorder, license collector, tax collector, public administrator, coroner, surveyor, district attorney, auditor, assessor, and superintendent of schools. These officers, however, may be either elected or appointed, the method of their selection being left to charter determination.

In delegating to local governmental units certain powers by direct constitutional provision, constitutional home rule introduces an element of federalism into what is otherwise a unitary state-local relationship.[46] The federal element, of course, is much more pronounced in the case of municipal home rule, involving as it ordinarily does a broad grant of authority to regulate municipal affairs generally, than in that of county home rule, which is restricted for the most part to matters of structural organization. Beginning with Missouri in 1875, some 20 states have made constitutional home rule available to some or all municipalities. County home rule did not develop until later, and as yet is not far advanced. Six states, however, now grant charter-making power, by constitutional provision, to some or all counties.[47]

COUNTY HOME-RULE PROVISIONS

California, Maryland, Texas, Ohio, and Washington have amended their state constitutions to provide for county home rule, and Missouri included a home-rule provision in her new constitution of 1945. The date of adoption for each state's provision, the counties to which the provision is applicable, and various data concerning the establishment and composition of charter commissions and the ratification and amendment of charters are set forth in Table 2. In all, somewhat more than 200 counties in the six states are empowered to frame and adopt home-rule charters, yet only 13—ten in California, two in Maryland, and one in Missouri—have actually done so. This number, however, is not fully indicative of the interest in

[46] See above, chap. 2, "The State-local Relationship." It is to be noted, however, that whereas the United States Constitution, in establishing a federal system, delegates certain powers to the general (national) government and reserves all others to the subdivisions (states), under home-rule provisions of state constitutions the general (state) government is the agency of reserved powers, possessing all authority not delegated to the subdivisional (local) governments.

[47] In addition, constitutional amendments approved in 1956 authorize the adoption of charters by Dade County (Miami), Fla., and Jefferson Parish (adjacent to New Orleans), La. The charter-making body for Jefferson Parish is established by constitutional provision, but that for Dade County is to be created by the legislature. The grant of power to Dade County appears to include substantial authority to legislate concerning the "affairs, property, and government" of the county. Idaho's constitution confers certain local legislative powers upon counties but no charter-making authority.

TABLE

Constitutional Provisions

State	Date adopted	Counties to which applicable	CHARTER COMMISSION: How obtained	Official title	Number of members
California	1911	All	Referendum election called by (*a*) board of supervisors (3/5 vote) or (*b*) petition (voters equal to 15% of those voting in county for governor in last election)	Board of freeholders	15
Maryland	1915	All	Referendum election called by petition (20% of county's registered voters).	Charter board	5
Ohio	1933	All	Referendum election called by (*a*) board of supervisors (2/3 vote) or (*b*) petition (10% of county electors)	Charter commission	15
Texas	1933	Those with population of 62,000 or more. Legislature, by ⅔ vote, may extend to any county of smaller population.	Petition to commissioners' court by voters who are owners of real estate (number of required signers varies with county population) *	Charter-drafting commission *	3-15 * †
Missouri	1945	Those with population over 85,000	Petition to county governing body (electors equal to 20% of those voting in county for governor in last general election)	Commission of freeholders	14 ‡
Washington	1948	All	Referendum election called by (*a*) county legislative authority or (*b*) petition (voters equal to 10% of those voting in county in last general election)	Board of freeholders	15-25 §

* Statutory provisions.
† Determined, within these limits, by county charter convention.
‡ Equally divided between the two major political parties.
§ Determined, within these limits, by county legislative authority or petition, as the case may be, in the call for election of a board of freeholders.

county home rule, since several other counties—more, as a matter of fact, than those securing adoptions—have drafted charters but failed to obtain the required popular vote for ratification. A general description of the procedures involved in the adoption and amendment of home-rule charters was given in the preceding chapter.[48] At this point, a glance at experience with charter drafting and adoption in the various home-rule states will serve to indicate the extent of the movement and some of the obstacles encountered.

THE CHARTER MOVEMENT

California. California was the first state to provide for county home rule, and it is there that the plan has achieved its greatest popularity. The home-rule amendment to the California constitution was originally adopted in 1911 and, as modified in 1914, still serves as the basis for county charters. Of the state's 57 counties, ten have adopted charters under those provisions and are now operating thereunder: Los Angeles (adopted 1912), San Bernardino (1912), Butte (1916), Tehama (1916), Alameda (1926), Fresno (1933), Sacramento (1933), San Diego (1933), San Mateo

[48] See above, chap. 3, "Home-rule charters."

2

ᵌor County Home Rule

CHARTER COMMISSION		
How members chosen	*How charters ratified*	*How amendments proposed*
Elected	Popular vote (majority of those voting on question) and approval by state legislature (majority of members of each house)	By board of supervisors or petition
Elected	Popular vote (majority of votes cast on proposition)	By county council or petition
Elected	Popular vote (majority of electors voting thereon. If municipal powers are vested in county, favorable majorities are required also (*a*) in largest city of county, (*b*) in area outside largest city, and (*c*) in majority of county's municipalities and townships)	By county legislative authority or petition
Selected by county charter convention composed of delegates from precinct conventions *	Popular vote (majority of electors voting thereon. Unless legislature provides otherwise by 2/3 vote, *separate* favorable majorities are required (*a*) within incorporated municipalities and (*b*) in unincorporated areas)	As provided in charter
Appointed by circuit and probate judges	Popular vote (majority of votes cast on question)	As provided in charter
Elected	Popular vote (majority of votes cast on question)	By county legislative authority

(1933), and Santa Clara (1950).[49] Three of these—San Diego, Sacramento, and Santa Clara—succeeded in adopting charters only after one or more unsuccessful attempts. In addition, at least nine other counties—Kern, Mendocino, Merced, Napa, Plumas, San Luis Obispo, Santa Barbara, Siskiyou, and Stanislaus—at one time or another have established boards of freeholders and drafted charters, only to have them fall short of the necessary popular vote for ratification. Most of the operating charters have now been amended several times.[50] California alone among the home-rule states requires that a county charter, after ratification by the local voters, secure the approval of the state legislature. This requirement, which on its face might appear as a major hurdle in charter adoption, has not operated as such in practice. No county charter approved locally has been denied legislative sanction, the legislature's approval apparently being forthcoming as a matter of course.

Maryland. In Maryland, Baltimore County framed a home-rule charter soon after adoption of the enabling amendment in 1915 but failed to secure its ratification. It was not until 1948 that Montgomery County, after

[49] The consolidated city and county of San Francisco, considered for some purposes as an additional county and for others as a city, operates under a home-rule charter adopted under other provisions of the state constitution.

[50] John C. Bollens and Stanley Scott, *Local Government in California* (Berkeley, University of California Press, 1951), pp. 79-80; University of California (Los Angeles), Bureau of Governmental Research, *County Government in California* (Sacramento, County Supervisors Association of California, 1951).

defeating a proposed charter four years earlier, became the first Maryland county to ratify a home-rule charter and put it into effect.[51] Following a revival of interest in Baltimore County, a charter board elected in 1954 drafted a charter which was adopted by the county voters at the general election of 1956.

Ohio. Ohio's home-rule amendment was adopted in 1933, and in the following year eight counties voted on the question of establishing charter commissions. In four of the eight the proposition was defeated.[52] The other four counties—Hamilton (Cincinnati), Lucas (Toledo), Mahoning (Youngstown), and Cuyahoga (Cleveland)—elected charter commissions, framed charters, and submitted the documents to the voters for approval. In the first three of these, the charters were clearly defeated at the polls, since they failed to receive a favorable majority in the county-wide vote. The Cuyahoga charter, on the other hand, received a favorable majority in the county at large, and for a time it was generally assumed that the instrument had been legally ratified. However, when the validity of the charter was contested in a mandamus proceeding before the Ohio supreme court, that tribunal held that it had not met all ratification requirements. According to the Ohio constitutional provision, a charter which vests in the county government only the usual county powers requires for ratification only a simple majority vote in the county as a whole, and it is this type of charter that the Cuyahoga charter commission had attempted to frame. If, however, a charter proposes to confer municipal powers upon the county, it must receive not only that general majority but three special majorities as well: (1) in the county's largest city, (2) in the county area outside the largest city, and (3) in a majority of the municipalities and townships of the county. In the opinion of the court, though contrary to the intent of the charter commission, the Cuyahoga charter, in conferring ordinance power upon county authorities, making it a duty of the county to enforce city and village ordinances, and providing for county use of a civil service system and the initiative and referendum, operated to vest municipal powers in the county government and therefore required for ratification all four of the specified majorities. Although the charter had obtained, in addition to the favorable majority in the county at large, the first of the three special majorities (that is, in the city of Cleveland), it had failed to receive the second and third, and, therefore, according to the court's ruling, had not met the constitutional requirement for ratification.[53]

[51] Cf. Richard D. Andrews, "County Home Rule in Maryland," *The County Officer,* Vol. XVI, pp. 95-96 (April, 1951).

[52] Harvey Walker, "County Home Rule in Ohio," *Ohio State University Law Journal,* Vol. I, pp. 11-14 (January, 1935).

[53] State *v.* Krause, 130 Ohio St. 455 (1936); Earl L. Shoup, "Judicial Abrogation of County Home Rule in Ohio," *American Political Science Review,* Vol. XXX, pp.

This supreme court decision was a severe blow to the home-rule movement in Ohio. If provisions such as those so considered in this case are to be consistently interpreted by the court as constituting a grant of municipal powers to the county, it is difficult to see how any charter could be drawn, particularly for a large urban county, which would avoid the necessity of clearing the four-majority hurdle.[54] In a populous county such as Cuyahoga, the movement for governmental reform is likely to center in the more highly urbanized areas, and the requirement of the majorities which the proposed charter failed to obtain operates to place a veto power in the hands of the rural voters. Despite this judicial setback, the movement for a county charter has continued in the Cleveland area, though thus far without success. After twice defeating proposals to elect a new charter commission, the Cuyahoga voters chose such a commission in 1949, but the charter drafted by that body was defeated in the 1950 general election. Thus, after more than two decades of experience under its home-rule amendment, Ohio remains without a single charter county.

Texas. In Texas several counties have shown varying degrees of interest in adopting home-rule charters, and about a half dozen have proceeded to the point of establishing charter commissions. Some of these commissions, however, failed to prepare charters or to do so within the allotted time, and in one case a commissioners' court failed to submit a completed charter to referendum. Only a single charter—that for El Paso County—has actually been submitted to popular vote, and it failed to secure the required majorities. Like Ohio, therefore, Texas is a home-rule state that still is without a charter county.[55]

Under the terms of the Texas amendment the popular vote on a proposed charter, unless the legislature by two-thirds vote determines otherwise, is to be canvassed separately within and outside incorporated municipalities, respectively, and for ratification the charter must receive a favorable majority *both* within the municipalities and in the unincorporated areas of the county. When the El Paso charter was submitted to referendum in 1934, it received a favorable majority in the county at large as well as within the city of El Paso, but it did not obtain the neces-

540-546 (June, 1936). Cf. S. Gale Lowrie, "Interpretation of the County Home Rule Amendment by the Ohio Supreme Court," *University of Cincinnati Law Review,* Vol. X, pp. 454-466 (November, 1936).

[54] Professor Earl Shoup has suggested that the question of what constitutes a vesting of municipal powers within the meaning of the constitutional provision is deserving of re-examination by the court. See Earl L. Shoup, "Constitutional Problems of County Home Rule in Ohio," *Western Reserve Law Review,* Vol. I, pp. 111-132 (December, 1949).

[55] Roscoe C. Martin, "The County Home Rule Movement in Texas," *Southwestern Social Science Quarterly,* Vol. XV, pp. 307-317 (March, 1935).

sary vote in the unincorporated area and therefore failed of adoption.[56] As in the case of Cuyahoga County in Ohio, the El Paso charter fell victim to the rural veto permitted under the constitutional requirement of special majorities, in addition to the general county-wide majority, for ratification. Although the constitutional grant of home-rule authority in Texas applies directly only to counties having a population of 62,000 or more, provision is made that the legislature by two-thirds vote may extend the charter-making privilege to any county of smaller population. Pursuant to legislative permission granted in this manner in 1947, a charter was drafted for the small rural county of Delta. However, upon the charter's submission to the state attorney general for an opinion regarding its validity, certain of its sections were ruled by that official to be invalid as conflicting with the home-rule amendment, and the document was never submitted to popular vote.[57]

The Texas home-rule amendment, though itself long and verbose, differs from the constitutional provisions of other home-rule states in that it leaves to legislative determination such matters as the method of establishing charter commissions, the composition of such commissions, and how commission members shall be chosen. The enabling legislation enacted to implement the amendment in these and other respects seems unnecessarily long and complicated. Though the El Paso charter was defeated by an adverse vote in rural areas, it appears that the failure of charter movements in other counties has been due in large measure to the complexity, vagueness, and ambiguity of the constitutional provisions and implementing legislation.

Missouri. Missouri's home-rule provision applies only to counties having more than 85,000 inhabitants and, at the time of its adoption in 1945, only four of the state's counties contained this required population. These were Jackson (Kansas City), St. Louis (a suburban county adjacent to the city of St. Louis), Greene (Springfield), and Buchanan (St. Joseph). Of the four, three acted promptly to establish freeholders' commissions and to draft charters and, though the proposals were defeated in Jackson and Buchanan, the St. Louis County charter was ratified and became effective at the beginning of 1951.

Washington. In Washington, active interest in the home-rule privilege extended by the 1948 amendment seems thus far to have been confined, at least for the most part, to King County (Seattle). A board of freeholders was chosen in that county in 1950, but the charter drafted by the board was rejected by the voters in 1952.

[56] *Ibid.* See also John P. Keith, *City and County Home Rule in Texas* (Austin, University of Texas Institute of Public Affairs, 1951), chap. 5.

[57] W. E. Benton, "The County Home Rule Movement in Texas," *Southwestern Social Science Quarterly*, Vol. XXXI, pp. 108-120 (September, 1950).

PROVISIONS OF COUNTY CHARTERS

Though the 13 home-rule charters vary considerably in length and in the details of their provisions, there are several respects in which they show a substantial degree of similarity. Each charter provides for an elective county governing body, the members of which are chosen in most cases from single-member districts. This governing body consists of five members in the California counties and seven in Baltimore, St. Louis, and Montgomery counties. Most of the charters provide a merit system for the selection of county employees and a majority establish budget procedures. Usually there has been some reduction in the number of elective offices. But perhaps the most distinctive feature of government in the home-rule counties lies in the fact that, in 11 of the 13, provision has been made for some sort of chief executive officer, charged in varying degrees with general administrative authority and responsibility. County managers are provided by charter provision in Sacramento, San Mateo, Santa Clara, and Montgomery counties, and an elective chief executive is similarly provided in Baltimore and St. Louis counties. In five additional counties in California a central administrative office has been established by the board of supervisors and charged with responsibility for administration of various functions vested by charter in the board. In Los Angeles and San Diego counties this official is called the "chief administrative officer" and in most respects approximates a genuine county manager; in Alameda, Butte, and San Bernardino his authority is more restricted.[58]

As indicated earlier, it is ordinarily not possible for a home-rule county, under existing constitutional provisions, to exercise a completely free hand in revamping even the structure of its government. Nevertheless, the range of discretion conferred has enabled charter counties to effect substantial improvement in their governmental machinery. In shortening the ballot, integrating administrative responsibility, and inaugurating the merit system and scientific budgeting, counties strike at the very heart of long-standing weaknesses in traditional organization; and a majority of the home-rule charters have included most or all of these reforms.

CONCLUSIONS

One of the most striking facts concerning the home-rule movement is that nearly all of the counties adopting charters have included urban or suburban communities of considerable population. This, of course, is not

[58] Bollens and Scott, *op. cit.*, pp. 80-87; *County Government in California,* pp. 30-31; John C. Bollens, *Appointed Executive Local Government: The California Experience* (Los Angeles, Haynes Foundation, 1952), pp. 37-38. See below, chap. 7. Fresno County also has experimented briefly with a chief administrative officer.

surprising, since it is in such counties that the multiplicity of public functions and the overlapping and conflict of local jurisdictions have pointed up most clearly the need for reorganization. Of California's ten charter counties, eight have populations of more than 200,000, with that of Los Angeles County exceeding 4,000,000. St. Louis, Baltimore, and Montgomery counties all fall in the populous category, St. Louis having, by the 1950 census, 406,000 inhabitants, Baltimore 270,000, and Montgomery, suburban to Washington, D. C., 164,000. Furthermore, a majority of the counties that have framed and rejected charters or given evidence of substantial interest in charter making without reaching the drafting stage have been relatively populous. This greater interest on the part of the more populous counties, even in those states where the charter-making privilege is extended to counties generally, suggests that the home-rule principle is best adapted to the needs of such communities. To be sure, rural counties in sparsely settled areas have varying needs with respect to governmental organization, but these can be met, and in some measure are being met, through optional legislation. And if, as seems clear, home-rule charters are most needed in urban and suburban communities, one may well question the propriety of ratification requirements, like those in Texas and Ohio, which operate to reserve a veto to the rural minority.

It is sometimes argued that since county functions are for the most part those which the state will control in any circumstance, and since needed variety in structural forms might be provided through optional legislation, home rule as applied to counties has no legitimate place in our governmental system. But, notwithstanding that county home rule is limited largely to matters of structure, its greater flexibility in such matters, as compared with optional legislation, may be advantageous. Even urban counties are by no means all alike with respect to their organizational needs, and home rule can provide a maximum latitude for experimentation. Furthermore, though the proposition does not readily lend itself to conclusive demonstration, something may be said for the argument that home rule, whether municipal or county, stimulates local interest and initiative in matters governmental. Certainly the drafting of a home-rule charter requires more resourcefulness than the mere adoption of the provisions of an optional statute.[59]

In any event, the counties adopting charters up to the present, in general, *have* bettered their organization thereby, and in some cases they might have achieved even greater improvement but for limitations in the constitutional grants. Existing home-rule provisions could be improved; and other states might well consider adopting provisions applicable either to their more populous counties or to counties generally. In the case of provisions of general application it may be assumed, if past experience

[59] Cf. Arthur W. Bromage and Kirk H. Porter, "County Home Rule: Pro and Con," *National Municipal Review*, Vol. XXIII, pp. 514-519, 535 (October, 1934).

is a reliable basis for prediction, that although some rural counties may wish to adopt charters, it will be the urban and suburban counties which are most likely to avail themselves of the home-rule privilege. States seeking to frame constitutional provisions and implementing legislation will find, even in the limited experience to date in a half-dozen states, much to underscore the desirability of conciseness and clarity of statement, as well as some indication of what is feasible and what not in the way of substantive content.

REFERENCES

Books and Special Studies

ASSEFF, Emmett, HIGHSAW, R. B., and LOOPER, C. E., *State Supervision of Local Finance in Louisiana* (Baton Rouge, Louisiana State University Bureau of Government Research, 1951).

BATES, Frank G., "State Control of Local Finance in Indiana," in Charles G. Haines and Marshall E. Dimock, eds., *Essays on the Law and Practice of Governmental Administration: A Volume in Honor of Frank Johnson Goodnow* (Baltimore, The Johns Hopkins Press, 1935).

BENSON, George, C. S., *The New Centralization* (New York, Farrar and Rinehart, 1941).

BETTERS, Paul V., ed., *State Centralization in North Carolina* (Washington, Brookings Institution, 1932).

CARR, Robert K., *State Control of Local Finance in Oklahoma* (Norman, University of Oklahoma Press, 1937).

Council of State Governments, *State-local Relations* (Chicago, 1946).

GRIMES, Marcene, *State Supervision of County and City Revenues in Kansas* (Lawrence, University of Kansas Governmental Research Center, 1956).

HEIN, Clarence J., *State Administrative Supervision of Local Government Functions in Kansas* (Lawrence, University of Kansas Governmental Research Center, 1955).

KEITH, John P., *City and County Home Rule in Texas* (Austin, University of Texas Institute of Public Affairs, 1951), chap. 5.

KILPATRICK, Wylie, *State Supervision of Local Budgeting* (New York, National Municipal League, 1939).

———, *State Supervision of Local Finance* (Chicago, Public Administration Service, 1941).

VAN DE WOESTYNE, Royal S., *State Control of Local Finance in Massachusetts* (Cambridge, Mass., Harvard University Press, 1935).

Articles

ALDERFER, H. F., "State Control of County Finance Increases," *National Municipal Review*, Vol. XXVIII, pp. 105-110 (February, 1939).

ANDREWS, Richard D., "County Home Rule in Maryland," *The County Officer*, Vol. XVI, pp. 95-96 (April, 1951).

BECK, Walter, "A Home Rule Experiment in Texas," *National Municipal Review*, Vol. XXIII, pp. 302-304 (June, 1934).

BENTON, W. E., "The County Home Rule Movement in Texas," *Southwestern Social Science Quarterly*, Vol. XXXI, pp. 108-120 (September, 1950).

Bromage, Arthur W., and Porter, Kirk H., "County Home Rule: Pro and Con," *National Municipal Review,* Vol. XXIII, pp. 514-519, 535 (October, 1934).

Dortch, Carl R., "The 'Indiana Plan' in Action," *National Municipal Review,* Vol. XXVII, pp. 525-529 (November, 1938).

Fairlie, John A., "Judicial and Administrative Control of County Officers," *Michigan Law Review,* Vol. XXVIII, pp. 250-275 (January, 1930).

Fesler, James W., "North Carolina's Local Government Commission," *National Municipal Review,* Vol. XXX, pp. 327-334 (June, 1941).

Fleming, John W., and Owsley, Roy H., "Maine's Emergency Municipal Finance Board," *National Municipal Review,* Vol. XXVII, pp. 143-147, 184 (March, 1938).

Hoffman, Samuel D., "A State Department of Local Government," *National Municipal Review,* Vol. XXVIII, pp. 348-354 (May, 1939).

Keith, John P., "County Home Rule for Michigan," *The County Officer,* Vol. XVII, pp. 234-240, 245, 252 (August, 1952).

Kenney, David T., "County Home Rule Today," "*The County Officer,* Vol. XVI, pp. 74-76, 81 (March, 1951).

Kneier, Charles M., "Some Legal Aspects of the Governor's Power to Remove Local Officers," *Virginia Law Review,* Vol. XVII, pp. 355-368 (February, 1931).

Lowrie, S. Gale, "Interpretation of the County Home Rule Amendment by the Ohio Supreme Court," *University of Cincinnati Law Review,* Vol. X, pp. 454-466 (November, 1936).

MacCorkle, Stuart A., "State Control over Counties in Texas," *Southwestern Social Science Quarterly,* Vol. XVII, pp. 161-177 (September, 1936).

Martin, James W., "State Supervision of County Finance in Kentucky," *National Municipal Review,* Vol. XXVIII, pp. 149-155 (February, 1939).

Martin, Roscoe C., "The County Home Rule Movement in Texas," *Southwestern Social Science Quarterly,* Vol. XV, pp. 307-317 (March, 1935).

Masslich, Chester B., "North Carolina's New Plan for Controlling Local Fiscal Affairs," *National Municipal Review,* Vol. XX, pp. 328-334 (June, 1931).

Mauck, Elwyn A., "Home Rule for Counties Continues Its Progress," *National Municipal Review,* Vol. XXVIII, pp. 89-95, 179 (February, 1939).

Miller, E. J., "A New Departure in County Government: California's Experiment with Home Rule Charters," *American Political Science Review,* Vol. VII, pp. 411-419 (August, 1913).

Ratchford, B. U., "The Work of the North Carolina Local Government Commission," *National Municipal Review,* Vol. XXV, pp. 323-327, 368 (June, 1936).

Satterfield, M. H., "State Appointment and Removal of Local Law Enforcement Officers," *Southwestern Social Science Quarterly,* Vol. XII, pp. 277-295 (March, 1932).

Shoup, Earl L., "Judicial Abrogation of County Home Rule in Ohio," *American Political Science Review,* Vol. XXX, pp. 540-546 (June, 1936).

———, "Constitutional Problems of County Home Rule in Ohio," *Western Reserve Law Review,* Vol. I, pp. 111-132 (December, 1949).

Snider, Clyde F., "State Control over Counties and Townships in Indiana," *John Marshall Law Quarterly,* Vol. III, pp. 556-569 (June, 1938).

Turck, Charles J., "The Governor's Power to Remove County Officials," *Kentucky Law Journal,* Vol. XIV, pp. 330-337 (May, 1926).

WAGER, Paul W., "State Control in North Carolina," *National Municipal Review*, Vol. XXIII, pp. 526-530 (October, 1934).

WALKER, Harvey, "County Home Rule in Ohio," *Ohio State University Law Journal*, Vol. I, pp. 11-14 (January, 1935).

WARNER, Edwin E., "A Study of the Indiana Plan of Budgetary Review," *Legal Notes on Local Government*, Vol. IV, pp. 279-295 (March, 1939).

WEIDNER, Edward W., "State Supervision of Local Government in Minnesota," *Public Administration Review*, Vol. IV, pp. 226-233 (Summer, 1944).

PART TWO

Organization

CHAPTER 5

County Governing Bodies

COUNTY GOVERNMENT IN GENERAL

American county government is so complex and lacking in uniformity that its analysis and description become no easy task. County organization varies from state to state, and often among counties of the same state. It includes numerous officers, boards, and commissions, the titles and functions of which are far from standardized. Some of these agencies are established by constitutional provision and others by statute; some are elected by the voters, others appointed, and still others constituted on an ex officio basis. In addition to the county officers and members of boards and commissions, the personnel of county government includes an imposing array of deputies, assistants, and employees. Though reasonably definite relationships between the various agencies have been worked out in some instances, there are many cases in which a particular county agency so lacks proper supervision, as well as co-ordination with related agencies, that it operates virtually as a "little government" in and of itself. One writer, indeed, has gone so far as to suggest that if American county government is established on any principle at all, it is the principle of confusion.[1]

Yet, notwithstanding wide diversity in detail, the government of most counties throughout the country is organized to a considerable extent along the same broad lines and may be said to consist of (1) some sort of general governing body, charged with various policy-determining and administrative functions and exercising at least a modicum of supervisory authority over county affairs generally, and (2) a considerable list of officers, boards, and commissions charged with more specific tasks. The present chapter is concerned with the nature, organization, and functioning of

[1] Roger H. Wells, *American Local Government* (New York, McGraw-Hill, 1939), p. 80.

agencies in the first of these categories. Other officers, agencies, and county employees will be considered in the chapter which follows.

NATURE AND TITLES OF COUNTY GOVERNING BODIES

Every fully organized county government is built in some measure around a central governing agency. In a few instances this agency is a single official. In Arkansas, for example, most nonfiscal functions normally exercised by a county governing body are performed by the county judge; and single nonjudicial officers perform the functions of governing bodies in several counties in Georgia and South Carolina. Generally, however, the governing body is a multimember agency. In common parlance, the body is frequently referred to merely as *the county board,* and that term, in a generic sense, will often be used in this book. The official title of the agency, however, varies widely. Most common by far is that of board of commissioners, which is used for all counties in 20 states and for some counties in a number of others. Next in frequency is the title of board of supervisors, used for all counties in seven states and for certain counties elsewhere. In Missouri, Arkansas, West Virginia, and most counties in Oregon and Tennessee, the governing body is called the county court. The title is fiscal court in Kentucky, commissioners court in Texas, police jury in Louisiana, levy court in Delaware, board of chosen freeholders in New Jersey, and board of commissioners of roads and revenue in more than a hundred Georgia counties. Each of some 18 other titles is used in one or more counties in various states (see Table 3).[2]

Whatever its title, the governing body in large measure personifies the county. It is the agency which, in official matters, acts for the county and on its behalf. It "is clothed with authority to do whatever the corporate or political entity, the county, might do if capable of rational action, except in respect to matters the cognizance of which is exclusively vested in some other officer or person. It is in an enlarged sense the representative and guardian of the county." [3] In the words of the appellate court of Indiana: "The county is known in law only by its board of commissioners, and acts, as a county, through its board." [4]

Where the governing agency consists, as it typically does, of several members, the general rule is that official action can be taken only when the body is legally in session, since members cannot bind the county by their individual actions, or even by action concurred in by a majority or all of the members if taken successively and separately. In many states the county governing body is accorded the status of a corporation. Like

[2] United States Bureau of the Census, *County Boards and Commissions* (Washington, Government Printing Office, 1947), pp. 4-5, 17-19.

[3] 11 *Cyc.* 389.

[4] Board of Commissioners of Newton County *v.* Wild, 37 Ind. App. 32, 35 (1905).

other corporations it is, in the eyes of the law, a continuous body, notwithstanding changes in its membership.[5]

TABLE 3

Titles of County General Governing Bodies *

Title of governing body	*Number of counties having*
Total	3,050
Board of commissioners	1,271
Board of supervisors	673
County court	369
Commissioners court	254
Fiscal court	120
Board of commissioners of roads and revenue	118
Police jury	63
Court commissioners	37
Commissioners of roads and revenue	30
Board of freeholders	21
Board of revenue	20
County commissioners	15
Assistant judges	14
Ordinary	11
Board of directors	8
County commissioners	8
Levy court	3
Advisory commission	2
Board of managers	2
Board of revenue and control	2
Governing commission	2
Supervisor	2
Board of auditors	1
Board of finance and control	1
Board of revenue and road commissioners	1
County council	1
Highway commission	1

* From United States Bureau of the Census, *County Boards and Commissions* (Washington, Government Printing Office, 1947), p. 2.

TYPES OF GOVERNING BODIES

The official title of a governing body frequently gives little indication of the agency's basic character. Disregarding official titles, the United States Bureau of the Census, on the basis of the character of their membership, distinguished nine types of governing body as operating in American counties in 1945—four major types and five minor.

[5] 20 *Corpus Juris Secundum,* "Counties," secs. 74, 87; Clyde F. Snider, "The Organization and Functions of County Boards in Indiana," *Indiana Law Journal,* Vol. XII, pp. 281-315 (April, 1937).

The major types, which together served more than 93 per cent of the nation's counties, were characterized as follows:

1. Board of commissioners or supervisors.
2. Board composed of township supervisors.
3. Board composed of a judge and commissioners.
4. Board composed of a judge and justices of the peace.

Boards of the first type are composed of members whose primary function and accountability are as members of the county governing body. In other words, all members of the board are ordinarily elected *as* such and are neither responsible to any other local unit nor charged with the performance of any noncounty functions. About two thirds of all county governing bodies in the country are of this nature. Members of boards of the second type are chosen from the various townships of the county, and at least some of these members have dual functions and accountability—as county board members and as officers of their respective townships. In some instances, municipalities as well as townships are accorded representation on these boards. Boards of the third type have as their presiding officer an official who acts both as chairman of the county governing body and as a judicial officer, usually judge of probate; but their other members function primarily as members of the governing agency. In the case of boards of the fourth type, found in most counties in Kentucky and Tennessee, not only does the presiding officer act both as chairman of the governing body and as a judicial officer, but other members also act both administratively and judicially, serving in the dual capacity of governing-body members and justices of the peace. Boards of the second, third, and fourth major types are therefore alike in that some or all of their members, in addition to their county duties, are charged with public responsibilities as judicial or township officers.

Minor types of governing body include: [6]

1. A single judge.
2. A plural-member court.
3. A single nonjudicial officer.
4. A nonjudicial ex officio body.
5. An executive and township supervisors.

The number of counties served by boards of each of the nine types is indicated in Table 4.

In some states all counties are provided with a uniform type of governing body; in others, however, though some one type usually predominates, one or more variant types will be found. Each California county, for example, has a board of supervisors of five members,[7] and every Indiana

[6] *County Boards and Commissions*, pp. 2-5; Cf. Edward W. Weidner, "The Confused County Picture," *National Municipal Review*, Vol. XXXV, pp. 166-171 (April, 1946).

[7] Exclusive of the consolidated city and county of San Francisco.

county a three-member board of commissioners. In Illinois, on the other hand, 84 counties have boards of varied size composed of township supervisors, 17 have three-member boards of commissioners, and Cook County has a board of commissioners of 15 members, ten elected from the city of Chicago and five from the townships outside the city.

TABLE 4

Number of Members of County General Governing Bodies by Official Character of Membership *

Character of membership	*Number of counties*	*Number of members*	*Average number of members per county*	*Number of members per 10,000 inhabitants*
Total	3,050	21,080	6.9	1.8
Board of commissioners or supervisors	2,012	7,993	4.0	1.0
Board composed of township supervisors	297	7,616	25.6	5.1
Judge and commissioners	350	1,666	4.8	1.8
Judge and justices of the peace	193	3,300	17.1	8.0
Single judge	86	86	1.0	2.5
Plural-member court	75	359	4.8	.7
Single nonjudicial officer	32	32	1.0	.5
Nonjudicial ex officio body	4	21	5.3	.6
Executive and township supervisors	1	7	7.0	.2

* From United States Bureau of the Census, *County Boards and Commissions* (Washington, Government Printing Office, 1947), p. 4.

SELECTION AND TERMS OF MEMBERS

County commissioners in Connecticut are appointed by the state legislature,[8] and in a few counties in other states some form of appointment is provided.[9] With these exceptions, the members of county governing bodies are everywhere popularly elected. Nomination of candidates is most often by direct primary election, though in some instances it is by caucus, convention, or petition.

Within the general framework of popular election, methods of choosing members show wide variation. In some counties all commissioners or supervisors are elected by and from the county at large; in others all are elected by districts; and in still others part of the board membership is chosen at large and part by districts. In some instances, though election is at large, there is a requirement of district residence. Thus, in Indiana all three commissioners are elected *by* the voters of the county at large, but one must be chosen *from* each of the three commissioner districts into which the county is divided. Considering the entire country, the most

[8] Henry J. Faeth, *The Connecticut County* (Storrs, University of Connecticut Institute of Public Service, 1949), p. 12.

[9] *County Boards and Commissions,* p. 7.

common method of selection by far is election from districts or governmental subdivisions of the county. Of the more than 2,000 counties having boards of the "commissioners or supervisors" type, less than 400 elect all board members at large. More than 800 choose all members by districts, and the remaining counties in the group make some use of the district principle. The districts by or from which members are elected are sometimes merely commissioner districts laid out for this purpose exclusively; at other times they are geographical subdivisions of the county, serving other administrative purposes in addition to that of election districts. Sometimes the election areas bear official titles other than that of district, being known, for example, as beats in Mississippi and wards in Louisiana.

In the case of boards of the "township supervisors" type, all members are elected from the county's townships or municipalities. Justices of the peace serving as members of county governing bodies are regularly elected from subdivisions of the county, as are a majority of the commissioners serving with judges on boards of the "judge and commissioners" type. As indicated in Fig. IV, half of the nation's counties elect all or part of their board members by districts; an additional 21 per cent require district residence; and in another 10 per cent members are chosen from townships and municipalities. Thus, less than one fifth of the counties elect all board members at large. From the standpoint of individual board members (Fig. V), only 11 per cent are elected at large without requirement of district residence.

Election of county board members by districts or townships rather than at large is sometimes defended on the ground that in assuring that board membership will be spread geographically, it makes possible the representation of any special interests peculiar to particular localities. Although this may serve a useful purpose in some instances, especially in the case of counties having highly urbanized as well as rural areas, it seems clearly unnecessary in counties that are predominantly rural and have populations and economic interests that are essentially homogeneous. Moreover, members elected from districts or townships may be inclined to favor policies and actions which are primarily advantageous to their respective localities rather than to the county at large and, through vote-trading tactics, may secure the adoption of many such measures by the board. District or township election does have the advantage of a shorter ballot, since under such a system each voter votes only for one or a few, rather than all, board members. But in a large majority of the counties the board is small enough to permit all members to be elected at large without lengthening the ballot unduly, especially where terms are staggered so that only a part of the membership is chosen at any one election. Furthermore, as will be pointed out later,[10] many of the larger boards should be reduced in size,

[10] See below, "Size of Membership," "Relative Merits of Large and Small Boards."

and such action would facilitate election at large. With respect to most counties, election at large seems preferable to choice from districts or townships. Certainly many counties now operating under small boards constituted on the district principle could benefit from a shift to election at large, thereby making each member of the governing body accountable to the voters of the entire county rather than to those of a particular subdivision.

FIG. IV

Per Cent Distribution of County Governing Bodies, by Method of Membership Selection

FIG. V

Per Cent Distribution of Members of County Governing Bodies, by Method of Selection

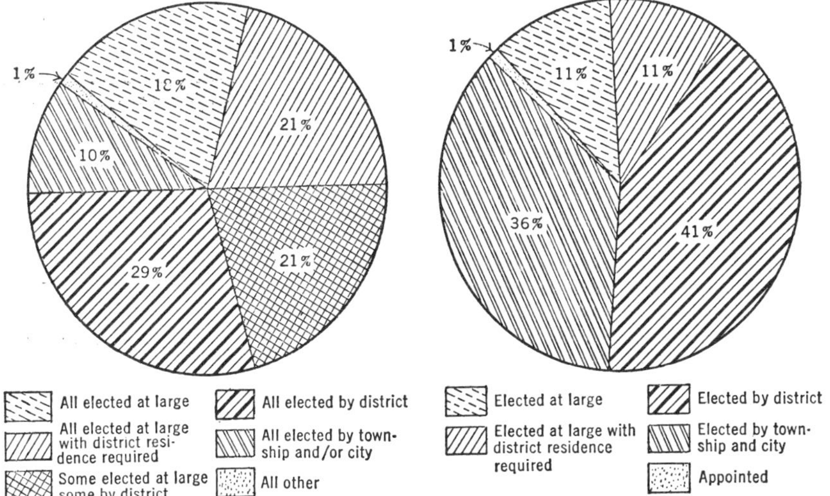

SOURCE: United States Bureau of the Census, *County Boards and Commissions* (Washington, 1947), p. 6.

Terms of county board members vary from a single year, in the case of township supervisors in Michigan, to eight years in the case of county judges in Tennessee. Most members have terms of two, three, four, or six years, with the four-year term by far the most common. Ordinarily, all board members in a given county have terms of the same length, though there are some exceptions. In counties of a few western states, for example, some members are elected for two years and others for four; and in a number of instances elsewhere, particularly where the county judge serves in that capacity, the chairman's term is longer than that of other members. In a slight majority of the counties throughout the country terms of board members are staggered, so that those of only a part of the membership expire in any one year.[11]

[11] *County Boards and Commissions,* pp. 7-8, 36-38.

SIZE OF MEMBERSHIP

Slightly more than a hundred counties in Arkansas and elsewhere have single-member governing authorities, and a few, principally in Vermont, have two-member agencies. With these exceptions, county boards range in membership from three upward. In counties with boards of the "commissioners or supervisors" type, the three-member board is most common and the five-member board next in frequency, with an average of four members for the 2,000 agencies of this type (see Table 4). Boards of the "township supervisors" type are the largest in size. The membership of these ordinarily reflects both the number of townships in the county and the number of inhabitants. In the first place, each township is usually represented on the board by its principal township officer, known in most instances as the supervisor. Though occasional counties have only a half-dozen townships or less, the average number is around 17, many have from 20 to 25, and a few have 30 or more. After according membership to the supervisor from each township, additional representation on the board is ordinarily provided for the more populous communities of the county. This is done in some states merely by allotting additional members to the populous townships. In Illinois, for example, every township having more than a specified number of inhabitants is entitled to elect, on the basis of a prescribed population formula, one or more additional members of the county board. Though they are called assistant supervisors, these additional members have no powers or duties as township officers but serve solely as members of the county governing body, their status differing markedly in this respect from that of the supervisors, who have both township and county responsibilities. Other states, after making each township supervisor a member of the county board, assign additional members to cities and villages. Thus Wisconsin provides that the board of supervisors, in addition to the chairman (supervisor) of each township, shall include elected representatives from cities and villages; and on Michigan boards municipalities are variously represented by elective, appointive, and ex officio members.[12] Whether board members, in addition to the township supervisors, are assigned to the townships themselves or to their municipalities, the result in either case is to give additional representation to the more populous places. By the time each township is given one board member in the person of its supervisor and the populous localities are provided with additional members, the boards composed of township supervisors frequently run to considerable size. Though occasional boards of this type have fewer members than some of the boards of commissioners or supervisors, in general their membership is much larger. Ranging upward in exceptional instances to 80 and

[12] Some of the city members in both Michigan and Wisconsin are elected by wards.

more, a membership of 40 to 50 is not unusual, and the average membership for all boards of this type is in the neighborhood of 25.[13] The large size of boards composed of township supervisors, as compared with governing bodies of other types, is shown in Figs. IV and V. There, it will be noted that although boards with their membership elected by townships and cities comprise only 10 per cent in number of all county governing bodies, they account for 36 per cent of all governing-body members.

In the country as a whole, and regardless of type, 1,363 counties were reported, as of 1945, to have governing boards of three members and 872 counties to have five-member boards. A total of 389 counties, consisting almost entirely of units employing boards of the "township supervisors" or the "judge and justices" type, had governing bodies of more than ten members, with 21 of these having memberships in excess of 50.[14] The geographic distribution of county governing bodies of different sizes is shown in Fig. VI.

FIG. VI

Size of County Governing Bodies: Geographical Distribution

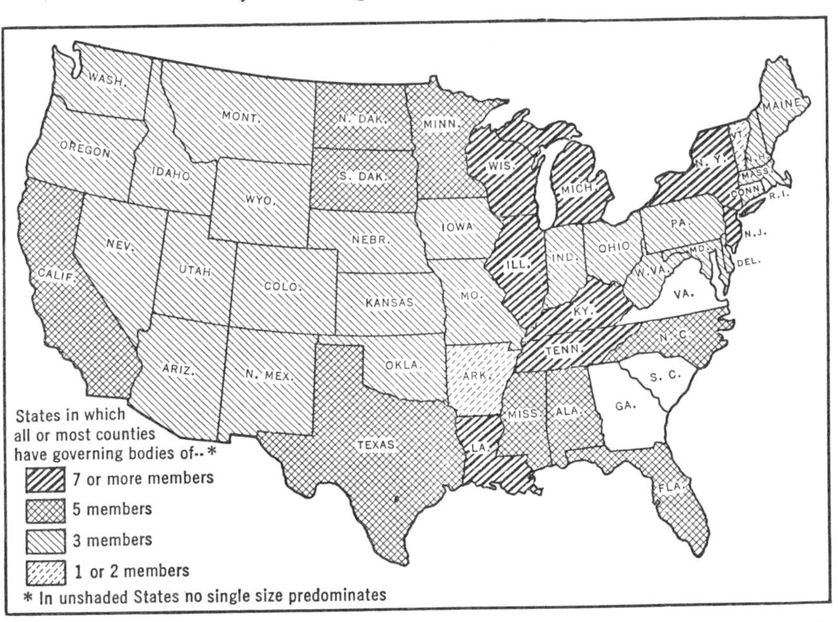

SOURCE: United States Bureau of the Census, *County Boards and Commissions* (Washington, 1947), p. 1.

[13] *County Boards and Commissions,* pp. 5, 32-35. The board of Wayne County (Detroit), Mich., was reported, in 1952, as having 97 members; see John P. Keith, "County Home Rule for Michigan," *The County Officer,* Vol. XVII, pp. 234-240, 245, 252 (August, 1952).

[14] Weidner, *loc. cit.*

ORGANIZATION

Presiding Officer. The principal officers of the county board are the chairman or president and the clerk. In some instances the chairmanship or presidency is an ex officio position. This is typically the case, for example, in boards of the "judge and commissioners" and "judge and justices of the peace" types, where the county judge serves as chairman; and it is also found in some counties with other types of governing bodies. Occasional county boards have a presiding officer elected as such by the voters. Most frequently, however, the chairman or president is elected by the board members from among themselves. With only a few exceptions, this is the plan followed by boards of commissioners or supervisors and boards composed of township supervisors, and these include well over two thirds of all county governing bodies.[15] Where the presiding officer is elected by the board, a one-year term is fairly common, with election taking place at the board's first regular session of the year, sometimes referred to as the organization session.

In general, the powers of the chairman or president are limited to serving as the board's presiding officer and signing official documents on behalf of the county. Where, as is usually the case, the chairman himself is a member of the board, he may vote on any issue, as do other members, but having done so, he has no casting vote in case of a tie. His status as presiding officer may carry some prestige and place him at times in a strategic position where he may be more influential than other board members. Furthermore, his influence is augmented in some instances by his power to appoint board committees. But he ordinarily lacks completely the power to appoint or remove administrative personnel on his own authority, as well as the veto power, and thus is not, in any true sense of the term, a chief executive officer of the county.

Clerk. The clerk of the county board is usually one of the regular elective county officers designated by law to serve in that capacity. Where the office of county clerk exists, that official serves as clerk of the board; elsewhere the function devolves upon the auditor or some other officer. Whoever performs them, the principal duties of board clerk are those of preparing agenda for board meetings, attending meetings and keeping minutes thereof, and making a formal record of ordinances, resolutions, and other forms of board action.[16]

Committees. Small boards of commissioners or supervisors make little or no use of committees; but in many of the larger governing bodies, particularly boards composed of township supervisors, an elaborate system of standing committees, patterned after that of state legislatures

[15] *County Boards and Commissions,* pp. 8, 17-19.

[16] For further discussion of the office of county clerk, see below, chap. 6, "Officers of General Administration," p. 152.

and city councils, is a major feature of board organization. Committees are ordinarily appointed by the board chairman or president. Though political parties, by and large, play a less important role in county boards than in state and municipal legislative bodies, board committees are frequently constituted along party lines, with the majority party being awarded the chairmanship and a majority of the members of each committee. The number of committees provided varies widely from county to county, reflecting in some measure the size of board membership. In boards with as many as 20 members there are often a dozen or more committees, and in some of the largest boards the number exceeds 30. Among the committees most commonly provided for are those on claims, ways and means, fees and salaries, almshouse, jail, public assistance, judiciary, licenses, roads and bridges, public buildings and grounds, and public health. The committees to be appointed, their titles, and the number of members on each are usually determined by each board through its procedural rules or bylaws. Where the committee system prevails, problems and proposals for action in any given field, before being considered by the full membership of the board, are ordinarily referred to the appropriate committee for its consideration and recommendation.

SESSIONS

Regular Sessions. Regular sessions of county governing bodies are held at intervals and at times prescribed by statute or board rule or, less commonly, by constitutional provision. Many boards meet monthly, and some, particularly in the more populous counties, more frequently. On the other hand, provision is made in some instances for only two or three regular meetings per year or even for a single annual meeting. Generally speaking, small boards meet more frequently than large. Illinois law, for example, provides for five regular meetings per year in the case of three-member boards of commissioners but only two in the case of boards composed of township supervisors. This is not without some justification since much of the administrative work performed in the case of small boards by the entire membership is, in the larger bodies, carried on by committees, and infrequent meetings of the entire board may suffice for the review and approval of committee action.

Adjourned Sessions. If the members of a county board, in regular session, feel that the proper dispatch of county business requires that they convene again prior to the date of the next regular meeting, this can ordinarily be accomplished through the adjourned session. Under this procedure the board, having met in regular session and disposed of the business at hand, adjourns to whatever date, earlier than that of the next regular meeting, it deems feasible. Upon reconvening on the designated day, the board proceeds to do business as an adjourned meeting, that is, a continuation, of the regular session which began on the earlier date. Adjourned sessions are rather commonly employed by boards that are limited by law to widely spaced regular sessions as a means of securing more frequent meetings. Thus a number of the larger boards in Illinois, provided by law with only two regular sessions per year, in June and September, in practice convene monthly through the adjournment device. In the eyes of the law, of course, the so-called "July meeting" and "August meeting" are in reality adjourned meetings of the June session, and those falling between September and June are adjourned meetings of the September session.

Special Sessions. Special sessions of the board, as distinguished from regular and adjourned sessions, may be called in various ways: by the presiding officer, by a specified number or proportion of the board members, or by a designated county officer on his own authority. Frequently, alternative methods are provided in a single state. Thus, special sessions may be called in Mississippi by the board president or any three members; in Iowa by the chairman or a majority of the members; and in Indiana by the county auditor, the clerk of the circuit court in case of the death or disqualification of the auditor, or the recorder in case of disqualification of both the auditor and the clerk.[17] Determination of when the public interest requires a special session of the board is usually left to the officer or members authorized to issue the call. In some instances special sessions are limited to the transaction of business specified in the call; but in others they may accomplish any act not required by law to be performed at a regular session.

Procedure. Board meetings in some instances are conducted in an orderly and business-like manner. Rather commonly, however, and particularly in the case of the smaller boards, proceedings are extremely informal, with little attention being paid to the fundamentals, not to mention the niceties, of parliamentary law. It is not unusual, during the course of a session, to find various officials and citizens engaging different board members in conversation simultaneously and the atmosphere one of general confusion and hubbub. Indeed, a visitor entering the commissioners' room in the courthouse while discussions are in progress may find it difficult to determine whether the board is officially in session or in recess.[18] To a greater extent than in the case of larger governing bodies, sessions of small boards tend to become mere perfunctory meetings held to regularize decisions previously arrived at in informal discussion. "Meetings of small boards are perfunctory," says Professor Kirk Porter,

[17] Huey Blair Howerton, *A Guidebook of the Board of Supervisors* (University, University of Mississippi Bureau of Public Administration, 1948), p. 8; Dean Zenor, *A Handbook for County Supervisors* (Iowa City, State University of Iowa Institute of Public Affairs, 1950), pp. 10-11; Snider, *loc. cit.*, p. 286.

[18] Snider, *loc. cit.*, p. 288.

"because it is possible for three or five men to determine policies beforehand in a very informal manner. Important matters can be decided on the courthouse steps, in a hotel lobby, or on the street corner . . . and they go into formal session merely to legalize decisions which in effect have already been made."[19] Larger boards, by their very nature, find it imperative to follow somewhat more closely procedural rules regarding decorum and debate, though even here informality and confusion are by no means unknown. Board meetings are generally open to the public, but, except in occasional instances when matters of unusual interest are being considered, few citizens ordinarily attend.

COMPENSATION OF MEMBERS

Members of county governing bodies are usually paid either an annual salary or a per diem allowance, the amount of which is fixed in some instances by law and in others by the board itself within constitutional or statutory limitations. Annual salaries range from a hundred dollars or so in some small rural counties to several thousand dollars in a few populous counties. In some of the latter, board membership is considered a full-time job, and there are other instances in which members are required by law to devote a specified number of hours per day or week to county business. Under the per diem form of compensation, members receive a fixed sum per day for time spent in attendance at board sessions or on committee work, subject to a legal limit in many instances on the maximum number of days per month or year for which compensation may be allowed. The per diem allowance varies widely, but in many cases at present it is in the neighborhood of $5, $8, or $10. In addition to salary or per diem, members are sometimes allowed mileage for travel to and from board sessions and committee meetings and for other travel necessary to the conduct of county business.

POWERS

As the central governing agency of the county, the board is vested with a wide variety of powers. Though in some instances certain authority is conferred upon the board by constitutional provision, most of its powers

[19] Kirk H. Porter, *County and Township Government in the United States* (New York, Macmillan, 1922), p. 115. Concerning board meetings in a Minnesota county, where the governing body is a seven-member board of commissioners, it has been reported: "There is a total absence of discussion in open meeting. Any important question is settled by conference before the meeting. If any matter comes up during the meeting, which has not previously been settled, the board solemnly adjourns to executive session to settle the question. Meetings have been held in which at least a dozen executive sessions have been interposed, during which time the interested spectators wait for the side show to adjourn, and the principals to return to the main tent"—R. M. Goodrich, "The County Board in Minnesota," *National Municipal Review*, Vol. XIII, pp. 684-690, 688 (December, 1924).

are delegated by statute. State statutes ordinarily set forth a long list of powers to be vested in the board. In addition, as the corporate authority of the county, the board is the repository of all powers conferred by law upon the county without designation of the officers through which they shall be exercised. But even though their authority is broad and varied, county boards, like other local government agencies, are strictly limited in their legal competence. As creatures of the law, they possess no inherent authority whatsoever but only those powers that have been delegated to them by law, either in express words or by reasonable implication. Any action taken by a county governing body in excess of its legal authority is void. Furthermore, when the law prescribes the procedure to be followed in the exercise of a particular power, this procedure must be adhered to in its essential aspects or the action taken will be held invalid.

County government, it should be noted, finds little application of the separation-of-powers principle which is a standard feature of our national and state governments and city governments of the mayor-council type. The county governing body, whatever its title and nature, ordinarily serves the county in both legislative and administrative capacities and, in some instances, possesses minor judicial powers as well. Though the following paragraphs suggest certain powers and duties as falling within each of the three categories, legislation, administration, and adjudication are so intertwined in the actual conduct of county activities as to make classification difficult and in some respects arbitrary.

Legislative Powers. The county board is sometimes referred to as the legislative body of the county, and it is true that such powers of a legislative nature as the county possesses are ordinarily vested in the board. But the title *legislative body* may be misleading unless two important facts are kept in mind. In the first place, it must be remembered that the county, as a quasi-municipal corporation, serves primarily as an agency of the state government in carrying out public functions of state-wide interest, and that the powers of a legislative or policy-determining nature that are conferred upon counties are relatively few. Secondly, while the board *is* a legislative body, though one of very limited authority, it is by no means exclusively legislative in character. On the contrary, it is also the principal administrative agency of the county—indeed, is generally regarded by the courts as *primarily* an administrative body—and at times is charged with duties of a judicial nature.

The legislative powers most commonly conferred by law upon county governing bodies fall into two categories: fiscal and regulatory. On the fiscal side, it is ordinarily the county board which, under authority conferred by the state and subject to state-imposed limitations, levies county taxes, makes appropriations, and incurs indebtedness.[20] Normally, these

[20] In some instances fiscal authority is vested in some agency other than the general governing body. See below, "Collateral Fiscal Agencies."

powers over local finance constitute the most important segment of county legislative authority. County regulatory powers are not extensive and generally are limited in their application to those portions of the county that are outside incorporated municipalities. Many counties are authorized to license and regulate certain forms of business enterprise in unincorporated areas. Perhaps the business most commonly subject to county regulation is the retail liquor establishment. Various forms of commercial amusement, such as circuses, carnivals, dance halls, amusement parks, and wrestling and boxing arenas, frequently are within county regulatory jurisdiction. Other enterprises subject to county regulation in various states include tourist camps, used-car lots, and the sale of fireworks. Some county boards may enact local health ordinances; and some or all counties in a number of states are empowered to enact zoning ordinances regulating the use of suburban and rural lands.

Occasionally, counties are authorized by constitution or statute to make and enforce any police, sanitary, or other local regulations that do not conflict with the general laws of the state. This seemingly broad grant of police authority, however, has not been of much significance in practice. For the most part, matters that might properly be the subject of county police ordinances are adequately covered by state law. Ordinances in conflict with the state legislation would, of course, be invalid, and the duplicating of state regulations would be superfluous. On the whole, county regulatory authority during recent years has been somewhat broadened, particularly in relation to zoning and the regulation of suburban business. Nevertheless, as compared with the regulatory power of municipalities it is still extremely meager.[21]

Administrative Powers. Administrative powers and duties of county boards are extremely numerous and varied. Many activities in this category center about the board's control over, and responsibility for, the courthouse, jail, almshouse, and other county property. In this connection the board ordinarily is empowered to purchase real estate, to construct and equip necessary buildings, to keep county property insured and repaired, to make appropriate rules concerning the use of public grounds and buildings, and to sell or lease property no longer needed for county purposes. The board makes contracts on behalf of the county and examines and settles claims against the county. Quite commonly the board appoints certain county officers, various assistants and deputies to other officers, and a considerable number of county employees; and not infrequently it is empowered to fill vacancies in elective offices. In some cases

[21] County zoning is discussed below, chap. 18. Concerning the constitutional competence of state legislatures to confer local legislative powers upon counties, see Herman Walker, Jr., "The Delegation of Police Power to Counties," *Louisiana Law Review*, Vol. III, pp. 522-558 (March, 1941), and "Police Power for Counties," *Journal of Land and Public Utility Economics*, Vol. XVII, pp. 367-372 (August, 1941).

the board fixes, usually within statutory or constitutional limits, the compensation of county officers and employees. Some county boards exercise important functions in connection with the holding of elections, such as laying out election precincts, providing polling places, and appointing precinct election officials. Frequently the board is charged with a major role in the construction of roads and bridges and the administration of public assistance. All in all, the administrative work of the board constitutes by far its greatest task.

Judicial Powers. The judicial powers of county governing bodies are today of minor importance. Some boards, however, continue to possess certain powers of a judicial nature which may be used either to implement legislative or administrative action or in separate and distinct proceedings. Reminiscent of earlier days when "county business" was conducted by local courts, county boards in some states are even accorded the legal status of judicial tribunals. Such status, however, bears no necessary relationship to the title of the official agency concerned. The governing body of Indiana counties, for example, though officially designated the board of county commissioners, is, in the eyes of the law, not only a corporation but a court of record.[22] As such it is empowered to punish contempt by fine or imprisonment and to enforce obedience to its orders by attachment or other compulsory process. The board has also been held to act judicially in various other matters, such as passing upon the public utility of proposed drainage or highway projects.[23] On the other hand, the county governing body in Missouri, though called the county court, does not now have the status of a judicial tribunal. Under the state constitution of 1875 that agency was a constitutional court of record with authority, among other things, to punish for contempt, issue writs of habeas corpus and hold hearings thereon, and, under some circumstances, issue injunctions.[24] But under the 1945 constitution the county court, though still existing by constitutional provision, lost its judicial status and became simply a county governing body with administrative and legislative authority. According to the Missouri supreme court the county court is no longer vested, nor can it be vested, with judicial power.[25]

In some instances, as we have seen, county boards are composed partly or wholly of judges or justices of the peace who, in their capacity as individual officers, are charged with judicial duties. But the judicial powers of county boards as such have declined to a point where today, generally speaking, they are of relatively little significance.

[22] Paul *v.* Walkerton Woodlawn Cemetery Association, 204 Ind. 693 (1933).

[23] Bryan *v.* Moore, 81 Ind. 9 (1881); Forrey *v.* Board of Commissioners of Madison County, 189 Ind. 257 (1920).

[24] William L. Bradshaw, "History of the Missouri County Court," *Missouri Historical Review*, Vol. XXV, pp. 387-403 (April, 1931). At one time the body also possessed probate jurisdiction.

[25] *In re* City of Kinloch, 362 Mo. 434 (1951).

FORMS OF BOARD ACTION

Procedural questions are ordinarily decided by the county board, and minor substantive matters frequently determined, on simple motion. Board action on major substantive matters, however, usually takes one of two forms: the ordinance or the resolution. In the usage of city councils, the ordinance is the higher and more authoritative form of action. Enacted by a more formal procedure than that followed in the case of a resolution,[26] the ordinance is ordinarily employed to effect action of a legislative character, while administrative action is commonly accomplished by resolution.[27] As applied to county boards, this distinction would suggest use of the ordinance for legislative purposes, such as the appropriation of money and the enactment of zoning regulations, and use of the resolution in administrative matters, such as letting contracts and ordering the construction of a highway or the repair of a county building.

In practice, any distinction made by county boards between ordinances and resolutions is frequently merely nominal, with the basic difference in their character being largely ignored. Thus, some boards employ the ordinance almost exclusively, and others the resolution, to accomplish action either administrative or legislative in nature. Others appear to use the two interchangeably, even to the point at times of adopting a resolution to effect the amendment or repeal of an ordinance. In general, any action within the authority of the board may lawfully be taken by resolution unless the statutes require action by ordinance or in some other specified manner,[28] and therefore use of the resolution where the ordinance would be more appropriate may not invalidate board action. However, a clearer differentiation in board rules and practice between the ordinance and the resolution would serve to accentuate the distinction between legislation and administration and would better assure adequate deliberation and the observance of minimum procedural safeguards in the case of action involving policy determination.

RELATIVE MERITS OF LARGE AND SMALL BOARDS

Having considered the various types of county governing body and the powers and duties devolved upon such agencies, the question may well be raised at this point as to what form of governing board is, generally speaking, preferable. Though, as we have seen, county boards exist in many different types and in extensive size gradation, the great majority

[26] Ordinances, for example, are commonly required to be given two readings, or more often three, on different days.

[27] Cf. William Anderson and Edward W. Weidner, *American City Government*, rev. ed. (New York, Holt, 1950), pp. 424-425.

[28] Gale *v.* Board of Supervisors of Oakland County, 260 Mich. 399 (1932).

may be grouped roughly into two major classes: (1) small boards of commissioners or supervisors, typically composed of three to five members elected by districts or at large; and (2) large boards composed of supervisors or justices of the peace elected from townships or other subdivisions of the county. Which of these two broad types, the large board or the small, is better adapted to serving the county as a general governing body?

In reality, each type of board possesses certain advantages over the other, yet neither is completely satisfactory. The large board, though permitting broader representation, is likely in populous counties to reach a size unwieldy for administrative purposes. Because of its numerous membership, the board must rely heavily upon the work of committees; and although committee action is nominally subject to control by the entire board, the system is likely in practice to result in a high degree of decentralization in administrative responsibility. Different committees may work at cross-purposes, yet the full board has little choice but to ratify their action—a situation flowing in part from the time element and in part, in some instances, from partisan politics. Election of board members by townships or other districts means that members are close to local residents for receiving their complaints and hearing their problems and are later present at board meetings to see to it that those problems are given attention. On the other hand, this method of election, as regards legislative matters, tends to emphasize local rather than county-wide interests and to encourage logrolling tactics. The small board, in contrast with the larger, is better adapted to the performance of administrative functions but is believed by some to provide inadequate representation for legislative purposes. As regards relative cost, comparative studies in Illinois, where some counties have three-member boards of commissioners and others boards composed of township supervisors, indicate that in counties of similar size and population in that state, the large-board system makes for higher overhead costs in county government.[29] Similarly, studies which have compared costs as between different states, some having large and others small county boards, lead to the conclusion that the cost of maintaining the larger boards is distinctly greater than that of the smaller.[30]

By and large, it appears that most of the difficulties arising from either type of board result from the fact that both administrative and legislative

[29] M. H. Hunter, *Costs of Township and County Government in Illinois* (Urbana, University of Illinois Bureau of Business Research, 1933); H. K. Allen, *Costs and Services of Local Government in Selected Illinois Counties* (Urbana, University of Illinois Bureau of Business Research, 1936).

[30] Cf. M. Slade Kendrick, *Comparison of the Cost of Maintenance of Large and of Small County Boards in the United States* (Ithaca, N. Y., Cornell University Agricultural Experiment Station, 1929).

duties are imposed upon the same agency. If county administrative functions were centered in a single official,[31] the county board might be limited to policy-determining functions, and a membership somewhat larger than that of our smallest boards as presently constituted, but considerably smaller than the largest, would probably be most satisfactory.[32] As matters stand today, the small board seems clearly preferable in the great majority of American counties. In most counties social and economic interests are sufficiently homogeneous to enable a board of three to five members, whether elected by districts or at large, to be adequately representative for performance of its limited legislative functions; and the small board is distinctly advantageous for administrative purposes. The desirability of a manageable board for administration is emphasized by the fact that the county governing body serves *primarily* as an administrative agency and only secondarily as a local legislative organ. Fortunately, two thirds of the nation's counties are now provided with relatively small boards of commissioners or supervisors, and a number of others have governing bodies of moderate size. But there still remain many counties, particularly among those of a rural or semirural character, where a reduction in board size would facilitate administration without impairing the effectiveness of the body as a minor legislative agency.

COLLATERAL FISCAL AGENCIES

County governing bodies, as we have seen, are generally charged, among their principal powers and duties, with the levying of taxes, the making of appropriations, and the borrowing of money on behalf of the county. Indeed, control of county fiscal affairs ordinarily constitutes the very core of the board's over-all authority and responsibility and, certainly, its most important power of a legislative character. But there are a number of instances in which county monetary powers, or certain aspects thereof, are taken out of the hands of the general governing board of the county and vested in a special fiscal agency operating at either the state or the county level. Where this is the case, the general governing body, except for its limited authority of a regulatory nature, becomes almost exclusively an administrative organ.[33]

[31] See below, chap. 7.

[32] Cf. John A. Fairlie, *Town and County Government in Illinois,* Report of the Joint Legislative Committee, 47th General Assembly of Illinois (Springfield, Ill., 1913), Vol. II, pp. 85-86.

[33] *County Boards and Commissions,* pp. 8-9; Faeth, *op. cit.,* pp. 7-9; Harold C. Grinnell, *Studies in Local Government and Taxation in Rural New Hampshire* (Durham, University of New Hampshire Agricultural Experiment Station, 1943), p. 29; Columbus Andrews, *Administrative County Government in South Carolina* (Chapel Hill, University of North Carolina Press, 1933); Snider, *loc. cit.,* pp. 306-315; Anne King Gregorie, "Legislators Usurp Counties," *National Municipal Review,* Vol. XXXVII, pp. 361-363, 376 (July, 1948).

Four New England states and South Carolina vest control over some or all county fiscal affairs in the state legislature or the members thereof—representatives and senators—from the respective counties. County taxes in Maine and appropriations in Massachusetts are authorized directly by the legislature. In Connecticut and New Hampshire, power to tax, appropriate, and borrow for county purposes rests with the delegations from the respective counties in the legislature, the New Hampshire delegations, when meeting as county fiscal bodies, being known as county conventions. South Carolina counties have their levies and appropriations made nominally by the state legislature, but under a system of reciprocal "courtesy" among the respective county legislative delegations which operates to make those delegations the bodies that in fact control county finance.[34] Two states—Arkansas and Indiana—provide each county with a local fiscal agency in addition to the general governing organ of the county. In Arkansas, where the county judge functions as a general governing agency, a quorum court composed of the judge and a majority of the justices of the peace of the county is charged with levying taxes and making appropriations. In Indiana, where a three-member board of commissioners is the principal administrative agency of the county, the taxing, appropriating, and borrowing powers are vested in a county council of seven members, four elected from districts and three at large. Four counties in Tennessee, three each in Florida and Georgia, and Wayne County, Mich., were also reported by the Census Bureau as being provided, in 1945, with local fiscal agencies apart from their general governing boards. In all, some 270 counties, or one in 11 for the country as a whole, have their governing authority divided between a general governing body and some sort of collateral fiscal agency.[35]

The use of a special fiscal agency, insofar as it effects a separation of the policy-determining function from that of administration, is in line with the separation-of-powers principle which, as we have noted, is for the most part nonexistent in county government. In placing the appropriation and the actual spending of county funds in different hands, the plan is all to the good; but in other respects there are disadvantages. Where the state legislature itself exercises county fiscal authority, the local government is deprived of powers and relieved of responsibilities essential to genuine local autonomy. Special county-level agencies, on the other hand, mean the use of two county governing bodies instead of one. This has the effect of rendering even more complicated an organizational setup already unduly complex and of further dispersing local authority.

[34] An exception exists in the case of Charleston County, where, under a new plan of government inaugurated in 1949, fiscal authority rests with the county governing body; see William F. Larsen, "Tradition Bows to Efficiency," *National Municipal Review*, Vol. XXXIX, pp. 497-500 (November, 1950).

[35] *County Boards and Commissions*, p. 8.

An additional disadvantage in the case of county fiscal boards whose members, like those of the Indiana county council, are popularly elected, is a further lengthening of the ballot. There is great need in county government generally for a single board or council charged with policy determination and an elected or appointed executive officer in charge of administration.[36] However, as long as we provide one multimember agency for both administrative and regulatory purposes, there appears to be little reason, under most circumstances, why the same body should not be vested with fiscal authority as well. On the whole, the collateral fiscal agency, whether of the state-level or county-level type, appears to create more problems than it solves.

REFERENCES

Books and Special Studies

BRADSHAW, William L., *The Missouri County Court: A Study of the Organization and Functions of the County Board of Supervisors in Missouri* (Columbia, University of Missouri, 1931).

City Representation on County Boards of Supervisors [*in Michigan*] (Ann Arbor, Michigan Municipal League, 1933).

HOWERTON, Huey Blair, *A Guidebook of the Board of Supervisors* [*in Mississippi*] (University, University of Mississippi Bureau of Public Administration, 1948).

KENDRICK, M. Slade, *Comparison of the Cost of Maintenance of Large and of Small County Boards in the United States* (Ithaca, N. Y., Cornell University Agricultural Experiment Station, 1929).

League of Virginia Counties, *Virginia County Supervisors' Manual* (Charlottesville, University of Virginia Bureau of Public Administration, 1953).

United States Bureau of the Census, *County Boards and Commissions* (Washington, Government Printing Office, 1947).

VAN EK, Jacob, "The County Board of Supervisors" in Benjamin F. Shambaugh, ed., *County Government and Administration in Iowa* (Iowa City, Iowa State Historical Society, 1925), pp. 19-76.

ZENOR, Dean, *A Handbook for County Supervisors* [*in Iowa*] (Iowa City, State University of Iowa Institute of Public Affairs, 1950).

Articles

BRADSHAW, William L., "History of the Missouri County Court," *Missouri Historical Review*, Vol. XXV, pp. 387-403 (April, 1931).

BUTTS, A. B., "The County Board in Mississippi," *National Municipal Review*, Vol. XIII, pp. 554-559 (October, 1924).

COLE, Taylor, "The Police Jury in Louisiana," *Southwestern Political and Social Science Quarterly*, Vol. XI, pp. 55-67 (June, 1930).

CRANE, Wilder Willard, Jr., "Reflections of a County Board Member," *The County Officer*, Vol. XXI, pp. 202, 204 (September, 1956).

FAIR, Eugene, "The Missouri County Board—Its Personnel and Procedure," *National Municipal Review*, Vol. XIV, pp. 680-686 (November, 1925).

[36] See below, chap. 7.

GOODRICH, R. M., "The County Board in Minnesota," *National Municipal Review,* Vol. XIII, pp. 684-690 (December, 1924).

GREGORIE, Anne King, "Legislators Usurp Counties," *National Municipal Review,* Vol. XXXVII, pp. 361-363, 376 (July, 1948).

HOLLAND, L. M., "Legislative Authority of County Government in Georgia," *The County Officer,* Vol. XX, pp. 16-18 (January, 1955).

PIDGEON, Mary Elizabeth, "The Power and Practice of Virginia County Boards," *National Municipal Review,* Vol. XIV, pp. 240-246 (April, 1925).

SNIDER, Clyde F., "The Organization and Functions of County Boards in Indiana," *Indiana Law Journal,* Vol. XII, pp. 281-315 (April, 1937).

WALKER, Herman, Jr., "Police Power for Counties," *Journal of Land and Public Utility Economics,* Vol. XVII, pp. 367-372 (August, 1941).

———, "The Delegation of Police Power to Counties," *Louisiana Law Review,* Vol. III, pp. 522-558 (March, 1941).

WEIDNER, Edward W., "The Confused County Picture," *National Municipal Review,* Vol. XXXV, pp. 166-171 (April, 1946).

CHAPTER 6

County Officers and Employees

FROM A CONSIDERATION of general governing agencies we now turn to the various officers and board members who, together with the governing bodies, comprise county officialdom. The functions of the different officers, for the most part, will be described in succeeding chapters dealing with local services. It is the purpose of the present chapter to give an over-all picture of county organization, to describe the duties of certain officers of general administration not falling within the scope of the functional chapters, and to consider some aspects of county employment and personnel problems.

The number of county officers and boards varies widely from state to state and from county to county, but in a typical county, excluding those of only minor significance, it is likely to run to a dozen or more. Generally speaking, governmental agencies tend to be more numerous in the more populous counties than in others. For convenience in discussion, county agencies may be considered as falling into three categories: (1) elective officers; (2) appointive and ex officio officers; and (3) special-function boards and commissions, so called to distinguish them from the agencies of general government discussed in the preceding chapter. It must be borne in mind, of course, that methods of choosing officers are by no means uniform and, therefore, that an office that is elective in one state or county may be appointive or ex officio in another. Though there are numerous exceptions, elective offices are most frequently established by constitutional provision, and appointive and ex officio offices by statute.

ELECTIVE OFFICERS

The county offices most commonly filled by popular election are those of clerk, treasurer, sheriff, coroner, recorder or register of deeds, superintendent of schools, assessor, attorney, surveyor, auditor, and judge. Other offices in considerable variety are occasionally elective. Frequently, constitutional provisions or statutes require the election of certain officers in every county of the state and of others in some counties. In Illinois, for example, every county elects a clerk, a treasurer, a sheriff, a coroner, a county judge, a clerk of the circuit court, a state's attorney, and a superintendent of schools; other elective offices found in one or a few counties of the state include those of assessor, auditor, probate judge, probate clerk, superior judge, clerk of the superior court, and clerk of the criminal court. The number of states providing by general law for each of the more common elective offices, though not necessarily requiring them in every county, is shown in Table 5.

TABLE 5

County Elective Offices *

Office	*Number of States*
County clerk	25
Court clerk	33
Treasurer	37
Sheriff	47
Coroner	30
Recorder or register of deeds	25
Superintendent of schools	26
Assessor	28
Attorney or solicitor	36
Auditor or comptroller	16
Surveyor or engineer	31
County court judge	20
Probate judge	19

* From United States Bureau of the Census, *Elective Offices of State and County Governments* (Washington, 1946).

Less frequently provided for, but existing in some instances on an elective basis, are such offices as those of tax collector, public administrator,[1] register of probate, register of wills, road commissioner, and public weigher. In addition, constables and justices of the peace are elected as county officers in many states, though ordinarily chosen by districts rather than from the county at large.

The term of office for elective county officials is usually two years or four, with the present tendency in favor of the longer term. Several states during recent years have amended their constitutions or statutes to lengthen the term of office from two years to four. A 1954 survey by the Institute of Public Affairs of the State University of Iowa indicated that

[1] The public administrator, where that office exists, administers the estate of any decedent who does not leave any relative or other person having a prior right to appointment as administrator.

most or all elective county officials in 25 states were chosen for four-year terms and that the two-year term predominated in 15 states. In a few states the terms of office are almost evenly divided between two years and four. The term is three years in New York and six years in Massachusetts, with New Jersey offices divided between three-year and five-year terms.[2]

Examination of the list of elective county offices readily suggests that most of the positions are strictly non-policy-determining in nature and therefore should be filled by appointment rather than by popular election. In many instances, however, election is prescribed by the state constitution and consequently could be abandoned only by constitutional amendment.

APPOINTIVE AND EX OFFICIO OFFICERS

Appointive and ex officio offices are less standardized than elective. About the only generalization that can be made concerning them is that some offices of one or both categories are to be found in most counties. Road commissioners, welfare superintendents, and health directors are among the county officers more commonly appointed. Some of the officers that are usually elective, such as the coroner, assessor, attorney, comptroller, and surveyor, are appointive in some instances. The county agricultural agent and the home demonstration agent, though not county officers in the strictest sense, are important functionaries at the county level in whose appointment and support county government in many states plays a part.[3] Various county offices of miscellaneous nature are filled by appointment in occasional states or in individual counties. Typical of the offices in this group are those of county veterinarian, mine inspector, inspector of weights and measures, apiary inspector, horticultural inspector, weed commissioner, public defender, and probation officer.

In some cases, as explained in Chapter 4, the governor or a state administrative department appoints certain county officers or shares in their appointment. At the local level, the appointing power is most commonly vested in the general governing body of the county, though for some offices it rests at times with the courts or with other local officers or agencies. In those counties, still few in number, which have a county manager or an elected chief administrator, the local appointing power centers in considerable measure in that officer. In Henrico County, Va., for instance, where manager government has been adopted under an optional law, the manager appoints all administrative officers and employees except the clerk, sheriff, and commonwealth's attorney; and

[2] John Wood and Clayton L. Ringgenberg, *Terms of Office of Elective County Officials in the 48 States* (Iowa County Officers Association, 1954).

[3] See below, chap. 18.

this was the case also in Warwick, Va., while that community, now a city, operated as a county under the manager plan.[4] Rarely, however, is a county executive officer vested with so extensive appointing authority.

Ex officio relationships are widely varied. Perhaps most common is the provision that the county treasurer shall serve ex officio as tax collector. On the other hand, it is sometimes the sheriff rather than the treasurer who is ex officio collector; and in some instances the treasurer is ex officio assessor. Individual county officers frequently serve ex officio as members of county boards or commissions of the kind discussed in the succeeding section.

Generally speaking, the ex officio method of servicing an office is open to criticism. An official assigned to serve a second office is likely to concentrate his efforts on the primary office and may have little time for, or interest in, the one served in an ex officio capacity.[5] Furthermore, a person chosen for a particular office may not be properly qualified for filling another unless the duties of the two are essentially similar. At the county level, nevertheless, in cases where formal merger is impracticable, the ex officio system has sometimes afforded a means of securing virtual consolidation of two or more offices that do not require the services of a full-time official. Under such circumstances, and as long as the ex officio duties have some reasonable relationship or similarity to the primary responsibilities of the official to whom they are assigned, the plan may be used to some advantage.

SPECIAL-FUNCTION BOARDS AND COMMISSIONS[6]

Superimposed upon the general governing body and individual officers in the organizational pattern of county government are numerous boards and commissions charged with designated administrative functions. Disregarding authorizations of such agencies contained in special and local legislation, the United States Bureau of the Census, as of 1944, reported no less than 761 authorizations in the general laws of the states for the mandatory or optional creation of special-function bodies of this character

[4] George W. Spicer, *Fifteen Years of County Manager Government in Virginia* (Charlottesville, University of Virginia Extension, 1951).

[5] On the other hand, the converse situation is occasionally found. In Illinois, for example, where justices of the peace are ex officio members of the township board of auditors, it is not unusual for a candidate to seek election as justice because of a desire for membership on the township board, though he may never intend to qualify and function in a judicial capacity. See below, chap. 12, "Justices of the Peace," p. 307.

[6] These special-function agencies, constituting a part of the county government organization, are not to be confused with the special-purpose *districts* considered in chap. 10. The latter are separately incorporated governmental units established for the provision of designated services, having their own governing agencies, and operating, for the most part, independently of the county and other local units.

in some or all counties.[7] Some states make much more use of special-function agencies than others. Generally speaking, such boards and commissions are used least in New England and most in states having populous metropolitan areas and those with governing bodies composed of township supervisors. Three New England states—Rhode Island (which is without organized county government), Maine, and New Hampshire—made no authorization of special-function bodies by general law; among the remaining 45 states, the other extreme was represented by New Jersey, with 47 authorizations relating to 19 functions, and New York, with 41 authorizations affecting 24 functions. The extent to which authorizations occur in the various states is shown further, in a general way, in Fig. VII.

FIG. VII

State Authorizations for Creation of County Special-Function Boards and Commissions

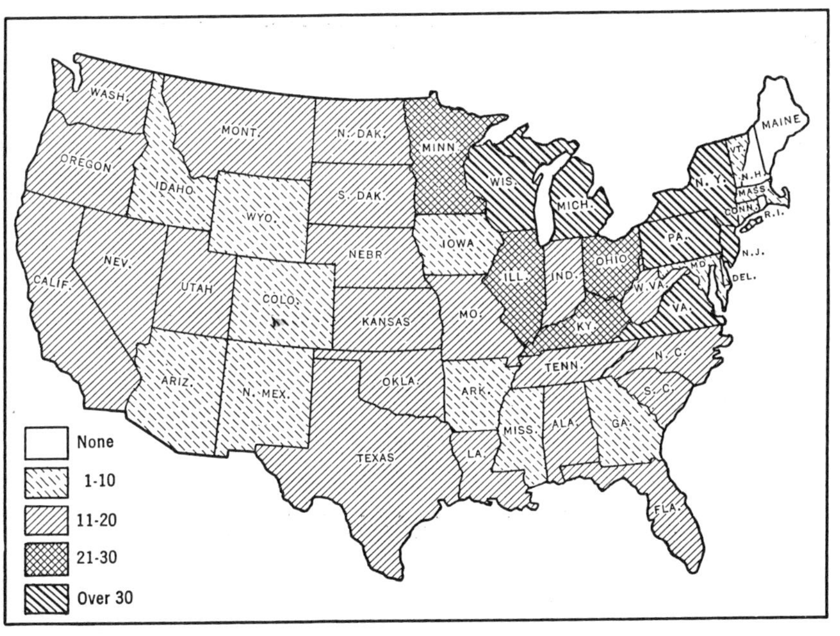

SOURCE: United States Bureau of the Census, *County Boards and Commissions* (Washington, 1947), p. 11.

Special-function boards and commissions are constituted in a variety of ways. Most commonly members are appointed by the county govern-

[7] United States Bureau of the Census, *County Boards and Commissions* (Washington, Government Printing Office, 1947), pp. 9-13, 14-16, 39-91. The discussion in the present section is based principally upon this Census Bureau report. For a summary of the relevant data therein, by the person primarily responsible for preparation of the report, see Edward W. Weidner, "Confused County Picture II," *National Municipal Review*, Vol. XXXV, pp. 228-232, 239 (May, 1946).

ing body, but this method is merely first among several. Some agencies are appointed by state authorities and some by the local courts. Many are composed of the members of the general governing body, and some of other county officers, ex officio. Not infrequently, the membership of a particular board is selected in part by one method and in part by another, the combination of appointive and ex officio members being especially common. In relatively few instances is a part or all of the membership elective. Terms of board members are in most instances two, three, four, or five years, and for members serving in other than an ex officio capacity they are generally staggered.

The authorizations reported by the Census Bureau provided boards and commissions for the performance of 72 different functions. Functional fields in which such bodies are most commonly employed include those of agriculture, airports, assessment, elections, finance, health, highways, hospitals, libraries, penal institutions, personnel administration, planning, recreation, schools, and welfare.[8] Within a given field the powers and duties of special-function agencies are by no means uniform. In the field of agriculture, for example, half of the authorized boards have jurisdiction over county fairs; but the others have varied purposes, such as land advice, livestock sanitation, and agricultural aid. Assessment boards, in some instances, are charged with the original assessment of property, but more commonly they are concerned with the review or equalization of assessments made by other officials. Most boards in the election field are canvassing bodies, though some are charged with general election administration. Special county finance boards in Indiana, Michigan, Ohio, and Oklahoma administer tax-limitation laws;[9] while boards in a number of other states perform various other fiscal functions, such as budget preparation and the selection of county depositories. Some welfare boards are concerned with the categorical programs of outdoor assistance, and others with institutional care.

The number of boards and commissions actually established under legislative authorization varies widely from county to county. Where the authorizing legislation is optional in character the agency contemplated may be established in only one or a few counties of the state, or in none at all. Indeed, optional statutes general in their terms are sometimes designed to meet the special needs of a single county or, at most, a few counties; and under such circumstances it is not to be expected that adoptions of the law's provisions will be numerous. Agencies provided by general law on a mandatory basis would normally be found in every county of the state concerned; but even here law and practice may be at variance, and some counties may not actually set up the agencies. Finally, in addi-

[8] Cf. Weidner, *loc. cit.*

[9] Cf. Clyde F. Snider, "Fiscal Control at the County Level," *National Municipal Review*, Vol. XXX, pp. 579-586 (October, 1941).

tion to boards and commissions established under general-law authorization, there are many others provided for by local or special laws.

In the light of these factors, it is not surprising that the total number of special-function county boards in existence throughout the country has never been determined. However, since most county governments include several agencies of this character, it may reasonably be assumed that the total number runs far into the thousands. The administrative picture is further complicated by the fact that it is not unusual to find, in a given county, two or more boards operating in a single functional field. As Weidner points out, "one hospital board may administer the county general hospital while another administers the tuberculosis hospital.... The county library and the county law library are sometimes under the control of different boards. Two boards in the welfare field are common, one to administer the categorical aid program and one to supervise the county's institutions." [10]

These special-function boards and commissions constitute one of the most serious obstacles in the path of administrative integration in county government. Some such bodies, it is true, are wholly or partially integrated into the general county structure through the appointment of their members by county authority or through fiscal control or administrative supervision; but many enjoy a large degree of independence. Until the number of such semiautonomous agencies is substantially reduced, an integrated county administration will remain, for the most part, an ideal rather than a reality.

NEED FOR ADMINISTRATIVE INTEGRATION

Lack of administrative integration, however, by no means flows entirely from the independence of boards and commissions. Most counties have no chief administrative officer charged with general co-ordination of administrative activities; [11] and the constitutional elective officers are, in many respects, independent of even the general governing body. Furthermore, little has been done at the county level in the direction of departmentalizing activities on a functional basis. Instead of a small number of major departments, each performing all county services within a given field and responsible to a common executive officer, county administrative organization ordinarily consists of numerous lesser agencies that are largely independent both of a common supervising authority and of each other; and frequently several such agencies are operating in the same functional field.

In a particular county, for example, the almshouse, outdoor relief, children's aid, and old-age assistance programs may each be administered

[10] Weidner, *loc. cit.*, p. 231.
[11] See below, chap. 7.

by a different agency instead of all through a single county welfare department.[12] Instead of being co-ordinated under a single department of public works, engineering and related activities may be scattered among various agencies such as a highway superintendent, surveyor, drainage commissioner, park board, and airport commission. Provision for a small number of major administrative departments to displace more numerous smaller agencies is desirable as a means of reducing duplication and overlap and fostering co-ordination of related activities.

The number of administrative departments which it is desirable to have is not likely to be uniform even for all counties of the same state. In general, more populous counties will require more departments because their governments engage in a greater variety of activities. This being the case, it would seem wise to establish by statute, for all counties, only a few basic departments which every county, regardless of its character and population, will need. These should probably include departments of finance, public welfare, public works, law enforcement, and, in those states where the county is the principal unit for school administration, a department of education. The county board in each county should then be empowered to establish whatever additional departments local needs may require.[13]

COMPENSATION OF COUNTY OFFICERS

The amount of compensation to be paid county officers is variously determined by constitutional provision, by statutory enactment, or, ordinarily within limitations prescribed by constitution or statute, by the county governing body. Since the pay of public officials should vary upward or downward with the general level of wages and prices, the practice of freezing or limiting compensation schedules in state constitutions is unwise. In the past, as price levels have risen, counties with absolute or maximum salaries fixed by constitutional provision have had to choose between acquiescence in underpayment of their officials and circumvention of the constitutional limitations by subterfuge. A favorite means of circumvention has been that of paying officers, over and above their regular official salaries, for services performed in designated special capacities. Until recently, for example, this practice was widespread in Illinois, where a constitutional provision of 1870 prescribing maximum county salaries was not repealed until 1952. In 1950, one county in that state, in addition to the maximum salaries permitted by the constitution, paid substantial sums to the county recorder as "superintendent of the

[12] Under the stimulus of federal-aid requirements, many states have now integrated the administration of some or all of the local welfare activities that are supported in part by the federal government.

[13] Cf. R. C. Atkinson, "Principles of a Model County Government," *National Municipal Review*, suppl., Vol. XXII, pp. 469-486 (September, 1933).

photostat machine," to the treasurer as "superintendent of the addressograph machine," and to the clerk of the circuit court as "custodian of escrow funds." As a means of increasing sheriffs' compensation, the Illinois legislature, in 1951, established in each county the office of "supervisor of safety," charged with enforcing the motor-vehicle traffic laws, and provided that this office be held by the sheriff. County boards were authorized to grant compensation for the performance of traffic duties, a device whereby the maximum salaries fixed for sheriffs by the constitution could be doubled.

Measures such as those just described are not necessarily to be condemned. Taken in an open and forthright manner, they may represent practicable means of providing a living wage for public servants despite outmoded provisions of a rigid constitution. A much better means of providing flexibility in compensation schedules, however, is that of omitting salary provisions entirely from state constitutions. Then the legislature is free to regulate the compensation of county officials or to delegate authority in such matters to county governing bodies subject to whatever safeguards it sees fit to impose by general law. On the whole, the most satisfactory plan is probably that whereby the compensation of county officers is determined by county authority subject to appropriate legislative limitations.

THE FEE SYSTEM

Compensation of county officers may take the form of a straight salary from the county treasury or fees collected by the respective officials as payment for specific services performed. Some officers are paid in part on a salary basis and in part by fees. As noted in the preceding chapter, members of county governing bodies are frequently paid on a per diem basis; and per diem compensation occasionally is used also for certain other officers, such as county surveyors, whose duties do not require everyday service. Most county officials, however, are compensated through salaries or fees, or a combination of the two.

Though the present tendency is distinctly toward salary compensation, the fee system still prevails for some or all officers in many states. State statutes establish elaborate schedules of fees to be charged for various services, frequently classifying counties on the basis of population and providing a different fee schedule for the counties of each class. Some fees, such as those for the recording of deeds and other legal documents, are paid by the individuals for whom the service is performed; others, such as fees received by the sheriff for serving various forms of court process, are a charge upon the county treasury. Some fee officers are permitted to retain as compensation whatever fees they collect, regardless of amount; others are entitled to retain only a specified maximum "salary" and are required to pay any excess collections into the county treasury;

still others may deduct from the amount paid into the treasury both their official compensation and the cost of administering their offices.

The fee system of compensation is unsatisfactory for several reasons.[14] In the absence of adequate accounting, it is frequently impossible to determine the amount actually collected as compensation by the various fee officers. If permitted to keep all fees collected, some officers are likely to be grossly overpaid and others underpaid. Where office expense is deductible from fees, the result in many cases is extravagant, if not actually padded, expense accounts. The fee system in theory provides compensation commensurate with the amount of work performed by the collecting officer; yet in practice there may be little relation between services performed and amounts collected. Fee officers may neglect or refuse to perform duties for which they consider the fees inadequate, preferring to devote their time and efforts to the more highly remunerative activities. Fees may be waived in return for political support or other favors, and the system thus perverted to the officer's partisan or personal advantage. In cases where an officer is allowed a specific salary, but with the provision that it shall be paid only from fees, if fees properly payable are less than the designated amount, the officer must suffer the loss or resort to devious means of augmenting collections. If properly administered, the fee system involves excessive bookkeeping, particularly with respect to fees payable by the county. In Illinois, for example, where fee officers deduct their salaries from fee collections and pay excess amounts into the treasury, sums paid by the county must be recorded by the receiving officer, reported to the county board, and, after deduction of the official salary, returned to the county treasurer. Finally, with regard to fees paid by the county, the system operates to confuse the public. "The result is that a particular office appears to be making its own way when in reality it is simply a case of juggling county funds."[15] As applied to justice-of-the-peace courts and jail administration, fee compensation is productive of additional evils which are considered in subsequent chapters.[16]

[14] See Virginia Commission on County Government, *Report on Progress in County Government, County Consolidation and the Fee System in Virginia and Other States* (Richmond, Va., 1934), chap. 4; Kentucky Legislative Council, *The Fee System as a Method of Compensating County Officials* (Frankfort, Ky., 1938); Kenneth E. Vanlandingham, *The Fee System in Kentucky Counties* (Lexington, University of Kentucky Bureau of Government Research, 1951); Florida State University Bureau of Governmental Research and Service, *The Fees System in Florida Counties* (Tallahassee, 1953). Since publication of the Virginia report, that state has eliminated the fee system for all county officers but the county clerk. George W. Spicer, "Virginia," in Paul W. Wager, ed., *County Government across the Nation* (Chapel Hill, University of North Carolina Press, 1950), p. 359.

[15] Henry C. Pepper, *County Government in Colorado* (Fort Collins, Colorado Agricultural College Experiment Station, 1934), p. 42.

[16] See below, chap. 12, "Weaknesses of Justice-of-the-peace System"; chap. 13, "The County Jail."

Students of public affairs now generally agree that fee compensation is cumbersome, inequitable, and outmoded. It is conducive to waste, poor administration, and even dishonesty. Payment to county officers of a straight salary from the county treasury, with the requirement that all fees collected be paid into the treasury, is simpler and more businesslike, reduces bookkeeping, and, in general, conforms to modern accounting practice. Under such a plan, many or all fees now paid from the county treasury might well be abolished entirely, thus eliminating, in some states the present duplicate transaction whereby fees are paid by the county to the official and subsequently returned by him to the county. Fortunately, fee compensation of county officials, though still extensive, is not so widespread as in former years and is steadily losing ground. Its complete abolition at an early date should be given high priority in plans for reorganizing local government.

OFFICERS OF GENERAL ADMINISTRATION

County officers may be considered as falling into two broad classes: functional officers and officers of general administration. Officers in the first of these categories are concerned with the actual performance of the functions or services for which county government exists—law enforcement, administration of justice, health and welfare administration, construction and maintenance of highways, recording of legal documents, and the like. Included in this group, among others, are the sheriff, coroner, county judge, welfare superintendent, highway commissioner, surveyor, recorder or register of deeds, and superintendent of schools.

Officers of general administration, on the other hand, are primarily concerned, not with the *ends* of government themselves but with providing the *means* whereby the functional officers and departments will be enabled to operate in achieving governmental ends. They carry on a wide variety of internal or "housekeeping" activities, such as the keeping of county records and accounts; the administration of elections; the collection, custody, and disbursement of county funds; the auditing of financial transactions; and the providing of legal advice and conducting of county litigation. None of these activities is in itself an object for which county government exists, yet each must be carried on in order that governmental ends may ultimately be obtained. Among the more important county officers charged with duties of general administration are the clerk, the treasurer, the auditor, and the county attorney. A particular officer, of course, need not be charged with either functional or general administrative duties *exclusively*. Thus, the county clerk, though performing duties of general administration primarily, is sometimes charged with certain responsibilities, for example, the licensing function, which might properly be considered functional in character.

Except for the recorder and the surveyor, whose offices are considered in subsequent sections of the present chapter, the various functional officers will be considered in later chapters dealing with the governmental functions which they perform. The officers concerned primarily with general administration will be considered at this point.

County Clerk. The office of county clerk, existing in slightly more than half of the states, is ordinarily filled by popular election. The clerk's principal duty is that of serving as secretary to the county board, and for this reason it would be more logical if he were appointed by that body.[17] Where there is no auditor or comptroller, claims against the county are filed with the clerk for examination and allowance by the county board; and, when claims have been allowed, warrants are drawn upon the county treasury by the clerk for countersignature and payment by the treasurer. Though the clerk does not share with the county board the legal power of allowing claims, any recommendations that he may make are likely to carry considerable weight, since he ordinarily will have gone over the claims prior to the board meeting and will have sought to determine whether the goods concerned have been delivered or the services performed. In some states the county clerk, in addition to serving as secretary to the county board, acts as clerk of one or more of the county's courts of record.

Other duties, varying from state to state, are frequently imposed upon the clerk. In some states he performs important functions in connection with elections, such as receiving nominating petitions, supervising the preparation of ballots, and acting as county registrar of voters. It is not unusual for the clerk to be charged with the issuance of various licenses, such as those for hunting and fishing, marriage licenses, and permits to operate dance halls and other amusement establishments outside municipal corporations. Because of his relation to the county board and his miscellaneous duties, the clerk's office tends to become a sort of clearinghouse for county business in general.

County Treasurer. County treasurers are provided in some or all counties in most states, and in three fourths of the states they are popularly elected. The primary duties of the treasurer are those of (1) receiving county revenues, (2) acting as custodian of county funds, and (3) disbursing county moneys according to law. As collector of the property tax, in which capacity he serves in most states,[18] the treasurer ordinarily collects not only the tax due the county itself but the amounts due the various governmental subdivisions within the county as well as that, if any, due the state. After collecting the total tax, he remits to the various other local governments and to the state their respective shares.

[17] See above, chap. 5, "Organization," p. 128.

[18] In some states the property tax is collected by the sheriff, and a few other states provide for a county collector other than the treasurer.

To protect the public against loss of funds through dishonesty, negligence, or mistake on his part, the county treasurer is usually required to provide an indemnity bond in an amount sufficient to cover any such losses. At one time it was a common practice for treasurers to keep as their own property any interest paid by banks on county deposits. More recently, however, many states have enacted "county depository" laws which (1) provide for designation by the county board or a special finance board of banks which may serve as depositories for county funds, (2) require the county treasurer to deposit in those banks public funds in his custody, and (3) stipulate that interest paid on the funds shall be public property.

Some states, by constitutional provision, either prohibit the county treasurer from succeeding himself or provide that he shall not serve more than two successive terms. These provisions apparently were inserted in state constitutions to insure a careful audit of the treasurer's books at frequent intervals, for a complete audit ordinarily is made whenever there is a change of incumbent of the office. Today, however, more and more states are adopting the practice of requiring a thorough audit at regular intervals, regardless of whether there is a change of incumbent. When this is done, the provisions limiting re-eligibility are quite unnecessary as far as proper auditing is concerned and, in practice, serve only to insure that the treasurer will be, at any given time, a person relatively inexperienced in the duties of his office.[19]

The treasurer's duties, it will be observed, are essentially of a ministerial and bookkeeping nature. He is vested with little or no discretion, being required merely to receive revenues, keep public funds safely, and make payments therefrom upon proper warrant. Moreover, the treasurer's records are often duplicated, to a large extent, by those of some other county officer, particularly the clerk or auditor.[20] When these facts are considered, it is difficult to justify retention of the office of county treasurer in many of the counties where it now exists. A few states have merged the treasurer's office with some other county office; and, in some counties in Georgia and elsewhere, the office has been entirely abolished and provision made for the designation of banks to serve as county depositories and disbursing

[19] Some degree of experience in the office of treasurer, notwithstanding constitutional prohibition of a second consecutive term, results at times from the operation of "rotation agreements" whereby each of two members of the dominant party organization of a county runs for every other term as treasurer and, upon being elected, appoints the other as his chief deputy. Thus, each of the two persons concerned is continuously active in the work of the treasurer's office, alternately as treasurer and as deputy. A similar practice exists in some counties in relation to other offices—especially the office of sheriff—for which there is a constitutional bar to immediate re-election.

[20] In Ohio, for example, "The principal records of the treasurer's office are an exact duplicate of records kept by the auditor"—Ohio Institute, *County Organization and Government in Ohio* (Columbus, 1932), p. 3.

agents.[21] Both of these plans deserve more widespread consideration, particularly as applied to small rural counties. Where the office is retained, the treasurer, because of the non-policy-forming character of his duties, should be appointed by the county board rather than elected as at present.

County Auditor. The office of auditor is found in some or all counties in a number of states. Though usually elected, the auditor, in some instances, is appointed by the county governing body or the courts or selected in some other manner. The primary function of the auditor, in most cases, is the examination of claims against the county and the recommendation of their payment or rejection. As indicated above, something of this nature is commonly done by the county clerk where the office of auditor does not exist. The type of audit here referred to is known in accounting parlance as the *preaudit,* since it is made *before* the actual disbursement of public funds. Its purpose is to determine whether a proposed expenditure has been duly authorized by the appropriating body and, if so, whether funds in the required amount are available for payment. The preaudit is most properly performed by an official responsible to the principal administrative authority of the governmental unit concerned, and, in the case of the county, this would suggest his appointment by the county board or, where such exists, the chief executive officer of the county. Though the title of auditor is commonly used at the county level, that of comptroller is more accurately descriptive of the duties involved in the preaudit. Where the official performing the preaudit is responsible to the principal administrator, he should be empowered to pass upon the wisdom and necessity of proposed expenditures as well as the fact of their legal authorization and the availability of funds, since expenditures, even though authorized in appropriation measures, should not be made if unwise or inexpedient.

Some county auditors, in addition to preauditing, are charged with the *postaudit* function. So called because it occurs *after* disbursement, the postaudit involves a periodic examination of the accounts of county officers handling public funds to determine whether expenditures made have been within the legal authority of the spending unit and whether all required procedures have been observed. Though the period between audits of this nature varies, annual audits are most common. Since the purpose of the postaudit is to determine matters of legality and to detect mistakes and defalcations on the part of administrative officers, its performance is properly a responsibility of an officer independent of the local administration. Since one means of obtaining the desired degree of independence is through popular election, this method of choosing the county officer charged with the postaudit is unobjectionable. But the combining of preaudit and postaudit duties in the hands of a single official, however

[21] See, for example, Melvin Clyde Hughes, *County Government in Georgia* (Athens, University of Georgia Press, 1944), pp. 25-26.

chosen, is inadvisable, since the officer is then placed in the position, at the latter stage, of examining his own accounts.

In governments generally, appointment of the postauditing officer by the legislative body has much to commend it. This method of selection shortens the ballot, provides the requisite independence, and makes the auditing officer directly responsible to the body whose wishes and authorizations, as expressed in appropriation measures, it is his duty to enforce. In those instances where administrative functions have been taken from the general governing body of the county and placed in the hands of a chief administrative officer, the county officer charged with the postaudit might well be appointed by the governing body; but the situation in most counties is complicated by the fact that the governing body is both legislative and administrative in character. What is needed today in most counties is a more effective preaudit by the clerk or secretary of the county board or, in more populous counties, by an appointive comptroller, and a regular and adequate postaudit by an elective county auditor, private accountants employed under state supervision, or state examiners.[22]

County Attorney. Members of county governing bodies and other county officers frequently require legal advice concerning their powers and duties, and most counties on occasion find themselves parties, as either plaintiff or defendant, to civil suits. In some states the prosecuting attorney, in addition to his duties in the enforcement of criminal law, supplies this legal counsel and represents the county in civil actions. In other instances such civil-law functions are in the hands of another law officer, usually known as the county attorney.[23] Ordinarily appointed by the county governing body, the county attorney has as his principal duties the advising of county officers in official matters, the instituting and conducting of civil suits on behalf of the county, and the defending of the county when civil actions are brought against it.[24] Other functions are also sometimes performed, such as assisting in the preparation of county bonds and tax-anticipation warrants and examining the title to real estate which the county proposes to purchase.[25]

Provision for a county attorney in addition to the prosecutor has the advantage of separating the civil and criminal phases of legal work and permitting specialization in each. The plan is probably advisable in coun-

[22] See below, chap. 19, "Accounting and Auditing"; also, concerning state audit of local accounts, above, chap. 4, "Inspection."

[23] The official title of the office is not uniform, and in some cases county attorney is the title of the prosecutor.

[24] The elective "attorney or solicitor" referred to in Table 5 is apparently the prosecuting officer.

[25] For an account of the multifarious duties of the county attorney in a populous New York county, see Elmer R. Weil, "What Are the Duties of Erie County's Law Office?" *The County Officer,* Vol. XIX, pp. 166-169 (August, 1954).

ties having sufficient legal business to require the full-time service of two lawyers; though even when the prosecuting attorney is charged with civil as well as criminal-law duties, a degree of specialization may be achieved in populous counties by the prosecutor's appointment of certain assistants to work in each field. In small counties, however, there is not likely to be enough civil-law work to warrant paying more than a meager salary, and an underpaid position rarely attracts a high type of talent. In such cases, it may be desirable to combine prosecuting and civil duties in a single office, particularly since many prosecuting attorneys now receive salaries so small that they must be supplemented by private practice.[26] One well-paid full-time county law officer may offer better value in services than two officials who are underpaid or are serving on a part-time basis. Perhaps as good a solution as any, in the light of varying needs, would be a law providing for a county attorney only in the more populous counties, or one making the appointment of such an officer optional with the respective governing bodies.

THE RECORDER OR REGISTER OF DEEDS

About half of the states provide for an elective county recorder or register of deeds[27] whose duty consists in making and preserving public records of various kinds of legal documents.[28] The documents for which recording facilities are almost always provided are those relating to real estate titles, such as deeds, mortgages, leases, and instruments showing the satisfaction of mortgages and leases. Records of this nature are designed to protect landowners by providing them with a complete history of the title to their properties, and also, to protect prospective purchasers or mortgagees by making it possible for them to detect any flaws in land titles. It is now the definite policy in most states that the title to all interests in land shall be apparent on the records; and practically all documents affecting title to real estate must be recorded to be valid against an innocent third party.

Recorders usually are required to prepare indexes of the land records in their offices. At best, however, the task of searching the records to verify the title to any parcel of land is tedious and expensive; and, as the recorded documents establish only a presumptive title and are not con-

[26] See below, chap. 13, "The Prosecuting Attorney."

[27] In other states the recording function is devolved upon other designated county or town officers.

[28] On the recorder's office and problems of records management, see Frank W. Kroeger, "County Recorders," *The County Officer,* Vol. XV, No. 3, pp. 17-19 (June, 1950); Wayne Grover, "Records at the Grass Roots," *ibid.,* No. 5, pp. 9-12, 25 (August, 1950), and "The Disposition of County Records," *ibid.,* Vol. XVII, pp. 164-166, 188 (June, 1952); Vernon L. Beal, "Records Management in Local Government," *ibid.,* pp. 280-282 (September, 1952).

clusive, persons relying upon them take the risk of defects being disclosed at a later time. To avoid the expense and delay of repeated examinations of the records for each purchase or mortgage, and to escape the uncertainty of the results, abstract and title-guaranty companies have developed. Furthermore, there has been established in some jurisdictions a simplified plan of land-title registration known as the Torrens system. Devised by Sir Robert Torrens, a British economist, and first successfully employed in Australia, this system provides for registration of the land *title* itself rather than registration or recording of mere documentary *evidence* of title. The basic object of the plan is to make the land-transfer transaction as simple and as safe as the transfer of other types of property. Effective with respect to a particular piece of property on its first transfer after establishment of the system, the plan involves an official examination of title and, if the title is found to be good, the issuance by a court, or by an administrative official pursuant to court order, of a title certificate. A copy of this certificate is filed with a registrar of titles, who in some instances is the county recorder ex officio, and any subsequent transfer of the property is effected by merely assigning the certificate and recording the assignment. An essential element in the Torrens plan is a system of state title insurance financed by moderate fees assessed for the issuance of title certificates and the recording of certificate transfers. From the insurance fund thus provided, indemnification is made to any person who may suffer loss because of misdescription or other error in the title certificate, as well as to anyone who may subsequently show that an interest of his in the property was erroneously foreclosed by the registration proceedings.[29] Now authorized in some 19 states, establishment of the Torrens system in some instances is optional with the respective counties, and in any event original registration under the system is optional with individual landowners. As a result, actual use of the plan is much more limited than the extent of its authorization might suggest. Notwithstanding that the system offers some significant advantages, title insurance generally can be secured more quickly than initial registration under the Torrens plan, and this may well be one reason why Torrens registration has not made greater progress.[30]

[29] "Torrens System," *The Encyclopedia Americana* (New York, 1955), Vol. XXVI, pp. 708-709; R. G. Patton, "The Torrens System of Land Title Registration," *Minnesota Law Review,* Vol. XIX, pp. 519-535 (April, 1935); "The Torrens System in Illinois," *Illinois Law Review,* Vol. XLV, pp. 500-509 (September–October, 1950). See also, William C. Niblack, *An Analysis of the Torrens System of Conveying Land* (Chicago, Callaghan, 1912); Jerome Beatty, "Is Your Title Clear?" *Reader's Digest,* Vol. XXVIII, No. 166, pp. 85-87 (February, 1936).

[30] Cf. "The Torrens System in Illinois," *loc. cit.* Another possible reason for preferring title insurance is the fact that the Torrens system, though reducing the difficulties and inaccuracies of title examination, does not eliminate the necessity for an accurate ground survey—a service ordinarily provided by reputable title companies. See Philip Kissam, "A Solution for Land Transfer Difficulties," *Scientific Monthly,* Vol. XLVII, pp. 44-47 (July, 1938).

Land records, though comprising the most important single group of documents recorded in the office of the county recorder, are by no means the only ones. Some states provide for recording documents concerning title to personal property. Among these are chattel mortgages; releases, extensions, and assignments of such mortgages; and bills of sale. Other instruments, the recording of which is provided for in some states, include liens of various kinds, articles of incorporation, marks and brands of livestock, and city street plans and real estate subdivisions.

Records in the recorder's office most commonly take the form of full and complete copies of the documents concerned. Traditionally, recording was done by longhand in heavy bound volumes, and this practice is still followed to a considerable extent. Today, however, some states authorize the use of loose-leaf books and typewriting. Even more significant is the growing tendency to provide for recording by photostating and microfilming. Photostatic recording, as compared with the old longhand method, has the advantages of speed and indisputable accuracy. Photographic equipment is costly, but a compensating factor is found in the smaller number of employees required to perform the recording work. Microfilming has the additional advantages of saving space and, by making it practicable to store duplicate sets in some place outside the courthouse, affording a means of insuring against loss of records.[31] Microfilmed copies of records have been found to require only about 2 per cent of the storage space required for the originals.[32] With the increasing pressure for courthouse space, it is not surprising that some counties are microfilming many of their old records and destroying the originals, and that more and more states are authorizing the microfilming of current records and the destruction of the originals after a designated number of years. Even where original records are not to be deliberately destroyed, the making of microfilm copies provides a means of insuring against the complete loss of records through fire, flood, or other catastrophe. In Illinois, for example, where at least 80 per cent of the state's counties have lost part or all of their records at one time or another through courthouse fires,[33] a number of counties have recently inaugurated programs of microfilming their records and depositing the film copies with the state library. Microfilm records in the recorder's office are made readily available for examination through the use of appropriate projection apparatus. Laws authorizing

[31] See Walter H. Wickins, "Five County Record Books on a Hundred Feet of Film," *American City*, Vol. LIX, No. 1, pp. 59-60 (January, 1944); Margaret C. Norton, "Microphotography and County Records," *Illinois Libraries*, Vol. XXVI, pp. 505-509 (December, 1944); Earl R. Hogan, "The County Recorders: Microfilming," *The County Officer*, Vol. XVII, pp. 116-117 (April, 1952); Kenneth T. Power, "Microfilm in Operation," *ibid.*, Vol. XVIII, pp. 218-221 (September, 1953).

[32] "Microfilming of Detroit Court Records Reduces Storage Space by 98 Per Cent," *Journal of the American Judicature Society*, Vol. XXXVII, pp. 42-43 (August, 1953).

[33] Norton, *loc. cit.*

microfilming ordinarily stipulate that the microfilm reproduction shall be deemed to be an original record, and that it may be so introduced as evidence before courts or administrative agencies. A uniform act pertaining to photographic copies of records as evidence was recommended in 1949 by the National Conference of Commissioners on Uniform State Laws and has now been adopted by a considerable number of states.

THE COUNTY SURVEYOR

A county office of long standing, but of very minor importance today, is that of the surveyor. This office exists in most states outside New England. The surveyor is usually popularly elected and compensated by fees. His primary duty is that of making land surveys and determining boundary lines and corners, when ordered to do so by the courts or upon the request of individual landowners.[34] Since, however, the boundaries of landholdings have now become relatively stabilized, there is little call for his services. The office might well be abolished and such surveys as are required made by licensed private surveyors.

ORGANIZATIONS OF COUNTY OFFICERS

County officers in many states are banded together in state-wide organizations for protecting and promoting their common interests and the interests, as they interpret them, of county government. In various states will be found state associations of county commissioners or supervisors, county clerks, county treasurers, sheriffs, coroners, recorders, highway commissioners, surveyors, assessors, prosecuting attorneys, and other county officers. In some instances there is a separate organization for the incumbents of each office, and in others a single association serves two or more offices. The principal activities of these associations ordinarily consist of an annual convention and concerted action with respect to proposed legislation. In some states, the organizations serving individual county offices or combinations of offices are joined together, at times along with one or more associations of township officers, in a single state-wide federation. Examples are the Indiana County and Township Officials Association and the Illinois Association of County Officials. Federations of this nature usually hold annual conventions and sometimes publish official magazines. Some regularly maintain at the state capital, at least during legislative sessions, a "legislative representative" (lobbyist) charged with promoting proposed legislation favored by the association and opposing proposals deemed inimical to its interests.

In 1936 there was organized a National Association of County Officials

[34] In some instances the surveyor also serves ex officio as county highway engineer or supervisor.

with membership consisting of county officers in the 48 states; and by the early 1950's this organization had some 6,500 paid members. Whereas state associations of county officials are interested primarily in state legislation and state-local relations, the foremost concern of the national association is with federal-county relations. With its general offices now in Washington, D.C., the organization has been particularly active in such matters as intergovernmental fiscal relations, federal aid for highway programs, grants for public assistance, and federal grant-in-aid programs generally. Information is distributed to county officials concerning proposed federal legislation of interest to counties; and at times the association takes a definite stand for or against proposals. The national association holds an annual convention; is officially represented at many meetings of the state associations, with which it seeks to co-operate in every way feasible; and publishes an official monthly journal entitled *The County Officer.*[35] The various state and national organizations do much to increase the political strength of county and other local officers and to enhance their influence over the course of legislation. Though this influence is in many respects beneficial, the action of some organizations, in defending particular local offices and their powers against legislative curtailment, has operated at times to deter the effecting of desirable improvements.

In addition to organizations of the kind described in the preceding paragraphs, mention should be made of the professional associations of national, state, and local officials organized on a nation-wide basis. Some county officials, for example, particularly from among those of the appointive group, are affiliated with the American Public Welfare Association, the American Public Works Association, the Federation of Tax Administrators, the National Association of Assessing Officers, and the National Association of Housing Officials. County managers, when meeting the prescribed professional qualifications, are admitted to membership in the International City Managers' Association. Organizations such as these exercise a substantial influence in the improvement of local administration and the promotion of intergovernmental co-operation.

COUNTY EMPLOYEES

In addition to the various county officers and their deputies, the work of county government requires employees, the number of whom will depend partly upon the size and population of the county. Some of these employees perform duties of a clerical nature in the courthouse offices, but others, for example, certain highway and welfare employees, engage in work which may take them to all parts of the county. The total number

[35] Dean Z. Haddick, "NACO and Its Organization," *The County Officer,* Vol. XVII, pp. 231-233 (August, 1952); see also, M. Ward Forman, "President's Report for 1951-52," *ibid.,* pp. 228-230.

of county officers and employees in the United States, as of October, 1956, has been estimated by the United States Bureau of the Census at 620,000.[36]

Although the quality of personnel determines in large measure the success of administration in county government, the problem of recruiting and maintaining an efficient staff of employees has not received adequate attention. This may be accounted for in part by the feeling that in most counties the number of employees is not sufficiently large to warrant the effort and expense necessary to bring about needed improvements. The importance of the personnel problem is emphasized, however, by the fact that some 40 per cent of all county expenditures goes for salaries and wages and that even in small counties with few employees, the salary-and-wage item is of major significance.

Among the important considerations in personnel administration are recruitment, pay and treatment while in the service, on-the-job training, and retirement benefits for superannuated employees. Certain aspects of these problems will now be discussed.[37]

THE MERIT SYSTEM IN RECRUITMENT

In a consideration of public employment the problem of recruitment is of primary importance; and in connection with recruitment the use of the merit system of appointment has been the most significant development. But though the merit system has made substantial progress at the national, state, and municipal levels, it is still employed to only a very limited extent in county government. A bare two dozen counties were reported as operating under civil service laws in 1913,[38] and in the years that followed progress continued to be extremely slow. Writing in 1936, H. Eliot Kaplan, secretary of the National Civil Service Reform League, declared: "In no unit of government has the merit system been more neglected than in the county service.... In county governments we have generally had about the poorest kind of government. Politics has been exploited to the highest degree. Nepotism has been practiced to the limit. Patronage has been rampant.... Corruption, too, has found its place in the wake of spoils."[39]

[36] United States Bureau of the Census, *State Distribution of Public Employment in 1956* (Washington, 1957).

[37] For comprehensive discussions of the personnel problem in government, see Commission of Inquiry on Public Service Personnel, *Better Government Personnel* (New York, McGraw-Hill, 1935); O. Glenn Stahl, *Public Personnel Administration,* 4th ed. (New York, Harper, 1956); Leonard D. White, *Introduction to the Study of Public Administration,* 4th ed. (New York, Macmillan, 1955), chaps. 21-30.

[38] Robert W. Belcher, "The Merit System and the County Civil Service," *Annals of the American Academy of Political and Social Science,* Vol. XLVII, pp. 101-111 (May, 1913).

[39] H. Eliot Kaplan, "A Personnel Program for the County Service," *National Municipal Review,* Vol. XXV, pp. 596-600, 616, 596-597 (October, 1936). Concerning nepotism in Colorado counties, see Pepper, *op. cit.,* pp. 39-40.

More recently, extension of the merit system to additional counties has been at a somewhat better rate, though even yet scarcely more than a good beginning has been made.

Perhaps as many as 300 American counties, or some 10 per cent of the total number, are today provided in some manner with civil service machinery for making appointments on the basis of competitive examination. Some of these have their own civil service commissions, ordinarily appointed by the county governing body or, where such exists, by the county executive. A few counties have single personnel officers, and others, more numerous, are served by state personnel agencies. Only New York and Ohio among the states require all counties to operate under the merit system, this being a constitutionally imposed requirement in these two states. Under New York law each county may select, through action of its board of supervisors, any of three forms of civil service administration: (1) a county civil service commission, (2) a county personnel officer, or (3) administration by the state civil service department.[40] Most of the state's counties have elected to have their own local commissions, though each of the other methods of administration has been chosen in a few instances. Outside New York, application of the merit principle to county personnel is more spotty. Some 40 per cent of California's counties were reported in 1955 as having civil service departments or personnel officers.[41] Elsewhere a number of relatively populous counties scattered among several states have their own civil service agencies. Included, among others, are the counties of Jefferson and Mobile in Alabama, Fulton in Georgia, Cook in Illinois, Baltimore and Montgomery in Maryland, Wayne in Michigan, St. Louis and Ramsey in Minnesota, St. Louis in Missouri, Mecklenburg in North Carolina, Multnomah in Oregon, and Milwaukee in Wisconsin. A considerable number of counties, for the most part in New Jersey and Ohio, are served by the state civil service commission on either a compulsory or an optional basis. New Jersey permits any county, by popular vote, to adopt the merit system and thereby place its personnel under the jurisdiction of the state commission; and most of the state's counties have exercised that option. In Ohio statutory responsibility for county personnel services rests with the state commission. It appears, however, that staff inadequacies have made it impossible for the commission to provide anything approaching a complete merit system for county

[40] The few county offices in the five counties within New York City are provided with personnel service, under statutory mandate, by the state department. The state department also serves rural school districts, but service for towns and special districts is provided by the respective counties. See Henry J. McFarland, "Personnel Services for Local Government: The New York Program," *Public Personnel Review*, Vol. XVI, pp. 148-152 (July, 1955).

[41] Harry W. Graham, "County Personnel Administration—Wide Variety in California Systems," *The Tax Digest*, Vol. XXXIII, pp. 99-105 (March, 1955).

employees in that state.[42] Given the necessary staff and financing, state administration of the personnel function offers many advantages over local commissions as a means of meeting the needs of small rural counties; but, as long as many of the states are themselves without general civil service agencies, the method affords little promise of widespread adoption.

In the final analysis, of course, the extent of the merit system in county government cannot be measured solely by the number of counties having formal civil service machinery. For one thing, a county may be provided with a civil service agency at the local or state level but have so many positions exempted by law from the agency's jurisdiction that personnel standards are substantially weakened. Again, account must be taken of the relative effectiveness of administration with respect to positions within the commission's jurisdiction. It is quite possible to have the form of the merit system without its substance. Partisan sabotage of the system is by no means uncommon. Though there are innumerable ways in which the spirit of civil service may be violated while the letter of the law is still observed, one of the most common is through the abuse of temporary appointments. To prevent interruption in the public business civil service laws generally provide that when a vacancy occurs and no register of eligible candidates is currently in existence for the position concerned, the appropriate authority, with the consent of the commission, may appoint someone without examination to serve until an examination can be given and a list of eligibles established. Politically minded commissions, at times, have deliberately permitted registers to lapse so that they might authorize temporary appointments on a partisan basis. Though some laws limit the duration of a temporary appointment to 90 days or some other prescribed period, such an appointment may, in the absence of a prohibition of such practice, be renewed again and again. And in any event, experience derived from service on the job gives a temporary appointee substantial advantage over other candidates if he elects to take the examination for the position when it is offered. In view of these circumstances, it is not surprising that in "civil service" counties a large percentage of the classified positions may, at a given time, be filled on a temporary basis or that some incumbents retain their positions on that basis for an extended period. Indeed, one employee in the service of Cook County, Ill., is reported to have held his position as a "temporary" appointee for 20 years.[43]

[42] Under Ohio law, as an alternative to direct state administration in any county, the state commission may designate the civil service commission of the county's largest city to serve as its agent in administering the county civil service. This plan has been followed in at least one instance, with Cleveland's municipal civil service commission providing personnel service for Cuyahoga County.

[43] Joseph Pois, Edward M. Martin, and Lyman S. Moore, *The Merit System in Illinois with Special Reference to Chicago and Cook County* (Chicago, Joint Committee on the Merit System, 1935), p. 37.

On the brighter side of the picture is the fact that even in counties having no general civil service program, some welfare employees may be under the merit system. The Social Security Act requires that state and local employees administering federal aid for old-age assistance or other relief programs be selected on a merit basis. Where counties served by no regular civil service agency participate in administering such federal-aid programs, they have been provided with special merit systems, frequently operated by state "merit-system councils," for the selection of county welfare employees engaged in these functions.

Though the merit system in recruitment has thus made some headway in county government during recent years, approximately 90 per cent of the counties continue to be unserved by civil service agencies of general jurisdiction, and a large majority of county employees are still subject to appointment and dismissal on a patronage basis.[44] Indeed, apart from townships and nonschool special districts, no other class of governmental units remains today so permeated by the spoils system.[45]

PAY STANDARDS

The term *merit system* is commonly used, and was used in the preceding section, to mean the appointment of public employees on the basis of their qualifications for the job concerned, as demonstrated through competitive examinations, rather than on the basis of service to the controlling political party, as under the "spoils system." In a broader sense, however, the merit system of personnel administration involves much more than proper recruitment, though that is one of its basic aspects. Recruitment on the basis of fitness, though the original object of civil service reform, is now properly viewed as only the first of several elements in any comprehensive merit system. The system also involves such factors as a probation period, promotion on the basis of demonstrated capacity and performance, protected tenure with provision for removal where the good of the service requires, adequate and equitable compensation, in-service training, and a fair and adequate retirement system. As the merit-system concept broadens, civil service agencies, once concerned solely with recruitment, are constantly being charged with additional responsibilities for the development and administration of programs which include these newer features.

One of the most important problems in over-all personnel administra-

[44] Cf. Stahl, *op. cit.*, pp. 30-31.

[45] Except in New York, where it is required of all governmental units of whatever kind, the merit system appears to be practically nonexistent in township government. Though some special districts of nonschool varieties, especially among those in metropolitan areas, have merit systems, the large majority of such units are without civil service provisions. School districts do not ordinarily have civil service commissions, but state certification requirements operate as a kind of merit system for teaching personnel.

tion is that of compensation. If competent employees are to enter the public service and remain, the salaries offered must bear some substantial relation to those paid for similar types of work in private enterprise. This is not to say that public salaries must always equal or exceed those in private employment, but it does mean that any differential in favor of private salaries must not be excessive. In seeking personnel to man its offices, government is inevitably in competition with private employment; and, if private salaries are substantially higher than public, the most desirable workers will be drawn off by private establishments and government left with a second-rate working force. In the past, most county salaries have not been high enough to attract the most satisfactory type of employee. Even in counties where recruitment is by the merit system, the low salaries offered have frequently deterred able candidates from taking examinations for appointment.

Not only should county salaries be sufficient in amount to attract competent personnel, but the salary scale should also be equitable; that is, like pay should be provided for like work throughout the service. If the clerks in some county offices are paid less than those in other offices for the same kind of work, and if the lower-paid employees discover the fact, as they are certain to do, the morale of the service inevitably suffers. In many counties today there is a marked variation in the salaries paid employees engaged in similar activities. County positions need to be classified according to character of the work involved, so that all employees performing duties of the same type and grade will be placed in the same class and paid at the same rate. All too few counties, as yet, have attempted anything in the nature of a scientific job classification. When this fact is considered, along with the widespread inadequacy of salaries, the low standards prevailing in county personnel generally are by no means surprising. There is urgent need in county government today both for a general raising of the level of employee salaries and for a standardization of compensation through job classification.

IN-SERVICE TRAINING

One of the most encouraging recent developments in county personnel has been in the matter of on-the-job or in-service training. Traditionally, county officers and employees, usually inexperienced in their official duties prior to their election or appointment, have been left to learn those duties themselves by trial and error—a method which has often been costly to the public. On leaving office, incumbents have taken with them their hard-won knowledge, leaving their successors to gain their own experience in the same haphazard fashion. In some instances holdover deputies or clerks have provided the staffs of new officers with a degree of prior experience, but at other times there has been a "clean sweep" in office personnel and even this measure of continuity has been wanting.

During the past two or three decades, substantial recognition has been accorded the problem arising from the passing of local offices into inexperienced hands every two or four years; and a beginning has been made in many states in providing new officers and employees with instruction in their official powers and duties. This is ordinarily done through meetings or conferences, usually known as training schools, short courses, workshops, or institutes, conducted for the respective official groups—sheriffs, clerks, treasurers, assessors, and so on. These short courses, as we shall call them, are most commonly provided by state government departments, state university institutes, or state associations of county officials, or by two or more such sponsors in co-operation. Thus, a short course for county highway commissioners may be offered by the state highway department, the university institute, the state association of highway commissioners, or, collaboratively, by two of these agencies or all three. Designed primarily for new officers and their deputies, but with a welcome accorded all employees of the office concerned, short courses are commonly administered on a state-wide or regional basis, though sometimes county by county, and vary in duration from a single day to a week or more. Instructors are drawn from university faculties, from the state departments, and from the more experienced and successful local officers within the group concerned. Through lectures, discussion sessions, and demonstrations, the student officers acquire training in their legal powers and in appropriate practices and procedures in the management of their offices. Closely related to the short-course training are the manuals, or guidebooks, for local officers now frequently prepared by the various sponsoring agencies, particularly some of the university institutes. These guidebooks attempt to set forth in simple and nontechnical language, within the briefest compass practicable and so arranged as to be most readily usable, the law relating to the office concerned and, sometimes also, various methods and practices involved in the performance of official duties. The guidebooks are distributed to local officers throughout the state and, frequently, to other interested persons as well, and are sometimes used as textbooks in the short courses.

Among the state departments most commonly providing short-course training or guidebooks, or participating in their provision, are the department of health (for local health officers), the tax commission or equivalent agency (for tax assessors and collectors), and the highway department (for highway commissioners and engineers). University and college institutes providing short courses, guidebooks, or both are steadily growing in number. Examples, to mention but a few, are the Institute of Local Government of Pennsylvania State University, the Institute of Government and Public Affairs of the University of Illinois, and the University of Mississippi's Bureau of Public Administration. Especially noteworthy for its broad program and long record of service is the University of North Carolina's Institute of Government. Founded in the 1920's by Albert Coates, a law professor who has been its director from the beginning, the institute operated for a time under private auspices but since 1942 has been an integral part of the state university. The North Carolina institute offers numerous short courses for county and municipal officials, prepares practical guidebooks, and provides a variety of other services to state and local officers. In no small measure this pioneer organization has served as a prototype for several of the institutes more recently established.[46]

Short courses and guidebooks constitute a significant step toward reducing the inefficiency in local administration that results from rapid turnover and an inexperienced staff. Incidentally, it may be observed that members of academic faculties participating in short-course programs often learn as much from local officials, concerning the day-to-day administration of local offices, as they are able to teach those officials regarding the more theoretical aspects of government. Properly organized and conducted, such programs constitute a fruitful source of mutual helpfulness and understanding on the part of professional teachers and their officer students.

RETIREMENT SYSTEMS

It is now generally recognized that a suitable system of retirement on pension is an essential element in a sound personnel program—advantageous to employees and public alike. Such a system affords an inducement for better-qualified persons to enter the public service and for competent employees to remain therein. Without a formal retirement system, there is a tendency to keep aged employees on the payroll at full salary as long as they are able to report for duty and go through the motions of their job, even though younger persons must be hired to do much of their work. This situation results in both added cost and inefficiency; yet it is rarely feasible, from either a political or a humanitarian standpoint, to discharge an employee with a long record of faithful service who is without means of support. A retirement system offers a method whereby an employee, upon reaching a designated age (usually 65 or 70), may be separated from the service as a matter of course and awarded an annuity which, if his employment has been of considerable duration, should provide him with a reasonable subsistence. In thus relieving older employees

[46] The development and activities of the North Carolina institute are detailed by its founder and director in Albert Coates, *The Story of the Institute of Government* (Bloomington, Ind., National University Extension Association, 1944). For a brief account, see Paul W. Wager, "A North Carolina Experiment," *National Municipal Review*, Vol. XXXIII, pp. 75-80 (February, 1944).

of active duty, the system keeps lines of promotion open and thereby provides an additional incentive to younger persons of ability to enter and remain in the service.

Retirement systems are financed in various ways, but the most common plan, and in general the most satisfactory, is that whereby contributions are made by both employees and the employing government. Employees' contributions, ordinarily deducted from their pay, now amount in most instances to about 5 per cent of their respective salaries; and government contributions, made through appropriations, are usually at least equal to those of the employees and sometimes exceed them. Moneys from the two sources are pooled in a trust fund and invested at interest, with both principal and accumulated interest ultimately being available for payment of benefits. The amount of the pension received by a particular employee on retirement will depend upon the amounts contributed to his account during his employment, and these, in turn, depend upon the length of his service and his rate of compensation. In practice, the pension is often about half the amount of the employee's salary at the time of retirement.

Some counties, for the most part those in the more populous category, have had retirement systems for a number of years. However, the great majority of counties have been without retirement plans, and in small counties the administration of individual pension systems has been impracticable. In units with only a few employees administrative costs are high, retirements may not be adequately staggered, and it is difficult to diversify properly the investment of retirement trust funds. To facilitate retirement provisions for local employees in general, and particularly to meet the needs of small units, several states during recent decades have established state-administered retirement systems for local personnel and provided for participation therein by counties and other local units on either an optional or a mandatory basis. Other states, instead of providing a separate plan for local employees, have required or authorized the coverage of local personnel under the system maintained by the state for its own employees. In either case, pooling of the resources and needs of numerous governmental units has reduced administrative costs per employee, facilitated proper staggering of retirements, and made simple a wide diversification of trust-fund investments. Such plans for local participation in state-administered systems have gone far toward providing retirement benefits for local employees who would otherwise be without coverage; and states that have not yet enacted enabling legislation in this field would be well advised to do so. As of October, 1952, it was estimated that no less than 47.8 per cent of all nonschool county employees were covered by state or local retirement plans along with 24.7 per cent of nonschool township employees, 47.7 per cent of the nonschool employees of special districts, and 78.6 per cent of all local school employees.[47] Many retirement systems, whether administered locally or on a state-wide basis, also provide for death and disability benefits.

COUNTY EMPLOYEES AND SOCIAL SECURITY

Prior to 1950 government employees were excluded from coverage under the system of old-age and survivors insurance provided by the federal Social Security Act. Amendments of that year, however, permitted coverage of state and local employees not covered under existing state or local retirement systems, through voluntary agreements entered into by the respective states with the federal security administrator. Old-age and survivors insurance is administered by the federal government and, save in its application to self-employed persons, is financed by a payroll tax falling equally on the employer and the covered employee.[48] Retirement annuities are provided for covered workers at the age of 65 (62 in the case of women), as well as certain benefits for their dependent relatives and survivors.

Pursuant to the 1950 amendments, the states proceeded to make the benefits of the federal system available to their employees and those of their subdivisions. A majority of the states soon completed agreements with the security administrator for coverage of state or local employees, or both. Agreements in effect by the spring of 1952 covered some 10,000 employing units and at least 350,000 employees; and by that time at least 1,000 counties, or approximately one third of the total number, had placed some or all of their employees under the federal system.[49] As of October, 1952, according to Census Bureau estimates, federal old-age and survivors insurance had been extended to 22.5 per cent of all nonschool county employees, 5.3 per cent of nonschool township employees, 14.8 per cent of the nonschool employees of special districts, and 4.2 per cent of local school employees.[50]

In 1954 the Social Security Act was amended to eliminate the exclusion from coverage of public employees already covered by state or local retirement systems, thus enabling the states to provide for coverage under the federal system without dissolving existing state and local retirement plans. This change made many additional state and local employees eligible for old-age and survivors insurance and has served as a stimulus to the states to expand state and local coverage under the

[47] United States Bureau of the Census, *Retirement Coverage of State and Local Government Employees* (Washington, 1953).

[48] The present (1957) total rate of tax is 4½ per cent (2¼ per cent each on employer and employee), imposed on the first $4,200 of compensation received by the employee in any one year.

[49] Alvin M. David, "Effects of the 1950 Amendments in the Federal Old-age and Survivors Insurance Program," *The County Officer,* Vol. XVII, pp. 203-205, 213 (July, 1952).

[50] *Retirement Coverage of State and Local Government Employees.*

federal system. By late 1954, 44 states had entered into agreements with the security administrator for federal coverage of varying extent.[51] When social security coverage is considered along with coverage under state and local retirement plans, it is evident that counties and other local governments have made more progress in providing retirement benefits for their employees than in most aspects of personnel administration.

REFERENCES

Books and Special Studies

ASSEFF, Emmett, and HIGHSAW, R. B., *Civil Service in the Louisiana Local Units of Government* (Baton Rouge, Louisiana State University Bureau of Government Research, 1951).

COATES, Albert, *The Story of the Institute of Government* [*of the University of North Carolina*] (Bloomington, Ind., National University Extension Association, 1944).

Florida State University Bureau of Governmental Research and Service, *The Fees System in Florida Counties* (Tallahassee, Fla., 1953).

HOWERTON, Huey Blair, *A Guidebook of County Appointive Offices* [*in Mississippi*] (University, University of Mississippi Bureau of Public Administration, 1949).

Kansas Legislative Council, *Compensation of County Officials* (Topeka, Kan., 1956).

Kentucky Legislative Council, *The Fee System as a Method of Compensating County Officials* (Frankfort, Ky., 1938).

RINGGENBERG, Clayton L., comp., *County Salaries in Iowa—1954* (Iowa City, State University of Iowa Institute of Public Affairs, 1954).

SIKES, Pressly S., *A Manual for County Auditors of Indiana* (Bloomington, Indiana University Bureau of Government Research, 1946).

United States Bureau of the Census, *Elective Offices of State and County Governments* (Washington, 1946).

———, *Retirement Coverage of State and Local Government Employees* (Washington, 1953).

VANLANDINGHAM, Kenneth E., *The Fee System in Kentucky Counties* (Lexington, University of Kentucky Bureau of Government Research, 1951).

WOOD, John, and RINGGENBERG, Clayton L., *Terms of Office of Elective County Officials in the 48 States* (Iowa County Officers Association, 1954).

Articles

BEAL, Vernon L., "Records Management in Local Government," *The County Officer*, Vol. XVII, pp. 280-282 (September, 1952).

BELCHER, Robert W., "The Merit System and the County Civil Service," *Annals of the American Academy of Political and Social Science*, Vol. XLVII, pp. 101-111 (May, 1913).

CHRISTGAU, Victor, "The 1954 Social Security Amendments as They Affect State and Local Governments," *State Government*, Vol. XXVII, pp. 232-235 (November, 1954).

[51] Victor Christgau, "The 1954 Social Security Amendments as They Affect State and Local Governments," *State Government*, Vol. XXVII, pp. 232-235 (November, 1954).

"Coverage of State and Local Government Employees under Social Security Act–Amended," *The County Officer*, Vol. XVI, pp. 15-17, 28 (January, 1951).

DAVID, Alvin M., "Effects of the 1950 Amendments in the Federal Old-age and Survivors Insurance Program," *The County Officer*, Vol. XVII, pp. 203-205, 213 (July, 1952).

FREIBERG, Harry A., "A Successful County Treasurer's Office," *National Municipal Review*, Vol. XXIII, pp. 531-534 (October, 1934).

GAST, E. A., "Modernizing a County Surveyor's Office," *American City*, Vol. XXIII, pp. 500-502 (November, 1920).

GRAHAM, Harry W., "County Personnel Administration–Wide Variety in California Systems," *The Tax Digest*, Vol. XXXIII, pp. 99-105 (March, 1955).

GROVER, Wayne, "Records at the Grass Roots," *The County Officer*, Vol. XV, No. 5, pp. 9-12, 25 (August, 1950).

———, "The Disposition of County Records," *The County Officer*, Vol. XVII, pp. 164-166, 188 (June, 1952).

HADDICK, Dean Z., "NACO and Its Organization," *The County Officer*, Vol. XVII, pp. 231-233 (August, 1952).

HAYMAN, Donald B., "Recent Developments in County Personnel Administration in North Carolina," *The County Officer*, Vol. XXII, pp. 317, 322, 324 (January, 1957).

HOGAN, Earl R., "The County Recorders: Microfilming," *The County Officer*, Vol. XVII, pp. 116-117 (April, 1952).

HURD, T. N., "Training Schools for Town and County Officials in New York," *National Municipal Review*, Vol. XXVI, pp. 603-604 (December, 1937).

KAPLAN, H. Eliot, "A Personnel Program for the County Service," *National Municipal Review*, Vol. XXV, pp. 596-600, 616 (October, 1936).

KILPATRICK, Wylie, "County Officials Hold National Conference," *National Municipal Review*, Vol. XXXIII, pp. 490-491 (October, 1944).

KROEGER, Frank W., "County Recorders," *The County Officer*, Vol. XV, No. 3, pp. 17-19 (June, 1950).

MCFARLAND, Henry J., "Personnel Services for Local Government: The New York Program," *Public Personnel Review*, Vol. XVI, pp. 148-152 (July, 1955).

"Microfilming of Detroit Court Records Reduces Storage Space by 98 Per Cent," *Journal of the American Judicature Society*, Vol. XXXVII, pp. 42-43 (August, 1953).

NORTON, Margaret C., "Microphotography and County Records," *Illinois Libraries*, Vol. XXVI, pp. 505-509 (December, 1944).

PAUL, Winston, "The County Employee," *Annals of the American Academy of Political and Social Science*, Vol. XLVII, pp. 81-84 (May, 1913).

POWER, Kenneth T., "Microfilm in Operation," *The County Officer*, Vol. XVIII, pp. 218-221 (September, 1953).

RECORD, James R., "Pay Rates of the County Employee," *The County Officer*, Vol. XVII, pp. 118-119 (April, 1952).

VANDENBOSCH, A., "The Fee System Receives Setback in Kentucky," *National Municipal Review*, Vol. XVII, pp. 200-203 (April, 1928).

WEIL, Elmer R., "What Are the Duties of Erie County's Law Office?" *The County Officer*, Vol. XIX, pp. 166-169 (August, 1954).

WICKINS, Walter H., "Five County Record Books on a Hundred Feet of Film," *American City*, Vol. LIX, No. 1, pp. 59-60 (January, 1944).

CHAPTER 7

The Problem of a County Executive

GENERAL LACK OF A PRINCIPAL EXECUTIVE OFFICER

In preceding chapters mention has been made of the fact that most American counties have no single chief executive charged with over-all supervision of the county's administrative activities. On the contrary, the general governing body of the county, in addition to exercising the limited legislative authority vested in counties, ordinarily serves as the principal administrative agency. The national government has its president; each of the states has its governor; most cities have a mayor or manager as chief administrator; and even the townships in some states are provided with a principal administrative officer. In the typical county, however, there is no counterpart of these officials; the county board serves as a multimember administrative agency for general supervisory purposes.

APPROACHES TO SOLUTION OF THE PROBLEM

The lack of a single chief executive comparable to the officials found in the other units mentioned is regarded by some students of local government as perhaps the most serious weakness of present-day county organization; and in a number of counties steps have been taken, or are being taken, to provide such an officer. It is the purpose of this chapter to examine the different types of executive officer introduced in these counties, the extent to which officers of the various types are employed, and their respective merits. Though variations in detail are innumerable, four principal approaches to the problem of providing a county executive are discernible: [1]

[1] A considerable segment of the literature on the subject is summarized by Edward W. Weidner in "A Review of the Controversy over County Executives," *Public Administration Review*, Vol. VIII, pp. 18-28 (Winter, 1948).

1. Adoption of the county-manager plan.
2. Provision for some sort of quasi manager—an appointive executive with administrative authority less extensive than that of an orthodox manager.
3. Provision for an elective chief executive.
4. Strengthening the administrative position of the county clerk or one of the other traditional elective county officers.

THE COUNTY-MANAGER PLAN[2]

The county-manager plan, patterned after the manager form of government now employed in many American cities, is characterized by two essential features: (1) a relatively small county board serving as the policy-determining body of the county, and (2) an appointive manager as the principal administrative officer. The National Municipal League's Model County Charter, which includes provision for the manager plan, offers a choice between election of all board members at large and election of some members at large and some by districts.[3] Election at large seems generally preferable, though in a majority of the counties now operating under the manager plan some or all members are elected by districts. As the general governing body of the county the board is empowered to adopt ordinances and resolutions expressive of public policy on matters under county jurisdiction, including appropriations and taxes, and to appoint the manager. It is the duty of the manager:

1. To enforce the ordinances and resolutions adopted by the board.
2. To appoint and supervise his principal subordinates in the administrative branch of the government.
3. To prepare the annual budget for submission to the board.
4. To attend board meetings for the purpose of answering questions and providing information.
5. To make recommendations to the board concerning matters on which that body seeks his advice.

[2] A brief summary of the plan and of the experience of individual counties with manager government is provided in the National Municipal League's pamphlet, *The County Manager Plan,* new ed. (New York, 1950). See also, National Municipal League, *Digest of County Manager Charters and Laws* (New York, 1950); Arthur W. Bromage, *American County Government* (New York, Sears Publishing Co., 1933), chap. 6; George W. Spicer, *Fifteen Years of County Manager Government in Virginia* (Charlottesville, University of Virginia Extension, 1951); Charles M. Kneier, "The County Manager Plan," *Public Management,* Vol. XII, pp. 45-49 (February, 1930); Robert B. Highsaw, "City and County Manager Plans in the South," *Journal of Politics,* Vol. XI, pp. 497-517 (August, 1949); Margaret Rohrer, "County Manager Government in California," *The County Officer,* Vol. XV, No. 6, pp. 25-31 (September, 1950); George W. Spicer, "Manager Counties Evaluated," *National Municipal Review,* Vol. XLII, pp. 331-337 (July, 1953); and additional items among the references at the end of this chapter.

[3] National Municipal League, *Model County Charter* (New York, National Municipal League, 1956).

Appointed by the county governing board, the manager is responsible to that body and serves at its pleasure. According to the generally accepted theory of manager government, a manager should be selected solely on the basis of his ability, training, and experience. Political affiliation should be disregarded, and there should be no requirement of local residence prior to appointment. Although both legislative and administrative *powers* remain in the hands of the board, as under the traditional form of organization, the manager plan provides for a separation of the two types of *functions*. The board continues to exercise the legislative function; but the supervision of administration, instead of remaining with the board, becomes a responsibility of the appointive manager to be discharged through subordinates of his own choosing. Having determined county policy and selected a competent manager to administer that policy, the board is expected to allow the manager a free hand in matters essentially administrative in nature; and the manager, on his part, though serving as a source of advice and recommendations, should not attempt to dictate to the board in policy matters. Thus, the manager plan leaves policy determination in the hands of the popularly elected board but emphasizes the professional element in administration and places responsibility for administrative supervision upon a single official —the county manager. If at any time the manager fails to conduct the county administration in an efficient and economical manner, securing results which are reasonably satisfactory within the limitations of the funds provided, it is within the authority of the board, and indeed becomes its duty, to remove the manager and appoint another in his stead. The Model County Charter provides for removal of the manager by simple majority vote of the board after notice with statement of reasons and, if requested by the manager, a public hearing. Occasional charters and laws, however, require a larger vote for removal; and a few provide a definite term for the manager subject to the power of the board to remove an incumbent before his term's end. Since manager government envisages appointment by the manager of department heads or comparable administrative officers of high rank, the plan ordinarily results in a substantial shortening of the county ballot, though in none of the present manager counties are all administrative officers appointed. Several manager laws and charters provide some sort of merit system for selection of a large portion of the lesser administrative personnel.[4]

At the beginning of 1956 manager government was in operation in 15

[4] The terms *executive* and *administrative,* as distinguished from *legislative,* are applied to governmental powers in this chapter in a nontechnical sense and are employed interchangeably. Manager charters and laws generally stipulate that the manager shall be the chief *executive* officer of the county. The charter of Montgomery County, Md., however, declares that the county council (governing body) shall be the chief *executive* authority of the county and that the manager shall be the chief *administrative* officer.

American counties in eight states. In each case the chief executive's powers and his legal relations with the county board met the standards of the International City Managers' Association for manager government, and these counties were therefore recognized by the association as having the manager plan, notwithstanding that the official title of the executive officer in several instances was something other than manager.[5] Of the manager counties, some had adopted the plan under home-rule charter provisions; in others establishment had been effected by special legislative act, with or without requirement of approval in a local referendum; and still other adoptions had taken place under optional laws (see Table 6).

TABLE 6

Manager Counties: 1956 *

State and county	*Population 1950*	*Date plan effective*	*Form of law*
CALIFORNIA:			
Sacramento	277,140	1933	Home-rule charter
San Mateo	235,659	1951	Home-rule charter
Santa Clara	290,547	1951	Home-rule charter
GEORGIA:			
Fulton	473,572	1947	Special statute
MARYLAND:			
Anne Arundel	117,392	1949	Special statute
Montgomery	164,401	1948	Home-rule charte
MONTANA:			
Petroleum	1,026	1942	Optional statute
NEW YORK:			
Monroe	487,632	1936	Optional statute
NORTH CAROLINA:			
Durham	101,639	1930	Optional statute
Guilford	191,057	1942	Optional statute
TENNESSEE:			
McMinn	32,024	1947	Special statute
VIRGINIA:			
Albemarle	26,662	1933	Optional statute
Arlington	135,449	1932	Special statute
Fairfax	98,557	1952	Optional statute
Henrico	57,340	1934	Optional statute

* Data in this table, except for final column (Form of law), are from *The Municipal Year Book* (Chicago, International City Managers' Association, 1956), pp. 500-519.

The first of the present manager counties to adopt the plan was Durham County, N. C., where manager government was inaugurated as long ago as 1930; and several others in the list were added only a few years later. Yet today, a full quarter century after the first adoption, only about one half of 1 per cent of the more than 3,000 American counties operate under

[5] In California and Virginia, for example, some managers bear the official title of county executive.

the plan. Reasons for this slow spread of manager government appear to be several. The strength of tradition, particularly in rural areas, opposition by political machines, and apathy on the part of the general citizenry all act as deterrents to the modernization of governmental organization. Furthermore, constitutional barriers frequently must be removed before an appointive office of manager can be established. In Nebraska, for example, an optional county-manager act of 1933 was declared unconstitutional by the state supreme court as violating a constitutional requirement that all county officers be elected; [6] and, subsequently, the voters of the state have twice rejected proposals to amend the constitution to make possible the enactment of a manager law. Most of the states now having optional manager laws found it necessary first to adopt enabling amendments to their constitutions; and the privilege of providing manager government by home-rule charter, where it exists, has been conferred through the effecting of constitutional change. At the beginning of the 1950's it was reported that the constitutions of no less than 25 states still contained provisions for county government that would have to be altered before managers could be provided.[7] Finally, the fact that a number of counties, as we shall see, have achieved a substantial degree of improvement through quasi managers or executive officers of other kinds has doubtless retarded the spread of manager government in its orthodox form.

PROS AND CONS OF MANAGER GOVERNMENT

Proponents of the manager plan believe that there is a genuine need at the county level for a single executive officer to co-ordinate administration of the various county services, and that this need can be met most effectively through a professional manager appointed by and responsible to the elective governing body. With the ballot shortened, county voters no longer are confronted with the task of investigating and comparing the qualifications of candidates for a dozen or so elective offices; they merely mark their choices for membership on the board of commissioners or other governing body and perhaps for a few other offices, such as those of judge and prosecuting attorney. The governing body carries on from this point, hiring as manager a competent person who, in turn, selects qualified people to do the county's work.[8] As has been pointed out: [9]

> If the county manager picks able people and does his own job well, the county commissioners will keep him on the payroll. If he bungles his job, he will be

[6] State *v.* Tusa, 130 Neb. 528 (1936).
[7] *Digest of County Manager Charters and Laws.*
[8] National Municipal League, *The County Manager Plan,* p. 9.
[9] *Ibid.,* p. 10.

fired forthwith. A prime virtue of the county manager plan is that the minimum number of *qualified* people is hired to conduct the county's business. . . . The taxpayers are not obligated to spend unnecessary thousands of dollars to fill elective offices that serve no useful purpose. The taxpayers are not penalized for the costly blunders of unqualified officers, nor for the waste resulting from unco-ordinated and unplanned activities of many independent offices and boards.

Manager government "provides for orderly, intelligent operation of the public's business. Overlapping functions and jurisdictional conflicts are abolished. Buck-passing doesn't work. All responsibility is placed on the shoulders of one executive, the manager, whose performance can easily be judged by the commissioners and the public." [10] In sum, manager government separates legislation and administration, centralizes administrative responsibility in the hands of a single professional officer, and avoids an attempt to secure professional competence through popular election. By facilitating administrative co-ordination, say its advocates, the plan tends to promote economy in government, thereby giving the taxpayer more service for his money; and, at the same time, the shorter ballot stimulates popular interest in county affairs and thus makes for a more vigorous local democracy.[11]

The case in favor of manager government is strengthened further by the fact that the plan, generally speaking, appears to have enjoyed a gratifying measure of success where it has been tried. From Virginia, where the plan has been employed more extensively than in any other state, Professor George Spicer reports that manager government has resulted in greater efficiency and substantial money savings.[12] County services have been expanded and improved. At the same time, more effective methods of budgeting, purchasing, and accounting have reduced substantially the overhead costs of administration in relation to total county expenditures. Popular control over county government has been enhanced; and improved governmental reporting to the people has tended to stimulate popular interest in county affairs.[13] In Monroe County, N. Y., manager government was reported in 1953 to have reduced the county's indebtedness by more than 80 per cent in 16 years of operation and, save for enlarged welfare expenditures, to have held down the total cost of government to a modest increase, notwithstanding the pressures of infla-

[10] *Ibid.*

[11] Cf. Paul W. Wager, "The Case for the County Manager Plan," *Public Management,* Vol. XII, pp. 78-82 (March, 1930); F. H. Heller, "The Case for a County Manager," *Your Government,* bulletin of the University of Kansas Governmental Research Center, Vol. IX, No. 4 (December 15, 1953).

[12] As indicated in Table 6, four Virginia counties employed the manager system in 1956. A fifth county, Warwick, operated successfully under the plan from 1945 to 1952. In the latter year the county area was incorporated as a city but, significantly, retained manager government. See James E. Pate, "Virginia Counties Turn Cities," *National Municipal Review,* Vol. LXI, pp. 387-389 (September, 1952).

[13] Spicer, *op. cit.,* and "Manager Counties Evaluated," *loc. cit.*

tion and expanding services.[14] Reports in equally favorable vein come from other counties of the manager group. Significant also is the fact that only one of the counties adopting manager government has abandoned it to date, and in this single instance the plan has now been reestablished. Originally inaugurated in 1933, the manager government of San Mateo County, Cal., fell prey to political machinations and after four years was abandoned through a charter amendment providing that the executive should be elected. However, after a dozen turbulent years of operation under the 1937 provision, an amendment providing for reversion to an appointive executive was approved in 1948, and, under this provision, the manager plan was restored in 1951.[15]

Despite outstanding accomplishments in most of the counties which have adopted the plan, the county-manager form of government is not without its critics. One of the principal arguments against the plan is based on the fact that counties, to a greater degree than cities, are mere subdivisions of the state for administration of services in which there is a state-wide interest. Over the local performance of these services, so the argument runs, the states are certain in any event to exercise a high degree of supervision through their own administrative departments in such fields as those of education, highways, health, welfare, and finance. Hence, there is no logical place in the local organizational setup for an appointive manager charged with general oversight of county administration, since such an official would stand directly between county professional officers, such as the highway superintendent, school superintendent, and health officer, and the respective state departments with which these county officials should be closely associated.[16] Under these circumstances the manager plan, far from facilitating administrative co-ordination as intended, would, in the opinion of those adhering to this school of thought, actually operate as an obstruction to state supervision and to the proper integration of state and county activities in a common field.[17] The manager plan has also been criticized as being undemocratic in that it provides for a chief executive officer who is appointed rather than elected. This criticism, based upon the assumption that an appointive executive will be irresponsive to the public will and beyond popular control, ignores the fact that the manager is appointed by a governing board itself chosen

[14] W. Earl Weller and Craig M. Smith, "Sixteen Years of Progress," *National Municipal Review,* Vol. XLII, pp. 393-397 (September, 1953).

[15] See John C. Bollens, *Appointed Executive Local Government: The California Experience* (Los Angeles, Haynes Foundation, 1952), pp. 176-185.

[16] Kirk H. Porter, "A Wet Blanket on the County Manager Plan," *National Municipal Review,* Vol. XVIII, pp. 5-8 (January, 1929), and "County Government and State Centralization," *ibid.,* Vol. XXI, pp. 489-492 (August, 1932).

[17] Cf. Lane W. Lancaster, *Government in Rural America,* 2d ed. (New York, Van Nostrand, 1952), pp. 344-348.

directly by, and subject to the control of, the voters. Furthermore, a small county board is in a much better position than the general public to observe and evaluate the work of a chief executive, and an unsatisfactory manager may be dismissed by the board at any time.

THE PLAN IN RURAL COUNTIES

Some students of local government, though agreeing that the manager form of organization may be appropriate for highly urbanized counties with problems similar to those of municipalities, feel that the plan is ill adapted to sparsely populated rural counties. This point of view is based upon two principal contentions: (1) that there is not sufficient supervisory work in the typical rural county to require the services of a full-time manager, and (2) that such a county could not afford to pay the salary that would be required to attract a qualified manager. The argument that there is not enough for a manager to do is founded in part on the proposition that county services in rural areas are relatively few and simple and in part on the fact that various state departments already exercise, and will continue to exercise, a considerable degree of supervision over county activities. Howard M. Kline, for example, writing at the end of the 1930's, takes the position that in Maryland's rural counties the functions of county government are so elementary that a full-time manager is not needed to supervise them; and he emphasizes the fact that the state already has assumed primary responsibility for improved standards of county administration in such basic fields as justice, health, schools, roads, and welfare. It is his opinion, furthermore, that the manager plan would prove too costly for the poor counties of that state. Arthur C. Millspaugh has expressed the belief that the plan probably would be financially impracticable in from half to three fourths of the counties throughout the nation.[18]

Over against these arguments stands the actual success of manager government in Petroleum County, Mont., the only strictly rural county in which the plan has thus far been tried. With an area of 1,664 square miles and a population in 1950 of only 1,026, the county's population density is less than one inhabitant per square mile; and the assessed valuation of its taxable property is the lowest of any county in the state. At the end of the 1930's the county found itself in serious financial straits. Oil production in the area had declined, and there was a falling off in crop and livestock returns as a result of drought and depression. The maximum tax levy authorized by statute was failing to provide sufficient

[18] Howard M. Kline, "No Job for a County Manager," *National Municipal Review*, Vol. XXVIII, pp. 358-364 (May, 1939); Arthur C. Millspaugh, *Local Democracy and Crime Control* (Washington, Brookings Institution, 1936), p. 170.

revenue for current costs, and a sizable debt had accumulated. Faced with this situation, the county, in 1942, adopted the manager plan.[19] R. R. Renne has related how, during the first four years of the plan's operation, the number of county officers and employees was markedly reduced, administrative costs were pared, and the county debt was liquidated. Under the new system only the county attorney and the three county commissioners remained elective. The appointive manager assumed duties traditionally performed by several elective officers; and administrative costs were reduced by more than a third, notwithstanding that during the same four-year period similar costs in the other counties of the state showed a slight increase.[20] More recently, manager government has continued to give gratifying results in Petroleum County. To be sure, governmental costs have risen there as elsewhere, but the rise has been exceedingly modest in comparison with other Montana counties. For the fiscal year 1952-1953 administrative costs in Petroleum County showed an increase of only 10 per cent over those for 1941-1942, the last year before the manager plan became effective; whereas the rise in other counties of the state for the corresponding period was 68 per cent.[21]

Although it is doubtless true that "one swallow does not make a summer," and it is wise to avoid hasty generalization, the experience of Petroleum County seems clearly to indicate that the manager plan is not necessarily unworkable in a county of small population and meager tax resources. On the contrary, it may well be argued that the small rural county is the very one that can least afford the financial burden flowing from an excessive number of un-co-ordinated offices and the overlapping and waste that are likely to result therefrom. Though county services in rural areas are less numerous than in urban, there still is urgent need, despite a considerable degree of state supervision, for a simple and responsive organizational setup and efficient administrative practices at the local level. The superimposing of a manager's compensation upon existing administrative salaries might, it is true, unduly enlarge the county's operating expenses. But where the manager, as in Petroleum County, assumes the duties of one or more of the traditional officers, and especially where additional office consolidation is effected, the over-all salary budget may actually be reduced. And this takes no account of money savings that are likely to result from improved budgeting, purchasing, and other

[19] R. R. Renne, "Too Small to Be Efficient?" *National Municipal Review,* Vol. XXXVI, pp. 78-82 (February, 1947).

[20] *Ibid.* Cf. Harold G. Halcrow, *County Manager Government in Montana: Presenting a Case Study of Petroleum County* (Bozeman, Montana State College Agricultural Experiment Station, 1949).

[21] See "Petroleum County Thrives with Manager," *National Municipal Review,* Vol. XLIII, pp. 250-251 (May, 1954), reprinted from *Montana Taxpayer* (March, 1954).

administrative practices that a competent manager may be expected to introduce.

QUASI MANAGERS

More numerous than counties with authentic managers are those provided with appointed executives having some but not all of the powers vested in the manager under the orthodox plan. These quasi managers, as they may be called for purposes of classification, are known by various titles; indeed, in some instances they are officially designated managers, though they fail in one or more respects to qualify for recognition by the managers' professional organization. With respect to the range of their administrative authority, these officers also vary widely, all the way from executive secretaries vested by the county board with only a few managerial duties to the chief administrative officers of certain California counties who, save for formal authority to appoint and remove department heads and prepare the budget, have practically all powers ordinarily conferred upon the orthodox manager.[22] A few examples will serve to indicate the varied nature of the administrative posts held by these quasi managers.

Hamilton County (Chattanooga), Tenn., has operated since 1941 under a so-called manager plan which, despite the fact that appointing authority rests with the governing body rather than the manager, has achieved remarkable success in improving roads, schools, and other county services, and in reducing county indebtedness.[23] Charleston County, S. C., under a special permissive statute, adopted in 1948 a modified manager plan which became effective the following year. Under this plan an elective county council appoints a chief executive (called manager), who serves on indefinite tenure. Though, as necessitated by constitutional provisions, many of the traditional county officers remain outside the manager's jurisdiction, the new form of organization goes a long way toward providing the county with a responsible, nonpolitical executive officer. Achievements reported for the plan during its first year of operation include establishment of a central budgetary control system; inauguration of centralized purchasing; introduction of a merit system and training program in the county police department; creation of a department of public works and introduction of improved methods of public-works administration; and finishing the fiscal year with a substantial cash surplus.[24] The governing board of Clark County (Las Vegas), Nev., acting under an enabling statute of 1951 applicable to counties having

[22] See below, "California's Chief Administrative Officers."

[23] *The County Manager Plan*, pp. 15-17.

[24] William F. Larsen, "Tradition Bows to Efficiency," *National Municipal Review*, Vol. XXXIX, pp. 497-500 (November, 1950).

populations of 10,000 or more, was reported in 1952 to have provided for a county manager to perform such administrative duties as may be required of him by the board. The Nevada law requires that the person appointed manager "be a graduate from an accredited four-year college or university with a degree in public administration or business management," and that he have had "at least four years of progressively responsible experience in administrative management or related activities." [25]

In Cuyahoga County (Cleveland), Ohio, following the defeat of a proposed home-rule charter which would have established the manager plan, the board of county commissioners, early in 1952, created the position of county administrative officer, to be filled by board appointment with the incumbent serving at the board's pleasure. Because of statutory restrictions it was necessary to give the new officer the legal status of assistant to the clerk of the board. Actually, he functions as an administrative assistant to the board, aiding the county commissioners in the performance of their managerial and administrative duties. In this capacity the administrative officer assists in the supervision of budgeting, purchasing, and contracts, and in co-ordinating the work of the various county departments and offices. He attends meetings of the county board and participates in board discussions; confers with department heads and receives reports from them; makes reports and recommendations to the county commissioners; and in general assists the board in carrying out its policies and enforcing its resolutions.[26] After a year of experience under this plan, the Citizens League of Cleveland reported the feeling in the county that the new position had been a success, and it urged passage by the Ohio legislature of a pending bill to enable the commissioners of any county of more than 125,000 population to appoint a chief administrative officer to assist the board in its administrative functions.[27] However, the proposed measure, which would have given statutory basis to the Cuyahoga office and expressly authorized extension of the plan to other populous counties, failed of enactment. An analysis of the development and operation of the Cuyahoga office during its first two years, made by the Cleveland Bureau of Governmental Research at the request of the board of county commissioners, resulted in the conclusion "that the office has made a worthwhile contribution to an improved and expanding county government." [28]

[25] *Statutes of Nevada* (1951), chap. 221; see also, "Three Counties Appoint Chief Administrative Officers," *Public Management,* Vol. XXXIV, pp. 60-61 (March, 1952).

[26] "The New County Administrative Officer," *Greater Cleveland,* Vol. XXVII, No. 5 (January 29, 1952); "Cuyahoga County Gets Administrative Officer," *National Municipal Review,* Vol. XLI, pp. 205-206 (April, 1952); "Three Counties Appoint Chief Administrative Officers," *loc cit.*

[27] *Greater Cleveland,* Vol. XXIX, No. 2 (April 2, 1953).

[28] Cleveland Bureau of Governmental Research, *Development of the Administrative Officer in Cuyahoga County: A Report to the Board of County Commissioners of Cuyahoga County, Ohio* (Cleveland, Ohio, 1955), p. 27.

CALIFORNIA'S CHIEF ADMINISTRATIVE OFFICERS

Prominent among quasi managers are the appointed executives found in a number of California counties. Three of that state's counties, as previously noted, have orthodox managers; but a larger number have executive officers failing in some measure to meet the prescribed standards for inclusion in that category. Several of these have the official title of chief administrative officer,[29] and this designation may be applied in a generic sense to all in the group. The first California county to provide for an officer of this nature was Los Angeles, where the plan was inaugurated in 1938. Under the terms of the ordinance establishing the new post, the chief administrative officer, appointed by the board of supervisors, was charged with the following duties: [30]

1. To supervise county departments and services and carry out the policies of the county board in matters of administration.
2. To study departmental budgets and make recommendations concerning them.
3. To supervise county expenditures and purchases.
4. To co-ordinate county services through interdepartmental transfers of personnel, equipment, and supplies.
5. To approve purchase orders of $1,000 or more and all contracts before their presentation to the board.
6. To make recommendations to the board concerning the creation or abolition of positions in the county service.

Subsequent ordinances assigned additional powers and duties, including approval of any increase in the number of county employees, and the authority to receive the reports of county officers and determine which of them shall be transmitted to the board. Four departments—those headed by the elective sheriff, district attorney, and assessor, and the civil service commission, whose members are appointed by the board of supervisors—are not fully under the jurisdiction of the chief administrative officer, though that official is charged with controlling their expenditures. Furthermore, the heads of departments under the jurisdiction of the chief executive are not appointed by him but by the board of supervisors from civil service lists.[31] Notwithstanding these deviations from the principles of orthodox manager government, the Los Angeles plan has enjoyed a remarkable degree of success. Evaluating the plan's operation from its

[29] The abbreviated title "CAO" finds widespread popular application in California to both county and city executives of this general type. See Bollens, *op. cit.*, p. 19.

[30] Earl R. Strathman, "They Like Los Angeles Plan," *National Municipal Review*, Vol. XXXVII, pp. 428-432 (September, 1948), which summarizes the experience of the first decade under the plan. For a more extensive account, see Abraham Holtzman, *Los Angeles County Chief Administrative Officer: Ten Years' Experience* (Los Angeles, University of California Bureau of Governmental Research, 1948).

[31] Strathman, *loc. cit.*

adoption to 1948, Earl R. Strathman concluded "that the chief administrative officer idea has succeeded in Los Angeles County. There has been little change in the philosophy which established the plan ten years ago. It has been tested and found adequate by both taxpayers and government officials in providing efficient and economical government." [32] And during more recent years this initial satisfaction with the plan appears to have continued.

San Diego County, in 1947, provided for a chief administrative officer patterned closely after the Los Angeles plan; and Stanislaus County, in providing for a county administrator in 1950, also made substantial use of the same precedent. Most of the other counties adopting the system, though frequently benefiting from the Los Angeles experience, have tended to vary further from the original model.[33] In all, a dozen California counties by 1952 had provided for appointive executives falling somewhat short of the status of orthodox managers. Of those adopting the plan only two had abandoned it, one of these rescinding its provision for the office before the plan actually was placed in operation. Thus, as of 1952, ten California counties [34] were operating under the plan; and an eleventh county was reported to have established an appointive post of county administrator in 1953.[35] The counties having chief administrative officers are about evenly divided between those with home-rule charters and those operating under general state law. In no instance, however, has the plan been inaugurated by charter or statutory provision. On the contrary, the new office was established in one county by resolution of the board of supervisors and in the others by board ordinance. Although several of the counties with chief administrative officers are highly urbanized, the list also includes some that are predominantly rural.[36]

Though the authority granted to chief administrative officers is not everywhere the same, Professor John Bollens suggests that there are, generally speaking, only two important formal differences between managers and chief administrative officers in California cities and counties. In the first place, managers usually have specific authority to appoint and remove department heads and certain other personnel, whereas most chief administrative officers can only make recommendations to the governing body concerning appointments and removals. Secondly, managers ordinarily are authorized to prepare the annual budget for submission to the city council or county board, while chief administrative

[32] *Ibid.*, p. 432.

[33] Bollens, *op. cit.*, p. 17.

[34] Alameda, Butte, Contra Costa, Kern, Los Angeles, Monterey, San Bernardino, San Diego, Solano, and Stanislaus. Counties having abandoned the plan were Riverside (before operation) and Fresno—*Ibid.*, pp. 17, 38, 166.

[35] "Sonoma County Secures an Executive Plan," *National Municipal Review*, Vol. XLII, pp. 465-466 (October, 1953).

[36] Bollens, *op. cit.*, pp. 30-31. 38.

officers are usually limited to collecting departmental estimates and transmitting these to the governing body along with their own suggestions. With respect to the vital matters of personnel and budgeting, therefore, managers exercise a direct legal grant of administrative authority, whereas chief administrative officers must operate indirectly through the making of recommendations to the local governing body. In practice, however, as Bollens points out, even these legal distinctions sometimes become blurred, with chief administrative officers actually reviewing and revising budgetary estimates and having their personnel recommendations accepted and approved as a matter of course. And in enforcing the adopted budget and supervising purchasing, the formal authority of most managers and chief administrative officers is much alike. All in all, in the actual performance of their duties many chief administrative officers approximate managers more closely than their formal legal authority might indicate.[37]

The experience of California counties with chief administrative officers appears, on the whole, to have been a happy one. The small number of abandonments, notwithstanding that the plan has been in operation in several counties for a considerable period of time, would seem to indicate substantial satisfaction with it, especially since the post of administrative officer rests in every instance upon mere action of the county board and therefore could be abolished by the board at any time. Satisfaction with the plan is further evidenced by its spread to city governments, more than 30 California municipalities having adopted the system since its establishment in Los Angeles County.[38] As a means of achieving a substantial degree of administrative integration where it appears undesirable or impracticable to provide for an appointive executive vested with full managerial authority, the chief administrative officer plan, on the basis of the California experience, seems to offer considerable promise.

ELECTIVE EXECUTIVES

Several counties have been provided, under various titles, with elective chief executives occupying a position roughly comparable to that of a mayor under the mayor-council form of city government. Such officers, in addition to various administrative powers, ordinarily are vested with a suspensive veto over certain forms of action by the county board. Some of these elective executive positions have been in existence for a considerable period of time, though others have been established only recently.

One position of long standing, dating from the late 1800's, is that of

[37] *Ibid.*, pp. 119-123.

[38] See *ibid.*, pp. 37-38. Some of the municipal adoptions have been by charter provision rather than by council action.

president of the county board in Cook County (Chicago), Ill. The governing body of that county is a board of commissioners of 15 members, one of whom is elected to serve both as commissioner and as board president. The president is presiding officer of the board, as is the chairman of the board in other Illinois counties and generally in counties elsewhere, but is vested with important additional powers, prominent among which are those of appointment and veto. With the advice and consent of the board of commissioners the president appoints numerous county officers, including the county auditor, county attorney, director of public welfare, superintendent of highways, and warden of the county hospital. Members of the county civil service commission are appointed by the president without the requirement of board concurrence. Every motion or resolution which appropriates money or makes a contract or in any way creates a pecuniary liability on the part of the county must be submitted to the president for his approval after adoption by the board. If the president approves the measure, he signs it; if he disapproves, he may exercise the veto power by returning the measure, within five days, to the clerk of the board with his objections in writing. A veto may be overridden by a four-fifths vote of the board's members. In case the president takes no action within six days upon a motion or resolution presented for his approval, the measure takes effect without his signature. In acting upon appropriation resolutions, the president may veto certain items thereof while approving others. The president is also empowered to call special meetings of the board of commissioners whenever, in his opinion, such meetings are necessary.[39]

Since 1900 Hudson and Essex counties in New Jersey have had elective executives with the title of county supervisor. The supervisor is elected for a three-year term. As the principal executive officer of the county he is nominally responsible for supervising subordinate officers and employees, but actually his administrative authority is narrowly circumscribed, inasmuch as he lacks the power of appointment. Though he may suspend or remove county employees for insubordination or neglect of duty, this power is seldom exercised, since an aggrieved employee may appeal to the state civil service commission or to the courts. Furthermore, the supervisor is without a staff of his own, having to rely upon the general county staff for assistance; and he neither prepares the budget nor controls expenditures. On the legislative side, the supervisor has the duty of recommending to the board of freeholders (county governing body) measures which he deems necessary for the welfare of the county; he also makes annual reports to the board concerning the county's government and finances. Resolutions adopted by the board are presented to the supervisor for his signature or disapproval. Any such resolution upon

[39] Cf. Clyde F. Snider, *County Government in Illinois* (Springfield, Illinois Tax Commission, 1943), pp. 59-60.

which he fails to act within a period of ten days becomes effective without his signature. If the supervisor vetoes a resolution, it is returned to the board with his objections and becomes effective only if repassed by a two-thirds vote of all board members. As a matter of custom the supervisor attends all meetings of the board of freeholders and exercises all privileges of board membership except that of voting.[40]

The New York counties of Nassau and Westchester adopted, in the mid-1930's, special legislative charters providing for elective chief executives entitled, in each case, the county executive. The term of office in Nassau County is three years; and in Westchester it is four. Both officers are charged with supervision and direction of the county administrative departments. Both are empowered to appoint department heads, subject to confirmation by the county board, and to appoint, without confirmation, employees in their own offices. In both counties the authority of the executive to remove his appointees is relatively broad. The Westchester charter specifically declares that the executive shall be "the chief executive and administrative officer of the county and the official head of the county government," and that it shall be his duty to see that state laws pertaining to county affairs, and resolutions and ordinances of the county board, are executed and enforced within the county. In Nassau the executive prepares the annual budget for presentation to the county board; and in Westchester preparation is by a budget director appointed by the executive. Both charters make it the duty of the executive to file with the county board an annual report on county finances, to present to the county board from time to time such other information concerning county affairs as he may consider necessary, and to recommend to the board such measures as he may deem expedient. Resolutions and other acts passed by the county board are subject in both counties to executive veto, which can be overridden by the board only by a two-thirds vote. In Nassau County the executive serves as the county board's presiding officer, with the right to speak and a casting vote in case of a tie.[41]

St. Louis County, Mo., by the terms of a home-rule charter adopted in 1950, vests all legislative power of the county in a county council of seven elected members and provides for an elective county supervisor as the county's chief executive officer. Elected for a four-year term, the supervisor is empowered to appoint and remove the heads of the principal administrative departments. He appoints certain other county officers also, and himself serves ex officio as a member of various administrative boards. It is the duty of the supervisor to execute and enforce the pro-

[40] James M. Collier, *County Government in New Jersey* (New Brunswick, N. J., Rutgers University Press, 1952), pp. 16-17, and "Elected County Chief Executives in New Jersey," *The County Officer*, Vol. XX, pp. 47-48 (February, 1955).

[41] *Laws of New York* (1936), reg. sess., chap. 879 (Nassau); *ibid.* (1937), chap. 617 (Westchester).

visions of the county charter, the laws of the state pertaining to the county, and the ordinances, resolutions, and orders of the county council. He is charged with supervising and co-ordinating the work of the county departments and agencies subject to his control, and to this end he is empowered to make temporary transfer of deputies and employees from one office or department to another. The supervisor is county budget officer, and in this capacity he prepares the annual budget and submits it to the council. It is the supervisor's duty to attend regular meetings of the county council and participate in the discussions without vote; to attend such other meetings as the council may require; to recommend to the council such measures as might, in his opinion, improve the county government and the general well-being of the people; to submit to the council an annual report on county affairs; and to submit such other reports as may be requested by the council or any three members thereof. Ordinances passed by the council are presented to the supervisor for his consideration. Upon approval and signature by the supervisor, an ordinance is deemed enacted. If an ordinance is vetoed by the supervisor, it is returned to the council with his objections and becomes effective only if repassed by affirmative vote of five of the seven council members. Any ordinance not returned by the supervisor within 15 days after its presentation to him may be made effective, notwithstanding the supervisor's inaction, by council resolution.[42] All told the St. Louis county executive, though bearing the same title as the executive officers of the New Jersey counties previously mentioned, occupies a markedly stronger position than do those officials, particularly with respect to administrative affairs.

The home-rule charter adopted in 1956 by Baltimore County, Md., provides for an elective executive, officially entitled county executive, who is declared to be "the chief executive officer of the county and the official head of the county government." With approval of the county council (legislative body), the county executive appoints a county administrative officer, who, in turn, appoints department heads with the approval of the county executive. Legislative acts passed by the council may be vetoed by the executive, and an affirmative vote of five of the seven council members is required to override the veto.

Such evidence as is available indicates that the elective executive plans represent a distinct improvement over the un-co-ordinated county organizations which in several instances they replaced. In Westchester County, for example, after a decade of experience with elective executive government, it was reported that, though not achieving all that its sponsors had anticipated, the new plan had resulted in better and more efficient county government, slightly more responsive to the public will.[43] As respects

[42] *Charter for St. Louis County, Missouri* (1950), Arts. III, IV.

[43] Hugh W. Robertson, "Westchester Likes Executive," *National Municipal Review*, Vol. XXXVIII, pp. 219-223 (May, 1949).

municipalities, the mayor-council plan, when the mayor is given relatively broad authority over personnel and budgeting, is considered one of the better plans of city government; and there seems to be no reason why a similar plan should not operate satisfactorily at the county level. The elective form of local executive is not open to the charge frequently made against appointive executives, however groundless that charge may be, that it is undemocratic.[44] Furthermore, a chief administrator with a title such as that of executive or supervisor may be more acceptable to a portion of the local citizenry than one bearing the title of manager, since the latter to some minds conveys an implication of dictatorship.[45] For these reasons, and regardless of the respective merits of appointive and elective executives, some counties may find the elective form more practicable as regards securing its adoption and continued operation.

THE COUNTY CLERK AS EXECUTIVE

In counties having no formal provisions for a chief executive officer, elective or appointive, there is frequently a disposition to vest in one of the traditional elective officers some of the duties normally falling to a principal administrator. Where the office of county clerk exists, the clerk is often the official by whom such duties can most readily be performed. His position as secretary to the governing body and the fact that he keeps a record of county financial transactions and commonly makes an informal preaudit of claims against the county place the clerk in any event at the center of county administration; and county board members are likely to rely heavily upon his advice, especially in routine matters.[46] If a clerk has held his office for several terms, his influence in all probability will be correspondingly enhanced.

Among the states which have gone farthest in enlarging the administrative responsibilities of the clerk is Wisconsin. In that state the county clerk, in addition to serving as secretary to the county board and its committees, is the official county accountant, keeps the county financial records, preaudits all bills for board action, usually prepares the preliminary budget, and, in many counties, serves as purchasing agent.[47] By exploiting his secretarial and financial duties, a clerk is able to establish himself in a strong administrative position; and many Wisconsin county clerks have done just that. A survey study by L. H. Adolfson in 1942 re-

[44] See above, "Pros and Cons of Manager Government."

[45] Cf. Edwin A. Cottrell, "The Controlled Executive in Municipal Government," *City Manager Yearbook* (Chicago, International City Managers' Association, 1933), p. 92; Bollens, *op. cit.*, p. 18. Recognition of this fact may well be the reason why, under some manager charters and laws, the appointive chief administrator is given the title of county executive rather than that of manager. See above, n. 5.

[46] Cf. above, chap. 6, "Officers of General Administration," p. 152.

[47] L. H. Adolfson, "The County Clerk as 'Manager,'" *National Municipal Review*, Vol. XXXIV, pp. 125-128 (March, 1945).

vealed that the clerks of seven counties "performed all the functions of a full county executive," and that 23 additional clerks "were the key general administrators of their counties," though falling short of full executive stature. In all, therefore, the clerks in 30 of the state's counties "approximated, unofficially but none the less effectively, the position of county executive." [48]

STRENGTHENING OTHER ELECTIVE OFFICERS

Where the office of county clerk does not exist, and occasionally even where it does, another officer sometimes serves as a limited executive or at least functions to some extent as a central county officer. In Arkansas counties the administrative powers assigned in most states to a county governing board are exercised by the county judge, whose role in certain respects approaches that of a chief administrator, though a great deal of administrative authority is diffused among other elected officers.[49] In the 40 or so Georgia counties having either the county "ordinary" or a single commissioner of roads and revenues as their principal governing authority, those officers serve, in a measure, as elected county executives. However, their executive powers are sharply curtailed by the fact that most county functions are performed by other elective officers beyond their control; and, at the same time, some of the duties of the ordinary and commissioner are of a policy-forming nature.[50] The probate judge in some Alabama counties assumes, at times, a position substantially similar to that of a county chief executive, with the extent of his actual authority and influence depending both upon varying statutory provisions and upon the officer's individual personality and qualities of leadership.[51] In those counties of Wisconsin where the clerk's office has not attained the strength that it has in some, the chairman of the county board, in many instances, functions virtually as a general administrator; [52] and a few North Carolina counties have made the board chairman a full-time officer vested with the powers and duties of a chief executive.[53]

[48] *Ibid.* Milwaukee County was omitted from the analysis here reported. Of the remaining 40 of the state's 71 counties, the position of the clerk, in terms of executive management, was rated "fairly strong" in 17 and "weak" in 23.

[49] Cf. Edward W. Reed and Henry M. Alexander, *The Government and Finance of Counties in Arkansas* (Fayetteville, University of Arkansas Bureau of Business and Economic Research, 1953), p. 24.

[50] Melvin Clyde Hughes, *County Government in Georgia* (Athens, University of Georgia Press, 1944), pp. 20-23.

[51] Cf. Karl A. Bosworth, *Black Belt County: Rural Government in the Cotton Country of Alabama* (University, University of Alabama Bureau of Public Administration, 1941), pp. 33-39, 110-111, and *Tennessee Valley County: Rural Government in the Hill Country of Alabama* (University, University of Alabama Bureau of Public Administration, 1941), pp. 21-22.

[52] Adolfson, *loc. cit.*

[53] Paul W. Wager, ed., *County Government across the Nation* (Chapel Hill, University of North Carolina Press, 1950), p. 410.

In Indiana, where there is no county clerk,[54] the elective auditor functions in many respects as a general county administrator, serving as clerk to both the board of county commissioners and the county council (fiscal body), aiding in preparation of the budget, and performing many of the duties of a comptroller with respect to budget enforcement.[55]

CONCLUSIONS

From the foregoing discussion it is evident that in a substantial number of counties, scattered among many states, measures have now been taken to provide a central executive officer of one kind or another. Some counties have established appointive managers or quasi managers; a few have been provided with elective executives of the mayoral type; and in a large number varying degrees of administrative authority have been conferred upon one of the traditional offices of county government. Generally speaking, experience with these various plans seems to have been gratifying, with only a few counties having abandoned a plan for an executive officer once it has been inaugurated.

Although plans providing for appointive executives have been most common in populous urban counties, they have also been employed in rural counties, and they seem to have been fully as successful in these as in urban areas. Thus far, all of the counties having elective executives have been urban or suburban in character; yet there would seem to be no reason why the plan might not be used successfully in less populous communities. Where there has been a strengthening, by general law or otherwise, of the administrative position of one of the traditional county officers, the counties affected have in many instances been rural.

Both reason and experience seem to suggest that every county should be provided with some form of central executive officer or be enabled to provide such an officer for itself through adoption of a home-rule charter or the provisions of an optional statute. That counties interested in modernizing their organization have not been unmindful of the need for a chief administrator is clearly indicated by developments in home-rule counties.[56] Of the 13 counties operating under home-rule charters in the mid-1950's,[57] no less than 11 had provided for chief executive officers either

[54] The term *county clerk* is sometimes applied in that state, in popular parlance, to the clerk of the circuit court, but the latter is the official designation.

[55] Cf. Clyde F. Snider and Max M. Sappenfield, "County and Township Government in Indiana," *Report of the Indiana State Committee on Governmental Economy* (Indianapolis, 1935), pp. 103-104. The title of county auditor, in Indiana as in some other states, is somewhat of a misnomer. The accounting duties of the Indiana official are, for the most part, those of a comptroller, with the postaudit of county accounts being performed by state examiners.

[56] Cf. John C. Bollens, "Administrative Integration in California Counties," *Public Administration Review*, Vol. XI, pp 26-34 (Winter, 1951).

[57] See above, chap. 4.

through charter provision or by action of the county governing body. Of California's ten home-rule counties, eight had appointive executives—three managers and five quasi managers (chief administrative officers).[58] Montgomery County, Md., operated under the manager plan; and St. Louis County, Mo., and Baltimore County, Md., had elective chief executives. Though the appointive form of local executive offers some advantages over the elective, it is the opinion of this writer that the elective form deserves more widespread consideration for use at the county level than it has thus far been accorded. And where, because of constitutional obstacles, tradition, or other factors, the establishment of a separate executive office, elective or appointive, appears to be impracticable, a strengthening of the administrative position of the county clerk or some other of the traditional county officers may well offer the most feasible means of providing a degree of administrative co-ordination and supervision in rural counties.

The argument that state supervision of county activities renders a local executive inappropriate is scarcely convincing. Central supervision of local government is much more highly developed in various European countries than in the United States, yet in those countries, as occasional students of the problem have pointed out, the subdivisions roughly equivalent to the American county are commonly provided with executive officers charged with substantial degrees of administrative responsibility.[59] The form of executive which will be found most suitable and the extent of the authority to be conferred upon the office may well vary with circumstances. But available evidence seems clearly to indicate that county government generally could be improved by provision for some sort of chief executive officer charged with co-ordinating both the service functions of the county and such internal or "housekeeping" activities as those of budgeting, purchasing, and personnel.[60] Notwithstanding that the problem has now been solved wholly or in part in some American counties, taking the country at large, the need for an executive officer remains today one of the most vital needs of county government organization.

REFERENCES

Books and Special Studies

BOLLENS, John C., *Appointed Executive Local Government: The California Experience* (Los Angeles, Haynes Foundation, 1952).

Cleveland Bureau of Governmental Research, *Development of the Administrative Officer in Cuyahoga County: A Report to the Board of County Commissioners of Cuyahoga County, Ohio* (Cleveland, 1955).

[58] Bollens, *Appointed Executive Local Government,* pp. 37-38.

[59] See Rowland A. Egger, "The Manager Plan Appropriate for Counties," *National Municipal Review,* Vol. XVIII, pp. 237-241 (April, 1929); Weidner, *loc. cit.*

[60] Cf. Heller, *loc. cit.*

CRAPSEY, Arthur H., comp., *County Manager Government in Effect in the County of Monroe, State of New York,* 2d ed., (Rochester, N. Y., Monroe County Manager Administration, 1940).

HALCROW, Harold G., *County Manager Government in Montana: Presenting a Case Study of Petroleum County* (Bozeman, Montana State College Agricultural Experiment Station, 1949).

HOLTZMAN, Abraham, *Los Angeles County Chief Administrative Officer: Ten Years' Experience* (Los Angeles, University of California Bureau of Governmental Research, 1948).

MULLER, Helen M., *County Manager Government* (New York, Wilson, 1930).

National Municipal League, *The County Manager Plan,* new ed. (New York, 1950).

———, *Digest of County Manager Charters and Laws* (New York, National Municipal League, 1950).

OVERMAN, Edward, *Manager Government in Albemarle County, Virginia* (University, Va., Bureau of Public Administration, 1940).

SPICER, George W., *Ten Years of County Manager Government in Virginia* (Charlottesville, University of Virginia Extension, 1945).

———, *Fifteen Years of County Manager Government in Virginia* (Charlottesville, University of Virginia Extension, 1951).

Syracuse Governmental Research Bureau, *Executive Management for Onondaga County: A Plan for the Manager Form of County Government* (Syracuse, N. Y., 1950).

Articles

ADOLFSON, L. H., "The County Clerk as 'Manager,'" *National Municipal Review,* Vol. XXXIV, pp. 125-128 (March, 1945).

BOLLENS, John C., "Administrative Integration in California Counties," *Public Administration Review,* Vol. XI, pp. 26-34 (Winter, 1951).

BRADSHAW, William, "County Managerial Tendencies in Missouri," *American Political Science Review,* Vol. XXV, pp. 1008-1013 (November, 1931).

BROMAGE, Arthur W., "Wanted: A Chief Executive in Counties," *National County Magazine,* Vol. I, No. 1, pp. 5-6, 28 (April, 1935).

CALROW, Charles J., "County Manager Government in Virginia," *National Municipal Review,* Vol. XXVII, pp. 148-152 (March, 1938)

COLLIER, James M., "Elected County Chief Executives in New Jersey," *The County Officer,* Vol. XX, pp. 47-48 (February, 1955).

Committee on County Government of the National Municipal League, "A Model County Manager Law," *National Municipal Review,* suppl., Vol. XIX, pp. 565-579 (August, 1930).

COTTRELL, Edwin A., SPICER, George W., and RANKIN, Robert S., "The County Manager Plan Proves Itself," *National Municipal Review,* Vol. XXIII, pp. 505-513 (October, 1934).

DAY, Willard F., "The Management of a County," *Public Management,* Vol. XVIII, pp. 293-296 (October, 1936).

EGGER, Rowland W., "The Manager Plan Appropriate for Counties," *National Municipal Review,* Vol. XVIII, pp. 237-241 (April, 1929).

GILL, Norman N., "County Management: Its Pros and Cons," *National County Magazine,* Vol. I, No. 2, pp. 16-17, 26-27 (May, 1935).

———, "County Management: What Is Its Future?" *National County Magazine,* Vol. I, No. 3, pp. 16-17, 26-27 (June, 1935).

GOVE, Samuel K., "A County Executive Officer," *Local Government Notes,* publication of the University of Illinois Extension Service in Agriculture and Home Economics, No. 43 (November 30, 1953).

———, "A County Executive Officer," *The County Officer,* Vol. XIX, pp. 190-193 (September, 1954).

HELLER, F. H., "The Case for a County Manager," *Your Government,* bulletin of the University of Kansas Governmental Research Center, Vol. IX, No. 4 (December 15, 1953).

HIGHSAW, Robert B., "City and County Manager Plans in the South," *Journal of Politics,* Vol. XI, pp. 497-517 (August, 1949).

HOUSTON, Robert C., "County Manager Government in California," *National Municipal Review,* Vol. XXVIII, pp. 128-133 (February, 1939).

KLINE, Howard M., "No Job for a County Manager," *National Municipal Review,* Vol. XXVIII, pp. 358-364 (May, 1939).

KNEIER, Charles M., "The County Manager Plan," *Public Management,* Vol. XII, pp. 45-49 (February, 1930).

LARSEN, William F., "Tradition Bows to Efficiency [in Charleston County, S. C.]," *National Municipal Review,* Vol. XXXIX, pp. 497-500 (November, 1950).

LARSON, Cedric, "Six Years of Managership in Arlington County, Virginia," *National Municipal Review,* Vol. XXVI, pp. 531-537 (November, 1937).

PORTER, Kirk H., "A Wet Blanket on the County Manager Plan," *National Municipal Review;* Vol. XVIII, pp. 5-8 (January, 1929).

RENNE, R. R., "Rural County Can Be Efficient," *National Municipal Review,* Vol. XXXIII, pp. 448-451 (October, 1944).

———, "Too Small to Be Efficient?" *National Municipal Review,* Vol. XXXVI, pp. 78-82 (February, 1947).

ROBERTSON, Hugh W., "Westchester Likes Executive," *National Municipal Review,* Vol. XXXVIII, pp. 219-223 (May, 1949).

ROHER, Miriam, "The Patient Lived [Manager Government in Monroe County, N. Y.]," *National Municipal Review,* Vol. XXVIII, pp. 120-127 (February, 1939).

ROHRER, Margaret, "County Manager Government in California," *The County Officer,* Vol. XV, No. 6, pp. 25-31 (September, 1950).

SCOVILLE, H. F., "Los Angeles County Adopts Modified Manager Plan," *National Municipal Review,* Vol. XXVII, pp. 461-462 (September, 1938).

SPICER, George W., "Manager Counties Evaluated," *National Municipal Review,* Vol. XLII, pp. 331-337 (July, 1953).

———, "Virginia's Arlington County Manager System," *The County Officer,* Vol. XVI, pp. 289-293 (November, 1951).

———, COTTRELL, Edwin A., and SANFORD, Harold W., "Spotlight on the County Manager Plan," *National Municipal Review,* Vol. XXV, pp. 561-571, 595 (October, 1936).

STRATHMAN, Earl R., "They Like Los Angeles Plan," *National Municipal Review,* Vol. XXXVII, pp. 428-432 (September, 1948).

WAGER, Paul W., "The Case for the County Manager Plan," *Public Management,* Vol. XII, pp. 78-82 (March, 1930).

———, "County Managers and Near Managers in North Carolina," *National Municipal Review,* Vol. XXVI, pp. 521-523 (November, 1937)

WEIDNER, Edward W., "A Review of the Controversy over County Executives," *Public Administration Review,* Vol. VIII, pp. 18-28 (Winter, 1948).

WELLER, W. Earl, and SMITH, Craig M., "Sixteen Years of Progress [Manager Government in Monroe County, N. Y.]," *National Municipal Review,* Vol. XLII, pp. 393-397 (September, 1953).

CHAPTER 8

New England Town Government

THE TOWN MEETING

THE NEW ENGLAND town affords the outstanding example in the United States today of a governmental unit which operates as a direct democracy instead of employing a representative body for purposes of policy determination.[1] The principal governing authority of the town is the town meeting, a primary assembly which every qualified voter of the town is eligible to attend. A regular annual meeting is held in each town during the spring months, except in Connecticut where the meeting is usually in October; and there are such special meetings during the year as are found necessary for the transaction of town business. Special meetings may be called at the discretion of the selectmen, and in most states they must be called on application of a specified number or percentage of the town's voters. A special meeting must be called in Connecticut on the application of 20 voters, or of 50 voters if the town has by ordinance adopted the higher requirement. In New Hampshire it is called on the application of 50 voters or one fourth of the voters in the town; in Vermont on the application of 5 per cent of the town voters; and in Massachusetts on request by 200 registered voters or 20 per cent of the total number of registered voters of the town, whichever number is the smaller.[2] Each meeting, whether annual or special, is held in response to a warrant or "warning." This document, usually issued by the select-

[1] Township meetings, frequently in a somewhat degenerate form, are held in certain other states; and annual school meetings serve as the policy-determining organs of school districts in some states both within and outside New England. See below, chaps. 9, 10.

[2] *General Statutes of Connecticut* (1955 suppl.), secs. 205d, 206d; *Annotated Laws of Massachusetts* (1955 cum. suppl.), chap. 39, sec. 10; *New Hampshire Revised Statutes Annotated* (1955), sec. 39:3; *Vermont Statutes* (1947 rev.), sec. 3503.

men,[3] designates the exact time and place of the meeting and sets forth an agendum of the business to be transacted. The selectmen may include in the warrant whatever articles (that is, items of town business) they deem appropriate, and usually they are required to include other articles upon request by a prescribed number or percentage of voters. The warrant has been described as "a writing which warns of the meeting, that is, it gives notice of and authorizes the meeting." [4] To be valid the warrant must be signed by at least a majority of the selectmen; and only matters specified in the warrant may be acted upon at the meeting. In early times, the townsmen were notified of meetings by constables calling at each house, but nowadays notification is by publication or posting. In some towns the warrants continue to be addressed to constables for service upon the voters; in others, they are addressed directly to the voters, with the selectmen themselves being responsible for notification or service.[5] The warrant reproduced in the appendix to this chapter illustrates the form and contents of these documents.

The town meeting usually is held in a town hall. If a town has but a single village (as a trading center or hamlet is commonly called even though unincorporated), the town hall frequently is located there; but if there are several such settlements, the hall may be erected near the town's geographical center, which may not be within any village. If the town hall is too small to accommodate the number of voters likely to attend, the meeting may be held in a school auditorium or some other more commodious building.

The principal functions of the annual town meeting are:

1. To receive the reports of town officers.
2. To levy taxes.
3. To vote appropriations for the ensuing year.
4. To authorize necessary borrowing.
5. To elect town officers.
6. To enact bylaws, or take appropriate action in a less formal manner, for the general government of the town.

The presiding officer of the meeting is the moderator. Originally, each meeting was called to order by the town clerk and selected a moderator from its membership. This plan of selecting a citizen-moderator for each individual meeting was believed to lessen the possibility that the town officers might tend to dominate the meeting should one of their number

[3] In Rhode Island warrants for town meetings, both annual and special, are issued by the town clerk, the statutes requiring the call of a special meeting upon request therefor by 10 per cent of the town voters. Under Maine law, if the selectmen unreasonably refuse to call a meeting, a warrant may be issued by a justice of the peace on application of 10 per cent of the voters. *Revised Statutes of Maine* (1954), chap. 91, sec. 4; *Rhode Island General Laws* (1938), chap. 330, secs. 5, 6, 8.

[4] George H. Deming and Gilbert M. Cantor, *Selected Duties of New Hampshire Selectmen* (Durham, University of New Hampshire Bookstore, 1952), p. 18.

[5] Cf. *ibid.*, pp. 20-21.

preside, and the plan is still in widespread use. In some cases today, however, the moderator is elected for a definite term and presides over all meetings during that term. Vermont towns, for example, elect their moderators in annual town meeting for a one-year term.[6] In New Hampshire the moderator is elected at the regular biennial election for a two-year term; and under Massachusetts law a moderator may either be chosen for each meeting or elected for a term of one or three years.[7] In most Connecticut towns the moderator of the annual meeting is designated by the registrars of voters, though at any special meeting the voters select their own moderator.[8] Whatever the tenure and method of selection, it is a common practice for the same person to be chosen as moderator again and again over a period of years.[9] The town clerk serves as secretary of the meeting.

Business coming before the town meeting includes decisions upon a wide variety of matters, such as the amounts to be appropriated for support of the various town services; what taxes shall be levied and at what rates; whether to authorize the selectmen to borrow money and, if so, in what amount and on what terms; whether to improve a particular stretch of town road; whether to make a proposed purchase of road machinery; whether to permit the sale of alcoholic beverages within the town; and the amounts of the salaries to be paid town officials. As the articles in the warrant are taken up for consideration and action, any voter is entitled to speak to the question at hand, and in many instances a goodly number avail themselves of this privilege. Except for the election of town officers, which ordinarily is by some sort of ballot, voting is usually *viva voce* or by show of hands.

Town meetings are usually called for a morning hour, frequently ten o'clock, and, with a noontime recess, continue through a substantial portion of the day. Dinner, as the noon meal is commonly called in New England, is often served by the local Ladies Aid Society or some other women's organization, and the meeting thus serves as a social gathering as well as a political assembly.[10]

The election of officers in town meeting traditionally involved the pre-

[6] *Vermont Statutes* (1947 rev.), sec. 3509.

[7] Harold C. Grinnell, *Studies in Local Government and Taxation in Rural New Hampshire* (Durham, University of New Hampshire Agricultural Experiment Station, 1943), pp. 19, 21; Geoffrey Bolton, *A Handbook for Town Moderators* (Boston, Massachusetts Federation of Taxpayers Associations, 1950), p. 1.

[8] Max R. White and Shirley Raissi, *Forms of Town Government in Connecticut* (Storrs, University of Connecticut Institute of Public Service, 1952), pp. 5, 7.

[9] In the Maine town of Brunswick, according to recent report, the same person had been elected as town-meeting moderator for more than 50 consecutive years. Lincoln Smith, "Political Leadership in a New England Community," *Review of Politics*, Vol. XVII, pp. 392-409 (July, 1955).

[10] See John Gould, *New England Town Meeting: Safeguard of Democracy* (Brattleboro, Vt., Stephen Daye Press, 1940), pp. 29-30.

senting of nominations from the floor, with the voters then writing on slips of paper the names of their preferred candidates; and this election procedure still prevails in a large majority of the towns, including most of those in rural areas. In a considerable number of towns, however, particularly among those in urban communities, use is now made of the Australian ballot; and, where this is the case, the annual meeting may be envisaged as consisting of two parts—the election and the business meeting.[11] Polls are opened for election purposes as soon as the meeting has been organized, and voting continues throughout the day, even while the business session is in progress.[12] The business session is usually held in the afternoon.[13] Some voters, more interested in personalities than in issues, vote for officers but do not attend the business session. Not infrequently, the business included in the warrant for the annual meeting is so heavy that one or more adjourned sessions are necessary to dispose of it.

The New England town meeting has had an illustrious history, and it seems still to function effectively in many communities, particularly those in strictly rural areas. In general, however, popular interest in town meetings appears to be on the wane. From Vermont, for example, Professor Andrew Nuquist reports that whereas at one time nearly every qualified voter attended town meeting, recent years have witnessed a decline in attendance, with a mere handful of voters appearing in some instances. Some people attribute this decline to the fact that the Australian ballot, now used in some towns, tends to make voting more impersonal; others point out that Vermonters no longer need rely upon the town meeting for social contacts; and still others assign a variety of different reasons.[14] Whatever the cause, it seems clear that there is less interest in Vermont town meetings today than was the case a few decades ago; and reports from other states indicate that this decline of interest has been rather general throughout the region. This is not to say that the primary assembly of voters does not remain a vigorous instrumentality of popular government in many towns, but the evidence seems to leave no doubt that the institution has lost some of its pristine vitality.[15]

[11] Cf. Bolton, *op. cit.*, p. 3. In some instances town elections now occur on a date different from that of the town meeting; and in others the elections, though held as a part of the town meeting, occur only biennially, that is, at every other annual meeting.

[12] In some places caucuses are held prior to the town meeting to nominate candidates for office.

[13] In occasional towns the annual meeting is not opened for voting until after noon, with the business session being scheduled for an evening hour.

[14] Andrew E. Nuquist, "March Meeting," *Vermont Life*, Vol. I, No. 3, pp. 9-11, 39 (Spring, 1947).

[15] For an excellent statement of the respective cases for and against town-meeting government and of the conditions under which the meeting functions most effectively, see Lincoln Smith, "Town Meeting Government," *Social Science*, Vol. XXX, pp. 174-185 (June, 1955).

In populous urban towns special town-meeting problems have arisen.[16] The mere existence of a numerous population is likely to result in a large and unwieldy meeting, even if many voters absent themselves, and may well mean that no building is available which will accommodate all of those who may wish to attend. Operation of the town meeting in the more populous towns has been further complicated by European immigration, which has introduced population elements unaccustomed to democratic institutions and, especially in industrial communities, has fostered factionalism. These factors have caused most of the larger towns to consider how traditional town government might be modified to meet changed conditions. "Many towns," wrote Professor Orren Hormell some years ago, "after carefully installing turnstiles at entrance to the town hall on town meeting day, and furnishing admission to those able to get past policemen, with check lists, at the door, finally have realized that the unlimited town meeting is so unwieldy, and even unrepresentative, that it must be reformed."[17] In some instances the weaknesses of the town meeting in its original form, as they have developed in the more populous communities, have now been overcome, at least in part, by adoption of the limited or representative town meeting to be discussed presently.

Also confronted by a special problem are those rural towns of a resort character in which much of the taxable property is owned by nonresidents who have built or purchased homes for occupancy during the summer months only. Many owners of summer homes maintain their legal residence elsewhere and therefore do not qualify as town voters, and in any event they are usually absent from the town when the annual meeting is held.[18] Under these circumstances, a relatively small number of permanent residents are in a position, in the town meeting, to levy taxes and make appropriations from which they stand to benefit, but the burden of which must be borne in large part by nonresident taxpayers. A possible remedy for this situation, though requiring statutory and perhaps constitutional changes, has been suggested in the form of a referendum by mail in which nonresident taxpayers would be afforded an opportunity to vote for or against proposed appropriations of substantial amount.[19]

[16] Cf. Lane W. Lancaster, *Government in Rural America,* 2d ed. (New York, Van Nostrand, 1952), p. 42.

[17] Orren C. Hormell, *Maine Towns* (Brunswick, Me., Bowdoin College, 1932), p. 19.

[18] In Connecticut town meetings other than those for the election of officers any citizen is entitled to vote, even though not a qualified elector, if he is twenty-one years of age and owns real or personal property of a specified assessed value. White and Raissi, *op. cit.,* p. 4.

[19] Kendall Banning, "Is the Town Meeting Democratic?" *National Municipal Review,* Vol. XXIV, pp. 152-155 (March, 1935).

THE BOARD OF SELECTMEN

The principal administrative agency of the town is the board of selectmen (called the town council in Rhode Island). This board ordinarily consists of three, five, or seven members, with the three-member board most common. Selectmen are elected at the town meeting or at a separate town election where such is held. In some instances their term is a single year, but in others a longer term is provided. The towns of Vermont and New Hampshire, and some of those in Massachusetts, choose their selectmen for three-year staggered terms; some Connecticut towns elect their selectmen biennially; and in Maine terms of longer than one year are permissible. Whatever the term of office, re-election tends to be the custom. Lincoln Smith, in a recent study of political leadership in a Maine town, found an incumbent selectman who, with but a single one-year break in continuity of service, had held office for 41 years, and two former members of the board who had served for 32 and 18 years, respectively.[20] The compensation of selectmen, like that of most other town officers, is usually regulated by town bylaws and, except in the more populous communities, is relatively small. In Connecticut the board of selectmen is required to represent at least two political parties, with no party having more than a bare majority of the board members.

The selectmen carry on the business of the town between town meetings. Some boards meet weekly, monthly, or at other regular intervals; others hold only irregular meetings as their business requires.[21] The specific duties of selectmen, which are numerous and varied, are prescribed by state statutes and town bylaws. Their function in issuing warrants for calling town meetings has already been noted. They have charge of town property, construct and maintain town roads, and manage elections. They examine claims against the town and, if they approve them, issue orders for their payment. Where there is no finance committee, the board of selectmen may be charged with preparation of the annual town budget. Authority is usually vested in the selectmen to grant numerous kinds of licenses; and, in the larger towns, the granting of licenses and permits for building and construction purposes, and for regulating peddlers, lodging houses, gasoline stations, and various kinds of amusements, is a time-consuming function.[22] In some towns the selectmen serve in various ex officio capacities, such as those of assessor, overseer of the poor, highway commissioner, and health officer; in other instances, particularly in the larger places, additional officials fill those posts. The

[20] Lincoln Smith, "Leadership in Local Government—The New England Town," *Social Science*, Vol. XXIX, pp. 147-157 (June, 1954).

[21] Cf. Grinnell, *op. cit.*, p. 22.

[22] John F. Sly, *Town Government in Massachusetts* (Cambridge, Mass., Harvard University Press, 1930), p. 156.

selectmen are also charged with the appointment of various town officers. Professor Max White has recently listed 30 town officers and agencies whose appointment in this manner is specifically provided for by Connecticut statutes; and in Massachusetts the statutes provide for some 40 separate officers whose appointment, under specified circumstances, is vested in the selectmen.[23] In Rhode Island, town councils exercise jurisdiction in probating wills and granting letters of administration.

For the most part the powers of the selectmen are conferred upon them collectively and must be exercised by them acting as a board. In Connecticut, however, the board of selectmen consists of a *first selectman* and from two to six other selectmen, and in practice the position of first selectman has come to be predominant. Only a few powers are conferred by statute upon the first selectman individually, and those are relatively minor in nature. By custom, however, the first selectman in most towns tends to assume responsibilty for the day-to-day activities of the board. Indeed, "the first selectman may, with some accuracy, be called the chief executive of the town." [24]

Some dissatisfaction with the work of the board of selectmen has been expressed at times. It has been pointed out that in many instances the most desirable persons are not elected to the position of selectman. As summarized by one writer on the subject, "this board has too often been of the professional political element and bureaucratic in operation." [25] In the larger towns there is need for a full-time officer to supervise administrative work. The town-manager plan, discussed at a later point in this chapter, is designed to provide a solution to this problem.

THE TOWN CLERK

Apart from the board of selectmen, the most important town officer is the clerk. In a sense the clerk may be considered to outrank the selectmen, so fully does the conduct of town affairs center in his office. The clerk in most instances is elected annually, though in Connecticut his term of office is two years. In any case, re-election is common. It is not unusual for the same person to be retained in the office for 20 to 40 years, and occasionally the office remains in the same family for successive generations.[26] The writer recently talked with a New Hampshire town clerk who had held the office for 39 years, but who modestly pointed out that

[23] Max R. White, *Handbook for Connecticut Selectmen* (Storrs, University of Connecticut Institute of Public Service, 1951), p. 31; Sly, *op. cit.*, pp. 156-157. See below, "Other Town Officers."

[24] White and Raissi, *op. cit.*, p. 2; see also, White, *Handbook for Connecticut Selectmen*, pp. 6, 8.

[25] Edwin A. Cottrell, "Recent Changes in Town Government," *National Municipal Review*, Vol. VI, pp. 64-69, 65 (January, 1917).

[26] Sly, *op. cit.*, p. 157.

a clerk of his acquaintance in a neighboring town had served several years longer. A woman clerk interviewed in Vermont was serving her ninth term after succeeding her late husband who, at the time of his death, had served for 11 terms. In 1954 a town clerk died in Vermont who had first been elected in 1898 and re-elected every subsequent year. This individual had succeeded his father in office and, in turn, was succeeded by his son.[27] The town clerk of Rye, N. H., was reported in 1948 as being elected to his sixty-first term.[28]

The duties of the clerk are numerous and varied.[29] He keeps a record of the proceedings of town meetings and is custodian of the town archives in general. He registers births, marriages, and deaths; in Connecticut, Vermont, and Rhode Island he is recorder of deeds; and in the last-mentioned state he is clerk of the probate court. Not only is he charged by statute with a wide variety of duties but he is the person to whom other town officers and townsmen alike turn for all sorts of information and assistance. In a very real sense, he is the general factotum of the town.[30] The clerk is ordinarily paid a salary which is little more than nominal in amount, but this is supplemented in some measure by fees which he is entitled to collect for various services performed by his office.

OTHER TOWN OFFICERS

Numerous town officers, in addition to those of selectman and clerk, are provided for by the statutes of the New England states. Some of these are required in some or all towns, but many are permissive. Of the older offices, some are now largely obsolete and either go unfilled or, if filled, provide the incumbents with little or nothing to do. Some of the offices are filled by popular election and others by appointment by the board of selectmen.

A town treasurer receives town revenues, is responsible for their custody, and pays claims against the town on order of the selectmen.[31] Town assessors are charged with the assessment of real estate and personal property for purposes of state and local taxation. Overseers of the poor dispense public assistance to the town's indigent persons.

The elective peace officer of the town is the constable,[32] with duties

[27] This instance was reported to the writer by Professor Andrew E. Nuquist of the University of Vermont.

[28] *Time*, Vol. LI, No. 12, p. 25 (March 22, 1948).

[29] For enumerations of powers and duties in two states, see Max R. White, *Handbook for Connecticut Town Clerks and Town Treasurers* (Storrs, University of Connecticut Institute of Public Service, 1951); Gilbert Cantor, *The New Hampshire Town Clerk* (Durham, University of New Hampshire Bookstore, 1954).

[30] Cf. Roger H. Wells, *American Local Government* (New York, McGraw-Hill, 1939), p. 84.

[31] In Vermont the town clerk usually serves also as treasurer.

[32] In Rhode Island there is also a town sergeant, with duties similar in some respects to those of the constable.

corresponding in general to those of the sheriff in the county. As in the case of the typical sheriff, the constable today gives relatively little time to the enforcement of criminal law. He is chiefly a process server for the selectmen and justices of the peace, sometimes acting also as a tax collector. Though considered to be state rather than town officers, justices of the peace in some instances are elected by towns.[33]

An elective school board or committee is charged with management of the town schools.[34] Highway officers with various titles are elected or appointed. A town officer who at one time was of considerable importance but now has little to do is the fence viewer. The usual duties of fence viewers are those of settling disputes between neighboring landowners concerning the location of partition fences; assigning portions of partition fences to the respective owners for maintenance; and, if such fences are not kept in repair, doing the necessary work thereon and collecting costs from the delinquent owners. Formerly, it was common for each town to have several fence viewers. Today, however, a call for their services is infrequent, though it is reported from Vermont that many towns continue to appoint fence viewers each spring and to fill various other town offices, also now largely obsolete, such as those of coal weigher, tree warden, poundkeeper, and inspector of lumber. In some towns the conferring of these offices apparently is considered to be an appropriate means of honoring deserving citizens, while in others the appointment seems to be made as a practical joke.[35] Similar practices appear to prevail in other New England states.[36] Numerous additional offices of early origin, the work of which has for the most part ceased to exist or been assumed by the state, still are provided for by statute in one or more states and may be filled in some towns.[37] Among the town offices and agencies more recently authorized or established in one or more states may be mentioned those of aviation commission, planning board, civil service commission, library trustees, and town manager.

[33] Justice-of-the-peace courts are discussed below, chap. 12.

[34] In general, the town is the unit for local school administration in New England, functioning either through the regular town government or as a legally distinct school corporation. However, in Connecticut, Maine, New Hampshire, and Vermont, there are a few instances of smaller school districts organized within the towns and independent of the town school units. See below, n. 50.

[35] Lawrence M. Howard, "Wanted: Work for Fence Viewers," *Vermont Life*, Vol. VIII, No. 3, pp. 10-11 (Spring, 1954).

[36] See Grinnell, *op. cit.*, p. 20, concerning the situation in rural New Hampshire.

[37] A description of the powers and duties of more than 30 town officers in early Massachusetts is to be found in Samuel Freeman, *The Town Officer*, 7th ed. (Boston, Thomas & Andrews, 1808). Among the officers there considered, along with most of those previously mentioned in the text and still others, are sealers of weights and measures, firewards, field drivers (to take up and impound livestock running at large), tythingmen (to enforce the laws against engaging in trade or travel on Sunday), gaugers of casks, measurers of salt, measurers of charcoal, measurers of grain, inspectors of lime, cullers of fish, and weighers of onions.

From what has been said it will be apparent that town government does not suffer from any dearth of offices. The number of offices actually filled varies widely, reaching 50 or more in a few instances. Twenty-odd is perhaps the average. A study of 116 rural towns in New Hampshire revealed, as of 1939, an average per town of slightly more than 27 offices filled. With so many positions, it is not surprising that in sparsely settled towns the same person frequently holds two or more offices. In the New Hampshire towns studied, for example, with an average of 27 offices filled, the average number of persons holding town office was only 22, or approximately four different office holders for each five offices filled.[38]

RECENT DEVELOPMENTS

Town government in New England developed originally in a pioneer society in which simple governmental machinery sufficed to provide the meager public services which the times required. With social and economic change, however, certain phases of the original system came to operate less satisfactorily, and modifications have been made in some instances in an effort to modernize governmental institutions and bring them into line with the changing times. The industrialization of some areas brought to certain towns large populations composed of people with widely varied social and political backgrounds, and this situation, as previously suggested, complicated the operation of the plenary town meeting.[39] As town expenditures mounted, the need became apparent for improved financial planning. And, with the increase in the number and variety of town services, it has seemed wise, particularly in the larger towns, to provide for a trained administrator to take over much of the work otherwise performed by the lay selectmen. As means of providing partial solutions to these problems, three new town agencies have developed and gained substantial adoptions: the representative town meeting, the finance committee, and the town manager. Each of these agencies will now be considered in turn.

REPRESENTATIVE TOWN MEETINGS

Pure democracy, under which governmental authority is exercised directly by the voters in primary assemblies, is practicable only within limited areas having comparatively small populations. In extensive regions, or in smaller areas with large populations, direct democracy must give way to democratic institutions of the representative type. This has been the experience of New England, where several of the more populous towns of Massachusetts and occasional towns in other states have found it

[38] Grinnell, *op. cit.*, p. 20.
[39] See above, "The Town Meeting."

expedient to abandon the town meeting in its traditional form in favor of the representative or limited meeting.[40]

As this newer plan operates in Massachusetts, the town is divided by the selectmen into precincts, ordinarily numbering from four to nine. The voters of each precinct elect an equal number of delegates, usually between 30 and 40, to serve as "town meeting members." These elected members, together with various town officers designated as members ex officio, make up the town meeting. This representative meeting possesses substantially the same powers as the plenary meeting which it supplants. Any elector of the town is entitled to speak at meetings of the representative assembly, but voting is restricted to members.[41]

The first Massachusetts town to adopt the limited town meeting was Brookline, which did so in 1915 in pursuance of a special enabling act passed by the Massachusetts general court (legislature) earlier in the same year. By 1928, 14 other Massachusetts towns had followed Brookline's example and adopted the plan, in each instance by popular vote pursuant to legislative authorization. All of these 15 towns had relatively large populations—the smallest around 9,000. Prior to 1926, the state constitution, as interpreted by the courts, prevented the legislature from authorizing the adoption of the limited meeting by towns of less than 12,000 population; but a constitutional amendment of that year now provides that the plan may be authorized in any town of more than 6,000 inhabitants.[42] The fact that the legislature, between 1928 and 1940, authorized adoption of the limited meeting in some 18 additional towns would seem to indicate that the plan was giving general satisfaction in those communities which had adopted it earlier.[43] In 1931 a law was enacted providing a standard form of representative town meeting government that may be adopted by any Massachusetts town in which a limited town meeting has been established under a special statute. The standard act, when adopted by any such town, replaces the special legislative act under which the town previously operated.[44]

Five Connecticut towns were reported in 1952 as having representative town meetings.[45] These had been established by special legislative acts,

[40] The term *limited town meeting* is ordinarily used synonymously with that of *representative town meeting*, and it is so used in this discussion. Occasionally, however, the term is employed to designate a meeting which, as is the case in a few towns, has been subjected to a curtailment of its *powers*. Where limitations of this nature are imposed, it is usual to vest authority to enact ordinances and bylaws for the most part in an elected town council, restricting the town meeting to financial functions, such as approval of the budget and authorization of borrowing.

[41] Sly, *op. cit.*, chap. 7.

[42] *Ibid.*

[43] See Alexander Lincoln, "Some Notes on Representative Town Meetings," *Massachusetts Law Quarterly*, Vol. XXXIII, No. 1, pp. 30-46 (April, 1948).

[44] *Annotated Laws of Massachusetts* (1952), chap. 43a.

[45] White and Raissi, *op. cit.*, pp. 10-11, 17-18.

the first in 1933 and the last in 1951. In four of these towns—Greenwich, Fairfield, Westport, and Darien—the representative meeting, as a general policy-determining body, has much the same powers as plenary town meetings, save for the fact that ordinances, appropriations in excess of a specified amount, and bond issues are subject to popular referendum on voter petition. In Milford the principal function of the representative meeting is that of budget approval, with other legislative powers being vested in an elective town council. In all five towns, town meeting representatives are elected by districts. Nominations are made by petition, and elections are nonpartisan. The number of representatives from each district is determined by the number of registered voters therein, with the number of voters per representative ranging from 100 in Darien and Greenwich to 300 in Milford. "In 1952 there were 64 representatives from 3 districts in Darien, 65 representatives from 10 districts in Fairfield, 216 representatives from 11 districts in Greenwich, and 28 representatives from 6 districts in Westport."[46] In some of the towns, in addition to elective members of the meeting, there are ex officio members without vote. The term of elected members is two years, except in Milford, where a four-year term is provided.

The town of Sanford, Me., with a 1950 population of 15,177, has had a representative town meeting since 1935 under authority of a special enabling statute. The law provides for a meeting of from 150 to 200 members elected by districts for three-year overlapping terms. As of 1955 the meeting consisted of 175 members elected from seven districts, with one third of the membership being elected each year. The Sanford meeting, patterned in general after the Brookline plan, seems to have operated more satisfactorily than the plenary assembly which it supplanted. Apparently, however, it is not easy to find 175 qualified townsmen who are willing to accept the responsibilities of town-meeting membership and give the necessary time to performance of the duties involved. In the case of special meetings, difficulty is sometimes experienced in securing the attendance of a quorum. Perhaps, under these circumstances, a somewhat smaller town-meeting membership would be even more advantageous.

The representative or limited meeting, as a policy-determining organ, is a compromise between the plenary assembly and the relatively small elective council common in municipalities. Where large and heterogeneous populations render the old-style meeting no longer practicable, the most logical solution might seem to be incorporation as a municipality with a small council. In New England, however, the tradition of direct democracy is strong, and such a step would constitute a drastic break with the past. Where opposition to so great a change makes the small

[46] *Ibid.*, p. 10.

council unfeasible, the representative meeting affords a useful adaptation of a traditional institution. On the whole, experience with the representative meeting appears to have been gratifying.

FINANCE COMMITTEES

As an agency for determining fiscal policy, the town meeting has suffered from the need for consideration of the town's financial problems and the formulation of a tentative financial program by some smaller body prior to the annual meeting. This need, which exists in all towns but is more acute in the larger communities, has been met in a measure in some instances by requiring the board of selectmen to prepare a budget for submission to the meeting. Another approach to the problem is through the establishment of a special budget-making agency. Known variously by such titles as finance committee, finance board, and budget committee, agencies of this nature are now employed in many towns, including a substantial number in each of four states: Connecticut, New Hampshire, Maine, and Massachusetts.

The Connecticut statutes provide that any town, at any annual or special town meeting, may vote to establish a six-member board of finance; and a large majority of the towns of the state have now established such an agency. Members of the board are elected for overlapping terms of three years in towns having annual elections and six years in those where elections are biennial. It is the duty of the board, after a public hearing, to prepare the town budget for presentation to the town meeting. The finance board is in a particularly strong position, since the town meeting, though it may reduce or strike out items from the budget as prepared by the board, may not increase items or insert additional ones.[47]

Although the primary function of Connecticut finance boards is budget preparation, other duties have been added. The boards "now provide for and complete certain audits, set the amount of surety bonds for several officials, recommend action on deficiency and special appropriations, approve the transfer of unexpended balances from one appropriation to another, publish the annual town report and set the local tax rate. Some boards also have limited jurisdiction over personnel matters."[48] By the terms of a 1953 statutory amendment the budget submitted by the board of finance may include a recommended appropriation for a contingent fund in an amount not exceeding 2 per cent of the total estimated expenditures for the current fiscal year. If such an appropriation is made,

[47] *General Statutes of Connecticut* (1949 rev.), chap. 36; *ibid.* (1955 suppl.), chap. 36; *ibid.*, chap. 59a, sec. 683d; John E. Dever and Joseph M. Loughlin, "Financial Control through Boards of Finance," *Municipal Finance*, Vol. XXIV, pp. 97-100 (November, 1951).

[48] Dever and Loughlin, *loc. cit.*, p. 98.

no expenditure or transfer may be made therefrom without the approval of the board of finance.

Under the terms of a municipal budget law originally enacted in 1935, any New Hampshire town, by vote of the annual town meeting, may establish a budget committee.[49] This committee consists of: one member chosen by the school board of each school district within the town; [50] one member of the board of commissioners of each village district; [51] one member of the town board of selectmen; and three, six, nine, or twelve members at large. The school-district representatives, in practice, are usually chosen from among school-board members. The selectman and village-district commissioners are designated by their respective boards for service on the committee. Members at large are either appointed by the moderator or elected by the town meeting, with the method of their choice and their number within the statutory alternatives being determined by the meeting. One of the members at large is elected by the committee as its chairman.

It is the duty of the budget committee, after consultation with local officers and after public hearings, to prepare the annual budget of town, school, and village-district expenditures for submission to the annual meetings of the respective units. The law provides that no appropriation may be made for any purpose not included in the budget and that the total amount appropriated by the town, school district, or village district shall not exceed by more than 10 per cent the amount allocated to it in the budget. However, the budget committee may submit, without approval, items which its members do not wish to recommend but which they believe the voters should be allowed to act upon; and appropriations may be made for such items as long as total appropriations for each unit (town, school, or village district) do not exceed budgetary recommendations by more than the 10 per cent allowed.

As of 1955, more than one fourth of New Hampshire's towns were reported by the state tax commission to be operating under the terms of the 1935 law. Furthermore, it appears that in a majority of the rural towns not operating under the statute preparation of the budget nevertheless has been delegated to a special committee of some sort rather than to the selectmen. These special committees, known variously as budget, finance, appropriation, and ways and means committees, are in some

[49] *New Hampshire Revised Statutes Annotated* (1955), chap. 32.

[50] Each New Hampshire town is constituted by law a school district, with a school meeting corresponding to the town meeting in town government and with its own school board. However, school districts organized under special acts retain their organization and are not included in the town district, unless they vote to dissolve their corporate existence and unite with the town district—*New Hampshire Revised Statutes Annotated* (1955), secs. 194:1, 194:37.

[51] The New Hampshire village district is a special-purpose district established to provide one or more municipal services for its inhabitants. See below, chap. 10, "New Hampshire's Village Districts."

instances appointed by the selectmen or elected by the voters, but more often they are appointed by the town moderator. Altogether, the desirability of careful budgetary planning prior to the annual meeting is now widely recognized in New Hampshire town government.[52]

Many towns in Maine and Massachusetts have established finance committees or equivalent agencies by town bylaws. Some of these committees date from the late 1800's or the first decade of the present century. The Massachusetts statutes since 1910 have specifically authorized the establishment of such an agency in any town, and since 1923 they have required its establishment in every town with an assessed valuation of more than $1,000,000. Actually, it appears that committees of this nature have been established in practically all Massachusetts towns of over 6,000 inhabitants and Maine towns of over 3,000. Massachusetts committees are officially known by at least four different names—finance committee, appropriations committee, warrant committee, and advisory committee—and there is some variety of terminology in Maine also. The committees range in size from 3 members to more than 30, with 9 members or 15 most common. Members are ordinarily appointed by the moderator of the town meeting for overlapping terms. The committees are nonpolitical, their membership usually consisting of business and professional men who hold no public office. The principal duty of the finance committee is to study the town's finances and prepare the annual budget for submission to the town meeting. Additional duties, however, are imposed by the bylaws of some towns. Thus, the committee is usually expected, in those Massachusetts towns where the title of warrant committee is used, to consider and make recommendations concerning all articles, financial and otherwise, in the town-meeting warrant. Legally, the powers of the committee are advisory only, except for its authority in Massachusetts to make transfers from the reserve fund to meet extraordinary and unforeseen expenditures. In practice, however, committee recommendations are usually followed. All in all, it appears that the finance committee in both Maine and Massachusetts is steadily increasing in influence and is becoming more and more a wholesome and decisive factor in the formulation of town policies.[53]

TOWN MANAGERS

In New England town government, as in local government generally, need has developed for improvements in administrative organization and

[52] Grinnell, *op. cit.*, p. 37.

[53] Sly, *op. cit.*, pp. 208-212; Hormell, *op. cit.*, pp. 17-19; Danforth W. Comins, "Powers, Duties, and Procedure of Town Finance Committees," in Charles J. Rohr, Alfred A. Brown, and Vernon P. Helming, eds., *Local Government in Massachusetts* (Amherst, Massachusetts State College Bureau of Public Administration, 1941), pp. 7-12; Richard A. Atkins and Lyman H. Ziegler, "Citizen Budgeting in Massachusetts," *National Municipal Review*, Vol. XXX, pp. 568-573 (October, 1941).

practices. As long as town services were few and simple the board of selectmen functioned fairly satisfactorily in the supervision of administration, as it still does in some of the least populous towns. In the larger places, however, with the increase in the number and variety of services, a genuine need has arisen for a single qualified person to supervise and co-ordinate administrative activities. To meet this need, some towns have adopted the manager plan of government now operating in several hundred American cities and a few counties.[54] Under this plan the selectmen, instead of themselves supervising highway maintenance, public assistance, and other administrative functions, appoint a qualified manager to supervise those activities under the general direction of the board.[55] Though appointed in a few instances for a fixed term, the manager in most cases serves at the pleasure of the board of selectmen. Chosen on the basis of training and experience, and ordinarily devoting his full time to town affairs, the manager appoints his principal administrative subordinates, prepares the town budget (except insofar as this duty may fall to a town finance committee), and serves as adviser to the selectmen. Thus is achieved more centralization of administrative responsibility, as well as a greater degree of professional skill in matters of administration, than is possible where administrative supervision is exercised directly by the selectmen. Save for education, which is administered by an independent school board, the over-all administration of town services centers in large measure in the manager's hands. The town meeting retains its position as the policy-determining organ of the town. The manager, however, is responsible directly to the board of selectmen, and only intermediately, through that board, to the voters in town meeting.

Connecticut, Maine, Vermont, and New Hampshire have general permissive statutes authorizing adoption of the town-manager plan. The laws of Maine, Vermont, and New Hampshire permit any town to provide for a manager by vote of the town meeting; and a like privilege is extended by Connecticut to any town having a board of finance. Massachusetts has no optional town-manager law of general application but has granted manager government to certain towns by special legislative enactments. The usual procedure in that state, when a town desires to adopt the manager plan, has been for the town meeting first to set up a local committee to draft a manager charter. Once this charter has been drafted and approved at a town meeting, it is submitted to the state legislature with the request that it be enacted into law; and, in enacting such a special charter, the legislative body makes its effectiveness con-

[54] The operation of the manager plan in relation to counties is considered above, chap. 7.

[55] In a few towns the manager is appointed and controlled by an elective town council other than the board of selectmen.

tingent upon a final approval by the town meeting. Some of the present manager towns in Connecticut and Maine also are operating under special legislative charters rather than under the general permissive statutes of their respective states.[56] Rhode Island towns may adopt manager charters under constitutional home-rule provisions.

The specific powers and duties of managers, depending as they do upon diverse charters and laws, vary somewhat among the different towns. Maine's general town-manager enabling act will serve for illustrative purposes, since under the provisions of this statute some four fifths of the town managers in that state, comprising approximately three fifths of those in all New England, are currently operating.[57] After declaring that the manager shall be the administrative head of the town government, responsible to the selectmen for the administration of all departments over which the selectmen have control, the statute imposes the following duties:[58]

1. To see that state laws and town ordinances are enforced.
2. To act as purchasing agent for all town departments, except school departments, and to submit to bids any purchases involving more than $100 if the selectmen so order.
3. To attend the meetings of the selectmen, except when his own removal is being considered, and to recommend for adoption those measures he may deem expedient.
4. To keep the selectmen and the citizens of the town fully advised concerning the town's financial condition.
5. To perform such other duties as the selectmen may prescribe, including the duties or any part of the duties of the town treasurer, the road commissioner or commissioners, the tax collector, and the overseers of the poor. (Actually, it is common practice for the selectmen to assign to the manager the duties of one or more of these designated officers.)

At the beginning of 1956, according to the International City Managers' Association, 155 New England towns were operating under the manager

[56] Orren C. Hormell and Lawrence L. Pelletier, *The Manager Plan for Maine Municipalities* (Brunswick, Me., Bowdoin College, 1949); Massachusetts Federation of Taxpayers Associations, *The Town Manager Plan in Massachusetts*, rev. ed. (Boston, 1951); Sly, *op. cit.*, pp. 194-205; Richard A. Atkins, "The Old and the New in Massachusetts Towns," *National Municipal Review*, Vol. XXIX, pp. 361-366 (June, 1940); K. R. B. Flint, "Twenty Years of Town Management in Vermont," *ibid.*, pp. 473-479 (July, 1940); Thorsten V. Kalijarvi, "Town Meeting vs. Town Management [in New Hampshire]," *ibid.*, pp. 540-544 (August, 1940); Carter W. Atkins, "Manager Plan in Connecticut Towns," *ibid.*, pp. 593-595, 610 (September, 1940); Orren C. Hormell, "Maine a Pioneer in Town Management," *ibid.*, pp. 648-653, 678 (October, 1940); Lashley G. Harvey, "First Break in New Hampshire," *ibid.*, Vol. XXXV, pp. 521-524 (November, 1946); Lawrence Pelletier, "New England Pioneers Again," *ibid.*, Vol. XXXVIII, pp. 79-84 (February, 1949); Gerald E. McLaughlin, "Town Manager," *Vermont Life*, Vol. VIII, No. 3, pp. 19-24 (Spring, 1954).

[57] *Revised Statutes of Maine* (1954), chap. 91, secs. 16-19.

[58] See Pelletier, "New England Pioneers Again," *loc. cit.*

plan. Included within this number were 106 towns in Maine, 19 in Vermont, 15 in Massachusetts, 9 in Connecticut, 5 in New Hampshire, and 1 in Rhode Island.[59] Thus each of the six New England states had one or more manager towns, with Maine numerically far in the lead.

Although some of New England's manager towns are primarily urban in character, others are rural or semirural. Approximately one fifth of the manager towns in Maine have less than 1,500 inhabitants, and several have fewer than 500.[60] In the more populous communities the role of the town manager is quite similar to that of his city counterpart, consisting chiefly of planning, organizing, co-ordinating, and the other related activities commonly associated with the term *management*. But in the small rural town the manager must himself do much of the work which in larger places is assigned to department heads or other subordinates. In the carrying on of his manifold activities he may spend a considerable part of his time in the field, actually working with his road crews, investigating applicants for public assistance, and performing other on-the-spot services. The small-town manager, as Professor Lawrence Pelletier has written, "is a doer rather than a director, supervisor or rationalizer. He *is* town government." [61]

The manager plan of town government is no longer in the experimental stage in New England. Some towns have operated under manager government for more than 20 years, and many have used it for more than a decade. Experience with the manager system seems to have demonstrated quite amply that the plan is readily adaptable to the town form of organization and that it may be used advantageously in the small rural town as well as in more populous communities. The rapid spread of the manager system, particularly in Maine, has been one of the outstanding developments of town government in recent years. So numerous have been recent adoptions of the plan that some towns have had difficulty in securing competent managers. In an effort to alleviate this situation, the University of Maine has now inaugurated a specialized program of training in public management designed to provide a supply of qualified candidates for managerial positions.[62]

Towns too small to require the services and pay the salary of a full-time chief administrator have secured the advantages of manager government in some instances by joining with one or more other local units in the

[59] See the directory of manager municipalities in *The Municipal Year Book* (Chicago, International City Managers' Association, 1956), pp. 498-521. Six Maine plantations also were reported as having managers. The nature of the plantation as a unit of government is considered below.

[60] Pelletier, "New England Pioneers Again," *loc. cit.*

[61] *Ibid.*, p. 83.

[62] See Edward F. Dow, "School for City Managers," *National Municipal Review*, Vol. XXXVII, pp. 491-494 (October, 1948).

employment of a single manager to serve each unit on a part-time basis. In several Vermont communities, for example, a manager is employed jointly by a town and an incorporated village therein; and Maine affords several examples of a single manager serving two or more towns, or towns and plantations. Wider use of the joint appointment readily suggests itself as a practicable means whereby the manager plan might advantageously be extended to additional rural communities.

MAINE PLANTATIONS

Some Maine communities are organized as plantations rather than as towns. The plantation form of organization originated in early Massachusetts, where the terms *town* and *plantation* appear at first to have been used interchangeably. Later, however, a distinction between the two developed, with the plantation having a legal status intermediate between that of an unorganized tract of land and that of an incorporated town. Upon separating from Massachusetts, Maine continued the plantation as a unit of local government; and plantation organization has been retained in Maine to the present time, notwithstanding that it has long since been abandoned in the mother state.[63]

The present-day plantation in many of its features is exceedingly similar to the town. There are some statutory provisions pertaining specifically to plantations, but a general provision declares that laws relating to town meetings and to the election, appointment, powers, and duties of town officers "apply to plantations and their officers, so far as applicable thereto, except where specifically otherwise provided."[64] So nearly alike are the two that the United States Census Bureau, for purposes of its enumeration of governments, considers fully organized plantations as towns.[65] In certain respects, however, the organizational setup of the plantation is somewhat simpler than that of the town; and it is this greater simplicity that supposedly makes the plantation form attractive to some of the most sparsely populated communities. Justification for retention of the plantation seems to rest on the fact that it makes available to communities of very few inhabitants a simpler, and therefore presumably less costly, form of organization than does the town.

The policy-determining organ in plantation government is the plantation meeting. According to the statutes, the voters of the plantation, at the annual meeting, elect a clerk, three assessors, a treasurer, a collector of taxes, a constable, a superintending school committee, one or more

[63] Maine Historical Records Survey Project, Work Projects Administration, *Town Government in Maine* (Portland, Me., 1940), p. 19.

[64] *Revised Statutes of Maine* (1954), chap. 101, sec. 8.

[65] See United States Bureau of the Census, *Governments in the United States in 1952* (Washington, Government Printing Office, 1953), p. 2.

surveyors of lumber, and two or more fence viewers.[66] One of the principal differences from town organization lies in the absence of a board of selectmen as such, the statutes providing that the plantation assessors shall be considered the selectmen of the plantation and shall perform the duties performed by the selectmen of towns.[67] The responsibilities of plantations for road maintenance, fire and police protection, health, and education are substantially the same as those of towns. However, only those plantations having populations in excess of 200 and property valuations of at least $100,000 are obligated to provide support for the poor.[68]

Though plantation organization at times has been looked upon as a prelude to town incorporation, some communities have now retained plantation status for many years and are likely to continue it indefinitely. As of 1936, the number of Maine plantations in existence was reported as 65, ranging in population from 30 to 1,500 but with approximately 55 having fewer than 1,000 inhabitants.[69] As the years go by, occasional towns, faced with declining populations and property values, reincorporate as plantations; on the other hand, some plantations, finding the cost of even so simple a local organization burdensome, surrender their charters and revert to unorganized or wildland status.[70] Altogether, there has been little net change in the total number of plantations during the past two decades, though the over-all tendency appears to be in the direction of reduction. Publications of the Maine Bureau of Taxation report the existence of 58 plantations as of 1954.[71]

REFERENCES

Books and Special Studies

BOLAN, Robert P., *Handbook for Massachusetts Selectmen* (Amherst, University of Massachusetts Bureau of Government Research, 1956).

BOLTON, Geoffrey, *A Handbook for Town Moderators* [*in Massachusetts*] (Boston, Massachusetts Federation of Taxpayers Associations, 1950).

CANTOR, Gilbert, *The New Hampshire Town Clerk* (Durham, University of New Hampshire Bookstore, 1954).

66 *Revised Statutes of Maine* (1954), chap. 101, sec. 6.

67 *Ibid.*, sec. 9.

68 *Town Government in Maine*, p. 21. Any plantation not required by law to support its poor may assume that responsibility voluntarily.

69 *Ibid.*, p. 19.

70 See William S. Carpenter, "Deorganization in Maine," *American Political Science Review*, Vol. XXXII, pp. 1139-1142 (December, 1938); and below, chap. 20, "Local Deorganization."

71 Maine Bureau of Taxation, *Maine State Valuation: 1954* (Augusta, Me., 1954). Apparently some plantations function as little more than areas for tax administration, lacking a full complement of local officers and not purporting to provide most of the services ordinarily expected of town and plantation governments. See Hormell, *Maine Towns*, pp. 11-12.

CANTOR, Gilbert, *The Tax Collector and the Town Treasurer in New Hampshire* (Durham, University of New Hampshire Bookstore, 1955).

CARTER, Robert M., *The Development and Financing of Local Governmental Institutions in Nine Vermont Towns* (Burlington, University of Vermont Agricultural Experiment Station, 1946).

DALTON, John J., and WILLIAMS, Sheldon W., *An Economic Study of Local Government in Fifty Vermont Towns* (Burlington, University of Vermont Agricultural Experiment Station, 1946).

DEMING, George H., and CANTOR, Gilbert M., *Selected Duties of New Hampshire Selectmen* (Durham, University of New Hampshire Bookstore, 1952).

DEWOLF, Austin, *The Town Meeting: A Manual of Massachusetts Law* (Boston, Geo. B. Reed, 1890).

FREEMAN, Samuel, *The Town Officer,* 7th ed. (Boston, Thomas & Andrews, 1808).

GOULD, John, *New England Town Meeting: Safeguard of Democracy* (Brattleboro, Vt., Stephen Daye Press, 1940).

GRINNELL, Harold C., *Studies in Local Government and Taxation in Rural New Hampshire* (Durham, University of New Hampshire Agricultural Experiment Station, 1943).

HORMELL, Orren C., *Maine Towns* (Brunswick, Me., Bowdoin College, 1932).

———, and PELLETIER, Lawrence L., *The Manager Plan for Maine Municipalities* (Brunswick, Me., Bowdoin College, 1949).

Maine Historical Records Survey Project, Work Projects Administration, *Town Government in Maine* (Portland, Me., 1940).

Massachusetts Federation of Taxpayers Associations, *The Town Manager Plan in Massachusetts,* rev. ed. (Boston, 1951).

National Municipal League, *Town Management in New England* (New York, 1940), a collection of articles from the *National Municipal Review.*

SLY, John F., *Town Government in Massachusetts* (Cambridge, Mass., Harvard University Press, 1930).

TRAFFORD, John E., *The Town Highway Agent in New Hampshire* (Durham, University of New Hampshire Bookstore, 1955).

WHITE, Max R., *The Connecticut Town Meeting: A Handbook for Moderators and Other Town Meeting Officials,* rev. ed. (Storrs, University of Connecticut Institute of Public Service, 1951).

———, *Handbook for Connecticut Selectmen* (Storrs, University of Connecticut Institute of Public Service, 1951).

———, *Handbook for Connecticut Town Clerks and Town Treasurers* (Storrs, University of Connecticut Institute of Public Service, 1951).

———, and RAISSI, Shirley, *Forms of Town Government in Connecticut* (Storrs, University of Connecticut Institute of Public Service, 1952).

WORCESTER, Alfred, *The Origin of the New England Townmeeting,* Waltham Historical Society Publication, No. 2 (Waltham, Mass., 1925).

Articles

ALEXANDER, John W., and BERGER, Morroe, "Is the Town Meeting Finished?" *American Mercury,* Vol. LXIX, pp. 144-151 (August, 1949).

ATKINS, Carter W., "Manager Plan in Connecticut Towns," *National Municipal Review,* Vol. XXIX, pp. 593-595, 610 (September, 1940).

ATKINS, Richard A., "The Old and the New in Massachusetts Towns," *National Municipal Review,* Vol. XXIX, pp. 361-366 (June, 1940).

Atkins, Richard A., and Ziegler, Lyman H., "Citizen Budgeting in Massachusetts," *National Municipal Review*, Vol. XXX, pp. 568-573 (October, 1941).

Banning, Kendall, "Is the Town Meeting Democratic?" *National Municipal Review*, Vol. XXIV, pp. 152-155 (March, 1935).

Brisbin, Willsie, "Town Meeting," *Vermont Life*, Vol. IV, No. 3, pp. 48-49 (Spring, 1950).

Coit, Margaret L., "The Small Town under Big Pressure," *New York Times Magazine*, pp. 20-22, 24 (February 24, 1952).

Cottrell, Edwin A., "Recent Changes in Town Government," *National Municipal Review*, Vol. VI, pp. 64-69 (January, 1917).

Dever, John E., and Loughlin, Joseph M., "Financial Control through Boards of Finance," *Municipal Finance*, Vol. XXIV, pp. 97-100 (November, 1951).

Fleming, John W., "Maine's Unorganized Territory Creates Few Problems," *National Municipal Review*, Vol. XXVIII, pp. 228-233, 237 (March, 1939).

Flint, K. R. B., "Twenty Years of Town Management in Vermont," *National Municipal Review*, Vol. XXIX, pp. 473-479 (July, 1940).

Googins, George E., "The Town-meeting," *Outlook*, Vol. LXXXII, pp. 561-565 (March 10, 1906).

Harvey, Lashley G., "First Break in New Hampshire," *National Municipal Review*, Vol. XXXV, pp. 521-524 (November, 1946).

Heilman, Grant, "Town Meeting Time," *Vermont Life*, Vol. IX, No. 3, pp. 6-11 (Spring, 1955).

Hormell, Orren C., "Maine a Pioneer in Town Management," *National Municipal Review*, Vol. XXIX, pp. 648-653, 678 (October, 1940).

Howard, Lawrence M., "Wanted: Work for Fence Viewers," *Vermont Life*, Vol. VIII, No. 3, pp. 10-11 (Spring, 1954).

Kalijarvi, Thorsten V., "Town Meeting vs. Town Management," *National Municipal Review*, Vol. XXIX, pp. 540-544 (August, 1940)

Lagemann, John K., "Democracy in Our Town," *Collier's*, Vol. CXIX, No. 10, pp. 13-15, 43 (March 8, 1947).

Lincoln, Alexander, "Some Notes on Representative Town Meetings," *Massachusetts Law Quarterly*, Vol. XXXIII, No. 1, pp. 30-46 (April, 1948).

Lord, Arthur, "The Representative Town Meeting in Massachusetts," *Massachusetts Law Quarterly*, Vol. IV, pp. 49-74 (February, 1919). On the same subject, see the remarks of Alfred D. Chandler, *ibid.*, pp. 77-91.

McLaughlin, Gerald E., "Town Manager," *Vermont Life*, Vol. VIII, No. 3, pp. 19-24 (Spring, 1954).

Nuquist, Andrew E., "March Meeting," *Vermont Life*, Vol. I, No. 3, pp. 9-11, 39 (Spring, 1947).

Pelletier, Lawrence, "New England Pioneers Again," *National Municipal Review*, Vol. XXXVIII, pp. 79-84 (February, 1949).

Robbins, L. H., "Democracy, Town Meeting Style," *New York Times Magazine*, pp. 24, 35, 38 (March 23, 1947).

Sly, John F., "Contemporary Town Meeting Government in Massachusetts," *National Municipal Review*, Vol. XV, pp. 444-446 (August, 1926).

———, "Massachusetts Town Meeting Bends but Does Not Break," *National Municipal Review*, Vol. XV, pp. 681-685 (December, 1926).

Smith, Lincoln, "Town Meeting Government," *Social Science*, Vol. XXX, pp. 174-185 (June, 1955).

Williamson, Samuel T., "Town Meeting at Salt Harbor," *New York Times Magazine*, pp. 16, 29-31 (March 21, 1948).

APPENDIX

A Town-meeting Warrant *

State of Maine
County of Waldo, S. S.

To George Nichols, a Constable in the Town of Lincolnville, in said Waldo County.

GREETINGS:

In the Name of the State of Maine you are hereby required to notify and warn the inhabitants of the Town of Lincolnville, qualified by law, to vote in Town affairs, to assemble at Tranquility Grange Hall in said Town on Monday, the Eighth Day of March, A.D. 1954 at ten o'clock in the forenoon, then and there to act on the following Articles, namely:

1. To choose a Moderator to preside at said meeting.
2. To choose a Town Clerk for the ensuing year.
3. To hear the reports of the Selectmen, Assessors, Overseers of the Poor, Treasurer, Collector of Taxes, Supt. of Schools, and other Town Officers.
4. To choose three or more Selectmen for the ensuing year and determine their Compensation.
5. To choose three or more Assessors for the ensuing year and determine their Compensation.
6. To choose three or more Overseers of the Poor for the ensuing year.
7. To choose three or more Fence Viewers, Surveyors of Lumber, Wood and Bark, Constables, Sextons, and Budget Committee, and any other officers deemed necessary.
8. To choose one or more Road Commissioners for the ensuing year.
9. To choose a Collector or Collectors of Taxes for the ensuing year and determine the Compensation for the same.
10. To choose a Treasurer for the ensuing year and determine Compensation for the same.
11. To choose a member for the School Committee for three years.
12. To choose a member of the School Committee for one year.
13. To choose a member for the Board of Trustees for the Lincolnville School District for five years.
14. To hear the report of the committee on revaluation.
15. To see what sum of money the Town will vote to raise and appropriate for revaluation or Assessors' Maps.
16. To see if the Town will vote to place the management and care of the Town's cemeteries in the hands of a board of five (5) cemetery trustees, the said trustees to be elected initially as follows: two for one year, two for two years, and one for three years; and thereafter to be elected for three-year terms; such board of cemetery trustees to expend such sums as the Town may hereafter make available for maintenance and care of cemeteries and also such income as may be derived from funds given the Town in trust for the perpetual care of individual lots or for the general maintenance and improvement of cemeteries.
17. To see if the Town will authorize and instruct the superintending school committee to pay the tuition charges of secondary school pupils attending preparatory schools and academies of their choice so long as the amount actually charged for tuition is less than the tuition charged at the high school in either Camden or Belfast.

* From *1953 Annual Report for the Town of Lincolnville, Maine,* pp. 44-48.

18. To see what sum of money the Town will vote to raise and appropriate for General School Maintenance.

A—Repairs and Equipment

19. To see what sum of money the Town will vote to raise and appropriate for permanent improvement of the following Roads and Bridges:

A—Moody Mt. Road to Wiley's Corner
B—Moody Mt. Road to Hope line
C—Lee Thurlow's Road
D—Masalin Road
E—Cobb Town Road
F—Butler Road
G—Hope Road to Moody Mt. Road
H—Old Town House Road
I—Fernald's Neck Road
J—Slab City Road
K—Belmont Corner Road
L—High Street

20. To see what sum of money the Town will vote to raise and appropriate for the following purposes:

A—Maintenance of Highways and Bridges
B—Snow Removal and Sanding
C—Surface and Tar
D—Repair of Sidewalks

21. To see if the Town will vote to raise and appropriate $1,066.00 for State Aid Construction under provisions of Sec. 25 and 29 of Chapter 20 R. S. 1944 as amended.

22. To see if the Town will vote to have its Selectmen ask the Highway Commission to designate the road leading from Wiley's Corner to the Searsmont town line over Moody Mt. as State Aid.

23. To see what sum of money the Town will vote to raise and appropriate for the Town Lot at Lincolnville Beach.

24. To see what sum of money the Town will vote to raise for each of the following purposes:

A—Officers' Salaries
B—Incidentals
C—Street Lights
D—Memorial Day
E—Schoolhouse Lot Grading
F—Civilian Defense
G—Care of Shade Trees
H—Support of Poor
I—Aid to Dependent Children
J—Public Health Nursing
K—State of Maine Publicity Bureau
L—Lincolnville Library

25. To see if the Town will vote to raise and appropriate the sum of $200.00 for the Fire Department.

26. To see if the Town will vote to raise and appropriate the sum of $400.00 for the Lincolnville Volunteer Fire Department, Inc., for fuel and lights.

27. To see what action the Town will take in regard to the Alewive privilege.

28. To see if the Town will vote to authorize the Selectmen in behalf of the Town to sell and issue quit claim deeds for the following lots of land.

A–Old Town House and Lot.
B–Schoolhouse Lot, so called.
C–Land acquired for the non-payment of Taxes thereon.

29. To see if the Town will vote to authorize the Selectmen to procure a Temporary Loan or Loans not exceeding in aggregate amount the sum of $15,000.00 in anticipation of the receipt of Taxes for the current municipal year, the proceeds of said loans to be used for necessary Town expense and to execute and deliver in the name of the Town its notes or note thereof, said loan to be paid during the municipal year out of money raised by Taxes during such current year.

30. To see if the Town will vote to ratify the action taken by the Lincolnville Volunteer Fire Department, namely: voting to appoint Bertrand I. Eugley Fire Chief and Virgil Hall Assistant Chief.

31. To see what wage the Town will vote to pay men, trucks and equipment on Town work.

32. To see what action the Town will vote to take in regard to Snow Removal for the ensuing year or next three years.

33. To see if the Town will vote to fix a date when taxes shall be due and payable and fix a rate of interest to be charged on taxes unpaid after date.

34. To see what sum of money the Town will vote to raise and appropriate for a public dump.

35. To see if the Town will vote to accept the following Cemetery Trust Funds:

$300.00 from Roger Libby for Arthur Libby lot
$200.00 Leslie D. Ames lot
$500.00 half for Charles Marriner lot and half for Charles Thomas lot.

36. To see if the Town will vote to raise and appropriate the sum of $175.00 for the Knox County General Hospital.

The Selectmen hereby give notice that they will be in session at the above named hall and place of meeting on Monday the 8th day of March for the purpose of correcting the list of Voters from 9:30 A.M. until the polls are closed.

Given under our hands this 13th day of February, 1953.

MALCOLM E. JOY
ALLEN MORTON
WILLARD HARDY
Selectmen of Lincolnville

CHAPTER 9

Township Government

As INDICATED IN AN earlier chapter, 16 states outside New England employ the township as a unit of government throughout some or all of their respective areas.[1] Though these states are scattered from the Atlantic coast to the Pacific, township organization tends to center in the north central region of the country commonly referred to as the Midwest. For this reason the term *midwestern* township is often applied to the county subdivision in the so-called township states to distinguish it more clearly from the New England town. In structural organization township government varies from state to state. Governmental agencies of the unit include a general governing board, variously constituted, a number of additional township officers, elective and otherwise, and, in some states, a township meeting.

TOWNSHIP MEETINGS

Of the 16 township states, eight make statutory provision for a township meeting, patterned after the town meeting of New England, as the policy-determining organ of the township. These township-meeting states are Illinois, Michigan, Minnesota, Nebraska, North Dakota, South Dakota, Washington, and Wisconsin.[2] All qualified voters of the township are potential members of the meeting. Some townships have township halls, and in such townships the meeting ordinarily is held therein. In other cases the meeting is held in any suitable building which the community may afford and which is designated for that purpose by the voters.[3] The

[1] See above, chap. 2, "Towns and Townships."

[2] The township meeting was used in New York down to the early 1930's.

[3] In Illinois, for example, where some townships have halls and others do not, the statutes provide that the meeting shall be held at "some convenient place in the town, to be fixed by the electors, at their annual town meetings."

usual practice is for the meeting, like its New England prototype, to elect a moderator to preside over its deliberations, though in Michigan the supervisor serves as moderator and in Wisconsin the chairman of the township board is chairman of the meeting. Provision is made by statute for a regular annual meeting in late winter or early spring and for the calling of special meetings whenever town business makes such action desirable. Requirements for calling special meetings differ from state to state. In Wisconsin, for example, such meetings are called on written request of 12 qualified voters; while in Illinois a special meeting is called whenever the supervisor, the clerk, and a justice of the peace, or any two of those officers, together with at least 15 town voters, file in the clerk's office a written statement declaring that such a meeting is necessary and setting forth its objects. Public notice of meetings, whether regular or special, must ordinarily be given by the township clerk, by posting and sometimes by publication as well. In some cases, however, notice of the annual meeting is not required where the day and hour are fixed by law.

The principal powers usually conferred upon the township meeting are those of (1) electing township officers, (2) levying taxes and making appropriations, (3) authorizing the borrowing of money, and (4) enacting bylaws for the management of township affairs. Bylaws may deal with a variety of subjects, depending upon the state concerned, such as weed eradication, protection of trees along highways, fence regulation, prohibition of livestock from running at large, and establishment of dog pounds. Other powers delegated to township meetings in some instances include making orders for the sale or use of township property; giving directions concerning exercise of the township's corporate powers, such as the powers to sue and be sued, acquire property, and make contracts; authorizing the erection of township buildings; and fixing, usually within statutory limits, the compensation of certain township officials. Special meetings in some states are more limited than regular meetings in respect to the matters with which they may deal; and sometimes, as in Illinois, they may consider only the business set forth in the request and notice therefor.[4] In general the powers of the township meeting in the Midwest, though broad, are less extensive than those of the New England town meeting. Actually, even one or more of the major powers mentioned above may be lacking in a particular state. Thus, township officers are elected, in some instances, in a regular township election rather than in the township meeting; and some states require that voter approval of the incurring of township indebtedness be given in a referendum election.

Although the township meeting, in many respects, bears a close resemblance to the New England town meeting with regard to legal compo-

[4] Cf. N. G. P. Krausz, *Handbook for Illinois Township Officers*, rev. ed. (Champaign, Ill., Garrard Press, 1956), p. 10.

sition and powers, it does not possess the vitality of its New England counterpart. This is the case even when one considers that the New England meeting, as pointed out in the preceding chapter, has lost some of its vigor in recent years. There are, here and there, communities where the township meeting is well attended, but this appears to be distinctly the exception rather than the rule. Some or all of the township officers, it is true, are usually in attendance. It is commonly provided that the township clerk shall call the meeting to order, preside until a moderator has been chosen, and serve as secretary; and, frequently, various officers of the township are required to present their annual reports at the regular meeting. Furthermore, the direct concern of the officers with township affairs would in itself induce some of them to attend. But attendance on the part of other citizens, except on rare occasions when some particular issue generates unusual interest, is astonishingly small. In townships of several hundred voters, or even several thousand, it is not unusual for attendance at the annual meeting to be no more than a dozen or so, and often it is even smaller. "Many citizens, some of them otherwise well-informed, seem to be completely unaware of the meeting's very existence, to say nothing of its importance." [5] Press accounts in township-meeting states are replete with reports of meetings, some of them in relatively populous townships, that are attended by a mere handful of voters. In many Illinois townships the 1956 meeting was reported as attended by five persons or less. When, as is often the case, the number of other voters in attendance is less than the number of township officers present, the latter are in a position to dominate the meeting and control its action. And if, as sometimes happens, *only* township officers attend, they constitute the meeting—not, to be sure, in their official capacity, but as voting citizens. In these circumstances, the township meeting fails utterly to operate on anything approaching a broadly democratic basis, township affairs actually being controlled by a small group. And when township officers constitute all or a majority of those in attendance at the meeting, the determination of township policy for all practical purposes slips by default into their hands, though responsibility for this policy rests by statute with the voters. Thus is violated one of the cardinal principles underlying town-meeting government in New England and elsewhere, namely, that the local voters themselves, and not their elected representatives, are responsible for the determination of basic policies.[6] All in all, it may fairly be said that the spirit of town-meeting government has failed to "take root" in most of the midwestern townships in which the meeting has been established by law.

Although nonattendance is perhaps the most serious weakness of the

[5] Clyde F. Snider, "The Illinois Town Meeting," *Illinois County and Township Official*, Vol. VIII, No. 12, pp. 5-7 (February, 1949).

[6] Cf. *ibid.*

township meeting as it generally operates, a different type of problem is occasionally encountered in some of the more populous townships in the form of the packed meeting. A group interested in securing a particular course of action from the meeting, by encouraging like-minded persons quietly but systematically to go early to the meeting, may fill up the hall with their partisans well in advance of the hour at which the meeting begins. In the case of a two o'clock meeting, for example, the hall may be filled to overflowing by one o'clock with persons who, by thus virtually excluding citizens of opposite views, will be in a position to command the votes necessary to determine meeting action. In this manner proposed budgetary items may be changed or other courses of action forced upon the meeting by a group whose views may be quite at variance with those of a majority of the township voters.

In view of the widespread failure of the township meeting to function as an effective agency for the management of local affairs, it has at times been suggested that the meeting system be completely abolished, as indeed has been done in New York. A less drastic, and perhaps preferable, course of action might seek to preserve the meeting in those few townships where the system actually functions and to abolish it elsewhere. Although a plan of this nature would present some difficulties of application, the desired end might conceivably be attained by providing for the transaction of township business in meeting if a specified percentage of the township voters are in attendance, and stipulating that otherwise the powers of the township meeting shall vest legally in the township board.[7] If the meeting is to be retained in some form in urban areas, in order to prevent the packing of meetings in populous townships it would seem desirable to abandon the plenary assembly in favor of a representative meeting along the lines of the system now operating in a number of New England towns.[8] Under a plan of this nature the meeting would consist, not of the township voters as such, but of a fairly numerous group of representatives elected by them. A meeting place, with facilities for seating all duly elected members, could then readily be provided; and, since it might reasonably be expected that most elected members would attend, the attendance at meetings might actually be larger, under normal circumstances, than is usually the case where the traditional form of meeting is employed. In the large majority of rural townships, however, unless the meeting can be invigorated and its attendance increased—conditions that seem unlikely of fulfillment—it would appear wise to abandon the primary assembly entirely and to place re-

7 Cf. Illinois Tax Commission, *Receipts and Disbursements of Townships and Road Districts, 1925-1936,* Survey of Local Finance in Illinois (Springfield and Chicago, 1939), Vol. IV, p. 12, published in co-operation with the Work Projects Administration.

8 See above, chap. 8, "Representative Town Meetings."

sponsibilty for financial and other policy matters squarely upon the shoulders of the elected township officers, who tend, in any event, to exercise policy-making powers under the meeting system as it now operates.

TOWNSHIP BOARDS

Every township state, including those with and those without township meetings, provides by statute for some sort of township governing board. The official title of this agency varies from state to state. In some instances it is designated merely as the town or township board. Several states use the title board of supervisors or board of trustees. The title is township committee in New Jersey, advisory board in Indiana, board of directors in Missouri, and board of auditors in Illinois. In this discussion the title *township board* will be used in a generic sense, as applicable to any such agency, whatever its official designation.

Most commonly, though by no means always, the township board consists of three members. In approximately half of the township states the board is strictly an elective body, composed of persons elected *as* board members; elsewhere, however, the composition of the board is wholly or in part ex officio.[9] Thus, the board consists in Illinois of the supervisor, the clerk, and the justices of the peace of the township; in Nebraska of the clerk, the treasurer, and one justice of the peace; in Michigan of the supervisor, the clerk, the treasurer, and two justices of the peace, with two additional justices being optional in the more populous townships; and in Missouri of the trustee and two elective members. Where there is a principal administrative officer of the township, such as the supervisor or trustee in several states,[10] who is ex officio a member of the board, that official usually is designated by statute as the board's chairman. In other instances the board chooses its own chairman from among its members. The township clerk, whether a member of the body or not, ordinarily serves as board clerk, though in Indiana the board chooses a secretary from its membership.

Terms of board members, as of township officers generally, are usually two years or four, but re-election is common.[11] Board membership in practice frequently includes one or more local political leaders, with the chairmanship in particular often being filled by such a person. Occupationally, board members in rural townships are predominantly farmers or

[9] In one of South Carolina's two townships, three of the five members of the governing township commission are appointed by the governor—United States Bureau of the Census, *Local Government Structure in the United States* (Washington, Government Printing Office, 1954), p. 71.

[10] See below, "Chief Township Officer."

[11] Concerning re-election in Kansas, see James W. Drury, *Township Government in Kansas* (Lawrence, University of Kansas Governmental Research Center, 1954), pp. 31-33.

local business men closely associated with farming. In this respect, as well as in the matter of members' age, Missouri's township boards probably are reasonably typical, and Bradshaw and Garrison report on them as follows: [12]

> First-hand data from representative townships indicate that generally the boards are composed of elderly men, the trustee usually being the oldest in years as well as the senior member. As would be expected, about 90 per cent of them are farmers or retired farmers. The others are small town, farmer-minded business men, such as a produce dealer, a butcher, a general merchant, a manager of an oil station, or an operator of a threshing machine.

State statutes ordinarily provide for a designated number of regular meetings of the township board each year and for the calling of special meetings as the township's business may require. The number of regular meetings, for example, is two in Illinois and Indiana, and three in Missouri. Though provisions for special meetings vary considerably, it is fairly common to permit the convening of such meetings at the discretion of the board chairman, a specified number of board members, or, where one exists, the township executive officer. In Indiana, for instance, special meetings may be called by the township trustee, the chairman of the board, or two board members; while in Illinois call for such meetings is issued by the township clerk at the request of the supervisor or of any two members of the board. In general, special meetings appear to be held rather frequently. Thus, in Missouri, though there are only three regular sessions each year, many boards meet monthly.[13] In townships having a township hall board meetings ordinarily are held in that building. Elsewhere meetings are held in public or private buildings of various kinds—frequently at the township clerk's office or the home of the board's chairman or clerk. In Missouri, for example: [14]

> While the statutes specify that the board shall meet at the office of the township clerk, this is seldom the practice. Indeed a clerk rarely has an office. The board may meet in a store, a bank, the residence of a board member, or some other convenient place. The court house usually furnishes the meeting place for a board when the county seat is in that township.

Board members ordinarily are compensated on a per diem basis for their services in attending meetings.

The powers of the township board vary from state to state, particularly between those states that have the township meeting and those that do not. In states having no meeting, the board is the general governing authority of the township and commonly possesses the taxing and other

[12] William L. Bradshaw and Milton Garrison, *Township Organization in Missouri* (Columbia, University of Missouri, 1936), p. 31.

[13] *Ibid.*

[14] *Ibid.*

financial powers. Also, it usually has some licensing and regulatory authority. Where the township meeting exists the board ordinarily prepares the annual budget for submission to the meeting. A power of the board in practically all states, whether or not there is a township meeting, is that of auditing and allowing claims against the township.[15] The board frequently is vested with some appointing power, the officers most commonly appointed being overseers or commissioners of highways. In addition to granting authority over specific matters, the statutes of several states provide that the board shall have charge of all township affairs not committed by law to other officers. The township board frequently serves ex officio as a township board of health, and sometimes, as a board of tax review or equalization. In some instances individual board members serve ex officio in various capacities, such as those of fence viewer and overseer of the poor.[16]

CHIEF TOWNSHIP OFFICER

Approximately half of the township states, including some with and some without the township meeting, confer upon a single official powers sufficiently broad to justify his being considered the head officer of the township. In such states the management of township affairs may be said to vest in this officer, assisted and checked in some matters by the township board, rather than in the board itself. The chief officer is known in Illinois, Michigan, and New York as the supervisor; in Indiana, Kansas, and Missouri as the trustee; and in Wisconsin as the town chairman.[17] Except in Indiana, the chief officer is a member of the township board; and in Illinois, Michigan, New York, and Wisconsin he is also a member of the county board. Furthermore, he usually serves in various ex officio capacities, such as those of township treasurer, assessor, and overseer of the poor.

Perhaps the authority of the chief township officer reaches its maximum in the case of the township trustee in Indiana. That official serves his township ex officio as clerk, treasurer, overseer of the poor, inspector of elections, fence viewer, and, in the less populous townships, assessor. He is also trustee, clerk, and treasurer of the school township, which serves as the principal local unit for school administration. In these various legal capacities the trustee serves as the chief administrative officer of his township for both civil and school purposes. He has charge of township property, prepares civil and school budgets, examines and settles claims against the township, administers public assistance, and manages the

[15] In Indiana, however, the allowance of claims is a function of the trustee.

[16] The title of the latter office has recently been changed in some states to supervisor of public assistance.

[17] Cf. Kirk H. Porter, *County and Township Government in the United States* (New York, Macmillan, 1922), pp. 312-313.

rural schools of his township even to the hiring of teachers. Until 1932, when township roads in Indiana were transferred to the county, the trustee also performed important functions in the field of highway construction and maintenance. The taxing, appropriating, and borrowing powers of the township, however, are in the hands of the township advisory board.[18]

THE TOWNSHIP CLERK

The office of township clerk is filled in some states on an ex officio basis but more commonly is elective. The clerk is charged with a wide variety of duties, some clerical, some custodial, some of a recording nature, and still others of miscellaneous character. He is official custodian of township records and documents and provides certified copies thereof upon proper application. He usually is clerk to the township board and, in states having township meetings, is secretary of the meeting. In these capacities it is his duty to make official record of all ordinances, resolutions, and bylaws adopted by the board or meeting. In some jurisdictions the clerk is registrar of vital statistics, and in some he is registrar of voters. Frequently, the clerk is a member ex officio of one or more boards or commissions in the township government, and, at times, he is appointed to membership on still other agencies. In Michigan, for example, the township clerk serves as a member of the township board, the township board of health, the board of township building inspectors, the township board of park commissioners, and the board of township canvassers, and he may also be appointed a member of the township board of election inspectors by the township board.[19] Considering the wide range of his duties, it is not surprising that the clerk's office tends to become a general clearinghouse for township information and activities. Where the office is elective, re-election is common. One township clerk in Illinois was recently reported to have served for 50 consecutive years, and another for 48. Though tenure of such prolonged duration obviously is extraordinary, re-election occurs with sufficient frequency that a substantial percentage of the incumbents, at any given time, are persons who, as the result of experience, "know their way about" in township affairs.

OTHER TOWNSHIP OFFICERS

The office of township treasurer, like that of clerk, is usually elective, though in some cases it is ex officio. The treasurer receives township taxes

[18] See Clyde F. Snider, *Township Government in Indiana* (Bloomington, Indiana University Bureau of Business Research, 1932), chaps. 1, 2; Frank G. Bates, "The Indiana Township—An Anachronism," *National Municipal Review*, Vol. XXI, pp. 502-504 (August, 1932).

[19] Claude R. Tharp, *A Manual of Township Government in Michigan* (Ann Arbor, University of Michigan Bureau of Government, 1948), p. 40.

and other revenues, has custody of these, and pays out the same on order of the township board. Sometimes he is required to keep the funds in his custody on deposit in a bank or banks designated by the township board as township depositories. Though less often than in the case of the clerk, the treasurer sometimes serves ex officio as a member of the township governing board and of other township boards or commissions.

Another elective township officer in some states is the assessor, whose duty it is to assess, usually under some degree of county or state supervision, real and personal property within his township for purposes of taxation.[20] Occasionally, there is also an elective township collector who collects taxes and pays over the money to the treasurer. There is a tendency at the present time, however, to abolish these two offices and to make the county the primary unit for tax assessment and collection.

The office of overseer of the poor or supervisor of public assistance is filled in a number of states by the township supervisor or trustee ex officio, but in others it is elective. It is ordinarily the duty of this official to dispense outdoor assistance—principally in the form of food, clothing, rent money, and medical care—to indigent persons residing within his township, and to determine what persons from the township are entitled to admission to the county almshouse. In the relatively few instances in which a township almshouse is maintained, this institution is under his supervision.

A township officer who is more commonly appointed by the township board than elected is the highway overseer or commissioner, of whom there may be more than one in a single township. This officer is charged with the construction and maintenance of minor roads and bridges. Townships generally serve as districts for the election of justices of the peace and constables, the functions of whom are considered at some length in the chapters on judicial administration and law enforcement.[21] As previously noted, there are several states in which some or all justices of a township serve as members of the township board. Miscellaneous township officers for which provision is made in various states include poundkeepers, weed commissioners, and fence viewers. These officers are usually appointive or ex officio, but in some instances they are elective. Poundkeepers operate pounds for the detention of stray dogs and livestock; weed commissioners are charged with eradicating noxious weeds on private premises in cases of owner inaction; and fence viewers settle disputes between adjoining landowners concerning the maintenance of divisional fences.

[20] The township assessor in some instances serves ex officio in capacities having little or no direct relation to his primary duty, as in Illinois, for example, where he is ex officio a fence viewer and a member of the township board of health.

[21] See below, chaps. 12, 13.

DECLINING IMPORTANCE OF THE TOWNSHIP[22]

The midwestern township is a product of a frontier civilization. Representing in part a transplanting to the westward of New England's system of town government,[23] its structure, as will be explained in the following section, has also been influenced in a substantial measure by the congressional township, which was introduced into federal territories at an early date as a feature of the public land survey system. In pioneer days, with their primitive facilities for communication and transportation, the township served as a convenient subdivision of the county for the performance of local public services. Justices of the peace and constables elected from the township dispensed simple justice in neighborhood disputes and dealt with minor infractions of the criminal law; overseers of the poor saw to it that destitute members of the community did not go cold or hungry; highway commissioners opened and maintained local roads to provide township residents with access to schools, churches, and markets; and township assessors appraised real estate and personal property for purposes of taxation. Other functions, most of them minor, were assigned to townships in various states. Generally speaking, however, except in an occasional state where the township has served as the basic school unit, major functions of township government have never exceeded four: law enforcement and judicial administration, road maintenance, assistance to the poor, and property assessment.

For a considerable period of time the township operated with a reasonable degree of satisfaction in providing local services in rural areas. More recently, however, and particularly beginning with the 1930's, township government has tended to fall into disfavor and, indeed, in some instances, has been largely or wholly abandoned. For this trend three principal reasons may be assigned. In the first place, improvements in communications and transportation have made it no longer necessary that local officials be stationed in subdivisions of the county in order to be readily accessible to the citizenry. Secondly, the expansion of governmental services at all levels has brought into the spotlight the duplication, waste, and inefficiency flowing from governmental operations in minuscule township areas. In every major field wherein townships operate, county government in most states is charged also with responsibilities; and in this situation, if actual overlapping of functions does not occur, at least there is duplication of governmental machinery. In many rural townships over-

[22] This section includes several extracts, some of them with slight modification, from Clyde F. Snider, "The Twilight of the Township," *National Municipal Review*, Vol. XLI, pp. 390-396 (September, 1952) Reproduction here is by permission of the *Review*.

[23] See above, chap. 8.

head costs—costs of merely "keeping the township going" as distinguished from expenditures for the direct accomplishment of township functions —absorb an unduly large proportion of the local budget.[24] Included in overhead costs are items such as officers' per diem, premiums on official bonds, office supplies, publication expenses, and rent for (or maintenance of, if publicly owned) office space and official meeting places. Professor James Drury reports, for example, that in those Kansas townships where the highway function has been transferred to the county some 40 per cent of all township expenditures, as of the early 1950's, went for overhead, with many such townships having budgets showing no expenditures except for overhead costs.[25] In Illinois, where some counties have townships and others do not, comparative studies strongly indicate that residents of nontownship counties receive local services as good as, or better than, those provided in counties served by both county and township governments, and at substantially lower total cost.[26] The general inadequacy of the present-day township as a judicial, highway, welfare, and assessment unit is considered in subsequent chapters of this book dealing with local functions and finance.[27] A third reason for township decline is found in the fact that in years of depression, war, and threat of war, increased costs of government have intensified tax-consciousness and stimulated popular demand for the elimination of waste and inefficiency. As a result of these and other related factors, there has been a consistent tendency to de-emphasize the township in the over-all governmental pattern.

One aspect of the declining importance of the township is seen in the widespread transfer of township functions to the county. State after state has made complete transfer to county jurisdiction of one or more of the major township functions. Thus, all township roads have been transferred to the counties in Indiana and Michigan, and all poor-relief functions in Kansas. In other instances some of the counties of a given state have effected functional transfer under optional laws, such as the Kansas statute under which approximately half of the counties have taken over township roads. In two states the transfer of functions has been so comprehensive as to eliminate township government entirely or to reduce the township to a mere empty shell. These are Oklahoma, where townships in the 1930's were deprived of the taxing power and had all of their remain-

[24] Cf. Drury, *op. cit.*, pp. 37, 39.

[25] *Ibid.*, pp. 36-39, 65.

[26] M. H. Hunter, *Costs of Township and County Government in Illinois* (Urbana, University of Illinois Bureau of Business Research, 1933); H. K. Allen, *Costs and Services of Local Government in Selected Illinois Counties* (Urbana, University of Illinois Bureau of Business Research, 1936).

[27] See below, chap. 12, "Weaknesses of Justice-of-the-peace System"; chap. 14, "Results of Small [Road] Units"; chap. 16, "General Outdoor Assistance"; chap. 19, "Property-tax Administration," pp. 499-500.

ing functions transferred to the counties; and Iowa, where so little is left to township government that the Census Bureau no longer includes the townships of that state in its enumeration of governmental units. Some individual townships in Minnesota and a few other states have been legally deorganized, and their functions have been transferred to the overlying counties. And in some instances where townships continue legally to exist their governments are in a moribund state, if not wholly inactive. Thus, in Kansas counties which have adopted the county-unit road system little is left to the townships except, if they choose to perform them, certain minor functions, such as cemetery maintenance, prairie-dog eradication, and weed control.[28] It is clear, therefore, that the midwestern township as a governmental unit is losing ground in two directions. In the first place, some township governments are being eliminated, either completely, through formal legal action, or virtually, through disuse of authority. And secondly, even where an "active" township organization is maintained, the importance of the township is continually being lessened through the transfer of functions to the county.[29]

The decline of the township as an instrumentality for local self-government is further evidenced by the lack of popular interest in township affairs and the dearth of candidates for township office. The general indifference toward township meetings has been noted in an earlier connection, and the vote cast in township elections often is pitifully small.[30] Notorious also is the reluctance of qualified citizens to accept township office. Some elective offices, in the absence of avowed candidates, are filled from persons nominated by write-in votes in the primary; and others, for want of nominated candidates, are filled by write-in votes in the general election. Where no one is elected to an office, or where the person elected fails to qualify, the office may be filled by appointment; or, in some instances, an incumbent officer, after his regular term has expired, may continue to serve until a successor is elected and qualifies. Notwithstanding these various means of filling offices to which no candidate seeks election, many township offices in practice remain vacant for long periods of time.

In the 1952 Kansas primary, according to Professor Drury, 45 per cent of that state's townships had not a single candidate filing for the office of trustee—the principal township office. Almost as large a number of townships had but one candidate filing; and less than 1 per cent of the townships had two or more candidates filing for each of the major parties. Except for such write-in contests as might develop, fewer than

[28] See Drury, *op. cit.*, chap. 4.

[29] See below, chap. 20, "Township Abolition"; "Local Deorganization"; "Transfer of Functions."

[30] See above, "Township Meetings."

10 per cent of the Kansas townships gave promise of any contest for the office of trustee in the subsequent general election. In the same primary, 90 per cent of the townships were without any candidate filing for the office of justice of the peace; and in only one township in the state did a full slate of candidates—two from each party—file for the office of justice.[31] Observation indicates that in many other areas where township government prevails, the situation is not basically different from that in Kansas.[32]

All in all, available evidence points to the conclusion that the midwestern township as a governmental institution is on the way out and, furthermore, that this fact is not to be regretted. From North Dakota, for example, where more than half of the counties have some nontownship territory, it is reported that even where township organization remains, functions of the township board of health have been largely taken over by the county physician and the school nurse; the construction of extensive systems of state and county highways has relieved townships of much of their responsibility for road maintenance; and the major burden of caring for the needy falls upon the county and unofficial organizations.[33] Commenting upon this situation as of the early 1930's, James McCrae declares: [34]

> The original functions of the civil township have been largely taken over by other organizations. Those which do remain to the township it can no longer perform efficiently; yet township organization costs the rural people of North Dakota from one and one-half to two million dollars per year. Approximately 15,000 people are drawing pay for the performance of duties which are of little significance. . . . State-wide elimination of township organization would be a forward step in the development and prosperity of the State.

In several states where township organization is optional with the respective counties competent scholars, on the basis of observation and investigation, have concluded that nontownship organization is preferable. Thus, the Illinois township has been characterized as "neither a necessary nor an economic governmental unit." [35] Township organization in Missouri has been found to be more expensive, less efficient, and generally less desirable than nontownship.[36] And the Nebraska township has been declared to be "losing its vitality and its significance as a unit of local government," with its "complete extinction . . . predicted by some authorities on the subject." [37]

[31] Drury, *op. cit.*, pp. 28-31.

[32] Cf. below, chap. 12, "Justices of the Peace," p. 305.

[33] James A. McCrae, "Township Government in North Dakota," *Quarterly Journal of the University of North Dakota,* Vol. XXIII, pp. 185-201 (1932-1933).

[34] *Ibid.*, p. 200.

[35] Hunter, *op. cit.*, p. 30.

[36] Bradshaw and Garrison, *op. cit.*, pp. 69-70.

[37] Roger V. Shumate, *Local Government in Nebraska* (Lincoln, Nebraska Legislative Council, 1939), p. 26.

In Kansas, though the legal forms of township organization remain and the township continues as an active unit in some places, township government in parts of the state is reported to have "almost died of atrophy." [38] As long ago as the 1920's, an Ohio legislative committee reported:

> There can be no question as to the decline of the township in Ohio. The last fifteen years have witnessed a gradual paring away of its functions and a shifting of authority to the county. . . . The process of decay which has been particularly evident in the last decade and a half is due to a fundamental cause, namely, the fact that the township is no longer suited to the requirements of local government in rural areas. The conditions which were originally responsible for its creation have ceased to exist. Its ultimate elimination seems practically certain.

On the basis of its findings the committee recommended "the immediate abolition of the township and the transfer of its remaining functions to the county." [39] As the Ohio report pointed out, evidence of township decline even then was not confined to any single state but was apparent generally throughout the Midwest. In the years since the report the importance of the midwestern civil township has continued to wane, with the rate of decline tending to be accelerated rather than retarded.[40]

THE CONGRESSIONAL TOWNSHIP: ITS INFLUENCE ON LOCAL GOVERNMENT

The congressional or survey township derives its name from the fact that it is established under laws enacted by the national Congress to provide a system for surveying the lands constituting the public domain. Though not in itself a unit of local government, the congressional township deserves consideration in a book of this nature for three reasons: (1) the student of rural government should have some knowledge of the basic features of a system of legal land description employed in rural areas throughout a large portion of the United States; (2) the congressional and the civil or governmental townships are frequently confused by the uninformed; and (3) the congressional township has had a substantial influence in determining the size and shape of civil townships.

The congressional township had its origin in the Ordinance of 1785 enacted by the Congress of the Confederation for the survey of public

[38] Drury, *op. cit.*, p. 66.

[39] *Report of the Joint Legislative Committee on Economy and Taxation of the Eighty-sixth Ohio General Assembly* (Columbus, 1926), pp. 251, 254.

[40] For a recent defense of the Ohio township, in which it is contended that the institution has actually gained in vigor since the 1926 report, see William B. Guitteau, *Ohio's Townships: The Grassroots of Democracy* (Toledo, Toledo Printing Co., 1949). This monograph is an account of the organization and activities of the Ohio State Association of Township Trustees and Clerks, distributed by the association to the trustees and clerks of the state's townships.

lands in the Northwest Territory—that vast region north of the Ohio River and east of the Mississippi from which eventually were carved the states of Ohio, Indiana, Illinois, Michigan, and Wisconsin.[41] Antedating by two years the famous Northwest Ordinance or Ordinance of 1787, providing a form of governmental organization for the territory, the Ordinance of 1785 established a plan for public land surveys which, after adoption of the Constitution, was continued by the Congress with minor modifications and extended to other federal territories as these were acquired and surveys were instituted. As a result, the survey system inaugurated in 1785 has now been applied, or is being applied, to all those lands in 29 states that constitute or have constituted the federal public domain, and congressional townships are found therefore in all of these states whether or not civil townships exist for governmental purposes.[42]

According to the terms of the survey law, the public lands are "divided by north and south lines run according to the true meridian, and by others crossing them at right angles, so as to form townships of six miles square." In this rectangular plan the township boundary lines running north and south are termed *range lines,* and those running east and west are called simply *township lines.* Horizontal tiers of townships are numbered north and south from established *base lines* running east and west; and vertical tiers are numbered east and west from *principal meridians* running north and south, each meridian being assigned a distinctive name or number. A particular township is identified for purposes of land records, patents, deeds, and other legal documents by the number of its tier north or south from base line and east or west from a designated principal meridian. Thus, Township 13 South, Range 41 East (abbreviated T. 13 S., R. 41 E.), of the Willamette Meridian, Ore., refers to that Oregon township situated in the thirteenth tier south of the pertinent base line and the forty-first tier east of the Willamette principal meridian.

The law also provides that each township "shall be subdivided into

[41] The following description of the public-land survey system is based, for the most part, on United States Bureau of Land Management, *Manual of Instructions for the Survey of the Public Lands of the United States* (Washington, Government Printing Office, 1947). Accounts briefer than that in the *Manual,* but considerably more extended than the one presented here, are to be found in Raymond E. Davis and Francis S. Foote, *Surveying Theory and Practice,* 3d ed. (New York, McGraw-Hill, 1940), chap. 23; Frank Emerson Clark, *A Treatise on the Law of Surveying and Boundaries,* 2d ed. (Indianapolis, Bobbs-Merrill, 1939), chap. 2. See also, Earl L. Shoup, *The Government of the American People* (Boston, Ginn, 1946), pp. 671-673; Arthur M. Weimer and Homer Hoyt, *Principles of Urban Real Estate,* rev. ed. (New York, Ronald Press, 1948), pp. 50-51.

[42] The 19 states wherein the congressional-township system has not been applied are the 13 original states; the five states of Maine, Kentucky, Tennessee, Vermont, and West Virginia, which were carved from original states; and Texas, which was an independent republic prior to admission to statehood. In each of these the state retained title to vacant lands within its borders and prescribed the method of their survey.

sections, containing, as nearly as may be, six hundred and forty acres each," and that these mile-square sections of each township "shall be numbered, respectively, beginning with the number one in the northeast section and proceeding west and east alternately through the township with progressive numbers till the thirty-six be completed" (see Fig. VIII).[43] Any particular section within a township can thus readily be identified by number. Each section is divided, in turn, into four quarter sections of 160 acres each, these being designated as the northeast, northwest, southeast, and southwest quarters, respectively (abbreviated N.E. ¼, etc.).

FIG. VIII

Congressional Township

6	5	4	3	2	1
7	8	9	10	11	12
18	17	16	15	14	13
19	20	21	22	23	24
30	29	28	27	26	25
31	32	33	34	35	36

6 miles (side) — 6 miles (bottom)

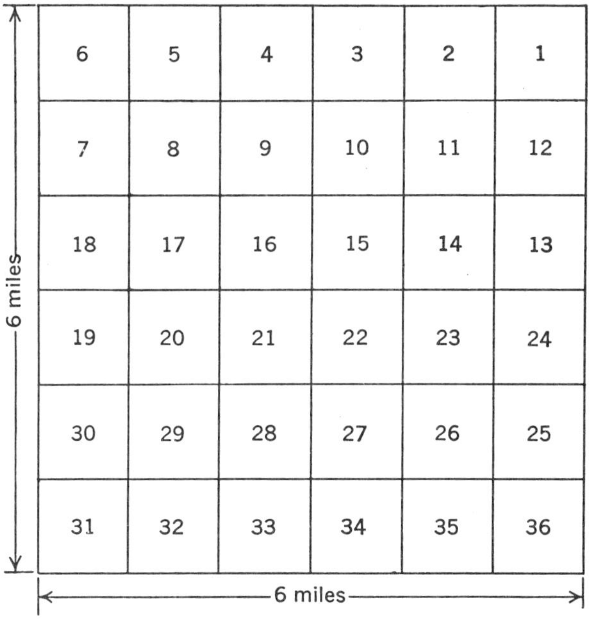

Quarter sections may be further divided, for description purposes, into half-quarters of 80 acres each and quarter-quarters of 40 acres. A 40-acre tract in the extreme northeast corner of a Colorado section, for example, might therefore be described as the Northeast Quarter of the Northeast Quarter of Section 22, Township 14 South, Range 81 West of the Sixth Principal Meridian, Colorado (N.E. ¼ of N.E. ¼ of Sec. 22, T. 14 S., R. 81 W. of 6th P.M., Colo.).

A prime objective of the congressional-township system of land survey is to facilitate the identification of particular parcels or tracts of land

[43] A different method of numbering sections was used at first under the Ordinance of 1785. See Clark, *op. cit.*, p. 28.

and to provide a reasonably simple and accurate method of describing real estate for recording and transfer purposes. This system of descriptions based on rectangular platting represents a distinct departure from the metes-and-bounds method of survey and description widely employed in states which have never constituted a portion of the public domain.[44] A metes-and-bounds description involves the establishment of a "point of beginning" at, or with reference to, some well-known natural object or landmark of record, which point ordinarily constitutes a corner of the tract of land to be described.[45] Proceeding from this point, the tract is bounded by detailing exact measurements of distance in specified directions until there is a return to the point of beginning. Though corner "monuments" of metal or stone planted in the ground by surveyors are frequently employed in metes-and-bounds descriptions,[46] widespread use is made also, both in establishing points of beginning and at intermediate points in the descriptions, of landmarks such as trees and buildings.

A serious disadvantage of the metes-and-bounds description lies in the fact that some or all of the landmarks used therein may be much less durable than the monuments and markers employed in connection with the public-land surveys. An extraordinary definition of a starting point in a Maine description is said to read: "commencing at a point on the River Road near the big hemlock tree where Philo Bates killed the bear."[47] Abstracters and registers of deeds have often encountered descriptions with such starting points as "the northeast corner of Gus Olson's barn"—and these descriptions must serve, of course, for legal purposes long after both Gus and his barn are gone.[48] A legislative act of 1901 reincorporating the town of Ripley, Tenn., describes the boundaries of the new corporation in part as follows: [49]

> Beginning at a stake in the west boundary line of the present limits of the old corporation, and in the north margin of the Ripley and Fulton road, running thence with said road in a western direction to the southeast corner of T. G. Gause's residence lot . . . thence north eighty-five degrees east to a blackgum marked with a cross and with mistletoe in the top, and with a blue bird sitting on a limb, which tree is a short distance east of Ed Johnson's horse lot; thence north twenty-four degrees east to cedar tree in G. W. Young's yard, a little east of his dwelling . . .

Though descriptions such as these, albeit amusing, happily are not typical, they serve to emphasize the difficulty of making a metes-and-

[44] "The term 'metes and bounds' comes from the old English words 'metes' meaning measurements, and 'bounds' meaning boundaries"—R. P. Boyd and David L. Uelmen, "Re-surveys and Metes and Bounds Descriptions," *Wisconsin Law Review*, pp. 657-687, 657 (July, 1953).

[45] Cf. *ibid.*, pp. 658-659.

[46] Cf. Clark, *op. cit.*, pp. 4-5.

[47] Quoted in Boyd and Uelmen, *op. cit.*, p. 659.

[48] *Ibid.*

[49] *Acts of Tennessee* (1901), chap. 223.

bounds description as clear, as concise, as accurate, and as enduring in character as a description in terms of township, range, section, and sectional subdivision, such as is possible under the congressional-township system.

The congressional township, as suggested above, is merely a six-mile-square geographic area for surveying purposes and ordinarily is without governmental organization of any kind. In some instances, it is true, congressional townships are, or at one time have been, incorporated as "school townships," but only for very limited purposes which do not justify their classification as distinct governmental units. Congress, in providing for the survey of the territorial lands, reserved Section 16 of each township for the support of public schools. Subsequently, whenever a new state was carved from federal territory, it was customary for Congress, in the enabling act or the statehood bill, to grant the Section 16 lands to the state for school purposes. The state government, in turn, commonly provided that these lands, or the proceeds therefrom when sold, should constitute a permanent fund, the income from which should be used for school support. Where the congressional township was constituted a "school township," it was usually for the purpose of performing certain duties in connection with the administration of the school lands and the distribution to the respective schools of income therefrom. Sometimes this "school township" has also been charged with other specific duties, such as the division of the congressional-township area into school districts, but it has not been charged with basic responsibility for local school finance and administration.[50] Not only does the congressional township thus fail to qualify as a unit of local government, but it fails even to constitute a true *geographic* subdivision of the county. County boundary lines frequently do not coincide with the township and range lines forming the boundaries of congressional townships; and some such townships overlap even the boundary lines of the states.[51]

Although not themselves governmental units, congressional townships nevertheless have been influential in determining the civil-township pattern. Where governmental townships have been established within areas already divided into congressional townships, there has naturally been some tendency on the part of the authorities laying out the civil townships to follow the boundaries of the pre-existing congressional townships. Some states require by statute that the boundaries of civil townships be made to conform "so far as practicable" to those of the congressional townships; and even in the absence of such a statutory requirement, the disposition toward conformity is frequently evident. Where the bound-

[50] "School townships" of this nature are to be distinguished from the Indiana school township, which is coterminous with the civil township and serves as the basic local unit for school purposes.

[51] Cf. Bradshaw and Garrison, *op. cit.*, p. 7.

aries of civil and congressional townships do not coincide, there is still some tendency to make the civil unit of substantially the same size and shape as the survey area. This influence of the congressional-township system upon the areal pattern of governmental townships has been more pronounced in some states than in others. In Missouri, for example, the influence appears to have been slight, with civil townships rarely coinciding with congressional and with the average area of the former about 50 per cent greater than that of the latter.[52] In various other states coincidence of boundaries is more common, and the average area of townships of the two types is approximately the same. Thus, the average area of civil townships in Indiana is 35.5 square miles, and in Kansas 36.6, as compared with the 36 square miles of the congressional township. All told, township states of the public-land group show considerable influence of the survey township upon the size and configuration of the governmental unit.[53]

REFERENCES

Books and Special Studies

BRADSHAW, William L., and GARRISON, Milton, *Township Organization in Missouri* (Columbia, University of Missouri, 1936).

Cincinnati Bureau of Governmental Research, *The Township Government in the State of Ohio with Particular Reference to Hamilton County* (Cincinnati, Cincinnati Bureau of Governmental Research, 1933).

DRURY, James W., *Township Government in Kansas* (Lawrence, University of Kansas Governmental Research Center, 1954).

GUITTEAU, William B., *Ohio's Townships: The Grassroots of Democracy* (Toledo, Toledo Printing Co., 1949).

KRAUSZ, N. G. P., *Handbook for Illinois Township Officers,* rev. ed. (Champaign, Ill., Garrard Press, 1956).

Michigan Township Officers' Guide (Lansing, 1938), compiled under supervision of the secretary of the Senate and the clerk of the House of Representatives.

SNIDER, Clyde F., *Township Government in Indiana* (Bloomington, Indiana University Bureau of Business Research, 1932).

THARP, Claude R., *A Manual of Township Government in Michigan* (Ann Arbor, University of Michigan Bureau of Government, 1948).

Articles

BATES, Frank G., "The Indiana Township—An Anachronism," *National Municipal Review,* Vol. XXI, pp. 502-504 (August, 1932).

BERNSTEIN, Harry E., "Our Township Government," *New Jersey Municipalities,* Vol. XXIX, No. 5, pp. 5-11 (May, 1952).

BROMAGE, Arthur W., "Recommendations on Township Government," Committee on County Government of the National Municipal League, Report

[52] *Ibid.*, pp. 7-8.

[53] Cf. above, chap. 2, "Towns and Townships."

No. 3, *National Municipal Review,* suppl., Vol. XXIII, pp. 139-145 (February, 1934).

EBERHARDT, John L., "Township Government in Kansas," *Your Government,* bulletin of the University of Kansas Governmental Research Center, Vol. IX, No. 2 (October 15, 1953).

DRURY, James W., "Townships Lose Ground," *National Municipal Review,* Vol. XLIV, pp. 10-13 (January, 1955).

———, "Changes in Township Government in Kansas," *The County Officer,* Vol. XX, pp. 30-31 (February, 1955).

McCRAE, James A., "Township Government in North Dakota," *Quarterly Journal of the University of North Dakota,* Vol. XXIII, pp. 185-201 (1932-1933).

SNIDER, Clyde F., "The Illinois Town Meeting," *Illinois County and Township Official,* Vol. VIII, No. 12, pp. 5-7 (February, 1949).

CHAPTER 10

Special Districts

NATURE AND VARIETY

THE SPECIAL DISTRICT, or special-purpose district as it is sometimes called, is a governmental unit empowered to perform but a single public service or, at most, a small number of services. In this respect it differs from general-purpose units, such as counties, townships, and municipalities, each of which is charged with the performance of a considerable variety of governmental functions.[1] The significance of special districts in the local government pattern, as Professor John Bollens suggests in his comprehensive study of special districts and their government,[2] is indicated, among other things, by their large number, their wide geographic dispersion, the amount of their expenditures, and the number of their employees. In 35 states, as of the mid-1950's, special districts, school and nonschool, were more numerous than local governments of any other type. Both school districts and soil-conservation districts, the two varieties which are geographically most widespread, included a large proportion of the national area, to say nothing of the extensive coverage of districts of other kinds. Expenditures of special districts exceeded the combined expenditures of counties, townships, and towns; and almost two of every five local government employees worked for special districts.[3]

Apart from the traditional school district, the rise of the special district as a major category among local governmental units is a development of relatively recent years. During the decade from 1942 to 1952 the number of nonschool special districts in the United States rose from about 8,300

[1] See above, chap. 2, "Classes of Units."

[2] John C. Bollens, *Special District Governments in the United States* (Berkeley, University of California Press, 1957).

[3] *Ibid.*, pp. 2-5, 29.

to more than 12,000, an increase of almost 50 per cent. Today, these districts make up the most varied area of local government in the nation and, at the same time, the one with which the general public is least familiar.[4] While nonschool special districts have been increasing in number, the number of school districts, as the result of active consolidation programs in many states, has been declining sharply. From 108,000 in 1942, the number of school districts dropped to 67,000 in 1952, and by 1954 had further declined to less than 60,000.[5] Nevertheless, school districts continue to outnumber not only nonschool special districts but the local governmental units of any other category. Every state has some nonschool special districts, and it is usual to find several varieties in a single state.[6] All but five of the states have school districts.[7]

The amount of state legislation relating to the organization and work of special districts is large and is constantly growing. Professor Frederic Guild found that as long ago as 1919, the legislatures of 34 states in a single year passed 1,096 acts, most of them amendatory of existing law, which directly concerned 82 varieties of special districts.[8] California alone now has on her statute books some 100 different laws relating to the organization and operation of such districts.[9] It is this basic legislation in the various states which authorizes the creation of special districts, prescribes the procedures to be followed in their establishment, determines what governing officials the districts shall have and how those officials shall be chosen, and confers district powers upon those officials. Usually procedures are also prescribed for the annexation of additional territory to districts as originally organized, for the detachment of territory therefrom, and for the dissolution of districts if desired.

The special districts authorized and established under the laws of the different states serve a wide variety of areas and purposes. Some districts serve urban or metropolitan areas, others operate exclusively in rural areas, and still others serve both urban and rural territory. Of the rural and semirural units, the school districts, of course, predominate in number. Several types of school districts may be found in a single state. In Illi-

[4] United States Bureau of the Census, *Special District Governments in the United States* (Washington, 1954), p. 1.

[5] United States Bureau of the Census, *School Districts in the United States in 1954* (Washington, 1955).

[6] A state-by-state listing of the types of district authorized by constitutional or statutory provision is provided in United States Bureau of the Census, *Local Government Structure in the United States* (Washington, Government Printing Office, 1954).

[7] The number of special districts, school and otherwise, existing in each individual state as of 1952 is shown above, chap. 2, Table 1.

[8] Frederic H. Guild, "Special Municipal Corporations," *American Political Science Review*, Vol. XIV, pp. 286-291 (May, 1920).

[9] Stanley Scott and John C. Bollens, *Special Districts in California Local Government* (Berkeley, University of California Bureau of Public Administration, 1949), p. 8.

nois, for example, there are elementary districts, high school districts, 12-grade districts, and districts of other special varieties. Nonschool districts employed wholly or in part in the service of rural needs include, among others, drainage districts, reclamation districts, soil-conservation districts, water-conservation districts, levee districts, flood-control districts, irrigation districts, erosion-prevention districts, highway districts, cemetery districts, fire-protection districts, health districts, hospital districts, tuberculosis sanitarium districts, library districts, fencing districts, pest-control districts, predatory-animal-control districts, and weed-eradication districts. The number of nonschool special districts, rural and urban, by major functional class, as of 1952, is shown in Table 7.

TABLE 7

Number of Nonschool Special Districts
By Major Functional Class *

Functional class	*Number*	*Per cent of total*
U. S. total	12,319	100.0
Fire	2,272	18.4
Highways	774	6.3
Health and hospitals	371	3.0
Sanitation	429	3.5
Nonhighway transportation	159	1.3
Housing	863	7.0
Natural resources	5,224	42.4
Drainage	2,174	17.6
Soil conservation	1,981	16.1
Irrigation and water conservation	641	5.2
Other	428	3.5
Cemeteries	911	7.4
Urban water supply	665	5.4
Other	651	5.3

* From United States Bureau of the Census, *Governments in the United States in 1952* (Washington, Government Printing Office, 1953), p. 5.

Though some special districts have large budgets and carry on activities which are extensive in scope, the overwhelming majority are relatively small in scale of operations. Only 213 nonschool special districts, or 2 per cent of all such units, had revenue in 1952 amounting to $500,000 or more, and only another 5 per cent had revenue of from $100,000 to $500,000. At the other extreme, 74 per cent of all the nonschool units in 1952 had revenue of less than $10,000. Similarly, fewer than 600 nonschool special districts had more than 25 employees in 1952, with only 138—slightly more than 1 per cent of the total number—employing 100 persons or more. At the opposite end of the scale, 4,466 nonschool units, or more than one third of the total number, reported no paid employment for the year.[10] The size-class distribution, in terms of number of paid employees, of districts performing selected functions is indicated in Fig IX.

FIG. IX

Size-Class Distribution, by Number of Employees, of Special Districts Performing Various Functions: 1952

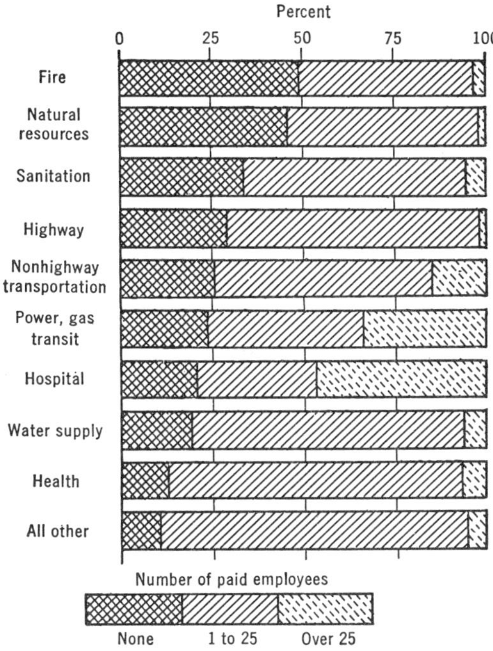

SOURCE: United States Bureau of the Census, *Special District Governments in the United States* (Washington, 1954), p. 1.

REASONS FOR CREATION

Reasons for the creation of special districts are many and varied. Some districts are established merely because existing general-purpose governments are unwilling to perform a particular service which the public desires. Such unwillingness may stem from various causes, including fear on the part of elective officials of the general-purpose unit that any increase in that unit's tax rate resulting from assumption of an additional function might militate against their re-election.[11] The system of small school districts, dating from early days, owes its origin mainly to the desire to provide educational facilities within reasonable walking distance

[10] United States Bureau of the Census, *Special District Governments in the United States,* pp. 1-2.

[11] Bollens, *Special District Governments in the United States,* pp. 9-10.

of every family. An important reason for establishing special districts of other types lies in the facts that many present-day governmental problems concern areas not coterminous with the traditional units of government, namely, county, township, and municipality, and that the special district affords a means of providing governmental units with boundaries coincident, or more nearly so, with problem areas. Thus, an area faced with an erosion problem may comprise several counties or parts of counties; or a rural community desiring fire protection may constitute only a portion of a county or township. Under such circumstances an erosion-prevention district on the one hand, and a fire-protection district on the other, may provide a practicable method of administering and financing the needed service within the territory concerned.

A further reason for the establishment of special districts is the desire to circumvent constitutional restrictions on local taxing and borrowing power. Many state constitutions impose strict limitations upon the power of local governments to tax and borrow, such limitations ordinarily being expressed in terms of a specified percentage of the assessed valuation of taxable property. Usually, however, *each* separate local entity is permitted, if authorized by the state legislature, to tax and borrow up to the designated limit, notwithstanding that several units may operate within the same area and therefore derive their revenue from taxation of the same property. Take, for example, a state whose constitution provides that no local government may become indebted to an amount exceeding 5 per cent of its assessed valuation. Now suppose that a county in this state wishes to establish a forest preserve for conservation and recreational purposes but finds that it has already exhausted its constitutional borrowing power. Under these circumstances, and provided that the state statutes permit such action, the inhabitants may organize a special forest-preserve district. The boundaries of this district may be substantially, or even exactly, coterminous with those of the county, yet the district has its own governing body and possesses, independently of the county, its own taxing and borrowing powers. Thus, the forest-preserve district, though embracing the same territory as the county, may proceed to issue the forest-preserve bonds which the county was unable to issue and to provide for retirement of the indebtedness from a tax levy imposed by the district. As another example, suppose that the constitution of a particular state imposes a limitation upon the property-tax rate which may be levied by counties and that a county in this state is finding it difficult, because of this limitation, to raise sufficient revenue for the adequate financing of highways, welfare work, and other county functions. The establishment under statutory authority of a highway district, coterminous with the county but endowed with its own taxing power, to take over the road function, will relieve the county government of responsibility in this field and thereby release for the more adequate support of welfare and other nonhighway services the county tax revenues formerly devoted to road purposes.

Still other factors account, wholly or in part, for the formation of special districts in particular instances. Two or more rural counties, unable individually to finance certain desired functions, such as library or health service, may join in establishing special districts to administer and finance such services on an area-wide basis.[12] Though services, such as fire protection and sewerage, might often be secured for unincorporated suburban areas through incorporation as municipalities or annexation to existing municipalities, local residents may favor the use of special districts, especially if they fear that incorporation or annexation would result in heavier taxes than those levied by the districts.[13] Professor Emmet Asseff has suggested, furthermore, that "the special district has a psychological attraction, for there a specific tax is applied to a specific function and area. The taxpayer is more willing to vote new taxes when he is certain of the purpose for which the money will be used and particularly if he is certain that it will be used in an area in which he is interested." [14] Finally, there appears to be a rather widespread belief that the special-district form of organization tends to "keep out of politics" the particular functions involved—in other words, that the directors or trustees of special districts are likely to be less subject to partisan influence than are the governing bodies of general-purpose units, such as counties, townships, and municipalities. This belief may well account in part for the durability of the district system of school organization and probably has been influential, in some instances, in bringing about the establishment of districts for nonschool purposes.

PROCEDURE FOR ESTABLISHMENT

Special districts, of whatever type, are established under state authority. In occasional instances establishment is effected or authorized directly by constitutional provision, but in most cases the pertinent law is statutory in form. Some districts owe their existence to special legislative enactments, which may or may not provide for a local referendum on the question of establishment. However, the large majority have been organized under statutes which are, at least in form, of general application. In states having constitutional prohibitions of special legislation, it is not uncommon to find that a statute which on its face applies throughout the state, or to all places within a stipulated classification, has, in reality, been

[12] This use of the special district is discussed below, chap. 20, "Functional Consolidation."

[13] John C. Bollens, "When Services Get Too Big," *National Municipal Review*, Vol. XXXVIII, pp. 498-503 (November, 1949).

[14] Emmett Asseff, *Special Districts in Louisiana* (Baton Rouge, Louisiana State University Bureau of Government Research, 1951), p. 3.

enacted at the request of a single community wishing to establish a district of the type concerned, but has been phrased in general terms so as not to violate the constitutional prohibition.

The procedure involved in establishing special districts under general enabling legislation varies in detail but in outline is fairly uniform. The first step, ordinarily, is the circulation of a petition requesting the creation of a district under the particular law concerned and describing the territory to be included. The petition must be signed by a specified number of local voters, or property owners, as the law may prescribe. Having received the required number of signatures, the petition is filed with a designated governmental agency, usually the county governing board or a local court. This agency examines the form and content of the petition and frequently holds public hearings on the question of establishing the district sought. The authority of the governmental agency, under the various statutes, ranges all the way from merely passing upon the legality of the petition to deciding upon the necessity and suitability of the proposed district and actually decreeing its establishment. Where there is a requirement of local referendum, as is most commonly the case, the proposal for establishment of the district, after approval by the local agency, is submitted to popular vote in a local election. As in the case of petitioning, the privilege of participating in this election extends in some instances to all qualified voters but is limited in others to property owners. If the election results in a vote favorable to establishment, the county board or court enters an order bringing the district into legal existence.[15]

DISTRICT POWERS

As Scott and Bollens have pointed out, special districts are vested with two kinds of powers: (1) various general powers common to practically all local governments, and (2) specific authority to carry on the activity or activities for which they are established.[16] Commonly included among the powers of a general nature are the power to sue and be sued, to make contracts, to hire employees, to acquire and dispose of real and personal property, to tax and borrow, and to take private property for public use under the right of eminent domain. The specific authority conferred varies, of course, with the type of district concerned. Highway districts, for example, would normally be empowered to lay out, construct, and maintain public roads; library districts would be authorized to provide books and other library facilities for use of the inhabitants of their territory. Like other units of local government, special districts possess and can exercise only those powers which have been conferred upon them by

[15] Cf. Scott and Bollens, *op. cit.*, pp. 3-4.
[16] *Ibid.*, pp. 4-5.

the state; and these must be exercised subject to whatever limitations have been imposed by constitutional or statutory provision.[17]

DISTRICT FINANCE

Sources of district revenue include local taxes, special assessments, service charges, and state and federal aid, with a few districts receiving grants from other units of local government. Most districts are empowered to levy property taxes or special assessments.[18] Some, however, are supported primarily or wholly from charges imposed for the services they provide. Irrigation districts, utility districts, and sewer districts are among those more commonly imposing service charges. State aid constitutes a major source of revenue for school districts, with school units also receiving small amounts of federal aid for special purposes, such as vocational education and school lunches. Districts for purposes other than schools sometimes are the recipients of state or federal aid, or both. Many special districts are authorized to borrow money, frequently with the requirement that bond issues be approved by the district voters. Borrowing is resorted to most commonly in anticipation of taxes or for the construction of improvements, with the bonds or other obligations being retired from local taxes and other revenues. Though it is usual for special districts to have either taxing or borrowing power, or both, there are some that possess neither. Thus, most soil-conservation districts may neither tax nor borrow, but rely for the support of their activities entirely upon contributions, in the form of money, materials, or services, from the national, state, county, and township governments, and from resident farmers.[19]

SCHOOL-DISTRICT GOVERNMENT

In 25 of the 48 states the principal unit for local school administration is the school district organized apart from, and generally independent of, other units of local government. In these "district states" the relatively small school district, rather than any larger governmental area, is the basic unit, both financial and administrative, for providing elementary and secondary education. Furthermore, in most of the states employing the county, town, or township as the principal area for school purposes, the territory within each of those general-government units is separately incorporated as a school district.[20] Though our concern at this point is primarily with the government of school districts in the "district states," much that is said would apply also to county, town, or township school districts.

[17] See above, chap. 3, "Local Powers."
[18] The nature of special assessments is considered below, chap. 19, "Nontax Revenues."
[19] See below, chap. 18, "Soil-conservation Districts."
[20] See below, chap. 17, "Local Responsibility."

School Meetings. Some states make provision, at least in rural districts, for an annual school meeting somewhat comparable to the town and township meetings discussed in previous chapters. The meeting consists of all resident voters of the district who choose to attend. It is in most cases held in the spring and presided over by the chairman of the district board. The usual powers of the district meeting include:

1. Electing members of the school board.
2. Making the tax levy.
3. Authorizing the acquisition or sale of real estate.
4. Fixing the length of the school term, subject to a minimum length required by statute.
5. Determining district policies in general, insofar as local discretion is allowed under state law.

As in the case of the New England town meeting, the school meeting may serve the community as a major social gathering as well as a governmental assembly. Sometimes it is an all-day affair, with a "basket dinner" at noon emphasizing its social characteristics.

School Boards. Every school district, whether it has a school meeting or not, is provided with a governing board. Usually bearing the official title of board of directors, board of trustees, or board of education, this agency is quite commonly referred to simply as the school board. In rural districts the board most commonly consists of three members, though in urban places it is ordinarily larger. Board members, as a rule, are elected by the voters of the district, at the district meeting, if such is provided, or at a regular school election. School elections in many instances are held separately from the general elections, and ordinarily they are nonpartisan in form. Nominations are variously made by primary election, petition, caucus, and self-announcement. Where election is in district meeting, nominations are usually presented from the floor. Exceptions to the elective method of choosing board members are more numerous in urban than in rural areas, with a considerable number of the larger city districts having appointive boards. The appointing power in such instances usually is vested in the mayor (sometimes to be exercised with the approval of the city council), but occasionally it rests with the council or the courts. Where appointment is used in the case of rural districts, the appointing authority is most likely to be the county superintendent or the county board of education. The term of board members varies, with the three-year staggered term being most common. Indeed, where the board consists of three members the three-year term is almost universal, one member being chosen annually.[21]

[21] Cf. Fred Engelhardt, *Public School Organization and Administration* (Boston, Ginn, 1931), pp. 59-62; Madaline Kintner Remmlein, *The Law of Local Public School Administration* (New York, McGraw-Hill, 1953), chap. 1, "The Legal Status of Local School Boards," *American School Board Journal*, Vol. CXXIV, No. 5, pp. 25-27, 83 (May, 1952), and *ibid.*, No. 6, pp. 29-30 (June, 1952).

The usual officers of the school board are a chairman (sometimes officially called president or moderator), a clerk, and a treasurer. In some states these officers are elected to their respective positions by the voters, but in others they are chosen by the board itself. The chairman is always a member of the board, and the other officers are usually members. Some states, however, permit district boards to select the clerk and treasurer from outside their membership. Occasionally, the same person serves as both clerk and treasurer; and in a few instances the county treasurer serves as treasurer of the various school districts within his county, with the office of district treasurer being dispensed with. The chairman presides at board meetings, exercises general management over board business, and serves as the board's spokesman. The clerk has custody of district records, keeps minutes of board meetings, and conducts the board's correspondence. It is the duty of the treasurer to receive district revenues; to keep district funds safely, commonly in depositories designated by the board; and to pay out district moneys on board order.[22]

The school board exercises broad authority over district affairs. It is charged with the care and maintenance of school property; purchases necessary supplies; hires teachers; provides transportation for pupils; determines the curriculum within statutory limitations; examines claims against the district, approving or disapproving their payment; and, in general, sees that the provisions of the state school law are complied with. In early days, with few trained teachers and no supervisors, "the board members visited classes, heard the children read and spell, questioned them about their work, and examined the writing and ciphering books."[23] Now, however, although some board members make occasional visitations, day-by-day management of the schools is left for the most part to the teaching staff, subject to supervision, in the larger districts, by principals, supervisors, and superintendents. Such supervision as exists in the case of the small rural districts is provided for principally through the office of the county superintendent of schools.[24]

In districts which employ the school meeting the board, in theory at least, functions primarily as an administrative agency charged with carrying out district policy as determined by the meeting. Where there is no school meeting, most functions performed by the meeting where it exists devolve upon the board, which thus becomes both the determiner and the administrator of district policy. In such instances it is the board that levies the district tax, authorizes expenditures, and borrows money on behalf of the district. In most cases, however, the issuance of bonds requires approval by the district voters.

[22] Cf. J. W. Diefendorf, *The School Board and the School Board Member* (Albuquerque, University of New Mexico Department of Government, 1947), pp. 17-19.

[23] *Ibid.*, p. 2.

[24] See below, chap. 17, "The County Superintendent."

GOVERNMENT OF OTHER SPECIAL DISTRICTS

Special districts for nonschool purposes almost invariably have some sort of board as their central governing agency. Members of these boards in most cases are known officially as trustees, directors, or commissioners. The number of members is most commonly three or five, though larger boards are not unusual. Some boards are elective, but in numerous instances a part or all of the membership is appointive or ex officio. In the case of certain types of districts, such as those for drainage or local improvement purposes, voting for the members of elective governing boards, as well as on such other district matters as the approval of borrowing proposals, is sometimes limited to landowners. With respect to irrigation districts, for example, the local electorate, instead of consisting of local residents, often consists of the owners of land within the district, without regard to their residence. Furthermore, each landowner frequently is accorded voting strength in proportion to his acreage.[25] Where governing boards are appointed, the appointing power ordinarily is vested in some local officer or body, such as the county board or judge or the mayor or council of a municipality, but rests occasionally with the governor or some other state agency.

The provisions in Illinois for the selection of the governing boards of different types of special districts illustrate the variety in methods of selection found even within a single state. The boards of most Illinois park districts are elective, though that of the Chicago district is appointed by the mayor with the consent of the council. Sanitary districts in most instances have boards appointed by the county judge, but the trustees of the Chicago district and one other metropolitan sanitary district are elected. Forest-preserve districts, where coterminous with counties, are governed by the county board of supervisors or commissioners ex officio, but districts embracing less than an entire county have boards of commissioners appointed by the president or chairman of the county board with the consent of that body. Fire-protection districts, tuberculosis sanitarium districts, and mosquito-abatement districts are under boards appointed by the county judge. Soil-conservation districts have boards of directors elected by the persons owning or occupying land within their respective areas. The governing authority of multitownship health districts is an ex officio board consisting of the supervisors of the various townships concerned and the chairman of the county board. Drainage commissioners are elected in some districts and appointed by the county judge in others. The officers of each road district are an elective highway commissioner and an elective clerk.

It will be noted that local appointment of district governing boards,

[25] Bollens, *Special District Governments in the United States*, pp. 145-147.

especially appointment by the county judge, is used rather widely in Illinois. Though Illinois practice provides no instance of state appointment, examples of that method of selection elsewhere are not wanting. Thus, commissioners of drainage districts in Massachusetts are appointed by a state reclamation board; and, in various states, a part of the membership of boards of directors of soil-conservation districts is appointed by a state soil-conservation committee.

Special-district governing boards are vested by statute with those powers which the state legislature has believed necessary for carrying out the purposes of the respective districts. These usually include the power to acquire property; to levy taxes or special assessments, or both; and to borrow on the credit of the district. However, there is ordinarily a statutory limit upon the tax rate; and it is commonly provided that the borrowing power may be exercised only with the approval of the district voters in an election. The board authorizes district expenditures and lets contracts for materials and services. Where a district is small and its tasks simple, the governing board itself may appoint all necessary employees and directly administer district affairs. On the other hand, where district operations are extensive or technical, the board may appoint a superintendent or general manager to serve as chief executive officer of the district and supervise its work under the board's general direction.[26] In the latter case, subordinate personnel may be appointed either directly by the board or by the executive officer with the board's approval.

A common practice is for a district governing board to choose a presiding officer, usually called president or chairman, from its own members. In many instances board members serve without compensation, and when compensation is provided, it is ordinarily nominal in amount.[27]

NEW HAMPSHIRE'S VILLAGE DISTRICTS

A somewhat unusual form of special district, often multipurpose in character, is seen in the village districts, known also as precincts, of New Hampshire. The settlements commonly referred to as villages are not incorporated as municipalities in New Hampshire but are governed as parts of the respective towns within which they are situated. In some communities, however, village districts have been organized over the years to perform some of the services ordinarily provided by municipal government.[28] As of 1952, according to the Census Bureau, 74 such districts were in existence in the state.[29]

[26] Cf. Roger V. Shumate, *Local Government in Nebraska* (Lincoln, Nebraska Legislative Council, 1939), p. 47.

[27] Bollens, *Special District Governments in the United States,* pp. 37-38.

[28] Lashley G. Harvey, "The Village District in New Hampshire," *American Political Science Review,* Vol. XL, pp. 962-965 (October, 1946).

[29] *Local Government Structure in the United States,* p. 55.

Some village districts have been created by special legislative act, but most have been formed under general enabling statutes. The usual statutory procedure calls for establishment of such districts by order of the selectmen of the town or towns concerned, upon petition and after approval by the voters of the proposed district at a special meeting. Under present statutory provision, a district may be established for any or all of the following purposes: [30]

> The extinguishment of fires, the lighting or sprinkling of streets, the planting and care for shade and ornamental trees, the supply of water for domestic and fire purposes, the construction and maintenance of sidewalks and main drains or common sewers, the construction, maintenance, and care of parks or commons, the maintenance of activities for recreational promotion, the construction or purchase and maintenance of a municipal lighting plant, and the appointing and employing of watchmen and police officers.

When a district has been established for any one of these purposes, any one or more of the other services may be added by vote of the annual district meeting, which, modeled after the town meeting, is the policy-determining organ of the district. The principal district administrative agency is an elective board of three commissioners. Other elective officers ordinarily include a moderator of the annual meeting, a clerk, and a treasurer. The village district is vested with all the powers possessed by towns with respect to the objects for which it has been established. It is empowered to levy property taxes, make appropriations for the services it is authorized to provide, issue bonds or borrow in anticipation of taxes, enter into contracts, and adopt necessary bylaws. The village district offers a means whereby the residents of a small settlement may provide themselves with services for which the entire town may be unwilling to be taxed. By having a single district supply numerous services, it becomes unnecessary to establish a large number of special districts, each independent of the others.[31]

PROS AND CONS OF SPECIAL DISTRICTS

The special district, as a form of local government, affords both advantages and disadvantages. Some of the advantages, actual or alleged, are suggested by the reasons accounting for the establishment of districts.[32] Thus, the special district provides a feasible means of supplying public services the need for which is not coterminous with the boundaries of general-purpose units. Use of special districts to expand local taxing or borrowing power may be regarded with favor or disfavor, depending upon individual circumstances and point of view. On the one

[30] *New Hampshire Revised Statutes Annotated* (1955), chap. 52, sec. 1.
[31] Harvey, *loc. cit.*
[32] See above, "Reasons for Creation."

hand, a special district may enable a local community to finance some desired public service which could not otherwise be provided; on the other hand, a district may be looked upon as an iniquitous device for circumventing reasonable constitutional limitations. Proponents of the special-district device argue that the general-purpose units of government are already overloaded with functions and that to impose additional responsibilities upon them will lower the quality of governmental services.[33] In contrast, the establishment of special districts for the performance of new functions will serve to maintain or raise service standards, since each new unit will be giving undivided attention to service in a particular field.

Opponents of special districts contend that their creation, by adding to the number of governmental units, increases the complexity and costliness of government at the local level. They maintain that the use of special districts, resulting as it does in an overlapping of jurisdictions, frequently causes duplication of functions and "buck-passing."[34] Insofar as special districts are provided with governing boards which are popularly elected, their existence imposes an additional task upon a voting public already overburdened. Furthermore, the special-district system, with its earmarking of certain revenues for particular services, makes for inflexibility in local financial administration.[35] According to Professor Asseff:[36]

> The use of the special district destroys, to a large extent, the necessary flexibility of financial policy which all governments must have today in order to handle most effectively and efficiently the changing and complex problems with which they are faced. The dedication of any revenue to a particular function, and this results when a special district is created, means that that revenue must be spent for that particular purpose even though at a later date there is a greater need for it elsewhere.

Thus, a particular county may find itself in serious financial straits at the same time that some of the special districts within its borders have surplus funds on hand.

All in all, it appears that a special district often is established merely as the "easy way out," when a more sensible course, in the long run, would be to impose the desired function upon one of the general-purpose governmental units, at the same time improving and strengthening the organization of the general-purpose unit in any manner that may be required to enable it to perform the additional service, and amplifying its taxing and borrowing power where necessary.[37] If special districts are

[33] Asseff, *op. cit.*, p. 8.

[34] *Ibid.*

[35] Cf. Kirk H. Porter, "A Plague of Special Districts," *National Municipal Review*, Vol. XXII, pp. 544-547, 574 (November, 1933).

[36] Asseff, *op. cit.*, p. 61.

[37] Cf. F. H. Guild, "Special Municipal Corporations," *National Municipal Review*, Vol. XVIII, pp. 319-323 (May, 1929).

thus to be absorbed into general-purpose units, service and financing differentials should be authorized, the general-purpose unit being empowered to provide special services for portions of its territory, in addition to the services provided throughout its entire area, and to levy special taxes or assessments for their financing within the areas receiving the additional services.[38]

COUNTY ADMINISTRATIVE DISTRICTS

Where the town or township does not exist as a subdivision of the county and a unit of local government, it is nevertheless common for counties to be divided into districts of some sort for such purposes as elections, the administration of minor justice, and road administration. Though mere administrative subdivisions of the county, and therefore not entitled to classification as autonomous governmental units, these various districts partake sufficiently of the nature of governmental units to deserve some attention at this point. Sometimes two or more sets or classes of districts are found within the same area, but where this is the case one set tends to be predominant in importance. The official designation of these primary districts varies widely. For example, they are called civil districts in Tennessee; militia districts in Georgia; beats in Mississippi; hundreds in Delaware; wards (subdivisions of the parish) in Louisiana; magisterial districts in Virginia, West Virginia, and Kentucky; and precincts in Alabama, Colorado, Idaho, and several other states. North and South Carolina, along with a few other states, employ the title of township; and in California the subdivisions are known as judicial townships. For convenience in discussion, the various county subdivisions of this nature may be referred to generically as county administrative districts. Since they ordinarily exist where town or township government does not function, such districts are most common in the southern and western states, though they are found also in other areas, as in the non-township counties of Illinois and Nebraska.[39]

County administrative districts are similar to the special districts considered earlier in this chapter in that districts of each class ordinarily serve but a single purpose or, at most, a few designated purposes. They are geographic subdivisions to facilitate certain aspects of county administration. Perhaps the most common function of the districts is that of serving as areas for the appointment or election of various local officers. Justices of the peace, constables, road commissioners, assessors, election officers, and members of the county governing body are among

[38] Bollens, *Special District Governments in the United States,* p. 259.

[39] See United States Bureau of the Census, *Minor Civil Divisions and Places of the United States: 1950* (Washington, 1953). The subdivisions in Illinois and Nebraska are known as precincts.

the officers so chosen in various places. As these office titles suggest, the local services with which the districts are most often concerned are those of law enforcement, justice, conduct of elections, road administration, and tax assessment.

A major difference between the county administrative districts and incorporated special districts lies in the fact that the former in most cases have no corporate capacity and no revenue-raising authority, but are simply convenient subdivisions for performing the functions of county government. Thus, the magisterial districts in Virginia, though among the more important of the county subdivisions in the several states, have been referred to as "subordinate divisions or precincts of a county, created for political and administrative purposes of exceedingly limited character. They are without that artificial personality possessed by corporate bodies." [40] And the supreme court of North Carolina, in considering the nature of the townships in that state, has declared that they are not corporate bodies but only "territorial sections of counties, upon which, for appropriate purposes, power is conferred to perform functions of government of local application and interest." [41]

Generally speaking, the number of administrative districts in a county is smaller than the average number of townships in counties under township organization. As a corollary, the average area of the districts is larger than that of the townships. In most instances cities and villages are included within the county administrative districts, though in some cases the larger municipalities either themselves form districts or are excluded from the district system. Although the county administrative districts in many areas are of considerable importance in the carrying on of county government, their over-all significance in the local government picture is quite minor in comparison with that of the New England towns, or of townships in those areas where township government still retains a substantial degree of vitality. In areas where the civil township has been deprived of most or all of its powers and functions, though perhaps nominally retaining its corporate form, that unit tends for all practical purposes to degenerate to the status of a county administrative district. This, for example, has been the situation in Oklahoma since the 1930's, when the townships of that state were deprived of taxing authority; and it would appear that the townships of Iowa, which have been so weakened that they have been dropped by the Census Bureau from its enumeration of local governments, today deserve classification as mere county administrative districts.[42]

[40] Moss *v.* Tazewell County, 112 Va. 878, 884 (1911).

[41] Wittkowsky *v.* Board of Commissioners of Jackson County, 150 N.C. 90, 95 (1908).

[42] See above, chap. 9, "Declining Importance of the Township."

OTHER CIVIL DIVISIONS

Other geographic divisions, unincorporated and without governmental organization but employed for such purposes as those of land description and tax administration, exist in various states, particularly among those in the New England group. In Maine there are, in addition to some 400 unorganized townships, nearly 200 other unincorporated divisions within which property is assessed and taxes are collected directly by the state. These divisions are variously designated as gores, grants, islands, patents, points, strips, surpluses, and tracts.[43] The varying terminology, as Professor Orren Hormell has pointed out, has its origin in historical factors and is not of governmental significance. Surpluses, gores, strips, and tracts "are parcels of land left out of the regular townships on account of the inaccuracies of the original survey." Gores "were originally three cornered or wedge-shaped parcels of land omitted in the original survey," while surpluses, strips, and tracts "were narrow strips, so omitted, adjacent to the regular township." Eventually, however, this distinction between gores and other forms of omitted lands disappeared, and at present several narrow strips are designated as gores. Grants and patents "are so designated by reason of the original grant of the territory to some individual or educational institution." Islands and points are "geographical divisions, situated outside the limits of any town or incorporated plantation." [44] Vermont has a few gores and one grant; and several divisions in New Hampshire are variously known as grants, locations, and purchases.[45]

PUBLIC AUTHORITIES

Similar in some respects to special districts are the public *authorities*, which are being used in increasing number at both state and local levels for the construction and operation of revenue-producing facilities. An authority of this nature has been defined as "a governmental business corporation set up outside of the normal structure of traditional government so that it can give continuity, business efficiency and elastic management to the construction or operation of a self-supporting or revenue-producing public enterprise." [46] As employed at the local level the public authority is designed to meet three principal needs: [47]

1. The need for a means of financing certain public improvements without conflicting with constitutional debt limitations.

[43] See Orren C. Hormell, *Maine Towns* (Brunswick, Me., Bowdoin College, 1932), pp. 11-12; see also, *Minor Civil Divisions and Places of the United States: 1950.*

[44] Hormell, *op. cit.*, pp. 12-13.

[45] *Minor Civil Divisions and Places of the United States: 1950.*

[46] Luther Gulick, "'Authorities' and How to Use Them," *The Tax Review*, Vol. VIII, pp. 47-52, 47 (November, 1947).

[47] Council of State Governments, *Public Authorities in the States: A Report to the Governors' Conference* (Chicago, 1953), pp. 1, 7.

2. The need for "a flexible administrative instrument to manage what are essentially commercial enterprises."
3. The need for an effective agency for handling intercommunity problems.

Projects sometimes administered through the authority form of organization include, among others, toll roads and bridges, airports, housing developments, and utility systems. Authorities are usually managed by boards of trustees or directors the members of which are chosen in a variety of ways, sometimes being appointed by the governing body or bodies of one or more counties or municipalities within the area concerned. In most instances an authority is without taxing power but may impose charges for the services which it provides. Construction funds are obtained by the issuance of *revenue bonds.* Being payable solely from operating revenues of the project for which they were issued and not from local taxes, these obligations ordinarily are not subject to constitutional debt limitations. In addition to the flexibility in financing thus obtained, authorities commonly enjoy considerable flexibility in managerial matters because of the fact that although they are limited in their functions, they are largely unlimited in their methods of operation. "The mission of an authority is defined, but the methods which it may explore to achieve that end, are left undefined." [48]

Although some authorities serve the area of a single city or county, others operate within two or more of the traditional local units or cut across their boundaries as the public convenience may require. Some authorities possess sufficient autonomy to be classed by the Census Bureau as independent governmental units and included within its count of special districts. In many instances, however, the functions performed by authorities are in lieu of, or supplementary to, services ordinarily provided by city or county governments, with the traditional governmental units in numerous cases establishing the authorities under statutory provision and retaining a significant degree of administrative control over them. "Thus, most authorities are not sufficiently autonomous to be classed as separate governmental units but are, rather, instrumentalities of existing State, municipal or county governments for performance of certain public services with which charges for benefit rendered can reasonably be associated." [49] Some *state* authorities, it may be noted, are closely related to local government. Several states, for example, have recently established state school-building authorities to construct local school buildings and lease them to local school districts on terms under which the rentals thereon will retire the revenue bonds issued for construction financing.

[48] Gulick, *loc. cit.*, p. 48.

[49] United States Bureau of the Census, *Governments in the United States in 1952* (Washington, Government Printing Office, 1953), p. 5. See also, United States Bureau of the Census, *Special District Governments in the United States*, p. 1.

REFERENCES

Books and Special Studies

Asseff, Emmett, *Special Districts in Louisiana* (Baton Rouge, Louisiana State University Bureau of Government Research, 1951).

Bollens, John C., *Special District Governments in the United States* (Berkeley, University of California Press, 1957).

Colorado Legislative Council, *Special Districts,* Report to the Colorado General Assembly (Denver, Colo., 1955).

Diefendorf, J. W., *The School Board and the School Board Member* (Albuquerque, University of New Mexico Department of Government, 1947).

Krausz, N. G. P., *Economic and Legal Status of Fire Protection Districts in Illinois* (Urbana, University of Illinois Agricultural Experiment Station, 1950).

Parks, Robert W., *Soil Conservation Districts in Action* (Ames, Iowa State College Press, 1952).

Scott, Stanley, and Bollens, John C., *Special Districts in California Local Government* (Berkeley, University of California Bureau of Public Administration, 1949).

United States Bureau of the Census, *Special District Governments in the United States* (Washington, 1954).

———, *School Districts in the United States in 1954* (Washington, 1955).

———, *Minor Civil Divisions and Places of the United States: 1950* (Washington, 1953).

Wyoming Taxpayers Association, *Special District Government with Particular Reference to Wyoming* (Cheyenne, Wyo., 1955).

Articles

Bollens, John C., "When Services Get Too Big," *National Municipal Review,* Vol. XXXVIII, pp. 498-503 (November, 1949).

Brown, Robert H., "The Composition of School Boards," *American School Board Journal,* Vol. CXXIX, No. 2, pp. 23-24 (August, 1954).

Contalonis, George T., "Some Powers and Duties of School Boards," *American School Board Journal,* Vol. CXXIX, No. 4, pp. 27-28 (October, 1954).

Guild, Frederic H., "Special Municipal Corporations," *American Political Science Review,* Vol. XIV, pp. 286-291 (May, 1920).

———, "Special Municipal Corporations," *National Municipal Review,* Vol. XVIII, pp. 319-323 (May, 1929).

Harvey, Lashley G., "The Village District in New Hampshire," *American Political Science Review,* Vol. XL, pp. 962-965 (October, 1946).

Kettleborough, Charles, "Special Municipal Corporations," *American Political Science Review,* Vol. VIII, pp. 614-621 (November, 1914).

Morgan, Robert J., "A New Voice in Government: The Watershed District," *State Government,* Vol. XXVI, pp. 288-290, 293 (December, 1953).

Porter, Kirk H., "A Plague of Special Districts," *National Municipal Review,* Vol. XXII, pp. 544-547, 574 (November, 1933).

Remmlein, Madaline Kinter, "The Legal Status of Local School Boards," *American School Board Journal,* Vol. CXXIV, No. 5, pp. 25-27, 83 (May, 1952), and No. 6, pp. 29-30 (June, 1952).

Scott, Stanley and Bollens, John C., "Special Districts in California Local Government," *Western Political Quarterly,* Vol. III, pp. 233-243 (June, 1950).

PART THREE

Popular Control

CHAPTER 11

Politics and Elections

POLITICAL IMPORTANCE OF COUNTY AND TOWNSHIP

THROUGHOUT MOST OF THE United States the county is an important unit in the conduct of elections and in the organization and work of political parties. In nearly every state the county is an area for the election of a number of county officers, who are usually chosen at the time of the general state and national elections and, for the most part, on national party lines. In many states the county is a unit of representation in the state legislature. These circumstances tend to make the county the chief local area in campaign activities, not only for the local officials but for state and national elections as well. Important county officers and leaders in the county party organization are likely to have a good deal of influence in the primaries and conventions for the nomination of congressmen and state officers and the selection of delegates to the national nominating conventions. County offices are useful steps up the ladder of political progress, and success in these positions may lead to more important posts in the state and national governments. Furthermore, the election of administrative officials and the general absence of satisfactory methods of filling appointive posts in the county service open the way to patronage and spoils and make the county an important division of the party machine.[1]

The political importance of the county, though considerable almost everywhere, varies somewhat among different sections of the country. Thus, it has been pointed out that this importance is greater in the central and western states than in either New England or the South.[2] In the

[1] Charles E. Merriam and Harold F. Gosnell, *The American Party System,* 4th ed. (New York, Macmillan, 1949), pp. 192-193.

[2] Chester Lloyd Jones, "The County in Politics," *Annals of the American Academy of Political and Social Science,* Vol. XLVII, pp. 85-100 (May, 1913).

township states of the Midwest party committees frequently are organized in the townships, but the importance of the township organization usually is distinctly secondary to that of the county committees. In New England, on the other hand, the county is "little more than a formal division of government," and the town rather than the county is the primary unit in party organization. Since in the South the county "has always been the chief agency of local government," it might be supposed that southern counties also would have developed the greatest strength in the matter of party organization. This, however, has not been the case. Because of the long prevalence in southern states of what is virtually a one-party system, personal politics rather than party politics have characterized the political struggles of that region, and strong party organizations within the counties have not generally developed.[3] An extraordinary degree of political importance, however, attaches to the county as an election area in certain southern states which employ a county-unit system of nominating or electing state officers. Mississippi's governor and other executive officers are elected by a combination of popular vote and county electoral votes; [4] a county-unit system of voting is employed in primary elections in Georgia for nominating the governor and other state officers; [5] and in Maryland, where candidates for the governorship and other state offices are nominated by party conventions preceded by primary elections, the convention delegates from each county are required to cast their votes for the candidates receiving the largest popular vote in the primary.[6] These county-unit systems of voting, in addition to increasing the electoral importance of the counties, operate in most instances to give proportionally more electoral votes to rural counties than to urban, in relation to population, and thereby enhance the influence of rural areas in state elections.

In the discussion which follows we shall be concerned both with local government activities in the administration of state elections, and with politics, nominations, and elections within the local governmental units themselves.

PARTY ORGANIZATION

Political parties, though constituting the principal medium through which citizens influence their government, originally developed outside

[3] *Ibid.* See below, "Personal Politics."

[4] Robert B. Highsaw and Charles N. Fortenberry, *The Government and Administration of Mississippi* (New York, Crowell, 1954), p. 70; Coleman B. Ransone, Jr., *The Office of Governor in the South* (University, University of Alabama Bureau of Public Administration, 1951), p. 52, n. 27.

[5] L. M. Holland, *The Direct Primary in Georgia* (Urbana, University of Illinois Press, 1949), pp. 44-48; Albert B. Saye, "Georgia's County Unit System of Election," *Journal of Politics*, Vol. XII, pp. 93-106 (February, 1950).

[6] *Annotated Code of Maryland* (1951), Art. XXXIII, sec. 64.

the framework of constitutional and statutory law. Today, however, parties in most states have a definite legal status. About a third of the state constitutions contain provisions of one kind or another relating to political parties; but much more important is statutory regulation. Although in a few states, principally in the South, statutory regulation is meager or nonexistent, in a large majority party membership, organization, and activities are now regulated in some detail by direct primary laws and other statutes.[7]

Whether prescribed by state primary law or by party rules, the formal machinery of party organization is, in general pattern, fairly uniform throughout the country. This organization consists of a series of party committees, with ordinarily a committee for each area from which officers are elected and a "committeeman" for each voting district or precinct.[8] In each state there will usually be found a state central committee, congressional district committees, legislative district committees, county committees, township committees where township government exists, city committees, and precinct committeemen. Members of the different committees are selected in a variety of ways, but most often they are elected by the party voters in the primary election or chosen by party conventions. Sometimes, the members or chairmen of one set of committees serve ex officio as members of one or more higher committees. The tendency in recent years has been to make increasing use of elective committees, and, since the advent of woman suffrage, provision has been made in some instances for equal representation of the sexes in committee membership. Ordinarily, each committee selects a chairman from among its members.

Selection methods may be illustrated from rural Illinois, where party organization is fairly typical. Precinct committeemen in that state are elected biennially in the party primaries, and they comprise the membership of the county committees. Congressional district and state senatorial district committees are composed of the chairmen of the county committees from the counties comprising the respective districts. Members of state representative district committees and the state committee are, like the precinct committeemen, elected by the party voters in the primary. Precinct committeemen, in addition to constituting the county committee, comprise the county convention, which chooses delegates to the state convention and to nominating conventions in judicial districts.

Each major party in each state is represented on the party's national committee by two members—a man and a woman. These national com-

[7] Joseph R. Starr, "The Legal Status of American Political Parties," *American Political Science Review*, Vol. XXXIV, pp. 439-455, 685-699 (June and August, 1940).

[8] Edward B. Logan, ed., *The American Political Scene*, rev. ed. (New York, Harper, 1938), chap. 2; Merriam and Gosnell, *op. cit.*, chap. 8.

mitteemen are variously chosen, depending upon law or practice in the respective states, by the state delegation to the national convention, the state convention, the state central committee, or the party voters in the primary.[9]

The members of the committee hierarchy constitute the central working force of the party. Each committee is responsible for party affairs in the area where it functions. During the interim between elections it is the job of the various committees to keep the party, together with public officers whom it has sponsored and potential candidates for future office, in as favorable a light as possible before the voters. Sometimes "slates" of candidates to be supported by the "organization" for nomination in the primaries are prepared by the party committees; and, whatever candidates are nominated by the party, it is the duty of the committees to work for their victory in the general election. To this end, the committees are charged with planning and conducting the election campaign and getting out the vote on election day. When party nominees have been placed in public office, party committeemen are frequently active in advising those officers on appointments and matters of policy and in serving in a liaison capacity between officials and private citizens.

When local elections are held at a time apart from state and national, as is often the case in cities, primary responsibility for conducting the campaign falls upon the local committee of the area concerned, though higher committees may give financial or other assistance. Since county elections are ordinarily held concurrently with those of the state, both state and county committees are active at such times. In presidential years, national, state, and county committees are activated all along the line, and their energies are mobilized into one grand campaign effort. Though the committee hierarchy is organized in an extremely loose manner, with committees at one level having little or no formal responsibility to those above, the various agencies ordinarily co-operate with each other in their work, intercommittee harmony frequently being promoted by the overlapping of committee personnel.

Precinct Organization. The basic geographic area in the system of party organization and in the conduct of elections is the precinct or voting district—the area served by a single polling place. In most states the formation and alteration of precincts is regulated in some measure by law, but their actual establishment is a function of local authorities, usually the county governing body or a special county election board.[10] In urban communities the primary factor in determining the size of precincts is the number of voters. State laws commonly fix a maximum num-

[9] Senatorial and congressional committees also operate at the national level.

[10] Sometimes distinct sets of precincts for city and school elections are established by the respective officials of those governmental units.

ber of voters per precinct, ranging from a few hundred to perhaps a thousand, but providing for enlargement of the number if voting machines are used. In sparsely settled rural regions, on the other hand, area is the primary determinant, since precincts large enough to include several hundred voters would require many to travel inconvenient distances to the polls. Consequently, many country precincts, though relatively large in extent, include but a small number of voters; and Nevada, because of her widely scattered population, has gone so far as to make provision for "mailing precincts."[11] Where township organization exists a rural precinct often includes an entire township, with townships wholly or partly urbanized being divided into precincts according to the number of voters. Ordinarily, both major parties maintain an organization in each precinct. However, in some precincts where one of the parties is in a hopeless minority, that party maintains no organization.

In some states the precinct organization consists of a party committee of two or more members. More commonly, however, there is a single precinct committeeman, sometimes called the precinct leader or captain; and even where the organization is in committee form, one person is likely to be in actual charge.[12] The precinct committeeman, usually elected by the party voters in the primary, has been referred to as the "unit cell" in the party structure and the most vital unit in the party machine.[13] "He is the bone and sinew of the machine. He is its foundation and the real source of its strength. If he does not function, the machine decays. If he quits, the machine dies."[14]

Though the work of the precinct committeeman varies from place to place and from time to time, depending upon the strength of his party and upon local customs and needs, in general perspective his duties are everywhere much the same. He is the party official charged with responsibility for maintaining direct contact with the voters, and in doing this, he does not confine his activities to election time but continues working between elections as well. Many precinct committeemen hold minor public jobs, but, regardless of their regular vocation, they ordinarily spend a substantial portion of their time on activities connected directly or indirectly with politics. They aid precinct residents in securing employment, public or private; give temporary assistance to the needy without the red tape and delay incident to publicly administered relief; lend a helping hand to those who become involved with the law; and in countless other ways perform small services for ordinary people. In return for these services, the precinct committeeman naturally hopes that those whom he has befriended will remember him at election time and vote

[11] Howard R. Penniman, *Sait's American Parties and Elections,* 5th ed. (New York, Appleton-Century-Crofts, 1952), p. 328.

[12] Merriam and Gosnell, *op. cit.,* p. 175.

[13] *Ibid.*

[14] Frank R. Kent, *The Great Game of Politics* (New York, Doubleday, 1923), p. 1.

for the candidates sponsored by him and his party. It is the duty of the precinct committeeman to see to it that qualified voters in his precinct who are likely to support the slate or ticket endorsed by the party organization are properly registered and that they vote in the primaries and general elections. Members of precinct election boards ordinarily are appointed on nominations made by the precinct committeemen of the respective parties, and party watchers for the polling places are designated by the committeemen. If the precinct committeemen perform their many duties in a competent manner, the party organization tends to function smoothly and effectively; if they fall down on the job, the party cause is likely to be lost.[15]

The County Committee. Above the precinct committee or committeeman in the party hierarchy is the county committee. Outside New England the county committee is one of the most active and powerful of the party agencies. Most frequently, the committee is composed of the precinct committeemen of the county, though in some states its members are elected by the county convention. The term of county committeemen is usually two years, but in some instances it is four.[16] The principal function of the county committee is organizing the local campaign. However, the importance of the committee's work varies in different sections of the country and with the type of election involved.

The chairman of the county committee "is likely to be an important figure in local affairs, and may wield great influence in party councils." [17] He is the executive head of the party within the county and is held responsible for the success or failure of his party at the polls. Through his control of patronage the chairman is often able to build up a powerful party machine in his county, in which case he becomes a dominant figure in local politics and may attain the authority of a "benevolent despot." On the other hand, "he may be merely the henchman of the real county boss." [18]

In some states the county chairman serves ex officio as a member of the state committee, and, in any event, he acts as the connecting link between the local organization and the state and national committees. As a result, the local committees are an important factor in the development of strong state party organizations, the success of the party in the state depending upon the degree to which its organizations at the local level are able to deliver the vote on election day.

[15] For a study of precinct committeemen in ten rural Illinois counties, see Leon Weaver, "Some Soundings in the Party System: Rural Precinct Committeemen," *American Political Science Review*, Vol. XXXIV, pp. 76-84 (February, 1940). A study of Republican precinct committeemen in metropolitan King County (Seattle), Wash., is reported in Hugh A. Bone, *Grass Roots Party Leadership* (Seattle, University of Washington Press, 1952).

[16] Penniman, *op. cit.*, p. 332,

[17] Merriam and Gosnell, *op. cit.*, p. 175.

[18] Penniman, *op. cit.*, p. 332. See below, "Rural Bossism."

RURAL BOSSISM

From what has been said concerning the formal organization of political parties it will be noted that the basis of party organization is essentially democratic in law and in theory. Precinct committeemen are generally elected by the party voters in the primaries, and many of the higher committees are composed either of precinct committeemen ex officio or of other elective members. If the personnel of party committees is substandard, that is largely because too many citizens take little interest in the choice of party officials in the primaries and refuse to accept the responsibilities of party service. Those who habitually complain that the party organization is corrupt and inefficient would therefore do well to remember that ultimate authority rests with the party voters to "turn the rascals out" and elect in their stead persons who might have the public interest more at heart.

Yet, notwithstanding these democratic features of formal party organization, actual control of party affairs rests, at times, in the hands of a political boss, who may or may not hold public or party office but who, in any event, is able, through influence derived from various sources, to determine the personnel and policies of the organization. Though less publicized than the bossism of urban areas, rural bossism is by no means nonexistent. Many rural counties have bosses, and, as Hamilton Owens has pointed out, these county bosses may be far stronger than their city counterparts. When it is remembered that the power of a boss flows in large measure from his personal contact with the voters, the strategic position of the rural boss is readily apparent. Whereas a city boss can know at sight and have personal contact with only a small percentage of the city's voters, the county boss may know practically all of the voters of his county and have personal contacts with most of them during the course of each year.[19] As previously intimated, the county boss may be the county chairman of the predominant party; but this is not necessarily the case. Whether or not he holds party office, the boss is commonly a prominent business or professional man or public official. Mr. Owens suggests that an ideal position from which to operate as boss is that of the county treasurership. In rural areas taxes quite commonly are paid in person rather than by mail, and thus, the treasurer, as a matter of course, sees many taxpayer-voters at least once each year, with them coming to see him rather than requiring him to make the approach. As tax collector, furthermore, the treasurer has an opportunity to do innumerable favors for constituents. When taxpayers complain about the amount of their tax bills, the treasurer can sometimes secure adjustments;

[19] Hamilton Owens, "The County Boss," *American Mercury,* Vol. XVII, pp. 70-74 (May, 1929).

and he may grant extensions of time for payment when taxpayers are hard pressed for funds.[20]

In considering the differences between county and city political machines, Frank R. Kent concludes that there is some basis for the claim that county politics are cleaner, and county candidates better, than those in the larger cities. One reason for this is that in rural communities, where the population is smaller and people know each other, politics are more personal and closer to the people. Another reason is that the county leaders are generally men of some standing in the community, apart from their political position, and do not make their living exclusively out of politics. The county boss usually attains his position of leadership not by working his way up through machine politics but because he is already prominent in business, civic, or governmental affairs. Nevertheless, the county organizations are built on patronage; and, though in general they have to be more careful in choosing candidates, some of the candidates chosen are as ignorant and incompetent as any in the cities. In addition, proportionately more money is spent in the counties, because of the greater expense of bringing the voters longer distances to the polls and because more time and effort must be spent on discussing the issues of the campaign if rural voters are to be won over.[21]

LOCAL ELECTION OFFICERS

In New England, local control of general elections is normally vested in the towns, with the board of town selectmen functioning as the principal supervisory agency. Elsewhere throughout the country the county usually serves as an administrative district for the conduct of both county and state elections, with authority to establish election precincts, appoint precinct officers, and canvass election returns. Within the county government the function of conducting elections may rest with the general governing body of the county or may be vested in a county election board composed of appointive or ex officio members. In either case certain election functions may be delegated to county officers or boards other than those charged with general supervision, as, for example, where the county clerk is charged with preparing ballots and providing other election supplies. Supervision of general elections within municipalities, particularly the larger ones, is sometimes a function of city election boards rather than of county or town officials. City, school, and other local elections may be under the jurisdiction of the town or county authorities charged with management of general elections but, instead, are often conducted by officers of the particular units concerned. In some of the midwestern states, for example, township elections are held at a

[20] *Ibid.*

[21] Kent, *op. cit.,* chap. 12.

different time from state and county elections and are conducted by township officers.

REGISTRATION OF VOTERS

To facilitate identification of voters at the polls and thereby reduce election frauds, such as "repeating" and the voting of "floaters," nearly all of the states have established systems of voters' registration whereby eligible voters are required to enroll in advance in order to cast their ballots on election day.[22] Since frauds like impersonation and repeating are more readily perpetrated in large cities than in rural communities, where most of the voters are personally known to the election officials, many of the early registration laws applied only to the more populous urban places. Even today, rural areas are exempted from the registration requirement in some states, though the present tendency is distinctly toward a state-wide requirement. The local official charged with voters' registration is frequently the county or town clerk, though some jurisdictions are provided with special boards of registrars. As in the case of other phases of election administration, the larger municipalities are provided in some states with registration agencies apart from those serving rural areas.

Registration systems are of two general types: periodic and permanent. Under the former, existing registration lists are discarded at regular intervals and completely new lists compiled. The period between registrations varies from one year to ten, with biennial or quadrennial registrations most common. Under the permanent plan, on the other hand, a voter, once registered, remains registered until he moves his residence, dies, becomes legally disqualified, or fails to vote for a specified period.[23] Where the interval between registrations is comparatively short, the periodic system, if properly administered, has the advantage of being highly accurate and, at all times, relatively up to date. It is disadvantageous, however, in its costliness and in requiring that the voter present himself again and again for reregistration. Because it is more economical, and especially because of its greater convenience to the voter, the permanent plan is now generally preferred, provided that the registration lists are kept up to date by continuous revision; and most of the more recent statutes provide for registration of the permanent type. A number of states, however, still use either the periodic system or a "mixed" sys-

[22] The most comprehensive treatise on the subject is Joseph P. Harris, *Registration of Voters in the United States* (Washington, Brookings Institution, 1929). For more recent data, see Council of State Governments, *Registration for Voting in the United States*, rev. ed. (Chicago, 1946), and *The Book of the States: 1956-57* (Chicago, 1956), p. 85.

[23] Ordinarily reregistration is required also when a voter's name is changed by marriage or otherwise.

tem whereby the periodic plan is employed in certain localities and the permanent plan in others. Some laws require registration for voting in any election, whereas others exempt certain local elections from the registration requirement. Some of the states permit voters who are absent from their place of residence or are physically disabled to register by mail. In a few instances this privilege of absentee registration is confined to members of the armed services, but more often it extends to qualified electors generally.[24]

For identification of voters at the polls most of the earlier registration laws employed a personal description of the voter placed in the record at the time of registration and including such items as age, height, weight, and color of eyes and hair. A more effective method of identification now widely used is based upon signature comparison. Under this system, the voter is required to sign the registration record when he registers and an application for ballot when he presents himself at the polls on election day, with his identification then being made by the election officials through a comparison of the two signatures.[25]

Under registration systems of the permanent type, a major problem is that of keeping the lists of voters up to date. In the absence of effective procedures for constant revision, lists soon become loaded with the names of persons who have died, moved away, or become disqualified; and on election day these names may be "voted" by the party machines. The means which are employed, in sundry combinations, for the revision and purging of registration lists are numerous and varied. It is fairly common to require that official notices of deaths, and sometimes also of criminal convictions, be transmitted to the registration officials. Registrations may be challenged in most states by any voter, and in some, by registration officials and party watchers as well. Many states provide for suspension or cancellation of registrations for failure to vote for a specified period. Some jurisdictions provide for cancellation, after notice and opportunity for hearing, of the registration of persons believed by the registration officials, on the basis of inquiries mailed to all registrants, to have moved away or become ineligible.[26]

Under the earlier permanent registration laws it was usual for registration and the revision of registration lists to be confined to designated periods of time between elections. The more recent tendency, however, has been to provide for a system of continuous registration and revision, under which new registrations may be made, registrations cancelled, changes of address filed, and corrections made at any time, except during brief periods when the registration books are closed, as is commonly the

[24] *Registration for Voting in the United States;* James K. Pollock, *Absentee Voting and Registration* (Washington, American Council on Public Affairs, 1940).

[25] Cf. Harris, *Registration of Voters in the United States*, pp. 232-238.

[26] *Registration for Voting in the United States.*

case for a certain number of days preceding each primary and general election.[27] The spread of continuous revision, as of various other improvements in registration technique, has been due in no small measure to the influence of the model system of permanent registration prepared by a committee of the National Municipal League and first published in 1927.[28] Recent state statutes establishing permanent registration on a state-wide basis and making registration and revision a continuous process represent a striking advance over the early laws providing periodic registration, and that only for populous communities.

ELECTION ADMINISTRATION

The conduct of elections is primarily a local responsibility and one in which, as previously indicated, various county, town, and other local officials share.[29] State statutes prescribe in detail the procedures to be followed in general elections, and in most states in the primaries as well; but the actual management of elections is left to local authorities, and election expenses are usually a charge on local treasuries.[30]

Activities in the field of election administration are widely varied. Voting precincts must be laid out, polling places designated, booths and ballot boxes provided, ballots printed, and precinct officials appointed to preside at the polls on election day. For polling places the tendency today in many localities is to make use, wherever possible, of public buildings; and in rural communities this is likely to mean school buildings, town halls, and county courthouses. Since the rental for polling places ordinarily constitutes a substantial item in election costs where privately owned buildings are used, the use of public buildings may effect a considerable saving to taxpayers. Precinct election boards are usually required by law to be constituted on a bipartisan basis. Some states require an even division of board members between the two major parties; but most provide for precinct boards composed of an odd number of members, with the party controlling the election machinery being entitled to a majority of the officers.[31] The precinct board ordinarily consists of three members or five, though in some instances a larger membership is provided. Board members, variously entitled inspectors of election, election judges, election clerks, and the like, are formally appointed by

[27] O. Douglas Weeks, "Permanent Registration of Voters in the United States," *Temple University Law Quarterly*, Vol. XIV, pp. 74-88 (November, 1939).

[28] "A Model Registration System," *National Municipal Review*, suppl., Vol. XVI, pp. 45-86 (January, 1927). This report has now been revised three times, the fourth edition appearing as a pamphlet publication of the National Municipal League in 1954.

[29] See above, "Local Election Officers."

[30] A comprehensive treatise on the subject is Joseph P. Harris, *Election Administration in the United States* (Washington, Brookings Institution, 1934).

[31] *Ibid.*, p. 132.

public authority, with the appointing power in rural areas vested most commonly in the county governing body, a county election board, the county judge, or the town board of selectmen.[32] Law or custom usually decrees, however, that the official appointing agency, whatever it be, shall merely confirm nominations made by the local committees of the respective political parties. In effect, therefore, precinct officials are party appointees, and the positions are frequently regarded as minor patronage and used as rewards for party service.

Some states provide, at least in urban areas, for two election boards in each precinct—a receiving board to receive the ballots and a counting board to count them. Under this double-board system, voting and counting proceed concurrently. More commonly, however, a single precinct board receives ballots during voting hours and, after the close of the polls, serves as a counting board to determine and certify the results.

When the vote in the precinct has been counted and tabulated, the results of the count are certified to the appropriate canvassing officer or board. In the case of town or township elections, this is likely to be a town or township agency charged with making the final canvass and issuing certificates of election to the winning candidates. Where county and state offices are at stake, precinct certification is ordinarily to a county canvassing agency. This is usually the county governing body or county election board. In Illinois, however, the canvassing board consists of the county clerk and the chairmen of the Republican and Democratic county committees; and various other provisions for composition of the agency are found in other states. Whatever its composition, the county canvassing agency issues certificates of election to persons elected to county offices and certifies to a designated state officer, usually the secretary of state, the returns from the entire county on state offices. Finally, a canvass for state offices is made by a state canvassing board, which then issues election certificates to winning candidates.

Canvassing agencies, at whatever level, have no authority to examine or recount the ballots, but are limited in their function to a compilation and certification of returns on the basis of the precinct count. However, the result of an election as finally certified by the canvassing authorities is usually subject to contest through a procedure prescribed by statute, and in the course of determining a contest, a recount may be ordered and carried out. Election contests are heard and determined in some instances by the election authorities, in others by the courts, and, in the case of legislative office, ordinarily by the legislative body itself.[33]

Counties and towns must usually bear the cost, not only of their own

[32] In Pennsylvania and a few other states precinct officials are elected by the voters —*ibid.*, p. 138.

[33] V. O. Key, Jr., *Politics, Parties, and Pressure Groups*, 3d ed. (New York, Crowell, 1952), pp. 642-643.

elections but that of the state elections for whose administration they are responsible; and in rural counties and towns election costs frequently constitute a considerable budgetary item in election years. Township, school, and other special-district elections are commonly held separately from state and county elections, with their costs a charge upon the treasuries of the governmental units concerned.

VOTING MACHINES

In some areas voting machines have now replaced paper ballots in some or all elections.[34] Operating on the principle of the cash register or adding machine, the voting machine permits votes to be cast, recorded, and automatically counted without the use of ballots in the ordinary sense.[35] Candidates' names appear on the face of the machine, and a vote is cast by the manipulation of keys or levers, additional spaces and keys being provided for voting on policy propositions.

Most of the states have now enacted voting-machine laws of one kind or another. These statutes ordinarily make the use of machines optional with the various local units, though some of the laws are mandatory in character. In most of the states having permissive legislation, machines are actually used, if at all, only in some of the larger cities, though in some states they are employed in certain rural areas as well. In at least three states—New York, Rhode Island, and Louisiana—machines are used in all precincts, both urban and rural.

Voting machines offer certain advantages over paper ballots. The average time required for casting a vote, once the voters have become familiar with the operation of the machines, is somewhat reduced, and therefore it is practicable to use larger and fewer precincts. Invalid and defective ballots are eliminated, since the machines are so constructed as to make the casting of such ballots impossible. The count is automatic, accurate, and available promptly after the close of the polls, and recounts for the most part are avoided. Perhaps the most important advantage of all is in the fact that various types of voting fraud, especially ballot-box stuffing and fraudulent counting, tend to be reduced or eliminated.[36] It may be noted, however, that the evils which voting machines are designed to overcome are more prevalent in urban areas than in rural. This fact suggests that more is to be gained through the use of machines in urban communities than in rural and doubtless explains why adoption of the device has been more widespread in urban areas. It seems certain that,

[34] T. David Zukerman, *The Voting Machine* (New York, Republican County Committee of New York Political Research Bureau, 1925); Spencer D. Albright, *The American Ballot* (Washington, American Council on Public Affairs, 1942), chap. 4.

[35] Cf. Merriam and Gosnell, *op. cit.*, p. 439.

[36] Harris, *Election Administration in the United States,* chap. 7.

in the future, voting machines will find ever wider use in both urban and rural regions. But, in view of the fact that election fraud is less widespread in rural areas, and considering the large initial cost of voting machines, it appears unlikely that the machine is destined, at least for many years to come, to displace completely the paper ballot in sparsely settled country precincts.

NOMINATING METHODS

Caucuses. Prior to development of the direct primary system, nomination of candidates for county, township, and other local offices was made by a variety of local caucuses and conventions. The nominating caucus is a meeting of voters for the purpose of designating local candidates, and, in some instances, also for selecting delegates to nominating conventions serving larger areas. Though some caucuses are nonpartisan, consisting of voters who, without regard to party affiliation, seek to agree upon candidates to whom they will give their united support, the device is more generally used for making party nominations, each party holding a caucus of its own members for that purpose.

In its heyday the caucus system developed various evils, caucus control tending to fall into the hands of ruling cliques, or machines, within the parties. Typical of these evils, which were more widespread in urban areas than in rural but tended to bring the system into general discredit, were the *snap* caucus and the *packed* caucus. The snap caucus was held on such short notice that most of the party members were unaware of the meeting or could not arrange to attend, thus making it possible for the inner circle to control caucus deliberations and dictate nominations. Caucus packing was accomplished in a variety of ways. Under one method, the meeting was held in a small room or hall with word passed out in advance to members of the inner clique to come early with their friends and occupy the seats. Where, by such practices as these, party machines controlled caucus nominations, their control extended also to any nominations made by conventions composed of delegates selected at the caucuses. In an effort to eliminate these evils, many states enacted legislation designed to regulate caucus proceedings, but in practice means were usually found of circumventing the regulatory measures.

In as much as regulation proved generally ineffective, the caucus system was eventually supplanted to a large extent by the direct primary election, though candidates for township and various other local offices are still nominated in many instances by the caucus method. A variant form of caucus now found in some places is that in which polls are kept open at a designated place for several hours and party voters, instead of assembling together at a specified time, appear individually during the polling period and vote by ballot for the candidates of their choice. This type of caucus bears close resemblance to the direct primary election and, indeed, in some states and localities, is called a primary. It is, however, conducted in a less formal manner than the direct primary, as the latter term is generally employed in this chapter, and is subject to a lesser degree of public regulation.[37]

Conventions. Whereas party caucuses for nominating purposes are composed of the party voters themselves, nominating conventions consist of delegates representative of the voters. Convention delegates are variously chosen by caucuses, subsidiary conventions, or the party voters directly in primary elections. Once widely used for making both state and local nominations, the convention, like the caucus, readily lent itself to machine domination and, for this reason, ultimately declined in popular esteem. Since the turn of the century state after state has abandoned convention nomination, wholly or in part, in favor of the direct primary system.

The Direct Primary. Devised in an effort to overcome the evils of the caucus-convention system and to bring the nominating process under direct control of the voters, the direct primary election has now become the predominant means of nominating candidates for state and local offices. Though some states had experimented previously with the direct primary principle, the real movement for establishment of the primary system did not develop until the early years of the present century. The first state-wide primary law was enacted by Wisconsin in 1903. Thereafter, the plan was adopted by other states in rapid succession until, by 1917, 44 states had enacted primary legislation, mandatory or optional, applicable to nominations for some or all offices.[38] In 1955 Connecticut became the forty-eighth state to enact a primary law. However, primaries are to be held in Connecticut only on challenge of nominations made by the state convention or town committees; and several other states still employ the caucus or convention for the making of nominations to certain offices.

Some primaries, as will be noted shortly, are nonpartisan in character.[39] The great majority, however, are of the partisan type, serving as the means through which nominations are made by the respective political parties. As thus used for making party nominations, the direct primary is an *intraparty* election for the selection of candidates who will compete for public office in the succeeding general election with the nominees of other parties and with independent candidates. Primary laws ordinarily apply only to parties whose candidates received a specified percentage

[37] P. Orman Ray, *An Introduction to Political Parties and Practical Politics,* 3d ed. (New York, Scribner, 1924), chap. 4.

[38] Charles E. Merriam and Louise Overacker, *Primary Elections* (Chicago, University of Chicago Press, 1928), chap. 5.

[39] See below, "Nonpartisanship."

of the total vote cast in the last general election, this percentage varying widely but being frequently in the neighborhood of 5 or 10 per cent. In many states, because of these limitations, only the two major parties hold primary elections, with minor-party and independent nominations being made in some other manner, frequently by the petition method, which is discussed at a later point. Primary elections in some southern states are conducted by party committees, and the costs thereof are paid by the parties or candidates. In most states, however, the primaries are conducted at public expense, by publicly appointed election officials, and according to much the same procedure as that followed in general elections. Names of persons desiring to become candidates for nomination under the primary system are usually placed on the primary ballot pursuant to petition signed by party members in number as prescribed by statute and filed with a designated public official. In addition to serving as a nominating agency, the primary is the election in which elective party officials—committeemen and convention delegates—are chosen, and this function further enhances its importance.

The basic objective of the direct primary is a democratizing of the nominating process. In some measure this objective has been accomplished, yet the primary has developed certain problems of its own. Where the primary is used ultimate control of nominations is exercised directly by the party voters rather than by party leaders, and a larger proportion of party members vote in the primary than participated, under the former system, in the making of caucus and convention nominations. But it should not be supposed that primary nominees are always the choice of a majority of the party members or that machine domination of primaries is by any means nonexistent. Nonvoting is notoriously extensive in primary elections, and a small primary vote makes it relatively easy, in many instances, for an active group within the party to secure the nomination of candidates of their choice. In practice it is not unusual for groups of party leaders, who may or may not constitute the membership of the official party committees, to prepare slates of candidates whom they propose to support in the primary and then to work zealously in the primary campaign for the nomination of those candidates. Such a "regular" or "organization" slate, if endorsed and supported by influential party leaders, is likely to carry the primary and win nomination, notwithstanding any "rebel" opposition on the part of less influential leaders, or even minor uprisings within the party membership. Indeed, machine pressure may be exerted to prevent independents within the party from filing for nomination or to prevail upon such persons, after they have filed, to withdraw before the date of the primary and thereby leave the field clear for organization candidates. Thus, it is often possible, under the primary system, for the party leadership or machine to control nominations quite as effectively as under the old caucus-convention system and still, since nominations are formally made by the party members themselves, to escape even that degree of responsibility which was theirs in the public mind when nominations were made by procedures which the leaders more obviously controlled.

Most state primary laws make it extremely easy for any aspirant to nomination to have his name placed on the primary ballot. Under the petition plan used in most states, the required number of signatures is usually so low that it can readily be met by any party member, whether or not he has substantial backing. In a few states mere declaration of candidacy, without the filing of a petition, is sufficient to place a name on the ballot. Because of these lax requirements, primary ballots tend to become cluttered with the names of persons who have no conceivable chance of winning nomination, but who, for publicity purposes or other reasons, decide to become candidates. Not infrequently, a half dozen or more candidates will contend for a single nomination. This situation, of course, is not universal—indeed, in some instances there is actually a dearth of primary contenders [40]—but multiplicity of candidates appears to be a widespread concomitant of the primary system in this country. Primary ballots, as a consequence, often become so long that it is impossible for the average voter to express an intelligent choice of candidates.

Another common result of the multiplicity of candidates is minority nomination. In most states a mere plurality vote in the primary is sufficient to nominate, that is to say, the candidate who receives the largest number of votes for a particular office wins the nomination, regardless of how small that number may be. Where this is the case, and there are three or more contenders for a particular nomination, the vote is often so divided that the winning candidate is nominated by less than a majority, indeed, sometimes by a relatively small fraction, of the total vote cast. Under these circumstances, it not infrequently happens that a person is nominated to an office, notwithstanding that many more persons voted against him (that is, voted for other candidates) than for him. To prevent the occurrence of minority nominations some southern states employ a system of run-off primaries. According to this plan, if no candidate for a particular office receives a majority vote in the regular primary election, a second primary is held in which the two candidates polling the largest votes compete for the nomination. With only the two candidates contending, one is then certain of securing a majority vote. The plan has the disadvantage of calling the voters to the polls an additional time when no candidate receives a majority vote in the first primary; but in the South, where Democratic nomination is usually tantamount to election, this added requirement of the voter may well be justified.

[40] See, for example, Kirk H. Porter, "The Deserted Primary in Iowa," *American Political Science Review,* Vol. XXXIX, pp. 732-740 (August, 1945).

Whatever its shortcomings, the direct primary appears now to have been permanently established as the predominant method of making nominations for local office. Where the primary system has been adopted, it has rarely been abandoned. Occasional reversions to older nominating methods have occurred here and there, but the distinct tendency has been toward ever wider use of primary nominations. The primary system avoids some of the more serious abuses of the caucus-convention system and places ultimate authority and responsibility for nominations directly in the hands of the rank and file of party voters. All in all, it appears to be the most satisfactory system yet devised for nominating candidates to public office.

Nomination by Petition. Nomination by voter petition has been used to some extent in this country for many years and seems likely to be continued as a supplementary nominating procedure. A petition for nomination is to be clearly distinguished from a petition for a place on the primary ballot. The petition under the primary system results merely in placing the name of an aspirant on the primary ballot, whereas the names which appear on the general election ballot are there as a result of winning in the primary elections. Under the system of nomination by petition, on the other hand, the effect of the petition is to place the candidate's name directly on the general election ballot. Petition procedure is much the same in both cases, though the nominating petition ordinarily requires a larger number of signatures than the primary petition. The petition method of nomination is used for a wide variety of local offices, being especially prevalent in the case of school board members and members of the governing bodies of other special districts. It is also commonly employed for the nomination of independent candidates, as distinguished from party candidates, for both state and local offices; and, where use of the direct primary is confined to the major parties, it is frequently used for making minor-party nominations. Participation in a primary for the nomination of major-party candidates usually disqualifies a voter from signing nominating petitions for independent or minor-party candidates for the same offices; and some states provide that a person who has been defeated in a party primary may not then be nominated by petition as an independent candidate for the ensuing election.[41]

NONPARTISANSHIP

Most county and township elections are conducted on a partisan basis, with candidates nominated by the respective political parties, through primaries or otherwise, contending for office in the general elections.

[41] Cf. Austin F. Macdonald, *American State Government and Administration*, 4th ed. (New York, Crowell, 1950), p. 102.

However, there are some instances of elections that are nonpartisan in form. A few states conduct all county or township elections on such a basis. Thus, all county elections in California and Minnesota, and all township elections in Ohio, are of the nonpartisan type. In several other states elections for specific county officers, most frequently judges and superintendents of schools, are nonpartisan.[42]

The distinctive feature of the nonpartisan election lies in the fact that the names of candidates on the election ballot are not accompanied by any party designation. Candidates' names are placed on the ballot in some instances as the result of a nonpartisan primary and in others as the result of nominating petitions. Whereas, under the partisan type of primary previously discussed, a separate primary is held for each political party, the nonpartisan plan involves a single primary in which all candidates for nomination contend and all qualified voters are entitled to vote. The two candidates for each office polling the largest primary vote are considered nominated and oppose each other in the ensuing general election. Provision is made in some instances, however, that if any candidate receives in the primary an absolute majority of all votes for the office he is seeking, he shall be declared elected without the necessity of a subsequent run-off election.

In California a nonpartisan primary for making county and judicial nominations is held in June of even-numbered years. Names are placed on the primary ballot by petition and payment of a filing fee. Candidates receiving a majority of the votes cast in the primary for their respective offices are declared elected. If no candidate receives a majority for a particular office, the two leading candidates oppose each other in the November general election.[43] In practice, the majority of county and judicial offices in California are filled as a result of the June primary, without resort to a run-off election in November.[44] Candidates for nonpartisan township elections in Ohio are nominated by petition.[45]

Nonpartisan elections, in addition to their use for some county and township officers, are commonly employed in school districts and other

[42] Cf. Robert Eugene Cushman, "Non-partisan Nominations and Elections," *Annals of the American Academy of Political and Social Science,* Vol. CVI, pp. 83-96 (March, 1923).

[43] Allan R. Richards, "California," in Paul W. Wager, ed., *County Government across the Nation* (Chapel Hill, University of North Carolina Press, 1950), p. 793.

[44] University of California (Los Angeles) Bureau of Governmental Research, *County Government in California* (Sacramento, County Supervisors Association of California, 1951), p. 79.

[45] Herbert C. Smith, *Rural Local Government in Ohio* (Columbus, Ohio, School and College Service, 1940), p. 20. Under Ohio law township elections may be conducted on a partisan basis, with nominations made in party primaries; but it is reported that this method is never used. William B. Guitteau, *Ohio's Townships: The Grassroots of Democracy* (Toledo, Ohio, Toledo Printing Company, 1949), p. 92.

special districts. Indeed, the nonpartisan form of election is the rule rather than the exception in special districts of all types, with nominations most commonly made by petition.

As far as theory is concerned, nonpartisanship as applied to local government has much to be said in its favor. There is little reason for carrying over into local affairs national party allegiance determined, nominally at least, by one's views on such matters as national fiscal policy and international trade. As the friends of nonpartisanship so vigorously insist, there is no Republican or Democratic way of building a county bridge, administering a district school, or dispensing township assistance to the needy. But a so-called nonpartisan election may be distinctly less nonpartisan in actuality than in name. The forms of nonpartisanship may exist without the substance. Though it is true that no party designation appears on nonpartisan ballots, the party affiliation of aspirants to nonpartisan office is frequently a matter of common knowledge and an important factor in determining the voters' choice. Party affiliation or preference may be frankly acknowledged, or even emphasized, in campaign speeches and literature or in the press; and, indeed, the regular party organization at times plays an active role in the support of "nonpartisan" candidates whom it favors. Thus, it is reported that in Ohio, party caucuses frequently decide whom the organization will support in the nonpartisan township elections, and party workers then circulate nominating petitions for the persons so chosen.[46]

Not only is genuine nonpartisanship difficult to attain in practice but the nonpartisan plan of choosing local officers, insofar as it does operate effectively, poses certain problems of its own. Proponents of nonpartisan elections argue that the plan makes available for local office some outstanding citizens who would not be willing to become involved in party politics, and this may well be the case. On the other hand, as long as many state and local offices remain on a partisan basis, the application of nonpartisanship to some offices tends to divide potential official personnel into two groups—partisan and nonpartisan—and to make difficult a transfer from one group to the other, since the voters appear to look askance at any abrupt shift of an office seeker from a partisan to a nonpartisan candidacy or from nonpartisan to partisan. To the extent that this situation prevails, channels of recruitment for both partisan and nonpartisan offices tend to be restricted. Finally, it may be noted that nonpartisanship, to the extent that it functions as intended, nullifies any collective responsibility which a party organization might be expected to supply.[47]

[46] Smith, *op. cit.*, pp. 20-21.

[47] For further analysis of these and other aspects of nonpartisanship, see Charles R. Adrian, "Some General Characteristics of Nonpartisan Elections," *American Political Science Review*, Vol. XLVI, pp. 766-776 (September, 1952).

PERSONAL POLITICS

Whether elections are partisan or nonpartisan in form, politics in many rural counties and townships are highly personal in character. More important than a candidate's party affiliation, in determining voter support or opposition, are such matters as his church and lodge associations, his general reputation in the community, and what the local gossips say concerning him and members of his family. In discussing county politics and elections in northern Alabama, Professor Karl Bosworth has remarked that "Church loyalties are strong and political leaders do not avoid opportunities to teach a Sunday School class or help install a bath in the parsonage." [48] In rural counties generally, ability of a candidate to advertise "I was born and raised in this county and have lived here all my life" ordinarily is worth a good many votes. If his family was among the pioneer settlers of the locality, so much the better. Sometimes a candidate's financial need is a factor. Thus, a person unable to engage in most private pursuits because of some physical handicap, or one in financial straits because of extended sickness in his family, may make a deliberate appeal to the voters' sympathy in furtherance of his candidacy.[49] Though the rural candidate may make some campaign speeches, much of his campaigning commonly takes the form of merely "meeting the people" in an informal manner at civic gatherings, picnics, public sales, and the like. Dean R. Cresap, in contending that rural overrepresentation in the California senate contributes to lack of partisanship in that body, observes that "it is easier for the rural voters to know more about their candidates. There are fewer voters, and a candidate may more easily make himself known to many of them. They tend to vote for Tom Jones because they know he is a Methodist, a rancher, a Rotarian, and a man with a pleasant family, rather than because he is a Republican or a Democrat." [50] A similar statement would seem clearly applicable to elections for both legislative and nonlegislative offices in the rural areas of many other states.

Where, as generally throughout the South and in many communities elsewhere, a single party is strongly predominant, the nominating primary of that party becomes the only election of importance, and intraparty contests therein are waged largely on the basis of personal factors, such as those mentioned in the preceding paragraph. And where the two-party system prevails the personal nature of county politics may well account in part for the ticket-splitting that tends to be relatively widespread in

[48] Karl A. Bosworth, *Tennessee Valley County* (University, University of Alabama Bureau of Public Administration, 1941), p. 20. Concerning county politics in Alabama's "black belt," see Karl A. Bosworth, *Black Belt County* (University, University of Alabama Bureau of Public Administration, 1941), chap. 2.

[49] Cf. "Oldtime Campaigning," *Time*, Vol. LXII, No. 4, pp. 10-11 (July 27, 1953).

[50] Dean R. Cresap, *Party Politics in the Golden State* (Los Angeles, Haynes Foundation, 1954), p. 61.

rural areas. Ticket-splitting takes countless forms, but one of the most common is that in which the voter supports the candidates of one party for state and national office and those of another for local office. It is not unusual, for example, for the voters of a particular county to give a plurality to the presidential ticket of one major party and still elect one or more county officers from the other. Though the results of local elections are influenced by state and national election trends, they are not necessarily controlled by them. In reporting the results of a recent analysis of election data in Ohio, Professor V. O. Key makes some significant observations concerning the independence displayed in voting for local candidates: [51]

> Contrary to the belief that the presidential tide almost invariably carries with it the local candidates of the winning party, the Ohio record indicates a fairly high degree of independence of national party trends in the selection of county officers. Although in most instances a Republican county presidentially chooses Republican county officers and a Democratic county, Democratic county officers, the departures from this consistency are of sufficient magnitude to excite attention. . . . In periods of ascending Republican presidential strength, a goodly number of Democratic county candidates withstand the storm. At times of ascending Democratic presidential strength, Republican county candidates demonstrate staying power. . . . While the trend in party control of county government moves with the presidential trend, local candidates of both parties in considerable degree withstand the tides that batter their presidential ticket.

On the whole, such evidence as is available clearly suggests that individual friendships and other personal factors, as contrasted with party affiliation, are more influential in local politics than in state and national, and, at the local level, more so in rural communities than in urban.

INITIATIVE AND REFERENDUM [52]

The popular referendum on specific questions is employed to a considerable extent in the affairs of counties and other local government units.

[51] V. O. Key, Jr., "Partisanship and County Office: The Case of Ohio," *American Political Science Review,* Vol. XLVII, pp. 525-532, 525, 531 (June, 1953).

[52] Most of the literature concerning the initiative and referendum relates to the operation of those devices at the state level and gives little or no attention to their application in the field of local government. Among the more recent studies may be mentioned James K. Pollock, *The Initiative and Referendum in Michigan* (Ann Arbor, University of Michigan Bureau of Government, 1940); Colorado Legislative Reference Office, *The Initiative and Referendum in Colorado* (Denver, 1940); Claudius O. Johnson, "The Initiative and Referendum in Washington," *Pacific Northwest Quarterly,* Vol. XXXVI, pp. 29-63 (January, 1945); Winston W. Crouch, *The Initiative and Referendum in California* (Los Angeles, Haynes Foundation, 1950); Joseph G. LaPalombara, *The Initiative and Referendum in Oregon: 1938-1948* (Corvallis, Oregon State College, 1950). One study of operations at the local level, though dealing with municipalities rather than counties and other local units, is Winston W. Crouch, "The Initiative and Referendum in Cities," *American Political Science Review,* Vol. XXXVII, pp. 491-504 (June, 1943).

In a number of states constitutional or statutory provisions require referendum votes on such matters as the creation of new counties, changes in county boundaries and county seats, the adoption or discontinuance of township government, proposed tax levies or bond issues, and the construction of public buildings. Many states provide for county- or other local-option votes on prohibition of liquor sales. Questions concerning the erection of a county hospital, the establishment of a county or township library, the consolidation of neighboring school districts, and the adoption of the county-unit system of school administration are among the many and diverse matters that require submission to the local electorate in various states. Frequently, referendum approval is prerequisite to the establishment of special districts, such as health districts and soil-conservation districts.

Several of the states which provide for the general initiative and referendum for state legislation also authorize their use by counties and other local units. The initiative, where thus authorized, makes it possible to enact by petition and popular vote ordinances or bylaws which cannot be secured from the local governing body. The referendum enables local voters, by petition properly filed, to require that a measure enacted by the governing body be submitted to popular vote for approval or disapproval. Under the Utah constitution, for example, the powers of initiative and referendum are conferred upon the voters of any legal subdivision of the state; and some other states also extend the powers to local units generally. Some constitutions, such as those of California, Nevada, Arizona, Arkansas, and Oklahoma, refer specifically to counties, usually along with municipalities, as possessing the initiative and referendum. Whereas the initiative and referendum may be made applicable to state legislation only by constitutional provision, local initiative and referendum powers may be conferred either by constitutional provision or by statute.[53]

Procedures to be followed in exercising the local initiative and referendum are prescribed by constitutional provision in some states and left to statutory determination in others. In California, Oklahoma, and Utah the procedures are to be provided by law; although in California, until otherwise provided by statute, the legislative body of any county or other local district may provide for the manner of exercising the powers. Arizona cities, towns, and counties are empowered to prescribe procedures within the restrictions of general laws.

The scope of the powers conferred by initiative and referendum provisions is not uniform; nor is it always clearly indicated. The powers apply in Arkansas and Nevada "to all local, special, and municipal legislation of every character"; in Arizona, to all local matters on which local governments "are or shall be empowered by general laws to legislate"; and in Okla-

[53] Cf. Jefferson B. Fordham, *Local Government Law* (Brooklyn, N. Y., Foundation Press, 1949), p. 407.

homa, "to all local legislation, or action, in the administration of county and district government." Whether fixed by constitution or by statute, the number of signatures required for an initiative petition is usually larger than for a referendum petition. A fairly common requirement is 15 per cent of the voters in the case of initiative and 10 per cent for referendum. These are the percentage requirements prescribed by the Arizona constitution. The constitution of Nevada provides that the legislature may not establish requirements higher than these; and the California constitution forbids local governing bodies to prescribe higher requirements in regulating initiative and referendum procedures pending their regulation by state statute.

Little information is available concerning the actual use of the initiative and referendum by counties and other rural units. As long as the legislative authority of these local governments remains narrowly limited, there would appear to be relatively few occasions for their exercise. If, however, local legislative powers are eventually to be enlarged, as appears likely in the case of counties, opportunities for use of the devices will be increased, and there might be greater disposition to authorize their use in additional jurisdictions.

THE RECALL

Where the popular recall is provided a specified number of voters may, by petition, demand and secure a special election to determine whether a designated officer shall continue in office to the end of his term or be immediately removed therefrom. Ten states, in their constitutions, make direct provision for this method of removal; [54] and the Michigan constitution requires the legislature to establish the recall. In Louisiana recall provisions have been enacted by the legislature pursuant to specific constitutional authorization. In each of these 12 states the recall applies not only to state officers but to county officials (parish officials in Louisiana) and to the officers of various other local governments. In most instances the recall applies to all elective officers, although four of the states except judges from its application; [55] and Kansas makes the device applicable to both elective and appointive officials.[56] In several states the recall provision declares that every public officer in the state, with judges excepted in some instances, shall be "subject to recall by the legal voters of the state or of the electoral district from which he is elected." However, the constitutions of California, Colorado, Nevada, North Dakota, and Wisconsin specifically provide for the recall of county officers; and the Louisiana

[54] Arizona, California, Colorado, Idaho, Kansas, Nevada, North Dakota, Oregon, Washington, and Wisconsin.

[55] Idaho, Louisiana, Michigan, and Washington.

[56] The most thorough study of the recall, though with reference primarily to a single state, is Frederick L. Bird and Frances M. Ryan, *The Recall of Public Officers: A Study of the Operation of the Recall in California* (New York, Macmillan, 1930).

provision applies expressly to parish officers. Most state constitutions providing for the recall prescribe the procedure to be followed in its exercise. In California and Colorado, however, although the procedure applicable to state officers is set forth in the constitution, that for local officers is to be provided by law; and, until so provided, the legislative body of each county or other local district is authorized to designate the method of exercising the power.

Outside those states with constitutional provisions establishing the recall or specifically authorizing it, the device, of course, may be provided for local governments by the state legislature on its own authority, and this has been done in some instances. In Nebraska, for example, under general statutory provision, any county officer other than the county superintendent of public instruction may be removed by recall.

Recall proceedings involve two distinct steps: the petition and the recall election. Provisions concerning petitions, the time of holding the recall election, and the method of choosing a successor vary from state to state. A local recall petition must be signed by a specified percentage of the qualified voters of the governmental unit concerned. This percentage ranges from 10 to 55, with a requirement of 25 per cent being fairly common.[57] The percentage is based, in some instances, on the total number of votes cast in the last election for the office affected and, in others, on the vote within the local area for governor or another designated state officer. The petition must set forth a statement of charges against the officer whose removal is sought and a demand for an election to determine whether he shall continue in office. When the petition has been signed by the necessary number of voters it is filed with a designated election official, usually the county clerk or the clerk of the other local unit concerned. If the petition is found to meet all legal requirements as to form and signatures, the recall election is ordered.

Recall elections take various forms. Under one plan, the name of the official against whom the recall is directed merely appears on the ballot, along with the names of other candidates nominated by petition, as a candidate for the office for the remainder of the term. If the incumbent receives more votes than any other candidate, he retains his office; otherwise he is removed and succeeded by the winning candidate. A variant of this plan is that in which the voter votes separately on two questions: the recall of the incumbent and the choice of a successor from among candidates nominated by petition. Under this plan, if there are more votes for than against the recall of the incumbent, he relinquishes his office to the person who, as a candidate, has received the largest vote. If, on the other hand, more votes are cast against than for the recall, the incumbent remains in office. Both of these forms of recall election are open to criti-

[57] *Ibid.*, p. 17.

cism on the ground that the official whose removal is sought must, if he is to remain in office, overcome not only the criticisms of his own record but the personal and political popularity of opposing candidates. Another, and perhaps the most satisfactory, type of election is that in which the voter is asked to vote on the single question of whether or not the officer concerned shall be recalled. If the election goes against the incumbent, he is removed from office, and a second election is held to choose his successor; or, in some states, the vacancy created by his removal is filled in the same manner that would be used if the vacancy had occurred from any other cause.[58] The Kansas constitution, for example, provides that in case of the recall of an officer, a vacancy exists "to be filled as authorized by law"; and the Louisiana constitution declares that "the sole issue tendered at any recall election shall be whether such officer shall be recalled." Oregon, by constitutional amendment of 1926, abandoned the plan of having the recall determined by an election contest in which the person receiving the highest number of votes is elected, and provided that "if an officer is recalled from any public office the vacancy shall be filled immediately in the manner provided by law for filling a vacancy in that office arising from any other cause."

Whatever the form of recall election, provision is ordinarily made that an officer may not be recalled until he has held the office for a specified minimum length of time, varying from three months to a year. The purpose of such a provision is to give the official at least a brief opportunity, before subjecting him to a recall election, to demonstrate to the voters the manner in which he can and will conduct his office. Furthermore, regulations governing recall often provide that an officer who wins a recall election and thereby retains his office may not be subjected to another such election until the lapse of a specified period of time. In some instances, a second recall election within a single term of office is prohibited altogether.[59]

Notwithstanding its availability in more than a fourth of the states, the recall appears to have been used but little as a means of removing officers of counties and other local governments in rural areas. In general, it seems to have been used more sparingly in the rural governmental units than in municipalities. Frederick L. Bird and Frances M. Ryan, in a comprehensive study of the recall in California published in 1930, report that from 1911, when the device was applied to counties and other local units by constitutional amendment, down to the late 1920's, the recall was employed, as far as could be ascertained, by only 12 of the state's 58 counties. During this period, 26 recall petitions were filed against officers of those counties and of judicial townships therein, 23 of which resulted in the holding of recall elections. As a result of those elections, eight local offi-

[58] *Ibid.*, 18.
[59] *Ibid.*

cials—two county supervisors, a district attorney, three justices of the peace, and two constables—were removed from office.[60] Later reports indicate that recall attempts against local officials other than those of cities have continued to be infrequent in California;[61] and there appears to be no reason to suppose that the device has been invoked more extensively by rural local units in the other states where it is authorized.

The merits of the recall are problematical. There is substantial agreement, however, that this method of removal is best suited to officers charged with the determination of public policy. Since the present-day duties of most officials of counties and other rural units are primarily administrative rather than policy-determining in nature, there would seem to be little need to apply the recall to those governments. If reorganization of local government, particularly with respect to counties, should ultimately vest broad powers of policy determination in a relatively small number of elective officials, provision for the recall of those officials might be of service as a method of popular control to be used in exceptional circumstances.

THE TASK OF THE LOCAL VOTER

County, township, and special-district elections account for a large part of the heavy task imposed upon the American voter. The county ballot, to begin with, is too long. As indicated in an earlier chapter, county voters are called upon to elect a considerable number of administrative officers in addition to members of the general governing body.[62] The fact that county elections ordinarily are held concurrently with the biennial elections for state and national officers contributes further to the seriousness of the problem. Introduction of the direct primary, though having a wholesome effect upon the nominating process in general, has necessitated calling the voters to the polls more frequently; and the primary ballot, because of the large number of candidates for nomination, often is even more cumbersome than that in the general election.

Township, school, and other special-district elections are held in many states on a different date from that of elections for state and county officers, but it is not unusual to find several of these units conducting elections at the same time. In some Illinois communities, for example, township, municipal, and park-district elections are held concurrently, and on the same day, in election years, as the annual township meeting. The result almost inevitably is voter confusion and discouragement; yet the price of

[60] *Ibid.*, pp. 279-304. During the same period, several directors of irrigation districts also were recalled.—*ibid.*, pp. 305-312.

[61] Winston W. Crouch, Dean E. McHenry, John C. Bollens, and Stanley Scott, *State and Local Government in California* (Berkeley, University of California Press, 1952), p. 93.

[62] See above, chap. 6, "Elective Officers."

unscrambling these various local elections by holding them on different dates would be still more numerous trips to the polls.

Local elections, it must be remembered, are not merely a matter of choosing local officers. In addition to expressing his choice of candidates, the voter is commonly asked to pass upon proposed bond issues and tax levies as well as a variety of other public policy questions. To the extent that use is made of the initiative, referendum, and recall, the voter's assignment is further complicated.

The undue length of many ballots combines with the multiplicity of elections to deter popular participation in local government and to make virtually impossible intelligent action on the part of those who do have the courage to vote. Any program of county government reorganization should give high priority to a shortening of the county ballot by providing for the appointment, rather than the election, of non-policy-determining officers. Moreover, the number and complexity of local elections might well be reduced by eliminating some of the many special districts and assigning their functions to the counties and other general-purpose units. A reduction in both the number of elective offices and the frequency of elections should go far toward stimulating active and intelligent citizen participation in local public affairs.

REFERENCES

Books and Special Studies

BIRD, Frederick L., and RYAN, Frances M., *The Recall of Public Officers: A Study of the Operation of the Recall in California* (New York, Macmillan, 1930).

Council of State Governments, *Registration for Voting in the United States*, rev. ed. (Chicago, 1946).

FISHER, Marguerite J., and STARRATT, Edith E., *Parties and Politics in the Local Community* (Washington, National Council for the Social Studies, 1945).

HARRIS, Joseph P., *Election Administration in the United States* (Washington, Brookings Institution, 1934).

———, *Registration of Voters in the United States* (Washington, Brookings Institution, 1929).

KEY, V. O., Jr., *American State Politics: An Introduction* (New York, Knopf, 1956).

LOGAN, Edward B., ed., *The American Political Scene*, rev. ed. (New York, Harper, 1938).

MERRIAM, Charles E., and GOSNELL, Harold F., *The American Party System*, 4th ed. (New York, Macmillan, 1949).

See also the standard textbooks in the field of political parties.

Articles

JONES, Chester Lloyd, "The County in Politics," *Annals of the American Academy of Political and Social Science*, Vol. XLVII, pp. 85-100 (May, 1913).

KEY, V. O., Jr., "Partisanship and County Office: The Case of Ohio," *American Political Science Review,* Vol. XLVII, pp. 525-532 (June, 1953).

LINGERFELT, Edmund R., "GI Revolt Wins Manager Plan," *National Municipal Review,* Vol. XXXVII, pp. 196-200 (April, 1948).

OWENS, Hamilton, "The County Boss," *American Mercury,* Vol. XVII, pp. 70-74 (May, 1929).

POLLOCK, James K., "New Thoughts on the Short Ballot," *National Municipal Review,* Vol. XXIX, pp. 18-20, 47 (January, 1940).

SMITH, Lincoln, "Leadership in Local Government–The New England Town," *Social Science,* Vol. XXIX, pp. 147-157 (June, 1954).

———, "Political Leadership in a New England Community," *Review of Politics,* Vol. XVII, pp. 392-409 (July, 1955).

STARR, Joseph R., "The Legal Status of American Political Parties," *American Political Science Review,* Vol. XXXIV, pp. 439-455, 685-699 (June and August, 1940).

WEAVER, Leon, "Some Soundings in the Party System: Rural Precinct Committeemen," *American Political Science Review,* Vol. XXXIV, pp. 76-84 (February, 1940).

WHITE, Theodore H., "The Battle of Athens, Tennessee," *Harper's Magazine,* Vol. CXCIV, pp. 54-61 (January, 1947).

PART FOUR

Functions

CHAPTER 12

Judicial Administration

THUS FAR OUR CONCERN has been with the historical development of local governmental units, their legal nature, the laws through which they are established, their relations to the state and national governments and to each other, the means of popular control over them, and their internal organization and powers. But local governments, like governments generally, exist for the performance of services, and to that aspect of the subject we now turn. A description of all the manifold activities carried on by local governments in rural areas would be quite impossible within the limits of this work. However, in the group of chapters of which this is the first, consideration will be given to the major services performed by these governments as well as to certain selected functions of lesser significance.

Among the most basic of governmental functions are the making of rules concerning the relations of individuals to each other and to organized society and the providing of tribunals through which controversies may be settled in accordance with those rules. The rule-making function, involving as it does the enactment of civil and criminal law, is for the most part a responsibility of the states. On the other hand, in providing judicial tribunals and administrative agencies for enforcing state law, heavy reliance is had upon the counties, townships, and other units of local government. It is the purpose of the present chapter to examine the nature and work of the local courts in rural areas. In the following chapter attention will be given to administrative agencies and problems in the field of law enforcement.

THE JUDICIAL FUNCTION

The judicial function consists, in essence, of the hearing and deciding of legal controversies. Courts, local and otherwise, are designed as forums for the peaceful settlement, according to legal rules, of disputes arising among individuals and groups or between individuals or groups and the government. In a typical judicial proceeding the court must, first, determine the facts of the case; second, determine the relevant rules of law; and, finally, apply the law to the facts as a means of arriving at a decision or judgment. The controversies, or cases, which the courts are called upon to adjudicate in the course of their work fall into two general classes: civil and criminal.

CIVIL AND CRIMINAL CASES

A civil case is usually concerned with a dispute between private parties regarding their respective legal rights and duties. The party who institutes the suit is know as the plaintiff, and the party against whom the action is brought as the defendant. Civil suits, like civil law, are concerned with such matters as property rights, contracts, torts, and domestic relations.[1] Frequently, they are instituted in an effort to recover damages arising from breach of contract or from unlawful injury to the plaintiff's person or property. Thus, a person who has been struck by an automobile and injured, one who believes that his reputation has been impaired by slanderous statements, or one whose property has been subjected to trespass may institute a civil suit for damages. Again, civil action may be brought to collect unpaid rent, overdue grocery bills, or money due on a promissory note. The fact that the plaintiff in a civil case is successful in securing a judgment does not in itself make certain that he will actually obtain his money from the defendant, since the government in no way guarantees the payment of a civil judgment. However, certain law-enforcement officers attached to the courts—marshals, sheriffs, and constables—will give a successful plaintiff all possible assistance in his efforts to collect by such means as levy of execution upon the defendant's property or garnishment of his salary or wages.

It is to be noted that, in most instances, the government itself is not a party to civil cases but is concerned only with providing the judicial machinery through which persons who have suffered wrongs may secure appropriate redress. This is not to say, however, that governmental units are never parties to civil suits. Though the states, as an attribute of their sovereignty, may not be made defendants in their own courts except by their own consent, they may, as plaintiffs, institute civil actions. Furthermore, many states now make provision by law for permitting suits against themselves under some circumstances, either in the regular trial courts or in special courts of claims. Permission thus granted most commonly relates to cases based upon contract, but in some instances it applies to tort claims also. Some units of local government, notably counties and townships, are considered to be mere administrative subdivisions of the state and therefore partake of the state's immunity from suit. However, most

[1] Concerning the nature of tort, see above, chap. 3, n. 60.

states have now enacted general laws authorizing such units to sue in the regular courts and making them liable to suit. Cities, as municipal corporations, may sue and be sued in the same manner as natural persons and private corporations. In any event, the government, as a party to a civil suit, plays a role distinctly different from its function in a criminal case.

Criminal cases involve alleged infractions of the criminal law—that body of law which defines crimes and penalizes their commission. A crime, in turn, is any antisocial act which the legislative body has considered sufficiently dangerous to the public peace and safety to justify its prohibition and punishment. Crimes range all the way from minor misdemeanors (such as violations of traffic regulations or local health ordinances), through major felonies (such as robbery and homicide), to treason, which is the most serious offense against the state. It is the function of the court, in a criminal case, to determine whether the accused person actually committed the crime with which he is charged and, if his guilt is established, to impose an appropriate penalty as provided by law. In criminal cases, in contrast to those of a civil nature, the government not only provides judicial tribunals for their determination but is itself the prosecuting party corresponding to the plaintiff in civil suits. All criminal actions, even those in the minor courts, are instituted in the name of the state or the people against the suspected person as defendant. Such actions are usually instituted by the local prosecuting attorney, though occasionally they are begun by the attorney general or, when involving violations of municipal ordinances, by the city attorney. Most local courts exercise jurisdiction in both civil and criminal matters.

LOCAL COURTS IN THE STATE JUDICIAL SYSTEM

Strictly speaking, all nonfederal courts are component parts of the judicial systems of the respective states. Like agencies of local government generally, the so-called local courts are created by state law or under state authority and derive their powers from the state. To a greater extent than most local organs, however, the courts are closely associated with the state in other ways; and it is doubtless for this reason that even those of the lowest order are usually considered as being, in the eyes of the law, state tribunals. Though most local judges are popularly elected, state appointment is more common than in the case of nonjudicial offices. Although many court cases involve locally enacted ordinances, the great bulk of judicial business in all but the most minor of courts ordinarily concerns the application of state statutes and the common law of the states. Some local judges are paid wholly or in part from the state treasury. And, finally, judgments of local courts are usually subject to review, on appeal, by tribunals operating at the state level.

Despite their legal classification as state tribunals, however, the lower courts function in many respects as integral parts of the local government machinery. Most local judges are locally elected and are considered by those who choose them to be local officers; and their compensation is usually paid wholly or in part from local funds. The jurisdiction of the local courts is limited geographically to a prescribed local area, normally a township, city, or county. And, in addition to their regular judicial functions, these courts are frequently charged with duties of a local administrative nature, such as the appointment of certain local officers and the participation in various ways in election administration. As indicated in earlier chapters, there are several states in which local judges serve as members of the governing bodies charged with general management of county affairs, and others where justices of the peace are members of township governing boards.[2] In view of these various factors, it is clear that any discussion of local government organization which omitted a consideration of the local courts would be incomplete and unsatisfactory.

Judicial organization at the local level is quite lacking in uniformity among the states. However, two principal grades of local tribunals, under varying official names, are almost universal: (1) courts of general trial jurisdiction, manned by elective or appointive judges; and (2) courts of minor jurisdiction, presided over in most instances by elective justices of the peace. Several states provide for courts of additional kinds in some or all counties. Certain counties, for example, have tribunals of intermediate jurisdiction between the general trial and justices' courts, and some have special probate courts. In some urban areas justices of the peace have been supplemented or supplanted, as tribunals of minor jurisdiction, by police magistrates or special municipal courts; and in a few states, as will appear presently, justice-of-the-peace courts have been wholly or partially superseded by modernized systems of minor tribunals.[3]

GENERAL TRIAL COURTS[4]

Each state has a principal trial court or set of courts vested with broad jurisdiction over civil and criminal cases. In most instances these tribunals are known as circuit, district, or superior courts, though the title in Ohio and Pennsylvania is court of common pleas,[5] and in New York the trial

[2] See above, chap. 5, "Types of Governing Bodies"; chap. 9, "Township Boards."

[3] See below, "Alternatives to Justice-of-the-peace System."

[4] The discussion in this section is based in large part upon data presented in Council of State Governments, *Trial Courts of General Jurisdiction in the Forty-eight States* (Chicago, 1951). This excellent report of the council to the Conference of Chief Justices is a comprehensive analysis of the structure, jurisdiction, functions, and management of the trial courts.

[5] In Pennsylvania the common-pleas courts have civil jurisdiction only, but their judges also serve the trial courts of criminal jurisdiction.

tribunal is known as the supreme court.[6] In a few instances a single trial court of general jurisdiction serves the entire state, but more commonly the state is divided into judicial districts with one or more courts in each. Some half-dozen states provide that each county shall constitute a judicial district. More commonly, however, only the more populous counties constitute separate districts, with districts in rural areas comprising two or more counties each. Where a district includes more than a single county it is usually required by law that court sessions be held in each county at least annually. The general trial court is typically a one-judge court, as contrasted with state appellate courts, which ordinarily consist in each instance of a "bench" of judges. When, as is not uncommonly the case, a judicial district is provided with more than one trial judge, as many court sessions as there are judges may be held concurrently, in different courtrooms or at various places within the district.

Trial-court judges were reported, as of 1951, to be chosen by popular election in 38 states, elected by the legislature in four, and appointed by the governor, with the consent of the senate or the executive council, in six.[7] In a majority of the popular-election states, choice is by partisan ballot, with nominations being made by party primary or, in a few instances, by party convention. More than a dozen states, however, provide for nomination by nonpartisan primary or petition and election by nonpartisan ballot. Some additional states, from among those that retain the party ballot, seek to reduce partisan influence in the choice of judges by holding judicial elections at different times from those for the choice of other state and local officials. In three states where judges are appointed by the governor their tenure is for life (Massachusetts and Rhode Island) or to the age of seventy (New Hampshire). A fourth state that uses appointment—New Jersey—provides that initial appointments shall be for seven years but reappointments for life. Elsewhere, the judicial term varies from two years in Vermont to fifteen in Maryland, with terms of four or six years most common.

The jurisdiction of the general trial courts is extremely broad, but in many instances it is subject to some limitations. Although the jurisdiction of the typical court is subject to no maximum limits, extending to the most serious criminal cases and to civil cases involving the largest of amounts, limitations on the minimum side are quite common. Many courts are denied jurisdiction over civil controversies involving less than a specified

[6] The highest court in New York state is called the court of appeals.

[7] *Trial Courts of General Jurisdiction in the Forty-eight States*, pp. 26-29. The states with legislative election were Connecticut, South Carolina, Vermont, and Virginia; those with gubernatorial appointment were Delaware, Maine, Massachusetts, New Hampshire, New Jersey, and Rhode Island. Special methods of appointment were used also in three districts in popular-election states—one in Alabama and two in Missouri (*ibid.*, pp. 30-31).

sum, frequently $50 or $100; and some or all misdemeanors are often excluded from their criminal jurisdiction. Some states vest probate jurisdiction in special courts,[8] and a few have separate chancery courts for the trial of equity cases.[9] In addition to possessing broad original jurisdiction in civil and criminal matters, general trial courts are ordinarily empowered to hear appeals from justices of the peace and other inferior tribunals. Many such courts are also authorized to review, on appeal, the actions of certain administrative agencies.[10]

Notwithstanding that their jurisdiction may be subject to some limitations, the general trial courts constitute the very core of the state judicial system. Civil and criminal cases, exclusive of those distinctly minor in nature, are begun in those courts, and the great majority of such cases are finally determined there. Though appeal from trial-court judgments to higher state courts is permitted, the right of appeal is exercised in relatively few cases. Indeed, it has been estimated that 95 per cent of all cases heard by the trial courts probably end in the same tribunals.[11] Thus, these courts of broad original jurisdiction tend in practice to become also courts of last resort. In addition, since most major lawsuits begin and end there, they are the tribunals from which many Americans gain their concepts of courts and justice generally.

In view of these facts, it would be difficult to overemphasize the significance of the general trial courts in the over-all judicial system and the urgency of having them manned by honest and competent judges. The importance of the trial judge's position and the heavy responsibilities of his office have been admirably summarized by Justice Frank Hollingsworth of the supreme court of Missouri, himself formerly the judge of a trial court, in the following words: [12]

[8] See below, "Probate Courts."

[9] Equity developed in England, and later in America, as a body of jurisprudence supplementary to the common law. The most widely used form of equitable relief is the restraining order known as an injunction. Whereas the common law attempts only to provide reparation for a wrong after it has been committed, equity, by use of the injunction, seeks to prevent the commission of threatened wrongs in cases where the common-law remedy would be inadequate. Equity and common law were originally administered by two separate and distinct sets of courts, and this practice still continues in a few American states, notably Arkansas, Delaware, Mississippi, and Tennessee. Certain other states administer the two forms of jurisprudence through a single set of courts but preserve the distinction between law cases and equity cases. In a majority of the states today, however, even the distinction between law and equity cases has been abandoned, and both legal and equitable rules are administered by the same courts under uniform procedure. For a discussion of equity and its administration, see Clarence N. Callender, *American Courts: Their Organization and Procedure* (New York, McGraw-Hill, 1927), chap. 10.

[10] *Trial Courts of General Jurisdiction in the Forty-eight States,* p. 60.

[11] Jerome Frank, *Courts on Trial: Myth and Reality in American Justice* (Princeton, N. J., Princeton University Press, 1949), p. 33.

[12] Frank Hollingsworth, "That Beleaguered Gentleman: The Trial Judge," *Journal of the Missouri Bar,* Vol. VII, pp. 83-84, 83 (June, 1951).

> To the vast majority of the people he is the judiciary; the court of last resort. He is without question the keystone of the whole judicial edifice, the most important official in the entire judicial system. . . .
>
> To the people, the judge of the circuit court is the personification of all courts. To the extent that they respect him as a man; to the extent that they have confidence in his ability and integrity; to the extent that he metes out justice to those who appear before him; to that extent do they respect and repose confidence in all courts.
>
> The power he wields is almost beyond comprehension; and the responsibility of that power rests heavily on the shoulders of the judge who undertakes to perform his duties with a vision of justice before him as his pole-star.

Though they try many cases without juries, it is the general trial courts which make most extensive use of the jury as a fact-determining agency in both civil and criminal cases. It is therefore appropriate at this point, before proceeding to a discussion of other local courts, to give some attention to the trial jury.

THE TRIAL JURY

The jury here under consideration is the petit or trial jury, as distinguished from the grand jury, which is discussed in the following chapter. Whereas the grand jury is concerned solely with enforcement of the criminal law, the petit jury is widely used in connection with both civil and criminal cases. Practically all state constitutions contain broad guarantees of the right to jury trial. Though lesser cases are sometimes excluded from these guarantees, and in many other cases, particularly among those of a civil nature, jury trial is voluntarily waived by the parties involved, the trial jury nevertheless plays an important role in present-day judicial administration. This is the body which, on the basis of the evidence presented at the trial, the arguments of counsel, and the instructions of the court concerning the law involved, decides, in a criminal case, whether the accused is guilty of the offense charged, and, in a civil action, whether judgment should be awarded to the plaintiff or to the defendant. At common law the trial jury consisted of 12 persons. Today, many states provide for the trial of misdemeanors and of some or all civil cases by juries of less than 12 members.[13] The jury of 12, however, is still almost universally required in the trial of major crimes and is widely used in other cases as well.[14]

[13] Francis X. Busch, *Law and Tactics in Jury Trials* (Indianapolis, Ind., Bobbs-Merrill, 1949), p. 29.

[14] Many states now permit the drawing of one or more "alternate" jurors in addition to the regular panel. Alternate jurors hear the evidence and arguments along with the regular jurors and are available to replace any of the latter who may die or become disabled or otherwise disqualified during the course of the trial. The use of alternate jurors is desirable, particularly in long-protracted cases, as a means of avoiding mistrials and the expense and inconvenience which new trials involve. Cf. *ibid.*, pp. 30-31.

Legal Qualifications of Jurors. Constitutions or statutes in the various states prescribe qualifications for jury service. There is usually a lower age limit of twenty-one or twenty-five, and sometimes an upper limit of sixty-five or seventy. Citizenship or eligibility to vote is frequently required; residence qualifications are common; and there is sometimes a property-ownership requirement or taxpaying test.[15] With respect to other qualifications, the Illinois law may be taken as fairly typical. It prescribes that jurors shall be "in the possession of their natural faculties and not infirm or decrepit. . . . Free from all legal exceptions, of fair character, of approved integrity, of sound judgment, well informed, and [individuals] who understand the English language." There is usually a lengthy list of statutory exemptions covering especially professional people and public officers. Among the classes thus commonly exempted are clergymen, lawyers, physicians, school teachers, state and local officers, policemen, and firemen. Formerly, juries were constituted exclusively of men. During recent years, however, most states have modified their constitutional and statutory provisions to permit jury service by women, some merely making women *eligible* for jury duty but providing that they shall be excused upon request, and others imposing the same *liability* for service upon women as upon men.[16]

Selection. The first step in the selection of a jury is the preparation of a list of names from which a panel may be drawn. The duty of preparing this list is placed, in different states, upon the county board, certain town officers, jury commissioners appointed by the courts, or other designated officers. In most states names for the jury list are taken from either the local assessment rolls or voters' registration lists, though some jurisdictions make use of city directories, telephone directories, and census reports. From the list so prepared, names to the number prescribed by law are chosen, usually more or less at random, and placed in the jury box. When a new panel of jurors is needed, the court clerk draws a designated number of names from the box, and the persons so chosen are summoned to appear for service. The summoning of jurors has traditionally been a function of the sheriff, and is today in most states. In a few jurisdictions, however, summons is now made by registered mail, a practice which seems to be more efficient than the older method and also, since sheriff's fees are eliminated, more economical. When a particular case is called, the plan usually followed is to place in a box the names of all jurors present and not engaged and to draw therefrom, for presentation to the parties for

[15] For an analysis of jurors' qualifications in the respective states, see *ibid.*, pp. 86-88.

[16] Lists of states having voluntary and compulsory types of laws, respectively, may be found in Alice K. Leopold, "The Legal Status of Women," *The Book of the States: 1956-57* (Chicago, Council of State Governments, 1956), pp. 341-346.

examination and challenge, as many names as there are to be jury members. Each party ordinarily is entitled to a specified number of *peremptory* challenges—that is, challenges without cause stated—and an unlimited number of challenges *for cause,* such as bias or relationship to parties involved. Prospective jurors are examined and challenges made by the attorneys of the respective parties, the prosecuting attorney performing these functions on behalf of the state in criminal actions. When a prospective juror is dismissed on challenge another name is drawn, and this process continues until a jury has been obtained which is acceptable to both parties.[17]

Jury Personnel. The personnel of trial juries has long been the object of widespread criticism. We are told that the persons best qualified for jury duty by education, experience, and temperament usually avoid service by one means or another and that as a result, the qualifications of those who comprise our juries are, on the average, considerably below desirable standards. In some measure, this criticism appears to be justified. The required legal qualifications, mentioned above, are certainly not such as to assure the selection of *competent* jurors. Furthermore, the exemption of professional groups relieves many persons, otherwise well qualified, of any legal obligation to accept service. In some jurisdictions the practice is followed of omitting the names of exempt persons, insofar as they can readily be ascertained, from the original jury lists; and, in any event, such persons, if their names are drawn, are entitled as a matter of legal right to be excused from service when they so request. If the exempt categories were narrowed, many qualified persons could be added to those liable for jury duty and still be excused by the trial judge, as indeed can persons now subject to call, upon a showing that service would work an unreasonable hardship upon them personally or upon their employers or clients.

In addition to those in exempt classes, many qualified persons are probably lost to jury service today through undue leniency on the part of some trial judges in excusing nonexempt persons. Where service would involve genuine hardship, excuse, of course, is justified and desirable. All too many persons, however, when their names are drawn, hasten to seek excuse on any plausible pretext because they shrink from assuming the responsibilities which the office of juror involves or because they dislike to leave their private business or profession for the time required. This attitude on the part of large numbers of citizens cannot fail to weaken the functioning of the jury system. Confronted with one prospective juror who is well qualified but desires excuse, and another who, though less qualified, is willing or even eager to serve, perhaps primarily for the per diem com-

[17] This paragraph is based principally upon J. A. C. Grant, "Methods of Jury Selection," *American Political Science Review*, Vol. XXIV, pp. 117-133 (February, 1930).

pensation allowed, it is asking a great deal of a trial judge to expect him to displease both by requiring service of the one and denying it to the other.

The admission of women to jury service seems clearly to have raised somewhat the level of jury personnel. A narrowing of legal exemptions and less leniency on the part of trial judges in the granting of excuses are avenues through which further improvement might well be attained. But the ultimate solution to the problem of securing competent jurors very likely must be sought in a greater readiness on the part of citizens generally to accept and perform jury duty. If the jury is to be retained as a basic feature of our judicial system, it is certainly not demanding too much of any citizen to ask that he be prepared, except in cases of genuine and extraordinary hardship, to accept jury duty once or twice in a lifetime, even at the cost of some personal discomfort and financial sacrifice.

The Unanimous Verdict. Apart from the matter of personnel, criticism of the jury system is perhaps most commonly directed at the requirement of a unanimous verdict. The unanimity requirement is an application of the common-law rule that in either a civil or a criminal action, except in some of the most petty cases, a valid verdict must be agreed to by every member of the jury.[18] Failure to secure unanimous agreement results in a "hung" jury and a mistrial, with the consequence that the case must be dropped or its trial begun anew.

Today, about half of the states have modified the common-law rule to permit verdicts by less than a unanimous vote in civil cases, and a few have taken similar action with respect to the trial of lesser crimes. Where the unanimity rule has thus been abandoned, the vote required is most commonly five sixths or three fourths of the jurors, but in occasional instances it is only two thirds. Notwithstanding these modifications, the unanimity requirement remains the general rule in criminal proceedings. Apparently capital offenses are never excepted from the requirement, other felonies are rarely excepted, and in all but some half-dozen states the requirement applies to every crime, whether felony or misdemeanor.[19]

From a numerical standpoint, in the typical criminal case with a jury of 12, the requirement that the verdict be returned by unanimous vote makes it 12 times as difficult to secure as to prevent a conviction. In order to secure a verdict of guilty, the prosecutor must convince *every* member of the jury, beyond reasonable doubt, of the defendant's guilt; whereas the defense attorney may "hang" the jury by convincing a *single member* that there is reasonable doubt of guilt. Few would disagree with

[18] Cf. Busch, *op. cit.*, p. 33.

[19] "Five-sixths Jury Verdicts: New York Legislation of 1937," *Columbia Law Review*, Vol. XXXVII, pp. 1235-1238 (November, 1937); Glenn R. Winters, "Majority Verdicts in the United States," *Law Society Journal*, Vol. X, pp. 380-387 (November, 1942); Busch, *op. cit.*, pp. 34-35.

the principle of Anglo-American law that an accused person is to be presumed innocent until his guilt has been demonstrated and that the burden of proving guilt is upon the state. Nevertheless, the question is well raised as to whether the unanimity requirement does not place the prosecution under an *undue* handicap. Many students of criminal law enforcement are coming to believe that all reasonable rights of a defendant might be adequately safeguarded and, at the same time, the interests of society more fully protected, by permitting the return of a verdict, except perhaps in the case of capital offenses, by something less than a unanimous vote. The American Law Institute, in its model code of criminal procedure, has proposed that while retaining the unanimity requirement in capital cases, a verdict be permitted by five-sixths vote in other felony cases and by two-thirds vote in misdemeanor cases. Some such modification of the requirement is certainly deserving of serious consideration in the interest of fair and effective judicial administration.[20]

SPECIAL COUNTY COURTS

Several states, in addition to general trial courts and justices of the peace, provide for special courts of one kind or another in some or all counties. The title of these tribunals is not uniform, but that of county court is fairly common; and, like other local courts, they are ordinarily presided over by elective judges. Their powers and duties vary widely but usually include original jurisdiction in civil and criminal matters which, though much less extensive than that of the general trial courts, is substantially broader than that of justices of the peace. In addition to their original jurisdiction, they frequently have authority, concurrent with that of the general trial courts, to hear appeals from justices of the peace and other minor magistrates. Some such courts are vested with jurisdiction over equity or probate matters, or both; and in a number of instances they are charged with certain administrative duties in connection with the county government. In some states these county courts may be considered as constituting, for all practical purposes, a third level in the local judicial hierarchy, midway between the general trial courts and the justices of the peace.

Reasonably typical of the courts of this nature are the county courts of Illinois, found in every county of the state and presided over in each instance by a county judge chosen by popular election for a four-year term. These tribunals have jurisdiction, concurrent with that of the circuit (general trial) courts, over criminal cases where the punishment involved is not death or imprisonment in the penitentiary; certain civil cases where

[20] For further criticisms of the jury system and suggestions for its improvement, see Frank, *op. cit.*, chaps. 8, 9; Julius H. Miner, "The Jury Problem," *Journal of Criminal Law and Criminology*, Vol. XXXVII, pp. 1-15 (May-June, 1946).

the amount in controversy does not exceed $2,000; and appeals from justices of the peace and police magistrates. Assigned to their special purview are certain types of civil proceedings, such as those for the collection of taxes and special assessments. The county courts serve also as probate courts, except in those more populous counties of the state which have been provided with separate probate courts of the kind discussed in the following section. Other states having county courts somewhat similar in nature to those in Illinois, though with varied organization and jurisdiction, include Colorado, Mississippi, Nebraska, North Dakota, Oklahoma, South Dakota, and Wisconsin.

PROBATE COURTS

An important task of American courts, in large part administrative rather than strictly judicial in nature, is the supervising of the management and disposition of the estates of deceased persons. This probate function, as it is called, is performed in some states by the courts of general trial jurisdiction, in others by special county courts of the kind described in the preceding section, and in a few by chancery courts. In a considerable number of states, however, probate jurisdiction in some or all counties is vested in separate tribunals. Usually manned by elected judges, these are most frequently known as probate courts, though in a few states they are called surrogate courts or orphans' courts, and in Georgia they are known as courts of ordinary. Most probate courts have jurisdiction throughout a county, but in some instances in New England jurisdiction is confined to smaller districts. In Vermont, for example, some counties are divided into probate districts with a court in each; and probate judges in Connecticut serve small districts composed of one or more towns. In Rhode Island each town constitutes a probate district, with probate jurisdiction exercised by the town council or by a probate judge appointed by the council.[21]

In legal parlance a deceased person is known as a *decedent* and a will as a *last will and testament.* A decedent who leaves a will is said to have died *testate;* one who does not leave a will has died *intestate.* When a decedent dies testate, the will is presented to the court to be probated. If the instrument is found to be authentic and to meet all statutory requirements for validity, it is admitted to probate and *letters testamentary* are issued to an *executor* charged with carrying out its provisions. Usually the person who is to act as executor is designated in the will itself. In the case of a person dying intestate, an *administrator* is appointed by the court, and *letters of administration* are issued, directing that the estate be distributed in accordance with the inheritance laws of the state. Executors and administrators perform their duties under close supervision by the

[21] Cf. Callender, *op. cit.*, chap. 11, app.

court, rendering accounts and reports as directed. At the proper time, the court will order that distribution of funds or property be made to the heirs; and, when final distribution has been completed, the executor or administrator is discharged.

Though the chief function of probate courts is to probate wills and supervise the management and settlement of estates of decedents, they have been given some other duties. Usually they have control over the estates of minors and other persons, such as the insane, who are under special protection of the law. Adoption proceedings in a number of states take place in the probate courts, and in some instances the tribunals are vested with limited jurisdiction over civil and criminal cases.[22]

JUSTICES OF THE PEACE

Number and Selection. The lowest rung in the judicial ladder throughout most of rural America is the court of the justice of the peace. Though appointed by the governor in a few states, justices, in most instances, are chosen by popular election. The election district is usually the township or some other subdivision of the county; and the term of office, in most cases, is either two or four years. The number of justices to be chosen in each district is fixed by state constitutional or statutory provision or by the county board under statutory authority. This number, which may be uniform for all districts or vary with population, ranges from one to five or more. Often, however, there are actually fewer justices in a particular district than provided for by law. This may result either from a dearth of candidates for the office or from the failure of persons elected, many of them merely by "write-in" votes, to qualify by taking the necessary oath and filing bond. In Minnesota, for example, though the statutes provide for two justices in each township, city, and village, in a large percentage of the townships and municipalities no election takes place, and, of the justices elected, many fail to qualify. Thus, in 1947, according to reasonably reliable statistics, of a potential 3,571 justices in 56 of the state's 87 counties, only 690, or less than 20 per cent, had qualified.[23] And in Indiana, where it is possible under the statutes for as many as 3,000 justices to hold office, it was estimated in 1942 that the number actually serving was approximately 450.[24] Notwithstanding a provision of the Indiana constitution to the effect that "a competent number" of justices shall be elected in each township, these data indicate that more than half of the state's 1,010 townships were in fact without justices at that time.

[22] Cf. *Bouvier's Law Dictionary,* Rawle's 3d rev. (St. Paul, Minn., West, 1914), Vol. I, p. 712.

[23] Forrest Talbott, *Intergovernmental Relations and the Courts* (Minneapolis, University of Minnesota Press, 1950), p. 61.

[24] Gail M. Morris, *Justice of the Peace Courts in Indiana* (Bloomington, Indiana University Bureau of Government Research, 1942), p. 15.

Though justices of the peace are elected from smaller areas, their courts ordinarily possess jurisdiction throughout the county.[25]

Judicial Functions. The judicial functions of the justice of the peace fall into three categories. In the first place, he tries civil cases wherein the amount involved does not exceed a fixed sum. This maximum varies considerably from state to state but is commonly $100, $200, or $300. Though some of the civil actions in justice-of-the-peace courts arise out of torts, the majority of such suits are based upon contracts, express or implied. Common examples are actions seeking to collect unpaid bills or rents or to secure judgment on promissory notes.[26] In the second place, the justice tries minor criminal cases. The fines and jail sentences which he may impose are strictly limited by the constitution or by statute; and it is not within his competence to impose a penitentiary sentence. The criminal offenses most commonly tried by justices' courts are breaches of the peace, traffic-law violations, infractions of health regulations, and violations of local ordinances.[27] In either a civil or a criminal case appeal from the decision of a justice of the peace may ordinarily be taken to a local court of intermediate or general trial jurisdiction.[28] Finally, as a "committing magistrate," a justice may hold preliminary hearings in cases involving serious crimes. The purpose of such a hearing is not to determine the guilt or innocence of the suspected person but merely to decide whether there is sufficient evidence against him to justify his being held for further action. If a justice, as the result of a preliminary hearing, finds that the evidence against the suspected person is substantial, it is his duty to hold the suspect, pending action by the grand jury or the filing of an information by the prosecuting attorney. This he may do by requiring the suspected person to give bond for his appearance or, if the required bond cannot be furnished or the offense is nonbailable, by committing him to jail.[29]

Nonjudicial Functions. In addition to their judicial functions, justices of the peace are usually vested with certain powers or duties of a nonjudicial nature. One of these is the performance of the marriage ceremony, and the term *marrying justice* bears witness to the well-known fact that some

[25] There are some exceptions to this general rule. In Indiana, for example, though their jurisdiction in criminal matters is coextensive with the county, the civil jurisdiction of justices' courts is usually confined to their respective townships.

[26] See Callender, *op. cit.*, pp. 52-55.

[27] *Ibid.*, pp. 50-51. In rural Minnesota, violations of the fish and game code constitute a considerable portion of the criminal cases in justices' courts; see Talbott, *op. cit.*, p. 65.

[28] When appeal is taken, the higher tribunal does not act, strictly speaking, as an appellate court, but tries the case *de novo*, that is, without reference to the earlier proceeding before the justice. Though jury trial may be demanded in cases before justices of the peace, in practice juries are used in such tribunals only occasionally.

[29] Cf. Callender, *op. cit.*, p. 51. Grand jury indictment and the prosecutor's information are discussed in the following chapter.

magistrates specialize in this function. Justices may also administer oaths and take acknowledgments. In the townships of Illinois, Michigan, Nebraska, and the second-class townships in New York, some or all of the justices are members of the township board; in Kentucky and Tennessee justices in most counties are members of the county governing board, and in Arkansas they are members of the county fiscal body. Where election as justice of the peace carries with it membership on the county or township board, the office is sometimes sought for that reason by persons who may have no intention of serving in a judicial capacity. In Illinois, justices in the latter category are sometimes referred to in popular parlance as "nonpracticing" and thus distinguished from the practicing justices who try cases.

WEAKNESSES OF JUSTICE-OF-THE-PEACE SYSTEM

During recent years, the institution of the justice of the peace has been widely criticized. Of English origin, the office was established in the American colonies and early states in a rural society at a time when laws were relatively few and simple and when primitive facilities for transportation and communication made it desirable that some means of administering homespun justice be made available within a few miles of every citizen. As the country developed, the office came to be regarded as a normal part of the judicial system, being required by constitutional provision in most states. With the passing of time, however, an agricultural society changed into one which at many points was highly industrialized; social relations and the laws governing those relations became numerous and complex; and transportation progressed to a point where the county courthouse was more readily accessible to the average litigant than had been the residence of a neighboring justice a few decades earlier. Because of these facts, it is now widely believed that the justice-of-the-peace court in its traditional form has outlived its usefulness.

Personnel and Court Facilities. For one thing, it is clear that our present-day law, with its manifold technicalities, cannot be properly administered by laymen. Yet justices of the peace ordinarily are not required to have, and the great majority of them do not have, any legal training.[30] Two principal reasons account for the fact that justices are rarely lawyers. In the first place, lawyers usually reside and practice in the county seat or other municipalities of fairly substantial size, and there-

[30] Not only are most justices lacking in legal training, but their formal education of a general nature frequently is relatively meager. A 1942 study revealed that of 297 Pennsylvania justices responding to a questionnaire, 47 per cent had received only an elementary school education or less; only 19 per cent had attended college; and less than 15 per cent were college graduates—Pennsylvania Bar Association, Committee on Minor Judiciary, *Survey of the Minor Judiciary in Pennsylvania* (State College, Pennsylvania Municipal Publications Service, 1942), p. 83.

fore large numbers of rural townships have no lawyers resident therein. Secondly, most lawyers who are professionally active are not anxious to neglect their private practice for performance of the duties devolving upon a justice, and for that reason they do not desire or seek the office. The relatively few instances in which the office of justice is held by a lawyer are found, for the most part, in urban areas, and the incumbent is usually either a recent law-school graduate seeking experience or an older member of the bar who, for one reason or another, is not active in practice. Not only are most justices of the peace completely without legal training, but most of them hear so few cases that they gain no more than meager experience even in the dispensing of lay justice. In Illinois, for example, it has been estimated that, of some 2,800 justices in the state, only about 400 handled as many as 25 cases, or an average of two cases per month, during 1951.[31]

To serve properly the judicial needs of a community, a local tribunal not only must be manned by a competent magistrate but must be provided with appropriate facilities in the way of courtroom, law books, and clerical assistance. In commenting upon the inadequacy of the township as a unit for judicial administration, Professor Edson Sunderland, of the University of Michigan Law School, has said: [32]

> A satisfactory court should be open at convenient hours and at sufficiently frequent intervals to make it reasonably accessible to all persons having business to transact with it. It should be held in a courtroom reasonably well arranged for the purpose, and supplied with at least a few fundamental law books, and suitable facilities for making and keeping records. The office should carry a sufficient stipend to be attractive, and the judge should devote enough time to his judicial duties to acquire the skill and judgment which experience alone can give.
>
> None of these requirements can be met in an ordinary rural township.

Though some justices are provided with courtrooms in the county courthouse or in a town or village hall, many must hold court in their homes or at their private offices or places of business. The "law library" available to the justice often consists solely of a copy of the revised statutes of the state—and that at times of an outdated edition. Of 61 Minnesota justices replying to a questionnaire in the late 1940's, 30 reported that they had access, in the way of law books, to the statutes only or to nothing at all.[33] Official records, with respect to justices' courts, are frequently scanty and

[31] Tom Page, "Local Judicial Activity," *Local Government Notes,* publication of the University of Illinois Extension Service in Agriculture and Home Economics, No. 35 (September 2, 1952).

[32] Edson R. Sunderland, "A Study of Justices of the Peace and Other Minor Courts —Requisites for an Adequate State-wide Minor Court System," *Fifteenth Annual Report of the Judicial Council of Michigan* (Lansing, Mich., 1945), Pt. 2, p. 71.

[33] Talbott, *op. cit.,* p. 67.

inaccurate, if not completely nonexistent. Concerning this, Professor Sunderland writes:[34]

> The amount of judicial business done by individual justices of the peace has usually been too small to warrant the employment of a clerk to keep the records and transact the clerical work of the court. The justice has ordinarily been his own clerk. The results have been unsatisfactory. Lay justices, chiefly concerned with other businesses in which they have been chiefly engaged, have had neither the knowledge, skill, experience nor facilities to keep adequate and convenient records. Justices' dockets are frequently defective and incomplete in both form and substance, and are often temporarily misplaced or completely lost.

Also frequently wanting in completeness and accuracy are the justices' accounts of money collected from litigants as costs, fees, fines, or bail, and the disposition of such funds.[35]

Fee Compensation. Even more serious, perhaps, than the justices' lack of legal training and the inadequacy of their facilities and records are the evils arising from the fee system of compensation. Although there are some exceptions, particularly in urban areas, the large majority of justices are paid no salary but receive as compensation fees assessed as a part of the "costs" in the cases brought before them. It is therefore incumbent upon a justice, if he desires to derive any income from his "judgeship," to conduct his office in a manner that will attract business to his court. In a civil case, the plaintiff is usually free to bring his action before any of several justices within the county. The justice who is fortunate enough to be the one chosen, in gratitude for this piece of business and in the hope of securing other cases in the future, will likely be disposed to decide the case in the plaintiff's favor. Indeed, civil cases in justices' courts are so generally decided in the plaintiff's favor that it has been said facetiously that "J.P." (the usual abbreviation for justice of the peace) means "judgment for the plaintiff."

A study of justice-of-the-peace courts in six Michigan counties revealed that of 933 civil cases disposed of, 926, or 99.2 per cent of the total, resulted in judgments for the plaintiff.[36] According to a survey in Tennessee, of 25,088 civil cases tried by 67 justices, judgment was given for the plaintiff in 24,663 cases, or 98.3 per cent of the total.[37] Although the very nature of civil cases brought before justices' courts would lead one to expect that a large proportion of them would be decided in the plaintiff's favor, even

[34] Sunderland, "A Study of Justices of the Peace and Other Minor Courts," *loc. cit.*, p. 109.

[35] *Ibid.*, p. 110.

[36] Edson R. Sunderland, "The Efficiency of Justices' Courts," in Arthur W. Bromage and Thomas H. Reed, *Organization and Cost of County and Township Government* (Detroit, Michigan Commission of Inquiry into County, Township and School District Government, 1933), pp. 142-146.

[37] T. L. Howard, "The Justice of the Peace System in Tennessee," *Tennessee Law Review*, Vol. XIII, pp. 19-38 (December, 1934).

by the most impartial tribunal, the percentages of plaintiff judgments revealed by such studies as these seem clearly to be excessive. Enlightening on this point are the results of a study in Indiana, where several of the more populous counties have salaried justices operating in urban areas. A survey of civil cases disposed of in that state revealed that in those counties which had some salaried justices, only 53.6 per cent of all such cases resulted in judgment for the plaintiff, whereas in counties having all justices on a fee basis judgment was given for the plaintiff in more than 79 per cent of the cases.[38] Like the percentage of plaintiff judgments in civil cases, the percentage of convictions in criminal cases in justice courts is extremely high. Insofar as it has been possible to determine from official records and local investigations, it appears that on the average, some 98 per cent of all traffic-violation cases tried before justices of the peace result in convictions.[39] Though this high frequency of conviction doubtless flows in part from the fact that the defendant in a traffic case is usually a stranger to the justice while the arresting officer is known to him and is a potential source of future business, another factor may well be a belief on the part of the justice, perhaps based upon past experience, that his fees would be more easily recovered from the defendant, who would be liable for costs in the event of conviction, than from the county, to which he would have to look for the fee payment in case of acquittal.[40]

With respect to criminal cases, another notorious evil of the justice-of-the peace system is that of the speed trap. A justice desiring to make his office profitable establishes himself along a main highway in or near a small village that imposes a ridiculously low speed limit. He then allies himself with one or more constables having ambitions similar to his own. The constable makes wholesale arrests of unwary motorists and prefers charges against them in the justice's court. The justice imposes a small fine and assesses costs sufficient to cover his own fee and that of the arresting constable. If the motorist appears to be a person of meager means, or if he protests vigorously enough, the "court" may remit the fine and require only the payment of costs, which will generally be in the neighborhood of $3.00 to $5.00. In any event, the victim, with some grumbling, will usually pay the amount demanded and be on his way rather than attempt to present a defense. Thus, the justice and the constable, through cooperative effort, are able to build up a lucrative business. Fortunate indeed is the motorist who travels widely and has not, at some time, fallen prey to the nefarious speed trap.[41]

Another evil growing out of the fee system of compensation is that of

[38] Morris, *op. cit.*, pp. 25-26.

[39] George Warren, *Traffic Courts* (Boston, Little, Brown, 1942), pp. 217-219.

[40] See below, p. 311.

[41] With regard to the speed-trap evil in Indiana, see Morris, *op. cit.*, pp. 17-18.

fee-splitting. According to this practice, justices competing for criminal cases may seek to attract business to their respective courts by offering to divide their own fees with constables or other arresting officers bringing cases before them. Though it is impossible to ascertain the extent of this pernicious and illegal practice, it certainly has existed in numerous instances, and there is reason to believe that it is relatively widespread.[42]

In civil suits the court costs, including justices' fees, ordinarily "follow the judgment" and become a charge on the losing party; and in criminal actions the costs are ordinarily assessed against the defendant in the event of conviction. On the other hand, if the defendant in a criminal case is acquitted or if, though convicted, he is unable to pay the costs, the fees of the trying justice, along with other cost items, usually become a public charge and are most commonly assessed against the county treasury. A few states, in regulating the fees of justices in criminal cases, provide that the justice shall be entitled to a fee only if he finds the defendant guilty. The United States Supreme Court, however, has held that such a provision with respect to a mayor's court is invalid as endangering judicial impartiality in violation of the due-process clause of the Fourteenth Amendment;[43] and it seems probable that provisions of this nature relating to justice-of-the-peace tribunals, if challenged in the federal courts, would be likewise declared unconstitutional. Even where justices' fees in cases of acquittal are legally a charge on the county treasury, county boards sometimes fail to make adequate appropriations for their payment. Such circumstances may still afford a strong incentive to a justice to make a finding of guilt where he believes that his fees would more readily be recoverable from a convicted defendant than from the county.[44]

After examining the weaknesses of the justice-of-the-peace system, one writer declares:[45]

> The justices of the peace as a class are wholly unqualified for the positions they occupy. The pernicious fee system and local politics break down their integrity

[42] For a discussion of alleged fee-splitting in one Tennessee county, see J. W. Manning, "In-justices of the Peace," *National Municipal Review*, Vol. XVIII, pp. 225-227 (April, 1929).

[43] Tumey *v.* Ohio, 273 U.S. 510 (1927).

[44] On the civil side, a pernicious practice sometimes encountered, and one which might well impair judicial impartiality, is that in which a justice of the peace operates a collection business and, if accounts turned over to him are not otherwise settled, files suit thereon in his own court. Such a situation, of course, places the justice in the position of representing the plaintiff and, at the same time, sitting as judge in the controversy. See Eugene Quay, "Justices of the Peace," *Illinois Bar Journal*, Vol. XXIII, p. 82 (November, 1934); Paul F. Douglass, *The Justice of the Peace Courts of Hamilton County, Ohio* (Baltimore, The Johns Hopkins University Press, 1932), pp. 38, 42.

[45] Chester H. Smith, "The Justice of the Peace System in the United States," *California Law Review*, Vol. XV, pp. 118-141, 140 (January, 1927).

and lead to corruption. They are often ignorant and wholly uncontrolled by statute or constitution. Their decisions are purely personal. The administration of justice by these lay magistrates is uncertain, unequal and unstable, and in truth, the system as such, is a denial of justice according to our highest conception of that term.

ALTERNATIVES TO JUSTICE-OF-THE-PEACE SYSTEM

In view of its many shortcomings, the justice-of-the-peace system today is thoroughly unsatisfactory as the foundational unit of state judicial organization. Many civic groups, crime commissions, and students of judicial administration have called for abolition of the system and its replacement by courts of minor jurisdiction organized along more modern lines.[46] What is needed is a system of minor courts county-wide in jurisdiction and presided over by salaried magistrates. Preferably, these magistrates should be appointed rather than elected and should be chosen from the legal profession. The number of magistrates should be small enough, and they should be so located geographically, that each would have sufficient business to justify his service on a full-time basis, the provision of a suitable courtroom and necessary law books, and the employment of a clerk to keep the court records. Fortunately, progress in the direction of reorganization has already begun. Several states during recent years have provided or authorized, in some or all counties, local tribunals embodying at least some of the features indicated as desirable.

Virginia's Trial Justices. Of the various states to act, Virginia led the way with the establishment of her *trial-justice* system. Early in the present century trial justices were provided in a few of the state's more populous counties, and a general law of 1934 established a trial-justice system for counties not covered by previous acts. Under the terms of the general statute, as subsequently amended, a full-time trial justice is appointed by the circuit judge in each county. The justice serves for a four-year term and is paid a regular salary by the state. Though they are not required to be lawyers, it appears that in practice most trial justices have been chosen from the legal profession. Each is authorized to appoint a clerk of his court, whose duty it is to keep the court docket and accounts and to perform whatever other duties may be prescribed by the justice. A single trial justice may be, and sometimes is, appointed to serve two or more counties.

The trial justice has original jurisdiction over violations of local ordinances and bylaws, as well as most other misdemeanors, and may hold preliminary hearings in more serious criminal cases. In the civil field, he has exclusive original jurisdiction over cases involving $200 or less, and con-

[46] Cf. W. F. Willoughby, *Principles of Judicial Administration* (Washington, Brookings Institution, 1929), chap. 22.

current jurisdiction with the circuit court where the amount involved is more than $200 but does not exceed $1,000. He is also judge of the juvenile and domestic relations courts of his county or counties. Justices of the peace are retained with authority to issue warrants and subpoenas and certain other forms of process, but they are deprived of jurisdiction to try civil or criminal cases.

The trial-justice system has now operated in Virginia, on a state-wide basis, for two decades, and apparently its results have been most gratifying. Lawyers of character and ability have generally been secured as justices, simple procedures have been retained, and costs of litigation have actually been less than under the former system.[47] A committee of that state's chamber of commerce has made the following observation: [48]

> Virginia has been widely commended for substituting the trial justice plan for justice of the peace administration. The pay of the justices of the peace had been derived from fees paid by the litigants and by the prosecuted, a method that cast doubt on the impartiality of the court's decisions. The justices were part-time and often untrained officials and frequently the full quota of justices was not filled. Under the present plan the trial justice pays all fees into the county and state treasuries and receives an annual salary as compensation. The positions are full-time and the men holding them are trained for the work.

In short, the new plan seems to have resulted in securing a much higher grade of court personnel than under the old justice-of-the-peace system and in more efficient judicial administration at lower cost.

Tennessee's General Sessions Courts. Beginning in 1937, the Tennessee legislature has enacted a number of special laws abolishing justice-of-the-peace courts in particular counties and creating in their stead general sessions courts of county-wide jurisdiction. Judges of these tribunals are popularly elected, usually for an eight-year term, and are paid regular salaries. In most instances the judge is required to be a lawyer and to give full time to his judicial duties. The clerk of the circuit court usually serves ex officio as clerk of the general sessions court. By the late 1940's general sessions courts had been established in 27 of the state's 95 counties. Where the new courts are provided, justices of the peace continue to be elected, retaining their authority to perform marriages and serve as members of the county governing body, but they are deprived of the power to hold trials.[49]

Missouri's Magistrate Courts. Missouri's new constitution of 1945 abolished the justice-of-the-peace system in that state and established in each county one or more magistrate courts with county-wide jurisdiction. In

[47] Arthur F. Kingdon, "The Trial Justice System of Virginia," *Journal of the American Judicature Society*, Vol. XXIII, pp. 216-221 (April, 1940).

[48] Virginia State Chamber of Commerce, *Opportunities for Economy in County Government in Virginia* (Richmond, 1947), p. 52.

[49] Henry N. Williams, "General Sessions Courts in Tennessee," *Journal of the American Judicature Society*, Vol. XXXI, pp. 101-104 (December, 1947).

counties of 30,000 inhabitants or less the probate judge serves ex officio as magistrate; more populous counties are provided with one or more magistrates elected as such. Counties which have more than a single magistrate are divided into districts, with one magistrate being elected from each district but having jurisdiction coextensive with the county.[50]

As of 1950, under constitutional provision and implementing legislation, the probate judge was serving as magistrate in 94 of the state's 114 counties, with each of the 20 larger counties having from one to six full-time magistrates. Though popularly elected, magistrates must be licensed to practice law. They serve a four-year term, receive a fixed salary, and are required to pay into the state treasury all fees collected. Magistrate courts have original jurisdiction concurrent with that of the circuit courts in misdemeanor cases. In civil matters they have jurisdiction over cases involving less than $500 in the smaller counties and less than $1,000 in larger counties.[51]

Though it is perhaps a bit early to attempt a definitive appraisal of the new system, it would appear that Missouri's magistrate courts are getting off to a good start. In over-all operation, the new courts seem to be distinctly superior to the old justice-of-the-peace tribunals. "That the magistrate courts have already demonstrated an improvement over the old justice of the peace courts," concluded Professor Martin Faust of the University of Missouri in 1950, "is very definitely the general consensus. Certainly no one wants to return to the old . . . system. The establishment of the magistrate courts is without doubt one of the outstanding reforms inaugurated by the 1945 constitution."[52]

Other States. North Carolina, in 1937, and Indiana, in 1939, enacted optional legislation empowering counties to establish inferior courts of county-wide jurisdiction, presided over by appointive, salaried judges and designed to handle many of the cases formerly tried by justice-of-the-peace courts. A Maryland law of 1939 permits the establishment of similar tribunals in counties of that state. The new courts are called county civil courts in North Carolina, magistrates' courts in Indiana, and trial magistrates' courts in Maryland.[53] In New Jersey, pursuant to the state's new

[50] *Constitution of Missouri* (1945), Art. V, secs. 18-21.

[51] Martin L. Faust, *Five Years under the New Missouri Constitution* (Jefferson City, Missouri Public Expenditure Survey, 1950), p. 16. Incumbent justices and probate judges were excepted from the requirement that magistrates be licensed to practice law.

[52] *Ibid.*, pp. 16-17. For an early appraisal of the new courts in the city of St. Louis, where their organization and jurisdiction are somewhat different from elsewhere in the state, see Governmental Research Institute, *Magistrate Courts in St. Louis* (St. Louis, Mo., 1948).

[53] See John A. Perkins, "Judiciary up to Date," *National Municipal Review*, Vol. XXIX, pp. 736-742 (November, 1940); Morris, *op. cit.*, pp. 31-32; Forest E. Abbuhl, "Maryland Modernizes Its Justice of the Peace System," *The County Officer*, Vol. XVI, pp. 77-78, 81 (March, 1951). Indiana's optional law was amended in 1941 to apply only to the state's more populous counties.

constitution of 1947, elective justices of the peace have been supplanted by district and municipal courts under appointive magistrates.[54] California's constitution was amended in 1950 to reorganize the minor judiciary in that state. Under the new provision and implementing legislation, judges of justice courts, who are to be elected for six-year terms, will be required either to have been admitted to the practice of law or to have passed a qualifying examination and will be paid a regular salary.[55]

Conclusion. The constitutional and statutory provisions of the various states mentioned are indicative of the kind of action that might well be taken more generally. In states where the office of justice of the peace is established by the constitution, it can, of course, be completely abolished only by constitutional amendment. But, even in many of these states, the legislature has broad powers over jurisdiction and may render the justice-of-the-peace court largely innocuous by transferring most or all of its criminal and civil jurisdiction to county courts presided over by salaried judges. Experience suggests, however, that remedial legislation, if it is to be generally effective, must be mandatory rather than optional in character. Justices of the peace and other local officers are usually so well organized and so influential with the local electorate that they can successfully block the adoption by local vote of any proposal designed to curtail their authority.

REFERENCES

Books and Special Studies

Busch, Francis X., *Law and Tactics in Jury Trials* (Indianapolis, Ind., Bobbs-Merrill, 1949).

Callender, Clarence N., *American Courts: Their Organization and Procedure* (New York, McGraw-Hill, 1927), chaps. 2, 4, 11-13.

Council of State Governments, *Trial Courts of General Jurisdiction in the Forty-eight States* (Chicago, 1951).

Douglass, Paul F., *The Justice of the Peace Courts of Hamilton County, Ohio* (Baltimore, The Johns Hopkins University Press, 1932).

Frank, Jerome, *Courts on Trial: Myth and Reality in American Justice* (Princeton, N. J., Princeton University Press, 1949).

Governmental Research Institute, *Magistrate Courts in St. Louis* (St. Louis, Mo., 1948).

Howerton, Huey Blair, and McIntire, Helen Hyde, *A Guidebook of the Justice of the Peace [in Mississippi]* (University, University of Mississippi Bureau of Public Administration, 1950).

Morris, Gail M., *Justice of the Peace Courts in Indiana* (Bloomington, Indiana University Bureau of Government Research, 1942).

Ohio Legislative Service Commission, *Justices of the Peace in Ohio* (Columbus, 1955).

[54] Joseph Harrison, "Judicial Reform in New Jersey," *State Government*, Vol. XXII, pp. 232-236, 247-248 (October, 1949).

[55] *Journal of the American Judicature Society*, Vol. XXXIV, p. 58 (August, 1950); *ibid.*, p. 120 (December, 1950).

Pennsylvania Bar Association, Committee on Minor Judiciary, *Survey of the Minor Judiciary in Pennsylvania* (State College, Pennsylvania Municipal Publications Service, 1942), a study of the justices of the peace and aldermen conducted with the co-operation of the Pennsylvania State College Institute of Local Government.

SUNDERLAND, Edson R., "A Study of Justices of the Peace and Other Minor Courts—Requisites for an Adequate State-wide Minor Court System," *Fifteenth Annual Report of the Judicial Council of Michigan* (Lansing, Mich., 1945), Pt. 2.

TALBOTT, Forrest, *Intergovernmental Relations and the Courts* (Minneapolis, University of Minnesota Press, 1950).

WARREN, George, *Traffic Courts* (Boston, Little, Brown, 1942), chap. 13.

Articles

ABBUHL, Forest E., "Maryland Modernizes Its Justices of the Peace System," *The County Officer,* Vol. XVI, pp. 77-78, 81 (March, 1951).

ALLEN, H. K., "Administration of Minor Justice in Selected Illinois Counties," *Illinois Law Review,* Vol. XXXI, pp. 1047-1055 (April, 1937).

BOK, Curtis, "The Jury System in America," *Annals of the American Academy of Political and Social Science,* Vol. CCLXXXVII, pp. 92-96 (May, 1953.)

BUTTS, A. B., "The Justice of the Peace—Recent Tendencies," *American Political Science Review,* Vol. XXII, pp. 946-953 (November, 1928).

EWING, Albert, Jr., "Justice of the Peace—Bedrock of Democracy," *Tennessee Law Review,* Vol. XXI, pp. 484-497 (December, 1950).

GRANT, J. A. C., "Methods of Jury Selection," *American Political Science Review,* Vol. XXIV, pp. 117-133 (February, 1930).

HARRISON, Joseph, "Judicial Reform in New Jersey," *State Government,* Vol. XXII, pp. 232-236, 247-248 (October, 1949).

HOFFMAN, Harold M., and BRODLEY, Joseph, "Jurors on Trial" (with an introduction by Jerome Frank), *Missouri Law Review,* Vol. XVII, pp. 235-251 (June, 1952).

HOLLINGSWORTH, Frank, "That Beleaguered Gentleman: The Trial Judge," *Journal of the Missouri Bar,* Vol. VII, pp. 83-84 (June, 1951).

HOWARD, T. L., "The Justice of the Peace System in Tennessee," *Tennessee Law Review,* Vol. XIII, pp. 19-38 (December, 1934).

HUNTER, Robert M., "Law in the Jury Room," *Ohio State University Law Journal,* Vol. II, pp. 1-19 (December, 1935).

"J. P.," *State Government,* Vol. VII, pp. 69-71 (March, 1934).

KINGDON, Arthur F., "The Trial Justice System in Virginia," *Journal of the American Judicature Society,* Vol. XXIII, pp. 216-221 (April, 1940).

LANCASTER, Lane W., "Justice of the Peace in Connecticut," *National Municipal Review,* Vol. XIX, pp. 9-13 (January, 1930).

MCKENNA, William J., "Justice in the Minor Courts," *Temple Law Quarterly,* Vol. XXV, pp. 436-448 (April, 1952).

MANNING, J. W., "In-justices of the Peace," *National Municipal Review,* Vol. XVIII, pp. 225-227 (April, 1929).

———, "Kentucky Justices of the Peace," *American Political Science Review,* Vol. XXVII, pp. 90-93 (February, 1933).

MINER, Julius H., "The Jury Problem," *Journal of Criminal Law and Criminology,* Vol. XXXVII, pp. 1-15 (May-June, 1946).

PAGE, Tom, "Local Judicial Activity," *Local Government Notes,* publication of the University of Illinois Extension Service in Agriculture and Home Economics, No. 35 (September 2, 1952).

PERKINS, John A., "Judiciary up to Date," *National Municipal Review,* Vol. XXIX, pp. 736-742 (November, 1940).

SIMMONDS, James R., "Reform in the Jury System," *Tennessee Law Review,* Vol. XXI, pp. 389-395 (June, 1950).

SMITH, Chester H., "The Justice of the Peace System in the United States," *California Law Review,* Vol. XV, pp. 118-141 (January, 1927).

SUNDERLAND, Edson R., "Qualifications and Compensation of Minor Court Judges," *Journal of the American Judicature Society,* Vol. XXIX, pp. 111-116 (December, 1945).

———, "Territorial Jurisdiction of Minor Courts," *Journal of the American Judicature Society,* Vol. XXIX, pp. 147-155 (February, 1946).

TEMPLE, Ralph R., "What Ails County Justice," *National Municipal Review,* Vol. XXXVI, pp. 376-381 (July, 1947).

WALLACE, Warren L., "Constables and J.P.'s in Iowa," *National Municipal Review,* Vol. XIII, pp. 7-10 (January, 1924).

WILLIAMS, Henry N., "General Sessions Courts in Tennessee," *Journal of the American Judicature Society,* Vol. XXXI, pp. 101-104 (December, 1947).

WILLIS, Hugh Evander, "Are Justice of the Peace Courts Impartial Tribunals?" *Indiana Law Journal,* Vol. III, pp. 654-657 (May, 1928).

CHAPTER 13

Law Enforcement

Closely related to the function of judicial administration, which was discussed in the preceding chapter, is the enforcement of the criminal law. In the field of civil law, as we have seen, the function of government consists merely in laying down the rules that are to govern individuals in their relations with each other and in providing judicial tribunals in which controversies may be adjudicated. With respect to the criminal law, however, government assumes the additional duty of preventing, insofar as possible, violations of the law, and of punishing the infractions that do occur. In a broad sense, of course, the courts themselves may be regarded as law-enforcement agencies, since their task consists primarily in the application of legal rules to the controversies coming before them. As more commonly used, however, and as employed in this book, the term *law enforcement* is given a more restricted meaning, being confined to the work of those agencies concerned with such matters as the preservation of the peace, the arrest of persons known or suspected to have violated the criminal law, the preferring of formal charges against suspected persons, the prosecution of accused persons before the courts, and the enforcement of court judgments. As thus understood, law enforcement is a function of the executive or administrative branch of government, as distinguished from the judicial branch, though at many points law enforcement and judicial administration are distinctly interrelated. So closely, indeed, are law-enforcement and judicial officers associated in their activities that some attention will necessarily be given to the latter at certain points in this discussion.

LOCAL RESPONSIBILITY

Though there exists a considerable body of federal criminal law enforced by federal officers through the federal courts, American criminal law, for the most part, is state law supplemented to a limited extent by local ordinances. The enforcement of criminal law, like its enactment, is basically a function of state government. In actual practice, however, primary responsibility for law enforcement has now been delegated in large measure to the various units of local government, with the states themselves maintaining only a general and somewhat attenuated supervision over the local authorities. This being the case, it is the local administrative agencies which to a large degree determine the effectiveness of law enforcement in a particular community and set its general tone. If the local agencies are adequately staffed and equipped and are manned by honest and competent personnel, high standards of enforcement are likely to prevail. On the other hand, if local officers are corrupt or incompetent, or if they are provided with inadequate staff or equipment, weak and ineffectual enforcement is almost certain to be the result.

Traditionally, the problem of law enforcement has been more acute in urban than in rural areas, since it is in the more populous communities that opportunities for commission of criminal offenses against persons and property are most numerous. Today, however, good roads and the automobile facilitate the perpetration of crime in rural communities, as well as the escape to rural areas of criminals who have committed their depredations in the cities. Indeed, criminals committing offenses in municipalities with well-organized and vigorous police departments may be impelled to flee to the country by the belief that inadequate rural police organization and the distances involved will make their apprehension more difficult. Rural enforcement problems are further complicated by the current need for enforcing state motor-vehicle regulations on rural highways.

Every state now has a state police force of some kind, and these forces operate primarily in rural areas. Some states specifically prohibit the state police from acting within the limits of municipalities except at the request of the local authorities; [1] and elsewhere, as a matter of practice, the state force usually acts within municipalities only upon local request. In some instances the state police force is a special highway patrol charged only with enforcement of motor-vehicle regulations; but in a large majority of the states the force is vested with general jurisdiction to enforce all state laws. Even where clothed with general police authority, however, the state force is not provided with sufficient personnel to undertake the regular enforcement of all laws relating to crime; nor is it expected to do so. Primary responsibility for policing rural America rests today, as it always has in the past, with locally chosen officials—particu-

[1] David G. Monroe, *State and Provincial Police: A Study in Police Functioning in the United States and Canada* (Evanston, Ill., Northwestern University Traffic Institute, 1941), pp. 20-21. Published in co-operation with the International Association of Chiefs of Police.

larly the county sheriff and the township constable. In the following pages attention will be given to the role of these rural police officers and that of other local agencies and institutions which enter law-enforcement proceedings at subsequent points. Preparatory to a consideration of individual officers and agencies, the enforcement process itself may be briefly summarized. In this connection, local ordinances relating to misdemeanors and their punishment will be considered as constituting, as indeed strictly speaking they do, a part of the criminal law of the state.

THE ENFORCEMENT PROCESS

For convenience, the process by which the criminal law is normally enforced may be considered as falling into seven successive steps: maintenance of the peace, arrest of law violators, preliminary hearing, preferring of charges, arraignment, prosecution and trial, and punishment of convicted persons.

Maintenance of the Peace. The first duty in law enforcement is that of preserving the peace and preventing, insofar as possible, infractions of the law. To this end sheriffs, constables, and other "peace" officers patrol the highways and visit establishments and gatherings where disorder is likely to arise or law violations to occur. In this manner the officers seek, by their very presence, to encourage law observance.

Arrest. When, notwithstanding these precautions, an infraction of the criminal law takes place, it is the duty of the police officers to seek out and arrest the perpetrator of the criminal act. In their searching for criminals, local officers are assisted, where such exists, by the state bureau of criminal investigation and identification.[2] Rural officers also at times have access to files of fingerprints and other identification aids maintained by municipal police departments, and the extensive fingerprint files of the Federal Bureau of Investigation are available for their use.

Arrest has been defined as "the taking of a person into custody in order that he may be forthcoming to answer for the commission of an offense,"[3] and is made sometimes with and sometimes without a warrant.[4] A warrant of arrest is a court order directing the arrest of a designated person or persons, issued upon complaint of a private citizen—usually some person who has been injured by the crime complained of—or of a law-

[2] A number of states maintain a bureau of this nature either as a unit within the state police department or independent thereof.

[3] American Law Institute, *Code of Criminal Procedure* (Philadelphia, 1931), sec. 18. For a scholarly analysis of the law of arrest, see Rollin M. Perkins, "The Law of Arrest," *Iowa Law Review*, Vol. XXV, pp. 201-289 (January, 1940).

[4] Cf. Rocco Tresolini, Richard W. Taylor, and Elliott B. Barnett, "Arrest Without Warrant: Extent and Social Implications," *Journal of Criminal Law, Criminology, and Police Science*, Vol. XLVI, pp. 187-198 (July-August, 1955).

enforcement officer. As a general rule, an officer may arrest without a warrant any person who commits a crime, either misdemeanor or felony, in his presence. For offenses not committed in his presence a warrant is ordinarily necessary, except that in the case of a felony, arrest may be made without warrant if the officer has *reasonable cause* to believe that the person arrested has committed the crime. Private citizens possess much the same legal authority to make arrests as do police officers, but in practice this authority is seldom exercised. Few persons wish to incur either the personal danger or the legal responsibility that the making of an arrest might involve. And, in a civil damage suit for false arrest, a jury is likely to be less lenient toward a private individual than toward a public officer who believed himself to be acting in the course of duty.

Preliminary Hearing. Once an arrest has been made, the next step, which ordinarily follows within a few hours, is to take the arrested person before a court for a preliminary hearing. This proceeding usually takes place before a justice of the peace or the judge of some other minor court, and its purpose is to determine whether the evidence against the suspected person is sufficient to justify holding him for action by the grand jury or prosecuting attorney. It is a common practice at preliminary hearings to hear only evidence against the suspect, although the latter must be permitted to make a statement if he wishes to do so. To justify holding the suspect, the court must be convinced by the evidence submitted that the crime charged has been committed and that there is reasonable ground to believe that the defendant is guilty. If the magistrate is so convinced, he "binds over" the suspect to the grand jury or to await the filing of an information by the prosecutor. On the other hand, if the magistrate decides that the evidence does not show a case, he discharges the prisoner. Although a discharge at this point usually terminates the proceeding against the suspected person, it is no constitutional bar to his subsequent rearrest on the same charge.[5]

When a suspected person, on the basis of the preliminary hearing, is ordered held for further action, the magistrate who issues the order must, unless the offense is nonbailable (this is frequently true of capital offenses), permit the release of the suspect on bail pending such action. In doing this, the magistrate fixes the amount of the bail bond which the suspect must post as security for his future appearance at the prescribed time. The amount of the bond may be posted in cash or negotiable securities or, as is more frequently the case, bond is supplied by a friend or a professional bondsman. In most instances, the security offered is in the form of real estate. Adequacy of the security must be approved by the magistrate, who, in this connection, may have the assistance of the prose-

[5] Cf. Clarence N. Callender, *American Courts: Their Organization and Procedure* (New York, McGraw-Hill, 1927), pp. 171-173.

cuting attorney's office in an investigatory and advisory capacity. If the suspect is unable to supply the required bail, or if his offense is non-bailable, he is placed in jail to await further disposition of his case.

Preferring Charges. The next step in the law-enforcement process is the preferring of formal charges against the suspected person. This is done either by grand jury indictment or by information filed by the prosecuting attorney.[6] These respective procedures will be explained in connection with our discussion of the grand jury and the prosecutor's office, after which an attempt will be made to evaluate their relative merits.

Arraignment. When formal charges have been preferred, the accused is next arraigned before the trial court. At this point, the indictment or information is read to the accused, and he is given opportunity to plead guilty or not guilty to the charges contained therein. Should he decline to plead, a plea of not guilty is entered by the court. When a plea of guilty is made, trial in most instances is dispensed with, and the court proceeds to pronounce judgment and sentence. Some states, however, have statutes relating to capital offenses which either prohibit the entry of a plea of guilty or provide that notwithstanding such plea, the court shall proceed with trial by jury.[7] A plea of not guilty brings the case to trial.

Prosecution and Trial. Though misdemeanors are often tried, in the first instance, in justice-of-the-peace courts or other minor tribunals, prosecutions for felony are ordinarily instituted in the general trial courts.[8] In the trial court it is usually the prosecuting attorney who conducts the state's case against the defendant. The defendant is represented by private counsel, counsel assigned by the court, or a public defender. The right to be tried by jury is generally guaranteed to defendants in criminal actions by constitutional provision; and, although jury trial may be waived in some jurisdictions and under some circumstances, waiver in felony cases is rare.

Punishment. When a verdict of guilty has been returned by the trial jury, the defendant may move to "arrest the judgment" or for a new trial. If such motions are not made, or are made and denied, the court pronounces sentence as provided by the statutes for the offense concerned.[9] The sentence may take the form of a fine, a term of imprisonment, or

[6] Indictment may, and sometimes does, precede arrest. This is likely to be true, for example, where indictments are returned as the result of investigations of such matters as election frauds, and it may occur in the case of any individual suspect who has not yet been apprehended. In these instances, "bench warrants" for arrest of the accused are issued by the trial court on the basis of the indictments.

[7] See 22 *Corpus Juris Secundum,* "Criminal Law," sec. 422.

[8] See above, chap. 12.

[9] Cf. Callender, *op. cit.,* pp. 195-198. A convicted defendant will usually be able to find statutory grounds upon which appeal may be taken to a higher court. If the higher court consents to review the case, this operates to stay the imposition or execution of sentence until the appeal is disposed of—*ibid.*

both.[10] At one time the punishment of criminals was looked upon as a matter of retribution or the wreaking of vengeance. Modern ideals, however, demand that reformation rather than vengeance constitute the principal consideration in the treatment of convicted persons. Imprisonment of criminals finds its justification today in (1) the protection of society against persons who would be dangerous if at large and (2) the attempted reform of those persons.

Prison sentences for felonies are served in state penal institutions. The county jail, however, is the usual institution for the detention of persons suspected or formally accused of crime but not yet tried and for the imprisonment of convicted persons sentenced to short terms for misdemeanors.[11] The nature and problems of jail administration are considered in the final section of this chapter.

THE SHERIFF

Among individual agencies concerned with law enforcement the county sheriff, as the principal police officer in rural areas, deserves first consideration. The office of sheriff is one of the oldest known to the English common law. Although the date of its origin cannot be fixed with exactness, the shire reeve, precursor of the sheriff, apparently existed as an officer of the English shire (county) as early as the middle of the tenth century, thus indicating that the present office, with due allowance for modernization in title, has a history extending back for a full thousand years. At one point during the early development of the office, the English sheriff, in addition to conserving the peace and performing functions closely related thereto, was charged with a number of other duties variously fiscal, judicial, administrative, and military in nature. Eventually, however, most of these extraneous functions were taken from the sheriff and assigned to other agencies—some of them to the newer offices of coroner and justice of the peace. By the time of the English migration to America in the seventeenth century, the sheriff had been stripped of practically all functions except the preservation of the peace, the serving of court process, and the keeping of public prisoners—duties which he has generally retained in this country to the present.[12]

[10] Imprisonment was originally used only for the temporary detention of persons awaiting trial or execution of sentence. Not until the latter half of the eighteenth century was the practice adopted of incarcerating prisoners for the purpose of punishment. Sanford Bates, *Prisons and Beyond* (New York, Macmillan, 1936), p. 31.

[11] Some municipalities maintain city jails for purposes similar to those served by the county institutions.

[12] Theodore F. T. Plucknett, "Sheriff," *Encyclopaedia of the Social Sciences* (New York, Macmillan, 1934), Vol. XIV, pp. 20-22; Ben W. Palmer, "The Vestigial Sheriff: The Shrunken Giant of the Present Day," *American Bar Association Journal*, Vol. XXXVI, pp. 367-369 (May, 1950). The English sheriff has traditionally served, and continues to serve today, as a returning officer in parliamentary elections.

The office of sheriff exists today in all of the 48 states. Contrary to the English practice of appointing to the office, American sheriffs are usually elected by the voters of the county. Indeed, this is now the method of choice in every state except Rhode Island, where appointment is by the governor.[13] The term of office, commonly prescribed by the state constitution, is usually either two or four years.[14] Choice by popular election makes it by no means certain that a sheriff will be fitted by training or past experience for the duties of his office; and, in several states, constitutional provisions to the effect that a sheriff may not succeed himself or may not serve more than two consecutive terms,[15] render it all but impossible for him to improve his qualifications through long tenure.[16] For these reasons, most incumbents of the sheriff's office are in no sense law-enforcement officers of the trained, professional type. The sheriff receives compensation for his services in the form of fees, a salary, or both, the modern tendency being to provide a fixed salary and to require the sheriff to turn into the county treasury whatever fees he collects. In the performance of his duties the sheriff is assisted by deputies, whom he appoints and for whose official acts he is responsible.

The usual duties of the sheriff fall into three principal categories: (1) he is conservator of the peace within his county; (2) he is an officer of the court or courts of record in the county; and (3) he is keeper of the county jail.[17] In addition, the sheriff in some instances serves ex officio as tax collector; and other duties of miscellaneous nature, some of them only remotely connected with law enforcement, are imposed upon him in various states.

As a peace officer, it is the duty of the sheriff to maintain the peace, to seek out and arrest lawbreakers, to quell disorders, and to suppress riots. Since cities and villages are usually provided with their own organized police forces, the police activities of the sheriff are largely confined to rural areas. If a situation arises which cannot be adequately dealt with by

[13] In the five counties within New York City the office of county sheriff has been abolished, and a single city sheriff is appointed by the mayor under civil service provisions. See *New York City Charter,* secs. 1031, 1032.

[14] As of 1952, the sheriff's term was reported to be two years in 19 states, four years in 26 states, three years in New York and New Jersey, and six years in Massachusetts—"Sheriffs' Terms and Tenure of Office," *The National Sheriff,* Vol. IV, No. 12, p. 9 (September, 1952).

[15] Three in Tennessee.

[16] Fortunately, there is at present a rather clear tendency in the direction of lifting restrictions on re-eligibility, a number of states having recently taken action to this end. Experience in the office is also fostered in some instances, notwithstanding limitations on re-eligibility, by informal arrangements whereby each of two persons serves alternately as sheriff and deputy sheriff. Regarding arrangements of this nature as applied to the office of county treasurer, see above, chap. 6, n. 19.

[17] In Kentucky, except in Jefferson County (Louisville), jail administration is in the hands of a county jailer, who is a separate and distinct officer popularly elected as such.

him and his deputies, the sheriff is authorized to summon to his aid the *posse comitatus*, or "power of the county." The posse, on any given occasion, consists of such able-bodied men of the county as the sheriff may call upon to assist him in enforcing the law; and state statutes provide penalties for failure to serve at the sheriff's call. In extreme emergencies, the sheriff may ask the governor of the state for assistance from the National Guard.[18]

In his capacity as a court officer, it is the sheriff's duty, personally or by deputy, to attend sessions of courts of record and to serve legal process issuing therefrom. Such process includes, for example, various writs, warrants of arrest, summonses to jurors, and subpoenas to witnesses. It is also a duty of the sheriff to execute court judgments. In criminal cases this may involve keeping in the county jail persons given short sentences for misdemeanors, or conveying felons to state penal institutions. It may even fall to the sheriff to execute death sentences, by hanging or otherwise, though in some states such sentences are now executed in state prisons. On the civil side, a common task of the sheriff is that of seizing and selling property, at the direction of parties entitled thereto, to satisfy money judgments.

As keeper of the jail, the sheriff is charged with supervision of the jail building and with the custody and feeding of prisoners. Where he is allowed a fixed sum per day for prisoners' board, he frequently finds it possible to make a substantial profit from this transaction.[19] It is the sheriff's legal duty to protect the life and health of his prisoners, and in some states he may be removed from office for permitting a prisoner to be taken from his custody and lynched.

During recent years, there has been a tendency for the sheriff's duties as court officer and jailer to overshadow his activities of a police nature. One reason for this, undoubtedly, is the fact that the sheriff's office is seldom provided with either the equipment or the personnel essential to a modern county-wide police system. Another reason, of perhaps even more significance, is the fact that the fees for the service of court process and the execution of judgments, and the opportunity to make a profit from the boarding of prisoners, make those aspects of the sheriff's work more lucrative than the tracking down of criminals.

In view of these circumstances some students of law enforcement have come to believe that the office of sheriff, in its present form, should be abolished.[20] Were this done, the sheriff's duties as a peace officer might

[18] The governor, of course, may order national guard units to duty in any community without request from the local sheriff.

[19] See below, "The County Jail."

[20] See, for example, R. E. Heiges, "Goodbye to the Sheriff," *Social Science*, Vol. XI, pp. 137-141 (April, 1936).

be transferred to the state police or to professionalized county constabularies such as have already been established in a few counties.[21] Other duties of the office, that is, the service of court process and keeping of the jail, being ancillary to the work of the courts, might be transferred to the clerk or clerks of the courts of record or imposed upon a newly created functionary appointed by the courts.

But the office of sheriff is of such antiquity and so intrenched in our political system and our state constitutions that its abolition or substantial curtailment in the near future is extremely unlikely.[22] A possible alternative to abolition which may merit consideration under some circumstances is that of making the office a more effective part of our law-enforcement machinery by establishing organized county police systems or highway patrols directly under the sheriff's control and supervision. Where such a plan is adopted, as it has been in a few urban counties,[23] it would seem well to relieve the sheriff of his civil duties so that he may be free to devote his undivided attention to law enforcement.

Whether or not the sheriff is relieved of all civil duties, any major function not closely associated with enforcement of the criminal law, such as that of tax collection, should certainly be placed in other hands. Where tax collection is a duty of the sheriff, it appears almost without exception to consume that officer's time and attention to the neglect of his primary functions. Since collection of taxes is both less hazardous and more remunerative than police activities, this is not surprising. In Kentucky, where the sheriff not only serves as tax collector but is charged with numerous additional duties largely foreign to law enforcement, policing activities seem clearly to suffer from the loss of official time to other matters.[24] And in Illinois, where the sheriff is ex officio tax collector in nontownship counties, several sheriffs reported some years ago that 100 per cent of their regular time was devoted to tax collection and process serving, thus relegating to after-office hours any work in criminal investigation.[25] In the principal police office of the county, such a situation is scarcely to be tolerated. If the sheriff is to serve with even moderate satisfaction as a

[21] See Bruce Smith, *Rural Crime Control* (New York, Columbia University Institute of Public Administration, 1933), chap. 4.

[22] The charter of St. Louis County, Mo., was amended in 1954 to establish a county police department under a bipartisan board of police commissioners and to limit the duties of the sheriff to those of keeping the jail and serving court process. See *National Municipal Review*, Vol. XLIII, p. 487 (October, 1954); *ibid.*, Vol. XLIV, p. 479 (October, 1955).

[23] Smith, *Rural Crime Control*, chap. 4.

[24] See Kentucky Legislative Research Commission, *State-local Fiscal Relations*, A Report to the Committee on Functions and Resources of State Government (Frankfort, Ky., 1952), pp. 27-28.

[25] Illinois Department of Public Welfare, Division of Criminal Identification and Investigation, *Survey of the Personnel and Equipment of the Sheriffs' Offices in Illinois* (Springfield, Ill., 1940).

law-enforcement officer, he must not be overburdened with extraneous duties.

THE CONSTABLE

In townships and other civil divisions of the county, the counterpart of the sheriff is the constable.[26] Though sometimes appointed, constables are usually elected,[27] and the number provided for in each township or district is frequently the same as the number of justices of the peace.[28] Also as in the case of justices, the number of constables actually elected and qualified is commonly less than the number authorized by law. In West Virginia, for example, 47 per cent of all constables' offices were vacant in 1951, with three counties reporting no constables whatsoever and 24 having fewer than half the permitted number.[29]

The constable is charged with two principal duties: (1) as a conservator of the peace, it is his duty to preserve order within his township or district and to arrest law violators; and (2) as an officer of the justice-of-the-peace court, he serves summonses, warrants, and subpoenas and executes judgments of the court. These functions, it will be observed, closely parallel two of the main duties performed by the sheriff at the county level. Since subdivisions of the county rarely maintain institutions for detention of prisoners, the third principal function of the sheriff, that of jail operation, has no equivalent in the case of the township officer.

The constable as a law-enforcement official displays many of the same shortcomings as does the justice of the peace as a judicial officer. In discussing the Michigan situation, which appears to be fairly typical of that in the states generally, Professor Sunderland has said: [30]

> Constables suffer from many of the same disqualifications as township justices. Individual constables, other than those serving in cities large enough to sustain a municipal court, do so little business that they acquire only the smallest amount of knowledge or skill as the result of experience. They have no organization, no central office, no system of records, no established procedure, no traditions regarding standards of performance. Their income from official activities is usually so small and irregular that it would rarely attract men of ability. Their large numbers and the restricted extent of their individual activities divide and dissipate public attention. This confers upon them a certain anonymity which tends to withdraw their activities from public criticism.

[26] In Rhode Island towns provision is made not only for the constable but for a town sergeant whose duties are similar in some respects to those of the constable.

[27] See Smith, *Rural Crime Control,* p. 82.

[28] See above, chap. 12, "Justices of the Peace."

[29] Harold J. Shamberger, *County Government and Administration in West Virginia* (Morgantown, West Virginia University Bureau for Government Research, 1952), p. 31.

[30] Edson R. Sunderland, "A Study of Justices of the Peace and Other Minor Courts—Requisites for an Adequate State-wide Minor Court System," *Fifteenth Annual Report of the Judicial Council of Michigan* (Lansing, Mich., 1945), Pt. 2, p. 112.

As in the case of sheriffs, most constables give more attention to their court duties than to their duties as peace officers.[31] This is especially understandable in the case of the constable, inasmuch as he usually derives his sole compensation from the fees of his office and no fees are provided for patrol duty or other merely protective services. The replies of 61 Illinois sheriffs to a questionnaire some years ago indicated that in 56 of the 61 counties the constables were entirely inactive in police work.[32] Surveys in other states[33] lead to the conclusion that the utter ineffectiveness of the constable as a peace officer is not peculiar to Illinois but is prevalent throughout the country. Students of law enforcement and judicial administration seem in general to agree that the office of constable, like that of justice of the peace, has outlived its usefulness and should be abolished. Indeed, if justices of the peace were eliminated, no reason would longer exist for the office of constable, inasmuch as that official now functions almost exclusively as a process server for justices' courts. Significant in this connection is the fact that Missouri, in replacing justice-of-the-peace tribunals with a system of magistrate courts,[34] recently abolished the office of constable in 112 of the state's 114 counties and provided that in those counties the sheriff should serve as the officer of the new court.[35] Virginia, another state in which justice-of-the-peace courts have been eliminated, has also discontinued the office of constable and transferred its powers and duties to the sheriff.[36] In 1953 the office of constable was abolished in King County (Seattle), Wash., by action of the board of county commissioners, with the work of the constables being turned over to the sheriff's office.[37]

THE CORONER

Only slightly less ancient than the office of sheriff is that of the county coroner, with a common-law history in England dating at least from the twelfth century. The office of coroner does not exist so generally in present-day America as does that of sheriff but is provided for by con-

[31] Among the exceptions are those constables who team up with justices of the peace in operating speed traps. Concerning the speed-trap evil, see above, chap. 12, "Justices of the Peace."

[32] Illinois Association for Criminal Justice, *Illinois Crime Survey* (Chicago, 1929), p. 340.

[33] See Smith, *Rural Crime Control,* pp. 84-92.

[34] See above, chap. 12, "Alternatives to Justice-of-the-Peace System."

[35] Martin L. Faust, *Five Years under the New Missouri Constitution* (Jefferson City, Missouri Public Expenditure Survey, 1950), pp. 15-16. The constable was retained as an adjunct to the magistrate court in Jackson and St. Louis counties and in the city of St. Louis.

[36] *Acts of Virginia* (1942), chap. 285.

[37] *National Municipal Review,* Vol. XLII, p. 348 (July, 1953); *ibid.,* Vol. XLIII, p. 252 (May, 1954).

stitution or statute in about three fourths of the states.[38] Ordinarily, a county has but a single coroner, though there are some exceptions to this rule. Thus, provision is made for two coroners in each Michigan county and three in each county of New Jersey.[39] Though appointed by the courts in a few states, coroners, in most instances, are chosen by popular election. The term of office is usually either two years or four. A few states impose constitutional restrictions on re-eligibility to the office, though such limitations are found less frequently than in the case of the sheriff. In occasional instances the coroner is required to be a practicing physician, and, in any event, the voters seem to prefer physicians for this office. Next after physicians, undertakers constitute the occupational group most heavily represented among coroners, but there is scarcely any calling without some representation.[40] Regardless of his vocation in private life, the coroner is all too often a petty politician and a cog in the local political machine.[41] In most instances his compensation is in the form of fees.

The Coroner's Inquest. Early English coroners were charged with a variety of duties, including the keeping of records pertaining to matters

[38] In several states the holding of inquests is a duty of justices of the peace; and in some other jurisdictions, as will appear later, coroners have been supplanted by medical examiners. Cf. Smith, *Rural Crime Control,* pp. 199-217; Glenn W. Ferguson, "It's Time for the Coroner's Post-mortem," *Journal of the American Judicature Society,* Vol. XXXIX, pp. 40-46 (August, 1955).

[39] Some counties in each of these states now operate under the medical-examiner system.

[40] Smith, *Rural Crime Control,* pp. 190-191. A survey of the early 1950's revealed that of Minnesota's 87 counties, 50 had physicians as coroners and 26 had undertakers. Included among the coroners of the remaining 11 counties were three osteopaths, a dentist, a banker, a real estate man, a newspaperman, a restaurant man, a retired farmer, an insurance man, and an undertaker's helper. Victor Cohn and Charles W. Bailey, *"Hidden Murder?" A Shocking Report on How Sudden and Mysterious Deaths Are Investigated by Many County Coroners,* chap. 4, reprinted from the *Minneapolis Morning Tribune* (February, 1953). Cf. Minnesota Legislative Research Committee, *The Coroner System in Minnesota* (St. Paul, 1954), pp. 11-13. Of North Carolina's 100 county coroners in 1951, 22 were physicians, 40 were undertakers, and 38 were drawn from miscellaneous businesses and professions. Included among the latter were farmers, merchants, salesmen, druggists, insurance agents, carpenters, an osteopath, a dentist, and a plumber; see Richard A. Myren, *Coroners in North Carolina: A Discussion of Their Problems* (Chapel Hill, University of North Carolina Institute of Government, 1953), p. 18. In Kansas, according to a survey by the University of Kansas Bureau of Government Research, 101 coroners for whom 1948 data were available included 62 physicians or surgeons, 26 undertakers, two assistant undertakers, six osteopaths, one chiropractor, two pharmacists, one justice of the peace, and one store clerk; see George S. Blair, *The Office of County Coroner in Kansas* (Emporia, Kansas State Teachers College, 1953), p. 12. Of the 70 county coroners in Wisconsin (outside Milwaukee County) in 1950, 17 were doctors, 33 were in the funeral and undertaking business, and 20 were drawn from various other occupations; see Charles H. Johnson, "The Wisconsin Coroner System," *Wisconsin Law Review,* pp. 529-547 (May, 1951).

[41] Cf. Lane W. Lancaster, *Government in Rural America,* 2d ed. (New York, Van Nostrand, 1952), pp. 170-173.

of criminal justice; collection for the king of treasure trove, shipwrecks, the goods and chattels of criminals, and whatever valuables might be found on unidentified dead persons; and the keeping of records of inquests.[42] Today, the principal function of the American coroner is that of holding inquests in the case of deaths occurring by violence or under suspicious circumstances or, in some states, by accident.[43] An inquest involves an examination of the body and a study of all circumstances relating to the death. When deemed advisable, an autopsy may be performed. The purpose of the inquest is to determine, insofar as possible, the cause of death, whether or not a crime has been committed in connection therewith, and, where crime is believed to be involved, the perpetrator of the crime. Although his official findings are not admissible as evidence before a trial jury it is the duty of the coroner, in connection with his investigation, to secure and preserve all available evidence and information that might aid the grand jury or prosecuting attorney in determining whether criminal charges are to be preferred.

The Coroner's Jury. In conducting an inquest, the coroner in some states may, and in others must, make use of a coroner's jury.[44] This agency consists of a small number of members—frequently six—chosen by the coroner, often from among bystanders or from residents of the neighborhood. The coroner presides over the jury and in large measure dominates its proceedings. When presiding at an inquest, he plays a dual role: (1) as a medical examiner, he is supposed to be able to determine the effects of wounds, bruises, fractures, poisons, and the like, in producing death; and (2) as a magistrate, he must conduct the hearing, examine witnesses, and instruct the jurors with respect to their legal duties. Few coroners combine the qualifications of lawyer and physician needed for the proper performance of these functions.[45]

Coroners' Verdicts. At the conclusion of an inquest, the coroner's jury deliberates briefly and returns its verdict. Coroners' verdicts are of four principal types.[46] (1) When the jury believes that the victim came to his death under circumstances for which no one is criminally liable, it returns a verdict of natural death, accidental death, or suicide, as the case may be.

[42] *Ibid.*, p. 170; George S. Blair, "The Coroner's Office Never Dies: It Just Fades Away," *The County Officer*, Vol. XVII, pp. 152-154 (May, 1952).

[43] Smith, *Rural Crime Control*, p. 189. A contingent function of the coroner in most states is that of performing the duties of sheriff in the event of a vacancy in the sheriff's office or in any case in which the sheriff is disqualified. Likewise, if it should become necessary to arrest the sheriff, the warrant of arrest is directed to the coroner for service.

[44] When no jury is used, the coroner himself has sole responsibility for conducting the inquest and making the necessary findings.

[45] Cf. Smith, *Rural Crime Control*, p. 193.

[46] The first three of these are distinguished and discussed by Kirk H. Porter in his *County and Township Government in the United States* (New York, Macmillan, 1922), pp. 184-185.

A verdict of this nature ordinarily ends the case, though it does not prevent further investigation if such is desired by the prosecuting officials. (2) If the jury believes that the deceased met death by violence or by any other means involving criminal liability, but is unable to discover the perpetrator of the crime, it may return a verdict stating its opinion that the victim met death at the hands of some person or persons unknown to the jury. When a verdict of this type is returned, it becomes the duty of the police and prosecuting attorney, if they are not already doing so, to attempt to find and apprehend the criminal. (3) If the jury believes that it is justified in fixing responsibility for the death upon some specific person or persons, it renders a verdict naming the person or persons believed to be responsible. On the basis of such a verdict, the coroner has authority to issue a warrant for the arrest of the person or persons named. (4) Finally, there is the so-called open verdict, wherein the jury, though perhaps assigning a medical cause of death, makes no finding with respect to the existence or nonexistence of criminal liability. An example would be a verdict, in a case of death from injuries received in an automobile accident, stating merely that death was "due to a cerebral hemorrhage caused by a skull fracture received in an auto collision." [47] Such a verdict leaves entirely to police and prosecuting officers the task of deciding whether liability apparently exists and, in the event of an affirmative decision, instituting appropriate action.

In practice, coroners' verdicts, whether rendered by a coroner or a coroner's jury, are sometimes so vague or meaningless as to be of no assistance whatever to the prosecuting authorities. Some are even written in an illiterate manner. Actual examinations of coroners' records have, for example, revealed the following "verdicts": "Found dead"; "Head severed from body"; "Diabetes, tuberculosis, or nervous indigestion"; "Could be diabetes or poison"; "Died suddenly after taking medicine"; [48] "So far as I could ascertain I found She came to her death from A natur cause comenly caled hart failure and I found no cause to Suspect Eny foul play"; "I lerned the man while Under the Enfluence of Whiskey or white mule Just willfully drowned himself"; and "the deceased came to her death by Natural Causes Unknown." [49]

Criticisms of the Office. For some years the coroner's office has been the subject of considerable criticism. With choice by popular election, and in the general absence of any professional requirements of candidates, it is not surprising that most coroners are poorly qualified for their duties. Many coroners are not physicians, and those chosen from the medical pro-

[47] Cf. *Champaign-Urbana* [*Ill.*] *News-Gazette,* p. 3 (March 17, 1948).

[48] Herman M. Adler, "Medical Science and Criminal Justice," *Criminal Justice in Cleveland,* Cleveland Foundation (Cleveland, Ohio, 1922), Pt. 5, p. 467.

[49] Raymond Moley, "The Sheriff and the Coroner," *Missouri Crime Survey,* Missouri Association for Criminal Justice (New York, Macmillan, 1926), Pt. 2, pp. 95-96.

fession are usually general practitioners rather than pathologists specially trained in those aspects of medical science involved in the performance of autopsies.[50] The difficulty of securing professionally qualified coroners is further enhanced by the fact that the duties of the office are legal as well as medical in nature. Even when a coroner is *either* a physician or a lawyer, he is almost never *both*, for a member of one of these professions is seldom trained in the other. Some universities now offer specialized training in the medicolegal science known as forensic medicine or medical jurisprudence, in which are combined certain aspects of the traditional disciplines of law and medicine. However, the relatively few specialists emerging from these courses are promptly engaged by insurance companies and other commercial establishments and afford no reservoir for the recruitment of coroners. Though there are some outstanding exceptions, particularly in certain urban counties, the great majority of American coroners are ill qualified for the performance of either the legal or the medical aspects of their work, and the standard of service provided by the office suffers acutely from this lack of competence.

So far as the coroner's jury is concerned, quite commonly that body [51]

> consists of six persons, none of whom has had any medical training or experience in homicide investigations. It seems to have been founded on the theory that ignorance multiplied by six equals intelligence. The findings of a coroner's jury are not admissible in evidence at any future trial—if any prosecution follows a coroner's inquest, the entire investigation has to be repeated by the state's attorney.

All in all, there seems little doubt that perpetrators of many murders and other homicides each year escape detection and punishment through the blunders of incompetent coroners and coroner's jurors who overlook or ignore criminal implications and return verdicts of accidental death, suicide, or death from natural causes. Equally regrettable is the fact that the same incompetence sometimes results in the branding of innocent persons as killers.[52]

Apart from the matter of unqualified personnel, one of the most com-

[50] When a coroner who is not a physician believes that an autopsy is advisable, he has authority to designate a physician to make the examination at the expense of the county. Like physician-coroners themselves, the persons designated are ordinarily general practitioners and frequently those who have proper political connections, and the examinations are often performed in a most perfunctory manner.

[51] LeMoyne Snyder, "Justice and Sudden Death," *Journal of the American Judicature Society*, Vol. XXXVI, pp. 142-147, 145-146 (February, 1953).

[52] See James Finan and Frederic Sondern, Jr., "The Scandal of Our Blundering Coroners," *Reader's Digest*, Vol. LV, No. 331, pp. 111-115 (November, 1949); Thomas C. Desmond, "The Coroner Racket: A National Scandal," *Coronet*, Vol. XXVIII, No. 2, pp. 60-64 (June, 1950); Pete Martin, "How Murderers Beat the Law," *Saturday Evening Post*, Vol. CCXXII, No. 24, pp. 32-33, 46 ff. (December 10, 1949).

mon criticisms of the coroner's office concerns its frequent tie-in with a particular undertaking establishment. As previously noted, the coroner is often an undertaker, and it seems unquestionable that undertakers often seek the office primarily as a means of advancing their private business interests. Where the coroner is not an undertaker, he may be allied with some friend in the undertaking business whose establishment he is disposed to favor. In either case, the coroner is in a strategic position to promote the business of the favored establishment by sending to it bodies under his jurisdiction. Sometimes this is simply a matter of suggesting the funeral home concerned, perhaps at their request, to friends or relatives of the deceased. At other times a body is sent by the coroner to a designated establishment without prior consultation with the family, and, of course, in some instances, there is no opportunity for such consultation. When it is borne in mind that the coroner is called upon to view the remains of about one fifth of all dead persons,[53] the opportunity afforded by an undertaker-coroner to exploit the public office for private profit appears extensive indeed. Legally, the relatives of a deceased person are usually entitled to overrule any suggestions of the coroner and call in another undertaker. In practice, however, this is not ordinarily done, and the favored position of establishments operated by coroners or their friends often arouses bitter resentment on the part of competitors.[54]

Considering the numerous shortcomings of the coroner's office, students of the problem rather generally agree that the office, in its traditional form, has no place in a modern law-enforcement system. That abandonment or modification of the office has been and continues to be slow, is readily explained on two principal grounds. In the first place, constitutional amendment is necessary in many states to abolish the office or effect any major change in its nature. Secondly, even where constitutional obstacles do not exist, the coroner is part of a well-established political pattern in American counties and, as such, is firmly intrenched in local politics.[55] Notwithstanding these difficulties, some progress is being made in the direction of reform. Abolition of the office and transfer of its functions to justices of the peace—a step that has been taken in a number of states—accomplishes little, since both legal and medical functions remain in the same hands and justices are ordinarily no better qualified than the typical coroner for performance of the duties involved. The most promising approach to the problem yet offered is that of replacing the coroner with what is known as the medical-examiner system, a plan which

[53] Snyder, *loc. cit.*, p. 144.

[54] As an attack upon the problem here involved the Wisconsin legislature, in 1955, enacted a statute providing that no coroner shall perform any of the services of a funeral director or embalmer upon the body of any person whose death he is required by law to investigate. *Wisconsin Session Laws* (1955), chap. 225.

[55] Richard B. Henderson, "'Crowner's Quest' and the Maryland Examiner System," *The County Officer*, Vol. XVI, pp. 99-102 (April, 1951).

already has been made effective throughout several states and in some communities elsewhere.[56]

The Medical-examiner System as an Alternative. Under the medical-examiner system the legal and medical aspects of the coroner's work are separated and placed in different hands, and an effort is made to achieve higher standards in the performance of both.[57] Legal phases of the work are vested in the prosecuting attorney, thereby conferring upon that official, who must ultimately present to the trial court such evidence of crime as may be discovered, power to supervise the collection of that evidence from the beginning.[58] The medical work of the office, including the performance of autopsies, is placed in the hands of a medical examiner who is appointed rather than elected, is usually required to be a physician, and may serve either a single county or a district comprising several counties. The officer or agency vested with appointing authority varies under the respective systems. Examiners are appointed in Maine, Massachusetts, and New Hampshire by the governor and council; in Maryland and Virginia by ex officio state commissions on post-mortem examinations; in Rhode Island by a chief medical examiner who, in turn, is appointed by the attorney general; and in New York City by the mayor from civil service lists.[59] Insofar as is practicable, an effort is made to secure as medical examiners persons who are not only physicians but are trained pathologists; and, even within the field of pathology, those who have further specialized in legal medicine are preferred. The ordinary hospital pathologist, being concerned primarily with disease, is not necessarily an expert in legal medicine. To qualify as such an expert, a physician [60]

> must have a large background of experience with all types of death by violence. He must be infallible in determining the direction of a bullet through a body. He must know how to remove the organs of the neck in order to demonstrate

[56] For a recent account generally favorable to the present-day coroner system in California counties, see Henry W. Turkel, "Merits of the Present Coroner System," *Journal of the American Medical Association*, Vol. CLIII, pp. 1086-1092 (November 21, 1953).

[57] On the system generally, see Oscar T. Schultz and E. M. Morgan, *The Coroner and the Medical Examiner*, National Research Council Bulletin (July, 1928), No. 64; George H. Weinmann, *A Compendium of the Statute Law of Coroners and Medical Examiners in the United States*, National Research Council Bulletin (August, 1931), No. 83; American Academy of Forensic Sciences and others, *A Model State Medico-legal Investigative System*, (New York, National Municipal League, 1950), tentative draft. The last-mentioned publication is a joint report of the American Academy of Forensic Sciences, the American Bar Association (Criminal Law Section), the American Judicature Society, the American Medical Association, the National Civil Service League, and the National Municipal League. A model act drafted by the National Conference of Commissioners on Uniform State Laws was approved by that group at its 1954 annual conference. See National Conference of Commissioners on Uniform State Laws, *Model Post-mortem Examinations Act* (Chicago, 1954).

[58] In certain instances some of these functions are imposed upon judicial officers.

[59] In New Hampshire the examiner is officially entitled the medical referee.

[60] *A Model State Medico-legal Investigative System*, p. 3.

manual strangulation without destroying either the tissues to be examined or structures vital for subsequent embalming. He must know whether a hemorrhage in the brain caused the fall or whether the fall caused the hemorrhage. He must know how to determine whether death was due to drowning or whether the victim was dead when thrown into the water. He must know whether multiple fractures resulted from a fall or from being struck by a motor vehicle. If death resulted from a fall, he must know how to search for evidence to distinguish among accident, suicide and homicide. All these basic problems and many others, especially those concerning surreptitious poisoning, must be understood by the pathologist who is an expert in legal medicine.

In one form or another the medical-examiner system apparently now exists on a state-wide basis in at least seven states—Maine, Maryland, Massachusetts, New Hampshire, Rhode Island, Vermont, and Virginia.[61] Some additional states have authorized their counties to adopt the system; still others—notably Arkansas, Georgia, and North Carolina—have adopted some features of the plan or empowered their counties to do so. Most of New Jersey's counties have medical examiners. Among individual counties employing the system elsewhere are Wayne and several others in Michigan; Duchess, Nassau, and Westchester in New York; Bexar in Texas; and Milwaukee in Wisconsin. Various other states and communities are currently considering adoption of the plan. In general, the new system appears to have produced gratifying results. In New York City, for example, it has been estimated that since the elimination of elective coroners, the medical examiner and his staff have "uncovered an annual average of 50 otherwise unsuspected deaths by violence."[62] When organized on a county-by-county basis, it is not surprising that the plan appears to have worked more satisfactorily in urban communities where medical examiners have been trained pathologists employed on a full-time, salaried basis, than in rural counties where the examiners have been general practitioners paid by fees.[63] This fact merely emphasizes the desirability of pooling the needs and resources of areas adequate for the provision of qualified personnel. Proper laboratory facilities also constitute an essential element in the operation of the medical-examiner system, and the provision of such facilities is practicable, except in the case of the most populous counties, only on a regional basis or through a central laboratory serving an entire state. It appears that not more than 50 or so of the nation's counties, individually, would provide enough business for a medical examiner's office to justify the cost of expert staff and laboratory equipment.[64] Hence, if the medical examiner is to replace the outmoded coroner in rural America generally, the change must be sought through abandon-

[61] See Ferguson, *loc. cit.*

[62] Richard S. Childs, "Rubbing out the Coroners," *National Municipal Review*, Vol. XXXIX, pp. 494-496, 495 (November, 1950).

[63] Cf. Smith, *Rural Crime Control*, pp. 207-209.

[64] Cf. Childs, *loc. cit.*

ment of the county as the geographic unit for provision of this service in favor of larger medical-examiner districts.

THE GRAND JURY

Long a principal agency for enforcing the criminal law in Anglo-American countries, and still of major importance though used less extensively than in earlier times, is the grand jury. The primary function of the grand jury is to consider cases of law violation laid before it by the prosecuting attorney for the purpose of determining whether the evidence against suspected persons is sufficient to warrant bringing them to trial. It does not determine the question of whether a suspected person is guilty of the offense concerned. Since the grand jury proceeding is not a trial, the suspected person has no right to appear before the jury, which is concerned only with weighing the evidence against him. If the jury, after due deliberation, concludes that the evidence is sufficient to justify bringing the suspect to trial, it returns an indictment, which is a formal charge or accusation, in the name of the state, that the suspected person committed the crime concerned. If, on the other hand, the jury deems the evidence insufficient for indictment, the suspected person is not brought to trial unless charged with the crime in a subsequent proceeding.[65]

Another power of the grand jury is that of acting as a general investigatory body. In such a capacity, it sometimes conducts investigations of matters of public concern such as alleged election frauds and the conduct of public offices. Such investigations usually result in special reports, and sometimes also in the return of indictments.[66]

Grand jurors are usually chosen by lot, often in the same manner as members of the trial jury.[67] In some states, however, legally qualified persons are designated directly for service by the county board or other selecting agency without resort to a random drawing of names. The body varies in size in the different states from 5 to 23 members.[68] At common

[65] See below, "The Prosecuting Attorney"; "Indictment *v.* Information."

[66] Cf. W. F. Willoughby, *Principles of Judicial Administration* (Washington, Brookings Institution, 1929), pp. 193-194. See also, "The Grand Jury—Its Investigatory Powers and Limitations," *Minnesota Law Review*, Vol. XXXVII, pp. 586-607 (June, 1953).

[67] See above, chap. 12, "The Trial Jury," p. 300.

[68] Michigan employs a system, commonly known as a "one-man grand jury," under which a single official, and he a judge, performs investigatory functions in connection with alleged crimes similar in many respects to functions vested in grand juries in other states. See Glenn R. Winters, "The Michigan One-man Grand Jury," *Journal of the American Judicature Society*, Vol. XXVIII, pp. 137-151 (February, 1945); William H. Gallagher, "The One-man Grand Jury—A Reply," *ibid.*, Vol. XXIX, pp. 20-24 (June, 1945); John Barker Waite, "Michigan's 'One-man Grand Jury' before the Supreme Court," *ibid.*, Vol. XXXI, pp. 184-186 (April, 1948). The one-judge investigating agency was replaced in 1949 by a body composed of three judges, but two years later the one-man plan was restored; see *Public Acts of Michigan* (1949), No. 311; *ibid.* (1951), No. 276. Several other states now have, or in the past have

law there were 23 members, the vote of 12 being necessary for the returning of an indictment, and the common-law rule is still followed in some states. In several states the grand jury consists of 12 members, 9 of whom must concur in an indictment. In no instance does indictment require a unanimous vote.

THE PROSECUTING ATTORNEY[69]

So vitally important is the work of the prosecuting attorney that his office may well be termed the keystone in the arch of law enforcement. The official title of this officer varies from state to state—being in different instances prosecuting attorney, state's attorney, commonwealth attorney, district attorney, and so forth—but that of prosecuting attorney is most indicative of his principal duties and is used in a generic sense in this discussion. Strictly speaking, the prosecuting attorney is an officer of the state, but since he is usually chosen locally and serves a particular community, he may, for practical purposes, be considered a local official. In some states there is a prosecutor for each county, whereas in others a single official serves a district embracing two or more counties. Though occasionally appointed by the governor or the courts,[70] the prosecuting attorney, in most states, is popularly elected, the usual term of office being two, four, or six years. His principal powers and duties are concerned with two phases of law enforcement: the preferring of formal charges against persons suspected of having committed crimes, and the prosecution in the courts of persons against whom charges have been filed.[71] Whereas in sparsely populated rural counties the prosecutor's office is manned by the prosecuting attorney, with sometimes a deputy and a stenographer, in metropolitan counties the work of the office requires an extensive staff of assistant prosecutors, investigators, and clerical employees.[72]

---

had, statutes authorizing judicial inquiry into the commission of crime by procedures resembling those used in Michigan. See Winters, *loc. cit.*, pp. 139-141.

[69] An excellent series of articles on the office of prosecuting attorney by Newman F. Baker and Earl H. DeLong will be found in sundry issues of the *Journal of Criminal Law and Criminology* for the years 1933-1935. See also, Newman F. Baker, "The Prosecuting Attorney: Legal Aspects of the Office," *ibid.*, Vol. XXVI, pp. 647-678 (January-February, 1936).

[70] Austin F. Macdonald, *American State Government and Administration,* 4th ed. (New York, Crowell, 1950), p. 448.

[71] In some states the prosecuting attorney, in addition to his duties of criminal-law enforcement, has various duties of a civil nature, such as giving legal advice to the county board and other county officers and conducting civil cases to which the county is a party. Elsewhere, these civil functions are performed by another law officer, usually known as the county attorney. See above, chap. 6, "Officers of General Administration," pp. 155-156.

[72] Cf. Newman F. Baker and Earl H. DeLong, "The Prosecuting Attorney: The Process of Prosecution, I," *Journal of Criminal Law and Criminology*, Vol. XXVI, pp. 3-21 (May, 1935).

The prosecutor, as noted earlier, lays before the grand jury cases of law violation that have come to his attention and submits to the jury such evidence against suspected persons as he has been able to obtain. Prior to presenting a case to the grand jury for action, the prosecuting attorney usually drafts an indictment document, which he transmits to the jury with the evidence. If the jury votes to indict, this document is validated by the jury foreman, who endorses it with the words "a true bill" and signs his name. If the decision is against indicting, the endorsement is that of "no true bill" or "bill not found." Finally, the prosecuting attorney is the official adviser of the grand jury with respect to its powers and procedure. From these relationships, it will readily be seen that the prosecutor is in a position to exert a powerful influence—indeed, in most instances, a determining influence—upon grand jury action. The jury normally considers only matters submitted to it by the prosecuting attorney, and whether or not an indictment is returned depends almost entirely upon the prosecutor's diligence and skill in collecting and presenting evidence in the case.[73]

The grand jury is an ancient institution of the English law, and its use, especially in felony cases, is still widely required in the American states by constitutional or statutory provision. However, a majority of the states now permit at least some use of the information as an alternative to grand jury indictment in the preferring of criminal charges, particularly in cases of lesser crimes.[74] In many states prosecution of practically all cases may now be by information; [75] and in some it has become the practice to use this device almost exclusively.[76]

An information is a formal accusation or charge of crime filed against a suspected person by the prosecuting attorney. Its effect, in bringing the accused to trial, is the same as that of an indictment, and it differs from the latter only in that it is filed by the prosecutor, on his own initiative and responsibility, without grand jury action. Whether or not an information will be filed in a particular case is wholly within the discretion of the prosecuting attorney. In view of what was said above concerning his relationship to the grand jury, it will readily be seen that the prosecuting attorney exercises a momentous power in determining who shall and who shall not be charged with crime. Where the information is used, the deci-

[73] The grand jury may, to be sure, return indictments on its own initiative and authority in matters not laid before it by the prosecuting attorney, but in practice this is seldom done. When the jury does thus act on its own responsibility, the instrument through which charges are preferred is sometimes called a *presentment* to distinguish it from the usual indictment found upon recommendations of the prosecutor.

[74] For a comprehensive analysis of the requirement and use of the grand jury, see Wayne L. Morse, "A Survey of the Grand Jury System," *Oregon Law Review,* Vol. X, pp. 101-160, 217-257, 295-365 (February, April, June, 1931).

[75] Raymond Moley, "The Initiation of Criminal Prosecutions by Indictment or Information," *Michigan Law Review,* Vol. XXIX, pp. 403-431 (February, 1931).

[76] R. Justin Miller, "Informations or Indictments in Felony Cases," *Minnesota Law Review,* Vol. VIII, pp. 379-408 (April, 1924).

sion as to whether it shall issue is solely his; and in the case of grand jury action it is largely within his power to determine whether an indictment shall be found.

When a suspected person has been charged, either by indictment or by information, with the commission of a crime, it becomes the duty of the prosecuting attorney to prepare the case against the accused and to conduct the prosecution, in the name of the state, before the proper court. In performing this duty, it is the prosecutor who, personally or by deputy, participates in selection of the trial jury; gathers, organizes, and presents evidence against the accused; examines the state's witnesses; cross-examines defense witnesses; and makes the state's final plea to the jury. These functions require, for their effective performance, a high degree of legal knowledge and oratorical skill. Given a reasonable amount of evidence against the accused, the likelihood of securing a conviction depends almost entirely upon the ability and energy of the prosecuting attorney. A special power of the prosecutor of much potential importance is that of asking the court to enter a nolle prosequi or dismissal of the case. Motion for a nolle prosequi is usually made on the ground that the state has insufficient evidence to secure a conviction and that it would therefore be a waste of time and money to proceed with the prosecution. Though the motion has perfectly legitimate uses, as, for example, in a case where the state's key witness has died, it may also be used by a prosecuting attorney who is so minded to bring about the dismissal of cases for personal or political reasons.

The paramount importance of the prosecuting attorney in law enforcement suggests that the office should be filled by one of the most able and experienced members of the local bar. Unfortunately, in many instances it is not so filled. The salary of the prosecutor is usually insufficient to attract the best legal talent, and in many rural counties it is so small that it must be supplemented by part-time private practice. Such a division of interest and efforts results all too frequently in the neglect of public duties. Furthermore, popular election is scarcely an effective means of securing the services of the most able lawyers. The prosecutor's office, particularly in rural areas, is often held either by a young lawyer fresh from school, who seeks by this means to widen his acquaintance and at the same time gain some experience, or, less frequently, by an older attorney, whose career in private practice has not been outstanding.[77] In either case, the incumbent is likely to prove a poor match for experienced criminal lawyers of the class often retained by persons accused of major crimes.

[77] In Ohio, which is probably a typical state in this respect, it was reported some years ago that the prosecutor in rural counties was "frequently one of the youngest and least experienced members of the bar. At the salaries prescribed the office can have little appeal to an established attorney in the average county. Most of the younger men interviewed frankly stated that they had sought the office for the sake of the courtroom experience and the advertising it afforded"—Ohio Institute, *County Organization and Government in Ohio* (Columbus, Ohio, 1932), p. 22.

INDICTMENT V. INFORMATION

As previously indicated, formal charges of crime may be preferred by grand jury indictment or by information filed by the public prosecutor. Originating in England as a device to extract from the people of a community knowledge concerning matters of interest to the crown, the grand jury eventually developed into an instrument for protecting the people against arbitrary accusation and prosecution by the crown; and it was this latter purpose that the framers of American state constitutions had in mind when they incorporated in those documents the provision that felony prosecutions might be commenced only by grand jury indictment.[78] At the present time, however, with the office of public prosecutor what it is, the grand jury seems to be in large measure superfluous. It tends to be dominated by the prosecutor and to become a mere "rubber stamp" for his wishes. Yet, although the prosecutor may be able to control the grand jury in its determination of whether an indictment shall be returned, he cannot be held responsible for the jury's action. When, on the other hand, the information is employed, it is impossible for the prosecutor to shift responsibility in the matter of preferring charges to shoulders other than his own. Comparative studies seem to indicate that the information, in general, possesses the following advantages over the indictment: [79]

1. It saves time.
2. It is cheaper.
3. It results in fewer unsuccessful prosecutions.
4. It properly centers in the prosecutor responsibility for action which, in any event, he is likely to control.

Because of these advantages, it is coming to be widely believed that states which have not yet done so would do well to follow the example of those that have largely abandoned use of the grand jury as the normal agency for preferring charges in felony cases.[80]

But although insistence upon use of the grand jury as the regular and normal accusatorial agency appears to constitute a hindrance rather than an aid to effective law enforcement, the institution may well be retained for action in cases where, for special reasons, the court may see fit to summon a grand jury, and particularly as a general investigatory body. Among the thousands of public officials there are inevitably some who are

[78] H. L. McClintock, "Indictment by Grand Jury," *Minnesota Law Review,* Vol. XXVI, pp. 153-176 (January, 1942).

[79] Cf. Moley, "The Initiation of Criminal Prosecutions by Indictment or Information," *loc. cit.*

[80] The United States Constitution, in a provision (Fifth Amendment) applying to the federal government but not to the states, stipulates that "no person shall be held to answer for a capital or otherwise infamous crime, unless on a presentment or indictment of a grand jury." In view of this requirement, all major criminal offenses against the federal government are prosecuted on grand jury charges. Misdemeanors, however, may be prosecuted in the federal courts on information.

derelict or corrupt, and an independent citizen body like the grand jury is often in a stronger position than are fellow officers to investigate official corruption and, where necessary, prefer formal charges of crime. Occasionally, even the prosecuting attorney himself may so pervert the powers of his office as to violate the very law which it is his duty to enforce, and it is scarcely to be expected that he will charge himself with malfeasance or negligence. A grand jury may perform a valuable service in examining or "auditing" the work of public officers generally and law-enforcement officers in particular. The notion of the grand jury as auditor has been aptly expressed by a civic group in Cleveland, Ohio, apropos the situation in Cuyahoga County: [81]

> The very size and complexity of crime in such a county . . . make it increasingly important that we have a careful and more or less continuous audit of enforcement by representative citizens entirely independent of county or city officials.
>
> Few substantial business firms—however ably managed—would feel safe without an audit by individuals entirely unconnected with the organization. One objective of the Grand Jury as that of an auditor should be by its very existence to deter any lapse in morals or efficiency.

Somewhat similar in import is a proposal recently advanced by the Grand Jury Association of New York County relative to grand juries in the counties within New York City. The proposed plan envisages enactment of a law to provide for empaneling twice yearly in each county concerned a special "watch-dog" grand jury, composed in the same manner as regular grand juries and possessing the same powers of subpoena and indictment, but charged solely with the duty of investigating malfeasance and misfeasance in public office. In the opinion of its proponents, such a plan would operate as a strong deterrent to corruption, thereby tending to prevent, rather than merely correct, official misconduct. Though the need for an agency of this nature may be most acute in metropolitan communities, the use of the grand jury as a citizen body to examine the conduct of public office and call to account delinquent officials seems thoroughly sound, in general principle, in its application to rural counties.

DEFENSE OF THE INDIGENT

It is a cardinal principle of American justice that a person accused of crime shall have the right to be represented in court by a lawyer, and this right is guaranteed by constitutional provisions, both federal and state. Many defendants in criminal actions, however, are without private means of employing legal counsel for themselves. Indeed, it appears that more than 80 per cent of the persons accused of crime are without sufficient

[81] Public Safety Committee of the Citizens League, "A Study of the Functions of the Grand Jury System," *Greater Cleveland*, Vol. XXVII, pp. 74-76, 75 (August 12, 1952).

funds to secure proper counsel.[82] In the cases of indigent defendants it becomes the duty of government to provide defense lawyers. This may be done in either of two ways: by the system of assigned counsel or by that of the public defender.[83]

Assigned Counsel. Under the system of assigned counsel, which is the traditional method of dealing with the problem, the trial judge, at the time of arraignment or at some other designated stage in the proceedings, appoints some member of the local bar to represent the defendant. Since lawyers are considered to be officers or agents of the courts, it is their duty to accept such assignments whether or not any provision is made for their compensation. Courts apparently have inherent power to assign counsel to indigent defendants in criminal cases, and every state now has statutory provisions on the subject. Assignment in capital cases is provided for in all states; and some three fourths of the states provide for assignment in all felony cases. A majority of the states provide for assignment in misdemeanor cases as well, though it appears that in practice assignment in such cases is seldom made. Payment of assigned counsel from the public treasury is authorized, with respect to some or all cases, in somewhat more than half of the states. Of these, some provide for compensation in capital cases only, others in all cases of felony, and still others in both felony and misdemeanor cases. The amount of compensation is left to the discretion of the court in some states and fixed by statute at a definite lump sum or per diem in others.[84]

The system of assigned counsel appears to have worked fairly satisfactorily in capital cases for two reasons. In the first place, at least some compensation is usually paid in such cases; secondly, and probably of more importance, the publicity attendant upon a capital case is frequently of considerable advertising value to the lawyer.[85] In other than capital cases, unfortunately, the plan has been rather generally a failure. Compensation in such cases is either nonexistent or inadequate, and there is usually no compensating factor in the form of desirable publicity. The lawyers assigned to defendants are often young and inexperienced. Moreover, unscrupulous lawyers sometimes use defense assignments as a means of extorting money from relatives of the accused, ostensibly to pay expenses involved in locating witnesses and otherwise preparing an adequate defense. If the amount demanded for such alleged purposes cannot be raised

[82] J. Edward Lumbard, Jr., "For Equal Justice—A Public 'Defender,'" *New York Times Magazine,* pp. 17, 68 (November 2, 1947).

[83] The two systems are discussed and compared, along with privately financed defender organizations, in Emery A. Brownell, *Legal Aid in the United States* (Rochester, N. Y., Lawyers Co-operative Publishing Co., 1951), chap. 6.

[84] Reginald H. Smith and John S. Bradway, *Growth of Legal-aid Work in the United States,* rev. ed. (Washington, U. S. Bureau of Labor Statistics, 1936), pp. 75-77.

[85] *Ibid.,* p. 77.

by those concerned in a lump sum, the lawyer may accept payment in installments, care being taken, by securing from the court a series of continuances, that the case does not come to trial and, therefore, that the defendant remains in jail until the final installment has been paid.[86]

The Public Defender. In an effort to overcome the weaknesses of assigned counsel, the office of public defender has now been established in some communities. First created in Los Angeles County, Cal., in 1914, the office now exists in several California counties, all the counties of Connecticut, a number of the more populous counties in Illinois, and certain metropolitan cities or counties elsewhere. The public defender is an elective or appointive public officer[87] who is paid a salary from the public (usually the county) treasury, and whose duty it is to defend all indigent persons accused of crime who request the trial court to provide counsel for them.[88] The office finds justification in the principle that it is as much the duty of government to see that innocent persons are acquitted as to see that the guilty are convicted. Therefore, just as a public prosecutor is provided to conduct judicial proceedings against accused persons, so a regular public defender should be provided to represent the interests of the indigent accused.[89]

The most important advantage of the public-defender system over that of assigned counsel lies in the more effective defense secured by indigent persons from full-time, salaried government lawyers who specialize in defense work. But there are other incidental advantages. Many public defenders, while putting forth every effort on behalf of accused persons for whom any substantial defense can be offered, encourage clients whose cases are clearly hopeless to plead guilty. This saves not only the time of the court but the cost of juries. There is also a saving, in states which provide compensation for assigned counsel, of the money that would otherwise be spent for that purpose. Indeed, it appears that in some instances these various savings have more than offset the cost of the defender's office, thus resulting in a net cash saving to the taxpayers.[90]

Since rural counties seldom have enough criminal-court business to require the services of a full-time defense lawyer for the indigent, it is not

[86] See Philip J. Finnegan, "The Work of the Public Defender of Cook County," *Journal of Criminal Law and Criminology*, Vol. XXVI, pp. 709-718 (January-February, 1936).

[87] Appointment, where that method of selection is employed, is frequently by the judges of the courts of criminal jurisdiction.

[88] The court, under special circumstances, may make assignment of counsel other than the public defender.

[89] In theory, it is the duty of the prosecuting attorney to protect the innocent as well as to see that the guilty are punished. The very nature of the prosecutor's office, however, makes it inevitable that he will be concerned almost exclusively with preparing and presenting cases against accused persons. Indeed, a prosecutor's success as a public servant is judged in large measure by the percentage of convictions that he obtains.

[90] Cf., for example, Finnegan, *loc. cit.*, pp. 717-718.

surprising that the public-defender movement has made most progress in urban communities. Though progress even there has not been rapid, the results of the system where tried have generally been gratifying, and it may reasonably be expected that the office of public defender will become more common in the future. The fact that many rural counties would find it impracticable to provide individually for the office suggests that consideration may well be given to the feasibility of defender districts embracing two or more counties.[91]

THE COUNTY JAIL

A traditional institution of rural government in the law-enforcement field, and one still found in all but a few counties, is the county jail.[92] Controlled as property by the county board, the jail is under the immediate care and management of the sheriff or a jailer employed by him.[93] The jail is used for the detention of two principal classes of prisoners: (1) persons awaiting action by the grand jury or the trial court and held because they are unable to provide bail or are accused of nonbailable offenses, and (2) persons serving short sentences (normally of less than a year) for offenses of which they have been duly convicted. Minor elements in jail populations include, among others, convicted persons awaiting transfer to state penal institutions, insane persons awaiting transportation to mental hospitals, and important witnesses who it is feared might disappear or who have asked for protective custody.[94] The major

[91] On the office generally, see Mayer C. Goldman, *The Public Defender* (New York, Putnam, 1917); Smith and Bradway, *op. cit.*, chap. 11; Lumbard, *loc. cit.*; James V. Bennett, "To Secure the Right to Counsel," *Journal of the American Judicature Society*, Vol. XXXII, pp. 177-181 (April, 1949); Samuel Rubin, "Justice for the Indigent: The Need for Public Defenders," *American Bar Association Journal*, Vol. XXXIX, pp. 893-896, 931 (October, 1953); David Mars, "Public Defenders," *Journal of Criminal Law, Criminology, and Police Science*, Vol. XLVI, pp. 199-210 (July–August, 1955). The literature on the subject for the most part is favorable to the establishment of the defender's office. For presentations of the contrary point of view, see William Scott Stewart, "The Public Defender System Is Unsound in Principle," *Journal of the American Judicature Society*, Vol. XXXII, pp. 115-118 (December, 1948); Edward J. Dimock, "The Public Defender: A Step towards a Police State?" *American Bar Association Journal*, Vol. XLII, pp. 219-221 (March, 1956).

[92] For a comprehensive discussion of jails and jail problems, see Louis N. Robinson, *Jails: Care and Treatment of Misdemeanant Prisoners in the United States* (Philadelphia, Winston, 1944). A graphic account of earlier date is Joseph F. Fishman (in collaboration with Vee Perlman), *Crucibles of Crime: The Shocking Story of the American Jail* (New York, Cosmopolis Press, 1923).

[93] Kentucky provides for an elective county jailer; see above, n. 17.

[94] A breakdown of the population of New Jersey jails, as of 1933, showed the percentages of prisoners detained for various causes to be as follows: serving sentence, 50 per cent; held for grand jury, 15.7 per cent; held for trial, 29.6 per cent; held for transfer, 1.1 per cent; held as witnesses, 1.5 per cent; held for other causes, 2.1 per cent—New Jersey Department of Institutions and Agencies, *New Jersey Jail and Workhouse Survey* (Trenton, N. J., 1936), p. 20.

importance of county jails in our law-enforcement system is indicated by the fact that something like a million men and women "do time" in these institutions each year.[95]

Defects of Jail Administration. County jails have long been the subject of widespread criticism.[96] Most jails are said to be insanitary, and many downright filthy. In the late 1940's only 13 of 54 California county jails were given a "good" rating with respect to over-all general sanitation; 15 were rated as fair, and 26 as poor.[97] And a report on a 1940 survey of Missouri's 115 jails,[98] though there is no reason to believe that the institutions of that state are worse than those of most others, gave none a rating above that of "fairly good" on cleanliness and sanitation, and only four that high a rating. On the scale downward, 22 were rated as fair, 23 as poor, and 66 as bad. Of the institutions in the latter group the report declared:[99]

> They are foul-smelling, damp, dark, dingy, and dungeon-like. Most of these 66 jails are filled with trash, litter, rubbish, junk, bottles, cans, old newspapers and magazines, rags, garbage, filthy and tattered bedding alive with vermin and black from saturation of strong creosote disinfectants and human excretions. And into such an environment sometimes decent and clean men and women and even boys and girls are locked to stay for an average, taking the State as a whole, of 19.6 days.

In addition to being insanitary, many jails, from the standpoint of physical safety, are veritable firetraps. A 1946 survey revealed that 22 of West Virginia's 55 county jails were admittedly bad fire risks, and it indicated that some of those reported to be fire-resistant may not have deserved that classification.[100] Instances are not wanting of prisoners burning to death in flimsy and unattended jails.[101]

Another criticism of jail administration flows from the general lack of appropriate classification and segregation of prisoners. Convicted persons and those awaiting trial, first offenders and habitual criminals, juveniles and adults, the healthy and the diseased—all are too often herded together

[95] Cf. James V. Bennett, "The Medieval County Jail," *Forum,* Vol. C, pp. 260-264 (November, 1938).

[96] An admirable summary of jail shortcomings by James V. Bennett, Director of the United States Bureau of Prisons, will be found in the article cited in n. 95; see also, Robinson, *op. cit.,* pp. 20-21; Joseph F. Fishman and Vee Terrys Perlman, "Let's Abolish the County Jail," *Survey Graphic,* Vol. XXVIII, pp. 26-27, 39-41 (January, 1939).

[97] *A Study of the County Jails of California* (Sacramento, Cal., 1949), p. 11; prepared for the California State Board of Corrections and the Commission for the Study of Adult Corrections and Release Procedures.

[98] That is, 114 county institutions and the municipal jail of St. Louis.

[99] Roy Casey, "Missouri Jail Survey," *Proceedings of the Seventieth Annual Congress of the American Prison Association* (New York, 1940), pp. 402-410, 408.

[100] W. T. Hammack, *Survey of County Jails in West Virginia* (Washington, U. S. Bureau of Prisons, 1946), p. 38.

[101] See Bennett, *loc. cit.*

in close quarters. Again, the large majority of jail inmates are kept in absolute idleness, to their physical, mental, and moral detriment. To be sure, some prisoners are provided with work either within the jail or outside. Trusties sometimes are employed in the jail kitchen or are given cleaning assignments in the jail, the sheriff's residence, or the courthouse. In some states county prisoners are used for road work or on construction projects, such as hospitals or other county buildings. A few counties, in addition to their jails, maintain workhouses for the detention and employment of prisoners serving sentences or operate industrial farms or work camps. By and large, however, idleness remains the general rule. Few counties have anything approaching the programs of prison employment now commonly provided by state penal institutions. In California, though several counties of that state have special work programs, approximately 80 per cent of all jail inmates were reported to be idle in 1948.[102]

Laxity in jail discipline appears to be widespread. Some jailers permit prisoners—at least those considered as reasonably trustworthy—to come and go much as they please, even allowing them to spend weekends at home on slight pretext.[103] Instances are on record of prisoners who, given the "run of the grounds," have used their freedom to commit burglaries and other depredations in the community while technically in jail.

A deplorable institution found in some jails is the "kangaroo court," by means of which, under the guise of self-government, some of the inmates—often those of the lowest type—dominate and persecute their fellow prisoners.[104] "A kangaroo court . . . is an organization for maintaining discipline, which some jailers permit the prisoners to form among themselves. They make the rules and enforce them, and it must be said that in the majority of cases they do not temper justice with mercy." [105] Some jailers seem unable to prevent the organization of kangaroo courts, and others apparently welcome them as a means of "passing the buck" and relieving themselves of disciplinary responsibilities. Incoming prisoners are tried by the court for "breaking into jail," and other trials are held for infractions of court rules. Upon "conviction," prisoners are fined for the benefit of court members, required to perform menial tasks, and, in general, made subject to the will of the controlling group. Refusal to pay the fines levied or to carry out otherwise the orders of the court subjects a recalcitrant prisoner to rigorous disciplinary measures. Punishment meted out by the court sometimes extends to unspeakable brutalities, with instances being known of fatal beatings administered for refusal to obey court mandates.[106] The kangaroo court is one of the most serious forms of jail mismanagement.

[102] *A Study of the County Jails of California*, pp. 13, 24-25.

[103] Cf., for example, Fishman, *Crucibles of Crime*, pp. 55-58.

[104] See Robinson, *op. cit.*, pp. 21-22, 27; Fishman, *Crucibles of Crime*, pp. 73-75; Hammack, *op. cit.*, pp. 7-8, 49-52, 61-62; Bennett, *loc. cit.*

[105] Fishman, *Crucibles of Crime*, p. 73.

[106] Cf. Bennett, *loc. cit.*

"Fundamentally," says Louis N. Robinson, "the presence of this organization within the walls of a jail is a confession of poor prison management, of the inability of guards and officers to keep order and to prevent the stronger prisoners from imposing their will on the weaker."[107] In the words of the recent West Virginia report: "Any jail in which a 'Kangaroo Court' operates indicates such poor administrative control that it cannot be accepted as suitable for the confinement of prisoners."[108]

Some jails are overcrowded, while others are empty or nearly so, suggesting that fewer and larger institutions, operated on a regional basis, might better equalize the required facilities. Few jails provide hospitalization for sick prisoners, and many do not even make adequate provision for medical examinations and the service of physicians on "sick call." In West Virginia, according to the report mentioned above, "No admission examination is given prisoners who enter the county jail, except that in some instances, in a few of the larger jails, those suspected of having venereal disease are examined and required to take regular treatment."[109] This situation is probably typical of many states. "Prisoners in the county jails have tuberculosis, venereal disease, and other afflictions which make them a real danger to the community to which they are released unless they are given proper treatment while in prison. At very little additional cost, many of these cases could be given proper care and treatment, at least to the extent of giving the public better protection against contagion or infection."[110] The operation of a jail commissary, through which inmates are permitted to purchase such items as extra food, candy, cigarettes, soft drinks, and, at times, even liquor, has developed in some institutions into a virtual racket whereby the jailer or a favored concessionaire is able to fleece prisoners of any pocket money they may have. Recreational programs and provision for religious services in jails are generally inadequate or completely lacking.

A final criticism of county jails—and a weighty one—is directed against the widespread prevalence of the fee system in their administration. Some states provide that the sheriff shall receive a "turnkey" fee of a dollar or some such nominal amount for unlocking and locking the jail door each time a prisoner is admitted or discharged. Such an arrangement offers a temptation to arrest and jail persons for slight cause under guise of strict law enforcement.[111] Even more serious is the fee system as applied to the feeding of prisoners—a system whereby the sheriff or jailer is allowed a fixed sum per day for the board of each prisoner without regard to the quantity or quality of the food provided. The result of such a plan almost

[107] Robinson, *op. cit.*, p. 27.
[108] Hammack, *op. cit.*, p. 49.
[109] *Ibid.*, p. 40.
[110] *Ibid.*
[111] Cf. Robinson, *op. cit.*, p. 22.

inevitably is substandard meals, to which may be added an incentive on the part of the sheriff to keep the jail filled to capacity. Records seldom reveal with any accuracy the amount of profit derived by sheriffs from the boarding transaction, but in many instances it is undoubtedly large. One Missouri sheriff was reported to have had income in excess of $13,000 from the feeding of prisoners in 1939; [112] and local attorneys estimated in 1946 that the sheriff of a central Illinois county was making $5,000 a year or more from the same source.[113] Whatever the amount of such profits, the system is unjustified. Even if viewed merely as a means of supplementing the otherwise inadequate compensation of a public official, the fee method as here employed is highly improper. Any system offering, as does this, an incentive to make a profit through the exploitation of unfortunates who have run afoul of the law, is deserving of the strongest condemnation.[114]

Recent Improvements. Proposals for improving jail administration are many and varied, but most of them may be considered as constituting particular aspects of three central recommendations: (1) that individual county jails, except in the most populous counties, be abolished in favor of a system of regional detention homes operated by the state or by groups of counties co-operatively; (2) that such county and regional jails as are retained be improved with respect to both physical condition and management; and (3) that fewer persons be placed in jails.[115] During recent years some progress has been made, though slowly, in each of these directions.

In some instances counties have closed their jails and arranged for the care of their prisoners by neighboring counties or cities in return for a stipulated compensation. The principle of the regional or district institution is exemplified in Virginia, where 40 counties and 13 cities were recently reported to be co-operating in the use of 21 jails. In North Carolina, though county jails are retained for the detention of persons awaiting trial, short penal sentences are now served in state-operated prison camps; and Virginia has recently established two state jail farms for misdemeanants.[116]

The physical condition of jail buildings has been improved somewhat. During the 1930's, when federal loans and grants were available to local

[112] See Casey, *loc. cit.*, p. 407. The fee system was subsequently abolished in Missouri by provision of a new state constitution.

[113] *Champaign-Urbana* [*Ill.*] *News-Gazette*, p. 3 (March 5, 1946).

[114] Cf. Hammack, *op. cit.*, p. 28.

[115] Cf. Robinson, *op. cit.*, pp. 273-274; Bennett, *loc. cit.;* Fishman and Perlman, *loc. cit.*

[116] Virginia State Chamber of Commerce, *Opportunities for Economy in County Government in Virginia* (Richmond, 1947), pp. 27-28; Paul W. Wager, "Effects of North Carolina's Centralization," *National Municipal Review*, Vol. XXVI, pp. 572-577 (December, 1937). The mere fact of state or regional operation, of course, does not, of itself, guarantee improvement. This is demonstrated in Rhode Island where, though the jails in the various counties are state operated, "the level of jail administration does not rise above the average for the country as a whole"—Bruce Smith, *The Jails of Rhode Island* (Providence, Rhode Island Public Expenditure Council, 1945), p. 2.

governments through the Public Works Adiministration for the construction of public buildings, a number of counties replaced their antiquated jails with modern structures. In other instances, fire hazards have been removed and better sanitary facilities installed.[117] Improvements in jail management have also taken place. Many counties now maintain juvenile detention homes in which youthful prisoners are kept rather than in the jail; and others have established separate quarters in the jail for juveniles. As previously noted, some counties have inaugurated employment programs for prisoners. Finally, more and more counties, some pursuant to state mandate and others voluntarily, are abandoning the fee system of feeding prisoners in favor of a plan whereby the county board merely allows and pays bills incurred by the sheriff for the purchase and preparation of prison food.

More frequent release of minor offenders on probation has lessened somewhat the number of persons committed to jail, but further means of reducing the jail population are needed. Many persons now committed because they are unable to provide bail might well be released on their personal recognizance. Some thus released would undoubtedly violate their obligation to appear as stipulated; but occasional transgressions would be more than offset by the fact that many persons, some of them innocent, would escape the humiliating and demoralizing effects of jail environment. Another measure deserving of wider use is installment payment of fines. A substantial percentage of jail inmates are there because of inability to pay fines assessed against them on conviction of minor offenses. These persons normally have no alternative but to "lie out" their fines at the statutory rate of a dollar or so for each day served. Permitting the payment of fines in installments would empty the jails of many such prisoners with little or no additional hazard to society, to say nothing of the financial saving to the public in avoiding their support during a period of detention.

Present Status. Notwithstanding some gradual improvement in county jails and their management, the over-all situation remains far from satisfactory. Since jail mismanagement flows in no small measure from a lack of trained and experienced administrative personnel, progress is bound to be slow as long as jail administration is a function of elective county sheriffs. A step in the right direction would be to remove jail management from the sheriff's jurisdiction and to place it in the hands of a functionary appointed by and responsible to the courts. Such a change, however, would be contrary to long-established tradition and, in some states, would require constitutional amendment. The hope for any rapid and general improvement in jail personnel is therefore dim.

A generation ago the typical jail was characterized by a particularly

[117] Several of the better jails are described in Robinson, *op. cit.*, pp. 173 ff.

competent authority as an "unbelievably filthy institution . . . having no segregation of the unconvicted from the convicted, the well from the diseased, the young and most impressionable from the most degraded and hardened;" which, by maintaining even the able-bodied in complete idleness, "generally affords ample time and opportunity to assure inmates a complete course in every kind of viciousness and crime." [118] Though the exceptions to this general characterization have increased over the years, it appears, unfortunately, to afford a fair description of all too many institutions, even today. Periodic inspections of county and city jails are made by the United States Bureau of Prisons to determine which of them are fit for the housing of federal prisoners awaiting trial or serving short sentences. As recently as 1950 only 451, out of a total of more than 3,000 institutions, were accorded full approval for this purpose, with 365 others being authorized for use on an emergency basis.[119] Such a situation, wherein nearly three fourths of all jails fail to qualify even for restricted federal use, is little short of disgraceful. "Most jails as presently staffed, supported, and operated," declares the 1946 report on West Virginia, "are anachronisms in our social order. The majority of them are totally unfit for human habitation, and much of their underlying philosophy is futile. It is a heritage . . . in which we feel more shame than pride." [120] This statement would be equally valid for most other states.[121] Clearly, the improvement of jails and jail management is currently one of the most pressing problems of American county government.

REFERENCES

Books, Reports, and Special Studies

Adler, Herman M., "Medical Science and Criminal Justice," *Criminal Justice in Cleveland,* Cleveland Foundation (Cleveland, Ohio, 1922), Pt. 5.

American Academy of Forensic Sciences and others, *A Model State Medico-legal Investigative System* (New York, National Municipal League, 1950), tentative draft.

Anderson, Walter H., *A Treatise on the Law of Sheriffs, Coroners, and Constables* (Buffalo, N. Y., Dennis & Co., 1941), 2 vols.

[118] Fishman, *Crucibles of Crime,* pp. 13-14.

[119] United States Bureau of Prisons, *Federal Prisons: 1950,* Annual Report of the Director of Prisons (Washington, 1951), p. 33. The federal rating is based on a number of factors, such as administration and discipline, building and equipment, cleanliness and sanitation, personnel, and food. Such improvements in jails and jail management as have taken place have been the result in considerable part of federal inspection and the assistance and advisory services offered to the local governments by the federal bureau. See above, chap. 2, "Federal-local Relations."

[120] Hammack, *op. cit.,* p. 3.

[121] For a recent account of conditions in one southern jail—an institution probably all too typical of American jails generally—see "Life in a County Jail," *American Mercury,* Vol. LXVIII, pp. 55-63 (January, 1949).

BATES, Sanford, *Prisons and Beyond* (New York, Macmillan, 1936), chap. 3.

BLAIR, George S., *The Office of County Coroner in Kansas* (Emporia, Kansas State Teachers College, 1953).

BROWNELL, Emery A., *Legal Aid in the United States* (Rochester, N. Y., Lawyers Co-operative Publishing Company, 1951).

California State Board of Corrections, *Minimum Jail Standards including Standards for Feeding, Clothing, and Bedding*, rev. ed. (1952).

CASEY, Roy, "Missouri Jail Survey," *Proceedings of the Seventieth Annual Congress of the American Prison Association* (New York, 1940), pp. 402-410.

COHN, Victor, and BAILEY, Charles W., *"Hidden Murder?" A Shocking Report on How Sudden and Mysterious Deaths Are Investigated by Many County Coroners*. Reprinted from the *Minneapolis Morning Tribune* (February, 1953).

FISHMAN, Joseph F. (in collaboration with Vee Perlman), *Crucibles of Crime: The Shocking Story of the American Jail* (New York, Cosmopolis Press, 1923).

Florida Institute of Government, *The Florida Sheriff's Manual* (1947).

GOLDMAN, Mayer C., *The Public Defender* (New York, Putnam, 1917).

Grand Jury Association of New York County, *Forty Years of Progress in Increasing the Effectiveness of the Grand Jury System* (New York, 1953).

HAMMACK, W. T., *Survey of County Jails in West Virginia* (Washington, U. S. Bureau of Prisons, 1946).

HEICES, R. E., *The Office of Sheriff in the Rural Counties of Ohio* (Findlay, Ohio, Privately printed, 1933).

HIGHSAW, Robert B., and MULLICAN, Carl D., Jr., *A Guidebook of the County Sheriff [in Mississippi]* (University, University of Mississippi Bureau of Public Administration, 1948).

HOFFER, Frank W., MANN, Delbert M., and HOUSE, Floyd N., *The Jails of Virginia* (New York, Appleton-Century-Crofts, 1933).

Illinois Department of Public Welfare, Division of Criminal Identification and Investigation, *Survey of the Personnel and Equipment of the Sheriffs' Offices in Illinois* (Springfield, 1940).

Indiana University Institute of Criminal Law Administration, *Indiana Sheriff's Manual of Law and Practice* (Bloomington, Ind., 1945), published in co-operation with the Indiana Sheriffs' Association.

IRION, Frederick C., *Post-mortem Investigations in New Mexico* (Albuquerque, University of New Mexico Department of Government, 1953).

JACKSON, William A., *The Office of Sheriff in Iowa* (Cedar Rapids, Iowa, The Torch Press, 1924).

Kansas Legislative Council, *The Office of the County Coroner in Kansas* (Topeka, Kan., 1956).

MILLSPAUGH, Arthur C., *Local Democracy and Crime Control* (Washington, Brookings Institution, 1936).

Minnesota Legislative Research Committee, *The Coroner System in Minnesota* (St. Paul, 1954).

MOLEY, Raymond, "The Sheriff and the Coroner," *Missouri Crime Survey*, Missouri Association for Criminal Justice (New York, Macmillan, 1926), Pt. 2.

MYREN, Richard A., *Coroners in North Carolina: A Discussion of Their Problems* (Chapel Hill, University of North Carolina Institute of Government, 1953).

National Conference of Commissioners on Uniform State Laws, *Model Post-Mortem Examinations Act* (Chicago, 1954).

National Municipal League, *Coroners in 1953: A Symposium of Legal Bases and Actual Practices* (New York, 1953).

New Jersey Department of Institutions and Agencies, *New Jersey Jail and Workhouse Survey* (Trenton, N. J., 1936).

ORFIELD, Lester B., *Criminal Procedure from Arrest to Trial* (New York, New York University Press, 1947).

QUEEN, Stuart A., *The Passing of the County Jail* (Menasha, Wis., Banta Publishing Co., 1920).

ROBINSON, Louis N., *Jails: Care and Treatment of Misdemeanant Prisoners in the United States* (Philadelphia, Winston, 1944).

SCHULTZ, Oscar T., and MORGAN, E. M., *The Coroner and the Medical Examiner*, National Research Council Bulletin (July, 1928), No. 64.

SMITH, Bruce, *Rural Crime Control* (New York, Columbia University Institute of Public Administration, 1933).

———, *The Jails of Rhode Island* (Providence, Rhode Island Public Expenditure Council, 1945).

———, *Police Systems in the United States*, rev. ed. (New York, Harper, 1949), chap. 4.

A Study of the County Jails of California (1949). Prepared for the California State Board of Corrections and the Commission for the Study of Adult Corrections and Release Procedures.

United States Bureau of the Census, *County and City Jails: Prisoners in Jails and Other Penal Institutions under County or Municipal Jurisdiction, 1933* (Washington, Government Printing Office, 1935).

United States Bureau of Prisons, *Manual of Jail Management* (Washington, 1948).

WEINMANN, George H., *A Compendium of the Statute Law of Coroners and Medical Examiners in the United States*, National Research Council Bulletin (August, 1931), No. 83.

Wisconsin Legislative Reference Library, *Basic Data on the Office of Coroner in Wisconsin* (Madison, Wis., 1955).

Articles

BAKER, Newman F., "The Prosecuting Attorney: Legal Aspects of the Office," *Journal of Criminal Law and Criminology*, Vol. XXVI, pp. 647-678 (January–February, 1936).

———, and DELONG, Earl H., "The Prosecuting Attorney: The Process of Prosecution, I" *Journal of Criminal Law and Criminology*, Vol. XXVI, pp. 3-21 (May, 1935).

BENDINER, Robert, "The Man Who Reads Corpses," *Harper's Magazine*, Vol. CCX, No. 1257, pp. 62-67 (February, 1955).

BENNETT, James V., "The Medieval County Jail," *Forum*, Vol. C, pp. 260-264 (November, 1938).

BLAIR, George S., "The Coroner's Office Never Dies: It Just Fades Away," *The County Officer*, Vol. XVII, pp. 152-154 (May, 1952).

———, "Office of the County Coroner in Kansas," *The County Officer*, Vol. XVIII, pp. 250-254 (October, 1953).

BRECKENRIDGE, A. C., "Wanted: Uniform Law Enforcement," *Journal of Criminal Law, Criminology, and Police Science*, Vol. XLV, pp. 170-175 (July–August, 1954). Reprinted in *The County Officer*, Vol. XX, pp. 39-42 (February, 1955).

BUTLER, Amos W., "The County Jail and the Misdemeanant Prisoner," *Journal of Social Forces,* Vol. II, pp. 220-225 (January, 1924).

BUTLER, Willis P., "The Coroner's Office in Louisiana and Medico-legal Duties in General," *American Journal of Medical Jurisprudence,* Vol. II, pp. 214-221 (May–June, 1939).

CHILDS, Richard S., "Rubbing out the Coroners," *National Municipal Review,* Vol. XXXIX, pp. 494-496 (November, 1950).

DELONG, Earl H., "Powers and Duties of the State Attorney-general in Criminal Prosecution," *Journal of Criminal Law and Criminology,* Vol. XXV, pp. 358-400 (September–October, 1934).

DESMOND, Thomas C., "The Coroner Racket: A National Scandal," *Coronet,* Vol. XXVIII, No. 2, pp. 60-64 (June, 1950).

DIMOCK, Edward J., "The Public Defender: A Step towards a Police State?" *American Bar Association Journal,* Vol. XLII, pp. 219-221 (March, 1956).

ESSELSTYN, T. C., "The Social Rôle of a County Sheriff," *Journal of Criminal Law, Criminology, and Police Science,* Vol. XLIV, pp. 177-184 (July–August, 1953).

FERGUSON, Glenn W., "It's Time for the Coroner's Post-mortem," *Journal of the American Judicature Society,* Vol. XXXIX, pp. 40-46 (August, 1955).

FINNEGAN, Philip J., "The Work of the Public Defender of Cook County," *Journal of Criminal Law and Criminology,* Vol. XXVI, pp. 709-718 (January–February, 1936).

FISHMAN, Joseph F., "The American Jail," *Atlantic Monthly,* Vol. CXXX, pp. 792-805 (December, 1922).

———, "Our Comic-opera Hoosegows," *American Mercury,* Vol. LXIX, pp. 176-183 (August, 1949).

———, and PERLMAN, Vee Terrys, "Let's Abolish the County Jail," *Survey Graphic,* Vol. XXVIII, pp. 26-27, 39-41 (January, 1939).

GETTLER, Alexander O., "Why the Coroner System Has Broken Down," *National Municipal Review,* Vol. XIII, pp. 560-568 (October, 1924).

"The Grand Jury—Its Investigatory Powers and Limitations," *Minnesota Law Review,* Vol. XXXVII, pp. 586-607 (June, 1953).

HAYNES, Fred E., "County Jails in Iowa," *Iowa Journal of History and Politics,* Vol. XLIV, pp. 61-85 (January, 1946).

HEIGES, R. E., "Goodbye to the Sheriff," *Social Science,* Vol. XI, pp. 137-141 (April, 1936).

HENDERSON, Richard B., "'Crowner's Quest' and the Maryland Examiner System," *The County Officer,* Vol. XVI, pp. 99-102 (April, 1951).

HUNT, Ernest L., "Medical Examiner's Routine and Records," *American Journal of Medical Jurisprudence,* Vol. I, pp. 247-252 (December, 1938).

JOHNSON, Charles H., "The Wisconsin Coroner System," *Wisconsin Law Review,* pp. 529 547 (May, 1951).

KRAMER, Ralph M., "Crime Prevention in the County Jail," *Survey Midmonthly,* Vol. LXXXIII, pp. 249-250 (September, 1947).

"Life in a County Jail," *American Mercury,* Vol. LXVIII, pp. 55-63 (January, 1949).

LUMBARD, J. Edward, Jr., "For Equal Justice—A Public Defender," *New York Times Magazine,* pp. 17, 68 (November 2, 1947).

MCCLINTOCK, H. L., "Indictment by Grand Jury," *Minnesota Law Review,* Vol. XXVI, pp. 153-176 (January, 1942).

MALDEIS, Howard J., "Medical Examiner's System in the State of Maryland," *Southern Medical Journal,* Vol. XLI, pp. 840-844 (September, 1948).

MARS, David, "The Public Defender System in Connecticut," *State Government,* Vol. XXVII, pp. 29-30, 41 (February, 1954).

———, "Public Defenders," *Journal of Criminal Law, Criminology, and Police Science,* Vol. XLVI, pp. 199-210 (July–August, 1955).

MARTIN, Pete, "How Murderers Beat the Law" *Saturday Evening Post,* Vol. CCXXII, No. 24, pp. 32-33, 46 ff. (December 10, 1949).

MILLER, R. Justin, "Informations or Indictments in Felony Cases," *Minnesota Law Review,* Vol. VIII, pp. 379-408 (April, 1924).

MISHKIN, Charles, "The Public Defender," *Journal of Criminal Law and Criminology,* Vol. XXII, pp. 489-505 (November, 1931)

MOLEY, Raymond, "The Initiation of Criminal Prosecutions by Indictment or Information," *Michigan Law Review,* Vol. XXIX, pp. 403-431 (February, 1931).

MORSE, Wayne L., "A Survey of the Grand Jury System," *Oregon Law Review,* Vol. X, pp. 101-160, 217-257, 295-365 (February, April, June, 1931).

NORRIS, Charles, "The Medical Examiner versus the Coroner," *National Municipal Review,* Vol. IX, pp. 498-504 (August, 1920).

PAGE, James F., "A Study of Local Offenders in the Payne County [Oklahoma] Jail," *Southwestern Social Science Quarterly,* Vol. XXIX, pp. 232-239 (December, 1948).

PALMER, Ben W., "The Vestigial Sheriff: The Shrunken Giant of the Present Day," *American Bar Association Journal,* Vol. XXXVI, pp. 367-369 (May, 1950).

PERKINS, Rollin M., The Law of Arrest," *Iowa Law Review,* Vol. XXV, pp. 202-289 (January, 1940).

Public Safety Committee of the Citizens League, "A Study of the Functions of the Grand Jury System," *Greater Cleveland,* Vol. XXVII, pp. 74-76 (August 12, 1952).

RAFFERTY, Brae, "The Medical Examiner System in Connecticut," *Connecticut State Medical Journal,* Vol. XVII, pp. 114-116 (February, 1953).

ROBINSON, Louis N., "The Perennial Jail Problem," *Journal of Criminal Law and Criminology,* Vol. XXXV, pp. 369-374 (March–April, 1945).

RUBIN, Samuel, "Justice for the Indigent: The Need for Public Defenders," *American Bar Association Journal,* Vol. XXXIX, pp. 893-896, 931 (October, 1953).

SCHULTZ, Oscar T., "The Coroner's Office," *Annals of American Academy of Political and Social Science,* Vol. XLVII, pp. 112-119 (May, 1913).

———, "A Physician Examines the Coroner," *National Municipal Review,* Vol. XXV, pp. 577-584, 608 (October, 1936).

SNYDER, Le Moyne, "Justice and Sudden Death," *Journal of the American Judicature Society,* Vol. XXXVI, pp. 142-147 (February, 1953).

STEPHENSON, C. M., "County Jail Financing in Kentucky," *National Municipal Review,* Vol. XXV, pp. 271-277 (May, 1936).

TRESOLINI, Rocco, TAYLOR, Richard W., and BARNETT, Elliott B., "Arrest without Warrant: Extent and Social Implications," *Journal of Criminal Law, Criminology, and Police Science,* Vol. XLVI, pp. 187-198 (July–August, 1955).

TURKEL, Henry W., "Merits of the Present Coroner System," *Journal of the American Medical Association,* Vol. CLIII, pp. 1086-1092 (November 21, 1953).

VANCE, B. M., "The Work of a Medical Examiner's Office," *American Journal of Medical Jurisprudence,* Vol. I, pp. 95-100 (October, 1938).

VANCE, B. M., "A Critical Review of the Medical Examiner System," *American Journal of Medical Jurisprudence,* Vol. II, pp. 243-248 (July, 1939).

WHEELER, Ruth Dunlop, "The Problem of the County Jail," *Journal of Criminal Law and Criminology,* Vol. XV, pp. 620-630 (February, 1925).

"Why Coroners?" *Council Comments,* No. 628 (November 29, 1954), a publication of the Citizens Research Council of Detroit, Mich.

YOUNGER, Richard D., "The Grand Jury under Attack," *Journal of Criminal Law, Criminology, and Police Science,* Vol. XLVI, pp. 26-49, 214-225 (May–June, July–August, 1955).

CHAPTER 14

Highways

THE RURAL ROAD PROBLEM

FROM THE EARLY years of our national history, provision of ways for public travel has been one of the principal concerns of local government. As long as overland travel was on horseback or by horse-drawn vehicle, primitive roads sufficed. In our pioneer agricultural society, children walked to country school or, in bad weather, were transported by their parents on horseback or by horse-drawn buggy. The route of the rural mailman comprised but a few miles and, with only occasional exceptions, could be covered any day regardless of mud, snow, or dust. Farm families drove to market once a week, in the family carriage or "spring-wagon," to sell their eggs, cream, and other produce and to purchase supplies. On Sundays these light vehicles provided transportation to church. Livestock was driven to the local market or transported by horse-drawn wagons; and the same farm wagons were the usual means of transporting grain and hay produced for sale. For such travel and transportation the necessary roads could readily be provided by locally elected highway commissioners with the assistance of neighboring farmers. Down to 1890 almost all of the rural highways in the United States were dirt roads; and practically all of the relatively small mileage classed as "all-weather" highways was surfaced merely with gravel or crushed stone.[1]

A movement to provide better roads began in a small way during the late 1800's, but it remained for the advent of the automobile, at the turn of the century, to set in motion a virtual revolution in American highways and highway problems. With the general spread of automotive travel and transportation, and accompanying economic and social changes, came a demand for all-weather roads suitable for heavy vehicular traffic that has

[1] United States Bureau of Public Roads, *Highways in the United States* (Washington, Government Printing Office, 1951), p. 2.

not abated to the present day. As small school districts were consolidated, the transportation of children to consolidated schools called for highways that would carry heavy school buses regardless of weather conditions. Today, more than 6,000,000 children—approximately one fifth of all school children in the United States—ride daily in 100,000 buses to more than 40,000 schools. Rural mail carriers, numbering some 30,000, now travel 1,500,000 miles of rural roads every day by car or truck, providing service as regular as that of city carriers. Local creameries have been largely supplanted by heavy milk trucks, which ply the rural highways daily to pick up fluid milk from the farms; and many metropolitan areas now receive their entire milk supply in this manner. Trucks are used to haul away from the farms a large percentage of other agricultural products—eggs, fruit, vegetables, grain, hay, and cotton. The stockyards of the country now receive about three fourths of all their livestock by truck.[2]

Though heavy-duty trucks and buses pose the most serious problem from the standpoint of highway durability, all-weather surfacing is required no less for the vast amount of passenger-car traffic. Whereas the farmer of horse-and-buggy days usually journeyed to his neighboring village only once a week, the present-day farmer often makes the trip daily and sometimes more than once in a single day. Furthermore, whereas trips beyond the nearest market-place were once unusual, trips to the county seat and principal shopping centers, for business and entertainment, are now commonplace. Rural roads are widely used by city dwellers as well as by rural residents. Sunday afternoons, in particular, and evenings during the hot summer months, are likely to find country highways crowded with cars from neighboring municipalities. Vacation travel is also a major factor in the use of rural roads. It is estimated, for example, that 63,000,000 Americans went on vacation trips during 1950 in 31,000,000 cars, with the average car covering 1,000 miles in nine days of travel.[3] Thus, urban dwellers, as well as the rural inhabitants themselves, have a genuine stake in the condition of rural roads.

The importance of the present-day highway function is indicated in some measure by the amount of road mileage, the number of vehicles using the roads, the extent of travel thereon, and the amount of highway expenditures. Included in America's public highway system are some 300,000 miles of city streets and 3,000,000 miles of rural roads. Traveling on these thoroughfares are some 60,000,000 motor vehicles. As of 1950, 5,500,000 passenger cars and 2,500,000 trucks were owned by farmers; but, as previously noted, vehicles owned by city dwellers also make extensive use of rural highways. Total travel on American highways in 1950 was estimated at some 450,000,000,000 vehicle-miles, of which 235,000,000,000, or an average of almost 5,000 miles for every registered vehicle in the

[2] Cf. *ibid.*, pp. 11-12.
[3] *Ibid.*, p. 11.

country, was on rural roads.[4] By 1954 total travel had risen to an estimated 557,000,000,000 vehicle-miles, with 814,000,000,000 vehicle-miles anticipated by 1965.[5] Highway expenditures consistently bulk large in state and local budgets, and federal expenditures for highway purposes also are considerable. Of all functions carried on by the states and their subdivisions, only education and welfare services approach or exceed highways in costs; and in the case of rural counties and townships the road function often accounts for the largest item of expenditure. As of 1954 total highway expenditures—federal, state, and local—were estimated at more than $6,000,000,000, with rural local road units alone spending well over $1,000,000,000.[6] And future expenditures may be expected to show substantial increases, particularly in view of provisions of the Federal-Aid Highway Act of 1956 authorizing large appropriations, extending through fiscal 1969, for expenditure on interstate and defense highways.

Involved in the modern highway function are a wide variety of activities. Policy decisions must first be made concerning how much mileage shall be built, where the roads shall be located, and of what material they shall be constructed. Right of way must then be secured and plans and specifications prepared. Actual construction work must be performed by government employees or, if by private contractors, under governmental supervision. Once built, roadbeds must constantly be maintained in a reasonable condition for travel. Weeds and brush must be cleared from the shoulders to preserve the appearance of the roads and prevent the development of obstructions to vision. In the northern states, snow and ice must be removed during the winter months. Markers and signs must be erected to guide travelers and promote safety.[7] Quite obviously, the construction and maintenance of highways suitable for modern traffic has become a highly specialized engineering task which can no longer be left, as was pioneer road building, to part-time, nonprofessional personnel. Nothing less than a properly organized administrative agency of the government concerned, staffed by competent employees and supplied with adequate funds, will be able to provide the highway services now demanded by the motoring public.

[4] *Ibid.*, pp. 11-12.

[5] Lucius D. Clay, "For an Adequate Highway System," *State Government*, Vol. XXVIII, pp. 79-81, 95 (April, 1955).

[6] *Report of the Commission on Intergovernmental Relations* (Washington, Government Printing Office, 1955), p. 217; United States Bureau of Public Roads, *Highway Statistics: 1954* (Washington, Government Printing Office, 1955), p. 86.

[7] Cf. George D. Young, *County Road Administration and Finance in New York* (Ithaca, Cornell University Department of Agricultural Economics, 1952), p. 2.

ROADS AND RURAL LIFE

Extensive road improvements during recent decades have been one of the most important factors in raising the general standard of living in rural areas. Farm life is less isolated than formerly. Automobiles and good roads have facilitated the marketing of farm products and have provided farm families with ready access to schools, churches, shopping centers, and recreational facilities. Rural people have been enabled to participate in a wide variety of community activities, such as those of farm organizations, fraternal groups, clubs, and extension programs. Better local roads have been a major factor in the improvement of rural health facilities. Services of doctors and visiting nurses are more readily obtained, and hospitals are made more accessible. Mobile units of public health departments designed to combat specific diseases now travel the rural highways to furnish chest X rays, treatments, inoculations, and other medical services.[8] In addition to these advantages, road improvements increase the value of adjacent farm lands.[9] For all of these reasons, rural dwellers constantly have demanded better highways. The favorable response by government to this demand is indicated by the fact that two out of every three American farms are now on all-weather roads and 20 per cent more are within two miles of such highways.[10]

THE NATIONAL GOVERNMENT AND HIGHWAYS

There is in this country no national highway system in the sense of a nation-wide network of thoroughfares built and maintained by the central government. During the first half of the nineteenth century, the famous Cumberland Road, or National Pike, was built by the national government. With Cumberland, Md., as its eastern terminus, this road was officially projected as far westward as Vandalia, Ill. Construction, however, was not completed to that point, and the road was ultimately ceded to the respective states through which it passed.[11] The national government has built and maintains some 92,000 miles of highways in national forests, parks, and reservations [12] and, beginning in 1916, has made gen-

[8] United States Bureau of Public Roads, *The Local Rural Road Problem* (Washington, Government Printing Office, 1950), p. 15.

[9] *Ibid.*, pp. 18, 22. A New York study of the mid-1930's indicated that "in general, a gravel road increases the value of a farm 20 per cent and a hard-surfaced road increases the value over a dirt road by 50 per cent"—W. M. Curtiss, *Use and Value of Highways in Rural New York* (Ithaca, Cornell University Agricultural Experiment Station, 1936), p. 25.

[10] *Highways in the United States*, p. 11.

[11] For a brief historical account of the Cumberland Road, see T. R. Agg and J. E. Brindley, *Highway Administration and Finance* (New York, McGraw-Hill, 1927), pp. 4-21.

[12] *Highway Statistics: 1954*, p. 114.

erous grants of financial assistance to the states for highway purposes. Congress has also co-operated in the construction of the Pan-American Highway by providing funds for surveys, for construction of the Alaskan segment, and for loans to various other American countries through which the highway passes. But the construction and maintenance of highways in the continental United States has always been and remains today a responsibility primarily of the states and their local governments.

Since 1925, under a co-operative arrangement between the American Association of State Highway Officials and the United States Bureau of Public Roads, a nation-wide system of principal connecting thoroughfares selected by a Joint Board on Interstate Highways has been given a uniform system of marking and numbering. Roads in this so-called national highway system are marked with shield-shaped signs which bear the name of the state, the letters "US," and the number of the route. East-west highways are designated by even numbers, and north-south routes by odd numbers.[13] It should be emphasized, however, that these "U. S. highways," though financed in part by federal funds, are built and maintained by the respective states as parts of their state highway systems and are given uniform marking and numbering solely for the convenience of the traveling public.

STATE AND LOCAL RESPONSIBILITY

During pioneer days, and indeed to the end of the nineteenth century, most overland travel was local in nature, and the task of providing public highways was left by the states almost entirely to their local governmental units.[14] Practically all road work was done by local authorities and financed by whatever funds could be raised locally for highway purposes. The first step away from purely local support of roads came in 1891 when New Jersey initiated state aid to counties for road building. By 1900 six other states had enacted similar laws, and by 1917 every state made some provision for state participation in highway financing.[15] With the rapid increase in automotive travel and the demand to "get the farmer out of the mud" came a constant extension of state participation in the highway function. The inauguration of the federal-aid program in 1916 provided an additional impetus to state activity, and shortly thereafter every state had established a highway department or equivalent agency. State high-

[13] Cf. John H. Bateman, *Introduction to Highway Engineering,* 4th ed. (New York, Wiley, 1942), p. 6.

[14] During the early 1800's numerous toll-financed "turnpikes" were built and operated by private companies.

[15] United States Public Roads Administration, *Highway Practice in the United States of America* (Washington, Government Printing Office, 1949), pp. 1-7; *Highways in the United States,* p. 3.

way departments were originally organized primarily for the purpose of administering aid to local governments. Later, they undertook construction, often with local assistance, and turned the completed roads over to the local authorities for maintenance. "The final step, strongly supported by the rural population, was eventually taken in every State when the State highway department was charged with full responsibility for construction and maintenance of a system of primary highways with State funds." [16]

Legal responsibility for the construction and maintenance of rural highways today varies from state to state (see Fig. X). Four states—Delaware, North Carolina, Virginia, and West Virginia—have centralized in the state government itself administrative and financial responsibility for all or nearly all rural roads. Elsewhere, primary responsibility is apportioned by statute between the state and local governmental units of one or more types. In some 20 southern and western states, and in the midwestern states of Indiana, Iowa, and Michigan, most or all nonstate roads in rural areas are under county jurisdiction. Local road administration in the six New England states rests primarily with the towns, though in Maine and Massachusetts counties receive and expend some highway funds. Approximately a dozen other states make a three-way distribution of highway responsibility among the state, county, and township governments. Also participating in the local highway function in several states are special road districts; and in a few instances one or more toll-road authorities operate in rural areas. Road districts in some instances are superimposed upon the county or township road organization to provide special highway services for the area within district boundaries; in others they take the place of the townships as basic road units, where local responsibility is divided between the county and a lesser area. Toll authorities usually are established to finance special highway projects, such as toll bridges.[17]

Ordinarily, a particular scheme of distributing highway responsibility among the various levels and agencies of government is effective throughout a given state. This, however, is not always the case. In Virginia, for example, though state administration is the general rule, three counties—two rural and one urban—have retained control over their local roads under optional legislation; and in Alabama, where maintenance of secondary roads is generally a county function, the state, in 1951, assumed responsibility for their administration in three counties.[18] Several states

[16] *The Local Rural Road Problem*, p. 4.

[17] Cf. *ibid.*, pp. 40-41; United States Bureau of Public Roads, *The Financing of Highways by Counties and Local Rural Governments: 1942-51* (Washington, Government Printing Office, 1955), pp. 1-6.

[18] United States Bureau of Public Roads, *Highway Statistics: 1951* (Washington, Government Printing Office, 1953), p. 101.

have optional laws under which some counties maintain all nonstate roads on a county-unit basis, while in other counties the local highway function is shared with townships or road districts. In Illinois special road districts take the place of townships, for highway purposes, in nontownship counties.

In 1951 nearly 18,000 local governmental units were exercising some measure of jurisdiction over local rural roads. These included approximately 2,700 counties, 14,000 towns and townships, 1,100 road districts, and a dozen toll authorities.[19] The number of units of each type operating in each state is shown on the map in Fig. X. As of 1954 the nation's rural highway mileage, exclusive of roads under federal control, was distributed approximately as follows: highways under state control (including state-controlled local roads), 600,000 miles; county roads, 1,700,000 miles; and town, township, and district roads, 600,000 miles.[20]

CLASSES OF RURAL HIGHWAYS

On the basis of their predominant purpose, rural highways may be classified roughly as (1) primary highways, (2) secondary highways, and (3) farm-to-market or "tertiary" roads. The first of these classes consists largely of interstate thoroughfares connecting the principal population centers of the country. Secondary highways are of an inter-county character and serve to connect the various cities within the state. Farm-to-market roads are designed principally to provide rural dwellers with access to local trade centers, as well as to railroads, schools, and churches. It will readily be seen, of course, that this is by no means a hard-and-fast classification, since some highways serve more than a single purpose and overlapping of the respective classes inevitably results. In a general way, control over these three types of highways has been vested for some years past, and to a considerable extent still remains, in the three respective levels of government sharing in the highway function. Most of the primary-road mileage is included within the state highway systems. Both secondary and farm-to-market roads are controlled in some states by the counties and in others by the towns; but, where both counties and lesser subdivisions participate, secondary highways are ordinarily controlled by the former and farm-to-market roads by the latter. A current tendency to shift farm-to-market roads from township or district control to county jurisdiction and to transfer more and more secondary mileage to the state highway system is considered at a subsequent point in the chapter.[21]

[19] Cf. *The Financing of Highways by Counties and Local Rural Governments: 1942-51,* p. 2.

[20] For detailed mileage data, by states, see *Highway Statistics: 1954,* p. 113.

[21] See below, "Trend toward Centralization."

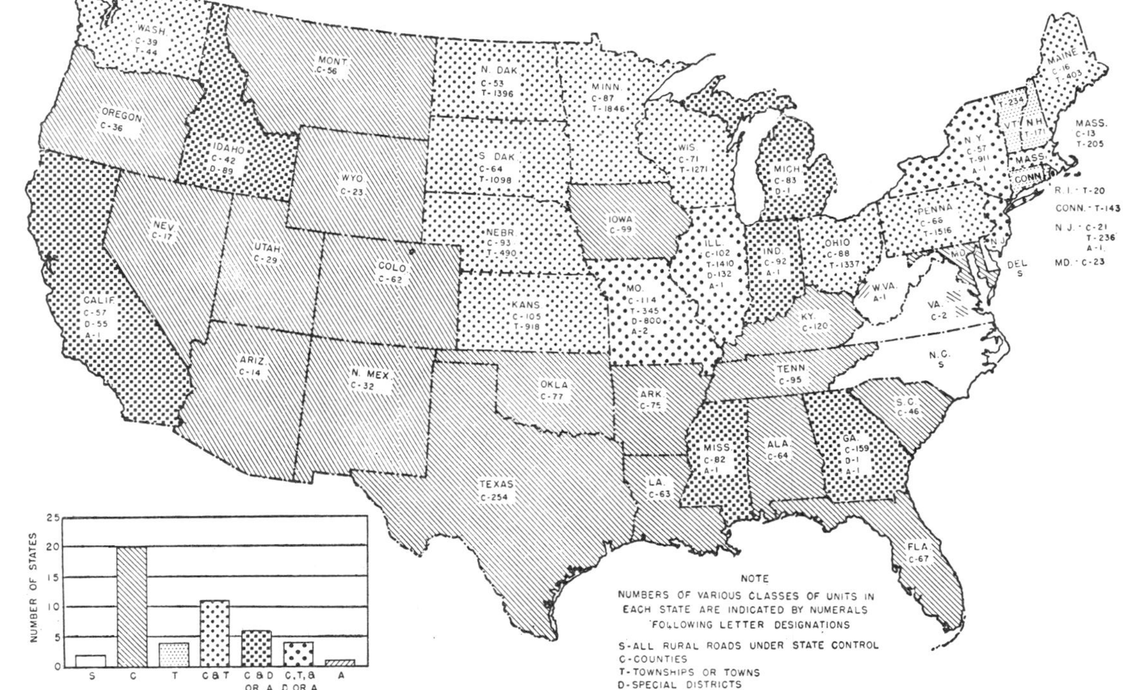

SOURCE: United States Bureau of Public Roads, *The Financing of Highways by Counties and Local Rural Governments: 1942-51* (Washington, Government Printing Office, 1955), p. 3.

FIG. X

Rural Local Road Units: 1951

CONDITION AND USE OF RURAL ROADS

Of the rural road mileage under state control, more than 90 per cent is provided with surfacing of one kind or another, nearly 40 per cent with Portland cement concrete, brick, or high-type bituminous pavement. In contrast, of the 2,300,000 miles of county, township, and district roads in 1954, slightly less than 60 per cent was surfaced. Furthermore, of the surfaced roads in the local systems, only 57,000 miles were of high-type pavement, the remainder being improved with gravel, stone, stabilized soil, and low-type bituminous materials. More than a million miles of local roads, constituting one third of the nation's rural mileage, were unsurfaced.[22] Many local roads, being unimproved or poorly surfaced and often inadequately maintained, are unfit for travel much of the time. Thus, a large part of Minnesota's township mileage was reported as of 1947 to be "made up of roads that are impassable during the winter and spring of the year and are quite unsatisfactory even during the drier part of the year." [23]

County, township, and district roads, though comprising three fourths of all rural mileage, carry less than one fourth of the total traffic. State roads constituting rural portions of the uniformly marked and numbered "national highway system" have an average traffic of more than 3,000 vehicles a day, and other state highways have an average of over 1,000 per day. On the more than 2,000,000 miles of local rural roads, on the other hand, average traffic is only 56 vehicles per day. "About 21 per cent of these local roads carry more than 50 vehicles a day, and another 39 per cent carry between 10 and 50. Approximately 40 per cent of the local rural roads, or about a million miles, are traveled by 10 or fewer vehicles a day." [24] These data clearly indicate the secondary character, from the standpoint of amount of traffic carried, of the rural roads under local management. Nevertheless, these local highways are vitally important both as farm-to-market roads and as "feeders" to the primary state systems. Their construction and maintenance today is, and will continue to be, one of the foremost concerns of local government in rural areas.

ADMINISTRATION AND PERSONNEL

General responsibility for locating, planning, and financing county roads and bridges usually is vested in the governing body of the county. In some instances the governing body not only determines such matters of policy but actually manages or supervises the details of construction

[22] *Highway Statistics: 1954,* p. 114.

[23] R. A. Gomez, *Intergovernmental Relations in Highways* (Minneapolis, University of Minnesota Press, 1950), p. 80.

[24] *Highways in the United States,* p. 13.

and maintenance operations. Elsewhere, however, the direct management of construction and maintenance, in accordance with policies laid down by the governing body, is in charge of a single administrative official, ordinarily called the county highway commissioner, superintendent, or engineer. This official in some instances is popularly elected, but more commonly he is appointed by the county governing body. The provision of such an administrative officer in the highway field is highly advisable. Members of elective governing bodies generally lack the training and experience to deal effectively with such technical matters as construction details and supervision of maintenance operations; and their attempt to do so, more or less directly, is a common cause of inefficiency in county road administration. Sound management practice suggests the desirability of restricting the highway functions of county governing bodies to those of policy formulation, with execution reposed in a qualified administrative officer. This official should be appointed rather than elected. Appointing authority is most properly vested in the county governing body or, where such a functionary exists, with the county chief executive. A requirement that the local appointment meet the approval of the state highway department is now found in a few states and is probably salutary in its general effect, particularly where the appointing agency is the county governing body.[25] In those states which divide local road responsibility between counties and townships or districts, it usually falls to the county governing authorities to select the roads to be included in the county highway system.

In townships serving as highway units, road affairs are most commonly under the jurisdiction of the regular township governing bodies. Many townships and road districts, however, are provided with elective road commissioners or supervisors. This is true, for example, in Illinois, where each township in counties under township organization and each road district in nontownship counties has an elective highway commissioner. In still other instances township or district roads are managed by an appointive superintendent or supervisor. Whatever the nature of township or district highway agencies, it is usually their duty to maintain all rural roads not under state or county jurisdiction. Responsibility of township or district officials ordinarily extends to the construction of bridges and culverts as well as to the maintenance of the roadbed, though in some states such structures, or at least those costing in excess of a designated sum, are built by the county highway authorities or under the supervision of county agencies.[26]

As of 1950, it was estimated that about 97,000 technical, skilled, and supervisory employees were participating in the conduct of local rural

[25] Cf. *The Local Rural Road Problem*, pp. 41-43.

[26] Cf. T. R. Agg, *American Rural Highways* (New York, McGraw-Hill, 1920), pp. 13-15.

road affairs throughout the country. Of this number, approximately 67,000 were full-time employees and 30,000 were seasonal. Those serving on a full-time basis included about 12,000 engineering employees, 44,000 equipment operators, and 11,000 superintendents or foremen. Of the 30,000 seasonal employees, some 11,500 were engaged in engineering work, 16,000 were equipment operators, and 2,500 were in the superintendent or foreman class. The average county was reported to have 22 technical, skilled, and supervisory road employees—18 full-time and 4 seasonal; while the average township had only two such employees—one full-time and one seasonal. It will be noted that in the case of engineering employees, about as many were seasonal as full-time, but that in other classes the proportion of seasonal workers was small.[27]

RESULTS OF SMALL UNITS

The extreme decentralization of rural road administration among thousands of small governmental units inevitably results in waste and inefficiency. Prior to the advent of the automobile, the dirt roads of the times were graded and maintained by simple horse-drawn machinery, the operation of which required a minimum of technical skill. Today, the construction and maintenance of all-weather highways is a highly technical task demanding the services of trained engineers in its planning and execution and the use of expensive motorized equipment manned by skilled operators. Some individual counties have too little road mileage to make practicable the provision of needed engineering services and mechanical equipment; and this is almost universally the situation in the smaller townships and road districts. The great majority of townships and road districts can ill afford either to employ a qualified highway engineer or to provide the machinery required for modern road maintenance. Where such machinery *is* purchased it is likely, because of the small mileage involved, to be idle much of the time. Furthermore, some townships and districts are financially able to provide better roads than others; and, where these small units serve as the basic administrative areas, there is no assurance that the local roads of the respective communities will be maintained as a co-ordinated highway system.[28]

In Illinois, where some three fourths of all local rural road mileage is under the jurisdiction of townships and road districts, a 1948 report by Griffenhagen and Associates declares that "One of the principal objections to the present plan lies in the fact that an elected highway commissioner is not likely to be skilled in the improvement and maintenance of roads

[27] *The Local Rural Road Problem,* p. 42.

[28] Cf. Clyde F. Snider, "The Twilight of the Township," *National Municipal Review,* Vol. XLI, pp. 390-396 (September, 1952).

and bridges. No technical or experience qualifications are required of him. The position is usually intended to be part-time so that an incumbent can continue his farming, trade, or other business while serving as highway commissioner. The salaries are very low, too low to attract anyone with qualifications for technical work in the highway field." It was found, furthermore, that "the very size of the townships and road districts as administrative units precludes any opportunity for a suitable organization for road improvement and maintenance." Though some of the wealthier units have modern motor graders and other essential machinery, a majority of the townships and districts "do not have enough equipment to be able to do their work efficiently. Often the equipment is worn out or obsolete, and generally there are too few pieces to permit all necessary operation. In each of many townships and road districts it would take the revenues for almost two years to pay for a heavy-duty motor grader. It is beyond the capacity of many local units to secure such equipment and still have anything left for current expenses." "On the other hand," the report continues, "the equipment which is purchased by townships and road districts can be used for only a limited time on the small mileage of road under any one jurisdiction. The result is that the equipment is idle a substantial part of each year. It is evident that local rural road administrative units of the present size are very much too small to own a minimum complement of equipment or to have a reasonable amount of use for it if it could be obtained." [29]

Along similar lines a road study committee of the Illinois Agricultural Association, reporting in 1949, pointed out that, in addition to the state's 102 counties, more than 1,600 Illinois townships and road districts, requiring some 5,000 road commissioners, supervisors, and district clerks in their administration, were charged with responsibility for local rural roads. This overorganization was believed to be responsible in considerable measure for the expensiveness of local road service in Illinois and the inadequacy of the service in many localities. "Expensive pieces of equipment are bought and used but a few days each year. Labor is ineffectively employed and directed. The wrong materials, or those which have not been tested, are used in many instances. Also, poor methods of repair, construction and maintenance are often followed. The results are a waste of tax money." [30] Such conclusions with respect to Illinois would

[29] Griffenhagen and Associates, *A Highway Improvement Program for Illinois*, Report to the Illinois Division of Highways for Transmittal to the Illinois Highway and Traffic Problems Commission (Chicago, 1948), pp. 223, 224. Each Illinois township and road district was reported to have an average of about 48 miles of road under its jurisdiction, with more than 200 such units, however, having less than 30 miles each.

[30] Illinois Agricultural Association, *Report of the Illinois Agricultural Association Road Study Committee* (1949), pp. 31, 32.

appear to be equally valid as applied to highway administration by townships and small road districts in other states.

TREND TOWARD CENTRALIZATION

Because of the general inadequacy of small local areas as financial and administrative units for road purposes, there has been a distinct tendency during recent decades toward greater centralization of the highway function. The centralization thus effected has taken three principal forms: (1) the complete transfer of the highway functions of some local governments to larger overlying units, with the result that the smaller areas have been eliminated entirely as units for road administration and finance; (2) the transfer of substantial amounts of mileage from the jurisdiction of smaller units to that of larger, while retaining the smaller areas as road units; and (3) the expansion of state administrative supervision over local road activities through such means as conditional grants of state financial assistance and state participation in the appointment of local road officials. State supervision through state aid and other measures is considered in subsequent sections of this chapter.[31] Attention will be given at this point to transfers of the highway function from smaller to larger governmental units and to the transfer of mileage to larger jurisdictional areas.

Notwithstanding that nearly 18,000 local governments still perform rural road functions, the number of local road units until recently was even larger by several thousand. As previously noted, the states of Delaware, North Carolina, Virginia, and West Virginia, which once divided the rural road function between the state and the counties, have now, but for a few exceptions in Virginia, completely eliminated the county as a highway unit and imposed full responsibility for rural roads on the state government.[32] This transfer of highway responsibility from county to state, occurring during the 1930's, removed some 250 counties from the list of local road units. Much larger is the number of townships, in states where those units have traditionally shared responsibility for rural roads with the state and county governments, which have now been eliminated as road units, with their functions in this field transferred to the county.

Iowa, Indiana, and Michigan, during the late 1920's and early 1930's, enacted statutes providing for the mandatory transfer of all township roads to county jurisdiction, thereby eliminating nearly 3,000 townships as road units.[33] Under the Iowa and Indiana laws the complete shift from

[31] See below, "Highway Finance;" "State Supervision and Control."

[32] West Virginia has one local toll authority.

[33] Michigan townships still may, and many of them do, contribute money to their respective counties to enable the county road commissions to provide better improvement of local roads than would be possible with funds otherwise available. See John E. Stoner, *Comparative County Highway Administration: A Study of Steuben County, Indiana; Branch County, Michigan; Williams County, Ohio,* Joint Highway Research

township to county jurisdiction was made at one time. Michigan, on the other hand, chose to make the shift gradually, providing for the transfer of 20 per cent of the township mileage each year for five years. Oklahoma, after a constitutional amendment of 1933 deprived townships of the taxing power and thereby virtually abolished the township as a governmental unit, enacted statutory provisions transferring road maintenance, along with such other functions as had previously been performed by the townships, to county jurisdiction.

Several states, instead of making mandatory the transfer of township or district roads to county jurisdiction on a state-wide basis, have enacted optional legislation under which individual counties may, if they wish, adopt the county-unit plan and thereby eliminate townships or road districts as highway units. Typical of such optional legislation is the Kansas statute, originally enacted in 1917 and subsequently amended in various respects. Under present provisions of the Kansas law the county-unit plan of local road administration *may* be adopted by the board of county commissioners of its own volition and *must* be adopted by the board on petition of 10 per cent of the qualified voters of the county. In either case, if 10 per cent of the county voters, within 90 days, file a petition with the county clerk protesting the board's action, a referendum election is held in the county in which the voters themselves approve or disapprove adoption of the plan. By early 1951, 52 of the state's 105 counties had adopted the provisions of the county-unit law.[34]

Still another means whereby road-maintenance activities may be shifted from township to county is through voluntary agreements between the governmental units concerned. Many townships in Wisconsin and Minnesota, as well as some in Kansas, Nebraska, and perhaps other states, have entered into contracts with the governing boards of their respective counties for county maintenance of township roads in return for stipulated payments from the township treasury.[35] Under arrangements of this nature the townships continue to function as financial units for road purposes and retain ultimate responsibility for administration, but they are relieved of the necessity of providing their own equipment and per-

---

Project (Lafayette, Ind., Purdue University, 1955), pp. 38, 44-48, 99-102. Township trustees in Iowa appear still to exercise certain vestigial road functions in the form of recommendations to the county board of supervisors. See Richard C. Spencer, "Iowa Townships Still Here"? *National Municipal Review*, Vol. XLI, pp. 397-399 (September, 1952).

[34] Walter Johnson, "Steady Trend in Kansas to County-unit Plan," *Better Roads*, Vol. XXI, No. 7, pp. 19-20, 32-34 (July, 1951). See also, Kansas State Highway Commission, *The County Road Unit System in Kansas* (Topeka, Kan., 1951).

[35] See, for example, Gomez, *op. cit.*, p. 99; Johnson, *loc. cit.;* Nebraska Legislative Council, *Report of the Committee on Reorganization of County Government* (Lincoln, Neb., 1950), p. 32. The existence of such contractual arrangements in Wisconsin and Minnesota was first called to the author's attention by C. M. Nelson, editor of the magazine *Better Roads.*

sonnel for maintenance work. A variant form of the contractual arrangement is that under which the work of maintaining township roads is let to private contractors. Either the county government or a well-equipped private operator is likely to be in a better position than is the average township to provide efficient maintenance service at reasonable cost.[36]

Even where smaller governmental units have retained financial and administrative responsibilities in the highway field, there has been a definite tendency to shift mileage to the jurisdiction of larger units. Ordinarily, state highway authorities are relatively free to incorporate county and other local roads into the state highway system as they see fit, and county authorities are likewise empowered to take over township or district mileage. Every year sees state highway systems enlarged at the expense of local mileage and a substantial shift of mileage from township or district control to county jurisdiction. When these mileage shifts are considered along with the complete transfers of road jurisdiction noted above, the progress of centralization in recent decades is remarkable. The transfer of roads from local to state control was most pronounced during the 1930's. During the six-year period from the close of 1930 to the end of 1936, more than 200,000 miles of highways were transferred from local to state control, state mileage thereby being increased by more than 64 per cent.[37] Though a major factor in bringing about this phenomenal increase in state-controlled mileage was the extensive transfer of local roads to the state in Delaware, North Carolina, West Virginia, and Virginia, the tendency toward a gradual increase in state mileage has been general throughout the country. Even more marked, when considered over a longer period, has been the removal of local roads from township and district jurisdiction. In 1920 it was estimated that probably as much as 70 per cent of the total road mileage in the United States was under township administration,[38] but today township roads constitute less than 20 per cent of the country's rural mileage.

Generally speaking, the shifting of responsibility for rural road administration from smaller to larger governmental units, in whatever manner accomplished, appears to have resulted in increased efficiency and reduced costs. In North Carolina, after several years of experience with state maintenance of secondary roads, a careful student of government

[36] A 1952 survey in Minnesota revealed that approximately one fourth of the townships of that state were currently contracting with their county governments for all maintenance work on township roads and that another one fourth had all such work performed by private contractors. In most of the remaining townships the maintenance function was performed in part by the county or private contractors or both, with only about 10 per cent of all the state's townships doing all of their own maintenance work. Minnesota Legislative Research Committee, *Local Road Maintenance in Minnesota* (St. Paul, Minn., 1952), pp. 3-4.

[37] Thomas H. MacDonald, "Financing of Local Roads and Streets," *Public Roads*, Vol. XIX, pp. 1-8 (March, 1938).

[38] Agg, *American Rural Highways*, p. 14.

concluded that at least 80 per cent of the counties had better roads under state maintenance, notwithstanding that the state had been spending less money for maintaining those particular highways than had been spent by the counties in earlier years.[39] The Virginia Advisory Legislative Council states in a recent report that upon state assumption of responsibility for Virginia's secondary highways, "tax levies were materially reduced throughout the State. At the same time a steady and continuing improvement began in the secondary road system." [40] Following the transfer of Michigan's township roads to county jurisdiction, it was reported from that state that the larger unit was proving superior to the township in making possible the employment of better technical personnel and more complete mechanical equipment.[41] And the experience of Kansas counties that have voluntarily abandoned township administration bespeaks general satisfaction with the county-unit plan. "Obviously," concludes a competent observer, "there are citizens in both county-unit and non-county-unit counties who are not entirely satisfied with the present management. But the trend in Kansas is toward the unit plan. Citizens are adopting it of their own choice, and the record shows that the trend is a progressive and wholesome one." [42]

HIGHWAY FINANCE

At one time many rural roads were built and operated by private turnpike companies and financed by tolls assessed against their users. But as the highway function attained full recognition as a public responsibility, construction and maintenance duties were gradually taken over by governmental agencies, and the roads were operated on a toll-free basis. Eventually, toll financing was almost universally abandoned, except for special highway adjuncts or facilities, such as bridges, ferries, and tunnels. Recent years have witnessed a revival of the toll system as a means of financing heavily traveled superhighways operated by various states. As a method of financing *local* roads, however, the toll principle continues to find very little use.

Another early method of financing rural roads, now largely obsolete, was the so-called road tax. Exacted of able-bodied men within certain age limits, this levy required the performance each year of a specified number of days' work on the highways or the payment of the money equivalent

[39] Paul W. Wager, "Effects of North Carolina's Centralization," *National Municipal Review*, Vol. XXVI, pp. 572-577 (December, 1937).

[40] Virginia Advisory Legislative Council, *Withdrawal of Counties from Secondary System of Highways*, Report to the Governor and the General Assembly of Virginia (Richmond, Va., 1951), p. 5.

[41] Murray D. Van Wagoner, "Township Roads," *Engineering News Record*, Vol. CXVII, pp. 649-652 (November 5, 1936).

[42] Johnson, *loc. cit.*, p. 34.

of the required work. Tolls and labor levies for road purposes were supplanted originally by the local property tax, and during one period of our history property taxation constituted almost the sole source of highway revenue. Today, however, the property tax has yielded first place to motor vehicle "user" levies, imposed and collected for the most part at the state level; and certain other nonproperty taxes provide road revenue in lesser amounts. Except for some very minor miscellaneous items, revenues for the support of local rural roads at the present time are derived from six sources: local property taxes; special assessments; local user levies; state-collected user taxes; grants from general state funds; and federal aid.

Local Road Revenues. The first three of the sources just mentioned—property taxes, special assessments, and local user levies—provide the bulk of road revenues strictly local in nature. Of the three, the local property tax provides by far the largest amount. Counties, townships, and special districts charged with highway responsibilities are authorized, in many instances, to impose upon property a special "road and bridge" levy for highway purposes. In addition, it is not unusual, in the case of counties and townships, for some portion of the revenue accruing from property levies for general governmental purposes to find its way into highway funds. Some local units, though imposing no levies specifically for highway purposes, finance their road and bridge activities from general funds derived in large part from property taxes. Altogether, local property taxes provide about 40 per cent of all the moneys expended on local rural roads.

Under the special-assessment plan of financing, part or all of the cost of constructing a highway is made a charge against property abutting thereon or in close proximity thereto. It is assumed that a road improvement, in addition to being of general benefit to the residents of the county, township, or district, confers an additional benefit upon nearby property and that it is equitable to levy against such property assessments commensurate with those special benefits. A so-called benefit district is laid out along the project, and the costs to be assessed are apportioned among individual properties therein on various bases, such as area and proximity. Though special assessments are widely used in financing the construction of city streets, they are employed only occasionally in the case of rural roads and even less frequently by counties than by townships and road districts. As a result, this source provides only a nominal portion of local revenues for rural road purposes.[43]

Highway-user taxes of the types commonly levied by the states are imposed by local governments in relatively few instances and are found even

[43] United States Bureau of Public Roads, *The Financing of Highways by Counties and Local Rural Governments: 1931-1941* (Washington, Government Printing Office, 1949), p. 22, and *The Financing of Highways by Counties and Local Rural Governments: 1942-51*, p. 21.

less frequently in the case of rural local units than in that of municipalities. A few counties, for the most part in the South, levy motor-fuel taxes, and there are occasional instances of county-imposed registration fees or "wheel taxes." As in the case of state user levies, local taxes of this nature are at times diverted to nonhighway purposes but for the most part are devoted to road services. Although local user levies produce substantial revenues for the individual units imposing them, those units are so few as to render virtually negligible, from a national standpoint, the importance of such taxes as a source of highway funds. Even where state law authorizes the imposition of local user levies, counties and other local units have appeared hesitant to use the power conferred. This fact seems attributable, in part at least, to the difficulty of administering such imposts at the local level. As the Bureau of Public Roads has pointed out: "Motor-fuel taxes restricted to a comparatively small area, such as a township or even the average county, can be easily avoided by purchasing gasoline in a neighboring unit of government. Local registration fees or wheel taxes also present enforcement problems which often cannot be dealt with effectively by local units." Furthermore, the common practice "of distributing a portion of the receipts from State-highway-user imposts to the local units undoubtedly tends to discourage the local units from entering this field of taxation."[44]

State Aid. State aid to local governments for support of the highway function takes two principal forms: (1) sharing with local governmental units the proceeds from highway-user taxes imposed and collected by the states; and (2) grants-in-aid to local units from general state funds. From the standpoint of amount received by the local governments, the sharing of user taxes is by far the more important.

Every state imposes a gallonage tax on gasoline used for highway travel or transportation. Ordinarily, the tax applies also to diesel and other forms of fuel oil, and, therefore, the designation *motor-fuel tax* is more accurately descriptive of the levy than the commonly used term *gasoline tax*. The rate of levy varies from state to state but today is most commonly in the neighborhood of four, five, or six cents per gallon.[45] A second form of user levy found in all states is the motor-vehicle license tax. Schedules of state charges for motor-vehicle licenses vary widely with respect to both bases and rates. Different schedules are commonly provided for passenger cars on the one hand and trucks and buses on the other, with further variations between private and commercial vehicles. Weight of vehicle, horsepower, and value are among the bases of charge employed in the various states singly or in combination. Annual license charges for private passenger

[44] *The Financing of Highways by Counties and Local Rural Governments: 1931-1941*, p. 24.

[45] The federal government also taxes the sale of gasoline—presently (1957) at the rate of three cents per gallon.

automobiles range upward from a few dollars to more than $200, with charges for buses and trucks in some instances exceeding $1,000.[46] Since heavy trucks and buses contribute through motor-fuel taxes substantially less than do passenger automobiles in relation to their wear and tear on the highways, there has been a tendency during recent years to increase the license charges for trucks and buses rather drastically in an effort to remedy this disparity. High license rates, however, may themselves occasion serious inequities as among different trucks and buses of the same weight or carrying capacity, since they fail to take into account the fact that some vehicles travel many times the number of miles that do others in the course of a year. This usage differential has now been taken into account in several states through the imposition of various forms of distance-weight or ton-mile taxes in lieu of further increases in license charges.[47] Still another state user levy, though one that yields relatively little revenue in comparison with the motor-fuel and motor-vehicle license taxes, is the charge for operators' licenses.

Although in some states a portion of the proceeds from highway-user taxes is diverted to nonhighway uses, revenues from such levies are devoted for the most part to highway services. Several states have constitutional provisions prohibiting the diversion of motor-fuel tax revenues to nonhighway purposes, and even where this is not the case, state legislatures have generally required that such revenues be used principally or solely for financing highway expenditures. Most states, instead of spending their user revenues on state highways exclusively, distribute a substantial portion thereof to local governmental units for construction and maintenance of local roads and streets. Such distribution is especially common with respect to motor-fuel taxes, which, of course, are by far the most lucrative of all the user levies, but it is frequently practiced also in the case of revenues from motor-vehicle and operators' licenses. Population, area, number of vehicle registrations, and road mileage are among the bases most commonly employed for making the distribution to local units. In determining allocations to *rural* units, the mileage factor is frequently accorded a predominant role.

In addition to distributing state user revenues to their local governmental units, or as an alternative thereto, the states at times make direct appropriations from their general funds to these units for highway purposes. Prior to 1951, for example, while providing for allocation of motor-fuel tax revenues only to counties and municipalities, the Illinois legislature at various times made direct appropriations to townships and road districts for highway purposes. When, in the year mentioned, the rate of the fuel

[46] William J. Shultz and C. Lowell Harriss, *American Public Finance*, 5th ed. (New York, Prentice-Hall, 1949), pp. 543-546.

[47] See Richard L. Neuberger, "Who Shall Pay for Our Roads"? *Harper's Magazine*, Vol. CCV, No. 1229, pp. 86-91 (October, 1952).

tax was increased and a share therein allocated to the townships and road districts, the grant-in-aid program was discontinued.

During 1952, counties in 41 states and towns or townships in 12 states were recipients of state aid of some sort for highway purposes.[48] Though the state grant-in-aid is of major importance at times to particular units, in the over-all national picture of local road revenues it is today of little significance in comparison with the sharing of state user levies.

Federal Aid. Prior to 1916, nonfederal highways in the United States were financed entirely from state and local funds. In that year Congress inaugurated a program of federal grants-in-aid to the states for highway purposes. Originally restricted to assistance in the improving of state primary highways, the federal-aid program was expanded during the depression years of the 1930's to include grants for urban extensions of federal-aid rural highways, for improving a limited mileage of secondary or "feeder" roads, and for the elimination of railroad grade crossings on highways of all classes.[49] During World War II federal-aid construction virtually ceased save for projects deemed essential to national defense; but with the cessation of hostilities the program was resumed in its broadened form, including grants for secondary roads. The Federal-Aid Highway Act of 1950, for example, authorized annual grants to the states of $150,000,000 (an amount which was increased substantially by subsequent federal-aid laws) for expenditure on "secondary and feeder roads, farm-to-market roads, rural mail routes, public school bus routes, local rural roads, county roads, township roads, and roads of the county-road class." Apportionment to the respective states is on the basis of area, rural population, and rural mail-delivery mileage. To qualify for federal assistance, construction projects must be selected by the state highway department and appropriate local officials in co-operation with each other; and only such roads may be built as can be maintained at reasonable cost to provide all-weather service. Though the grants are made to the states, a large part of the federal funds is channeled through the state departments to local governmental units charged with responsibility for the classes of roads concerned. By the beginning of 1955 federal-aid secondary road systems in the various states embraced a total of nearly 500,000 miles;[50] and the federal grants, though not constituting a major source of local road revenue, were by no means a negligible item.

Trends in Road Financing. Two trends, interrelated in nature, have been clearly discernible in the financing of rural highways during recent

[48] John R. Kerstetter, *Local Government's Share of State-collected Highway Funds and Revenues* (Washington and Chicago, American Municipal Association, 1955), pp. 3, 55.

[49] G. Donald Kennedy, *The Role of the Federal Government in Highway Development* (Washington, Government Printing Office, 1944), pp. 11-12; Thomas H. MacDonald, "Paving America," *State Government*, Vol. XVIII, pp. 78-80 (May, 1945).

[50] *Highway Statistics: 1954*, p. 117.

years: (1) the increased participation of the state and national governments in highway support, and (2) the progressive shifting of road costs to persons using the highways through the device of the user levy.[51] At one time, as we have seen, rural roads were financed almost entirely by the local governmental units through the property tax. For two decades now the national government has played a part, though as yet always a modest one, through grants-in-aid for use on secondary systems. Much more pronounced has been the growing participation of the state governments in local road financing, in some degree through state grants-in-aid but in much larger measure through the sharing of state user taxes. In 1931 state aid (grants and tax sharings) to local governments for rural roads amounted to less than half the amount raised for that purpose from local sources; whereas by 1941 the amount received from the states actually exceeded local road revenues.[52] Today, state aid accounts for more than half of the total sum expended by local governments on rural roads, with the greater part of this aid consisting of allocations from state motor-fuel levies.

Highway Borrowing. Whatever the ultimate source of local highway funds, it is commonly necessary, when new improvements involving heavy outlays are undertaken, to borrow money for the immediate defraying of construction costs. In such cases the local unit concerned ordinarily issues and sells interest-bearing bonds payable from revenues subsequently collected. Counties, townships, and road districts usually have statutory authority, within specified limitations, to issue bonds for road construction. In addition to being approved by the governing body of the local unit concerned, bond issues frequently require approval by the local voters in a referendum election. During the years of depression and World War II, the outstanding road debt of rural local units was reduced from an all-time high of $1,800,000,000 in 1929 to $879,000,000 in 1947—a reduction of more than 50 per cent.[53] A postwar resumption of construction activities has resulted in new borrowings somewhat exceeding debt retirement, with outstanding debt at the end of 1953 amounting to $934,000,000.[54]

STATE SUPERVISION AND CONTROL

Though responsibility for some 80 per cent of the nation's rural road mileage still rests with local governmental units, a substantial degree of supervision and control over the local road function is exercised by state

[51] Cf. Charles L. Dearing, *American Highway Policy* (Washington, Brookings Institution, 1942), p. 100.

[52] *The Financing of Highways by Counties and Local Rural Governments: 1931-1941*, p. 18.

[53] *The Local Rural Road Problem*, p. 36.

[54] *Highway Statistics: 1954*, p. 88.

highway departments. In the first place, submission to various control measures is usually exacted of local governments as a price for receiving state aid. When the state makes grants of money to local units for road purposes or shares with the local governments the proceeds from state user levies, it ordinarily requires the local units to comply with prescribed state standards and to submit to other measures of state control. Common provisions in this respect are that the projects on which state funds are to be expended shall be designated by joint action of local and state authorities, that specifications and contracts shall be subject to state approval, and that state authorities shall be permitted to inspect the work as it progresses to make certain that state requirements are being complied with. Frequently, there is a requirement that a prescribed percentage of improvement costs be defrayed by locally raised funds, and, at times, provision is made for a state audit of local road accounts. All in all, state supervision over local road projects financed wholly or in part from state funds is likely to be extensive and relatively thorough.

But state supervision is by no means limited to state-aid projects. Many states, for example, provide for advice and assistance by state agencies to local authorities on highway matters generally. Thus, state highway departments are frequently required to give advice and information, at the request of local road authorities, concerning the construction, repair, and maintenance of roads and bridges; and, in some instances, they must even prepare specifications for local improvement projects. Some state departments compile and publish statistics relating to local highways. A special means of giving advice and instruction is through the holding of road schools or institutes for local road officers. In several states regular annual meetings of this nature are held by the highway department, on a statewide or regional basis, at which county engineers and other local road officials are given practical instruction and demonstrations in road building and maintenance. Some states require local road officers to make periodic reports to the state highway department.

A control device of particular significance employed in some states involves state participation in the selection and removal of local road officers. In Illinois, for example, appointment of county highway superintendents is a joint responsibility of the respective county governing boards and the state department of public works and buildings. When an appointment is to be made, the county board submits to the state department a list of not more than five persons who possess the statutory qualifications for the office and whom the board considers to be desirable candidates. The state department, through its highway division, then determines by examination the person or persons best fitted for the office; and from among these the county board appoints a highway superintendent. If no person on the list is found by the state department to be eligible, the county board must submit additional lists until an eligible candidate is found.[55] In Kansas, appointments of highway engineers by boards of county commissioners are subject to approval by the state highway commission, and county engineers may be removed by the state commission for incompetence.[56]

State-local contacts in the highway field, it should be noted, are not confined to those specifically provided for by statute. Local road authorities often make use of the technical facilities of the state highway department, even where not required by law to do so; and state and local officials co-operate in numerous informal ways to effectuate common ends.[57] The present-day importance of state supervision over local roads is indicated by the fact that it is common to find a special "county division" or similar unit organized within the state highway department to carry on activities of this nature. Indeed, the Federal-Aid Highway Law now requires that every state receiving federal funds for expenditure on secondary roads maintain a secondary road unit in its highway department so organized as to discharge satisfactorily the duties imposed upon the states by federal law in connection with grants for secondary road systems.[58]

The need for central supervision over local road authorities is apparent when we consider the general state-wide interest in local road systems and the technical tasks involved in modern highway construction and maintenance. During past years the expansion of state supervision has been accompanied by a steady improvement in local road standards, and it seems beyond question that the improvement has been due in some measure to the increase in state control. Shortly before the transfer of Virginia's county roads to state administration, the New York Bureau of Municipal Research, in considering the matter of state supervision of county highway administration, concluded that recent progress in local administration in Virginia could be traced "almost entirely to the educational work conducted by the State aid engineer's office, coupled with authority exercised by that official." [59] This conclusion, broadened to cover the influence on local road administration of state supervision generally, would appear to have a large measure of applicability to other states at the present time.

[55] Clyde F. Snider, *County Government in Illinois* (Springfield, Illinois Tax Commission, 1943), p. 81; *Illinois Revised Statutes* (1955), chap. 121, sec. 8.

[56] Marvin Meade, "The County Engineer," *Your Government*, bulletin of the University of Kansas Governmental Research Center, Vol. VII, No. 7 (March 15, 1952).

[57] Cf. Gomez, *op. cit.*, pp. 84-85.

[58] In states where the local road function is divided between counties and townships, direct state contacts are for the most part with the counties, and state regulations are channeled through the county authorities to the lesser units. Cf. *ibid.*, p. 95.

[59] New York Bureau of Municipal Research, *County Government in Virginia*, Report on a Survey Made to the Governor and His Committee on Consolidation and Simplification (Richmond, Va., 1928), p. 72.

REFERENCES

Books, Reports, and Special Studies

AGG, T. R., *American Rural Highways* (New York, McGraw-Hill, 1920).

———, and BRINDLEY, J. E., *Highway Administration and Finance* (New York, McGraw-Hill, 1927).

BATEMAN, John H., *Introduction to Highway Engineering*, 4th ed. (New York, Wiley, 1942).

Council of State Governments, *Highway Legislation in 1955* (Chicago, 1956).

CURTISS, W. M., *Use and Value of Highways in Rural New York* (Ithaca, N.Y., Cornell University Agricultural Experiment Station, 1936).

DEARING, Charles L., *American Highway Policy* (Washington, Brookings Institution, 1942).

GOMEZ, R. A., *Intergovernmental Relations in Highways* (Minneapolis, University of Minnesota Press, 1950).

Griffenhagen and Associates, *A Highway Improvement Program for Illinois*, Report to the Illinois Division of Highways for Transmittal to the Illinois Highway and Traffic Problems Commission (Chicago, 1948).

Illinois Agricultural Association, *Report of the Illinois Agricultural Association Road Study Committee* (1949).

Illinois Legislative Council, *Local Road Administrative Units* (Springfield, Ill., 1956).

Kansas State Highway Commission, *The County Road Unit System in Kansas* (Topeka, Kansas State Highway Commission, 1951).

KENNEDY, G. Donald, *The Role of the Federal Government in Highway Development* (Washington, Government Printing Office, 1944), printed for use of the Special Committee on Post-war Economic Policy and Planning, 78th Cong., 2d sess.

KERSTETTER, John R., *Local Government's Share of State-collected Highway Funds and Revenues* (Washington and Chicago, American Municipal Association, 1955).

KRAUSZ, N. G. P., and SWANSON, Earl R., *An Analysis of Local Road Unit Costs in Illinois* (Urbana, University of Illinois Agricultural Experiment Station, 1957).

Local Rural Road Use and Benefits in Maryland (College Park, University of Maryland Agricultural Experiment Station, 1950).

MCMILLAN, T. E., Jr., *County Unit Road Administration in Texas* (Austin, University of Texas Institute of Public Affairs, 1954).

Minnesota Legislative Research Committee, *Local Road Maintenance in Minnesota* (St. Paul, Minn., 1952).

STONER, John E., *Comparative County Highway Administration: A Study of Steuben County, Indiana; Branch County, Michigan; Williams County, Ohio*, Joint Highway Research Project (Lafayette, Ind., Purdue University, 1955).

United States Bureau of Public Roads, *The Financing of Highways by Counties and Local Rural Governments: 1931-1941* (Washington, Government Printing Office, 1949).

———, *The Financing of Highways by Counties and Local Rural Governments: 1942-51* (Washington, Government Printing Office, 1955).

———, *Highways in the United States* (Washington, Government Printing Office, 1951).

United States Bureau of Public Roads, *Highway Statistics* (Washington, Government Printing Office, annually).

———, *The Local Rural Road Problem* (Washington, Government Printing Office, 1950).

United States Public Roads Administration, *Highway Practice in the United States of America* (Washington, Government Printing Office, 1949).

Virginia Advisory Legislative Council, *Withdrawal of Counties from Secondary System of Highways*, Report to the Governor and the General Assembly of Virginia (Richmond, Va., 1951).

YOUNG, George D., *County Road Administration and Finance in New York* (Ithaca, Cornell University Department of Agricultural Economics, 1952).

Articles

ANDERSON, Lynn F., "Centralized Road Administration in Texas," *The County Officer*, Vol. XIX, pp. 258-264 (December, 1954).

GARRETT, John H., "Our Secondary Roads: A County Responsibility," *The County Officer*, Vol. XVII, pp. 246-247 (August, 1952).

HUBER, Wendell P., "Engineering a County Highway Department," *Public Works*, Vol. LXXXVII, No. 3, pp. 104-106 (March, 1956). Reprinted in *The County Officer*, Vol. XXI, pp. 106-108 (May, 1956).

JOHNSON, Walter, "Steady Trend in Kansas to County-unit Plan," *Better Roads*, Vol. XXI, No. 7, pp. 19-20, 32-34 (July, 1951).

MACDONALD, Thomas H., "Financing of Local Roads and Streets," *Public Roads*, Vol. XIX, pp. 1-8 (March, 1938).

———, "Progress of the Federal-aid Road Program," *State Government*, Vol. XXIII, pp. 32-34, 40 (February, 1950).

MEISNER, James F., "The County Engineer," *Public Works*, Vol. LXXXVII, No. 3, pp. 93-94 (March, 1956). Reprinted in *The County Officer*, Vol. XXI, pp. 109-110 (May, 1956).

PEAK, George W., "Highway Financing," *The County Officer*, Vol. XV, No. 7, pp. 18-20, 29-30 (October, 1950).

SCHEFFER, Walter F., "State-county Administration of Highways in Wisconsin," *The County Officer*, Vol. XX, pp. 64-67 (March, 1955).

SEEGMILLER, Keith L., "Highway Laws from the County Point of View," *The County Officer*, Vol. XXI, pp. 22-24 (February, 1956).

STONER, John E., "General Manager and Professional Leader [The County Highway Engineer]," *Better Roads*, Vol. XXIII, No. 12, pp. 25-26, 28 (December, 1953). Reprinted in *The County Officer*, Vol. XIX, pp. 56-58 (March, 1954).

———, "The Governing Board and the County Engineer," *The County Officer*, Vol. XX, pp. 51-56 (March, 1955).

———, "The Board and the Engineer," *The County Officer*, Vol. XXI, pp. 99-101, 104-105 (May, 1956).

SWANSON, Earl R., "Rural Road Costs and Size of Road Unit," *Current Economic Comment*, publication of the University of Illinois Bureau of Economic and Business Research, Vol. XVIII, No. 3, pp. 25-32 (August, 1956).

VAN WAGONER, Murray D., "Township Roads," *Engineering News Record*, Vol. CXVII, pp. 649-652 (November 5, 1936).

CHAPTER 15

Health and Housing

SICKNESS AND ITS TOLL

ALTHOUGH RECENT DECADES have witnessed marked improvement in the nation's health record, sickness remains a major American problem. It has been estimated that every year sees in this country the death of 325,000 people whom we have the knowledge and skills to save and the loss to the nation of 4,300,000 man-years of work through bad health. The annual loss in potential production and wages occasioned by sickness and disability has been placed at $27,000,000,000, with the probability that an additional $11,000,000,000 is lost through premature deaths from preventable causes.[1] For the prevention and treatment of the illnesses and other conditions from which flow these vast losses, the nation's total expenditures for civilian medical and health services in 1951 were estimated at nearly $14,000,000,000, of which almost one fourth was paid from public funds—federal, state, and local.[2]

THE RURAL HEALTH SITUATION

The impression was once widespread that "the country" was a much more healthful place in which to live than were urban communities; and there was considerable ground for this impression at a time when the sunshine, fresh air, and open spaces of rural areas stood in sharp contrast to the filth and overcrowding that prevailed generally in large cities. But with advances in preventive medicine and municipal sanitary engin-

[1] Oscar R. Ewing, *The Nation's Health: A Ten-year Program* (Washington, Federal Security Agency, 1948), pp. 1, 28.

[2] *America's Health Status, Needs and Resources: Building America's Health,* Report of the President's Commission on the Health Needs of the Nation (Washington, Government Printing Office, 1953), Vol. II, p. 253.

eering and concurrent improvements in urban housing, the situation has changed substantially. City environments have gained greatly in healthfulness, with the contrast between urban and rural areas becoming less marked and tending to disappear altogether.

Death rates historically have been consistently higher in urban areas than in rural, and they remain so today; but the difference in rate is narrowing.[3] "While the general death rate of rural people is today still slightly less than that of city people, the decline in death rates has been much less in the country than in the cities."[4] In certain respects rural areas now actually make a less favorable showing than urban. Thus, deaths from various preventable diseases, such as typhoid fever and malaria, are more frequent in rural areas, and rates of maternal and child mortality are higher in rural communities. The wider prevalence of physical defects among farm people is indicated by the fact that in connection with selective service in World War II, draftees from farms showed higher rejection rates than the average for the country as a whole.[5] Farm accidents add to the toll of rural deaths. "Agricultural work is far more hazardous than most folks realize. In 1943, 4,500 persons working in agriculture were killed on their jobs; this accounted for 25 per cent of all persons killed at work in that year, although persons engaged in agriculture represent only 16 per cent of all working people."[6] Finally, it may be noted that the rural mortality situation is probably less favorable, in reality, than appears from the official statistics, since deaths of rural residents frequently occur in city hospitals and therefore are included in the urban data, and since, because of less adequate facilities for collecting vital statistics in rural areas, more rural deaths than urban go unreported.[7]

REASONS FOR LAGGING PROGRESS

When reasons are sought for the fact that rural communities are making slower progress than urban in the prevention and treatment of disease, various factors are found to be involved. In many areas one factor is that of low farm income. "Purchasing power for medical care has been lacking in much of rural America. Even in a prosperous year such as 1945 the net per capita income of persons living on farms was $743, whereas for

[3] George W. Bachman and others, *Health Resources in the United States* (Washington, Brookings Institution, 1952), pp. 16-17.

[4] United States Department of Agriculture, Interbureau Committee on Post-War Programs, *Better Health for Rural America* (Washington, Government Printing Office, 1945), p. 1.

[5] *Ibid.*, pp. 1-2.

[6] *Ibid.*, p. 1.

[7] Frederick D. Mott and Milton I. Roemer, *Rural Health and Medical Care* (New York, McGraw-Hill, 1948), pp. 50-51.

persons not on farms it was $1,259."[8] Although in prosperous farm areas income is relatively high, this differential in average income between farm and nonfarm people explains why many of the former just do not have the money necessary to provide themselves with adequate medical care. The high incidence in rural areas of some of the preventable diseases is due in no small measure to poor sanitation on farms and in small villages. Three out of every four rural families are without proper sanitary facilities; and the great majority of farm water supplies lack sanitary pumps and adequate protection against surface contamination.[9] But perhaps most outstanding of all reasons for the inadequacy of rural medical care, though one not unrelated to the others mentioned, is the shortage in medical personnel and facilities in rural areas.

LACK OF MEDICAL PERSONNEL AND FACILITIES

Virtually every type of personnel and physical facility involved in the provision of medical care, whether private or public, is less adequate in rural communities than in urban. In proportion to population, rural areas have fewer doctors, fewer dentists, fewer nurses, fewer hospital beds, and less adequate provision for public-health services. In 1940, in the country as a whole, there was one physician for every 831 persons. At that time nearly 11,000,000 Americans in the nation's most highly rural areas were served by only one physician to approximately 1,700 people. In 1941-1942, the nation's metropolitan counties boasted a dentist for every 1,368 inhabitants; but in the most rural counties each dentist was required to serve an average of 4,235 persons. Of the nation's graduate trained nurses in 1940, less than 20 per cent were located in the country's rural communities, though the latter included more than 40 per cent of the national population.[10] During World War II and more recently, the loss of doctors, dentists, and nurses to the armed services has been particularly serious in its effect on rural areas, aggravating still further the shortage in supply.[11] In 1942, 289 metropolitan counties had 4.7 beds in general hospitals per 1,000 inhabitants; but 1,785 of the nation's most rural counties, including one fifth of the national population, were served by only 1.5 beds per 1,000 persons. With respect to mental and tuberculosis hospitals, also, rural facilities lag behind those of urban areas.[12] According to an estimate of the mid-1940's, the bringing of rural hospitals up to a level of reasonable adequacy would require 70,000 additional general hospital beds, 23,000 additional beds in tuberculosis hospitals, and 2,000 additional beds

[8] National Health Assembly, *America's Health: A Report to the Nation* (New York, Harper, 1949), p. 142.

[9] *Better Health for Rural America*, pp. 4-5.

[10] Mott and Roemer, *op. cit.*, pp. 151-153, 186-187, 192.

[11] Cf. *ibid.*, chap. 12.

[12] *Ibid.*, chaps. 13, 14.

in mental institutions.[13] Notwithstanding substantial improvements during recent years in rural public-health departments, the services provided by such agencies continue, on the average, to be inferior to those of urban departments, with millions of rural Americans still lacking full-time service. Finally may be mentioned the fact that programs of voluntary medical-care insurance provided through policies issued by commercial insurance companies and through such nonprofit prepayment plans as the Blue Cross and Blue Shield, though now affording some degree of protection to nearly half of the nation's people, reach only a very small fraction of the rural population.[14]

RURAL DOCTOR SHORTAGE

At the very heart of the problem of providing adequate medical care in rural areas is, of course, the scarcity of rural physicians. Thousands of rural communities today have no local doctor whatsoever, or only one of advanced age, who, when removed from practice by death or retirement, is unlikely to be replaced. Young doctors generally are loath to establish themselves in rural communities, and for this there are various reasons. Many wish to specialize, and opportunities for specialization are better in the more populous centers. Those expecting to be general practitioners feel that in rural practice they would be professionally isolated, with too little opportunity to consult with their colleagues and to keep abreast of current developments in medical science. Another deterrent is the fact that doctors fresh from their medical training are frequently without the financial means of providing themselves with appropriate office and clinical facilities, whereas these would be readily available in urban localities through hospitals or clinics or through collaboration with established colleagues. A lone practitioner, upon whom an entire community is largely dependent for medical care, must work long hours and be subject to call at all times. It is exceedingly difficult for such a physician to get away from his post for needed vacation or study; and the educational and cultural opportunities for his family may compare unfavorably with those available in urban areas. In addition to considerations such as these is the fact that rural practice is likely to be less lucrative than practice in an urban community.[15]

[13] V. Webster Johnson, John F. Timmons, and E. Jay Howenstine, Jr., "Rural Public Works: Part I—Needed Improvements and Useful Jobs," *Journal of Land and Public Utility Economics*, Vol. XXIII, pp. 12-21 (February, 1947).

[14] Milton I. Roemer, "Rural Programs of Medical Care," *Annals of the American Academy of Political and Social Science*, Vol. CCLXXIII, pp. 160-168 (January, 1951); Margaret C. Klem, "Voluntary Medical Care Insurance," *ibid.*, pp. 90-105.

[15] Edmund de S. Brunner and J. H. Kolb, *Rural Social Trends* (New York, McGraw-Hill, 1933), p. 279; Nathan Bushnell, III, "How Can We Develop Medical Care in Rural Communities?" *The County Officer*, Vol. XVII, pp. 81-85 (March, 1952).

In an effort to overcome some of the disadvantages of country practice and to encourage young doctors to settle in rural communities, various experiments have been undertaken in recent years, some by state and local governments and others by private organizations or groups. Some state universities, such as the University of Kansas, have enlarged the facilities of their medical schools to increase somewhat the over-all supply of physicians; and, to lessen the professional isolation of rural practitioners, they have organized postgraduate refresher courses both at the university and in the field.[16] Various communities in Kansas and elsewhere, to meet the need of the beginning practitioner for initial capital outlay, have raised funds to provide modern office and clinical facilities, permitting the young doctor, after he has become established in practice, to amortize the cost over a period of years and on favorable terms. Fellowship programs have been employed in an effort to encourage young doctors to enter rural practice. During the 1930's, for example, the Commonwealth Fund awarded fellowships to a number of medical students on condition that they would practice in rural communities for a specified number of years after graduation. Though the results of this program were somewhat disappointing, most of the fellowship recipients leaving the rural areas as soon as the period of their obligation had expired, several states subsequently launched fellowship or scholarship programs in the form of grants or loans financed from legislative appropriations.[17] In Illinois the state medical and agricultural associations have co-operated in offering loans to medical students who will agree to practice for five years in rural communities in need of physicians. Certain small towns in New England have resorted to direct cash subsidy to attract physicians, guaranteeing a minimum annual income and paying from town funds the difference between the guaranteed amount and what the doctor earns from his practice.[18] Of these various programs designed to augment the supply of rural physicians, some appear to have enjoyed singular initial success. On the other hand, some have been discouraging in their results and still others have been inaugurated too recently to warrant appraisal. At best, however, efforts such as these cannot be expected to provide more than a beginning in the alleviation of the present shortage. So strong are the attractions of urban practice, and so small the number of graduating medical

[16] The Kansas program is described by Bushnell, *loc. cit.* See also, Clyde Hostetter, "How Some Towns Get Doctors," *Town Journal*, Vol. LXII, No. 8, pp. 22-23, 49 (August, 1955).

[17] Roemer, *loc. cit.* One such program is that of Virginia, under which cash scholarships are granted annually to a limited number of medical and dental students, the recipients agreeing to practice in a rural area one year for each year of the scholarship grant. Mack I. Shanholtz, "Supplying Rural Virginia with Doctors," *State Government*, Vol. XXVIII, pp. 105-106, 117-118 (May, 1955). For an account of the Mississippi program in its early years, see Julia C. McCoy, "Mississippi's Medical Education Loan Program" *ibid.*, Vol. XXVI, pp. 113-115, 125 (April, 1953).

[18] Roemer, *loc. cit.*

students, that the providing of physicians for rural areas promises to remain a major problem for many years to come. Furthermore, the problem of staffing rural communities is no less acute and scarcely less difficult of solution with respect to other types of medical personnel.

EARLY PUBLIC-HEALTH ORGANIZATION

Medical care in the United States has always been provided primarily through private practitioners. Government, however, from early days, has assumed a degree of responsibility for preserving and promoting community health. Interest by the state and national governments in health matters is of long standing, and the activities of those governments in the health field have tended to increase during recent years. But it is upon government at the local level that primary responsibility for public-health activities has been imposed.

Local boards of health appear to have been established in Massachusetts as early as 1797.[19] During the century that followed, health boards and health officers were introduced quite generally throughout the country. Nearly every city and village was provided with some sort of health organization. To serve rural areas, provision was made for township or county boards of health, and sometimes for both in a single state.[20] These early health boards were endowed with very meager authority, their powers being limited for the most part to the establishment of quarantine, the abatement of nuisances, and the appointment of a health officer to enforce their orders. Early health officers usually served on a part-time basis and, though sometimes physicians, were frequently laymen without any professional qualifications in health work.[21]

MORE RECENT DEVELOPMENTS

From these primitive beginnings, local public-health organization and functions have developed along three principal lines: (1) expansion of the powers and activities of local health authorities; (2) replacement, in substantial measure, of part-time, nonprofessional personnel by full-time,

[19] Wilson G. Smillie, *Public Health Administration in the United States*, 3rd ed. (New York, Macmillan, 1947), p. 425.

[20] In Illinois, for example, provision is made for township boards of health in counties which have adopted township organization and for county boards of health in nontownship counties. Minnesota provides for township health boards and also for county boards of health to serve the territory of any townships not organized for governmental purposes. Cf. Clyde F. Snider, *County Government in Illinois* (Springfield, Illinois Tax Commission, 1943), p. 77; Laurence Wyatt, *Intergovernmental Relations in Public Health* (Minneapolis, University of Minnesota Press, 1951), pp. 135-136.

[21] Cf. Allen W. Freeman, ed., *A Study of Rural Public Health Service* (New York, Commonwealth Fund, 1933), p. 1; Carl E. McCombs, *City Health Administration* (New York, Macmillan, 1927), p. 50.

trained officers and employees; and (3) substitution of larger for smaller geographic areas for the organization of health services. These various phases of development, of course, are closely interrelated, since only professional personnel is qualified to perform modern health functions and larger areas are frequently necessary to make feasible the provision of such personnel on a full-time basis.

The first local health department to provide full-time service on a county-wide basis appears to have been that of Jefferson County, Ky., which contains the city of Louisville. In 1908 that county placed its health officer on a full-time basis and provided him with a staff of sanitary inspectors. Three years later, full-time county-wide departments were established in Guilford County, N. C., and Yakima County, Wash. Each of these three counties contained cities of considerable size, and it remained for Robeson County, S. C., to become, in 1912, the first rural county to establish a full-time health department.[22] From this time on, state legislation permitting counties to establish full-time health departments spread rapidly, such departments usually seeking to provide as their minimum full-time staff a medical director, enough nurses and sanitary engineers to meet the county's needs, and adequate clerical personnel.

Inasmuch as many rural counties have neither the financial resources to support a full-time department nor a population large enough to make complete utilization of its services, many state laws also authorized the establishment of multicounty departments, the merging of city and county departments, or the organization of two or more counties, townships, or other local units into special public-health districts for the pooling of their resources and needs. By the early 1950's, 34 states had statutes permitting two or more counties to join in establishing a multicounty health department, and 15 states authorized the establishment of multitown or multi-township departments. A majority of the states permitted the formation of city-county departments, and some provided that townships might join with cities or counties in establishing an agency for health services.[23] In practice there are several means by which two or more local government units, if authorized by law to do so, may co-operate in maintaining a single health department to serve their common needs. Two neighboring counties, for example, might follow any of three courses:

1. They might provide by agreement that the department of one county will provide health service for residents of the other in return for payment by the latter of specified compensation.
2. They might provide by agreement for establishment and operation of a joint department, serving the residents of both counties, with each

[22] Haven Emerson and Martha Luginbuhl, *Local Health Units for the Nation* (New York, Commonwealth Fund, 1945), p. 12.

[23] Clifford H. Greve, "Provisions of State Laws Governing Local Health Departments," *Public Health Reports,* Vol. LXVIII, pp. 31-42 (January, 1953).

county participating in departmental administration and contributing from its own tax funds a specified proportion of the costs.

3. They might establish an overlying public-health district, embracing the territory within both counties and endowed with its own taxing power, to operate a district department serving the residents of the entire area.

As defined by the United States Public Health Service, "A full-time local health unit is one which is officially organized to provide medical, nursing, and sanitation public health services during all of the regularly scheduled work week of the governmental unit to which it is attached and which is under the full-time direction of a health officer or other designated administrative head." [24] The actual establishment of full-time departments under the various state enabling acts at first proceeded slowly but was accelerated as a result of federal grants-in-aid provided by the Social Security Act of 1935 for the establishment and maintenance of full-time local health services. Since then the formation of full-time departments has proceeded more rapidly, though their coverage still is far from complete. At the end of 1950, according to data reported to the Public Health Service, some 1,396 of the nation's counties were served by full-time local health units —672 by single-county departments and 724 by 298 multicounty or district departments. With an additional 135 counties receiving full-time local service directly from state-administered health districts, slightly more than half of the nation's counties, in all, were provided with local services from full-time health organizations.[25] The urban and rural areas reported in 1953 as being provided with full-time local health service by governmental agencies of various types are indicated in Fig. XI.

HEALTH BOARDS AND OFFICERS

County and township boards of health sometimes are constituted on an ex officio basis and in other instances are appointive. In some cases membership is partly ex officio and partly appointive. Where the ex officio board is used, it is not uncommon for the regular governing body of the county or township to serve also as the board of health. In the case of appointive members, the appointing power rests variously with the local governing body, a local administrative official, or, occasionally, the state board of health or state health officer. Representatives on district health

[24] United States Public Health Service, *Report of Local Public Health Resources: 1950* (Washington, 1952), p. ix.

[25] *Ibid.*, pp. 1-4. Prior to 1950 the Public Health Service considered a full-time health department any department served by a full-time health officer. In the year mentioned, however, the service adopted the definition noted above, requiring not only the presence of a full-time *officer* but the provision of full-time *services*. As a result of adoption of the more restrictive definition, the number of full-time local units here recorded is somewhat smaller than that reported for some preceding years. Cf. *ibid.*, p. ix.

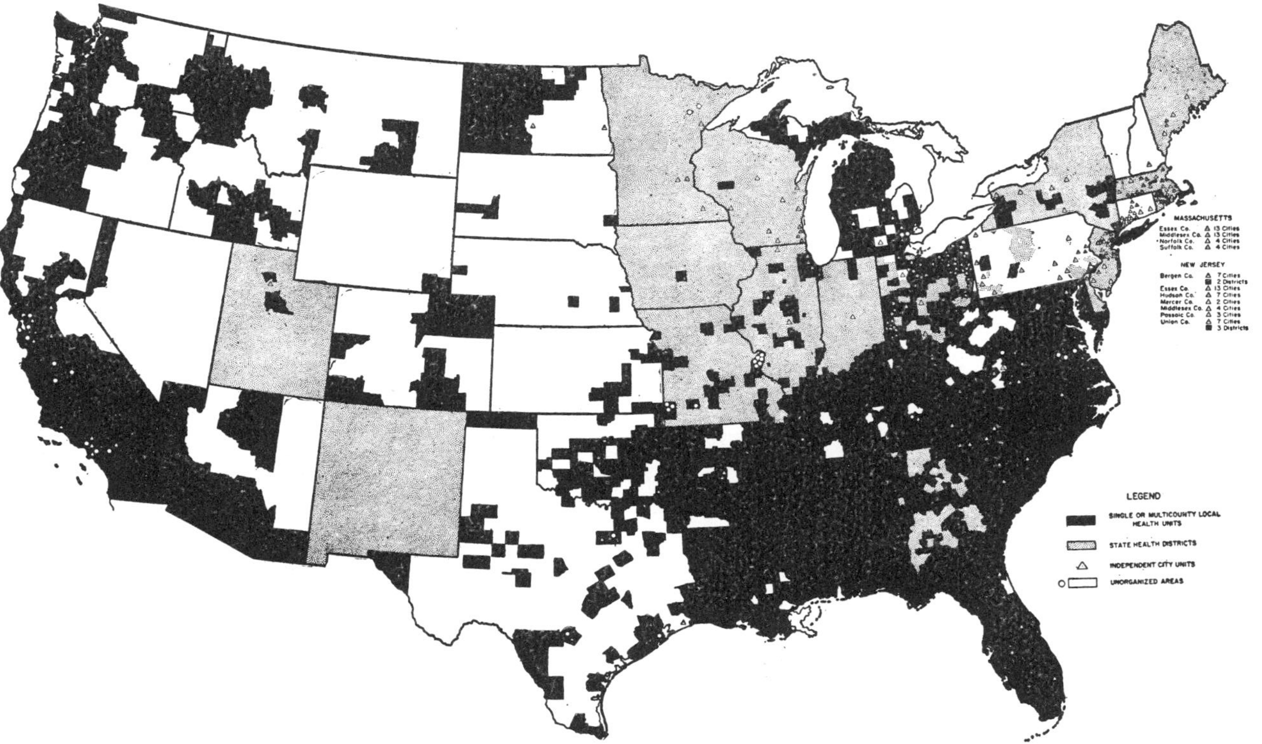

SOURCE: United States Public Health Service.

FIG. XI

Areas Reporting Full-Time Local Health Service: 1953

boards are usually appointed by the governing bodies or administrative officials of the counties, townships, or municipalities comprising the districts. Local health *officers* are appointed most commonly by the local boards of health, but sometimes by local governing bodies, local administrative officials, or state health authorities. Where appointment is vested in authorities at the local level, confirmation by the state health officer or state board of health is sometimes required.[26] Though the division of functions between health boards and health officers is by no means uniform or clearly drawn, the boards generally are vested with certain policy-making authority, including power to issue necessary orders and regulations, while health officers are concerned primarily with enforcement activities. Full-time health departments ordinarily are administered by appointive boards of health, which, in turn, appoint the chief medical officers of their departments. Such departments, where they exist, usually supplant other local health boards and health officers within their respective jurisdictions.

DECENTRALIZED ADMINISTRATION

Notwithstanding the elimination during recent decades of substantial numbers of local health units and boards, local health administration still suffers from excessive decentralization. A committee of the American Public Health Association, on the basis of a nation-wide survey, reported in 1945 that 18,000 or more local government jurisdictions—counties, cities, townships, villages, and special districts—were still responsible for providing local health service on a full-time or part-time basis.[27] As the kind of reorganization needed to remedy this situation, the committee recommended establishment of a comprehensive system of local health units covering the entire nation and having in each instance sufficient population and resources to support a basic minimum full-time health program. The specific suggestions submitted by the committee called for a total of 1,197 local units—318 single-county units; 821 multicounty units; 36 "county-district" units, including *parts* of one or more counties; and 22 city units. Seventy-eight per cent of these proposed units would have populations of at least 50,000, the minimum considered desirable for the support of a full-time department. The less populous districts would serve sparsely populated rural communities where districts of 50,000 persons would require unduly large areas. A system of units such as the one suggested should, in the opinion of the committee, make it possible to pro-

[26] Greve, *loc. cit.*

[27] Emerson and Luginbuhl, *op. cit.*, is the published report of this committee. For a summary of the principal findings and recommendations of the committee, see Martha Luginbuhl, "Local Responsibility for Health Service," *Public Administration Review*, Vol. VI, pp. 30-41 (Winter, 1946).

vide the entire population of the country with minimum full-time health service at reasonable cost. The committee, of course, had no thought of offering a definitive program; it sought merely to outline sound *principles* of reorganization which might be of helpfulness to the states and localities as they seek to improve their health administration. As such a statement of principles, the committee's recommendations deserve careful study. Though there has been some further reduction in the number of administrative units since issuance of the committee report, this has not been sufficient to alter the over-all situation in any substantial degree.

LOCAL HEALTH SERVICES

As previously suggested, the present tendency is toward enlargement of the powers of local health authorities and expansion of their functions. Local health boards originally were concerned with little beyond quarantine measures and nuisance abatement, and even today some part-time health agencies are almost as limited in their activities. But the trend of late has been toward emphasis of *services* rather than *control* measures, and this has been particularly true in the case of full-time health departments.[28] For some years there has been general agreement among public-health administrators that it is highly desirable to have local health departments provide a minimum of six essential services: [29]

1. Communicable-disease control.
2. Community sanitation service.
3. Laboratory services for local physicians.
4. Maternal and child health services.
5. Collection and analysis of vital statistics.
6. Health education.

To this list a seventh basic function has recently been added, namely, the prevention and control of chronic diseases.[30] "Accident prevention, the hygiene of housing, industrial hygiene, school health services, mental health, medical rehabilitation, and hospital and medical care administration are other areas of service and responsibility which have been incorporated into the programs of an increasing number of local health departments." [31] Deserving of note also is a current tendency, as yet not strongly pronounced but perhaps indicative of a future trend, to transfer from welfare to health authorities the duty of providing general medical care for the needy. As a result, the health departments in Maryland's 23 counties and in occasional counties elsewhere now administer general medical-

[28] Cf. Joseph W. Mountin and Evelyn Flook, *Guide to Health Organization in the United States: 1951* (Washington, U. S. Public Health Service, 1953), p. 57.

[29] Cf. Ewing, *op. cit.*, p. 165.

[30] Cf. *America's Health: A Report to the Nation,* p. 79.

[31] "The Local Health Department—Services and Responsibilities," *American Journal of Public Health,* Vol. XLI, pp. 302-307, 303 (March, 1951).

care programs.[32] Services provided under these programs are usually available to recipients of public assistance and to other low-income persons considered medically indigent. The care offered "may include the preventive, diagnostic and therapeutic services of physicians in home, office or clinic, hospital care, dental service, bedside nursing care, laboratory services, drugs and appliances, and other related services." [33] Some of the major aspects of the work of local health departments require further comment.

Disease Control. Many local health activities have to do with the control of communicable and preventable diseases. Physicians are required by law to report cases of communicable disease to the local health authorities, who then investigate and take appropriate control measures. Isolation and quarantine, once the core of public-health programs, continue to be important and, together with prohibition of public meetings, still constitute virtually the only forms of control in many rural areas without full-time health departments. Modern preventive medicine, however, is making constantly greater use of immunization. State health departments commonly supply physicians with free vaccines and sera of various kinds for use in their private practice, and local departments administer vaccines to the indigent and, sometimes, to the general public.[34]

In addition to control activities of a more general nature, special programs have now been inaugurated in various fields, of which those for the control of tuberculosis and venereal diseases are most widespread. Since early diagnosis plays so important a part in the control of tuberculosis, the programs in that field give much attention to case discovery. The older procedure of skin tests, followed by chest X rays for only those persons showing positive reactions, is now being generally supplanted by mass X-ray examinations administered by local health departments or traveling state clinics.[35] Persons found to be suffering from tuberculosis are advised with respect to hygiene, nutrition, and nursing and medical care and, to the extent that facilities are available, are provided with care in tuberculosis hospitals. Practically every local health department operates a clinic for venereal-disease control, necessary drugs sometimes being supplied by the state department.[36]

[32] Milton Terris and Nathan A. Kramer, *General Medical Care Programs in Local Health Departments* (New York, American Public Health Association, 1951). The Maryland programs are administered by the county departments as agents of the state health department's bureau of medical services.

[33] *Ibid.*, p. 41.

[34] Harry S. Mustard, *Government in Public Health* (New York, Commonwealth Fund, 1945), pp. 146-151.

[35] Bernhard J. Stern, *Medical Services by Government, Local, State, and Federal* (New York, Commonwealth Fund, 1946), pp. 56-57. Some local departments make a practice of mailing periodically to the families within their jurisdiction the suggestion that their members report to the clinic for routine chest X rays.

[36] Mustard, *op cit.*, pp. 157-162.

With the lengthened life span resulting from improved sanitation and advances in medical science, the chronic diseases of middle age and advanced years constitute progressively more serious problems. Some of these, such as heart disease and cancer, account for large proportions of present-day deaths. Others, such as the various forms of arthritis and rheumatism, though not major causes of death, take a heavy toll of working capacity, since they maim and disable their victims over long periods of time. Chronic diseases today constitute perhaps the greatest of all challenges to medical personnel, both private and public. Like the communicable diseases, many of the chronic disorders can be controlled in some measure. Some of them can be prevented through proper safeguards against occupational hazards. "Many can be arrested if they are recognized before they have run their course or have given rise to new and secondary conditions." [37] In the light of these facts, local health departments, along with other public-health agencies, are giving more and more attention to the problem of chronic diseases. Many local departments, spurred by state and federal grants-in-aid, have already inaugurated programs for the control of heart disease and cancer, and other chronic ailments are becoming the subject of ever greater concern.

Sanitation. Inspectional and regulatory activities for the promotion of sanitation comprise a major aspect of public-health work. Though problems of sanitation are particularly acute in densely populated urban communities, they are of no small concern in unincorporated suburban areas under county or township jurisdiction for health purposes. Local health officers inspect public water supplies and facilities for sewage and garbage disposal. If insanitary conditions are found, orders are issued for their correction, which orders, if they are reasonable and meet required procedural standards, are ultimately enforceable in the courts. Sanitary inspection is commonly provided also for such other community facilities as swimming pools and tourist and trailer camps.

Protection of the community's food and milk supply is an important function of the local health department. Hotels, restaurants, and food markets are inspected by sanitation officers, and insanitary conditions in such an establishment, if uncorrected, may be ground for revocation of its license to operate. Milk-control laws of one kind or another have now been enacted by most states, but these must ordinarily be supplemented by local regulation if the safety of milk and milk products offered for sale is to be adequately assured. Local ordinances regulating the production and distribution of milk are concerned with sanitary conditions of dairy farms, barns, and milk rooms, and with the cleanliness of cows and their handlers and of milk containers and distributing facilities. To enforce the standards prescribed, local health departments license producers and dis-

[37] Federal Security Agency, *Annual Report: 1952* (Washington, Government Printing Office, 1953), pp. 108-110.

tributors, inspect farms and plants, and test milk samples for bacterial count.[38]

Vital Statistics. If governmental authorities are to safeguard the public health through proper protective measures and be able to evaluate the effectiveness of control programs, they must have reliable information concerning births and deaths and the nature, location, and extent of illness.[39] To provide such information the collection and recording of so-called vital statistics has become a standard feature of local health work.

Statistical data of particular significance to public-health programs fall into three principal categories: (1) birth statistics, (2) morbidity (sickness) statistics, covering a wide variety of "notifiable" diseases; and (3) mortality statistics, relating to deaths and their causes. All three types of data are usually required to be reported by physicians, and births are reportable also by midwives, and deaths by undertakers and coroners. Of the various types, mortality statistics are most complete, since it is usually necessary that a death certificate be filed before a burial permit may be issued. Though the persons required by law to report births, sickness, and deaths are subject to penalty for failure to do so, such penalties are seldom imposed. As a result, there is much laxity in reporting, though less now than in earlier times; and in general it is in the rural areas that reporting is least complete.

During World War II, when birth certificates were widely required of persons seeking employment in government service or defense industry, the inadequacy of existing birth records, especially in rural areas, was forcefully impressed upon the public mind. In many instances it was found, particularly with respect to persons in the more advanced age groups, that births had never been recorded or that original records had been lost. To meet this situation a number of states which had not previously done so enacted laws providing for "delayed birth registration." Under such laws, a person for whom no birth record can be found is permitted to establish the date and place of his birth by documentary evidence supported by affidavits of persons having knowledge of the facts concerned. This having been done, a certificate of delayed birth registration is issued and recorded, which thereafter has the same standing in law as an original birth record.

State laws concerning vital statistics commonly provide that physicians and other persons required to do so shall file their reports with local "registrars," who enter the data on local records and then relay the reports to the state health department. Local registrars are frequently county, township, or city clerks serving ex officio as vital statistics officers. Where

[38] American Municipal Association, *Milk Control* (Chicago, Public Administration Service, 1937), pp. 10-26.

[39] Cf. Schuyler C. Wallace, *State Administrative Supervision over Cities in the United States* (New York, Columbia University Press, 1928), p. 136.

a full-time local health department is in operation, the duties of registrar sometimes devolve upon the department's health officer. In reporting and recording vital statistics, widespread use is now made of standard forms recommended by the United States Public Health Service.

Health Education and Public-Health Nursing. A regular function of full-time local health departments, and one constantly growing in importance, is that of health education. Through newspaper publicity, pamphlets, lectures, films, radio and television—indeed, through all possible channels of communication—efforts are made to make health knowledge available to the general public in simple and understandable form.[40] One of the most widespread of all health activities is public-health nursing, a service which is important both in itself and for its contribution to other health programs, such as that of maternal and child hygiene. Visiting nurses are employed locally by both public and private agencies. Those serving local health departments devote much of their time to health education, particularly among low-income families, but also render maternity service and, to some extent, bedside care for the sick. School nursing in some communities is a function of the local health department, and in others it is provided by nurses employed by the school district.[41]

RURAL HOSPITALS

In the providing of hospital facilities government plays a major role, especially in rural areas. In 1953, of the 6,840 hospitals registered with the American Medical Association, 4,704 were operated by nongovernmental agencies and 2,136 by governmental authorities. Yet the governmental hospitals, though comprising less than one third of the total number of institutions, provided more than two thirds of all hospital beds. In general, nongovernmental hospitals serve patients suffering from acute illnesses which require only short-term hospitalization; while the governmental institutions, though also serving many short-term patients, care for most mental and tuberculous patients and others requiring long-term treatment. Of the governmental hospitals reported in 1953, 392 were operated by the national government, 550 by the various states, 713 by counties, 396 by municipalities, and 85 on a city-county basis. Federal hospitals are maintained to provide care for certain special groups, such as members of the armed services, veterans, Indians, and inmates of federal prisons. With respect to the state and local governments, it is most common for the states to maintain institutions for mental patients and to impose upon local governmental units primary responsibility for providing general and tuberculosis hospitals. However, institutions of all types are maintained, in

[40] Cf. Mustard, *op. cit.*, p. 131.

[41] Committee on the Costs of Medical Care, *Medical Care for the American People,* Final Report (Chicago, University of Chicago Press, 1932), pp. 86-87.

some number, by governments at both levels. Included in the 713 county institutions in 1953 were 481 general hospitals, 164 tuberculosis hospitals, 35 institutions for the treatment of nervous and mental disorders, and 33 institutions of other types.[42]

Existing hospital service is inadequate generally throughout the country and, as previously noted, is especially so in rural communities.[43] During recent years, however, facilities have been expanded somewhat, and, fortunately, the expansion has been greatest in rural and semirural areas, where the shortage has been most acute. Between 1944 and 1953, for example, while nongovernmental, state, and municipal hospitals increased in number by less than 10 per cent, the increase in the case of county hospitals exceeded 40 per cent, and in that of city-county institutions it was more than 50 per cent. These additions to our hospital resources, both rural and urban, have been the result in no small measure of the Hospital Survey and Construction Act of 1946, commonly known as the Hill-Burton Act, providing for federal financial assistance to the states and localities as a means of stimulating needed construction. The 1946 statute provided $3,000,000 to aid the states in surveying their hospital needs and authorized grants-in-aid of $75,000,000 a year for five years to help build state, county, city, and private nonprofit hospitals and health centers. Each dollar of federal funds was to be matched by two dollars of state or local money for both survey and building costs. In recognition of the fact that some states are better able than others to provide their own facilities, the law specified that federal funds should be apportioned on the dual basis of population and per capita annual income, thus making the poorer states eligible for more federal money per person than the wealthier. Amendments adopted in 1949 extended the program to 1955; increased construction-grant authorization to $150,000,000 annually; and provided that the federal share of construction costs, instead of continuing at the uniform one third fixed in the original measure, shall vary from one third to two thirds, depending upon the per capita income of the recipient state.[44] More recent amendments have extended the program to 1959.

By 1954, more than 2,000 projects had been approved under the Hill-Burton program, and about two thirds of these were in actual operation.[45]

[42] The 1953 data in this paragraph are from F. H. Arestad and Mary A. McGovern, "Hospital Service in the United States," *Journal of the American Medical Association,* Vol. CLV, pp. 255-278 (May 15, 1954). See also, United States Senate Committee on Labor and Public Welfare, *Activities of Government in the Field of Health Services,* Sen. Rept. 359, Pt. 3, 82d Cong., 1st sess. (Washington, Government Printing Office, 1951).

[43] See above, "Lack of Medical Personnel and Facilities."

[44] United States Public Health Service, *The Hospital Act and Your Community* (Washington, Government Printing Office, 1947); *State Government,* Vol. XXII, p. 291 (December, 1949).

[45] United States Department of Health, Education, and Welfare, *Annual Report: 1954* (Washington, Government Printing Office, 1955), p. 130.

Included among the projects were a considerable number of modern county institutions to serve rural communities previously lacking hospital facilities. Prior to 1946, no fewer than 1,200 American counties—40 per cent of those in the entire nation—were reported as having no registered hospital whatsoever. Today, the picture is less dark, but even yet hundreds of rural counties are without hospitals. Incidentally, it may be observed that improvement of rural hospital facilities is probably one of the most effective of all possible means of attracting young physicians to rural practice.

RURAL HEALTH CO-OPERATIVES

Although consumer co-operatives are not, strictly speaking, governmental in nature, they resemble governmental enterprises in that they seek, through collective effort, to provide certain commodities or services to their members, and sometimes to nonmembers as well, on a nonprofit basis. In concluding our description of health services in rural communities, mention should be made of the part, small though it is, played by rural health co-operatives. As of 1949, at least 101 rural health co-operatives had been established in 21 states, for the most part west of the Mississippi River, and 54 of these were known to be currently operating health services of some kind or taking steps toward that goal. These co-operatives had been variously formed for one or more of three purposes: (1) to attract doctors to a community lacking or deficient in medical services; (2) to provide and operate a health-service center; and (3) to operate a prepayment plan for rural medical care.[46] Most numerous among the health co-operatives are those that have been established in various western states for the construction and maintenance of hospitals, of which there are some twenty in Texas alone.[47]

PRESENT DEFICIENCIES

Notwithstanding that local public-health organization is being constantly improved and full-time coverage steadily expanded, facilities still are far from adequate. Local health units remain too numerous, and most of them, including many full-time units, are too small. Of the 970 county and district units reported in 1950, 625 were serving less than 50,000 persons, and 393 fewer than 35,000. Even these full-time departments, in many instances, are sadly understaffed with respect to one or more of the four

[46] Helen L. Johnston, *Rural Health, Coöperatives* (Washington, Farm Credit Administration, 1950).

[47] Cf. Roemer, *loc. cit.* Consumer co-operatives also are used in rural areas, and much more extensively than in the health field, for the purpose of providing electric service to farms and other rural establishments. See below, "Rural Housing."

types of personnel required to provide adequate service—physicians, nurses, sanitarians, and clerical employees. Minimum staffing needs of existing full-time health departments, urban and rural, to say nothing of the problem of staffing newly organized units, was estimated, as of 1950, to approximate an additional 1,000 physicians, 10,000 nurses, 1,600 sanitation workers, and 1,400 clerical employees. And, finally, there must be faced the regrettable fact that nearly half of all American counties, including about one fourth of the national population, still have only part-time local health service or none at all.[48]

FUTURE OUTLOOK

In the foregoing pages a good deal has been said concerning the shortage in rural communities of medical personnel and facilities, both private and public, and mention has been made of the inability of many rural people, because of lack of purchasing power, to obtain proper medical care, even where the needed facilities are available. By various means, several of which have been considered in the preceding discussion, an endeavor is being made to augment private medical resources in rural areas; and, through voluntary prepayment plans, some rural inhabitants who could not otherwise do so are being enabled to purchase proper care. To supplement and undergird private resources, the coverage of full-time local health departments is being extended to embrace more and more communities, and effort is being made to provide these departments with proper staff and financing. Insofar as suitable medical care is made available to rural America through private initiative, local health departments may well continue to be limited in their services to those now generally performed by the more adequately staffed full-time units. To whatever extent private resources and voluntary prepayment programs fail to meet rural needs, it seems likely that there will be increasing demand for the assignment of additional responsibilities to public-health agencies, and perhaps for meeting a portion of the cost of medical care through some form of compulsory health insurance.

RURAL HOUSING

The level of general health in any community depends in some measure upon housing standards, and housing in many rural areas leaves much to be desired. Rural housing, by and large, has long been inferior to urban, and, despite recent improvements, it remains so today. Slum conditions are by no means confined to urban centers. Rural slums, though less concentrated and therefore less striking, are nonetheless real. Crowded,

[48] *Report of Local Public Health Resources: 1950,* pp. 5, 21-32, 51.

unsafe, and unhealthful farm housing is widely prevalent in various sections of the country, and particularly so among tenant farmers and sharecroppers, many of them Negroes, in some of the southern states.

In 1934, at a time when a third of the nation's total population was estimated to be ill-housed, a sampling survey directed by the Bureau of Home Economics of the United States Department of Agriculture revealed that about 60 per cent of all American farm people, comprising approximately 4,000,000 families, were living under substandard housing conditions. This survey indicated that fully a fourth of all farmhouses in the United States were in poor structural condition because of defective foundations, floors, walls, or roofs. More than half of all farmhouses were over 25 years old, and a fifth of them had stood for more than a half century. Many of these were shamefully run-down, unpainted shacks, some with holes in the roofs and some without doors or windowpanes.[49] Other investigations have disclosed extensive overcrowding in farm homes. During the 1930's many rural counties were reported to be without a single unoccupied habitable dwelling. As a result, large families often were compelled to live cramped up in shacks of two or three rooms, or several families to double up in a house that would have been substandard even for one.[50]

In the two decades since these reports, some improvement has been effected in farm housing, in part as a direct result of government housing programs but more largely because increased farm income has rendered possible the making of needed repairs and replacements. Yet rural housing continues to lag far behind urban. A sampling survey by the Census Bureau in 1947 indicated that about 19 per cent of all farm dwelling units were still in need of major repairs, as compared with 8 per cent in the case of nonfarm units; 67 per cent of the farm units, in contrast with 12 per cent of the nonfarm, lacked running water; 80 per cent of all farm homes, as against 25 per cent of the nonfarm dwellings, were without private bath and flush toilet; and 40 per cent of the farm units, as compared with 5 per cent of the nonfarm, lacked electric lights. Only 20 per cent of American farm dwellings, in contrast with 75 per cent of the nonfarm units, were equipped with all of the major conveniences ordinarily considered essential to a modern home.[51] The housing census of 1950 indicated that, as of mid-century, 16 per cent of owner-occupied farm dwellings and 29 per cent of those occupied by renters were overcrowded

[49] United States Department of Agriculture, *The Farm-housing Survey* (Washington, 1939). Cf. United States Housing Authority, *Annual Report: 1939* (Washington, Government Printing Office, 1940), p. 26.

[50] United States Housing Authority, *Annual Report: 1939,* p. 26.

[51] United States Bureau of the Census, *Housing Characteristics of the United States: April, 1947,* Current Population Reports (Washington, 1947), Series P-70, No. 1. Nonfarm units, as the term is used in these data, include both urban and rural nonfarm dwellings. Cf. Roy J. Burroughs, "Toward a Farm Housing Policy," *Land Economics,* Vol. XXIV, pp. 1-22 (February, 1948).

in the sense of having occupancy density in excess of one person per room.[52] Most spectacular of all recent improvements in rural housing has been the widespread electrification of farm homes, brought about in large measure through local electric co-operatives organized under the sponsorship of the federal Rural Electrification Administration. As of the mid-1940's, more than 900 rural electric co-operatives were serving 1,500,000 families in 46 states.[53] So rapid has been the extension of rural electrification that 80 per cent of all occupied farm dwellings were equipped with electric lights in 1950 as compared with only 32 per cent in 1940.[54] By 1954, 90 per cent of all American farms were supplied with electricity.[55]

LOCAL HOUSING AUTHORITIES

The most extensive program of public housing yet undertaken in this country, save for the provision of temporary wartime facilities, was inaugurated under the United States Housing Act of 1937. By the terms of this statute, which as amended by subsequent housing acts remains the basic public-housing law, federal financial assistance in the form of long-term capital loans and annual subsidy grants was offered to local public housing authorities organized under state law for the construction and operation of low-rent housing projects. Through such projects it is sought to provide subsidized housing for families which, because of low income, are unable to pay from their own funds the full cost of decent housing accommodations. The subsidy feature of the program is seen in the fact that the rent charged for a housing unit is determined by the income and size of the occupant family rather than by the cost of the facilities provided, the difference between the actual cost and what the family can afford to pay being met from government funds. To qualify for federal aid, local projects must meet prescribed standards with respect to such matters as maximum construction cost, acceptance of only low-income tenants, and local financial participation. It is also generally required that for each new dwelling unit constructed a slum unit be eliminated, though in times of acute housing shortage deferment of such elimination may be

[52] United States Bureau of the Census, *Census of Housing, 1950: Farm Housing Characteristics* (Washington, 1953), Vol. III, p. xxix.

[53] Frederick W. Muller, *Public Rural Electrification* (Washington, American Council on Public Affairs, 1944); United States Department of Agriculture, *Report of the Administrator of the Rural Electrification Administration: 1946* (Washington, Government Printing Office, 1946). Though a few electric co-operatives operate generating plants, most of them operate distribution systems only, purchasing their electrical energy wholesale from private utility companies, municipal plants, or federal power projects.

[54] *Census of Housing, 1950: Farm Housing Characteristics*, p. xxx.

[55] For percentages in individual states, see United States Department of Agriculture, *Report of the Secretary of Agriculture: 1955* (Washington, Government Printing Office, 1956), p. 49.

authorized by the federal administering agency. To administer the program at the federal level, the 1937 law initially established the United States Housing Authority. This agency subsequently was merged with the Federal Public Housing Authority, which, in 1947, was superseded by the Public Housing Administration—a unit in the newly established Housing and Home Finance Agency.

As a result of the federal legislation most states authorized the organization of local housing authorities by cities or counties, or by both, some also permitting the establishment of regional authorities serving two or more counties. These local housing authorities are governmental corporations empowered to build and operate low-rent housing projects and to enter into contracts with the national government and with local governments for financial assistance. They usually are vested with borrowing power and the power of eminent domain. However, they ordinarily have no taxing power but rely upon rental income and government subsidies for funds to repay construction loans and meet operating costs. Federal loans and grants are made in cash, but local government contributions more commonly take the form of land, services, or tax exemption. The governing body of the local housing authority is a board of directors, the composition of which varies from state to state. A fairly typical provision is for a board of five members, appointed by the mayor in the case of a city authority and by the county board in the case of a county authority. The board of directors usually appoints an executive director to supervise the authority's staff and execute board policies. In some instances there is a state housing agency which exercises supervisory powers over the organization and operation of local housing authorities, sometimes also participating in the appointment of the local boards of directors.[56]

FARM HOUSING PROGRAMS

Though the projects constructed by local housing authorities have been for the most part in urban areas, the original program envisaged improved farm housing as well. Public housing for farm families differs from urban projects in that, instead of multifamily apartment houses, it involves the construction of single dwellings on individual farms. As the farm housing projects actually established were usually administered, a farm owner unable to provide decent housing for himself, or for his tenant, sharecropper, or wagehand, made application to the local county or regional authority for the construction of a new dwelling. The application was referred to a representative of the Farm Security Administration for in-

[56] Cf. B. J. Hovde, "The Local Housing Authority," *Public Administration Review*, Vol. I, pp. 167-175 (Winter, 1941); Annette Baker Fox, "The Local Housing Authority and the Municipal Government," *Journal of Land and Public Utilities Economics*, Vol. XVII, pp. 280-290 (August, 1941).

vestigation of the farm and the income of the proposed occupant. If the farm was found potentially capable of sustaining the family and yielding sufficient income to pay the rent, and if all other requirements for eligibility were met, the application was approved. The farm owner then conveyed a small tract of land to the local housing authority as a building site. When a house had been erected thereon, it was leased to the owner of the farm at a low rental—usually in the neighborhood of $60 per year.[57] These farm houses, though not equipped with bathrooms and some of the other conveniences common in urban communities, nevertheless were sturdily built and provided with safe and adequate water supplies and outdoor toilet facilities.[58]

By 1941, rural housing authorities had been established to serve 352 counties, many of them in the South where housing conditions are particularly bad,[59] and contracts had been made by the United States Housing Authority with local authorities for building several thousand farm homes. With the outbreak of World War II, however, labor and materials which had been intended for low-rent housing projects were diverted to war housing, and work on most of the low-rent projects was suspended. As a matter of fact, only a few hundred of the projected farm homes were actually completed; and under the Housing Act of 1949 federal financial assistance ceased to be available for strictly farm housing. Pursuant to this change in policy, the federal government subsequently sought to promote the liquidation of the small farm program by encouraging the local housing authorities owning the projects concerned to sell their houses on liberal terms to the individual farm owners, and by 1955 all but a few of the houses had been disposed of in this manner.[60]

Notwithstanding the discontinuance of this program of farmhouse construction, two other modest programs of rural low-rent public housing are still being operated by local housing authorities. One of these consists of rural nonfarm projects built and owned by local authorities under the terms of the Housing Act of 1949. As of 1954, 277 of these projects, containing more than 10,000 units, had already been completed, and others were in the development stage. The second program comprises 38 farm

[57] Rupert B. Vance and Gordon W. Blackwell, *New Farm Homes for Old: A Study of Rural Public Housing in the South* (University, University of Alabama Press, 1946), pp. 32, 86. See also, M. H. Satterfield, "Mississippi Leads South in Rural Housing," *National Municipal Review*, Vol. XXIX, pp. 311-314 (May, 1940).

[58] Federal Public Housing Authority, *Public Housing: The Work of the Federal Public Housing Authority* (Washington, Government Printing Office, 1946).

[59] M. H. Satterfield, "Intergovernmental Cooperation in the Tennessee Valley," *Journal of Politics*, Vol. IX, pp. 31-58 (February, 1947).

[60] Housing and Home Finance Agency, *Eighth Annual Report: 1954* (Washington, Government Printing Office, 1955), p. 360; "A Rural Slum Clearance Program Comes to an End," *Journal of Housing*, Vol. XII, pp. 278-280, 292 (August–September, 1955).

labor camps, embracing 9,000 units, built by the United States Department of Agriculture in the late 1930's for migrant farm workers. Transferred to the Public Housing Administration under terms of the Housing Act of 1950, these camps became public projects for the housing of low-income farm workers, and by 1954 all but two had been conditionally sold to local housing authorities.[61] In addition to the programs of public housing, mention should be made of the credit extended to farmers at various times by the federal government for housing construction and repair. Under the Housing Act of 1949, for example, the secretary of agriculture is authorized to make loans to farmers unable to obtain necessary credit from private or co-operative sources for the provision of adequate housing for themselves or their farm workers. These loans, which under some circumstances may be supplemented by subsidies, are made through county offices of the Farmers Home Administration in the Department of Agriculture. By the end of 1950, approximately 6,600 farm housing loans, amounting to about $30,000,000 had been approved under these provisions.[62]

Through public housing and government credit, but to a greater extent from increased private outlay, housing conditions in the United States have improved substantially during recent years. Fortunately, the most conspicuous gains have been made in the farm areas of the country, where substandard conditions have been most widely prevalent. In 1948 alone, according to Department of Commerce estimates, outlays for new residential farm construction amounted to $275,000,000.[63] Yet, despite this progress, the farm housing situation remains far from satisfactory. Further improvement in housing continues to constitute a major problem of American rural life.

REFERENCES

Books, Reports, and Special Studies

America's Health Status, Needs and Resources: Building America's Health, Report of the President's Commission on the Health Needs of the Nation (Washington, Government Printing Office, 1953), Vol. II.

BACHMAN, George W., and others, *Health Resources in the United States* (Washington, Brookings Institution, 1952).

BEYER, Glenn H., *Rural Housing in New York State* (Ithaca, N.Y., Cornell University Agricultural Experiment Station, 1952).

Blue Earth County Council on Intergovernmental Relations, *A Study of Public Health Administration in Blue Earth County, Minnesota* (Mankato, Minn., ca. 1947.)

[61] Housing and Home Finance Agency, *Eighth Annual Report: 1954*, p. 360.

[62] Housing and Home Finance Agency, *A Summary of the Evolution of Housing Activities in the Federal Government* (Washington, 1950).

[63] Cf. Housing and Home Finance Agency, *The Housing Situation: The Factual Background* (Washington, 1949), pp. 8, 19.

Committee on the Cost of Medical Care, *Medical Care for the American People*, Final Report (Chicago, University of Chicago Press, 1932).

DAVIS, Michael M., *Public Medical Services* (Chicago, University of Chicago Press, 1937).

EMERSON, Haven, and LUGINBUHL, Martha, *Local Health Units for the Nation* (New York, Commonwealth Fund, 1945).

EWING, Oscar R., *The Nation's Health: A Ten-year Program* (Washington, Federal Security Agency, 1948).

FREEMAN, Allen W., ed., *A Study of Rural Public Health Service* (New York, Commonwealth Fund, 1933).

GOLDMANN, Franz, *Public Medical Care: Principles and Problems* (New York, Columbia University Press, 1945).

HISCOCK, Ira V., *District Health Administration* (Lancaster, Pa., Science Press Printing Co., 1936).

Housing and Home Finance Agency, *Annual Report* (Washington, Government Printing Office).

———, *The Housing Situation: The Factual Background* (Washington, 1949).

———, *A Summary of the Evolution of Housing Activities in the Federal Government* (Washington, 1950).

JOHNSTON, Helen L., *Rural Health Coöperatives* (Washington, Farm Credit Administration, 1950), published in co-operation with the U. S. Public Health Service.

MOTT, Frederick D., and ROEMER, Milton I., *Rural Health and Medical Care* (New York, McGraw-Hill, 1948).

MOUNTIN, Joseph W., and FLOOK, Evelyn, *Guide to Health Organization in the United States: 1951* (Washington, U. S. Public Health Service, 1953).

MUSTARD, Harry S., *An Introduction to Public Health*, 3d ed., (New York, Macmillan, 1953).

———, *Government in Public Health* (New York, Commonwealth Fund, 1945).

———, *Rural Health Practice* (New York, Commonwealth Fund, 1936).

———, "Local Health Administration: Rural," in Haven Emerson, ed., *Administrative Medicine* (New York, Nelson, 1941), pp. 311-323.

National Health Assembly, *America's Health: A Report to the Nation* (New York, Harper, 1949).

National Health Conference, *The Nation's Health* (Washington, Government Printing Office, 1939).

SMILLIE, Wilson G., *Public Health Administration in the United States*, 3d ed., (New York, Macmillan, 1947).

SOUTHMAYD, H. J., "Rural Hospitals," in Haven Emerson, ed., *Administrative Medicine* (New York, Nelson, 1941), pp. 19-37.

STERN, Bernhard J., *Medical Services by Government, Local, State, and Federal* (New York, Commonwealth Fund, 1946).

TERRIS, Milton, and KRAMER, Nathan A., *General Medical Care Programs in Local Health Departments* (New York, American Public Health Association, 1951).

United States Bureau of the Census, *Housing Characteristics of the United States: April, 1947*, Current Population Reports (Washington, 1947), Series P-70, No. 1.

———, *Census of Housing, 1950: Farm Housing Characteristics* (Washington, 1953), Vol. III.

United States Department of Agriculture, *The Farm-housing Survey* (Washington, 1939).

United States Department of Agriculture, *Housing Needs and Preferences of Farm Families* (Washington, Government Printing Office, 1952).

———, Interbureau Committee on Post-War Programs, *Better Health for Rural America* (Washington, Government Printing Office, 1945).

United States Department of Health, Education, and Welfare, *Annual Report* (Washington, Government Printing Office).

United States Public Health Service, *Report of Local Public Health Resources: 1950* (Washington, 1952).

———, *State Laws Governing Local Health Departments* (Washington, Government Printing Office, 1953).

VANCE, Rupert B., and BLACKWELL, Gordon W., *New Farm Homes for Old: A Study of Rural Public Housing in the South* (University, University of Alabama Press, 1946).

WINSLOW, C.-E. A., *Health on the Farm and in the Village* (New York, Macmillan, 1931).

WYATT, Laurence, *Intergovernmental Relations in Public Health* (Minneapolis, University of Minnesota Press, 1951).

Articles

BARNES, M. E., "The County, the Logical Public Health Unit," *National Municipal Review,* Vol. XXI, pp. 499-501 (August, 1932).

BLAIR, George S., "County Health Departments in Pennsylvania," *The County Officer,* Vol. XX, pp. 128-130 (June, 1955).

BURROUGHS, Roy J., "Toward a Farm Housing Policy," *Land Economics,* Vol. XXIV, pp. 1-22 (February, 1948).

BUSHNELL, Nathan, III, "How Can We Develop Medical Care in Rural Communities?" *The County Officer,* Vol. XVII, pp. 81-85 (March, 1952).

DORN, Harold F., "Rural Health and Public Health Programs," *Rural Sociology,* Vol. VII, pp. 22-32 (March, 1942).

GREVE, Clifford H., "Provisions of State Laws Governing Local Health Departments," *Public Health Reports,* Vol. LXVIII, pp. 31-42 (January, 1953).

HOVDE, B. J., "The Local Housing Authority," *Public Administration Review,* Vol. I, pp. 167-175 (Winter, 1941).

JOHNSON, V. Webster, TIMMONS, John F., and HOWENSTINE, E. Jay, Jr., "Rural Public Works," *Journal of Land and Public Utilities Economics,* Vol. XXIII, pp. 12-21, 132-141 (February, May, 1947).

KEITH, Nathaniel S., "Opportunities for Slum Clearance," *The County Officer,* Vol. XV, No. 7, pp. 14-17, 31 (October, 1950).

"The Local Health Department—Services and Responsibilities," *American Journal of Public Health,* Vol. XLI, pp. 302-307 (March, 1951).

LUGINBUHL, Martha, "Local Responsibility for Health Service," *Public Administration Review,* Vol. VI, pp. 30-41 (Winter, 1946).

MOLDENHAUER, Ruth M., and GREVE, Clifford H., "General Regulatory Powers and Duties of State and Local Health Authorities," *Public Health Reports,* Vol. LXVIII, pp. 434-438 (April, 1953).

MOTT, Frederick D., "A Public Health Program for Rural Areas," *Public Health Reports,* Vol. LXI, pp. 589-598 (April 26, 1946).

MOUNTIN, Joseph W., "Participation by State and Local Health Departments in Current Medical Care Programs," *American Journal of Public Health,* Vol. XXXVI, pp. 1387-1393 (December, 1946).

RADEMAKER, Lee A., "The County in Modern Public Health Services," *The County Officer,* Vol. XVII, pp. 174-177, 179 (June, 1952).

Roemer, Milton I., "Rural Programs of Medical Care," *Annals of the American Academy of Political and Social Science,* Vol. CCLXXIII, pp. 160-168 (January, 1951).

Rothrock, Roger L., "The Rôle of the County Hospital," *The County Officer,* Vol. XIX, pp. 2-4 (January, 1954).

"A Rural Slum Clearance Program Comes to an End," *Journal of Housing,* Vol. XII, pp. 278-280, 292 (August–September, 1955).

Satterfield, M. H., "Mississippi Leads South in Rural Housing," *National Municipal Review,* Vol. XXIX, pp. 311-314 (May, 1940).

Shanholtz, Mack I., "Supplying Rural Virginia with Doctors," *State Government,* Vol. XXVIII, pp. 105-106, 117-118 (May, 1955).

CHAPTER 16

Public Welfare

THE LOCAL WELFARE FUNCTION

LOCAL GOVERNMENTS IN rural America have, from earliest times, played an important role in the providing of public-welfare services. These, as the term is ordinarily understood, are services provided at public expense for certain disadvantaged groups in society, particularly the dependent, delinquent, and criminal classes, and persons suffering from physical or mental handicaps.[1] Institutional care for criminal, delinquent, and defective persons is provided, for the most part, by the states. In caring for the dependent poor, on the other hand, the local governments since colonial days have had a considerable part. Originally, providing the necessities of life for persons unable to support themselves was *solely* a local responsibility. Eventually, however, the states began to lend a hand; and during the depression years of the 1930's, particularly with enactment of the Social Security Act of 1935, the federal government embarked upon a program of participation. Today, therefore, both state and national governments share in the support of the needy, but the role of the local units, and especially that of the counties and townships, continues to be one of major significance. Responsibilities of the local governments in this field are discharged through administering and financing, or participating in the administration and financing of, various programs of poor relief, or public assistance as it is now coming to be called. Even in relatively prosperous times, the providing of public assistance constitutes one of the principal functions of many local governments in rural areas.

[1] Concerning the public welfare concept generally, see Marietta Stevenson, *Public Welfare Administration* (New York, Macmillan, 1938), pp. 1-2; E. C. Lindeman, "Public Welfare," *Encyclopaedia of the Social Sciences* (New York, Macmillan, 1934), Vol. XII, pp. 687-689.

CHANGE OF ATTITUDE TOWARD THE POOR

Evolution of the public-welfare function, insofar as it relates to care for the needy, has been characterized during recent decades not only by a partial shift of responsibility from the localities concerned to the state and national governments but by a distinct change in public attitude. "Recipients of relief once were objects of disgrace and humiliation."[2] Now, however, "We have come to realize that poverty, particularly in times of economic stress, is unavoidable and that the individual who needs help should not be subjected to indignity and public disgrace because of circumstances beyond his control."[3] This change in public attitude is nowhere seen more clearly than in the changes in terminology that are being adopted by welfare workers and officially incorporated into state statutes through amendments to, or codifications of, the welfare laws. In various states, for example, in an effort to remove any social stigma from recipients of public aid, "pauper laws" have become "public-assistance codes," "paupers" have become "needy persons," "poor relief" has become "public assistance," "overseers of the poor" have become "supervisors of public assistance," the "poorhouse" has become the "county home," and the "inmates" of that institution have become "residents" or "patients." Though the newer terminology is clearly indicative of a pronounced trend and seems generally preferable to the old, its adoption as yet is far from universal. Since the older nomenclature is still officially retained in some states, the old and the new will be used interchangeably in the following discussion.

PUBLIC-ASSISTANCE PROGRAMS

Public-assistance measures are classified in two principal ways. The first of these distinguishes between *indoor* and *outdoor* assistance. Indoor assistance is provided to poor persons within the doors of public institutions and is sometimes called institutional relief. Outdoor aid, on the other hand, is given outside public institutions, usually within the homes of the recipients, and is frequently referred to as home relief. Each of the two forms of assistance has its peculiar advantages and disadvantages. The indoor variety is almost essential for poor persons who because of sickness or other physical or mental handicap require constant attention and care. It is less difficult to provide proper care for these persons in an institution equipped for that purpose than elsewhere, and less expensive to care for several in a common institution than in their respective homes. Outdoor

[2] Tax Foundation, *Improving Public Assistance: Some Aspects of the Welfare Problem* (New York, 1953), p. 6.

[3] From a statement of Gov. Adlai E. Stevenson, accompanying his approval of the Public Assistance Code of Illinois, August 4, 1949, printed in *The Public Assistance Code of Illinois and Related Laws Affecting Public Aid: 1949-1951* (Springfield, Illinois Public Aid Commission, n.d.), pp. iii-iv.

assistance has the advantage of greater flexibility. In the case of an able-bodied poor person who has some income but not enough for his entire support, the simplest and often the most economical course is to supply him with supplementary funds that will enable him to maintain his home. Another alleged advantage of outdoor assistance is the fact that the social stigma of pauperism, though now removed in substantial measure from all forms of public aid, inheres even less in assistance of the outdoor type than in that of the indoor variety. Accepting public funds or grocery orders for use in one's own home is a very different thing from going "over the hill to the poorhouse." Yet it must be admitted that this very absence of social stigma may encourage some persons to apply for outdoor assistance who would make further effort to support themselves before seeking admission to an institution. When this occurs on a large scale, only the most vigilant administration will prevent the assistance rolls from being padded with the names of persons who are not actually entitled to public support.

Traditionally, indoor relief has been looked upon as the normal means of supporting persons who are permanent public charges, and outdoor assistance has been considered as intended primarily for those who require only temporary help. Today, however, the tendency is to confine indoor assistance to the sick and handicapped classes and to use the outdoor variety in other cases. One of the principal reasons for this trend is doubtless the fact that outdoor aid permits the recipients to lead more normal lives than is possible for inmates of institutions. Regardless of the respective merits of indoor and outdoor assistance, it is necessarily the latter which must be expanded in times of economic depression and widespread unemployment, if for no other reason than the physical inadequacy of public institutions to carry the relief load during such periods.

A second classification of public-assistance measures distinguishes between *general* and *categorical* assistance. According to this distinction, general assistance is that available to all whose support is a public responsibility and who are not eligible for aid under any of the special or categorical programs. Categorical assistance is designed to aid poor persons of special classes or categories. At the present time, five major outdoor-assistance programs are in operation. One of these, the general-assistance program, is administered and financed wholly by the state and local governments. The other four are the categorical programs of old-age assistance, aid to the blind, aid to dependent children, and aid to the permanently and totally disabled. These programs are administered by the state governments directly, or by local agencies under state supervision, and are financed in part by federal aid. The county home or almshouse, which is the principal institution for assistance of the indoor variety, has traditionally been a general relief agency, though in some states these institutions are now being converted into nursing homes for the infirm and chronically ill.

GENERAL OUTDOOR ASSISTANCE

Outdoor assistance of a general nature usually takes the form of food, clothing, shelter, fuel, utility service, and medical supplies, or of money grants for the purchase of these and other necessities. In a majority of the states this form of aid is primarily a county responsibility. Elsewhere, the unit most commonly charged with supplying this type of assistance is the township or, in New England, the town. A few states provide for county administration in some counties and township administration in others; and in several states the program is administered in some communities by municipalities.[4]

The demand for outdoor assistance fluctuates widely with changes in economic conditions and the extent of unemployment, and it also varies somewhat with the seasons, being heaviest during the winter months. Because of variations in eligibility requirements and available funds, assistance programs are quite uneven among the different states; and frequently there are also variations in adequacy between different localities within the same state.[5] In early 1935, at the depth of an economic depression and before the categorical-assistance features of the social security program had become operative, more than 5,000,000 cases—families and single individuals—were receiving general assistance from the state and local governments.[6] Subsequently, as cases were transferred to the federally aided programs of categorical assistance, and as employment opportunities were afforded in defense and war industries, drastic curtailment of the general-assistance program became possible. During the summer of 1954 the number of cases receiving general assistance was approximately 299,000, with average monthly payments per case being slightly more than $51.[7]

Generally speaking, it seems unwise to administer outdoor assistance through any governmental unit smaller than the county. The average township is too small to maintain a welfare department with trained caseworkers and other personnel. Moreover, under township administration assistance standards are likely to vary considerably, with the aid provided being adequate in some units and inadequate in others. Ordinarily, the townships with heavy case loads are the very ones which, because of low property valuations, are least able to support their poor from local taxes. This financial inequality is counterbalanced in some measure by state

[4] Cf. Arthur C. Millspaugh, *Public Welfare Organization* (Washington, Brookings Institution, 1935), pp. 278-282.

[5] Rose J. McHugh, "Public Assistance," *Social Work Year Book: 1947* (New York, Russell Sage Foundation, 1947), pp. 371-387.

[6] Council of State Governments, *The Book of the States: 1945-46* (Chicago, 1945), p. 327.

[7] United States Department of Health, Education, and Welfare, *Annual Report: 1954* (Washington, Government Printing Office, 1955), p. 43.

grants-in-aid to the poorer townships, but the inadequacy of the township as an administrative unit, even with state supervision, remains. Because of this fact there is some tendency at the present time, in states where township administration has prevailed in the past, to transfer responsibility for general assistance to the county, which, in many instances, is already administering the categorical programs.

THE CATEGORICAL PROGRAMS

Four programs of categorical aid—old-age assistance, aid to the blind, aid to dependent children, and aid to the permanently and totally disabled—now exist quite generally throughout the country. Though earlier legislation in some states provided limited benefits for needy persons in the first three of these categories, the major impetus for the establishment of such programs was afforded by provisions of the Social Security Act, which made federal grants-in-aid available for their support. As originally enacted in 1935, the federal law provided grants for the needy aged, the needy blind, and dependent children; and aid for the needy disabled was added by amendments of 1950. Today, practically all of the states operate the four programs; and with but an occasional exception, all of the state programs qualify for federal aid. As of 1954, for example, every state provided old-age assistance, aid to the blind, and aid to dependent children; and, except for Nevada's program for dependent children, all of the state plans were approved for federal assistance. At the same time, though scarcely four years had elapsed since authorization of federal support, 42 states already were administering aid to the disabled under federally approved plans, and others were preparing to inaugurate such programs.

In prescribing administrative standards which must be met by the states if they are to qualify for federal aid, the Social Security Act requires that the programs of categorical assistance be administered either by a central state agency or by local governmental units under state supervision. If administration is by local units, the programs must be mandatory upon them. Provision must be made for granting to any applicant whose claim for assistance is denied at the local level an opportunity for a hearing before the state supervisory agency; and methods of administration must be established, including merit-system principles of personnel management, that will meet the approval of the Social Security Administration. Federal aid originally was denied for any assistance payments to inmates of public institutions. Some state laws, however, provided for payments to such persons from state or state and local funds; and a 1950 amendment to the Social Security Act now permits federal sharing in assistance payments to needy aged, blind, or disabled patients in public medical institutions other than mental or tuberculosis hospitals, provided that such patients are otherwise qualified for aid under the categorical programs. As would be expected, statutory qualifications for receiving categorical assistance vary somewhat among the states, but as a result of federal-aid standards, they tend to be similar in essentials. Some states impose citizenship and residence requirements. The two universal qualifications, however, are (1) need, as that term is defined by statute, and (2) the existence, again in accordance with statutory definition, of old age, blindness, child dependency, or permanent and total disability.[8]

Old-age Assistance. Of the four categorical programs, that for the needy aged is by far the most extensive and the most costly. As the life span lengthens, older people constitute an ever larger proportion of our total population, and the problem of their care becomes correspondingly greater. In the early 1950's there were more than 13,000,000 persons sixty-five years of age or over in the United States—more than 8 per cent of the total population;[9] and it has been estimated that by 1980, barring unforeseen changes in existing trends, there will be some 22,000,000 such persons.[10] Dependency is inevitably more prevalent among persons in this higher age group than in the population generally. A very large number of older persons are without either savings or income and have no relatives to support them. Many suffer from some chronic disease, and those who are able-bodied frequently find it difficult to secure employment because of their advanced age. For these reasons, the provision of assistance to the needy aged has come to be recognized as a major problem calling for special measures in its solution.

The age requirement for receiving aid under the old-age assistance programs is almost universally sixty-five years.[11] The statutory definition of need, as a qualification for assistance, shows some variation in detail but is everywhere much the same in general purport. In about half of the states, a needy person is defined as one who does not have sufficient income or other resources to provide a reasonable subsistence compatible with decency and health; and in most other states substantially the same requirement is expressed in slightly different language. The amount of assistance granted to a qualified applicant depends upon his individual circumstances and is intended, together with his private income or resources, if any, to enable him to live in a decent and healthful manner.

[8] For a summary of conditions for the granting of federal aid to the states, and a tabular analysis of the various state laws governing the categorical programs, see United States Department of Health, Education, and Welfare, *Characteristics of State Public Assistance Plans under the Social Security Act* (Washington, Government Printing Office, 1956).

[9] Federal Security Agency, *Annual Report: 1952* (Washington, Government Printing Office, 1953), p. 42.

[10] Ollie A. Randall, "The Aged," *Social Work Year Book: 1947*, pp. 41-45.

[11] Colorado provides, in addition, for assistance payments from nonfederal funds to needy persons sixty to sixty-five years of age who meet prescribed conditions of long residence in the state.

There is usually, however, a provision that the award may in no case exceed a specified maximum amount. This maximum is fixed in most states as the maximum amount toward which the national government will contribute. A few states set a higher maximum and finance the excess from nonfederal sources, and a few others fix a maximum below that toward which federal contributions are obtainable. Several states, on the other hand, impose no fixed limitation on the amount of individual awards.

Old-age assistance is to be carefully distinguished from the program of old-age and survivors *insurance*, also provided for by the federal Social Security Act. The latter program, financed by a federal payroll tax falling equally on employer and employee, is administered entirely by the national government, with the states and local units having no part whatsoever therein. The insurance plan is designed to provide retirement benefits for covered workers upon their reaching the age of sixty-five (sixty-two in the case of women), as well as benefits, under certain circumstances, to the wives and dependent children of retired workers or to their widows and other dependent survivors. Whereas old-age assistance is a form of poor relief, paid as a gratuity and only to aged persons who are needy, benefits under old-age and survivors insurance are received by retired persons as a matter of right and without regard to their financial status.[12]

In 1954 recipients of old-age assistance throughout the country numbered more than 2,500,000—nearly one in five of the population age sixty-five or over—and assistance payments to individuals averaged about $51 per month.[13] As coverage under old-age and survivors insurance is extended to additional classes of workers, and as more and more workers, upon reaching the age of retirement, have been employed under that program for sufficiently long periods to provide substantial retirement annuities, the number of needy aged persons requiring public aid in the form of old-age assistance should show a corresponding decline. But until more extensive and adequate protection is afforded through the federal insurance system, old-age assistance will undoubtedly be continued as a major public program to care for those persons who reach advanced age without sufficient private income and resources for their support.

Aid to the Needy Blind. Aid to the blind is designed to provide financial assistance to needy persons who are completely blind or whose vision is so impaired as to prevent them from carrying on activities for which eyesight is essential. The definition of blindness that must be met by appli-

[12] In providing benefits for dependent wives, children, and survivors of insured workers, as distinguished from the primary benefits paid to retired workers themselves, the element of need does enter in some measure into the program. Under 1956 amendments provision is made for benefits to disabled workers at the age of fifty.

[13] United States Department of Health, Education, and Welfare, *Annual Report: 1954*, p. 41.

cants in order to qualify for assistance payments differs in some degree in the various states. Though in some instances stated in more general language, it is usually expressed in technical terms. A typical provision requires that central visual acuity in the better eye be 20/200 or less with correcting glasses or that there be a disqualifying field defect. The standard of need required of applicants is similar in general to that for old-age assistance, except that in determining need, the first $50 per month of earned income is disregarded.[14] As in the case of old-age assistance, a few states impose no limit upon the maximum amount of individual awards for aid to the blind. Most states, however, do set a maximum, and in many instances this is the same as for old-age grants. In 1954 recipients of aid to the blind numbered approximately 101,000, or about half of the estimated blind population, with individual assistance payments averaging approximately $56 per month.[15]

Aid to Dependent Children. At one time it was customary to care for dependent and neglected children either in the county almshouse along with adult paupers or in orphans' homes maintained by religious, social, or fraternal organizations or, less commonly, by county or state governments.[16] Today, though children in considerable number are still provided for in children's homes of various kinds, institutional care is less widely used than formerly. It has long been recognized that even the best of institutions cannot provide the normal home environment desirable for the rearing of children, and during recent years there has been a strong tendency to make constantly increasing use both of foster-home care and of financial assistance designed to enable mothers of dependent children to maintain their own homes.[17] The latter method of care is especially advantageous where a mother can demonstrate that she is a suitable person to retain custody of her dependent children. Not only does it enable the children concerned to grow up in their mother's home rather than in a public or private institution, but in many cases it is more economical. Often a mother will have some income of her own that will need merely to be supplemented from the public treasury to enable her to maintain her home, whereas if the home is broken up and the children placed in institutions, the cost of their entire support becomes a charge on public or private charity. Aid to dependent children, frequently referred to prior to the Social Security Act as mothers' pensions or mothers' aid,

[14] This exception is a qualifying requirement for federal aid.

[15] United States Department of Health, Education, and Welfare, *Annual Report: 1954*, p. 43.

[16] Martha P. Falconer, "Institutions for the Care of Children," *Encyclopaedia of the Social Sciences* (New York, Macmillan, 1930), Vol. III, pp. 410-412. The term *orphanage,* or *orphans' home,* has been widely applied to institutions for child care, notwithstanding that only a small percentage of the children cared for therein are actually orphans.

[17] *Ibid.*

seeks through public assistance to make possible the caring for dependent children in the homes of their mothers or other suitable relatives.

The Social Security Act defines a dependent child as a needy child who (1) is under the age of eighteen; (2) has been deprived of parental support or care by reason of the death, continued absence from the home, or physical or mental incapacity of a parent; and (3) is living with his father or mother, or with any other of a specified list of relatives, in a place of residence maintained by one or more such relatives as his or their own home. State definitions, though varying in some respects, tend to be substantially similar to that of the federal law. The general purport of the "need" requirement is that the private resources available for the support of the child must be insufficient to provide a reasonable subsistence compatible with health and well-being. Some states limit individual payments to the amounts toward which federal contributions are available. A few, however, set lower limits, but others impose higher limits or none at all. In the 47 states then having federally approved systems, payments were made in 1954 on behalf of 2,000,000 persons (children and adult caretakers), with the average monthly payment per person being approximately $24.[18]

Aid to Permanently and Totally Disabled. The newest of the categorical programs, inaugurated as a result of 1950 amendments to the Social Security Act, provides aid to needy persons eighteen years of age or over who are permanently and totally disabled. The definition of need in the various states is usually the same as that under the old-age assistance program. Definition of qualifying disability is not prescribed by federal law but is left to the respective states. Some states have adopted statutory definitions, but most have preferred to leave definition to administrative determination. A few states have adopted definitions so narrow as to confine assistance to persons who are bedfast or housebound. More common, however, are definitions sufficiently liberal to permit the granting of assistance to needy persons who, though not housebound, are permanently prevented by disease or other disability from engaging in useful occupations, including homemaking. Nearly half of those granted disability aid are suffering from heart disease, paralysis, or arthritis; with amputations accounting for another substantial group. Still other recipients suffer from a variety of impairments or diseases, such as mental deficiencies, tuberculosis, or cancer. State provisions concerning the amount of assistance payments are generally similar to, and in many instances identical with, those applicable to old-age assistance.[19] In 1954, in the 42 states

[18] United States Department of Health, Education, and Welfare, *Annual Report: 1954*, pp. 19, 43.

[19] Margaret Greenfield, *Permanent and Total Disability Aid* (Berkeley, University of California Bureau of Public Administration, 1953); United States Department of Health, Education, and Welfare, *Characteristics of Recipients of Aid to the Permanently and Totally Disabled: Mid-1951* (Washington, 1953).

which had then inaugurated federally approved programs, disability-aid payments averaging $53 per month were being made to 211,000 recipients.[20]

INDOOR ASSISTANCE: THE ALMSHOUSE[21]

The basic institution in the United States for providing indoor care for the poor is the public almshouse. This institution, in many instances, is known officially by other names, such as poorhouse, poor farm, infirmary, poor asylum, or county home; and the latter title, in view of the changing character of the institution and its population and because of a desire to lessen any social stigma that may attach to inmates, is currently gaining in favor. Several states have used the name county home for many years, and certain others have adopted that designation recently. Nevertheless, the term *almshouse* is still widely employed and in this discussion will frequently be used in a generic sense as applicable to the type of institution here under consideration, whatever its legal designation.

Almshouses are usually operated by counties, though there are numerous exceptions to this general rule. Some cities, particularly among those in the more populous group, maintain such institutions. In Delaware a single state welfare home has supplanted county almshouses. New Mexico, where public assistance has always been state administered, operates two homes for the aged and chronically ill. One or more state homes or infirmaries supplementary to local almshouses are found in several states, including Maryland, Michigan, Rhode Island, West Virginia, and Wyoming. In the New England states, with the exception of New Hampshire, the conduct of local almshouses is ordinarily a town function.[22]

In its traditional form the almshouse consisted typically of a single building divided into two wings, one for women and the other for men. The wings were often of equal size, notwithstanding that male inmates normally far outnumber female in such institutions, with the result that the men's ward was overcrowded.[23] Of antiquated construction, insanitary, and lacking in modern conveniences, the building frequently con-

[20] United States Department of Health, Education, and Welfare, *Annual Report: 1954*, p. 43.

[21] Portions of the following discussion of almshouses and nursing homes appeared originally, in substantially their present form, in Clyde F. Snider, "The Fading Almshouse," *National Municipal Review*, Vol. XLV, pp. 60-65 (February, 1956). Reproduction here is by permission of the *Review*.

[22] Cf. Millspaugh, *op. cit.*, pp. 282-283. In some places, where the almshouse is operated by the county, the cost of supporting a poor person therein is nevertheless a charge upon the township of his residence.

[23] Indiana county homes as recently as 1946 contained approximately two-and-one-half times as many male as female residents. Lynn Robertson, J. B. Kohlmeyer, and J. E. Losey, *Indiana County Homes and Their Adaptation to Present Conditions* (Lafayette, Ind., Purdue University Agricultural Experiment Station, 1948), p. 28.

stituted both a firetrap and a menace to the health of inmates. Lighting and ventilation were inadequate, and food was of poor quality and insufficient in quantity. Facilities for medical care were virtually nonexistent, the only doctor service available being that provided by a part-time "county physician" serving on a fee basis. In many instances a farm was operated in connection with the almshouse, on which was raised some of the food consumed at the institution and, occasionally, some additional produce for sale. The almshouse superintendent, ordinarily appointed by the county board, was usually a farmer, and frequently the superintendent's wife served as matron. All too often these managers had neither social service training nor a social outlook. The heterogeneous character of the almshouse population made practically impossible the provision of proper care for the inmates of any class. Into the single institution were commonly herded together, with little attempt at segregation, the old and the young, the able-bodied and the sick, the mentally normal and the feeble-minded, and, sometimes, even the insane. Virginia almshouses of a generation ago, though probably no worse than the general run, were characterized by that state's board of charities and corrections as a catch-all for the dregs of society. "The population of the average county almshouse," observed the board, "is composed of the aged and the infirm, the afflicted, the feeble-minded, the idiots, the blind, prostitutes, and children of all ages."[24] Happily, this situation, as we shall see, has now been remedied to some extent, though even today many almshouses make inadequate provision for segregating the different classes of inmates.

Another factor contributing in a large measure to the unsatisfactory nature of almshouse operation has been the small number of inmates for which, in many instances, an institution has been maintained. There have always been some governmental units which, although empowered to maintain almshouses, have provided otherwise for their poor requiring indoor care. For many years, however, there was a tendency for each county or other local unit to maintain its own institution whether or not the number of poor persons within its jurisdiction was large enough to justify such maintenance, and to some degree this tendency has continued to the present. Of 2,183 almshouses covered by a survey in the 1920's, made by the Bureau of Labor Statistics in the United States Department of Labor, 137 reported having no inmates, 787 others had ten or less, and fewer than a third of the total number had as many as twenty-five.[25] As recently as 1950, 32 of Tennessee's 70 almshouses had fewer than ten inmates and 26 others fewer than twenty.[26] An institutional population as

[24] Virginia State Board of Charities and Corrections, *Thirteenth Annual Report: 1921* (Richmond, Va., 1922), p. 11.

[25] Estelle M. Stewart, *The Cost of American Almshouses* (Washington, U. S. Bureau of Labor Statistics, 1925).

[26] William E. Cole and Russell R. Dynes, *Homes for the Homeless in Tennessee* (Knoxville, University of Tennessee Division of University Extension, 1951), p. 11.

small as that existing in many almshouses is clearly insufficient to permit economical operation. High per-inmate costs are almost inevitable, and, even then, the facilities and care provided are often substandard. In normal times, and especially in rural areas, the number of poor persons requiring institutional care in the typical county is usually insufficient to justify the maintenance of an almshouse; and in times of widespread unemployment and need, the extraordinary situation is generally met by expanding outdoor-assistance programs. Summarizing the situation as revealed by the Bureau of Labor Statistics survey, Estelle M. Stewart writes: [27]

> The unavoidable conclusion seems to be that dilapidation, inadequacy, and even indecency are the outstanding physical features of most of our small almshouses. Ignorance, unfitness, and a complete lack of comprehension of the social element involved in the conduct of a public institution are characteristic of a large part of their managing personnel. Among the inmates themselves insanity, feeblemindedness, depravity, and respectable old age are mingled in haphazard unconcern. It is idle, then, to imagine that social conditions in these institutions could be other than deplorable.

EFFECT ON ALMSHOUSES OF SOCIAL SECURITY PROGRAM

With the inauguration of the social security program, there was widespread belief that old-age assistance and aid to the blind would sound the death knell of the local almshouse. The Social Security Act, it will be remembered, originally denied federal aid for the payment of benefits to inmates of public institutions. Because of this fact, it was assumed that the aged and the blind in almshouses would leave those institutions and qualify for benefit payments under the new programs, and that since so large a proportion of almshouse inmates are sixty-five years of age or over, this exodus would permit the closing of many or most of the local institutions.

As a matter of fact, the new programs of categorical assistance did effect a considerable reduction in almshouse populations throughout the country, and substantial numbers of institutions were closed in various states.[28] The effect of the new programs in this direction, however, was less pronounced than had commonly been anticipated, because of the

[27] Stewart, *op. cit.*, p. 41.

[28] See "Effect of Social-Security Program on Almshouses," *Monthly Labor Review*. Vol. XLVII, pp. 518-524 (September, 1938); T. C. Pihlblad, "A Study of Missouri Almshouses," *Southwestern Social Science Quarterly*, Vol. XIX, pp. 201-210 (September, 1938); Loula Dunn, "Status of County Almshouses in Alabama," *Public Welfare News*, Vol. VI, No. 3, pp. 2-4 (March, 1938); Violet M. Fischer, "Kansas County Homes after the Social Security Act," *Social Service Review*, Vol. XVII, pp. 442-465 (December, 1943); Raymond M. Hilliard, "The Emerging Function of Public Institutions in Our Social Security Structure," *ibid.*, Vol. XX, pp. 479-493 (December, 1946).

high frequency among almshouse inmates of chronic diseases necessitating institutional care. The National Health Survey of 1935-36 indicates that one half of all persons in the United States age sixty-five or over suffer from some chronic disease, and the proportion is considerably higher among almshouse inmates than in the general population.[29] It has been estimated, for example, that 80 per cent of the inmates of county almshouses in Illinois in 1945 were in need of continuing nursing service.[30] Until more appropriate facilities for care of this nature are made available, it is likely to be provided in large measure through the continued operation of almshouses.

RECENT IMPROVEMENTS

Although conditions in many almshouses are still far from satisfactory, the general situation with respect to such institutions has improved considerably during recent decades. Certain classes of inmates have rather generally been removed from the almshouse population and provided with more appropriate forms of care. It has become common policy, for example, to provide care for dependent children, to the extent that such care is still institutional, in special children's homes, and to care for indigents who are insane or feeble-minded in appropriate state institutions. This policy has not only resulted in better care for the children and mentally handicapped but, by leaving a less heterogeneous population in the almshouses, has simplified the task of providing care for persons remaining therein. With the removal of children and defectives from the almshouse, that institution becomes principally an old folks' home. In 1946, for example, the average age of county-home residents in Indiana was sixty-eight years, with 63 per cent having reached sixty-five and 46 per cent being seventy or over.[31]

Gradual improvement is being made in physical plants. Some almshouse buildings have been replaced and others modernized. In both cases more attention is being given than formerly to proper lighting, heating, ventilation, and sanitary facilities, and to kitchen and medical equipment. In some instances there have been substantial improvements in structural plan. To lessen somewhat the "institutional" environment of the almshouse and to promote proper classification of inmates, some local governments have modified the traditional structure by providing, instead of a single large building, either a central building with several detached wings or a number of smaller separate buldings. Under this scheme, known as the cottage

[29] Cf. Ellen C. Potter, "State Responsibility for the Care of the Chronically Ill," *State Government*, Vol. XIX, pp. 39-42, 61 (February, 1946).

[30] *Interim Report of the [Illinois] Committee to Investigate Chronic Diseases among Indigents* (Springfield, Ill., 1945), p. 9.

[31] Robertson, Kohlmeyer, and Losey, *op. cit.*, p. 28.

system, the sick may be placed in separate quarters for special care, old couples may be given quarters together, and other desirable segregation measures may be carried out. Some of the most up-to-date almshouses of the country are now of the cottage type.[32]

Of late, as we have seen, many of the smaller almshouses have been closed. Census Bureau data for the year 1922 reveal the existence in the United States at that time of more than 2,300 public institutions for care of the indigent. From a questionnaire survey recently conducted by the present writer it appears probable that fewer than 1,400 such institutions are in operation today—a reduction of more than 40 per cent within a single generation. Furthermore, a goodly number of present-day institutions, far from being almshouses of the traditional type, are in the nature of modern nursing homes for the chronically ill.

When a county or town discontinues its almshouse, it must ordinarily make some other arrangement for the care of its poor, as has been necessary in the past in the case of those units which have never operated almshouses. Many states provide that one local governmental unit may contract with another for the care of its poor, and under this authority some of the counties and towns which have closed their almshouses have arranged to purchase such institutional care for their poor as is needed in almshouses of neighboring units. In other instances the county or town "boards out" its poor with private families.[33] Care in private nursing or convalescent homes is a newer development but is spreading. Among the states currently using this plan in some measure are Connecticut, Maine, Massachusetts, New Jersey, Utah, and Washington.[34] Where there is an appropriate state institution, local units in some instances arrange for the care of their poor therein. Whichever of these methods of providing institutional care is used, the cost must usually be paid from the funds of the county or town of the indigent person's residence. There are, however, some exceptions to this general rule of local financial responsibility. Care in state institutions ordinarily is provided partly or wholly at state expense; in Connecticut the state pays a part of the cost of supporting indigent persons in homes operated by towns other than those of their residence; and in Washington the entire operating cost of county infirmaries is borne by the state.

Still another approach to the problem of the small almshouse is afforded

[32] John L. Gillin, *Poverty and Dependency: Their Relief and Prevention,* 3d ed. (New York, Appleton-Century, 1937), pp. 183-184.

[33] Millspaugh, *op. cit.*, p. 284; Gillin, *op. cit.*, p. 186.

[34] As of the mid-1940's, approximately two thirds of Virginia's counties were reported as maintaining no almshouses, either individually or in co-operation with other counties or cities, but as boarding their indigent poor in private homes or institutions. Virginia State Chamber of Commerce, *Opportunities for Economy in County Government in Virginia* (Richmond, Va., 1947). By 1955 only eight Virginia counties were operating their own almshouses.

by the jointly operated institution serving two or more local units. Such joint operation, given the necessary enabling legislation, may be provided either through special almshouse districts embracing the territory of the towns or counties concerned or through intertown or intercounty agreement. A good example of the system is provided in Virginia, where in several instances old-style county and city almshouses have been replaced by modern district homes.[35] Under Virginia law district homes are established by the governing bodies of the counties and cities concerned and are managed in each instance by a district board whose members represent the co-operating units and are elected by their governing bodies. The district board appoints a superintendent and other necessary personnel for the home. Governing bodies of the co-operating units contribute to the cost of purchase or erection of the home and its equipment in proportion to the population of their units, and to operating costs in proportion to the number of inmates cared for from the respective counties and cities.[36] As of 1955, four district almshouses established under these provisions were serving a total of 24 counties and three cities. Among the joint institutions reported as operating at that time in other states were two bicounty homes and one four-county home in Minnesota; a bicounty home in Pennsylvania; a tricounty home in West Virginia; and two homes in Vermont, one serving three towns and the other five. Joint operation, by enlarging both the territory supporting a single institution and the population served thereby, promotes the economic feasibility of replacing numerous old-style almshouses with a smaller number of modern, well-managed homes.

COUNTY NURSING HOMES

Perhaps the most significant of recent developments has been the conversion of many old-style almshouses into modern nursing homes for care of the aged and chronically ill. As longevity increases with the progress of medical science and sanitation, older people constitute an ever larger proportion of our national population, and their care looms constantly larger as a governmental problem. Since the incidence of chronic diseases —cancer, arthritis, rheumatism, heart disease, and the like—is higher among older people than among the younger, the problem of providing institutional care for the indigent aged becomes largely one of supplying proper medical and nursing facilities.

As previously indicated, many almshouses were closed during the late 1930's and the following decade as a result of the outdoor assistance programs for the aged and the blind provided by the Social Security Act.

[35] Robert H. Kirkwood, *Fit Surroundings: District Homes Replace County Almshouses in Virginia* (Richmond, Virginia Department of Public Welfare, 1948).

[36] *Code of Virginia* (1950), secs. 63-308 to 63-318. See also, *ibid.* (1954), cum. suppl., secs. 63-309, 63-318.1.

Many others, however, notwithstanding their general inadequacy, found it necessary to continue in operation to provide a home for disabled inmates who required nursing care and who were unable to obtain this care, even with the aid of public subsidy, in the homes of relatives or friends or in private institutions. To encourage local governmental units to improve and modernize their facilities, some states provided that old-age assistance and aid to the blind might be paid to the inmates of the local institutions who were otherwise qualified to receive such aid, provided the institutions met certain standards prescribed by a specified state agency, usually the welfare department. Since federal grants-in-aid at this time were not available for benefits to such inmates, assistance payments were made wholly from nonfederal funds. The state standards which a county home or other public institution was required to meet in order to qualify its inmates for old-age assistance or aid to the blind concerned such matters as structural safety and convenience, sanitation, heating and lighting, ventilation, proper fire escapes, equipment, medical facilities, and staff. Inmates of approved institutions receiving old-age assistance or aid to the blind used the money to pay for their institutional care, and thus a considerable portion of the cost of their support was shifted from the local taxpayers to the state. The opportunity to effect this transfer of tax burden provided a strong incentive for county boards and other local authorities to make the necessary capital outlay to modernize their almshouses. In some instances, where existing institutions had been reasonably satisfactory, modernization was not a major task; but in other cases the construction, wholly or in part, of new buildings and the installation of new equipment were required.

Some local units modernized their almshouses even in the absence of state legislation of the kind noted in the preceding paragraph, but such legislation served as a potent stimulus to modernization. Many counties converted their old almshouses into adequately equipped and well-managed nursing homes, operated in some instances as wings or units of county hospitals but more often as separate institutions. Further impetus was given the nursing-home movement when, in 1950, the Social Security Act was amended to inaugurate a program of federal grants for aid to the permanently and totally disabled and to provide that henceforth the federal government would share in assistance payments to needy aged, blind, or disabled persons who were patients in public medical institutions other than tuberculosis or mental hospitals. At present, therefore, the states are at liberty to make old-age assistance, aid to the blind, and disability aid, including federal contributions, available to persons otherwise qualified who are patients in county or other publicly operated homes approved as public medical institutions.

The exact number of nursing homes currently operated by counties and other local governments is not known but undoubtedly is increasing steadily. Available information indicates that of the local welfare institutions now in operation, several hundred qualify as nursing homes. Among the states having such homes in largest numbers are California (where the homes are operated as parts of county hospitals), Illinois, Michigan, New York, and Wisconsin. A few states report that all their remaining county institutions are of nursing-home character and that the old-style almshouse has been completely eliminated. County nursing homes ordinarily are licensed and supervised in the same manner as private homes of similar character. The licensing and supervisory agency in most instances is the state health department, but in a few states it is the welfare department.

The quality of the facilities and care offered by county nursing homes, of course, is not uniform. On the whole, however, these institutions stand in refreshing contrast to the old-style almshouses they have supplanted. For the most part they are clean and well managed and properly equipped to provide nursing service. The farm land commonly associated with the traditional almshouse has been disposed of in most instances, since nursing homes provide no able-bodied inmates to perform farm labor; and the farmer superintendent has been superseded by qualified nursing and managerial personnel. Provision is made for the attendance of patients by physicians, and in many instances there are organized social and recreational programs. With regard to construction and physical equipment, some of the newer homes are ultramodern in design and border on the luxurious in their appointments. Stainless-steel kitchens, modern medical examining rooms, solariums, reading rooms, and nurses' living quarters are among the facilities sometimes provided, in addition to comfortable bedrooms and wards. When adequately staffed and competently managed, institutions of this nature are in a position to offer nursing care equivalent to that provided by the best of private nursing homes.

Considering the facilities offered and the quality of service maintained, it is not surprising that persons who are financially able to pay for their own care are frequently applicants for admission to county nursing homes. Indeed, it is not uncommon to find as patients in a single nursing home indigent persons whose care is paid for from the general-assistance funds of the town or county of their residence; persons who receive old-age assistance, aid to the blind, or disability aid, and who use these funds to purchase their care; and persons of private means who pay for their own care. Of 16 states for which recent data have been secured, all provide for admission to their publicly operated nursing homes of patients in the first two of these categories, and 12 provide for the acceptance of private patients as well. With the outdating of the old-style almshouse, the growing seriousness of the problem of chronic illness,[37] and the shortage of

[37] See above, chap. 15, "Local Health Services," p. 393.

private nursing homes offering suitable care at reasonable cost, the development of county nursing homes is one of the most encouraging present-day features of local welfare administration.

LOCAL WELFARE ORGANIZATION

In most states the principal agency for welfare administration at the local level is the county welfare department. Prior to the inception of the social security program, county government generally included no agency for the administration of an integrated welfare program. Poor relief, where a county function, was frequently administered directly by the county governing board or by overseers of the poor appointed by the board. Other welfare activities, where these existed, were managed in some instances by the county board and in others by some other county agency. Thus, systems of mothers' pensions, the forerunner of aid to dependent children, were administered in some states by the county court; children's homes were frequently administered either by the court or by a special board; and the almshouse or county home was, as it still is in many instances, managed directly by the county board. Nevertheless, there were some early attempts at partial integration. By 1933 about a third of the states had made provision, on either a mandatory or a permissive basis, for the establishment of agencies charged with administering two or more welfare services on a county-wide basis.[38]

When the Social Security Act stipulated, as a prerequisite to federal grants-in-aid, that programs of categorical assistance be administered either directly by a state agency or locally under state supervision, a considerable majority of the states chose the latter plan and established county welfare departments or similar county agencies in conformity with federal standards.[39] These newer county departments vary greatly in the details of their organization but usually include a welfare board and a director, who is the department's executive officer. Members of the welfare board are most commonly appointed by the county governing body, but in a number of states some or all members are appointed by the state welfare department, by the governor, or in still some other manner. The director in most states is appointed by the county welfare board, subject to qualifications and procedures prescribed by the state department, though in some instances the state department makes the appointment. Staff members of the county department are appointed according to merit-system rules, usually as the result of competitive examination. The principal duty of the county welfare department ordinarily consists in administering,

[38] Mary Ruth Colby, *The County as an Administrative Unit for Social Work* (Washington, U.S. Children's Bureau, 1933), pp. 23-36.

[39] In a few states, towns or municipalities participate in administering the federal-aid programs.

under state supervision, the programs of old-age assistance, aid to the blind, aid to dependent children, and (since 1950) aid to the permanently and totally disabled. The county department receives applications for these forms of aid, investigates the applicants, and determines, subject to appeal to the state welfare agency, whether aid should be granted and, if so, in what amount. After an award of assistance has been made, the county department keeps in touch with the recipient in order to be advised if and when a change in his circumstances warrants discontinuance of the assistance or a modification of its amount. Reports are made regularly by the county department to the state supervising agency. In many states, the county welfare department is charged with various functions in addition to administration of the four programs mentioned. Examples of additional duties are the administration of general assistance, supervision of probationers, and provision of child-welfare services. Some states have sought to place virtually all local public-welfare activities, or at least those in rural areas, under the department's jurisdiction.

Townships rarely have anything even approximating a welfare department, such welfare functions as are devolved upon those units usually being performed by the general township officers. The welfare function most frequently conferred upon townships is the administration of general outdoor assistance, a function which is performed in many states by the township trustee or supervisor, sometimes in an ex officio capacity as assistance supervisor. In New England towns this form of aid is usually administered through the town selectmen or, especially in the larger communities, by elected overseers of the poor.[40]

FINANCING PUBLIC ASSISTANCE

The cost of public assistance, once borne solely by local governmental units, now is shared by all three levels of government—national, state, and local. General assistance is financed from state and local funds, with no federal participation.[41] In some 16 states the local governments bear all of the cost, and in a few others the entire cost is paid from the state treasury. In a majority of the states, however, general-assistance payments are made in part from local tax funds and in part from state aid.[42] At

[40] The larger cities of the country commonly have their own public-welfare departments, some of which are elaborately organized and provide a wide variety of social services. For further discussion of local welfare organization, see Millspaugh, *op. cit.*, chaps. 8, 9; Stevenson, *op. cit.*, Pt. 2, chap. 3; R. Clyde White, *Administration of Public Welfare,* 2d ed. (New York, American Book Co., 1950), chap. 5.

[41] The federal government from time to time makes available, for distribution to persons on public-assistance rolls, certain food products purchased by the government in connection with its program for supporting farm prices.

[42] Public Administration Service, *Unemployment and Relief from the Local Government Point of View,* A Report of the W. E. Upjohn Institute for Community Research (Chicago, 1956), p. 139.

present, somewhat more than half of all expenditures for general assistance is met from state funds.[43]

The categorical-assistance programs are financed in part by the national government, in part by the states and, in some states, in part by the local units. The Social Security Act requires, as a condition to the granting of federal aid in support of the categorical programs, that there be some state participation in financing, but leaves it to each state to determine whether the state government shall bear all of the nonfederal portion of the costs or whether a part thereof shall be made an obligation of the local governments. Some states have chosen the first of these alternatives, but a majority provide for payment of a part of the cost of one or more of the programs from local funds.[44] The extent of federal participation in financing categorical assistance is determined by the Social Security Act and the tendency has been, with successive amendments to the law, to enlarge that participation. By the terms of 1956 amendments, federal contributions, in the case of old-age assistance, aid to the blind, and aid to the disabled, were fixed at four fifths of the first $30 of the average monthly assistance payment per recipient, plus half the balance of all expenditures up to $60 per month for individual payments. For aid to dependent children, federal funds would pay fourteen seventeenths of the first $17 of the average monthly payment per recipient, plus half the balance up to $32 for a needy adult caretaker, $32 for the first child, and $23 for each additional child. In addition to contributing directly to assistance payments, federal grants are available to cover a portion of the administrative costs of the various programs. For fiscal 1952, prior to the effectiveness of amendments of that year and of 1956 liberalizing federal participation, federal grants to the states covered 52 per cent of all expenditures for assistance and administration in the case of old-age assistance and aid to dependent children, 49 per cent in the case of disability aid, and 47 per cent in the case of aid to the blind—in other words, slightly more than half of the entire cost of the four programs.[45] Of the over-all cost of the categorical programs at that time, counties and other local governments contributed perhaps 8 per cent, with the remainder, in the neighborhood of 40 per cent, being borne by the states.[46]

The increasing participation of the state and national governments in public-assistance financing is indicated in an impressive manner when the percentage distribution of total expenditures in 1951 is contrasted with the distribution for ten years, and twenty years, earlier. In 1931, when all public assistance was still of the general variety, 82 per cent of all assist-

[43] Cf. *Improving Public Assistance,* p. 11.

[44] Federal Security Agency, *Social Welfare Administration in the United States of America* (Washington, 1950), p. 39.

[45] Federal Security Agency, *Annual Report: 1952,* p. 102.

[46] Cf. *Improving Public Assistance,* p. 11.

ance expenditures was from local funds, and only 18 per cent from state funds, with no federal participation. In 1941, with three federally subsidized programs of categorical assistance having been inaugurated under the Social Security Act, 34 per cent of all assistance expenditures came from federal funds, 45 per cent from state, and 21 per cent from local. By 1951, reflecting the initiation of a fourth categorical program and a liberalization of federal grants for all such programs, the national government's share in total assistance expenditures had risen to 48 per cent, with the states paying 41 per cent and the local governments 11 per cent.[47] In 1954, with 5,600,000 persons receiving public assistance of one kind or another and total expenditures for the various programs of $2,500,000,000, more than half of the total was paid from federal funds.[48]

The pronounced drop, since the depression years, in the percentage of over-all assistance expenditures contributed by the local governmental units, reflects both a decrease in the relative importance of general assistance and a growing disposition on the part of the states to assume an ever larger share of responsibility for financing the nonfederal portion of expenditures for categorical aid. Notwithstanding increased participation by the state and national governments, the financing of public assistance still accounts for a major item in local budgets, particularly those of counties, towns, and townships. In 1951, public-assistance expenditures from local funds amounted to $300,000,000 of which $126,000,000 was for general assistance and $174,000,000 represented local government contributions to the support of the four categorical programs.[49]

REFERENCES

Books, Reports, and Special Studies

ABBOTT, Grace, *From Relief to Social Security* (Chicago, University of Chicago Press, 1941).

BROWN, Josephine C., *Public Relief: 1929-1939* (New York, Holt, 1940).

BROWN, Roy M., *Public Poor Relief in North Carolina* (Chapel Hill, University of North Carolina Press, 1928).

BROWNING, Grace, *Rural Public Welfare: Selected Records* (Chicago, University of Chicago Press, 1941).

BRUNER, David Kenneth, *The Township and Borough System of Poor Relief in Pennsylvania* (Privately printed, 1937).

BURNS, Eveline M., *The American Social Security System* (Boston, Houghton Mifflin, 1949).

COLBY, Mary Ruth, *The County as an Administrative Unit for Social Work* (Washington, U. S. Children's Bureau, 1933).

[47] Data from *ibid.*, pp. 6-7.

[48] United States Department of Health, Education, and Welfare, *Annual Report: 1954*, pp. 40-41.

[49] *Improving Public Assistance*, p. 11.

COLE, William E., *Almshouse Policies and Almshouse Care of the Indigent in Tennessee* (Knoxville, University of Tennessee Division of University Extension, 1938).

———, and DYNES, Russell R., *Homes for the Homeless of Tennessee* (Knoxville, University of Tennessee Division of University Extension, 1951).

Federal Security Agency, *Social Welfare Administration in the United States of America* (Washington, 1950).

GILLIN, John L., *Poverty and Dependency: Their Relief and Prevention,* 3d ed. (New York, Appleton-Century, 1937).

HOFFER, Frank W., *Counties in Transition: A Study of County Public and Private Welfare Administration in Virginia* (University, University of Virginia Institute for Research in the Social Sciences, 1929).

JAMES, Arthur W., *The Public Welfare Function of Government in Virginia* (Richmond, Virginia Department of Public Welfare, 1934).

JOHNSON, Alexander, *The Almshouse* (New York, Russell Sage Foundation, 1911).

Kansas Emergency Relief Committee, *A Study of Kansas Poor Farms* (Topeka, Kan., 1935).

KIRKWOOD, Robert H., *Fit Surroundings: District Homes Replace County Almshouses in Virginia* (Richmond, Virginia Department of Public Welfare, 1948).

LANDIS, Benson Y., *Rural Welfare Services* (New York, Columbia University Press, 1949).

MARTZ, Helen E., *Citizen Participation in Government: A Study of County Welfare Boards* (Washington, Public Affairs Press, 1948).

Maryland Legislative Council, *Report on Almshouses in Maryland* (1940).

MILES, Arthur P., *An Introduction to Public Welfare* (Boston, Heath, 1949).

MILLSPAUGH, Arthur C., *Public Welfare Organization* (Washington, Brookings Institution, 1935).

Ohio Institute, *County Welfare Organization in Ohio* (Columbus, Ohio, 1928).

Public Administration Service, *Unemployment and Relief from the Local Government Point of View,* A Report of the W. E. Upjohn Institute for Community Research (Chicago, 1956).

RAUP, Ruth, *Intergovernmental Relations in Social Welfare* (Minneapolis, University of Minnesota Press, 1952).

ROBERTSON, Lynn, KOHLMEYER, J. B., and LOSEY, J. E., *Indiana County Homes and Their Adaptation to Present Conditions* (Lafayette, Ind., Purdue University Agricultural Experiment Station, 1948).

STEVENSON, Marietta, *Public Welfare Administration* (New York, Macmillan, 1938).

———, and MACDONALD, Alice, *State and Local Public Welfare Agencies* (Chicago, American Public Welfare Association, 1939).

STEWART, Estelle M., *The Cost of American Almshouses* (Washington, U. S. Bureau of Labor Statistics, 1925).

Tax Foundation, *Improving Public Assistance: Some Aspects of the Welfare Problem* (New York, 1953).

United States Department of Health, Education, and Welfare, *Annual Report* (Washington, Government Printing Office).

WHITE, R. Clyde, *Administration of Public Welfare,* 2d ed., (New York, American Book Co., 1950).

Articles

DUNN, Loula, "Status of County Almshouses in Alabama," *Public Welfare News*, Vol. VI, No. 3, pp. 2-4 (March, 1938).

"Effect of Social-security Program on Almshouses," *Monthly Labor Review*, Vol. XLVII, pp. 518-524 (September, 1938).

FISCHER, Violet M., "Kansas County Homes after the Social Security Act," *Social Service Review*, Vol. XVII, pp 442-465 (December, 1943).

HILLIARD, Raymond M., "The Emerging Function of Public Institutions in Our Social Security Structure," *Social Service Review*, Vol. XX, pp. 479-493 (December, 1946).

Indiana Department of Public Welfare, *Public Welfare in Indiana*, Symposium on County Homes, Vol. LVIII, No. 5 (May, 1948), entire issue.

PIHLBLAD, T. C., "A Study of Missouri Almshouses," *Southwestern Social Science Quarterly*, Vol. XIX, pp. 201-210 (September, 1938).

SNIDER, Clyde F., "The Fading Almshouse," *National Municipal Review*, Vol. XLV, pp. 60-65 (February, 1956).

CHAPTER 17

Education

IN TERMS OF CAPITAL investment, amount of expenditure, and number of employees, the most important function of local government in rural America is the provision of elementary and secondary schools.[1] Such considerations apart, few would dissent from the proposition that government in the United States, at whatever level and in whatever geographic area, performs no more vital service than the education of the nation's youth. In a democratic society widespread education constitutes the very foundation of free institutions, and it is therefore essential that educational opportunities be available to all of our country's inhabitants. For this reason, the provision of school facilities cannot safely be left to private individuals and organizations but must be undertaken as a public service. Though many private and sectarian schools exist throughout the nation, nearly 90 per cent of the country's school children now attend institutions maintained at public expense.

A MAJOR PUBLIC TASK

During the school year 1951-52 more than 26,000,000 pupils—a sixth of the total population of the nation—were enrolled in public elementary and secondary schools, and enrollments were continuing to rise. In the year mentioned the public schools of the country were manned by more than a million teachers. The total investment in public-school property was estimated at almost $14,000,000,000, or $525 per pupil enrolled; and expenditures for public-school purposes amounted to more than $7,000,000,000.[2] By 1955 public-school enrollments had passed the 30,000,000

[1] Cf. Edmund de S. Brunner and J. H. Kolb, *Rural Social Trends* (New York, McGraw-Hill, 1933), p. 168.

[2] Rose Marie Smith, "Statistical Summary of Education: 1951-52," *Biennial Survey of Education in the United States: 1950-52* (Washington, U. S. Office of Education,

mark, and it has been estimated that by 1960 enrollments will exceed 36,000,000.[3] Education regularly constitutes the largest single item of local government expenditure and occupies a prominent place in state budgets as well. These various facts give some indication of the gigantic proportions of the task of providing public-school facilities in the United States.

THE NATIONAL GOVERNMENT AND EDUCATION

In delegating powers to the national government, the United States Constitution makes no mention of education, and, consequently, provision of public educational facilities is left, by virtue of the Tenth Amendment, primarily to the states. The national government, it is true, has displayed an active interest in education. Early in our history there were federal grants of land and money to the states for school purposes, and, more recently, the national government has undertaken many activities concerned directly or indirectly with the promotion of education. Thus, the United States Office of Education collects and publishes educational statistics and various types of information concerning schools and colleges, conducts research studies on educational problems, and provides an advisory and consultative service to state and local school officials. Congress provides federal funds in aid of state agricultural colleges, vocational education in high schools, and various other special educational programs. Federal aid is granted also for support of local schools in communities where enrollments have been vastly increased because of military installations or other activities of the federal government; and currently there is a growing demand, as yet unfulfilled, for federal aid to elementary and secondary schools generally.[4] After World War II, funds made available to veterans for educational purposes under the so-called GI Bill of Rights encouraged millions of ex-service men and women to pursue academic training further than they would otherwise have done. Nevertheless, the providing of education remains primarily a function of the respective states, to be performed by the state governments themselves or passed on to the local governmental units. In practice, most states have chosen to impose basic responsibility for elementary and secondary schools upon their local subdivisions.

1955), chap. 1; Samuel Schloss and Carol J. Hobson, "Statistics of State School Systems: 1951-52," *ibid.*, chap. 2.

[3] Tax Foundation, *Public School Financing: 1930-1954* (New York, 1954), p. 8.

[4] For discussion of the issue in its various aspects, see Charles A. Quattlebaum, *Federal Aid to Elementary and Secondary Education* (Chicago, Public Administration Service, 1948); Frank N. Freeman, "For Federal Aid to Education," *State Government*, Vol. XXI, pp. 14, 19-20 (January, 1948); Carl H. Chatters, "Against Federal Aid to Education," *ibid.*, pp. 15, 21-22. In 1956 Congress considered but failed to enact proposals for federal aid in the construction of public-school buildings as a means of alleviating the acute building shortage.

STATE PUBLIC SCHOOL SYSTEMS

Only in Delaware are the administration and financing of local schools so highly centralized as to constitute what may properly be considered a state-unit system. In every state, however, the state government has assumed important functions in the field of elementary and secondary education. These functions, for purposes of convenience, may be grouped into three principal categories: (1) the enactment of legislation establishing and regulating a system of public schools; (2) supervision and control of local schools through state administrative agencies; and (3) contribution of financial support. State participation in the financing of local schools is discussed in a subsequent section of this chapter. Activities falling within the first two groups mentioned will be considered briefly at this point.

It is the state legislature which enacts the basic laws governing the public school system. Through a succession of statutes, sometimes referred to collectively as the state school code, the legislature determines what local units shall be responsible for providing schools, how those units shall be organized and governed, what officers the local units shall have and how they shall be chosen, and what taxing and other powers the local units shall possess. Various state officers and boards are commonly established with supervisory authority over local schools and school officers. Standards for teacher certification are fixed, and the minimum length of the school term prescribed. The subjects to be taught in the schools, and in some states the textbooks to be used, are determined in large measure by the state, either directly by statute or through the supervisory agencies. Compulsory attendance laws require school attendance by children of specified ages, with the age limits of seven to sixteen years being fairly common. A majority of the states have established minimum salary standards for public-school teachers, and all states now make provision for some sort of teacher retirement system.

Every state has one or more state boards with educational functions, and in about 40 states one such agency, generally called the state board of education, exercises some degree of control over elementary and secondary schools.[5] In each state there is also a chief state school officer. This official is most commonly known as the superintendent of public instruction, though commissioner of education or some other title is used in some instances. A great deal of variation exists among the states with respect to the powers conferred upon state educational agencies as well

[5] Special boards, sometimes several in a single state, deal with individual phases of educational work. Examples are vocational education boards, library commissions, textbook commissions, and teacher retirement boards.

as the division of those powers between the state board of education and the state superintendent. Functions commonly performed by one agency or the other include enforcement of various school laws, determination of educational policies, supervisory control over elementary and secondary schools, determination of courses of study, adoption of textbooks, certification of teachers, and distribution of state school funds.[6]

Over the years, the state governments have assumed ever broader responsibility in the field of elementary and secondary education. At one time decisions concerning the school facilities to be provided and also the financing of those facilities were left almost entirely to the local school authorities. Gradually, however, it has been realized that education in a democratic society is too important to be left solely to the whims of local communities.[7] Moreover, with increased mobility of population more and more persons live as adult citizens in other localities than those in which they received their schooling, and, hence, the educational standards of a given community cease to be of purely local interest. It is therefore no matter for surprise that state governments today, though in most instances leaving primary responsibility for school administration with the local governmental units, nevertheless prescribe and enforce minimum educational standards for local schools and provide state funds to assist the local communities in meeting those standards.

LOCAL RESPONSIBILITY

Each state legislature determines by law what governmental unit shall assume primary responsibility for the financing and administration of elementary and secondary schools, and there is considerable variation among the states with respect to the unit used. For purposes of discussion, it is helpful to classify the states into groups on the basis of the governmental area so employed. In Delaware, responsibility for providing schools is so far centralized in the state government itself as to justify characterization of that state's educational organization as a state-unit system. In all other states, primary responsibility for providing schools is imposed upon local governmental units of one kind or another. Of these 47 states, by rule-of-thumb classification,[8] 15 use the county unit as the predomi-

[6] W. S. Deffenbaugh and Ward W. Keesecker, *State Boards of Education and Chief State School Officers: Their Status and Legal Powers* (Washington, U. S. Office of Education, 1940).

[7] Cf. Ward G. Reeder, *The Fundamentals of Public School Administration,* 3d ed. (New York, Macmillan, 1951), pp. 50-54.

[8] Cf. National Commission on School District Reorganization, *Your School District* (Washington, National Education Association, 1948), pp. 258-261; Chris A. DeYoung, *Introduction to American Public Education,* 2d ed. (New York, McGraw-Hill, 1950), pp. 76-77.

nant type of administrative organization,[9] 9 use the town or township unit,[10] and 23 employ the district system.[11] It should be emphasized, however, that many states do not use a single type of unit to the exclusion of all others. For example, some independently incorporated school districts are frequently found in states where one of the larger units is more commonly employed as the basic administrative area. The suggested classification, therefore, is made on the basis only of the type of school unit which *predominates* in the respective states. It is further to be noted, as is explained more fully in the following section, that, where the county, town, or township unit prevails, the schools are frequently operated through separate school corporations, legally distinct from, but coterminous with, the general-purpose units and often known officially as school districts. As employed in this chapter, however, the term *district system* designates that plan of school organization under which the typical district is smaller in area than the overlying general-purpose unit, whether county, township, or town; and the term *district state* refers to a state wherein the district system, as thus defined, prevails.[12]

[9] Alabama, Florida, Georgia, Kentucky, Louisiana (parish unit), Maryland, Mississippi, Nevada, New Mexico, North Carolina, South Carolina, Tennessee, Utah, Virginia, and West Virginia. Though Mississippi and South Carolina have been classified at times as "district" states, the United States Census Bureau, in its 1952 enumeration of local governments, concluded that all but a few of the districts in those states were, in fact, mere dependent agencies of the county governments and therefore not entitled to consideration as separate governmental units—United States Bureau of the Census, *Governments in the United States in 1952* (Washington, Government Printing Office, 1953), p. 9. Nevada was added to the county-unit group by legislation enacted in 1955. The Nevada law provides that there shall be a single school district coterminous with each county, but stipulates that counties with fewer than 45 teachers may establish joint bicounty or multicounty districts by action of their respective boards—*Statutes of Nevada* (1955), chap. 402.

[10] Connecticut, Indiana, Maine, Massachusetts, New Hampshire, New Jersey, Pennsylvania, Rhode Island, and Vermont.

[11] Arizona, Arkansas, California, Colorado, Idaho, Illinois, Iowa, Kansas, Michigan, Minnesota, Missouri, Montana, Nebraska, New York, North Dakota, Ohio, Oklahoma, Oregon, South Dakota, Texas, Washington, Wisconsin, and Wyoming. The term *school district* is used in this chapter to mean an incorporated special-purpose unit charged by law with important powers and duties concerning the administration and financing of public schools. In a different sense the term is sometimes used to refer to a mere attendance area, within a county, township, or incorporated school district, which is served by a particular school building.

[12] Professor John Bollens, in a recent study, distinguishes between independent school districts, whether county-wide, township-wide, or of smaller area, and school systems administered by general-government units or agencies responsible to such units. On the basis of this distinction. Bollens found that, as of 1956, 28 states employed independent districts as the exclusive instrumentality for providing public education below the collegiate level, while ten additional states employed such districts as the predominant instrumentality. In only ten states were general-government units employed exclusively or predominantly in providing elementary and secondary schools. See John C. Bollens, *Special District Governments in the United States* (Berkeley, University of California Press, 1957), pp. 179-180.

RURAL SCHOOL UNITS[13]

Nearly half of the nation's children attend schools in rural areas, and it is with these pupils and the problems of their education that we are here primarily concerned.[14] From what was said in the preceding section, it is apparent that the duty of providing rural schools rests in varying degree in different states with (1) the county, (2) the town or township, and (3) the school district. Before considering each of these as a public-school unit, it will be well to recall two traditions that have been extremely influential over the years in American education. The first of these is the tradition of local self-determination in educational matters. Not only have the states imposed upon their local governments responsibility for providing schools, but they have allowed the local units rather wide discretion in the determination of school policies. Though this discretion has been somewhat narrowed during recent years with the broadening of state supervision and control, the feeling is still strong that local communities should enjoy a substantial degree of autonomy in school matters.

The second tradition concerns the separation of the school function, for financial and administrative purposes, from other local government services. It has been felt that the function of providing educational facilities is of such paramount importance to the community and to the state at large that it should be placed, as far as reasonably possible, above the considerations of partisan politics, which are likely to pervade the administration of most local services. For this reason, a system of administration and financing has been devised under which local officials concerned with governing the public schools generally enjoy a large degree of independence from those charged with administering other functions, such as roads and public assistance. Under the system of small school districts prevailing in nearly half of the states the independence of school authorities from other local agencies is virtually complete. Even where the town, township, or county is employed as the basic geographic area for school purposes, the school system is ordinarily accorded a large measure of autonomy in administration and usually also in matters of finance. This is accomplished by vesting operation of the schools in a special school corporation, which, though coterminous with the township

[13] For purposes of most of the rural-urban data presented in this chapter, rural areas, in conformity to the Census Bureau's traditional definition, include all territory outside municipalities of 2,500 or more inhabitants. For the definition employed by the bureau in connection with the 1950 census, see above, chap. 2, "Urban Units v. Rural."

[14] In the early 1950's, according to a report of the National Education Association, an estimated 43 per cent of all public-school pupils in the United States attended rural schools—National Education Association, *Rural Teachers in 1951-52,* Research Bulletin (Washington, 1953), Vol. XXXI, No. 1, p. 4. Cf. Rose Marie Smith, *Education in Rural and City School Systems: Some Statistical Indices for 1947-1948* (Washington, U.S. Office of Education, 1951), p. 4.

or county, is legally a distinct and separate entity, or by placing school government, in any event, in the hands of officials and agencies apart from the "regular" township or county officers. In the New England states, for example, where the town is the basic unit for school purposes, educational affairs are ordinarily managed through a special school board which possesses a large degree of autonomy, with annual school meetings sometimes being held separately from the regular town meetings.[15] In states where the township serves as the basic school area, the school system is ordinarily operated by a special school district, or "school township," coterminous with the civil unit.[16] And where the county unit is employed, whether or not the county area is separately incorporated for school purposes, the school system is administered by a special board of education which usually is fiscally independent of the general county government.[17]

THE DISTRICT SYSTEM

Under the widely prevalent district system, responsibility for providing elementary and high schools rests primarily upon small school districts organized and operated under state law. Notwithstanding a drastic reduction in the number of districts in preceding years, more than 67,000 such units were in existence in the United States in 1952. Among the individual states, Nebraska and Minnesota led the list, with more than 6,000 districts each; but seven other states—Illinois, Iowa, Kansas, Michigan, Missouri, South Dakota, and Wisconsin—had more than 3,000 each.[18] Though some districts in urban communities serve large school populations and the number of consolidated districts with substantial enrollments is steadily growing in other areas, the great majority of American school districts are still small rural units. This is clearly seen in the fact that

[15] Town school districts in Vermont and New Hampshire constitute distinct corporate entities, with the school-district meeting being held separately from the annual town meeting, though frequently on the same day. Concerning the latter state, see Harold C. Grinnell, *Studies in Local Government and Taxation in Rural New Hampshire* (Durham, University of New Hampshire Agricultural Experiment Station, 1943), pp. 26-29.

[16] In Indiana the "school township," though legally a distinct corporation, is served by the same set of officials as the civil township.

[17] *Your School District*, pp. 49-50. Under the township- or county-unit plan, schools in some or all municipalities are frequently governed by independent districts, with the jurisdiction of the township or county district confined wholly or in large part to rural areas. Notwithstanding the tendency to make local school authorities largely independent of other governmental agencies, the Census Bureau reported, as of 1952, that approximately one fourth of all public-school pupils in the country were enrolled in "dependent" school systems operated by city, county, town, or state governments. See *Governments in the United States in 1952*, p. 4; also above, n. 12.

[18] For further data concerning the number of districts in the respective states, see above, chap. 2, Table 1. See also, chap. 2, n. 30, and below, "The Consolidation Movement."

during the school year 1951-52, more than 44,000 districts—two thirds of the entire number—enrolled fewer than 50 pupils each and accounted together for only 3 per cent of the total district enrollment.[19]

In the typical school district the principal governing authority is an elective board, most commonly of three members, which has custody of school property, hires teachers, and exercises general administrative control over school affairs. District finances are controlled in some states by the school board and in others by the district's voters in annual school meeting. The organization of school-district government has been described at some length in an earlier chapter.[20]

INADEQUACY OF SMALL DISTRICTS

The district system was devised early in our national history with a view to making basic educational facilities reasonably available to all children of school age, notwithstanding primitive means of transportation and communication. As new states were organized, the system gained widespread favor as being well adapted to the needs of frontier communities. Under present-day conditions, however, the district system, though steeped in tradition, displays many serious weaknesses. The great majority of school districts in rural America are small both in area and in population. Most of them maintain but a single one-room school. In the early 1950's, notwithstanding that the number had been reduced by 60 per cent during the preceding two decades, there were still more than 50,000 one-room schools in the country educating 1,500,000 young Americans.[21]

The typical one-room school is housed in an antiquated building which lacks proper facilities for heating, ventilation, lighting, and sanitation. In this building a single teacher, who is often both inexperienced and underpaid, teaches all subjects in the eight elementary grades. In addition, she (the teacher is usually a woman) is responsible for whatever limited extracurricular activities are carried on, such as social events for school patrons, and frequently she must be her own school janitor as well.[22] Under such circumstances it is manifestly impossible to carry on a satisfactory educational program. The average teacher cannot be even moderately competent in a dozen different subjects. Class periods are necessarily limited to a few minutes each, and classes are held in the room where other pupils are expected to study. There is no place in the program for physical education, music, art, manual training, domestic science, and the various other subjects which at one time were considered luxuries but now are

[19] *Governments in the United States in 1952,* p. 4.

[20] Above, chap. 10.

[21] *Rural Teachers in 1951-52,* p. 4; Smith, *Statistical Summary of Education: 1951-52.*

[22] Less than 20 per cent of rural teachers are men.

accepted as essential parts of a properly balanced school program. Frequently, the number of pupils is so small that it is quite impossible to conduct group activities and provide desirable social relationships within the school. Yet, in spite of these gross inadequacies, the per-pupil cost of education in such schools, because of the small enrollments, is often amazingly high. Poor physical plant, burdensome teaching loads, and, frequently, inadequate financial support, conspire to foster inefficiency in one-room rural schools. Only the tireless energy, the resourcefulness, and the selfless devotion displayed by thousands of country teachers make possible anything approaching even tolerable educational standards. The matter for wonder is not that the work done by the country teacher is unsatisfactory but that under the circumstances she accomplishes as much as she does.

Another disadvantage of the district system lies in the inequality of financial resources available to the various districts for the support of schools. From the standpoint of value of taxable property, some districts are relatively wealthy and others are poor, and this without any reference to the number of school-age children within the respective units. In wealthy communities a relatively low tax rate for school purposes may produce sufficient revenue to provide the best facilities that other circumstances permit, whereas in poorer districts even a burdensome rate may fail to yield enough to provide the barest essentials. Thus it happens, when school financing is left entirely to the respective districts, that some children will have much better educational opportunities than others because of the merely fortuitous circumstance that they live in a district containing taxable property of relatively high value. In a country that emphasizes democratic ideals, such inequality of opportunity is deplorable, and, fortunately, it is now rectified to some extent by state financial assistance to the poorer districts.[23]

The weaknesses of the one-room elementary school are found also, in forms only slightly less extreme, in the small rural high school. Because of the small teaching staff in such institutions, instructors are required to teach subjects in which they are not properly prepared. Curricula are narrow, buildings and equipment are inadequate, and unit costs are likely to be high. The substandard nature of the work done in thousands of small elementary and high schools is readily seen when students from those schools enter college or university. Although there are exceptions, such students in general give evidence of training inferior to that of those from larger and more modern schools. Even more serious are the results of the inferior quality of the small schools when viewed from the standpoint of the millions of young Americans who receive all of their formal education there and never enter any institution of higher learning.

[23] See below, "School Finance."

THE CONSOLIDATION MOVEMENT

The most obvious means of overcoming the disadvantages of the small school district is, of course, the provision of larger units for educational financing and administration. One method of accomplishing this is through the consolidation of numerous small districts into fewer and larger units. During recent decades a number of states have carried through consolidation programs of varying comprehensiveness. Some of these programs have been compulsory in nature, but others have been voluntary in character, with merger effected by vote of the local inhabitants. Whether merger is to be compulsory or voluntary, several states have provided by law for county "school survey committees," or "school reorganization committees," to examine existing districts and district boundaries and prepare plans for reorganization and consolidation. Plans thus prepared may take the form of mere recommendations which the local voters are free to adopt or reject in referendum elections; or, on the other hand, the county committees may be empowered actually to put their plans into effect, after public hearings thereon, by compulsory order. One state in which compulsory consolidation has been used to a considerable degree is that of Kansas. Though the Kansas statute vesting compulsory authority in county committees eventually ran afoul of the courts and was declared unconstitutional, this did not occur until a large number of consolidations had been effected under its provisions.

By the terms of the Kansas consolidation act of 1945 a division of school reorganization was created in the state department of education; and a school reorganization committee, to be appointed by the board of county commissioners, was established in each county. The county committees were directed to prepare plans for reorganizing the elementary school districts within their respective jurisdictions and were empowered, after public hearings thereon, to issue orders placing those plans in effect. Persons dissatisfied with reorganization orders issued by any county committee might obtain a rehearing and, if dissatisfied with orders issued after rehearing, might apply to the district court for a review of the committee's plan and procedure. It was made the duty of the state division to become conversant with all factors affecting the determination of proper boundaries for elementary school districts in the state and to counsel and advise with the reorganization committees of the various counties.[24] In 1947 this

[24] *Kansas Session Laws* (1945), chap. 291. Cf. Clyde F. Snider and Neil F. Garvey, "County and Township Government in 1945," *American Political Science Review*, Vol. XLI, pp. 28-47 (February, 1947). An amendment subsequently provided that any county might, at its option, replace its appointive reorganization committee with a committee elected by a convention of delegates chosen at special school-district meetings.

legislation was declared unconstitutional by the Kansas supreme court as an attempt to delegate legislative power to the county committees.[25] Prior to the court decision, however, consolidation orders had already been issued eliminating large numbers of districts; and these consolidations were validated by subsequent legislative action which in turn was sustained by the court.[26] During this same period, furthermore, additional reductions were made in the number of Kansas districts through voluntary consolidations effected under previously existing school laws; and some consolidations under the older statutes have been made more recently.

Current consolidation procedures of the voluntary variety are typified by the program established in Illinois by a statute of 1945. This law creates a state advisory commission on school reorganization and provides that a school survey committee may be established in any county at the option of the members of the local school boards. Members of the county survey committee are elected by the school board members and work under the supervision of the state advisory commission and the state superintendent of public instruction. It is the duty of the county committee to study the existing organization of school districts and to recommend such reorganization as in the committee's judgment "will afford better educational opportunities for the pupils and inhabitants of the county, more efficient and economical administration of public schools, and a more equitable distribution of public school revenues." Tentative reorganization schemes prepared by county committees are considered at public hearings, after which a report of final recommendations is prepared. These final recommendations of the committees, however, must be approved by the voters of the communities concerned before becoming effective.[27] By the beginning of 1948 every Illinois county but one had established a school survey committee under the terms of the 1945 statute. By 1952 reorganization plans approved by local voters had served to reduce the number of Illinois districts from more than 12,000 to less than 4,000, and further reduction in the number has been made since that date.[28]

Inasmuch as the elimination of small school districts is primarily a problem of rural areas, it is usual to provide for rural control of the county committees charged with effecting consolidations or making recommendations with respect thereto. The Kansas law, for example, provided that all members of school reorganization committees should be appointed

[25] State *v.* Hines, 163 Kan. 300 (1947).

[26] State *v.* Common School District No. 87, 163 Kan. 650 (1947).

[27] *Laws of Illinois* (1945), p. 1608. Cf. Snider and Garvey, *loc. cit.*

[28] As of October 1, 1955, the number of Illinois districts stood at 2,242—Illinois Legislative Council, *Between Sessions*, Newsletter, No. 41 (November, 1955).

from areas outside cities of a population of 15,000 or more and that at least three of the five members of each committee must reside outside the corporate limits of any city. And in Illinois five of the nine members of each school survey committee are chosen by the members of the rural school boards in the county and four by the members of urban boards. Further to be noted is the fact that in several states having consolidation laws which are strictly voluntary *in form,* consolidations have been encouraged, or made virtually compulsory, by the application of economic pressure through provisions of state-aid laws. In Illinois, for example, a state-aid provision effective in the 1940's denied state aid to any elementary school having fewer than seven pupils in average daily attendance, unless both the state and county superintendents should certify that the transportation of pupils to other schools was impracticable; it also provided for a progressive increase in the minimum number of pupils required of a state-aid school. Since the mid-1950's state aid has not been available in Illinois, where transportation of pupils is feasible, to any elementary district with fewer than 15 pupils in average daily attendance or to any high school with an average daily attendance of less than 60 pupils. The large number of consolidations affected in Illinois under a statute which in itself is purely voluntary is clearly attributable in substantial measure to this denial of state financial assistance to schools too small to meet the attendance requirements.[29]

According to Census Bureau reports, the total number of school districts in the United States in 1952 was 67,346, as contrasted with 108,579 in 1942.[30] This represented a reduction, taking the country as a whole, of 38 per cent. Although flowing in some small measure from a reclassification of governmental units in certain states, the reduction for the most part was the result of consolidations. In practically every "district" state consolidation was under way, though the movement was more active in some states than in others. As would be expected, consolidations tended to be most numerous in states where small districts had previously existed in large numbers. During the ten-year period each of seven states—Arkansas, Illinois, Kansas, Missouri, New York, Oklahoma, and Texas—eliminated more than 2,000 districts. Together, these states eliminated a total of more than 28,000 districts, to account for 69 per cent of the decrease in number for the entire country. The number of districts in each of the seven states as of the beginning and end of the ten-year period, and the percentage of decrease during the period, are as follows:[31]

[29] At an earlier time the state-aid program in Illinois actually encouraged the retention of small districts by providing that per-pupil grants should be paid to every district for a minimum of 18 pupils, whether or not that many were in attendance.

[30] *Governments in the United States in 1952,* p. 1.

[31] *Ibid.,* p. 4.

State	*Number of school districts* 1942	1952	*Per cent decrease*
Arkansas	2,644	422	84.0
Illinois	12,138	3,484	71.3
Kansas	8,632	3,984	53.8
Missouri	8,613	4,891	43.2
New York	6,064	2,915	52.0
Oklahoma	4,518	2,100	53.5
Texas	6,159	2,479	59.8

The extent to which consolidation has been effected over a somewhat longer period of time is suggested by the fact that between the school year 1929-30 and that of 1951-52, the number of one-teacher public schools in the country decreased from 149,300 to 50,700, and the number of pupils transported increased from approximately 2,000,000 to more than 7,000,000, the figure in the latter year representing more than one fourth of all public-school pupils.[32]

Consolidated districts, with their greater financial resources and larger numbers of pupils, are able to provide better physical plants, broader curricula, and improved instruction, and in general to operate school systems superior to those of the smaller districts which they supersede. When all elements of cost are considered, including transportation of pupils to the consolidated school, it is doubtful whether school consolidation results in most instances in monetary savings. Indeed, until new buildings have been paid for, the modern consolidated schools may actually cost somewhat more. But costs are more equitably distributed, and there seems to be little doubt that the improvement in educational facilities fully justifies some small increase in school expenditures and the fact that some of the more distant pupils may have to spend a longer time than might otherwise be desirable in traveling to and from the consolidated school. An alternative to consolidation as a method of avoiding the shortcomings of the small school district is the adoption of one of the larger areas of local government—township or county—as the principal unit for school purposes.

THE TOWN OR TOWNSHIP UNIT

In the six New England states the town, and in New Jersey, Pennsylvania, and Indiana the township, is the principal area for school administration. Under the New England town system, educational affairs in each town are managed by a board of school directors or trustees chosen by the local voters at school or town meeting. Ordinarily, this board manages the schools within villages as well as those in strictly rural areas, though a few

[32] Smith, *Statistical Summary of Education: 1951-52.* For further consideration of the consolidation movement, see below, chap. 20, "School Consolidation."

of the larger municipalities have city boards of education.[33] In New Jersey and Pennsylvania, each township constitutes a school district, with a board of education for administering all schools except those within areas (for the most part municipalities) which are separately incorporated for school purposes. Each civil township in Indiana is incorporated also as a school township, and an elective township trustee is charged with management of the rural schools therein.[34]

It is to be noted that use of the town or township as the basic educational unit does not necessarily mean the elimination of the small one-room school. Even though managed and financed on a town or township basis, one-room schools serving small attendance areas may still exist if state laws permit and the local school authorities desire.[35] Nevertheless, the town or township plan of school administration tends to encourage use of larger attendance areas and the operation of larger, better-equipped, and better-staffed schools than are ordinarily found under the district system.

THE COUNTY UNIT

Fifteen states, principally in the South but including the western states of Nevada, New Mexico, and Utah, employ the county-unit plan of school administration. Under this plan, schools are managed and financed on a county-wide basis. Administrative organization for school purposes varies somewhat among these states, but usually there is a county board of education with a county superintendent of schools appointed by and responsible to the board. The superintendent, as the executive officer of the board, is charged with management of the rural schools of the county. City schools in some instances are under the jurisdiction of the county unit, but in others they are separate units with their own school boards and superintendents.

Outside the county-unit states, individual instances are to be found, and are becoming more numerous, in which high schools, or both elementary and high schools, are administered and financed through county-wide districts. As of 1947 New Jersey, a township-unit state, was reported as having six county high school districts, and one or more county school districts were reported as existing in each of eight district states.[36] More

[33] Cf. Ellwood P. Cubberley, *State School Administration* (Boston, Houghton Mifflin, 1927), p. 186; also, *Your School District,* p. 49.

[34] Indiana cities, and some of the state's lesser municipalities known as towns, are separately incorporated as school cities or school towns and are not included within the school township. Fiscal control in Indiana townships, both civil and school, is vested in an elective "advisory board" of three members.

[35] As of 1950, some 4,000 one-room schools were reported still in existence in the nine township-unit states. Rose Marie Smith, "Statistical Summary of Education: 1949-50," *Biennial Survey of Education in the United States: 1948-50* (Washington, U.S. Office of Education, 1953), chap. 1.

[36] *Your School District,* p. 262.

recently, five counties in Illinois, another district state, have established single school districts coterminous with the county through consolidation. These county districts, though bearing no closer relation to the regular county government than other school districts in the state, afford the same general advantages in school administration and financing that are provided by the county unit elsewhere.

Like the town or township unit, the county educational unit does not assure the elimination of small, inefficient schools. It does, however, provide a more equitable basis for school financing than the system of small districts or even the town or township plan. Because of both financial and administrative advantages, there is a distinct trend today toward larger school units than those commonly used in the past, and the county unit is steadily gaining in favor among educators and students of school administration. Even some of the present-day counties are too small for the most efficient and economical administration of educational affairs and might well be merged with others to form still larger school units.[37]

Many states which do not use the county-unit system of administration nevertheless provide for county boards of education, and a still larger number have county school superintendents charged with various supervisory functions with respect to rural schools.

COUNTY BOARDS OF EDUCATION

County boards of education are found in some 30 states. The size of the body varies from three members to more than twenty, with a five-member board most common. In a majority of the states providing for such an agency board members are chosen by popular election, though several states provide for appointment. Members are appointed, for example, in Georgia by the grand jury, in Maryland by the governor, in North Carolina by the state legislature, and in some Tennessee counties by the county court.[38] In Indiana the board is an ex officio body composed of the township trustees of the county, the chairman of the school trustees of each municipality separately organized for educational purposes, and the county superintendent of schools.[39]

The powers of county school boards vary widely, particularly between states where the county-unit system prevails and those in which the county serves merely as an area for the supervision of schools maintained by

[37] Cf. Alonzo O. Briscoe, *The Size of the Local Unit for Administration and Supervision of Public Schools* (New York, Teachers College Bureau of Publications, 1935), pp. 106-107.

[38] Council of State Governments, *The Forty-eight State School Systems* (Chicago, 1949), pp. 59-60, 196.

[39] The county superintendent serves as the board's presiding officer. In many counties, as a matter of practice, members representing municipal school corporations take no active part in board affairs.

townships or districts. Where the county is the primary unit for school purposes, the board is normally the chief policy-determining organ of the county school corporation, levying school taxes, authorizing expenditures, and deciding all questions of educational policy not determined by statute. In a majority of the county-unit states the board also appoints the county superintendent, who serves as the board's executive officer in charge of administrative matters. Where the county-unit system is not employed the position of the county board of education is much weaker. In some instances its function is limited almost entirely to that of acting in an advisory capacity to study the general needs of the schools of the county and make recommendations to the township or district authorities. At other times it is charged with duties relating to such matters as the appointment of attendance officers and the selection of textbooks, but in no event does its authority approach that of the typical board under the county-unit plan.

THE COUNTY SUPERINTENDENT

The office of county school superintendent exists in approximately 38 states.[40] In a majority of the county-unit states, the superintendent is appointed by a county board of education. Elsewhere the office is most commonly filled by popular election, though other methods of choice are found in some instances.

The powers and duties of the county superintendent vary considerably, especially between county-unit and non-county-unit states. In the former, the superintendent usually serves as the executive officer of the county board of education, being clothed with much the same administrative authority as that commonly possessed by city school superintendents. Where, on the other hand, the basic school unit is the township or school district rather than the county, the position of the county superintendent is considerably weaker. City school systems in such instances ordinarily are not under his jurisdiction, and he functions principally as an agent of the state department of education in exercising various forms of supervisory authority over the rural schools of the county and seeing that the rules and regulations of the state department are carried out.[41]

[40] Several other states, principally in New England, have "union superintendents" or "district superintendents" with supervisory functions corresponding in a general way to those of the county superintendent where the latter office exists in non-county-unit states. Concerning the office generally, see Julian E. Butterworth, *The County Superintendent in the United States* (Washington, U.S. Office of Education, 1932); N. William Newsom, *The Legal Status of the County Superintendent* (Washington, U.S. Office of Education, 1932); Robert B. Highsaw and Harold S. Thames, *A Guidebook of the County Superintendent of Education* (University, University of Mississippi Bureau of Public Administration, 1951); Minnesota Legislative Research Committee, *The Office of Superintendent of Schools* (St. Paul, Minn., 1952).

[41] Cf. Benjamin J. Burris, *The County School System: How Organized and Administered* (Indianapolis, Indiana State Department of Public Instruction, 1924).

One of the most important supervisory functions of the superintendent is that of visiting and inspecting the schools under his jurisdiction. Such inspection is necessary to determine whether the local schools are meeting state-prescribed standards generally and state-aid requirements in particular. In this connection, "the county superintendents inspect school buildings, playground facilities, sanitation facilities, educational supplies, and all aspects of the rural educational program." [42] The superintendent frequently assists local school boards in the selection of teachers. He is the official adviser of teachers and school officers and, through his visits and advice, attempts to raise the general standards of the schools and to improve instruction therein. In some states the superintendent serves ex officio as county attendance officer in enforcing state compulsory attendance laws; in others, however, an attendance officer is appointed by the superintendent. Other functions assigned to the county superintendent in various states include the calling and supervision of school elections; the distribution of state-aid funds to school districts; assisting in the preparation of school budgets; and the performance of specified duties with respect to the fixing of school-district boundaries, the licensing of teachers, the provision of pupil transportation, the supervision of school construction, and the purchase of school supplies and equipment.[43]

In the performance of his visitation and supervisory duties the county superintendent collects numerous statistical data concerning the schools of the county which he is required by law to report, in turn, to the state department of education. Indeed, one of the most helpful services performed by the superintendent is that of channeling to the state department local educational data to be used by the department in the administration of state aid and other supervisory programs and made available to the legislature for its guidance in the formulation of school laws. In a typical non-county-unit state "the proper role of the county superintendent has been defined as that of a planner, leader, stimulator, and promoter for the local rural schools and that of a field representative and administrator of the state office. When the office carries out these roles, it serves a purposeful and useful function in rural school administration." [44]

SCHOOL FINANCE [45]

At one time American schools depended for their support almost entirely upon the proceeds from a local property tax, and, taking the country as a whole, this tax is still the largest single source of local school revenue.

[42] *The Office of Superintendent of Schools,* p. 6.
[43] Cf. *Your School District,* p. 64.
[44] *The Office of Superintendent of Schools,* p. 2.
[45] On the subject in general, see Paul R. Mort and Walter C. Reusser, *Public School Finance,* 2d ed. (New York, McGraw-Hill, 1951).

During recent decades, however, in recognition of the state-wide interest in elementary and secondary education, the states have assumed a substantial part of the burden of school finance. Every state now provides some state aid for schools, and the tendency is toward a constant increase in the amount.[46] During the school year 1951-52, nearly 39 per cent of all local school revenues in the United States came from state sources, as compared with less than 17 per cent in 1929-30. Among individual states the percentage of total school revenues derived from state sources varies widely. In 1951-52 the range was from less than 10 per cent to more than 70 per cent, with the schools of a dozen states deriving more than half of their revenues from state sources.[47]

State financial grants enable local school units both to improve their educational facilities and to reduce the burden of the local property tax for school purposes. State grants may be made to the local units at a fixed rate per pupil in average daily attendance or on some other predetermined basis, or they may be apportioned according to need. When the latter plan is followed the term *equalization grant* is sometimes used, since the purpose of the state assistance is to equalize educational opportunities between the poorer and more wealthy communities. A system of equalization grants in common use provides that if a local school corporation levies a specified minimum rate of property tax for school purposes, the state will supplement the proceeds from this local levy by whatever amount is necessary to enable the local unit to maintain a school or schools of state-prescribed standards. State educational funds, equalization and otherwise, are usually distributed to the local school units, in accordance with the provisions of state law, by the state department of education, with the county superintendent in some states acting in an intermediary capacity. The amounts to which the respective local units are entitled are determined on the basis of reports, covering such matters as school attendance and local revenues and expenditures, which are made by local school officers to the state or county authorities. Some states distribute part of their school funds to the local units on a flat per-pupil basis and another part, as equalization grants, on the basis of need. As previously noted, the withholding of state aid from school districts having only a few pupils has been employed in some instances as a means of promoting district consolidation.[48]

In 1951-52, 58 per cent of all local school revenues in the country was derived from local sources—principally property taxation—and 3 per cent was supplied by the federal government.[49]

[46] Cf. Reeder, *op cit.*, p. 337.
[47] Smith, *Statistical Summary of Education: 1951-52.*
[48] See above, "The Consolidation Movement."
[49] Smith, *Statistical Summary of Education: 1951-52.*

RURAL SCHOOLS V. URBAN

Generally speaking, the educational standards of rural schools have always lagged behind those maintained in urban areas. A generation ago a publication of the United States Bureau of Education, after observing that about half of the nation's school children were enrolled in village and open-country schools, declared: [50]

> These twelve million children are laboring under distinct educational disadvantages. So far as the open-country schools are concerned, fully two hundred thousand of these schools may still be classed as one-room schools of the pioneer type, which but poorly meet the needs of modern agricultural life. Their teachers are largely immature, inexperienced, poorly trained, and of limited vision of rural needs and problems. The school year is much shorter than it ought to be, enrollment of school population is in many States low, daily attendance is often irregular, and compulsory-attendance laws are not always enforced as they should be. The course of study in the small schools is often badly planned and the courses poorly taught, and financially they are meagerly supported in comparison with what is invested in education elsewhere. Recent educational surveys have disclosed that in certain States the level of school education must be measured by about six and one-half years of school attendance for the villages and less than five years for the rural districts. Such limited education cannot furnish the intelligent leadership required at this present time of entrance upon the new era of scientific agriculture.

In the years following this statement the rural schools improved somewhat, yet after the lapse of two decades George Works and Simon Lesser were still justified in writing: [51]

> Every commonly employed statistical measure suggests that the quality of educational service provided by rural schools, considered as a group, falls far below national norms. School facilities and conditions clearly reveal the difficulties faced by the rural population in trying to educate a disproportionately large share of the nation's children on a disproportionately small share of the national income. . . . Although the nation's rural schools enrolled 50 per cent of all pupils in 1935-36, only 37 per cent of the funds for the support of public elementary and secondary schools were expended upon them.

During the 1940's and 1950's the improvement of rural schools has been more rapid. This has been due in no small measure to increased state aid and to the school-consolidation programs, which in several instances have been stimulated, in turn, by state-aid formulas. It is in the smallest schools, by and large, that substandard conditions, such as obsolete buildings, lack of proper equipment, and poorly trained teachers,

[50] H. W. Foght, *Rural Education,* U. S. Bureau of Education Bulletin (Washington, 1919), No. 7, pp. 3-4.

[51] George A. Works and Simon O. Lesser, *Rural America Today: Its Schools and Community Life* (Chicago, University of Chicago Press, 1942), pp. 24-25. Copyright, 1942, by the University of Chicago.

have been most widely prevalent;[52] and it is therefore not surprising that consolidation has brought improvements in both physical plant and instruction. Notwithstanding marked progress, however, rural schools, as a group, still compare unfavorably with urban. In the school year 1947-48, total current expenditure per pupil in 36 states for which data were available was only $173 in rural areas as compared with $206 in urban communities; and the average length of the school term was 172 days in rural districts as compared with 183 days in urban.[53] In 1951-52 less than half of all rural school buildings were of relatively modern construction; nearly 30 per cent of the rural teachers rated their buildings as unsatisfactory for up-to-date educational programs; and nearly 3 per cent of rural elementary teachers were teaching in churches, town halls, lodge halls, residences, or other buildings neither designed nor constructed for school use.[54] Though the estimated average salary paid rural teachers rose from $867 in 1936-37 to $2,484 in 1951-52, rural salaries were still substantially lower than urban.[55]

Today's rural schools, on the whole, provide elementary and secondary education at standards far above those of a generation ago. Schools are more adequately financed, physical facilities have been greatly improved, curricula have been broadened, and better-qualified teachers have been secured. The one-room school with all its shortcomings is still more prevalent than it should be, but the number of such schools has declined from 200,000 to less than 60,000 and is being further reduced as consolidation continues. Though additional improvement is needed to bring the rural schools more nearly up to urban standards, the progress of recent years has been gratifying and prospects for the future are encouraging. The present situation, with a note of optimism regarding the future, is well expressed in a recent publication of the United States Office of Education. After presenting comparative data, financial and otherwise, on rural and urban schools respectively, this study concludes:[56]

> The indices presented, both financial and non-financial, show the public elementary and secondary schools in city systems to be on the average somewhat better than those in rural systems. Urban schools pay higher salaries to their teachers; they spend more per pupil for education; they have a longer school term. All these factors suggest more adequate educational services. . . . Rural schools, however, are improving; the differences between rural and urban schools are gradually decreasing in such important items as teachers' salaries and per pupil expenditures. In some States the rural areas present a more favorable picture than the urban areas in other States, since large differences among the States still prevail.

52 *Rural Teachers in 1951-52,* p. 51.

53 Smith, *Education in Rural and City School Systems,* p. 3.

54 *Rural Teachers in 1951-52,* pp. 35-36; Sam M. Lambert, "Today's Rural Teacher," *The County Officer,* Vol. XVIII, pp. 156-158 (June, 1953).

55 *Rural Teachers in 1951-52,* p. 39.

56 Smith, *Education in Rural and City School Systems,* p. 5.

RURAL LIBRARY SERVICE

Closely related to the school system in providing educational facilities is the public library. "The concept of the library as an educational service is as old as the public library itself. . . . Today it is sufficiently clear that the library is an active ally of public education at all levels and an indispensable agency in adult education." [57] At one time the public library was concerned almost exclusively with the distribution of books. The modern library of the present day provides, in addition, magazines and newspapers in wide variety and, frequently, educational films and recordings. The larger and more progressive institutions also offer informational and advisory services.

Unlike public school facilities, public library service, being optional rather than mandatory, is far from universal.[58] Where service is provided there is wide variation in standards, but in general it is the rural areas that suffer most acutely from inadequate service or the complete want of library facilities. Almost every municipality of any considerable size maintains a library. On the other hand, notwithstanding the gradual broadening of library coverage during previous years, it was reported in the late 1940's that fully one fourth of the American people still lived in governmental units which did not maintain public libraries, and that 91 per cent of the people without libraries were residents of small villages or the open country.[59] When account is taken of the fact that rural library facilities, where they exist, are generally inferior in quality to those provided by municipalities, it is evident that only a small proportion of the rural people have library service comparable to that available in nearly every urban community.[60] Thus it becomes clear that the present-day problem of providing complete and adequate library service is essentially a rural problem.[61] To the extent that this problem is being solved—and, though progress is slow, it *is* being solved in constantly increasing measure—it is through library service provided by town and township libraries, county and regional libraries, and state library extension.

TOWN AND TOWNSHIP LIBRARIES

Most New England towns maintain libraries, though many of these are small and are open only during designated hours of the day or certain

[57] Carleton B. Joeckel, *Library Service*, Staff Study No. 11 for the Advisory Committee on Education (Washington, Government Printing Office, 1938), pp. 16-17.

[58] Cf. *ibid.*, p. 8.

[59] Carleton B. Joeckel and Amy Winslow, *A National Plan for Public Library Service* (Chicago, American Library Association, 1948), p. 19.

[60] Cf. American Library Association, *Rural Public Library Service* (Chicago, 1945), p. 3.

[61] Cf. Joeckel, *Library Service*, p. 9.

days each week. Typically, the town library is governed by an elective board of trustees. The amounts appropriated by towns for library purposes vary widely, with many of the institutions being financed in part by income from endowments or trust funds. Occasional townships in some midwestern states maintain libraries, and a somewhat larger number contribute to the financial support of public libraries operated by other governmental units. Outside New England, however, it is the county and regional libraries that are primarily responsible for providing library service to rural areas.

COUNTY AND REGIONAL LIBRARIES[62]

County libraries may be divided, according to governmental type, into three principal classes.[63] The first and most widely prevalent type may be called the independent county library. Libraries of this character are usually established by the county governing board, with or without popular approval at a referendum election as state law may require, and are operated as a part of the county government. Control of the library may be exercised directly by the county governing board or may be in the hands of a special library board, ordinarily consisting of lay members appointed by the county governing body and, save for the necessity of depending upon the governing body for financial support, enjoying a large degree of autonomy in its relations to the general county government.[64] Of the two forms of administration, the special board is the more common and is generally preferred on the assumption that it lessens political interference. A county library of the independent type may serve the residents of the entire county or only the inhabitants of those parts of the county not served by city or other publicly supported libraries. Where the latter plan is used, taxes for the support of the county library are usually imposed only upon property within the areas served by it. A second type of county library service that is fairly common is the contract variety. Under this plan, the county board enters into a contract with an already existing library for supplying library service to county residents. The institution agreeing to provide such service is occasionally the library of another county, but is most frequently a city library—usually one located in the county seat or the county's largest municipality. The amount to be

[62] A comprehensive discussion of the nature and operation of libraries in these categories will be found in Gretchen Knief Schenk, *County and Regional Library Development* (Chicago, American Library Association, 1954).

[63] Eleanor Hitt Morgan, "The County Library," in Carleton B. Joeckel, ed., *Library Extension: Problems and Solutions* (Chicago, University of Chicago Press, 1946), pp. 59-74. Cf. also Carleton B. Joeckel, *The Government of the American Public Library* (Chicago, University of Chicago Press, 1935), pp. 264-271.

[64] Concerning local library government, cf. Robert D. Leigh, *The Public Library in the United States* (New York, Columbia University Press, 1950), pp. 110-112.

paid by the county may be computed upon any one or more of various bases, such as population of the territory served, number of borrowers, or cost of providing the service. Yet a third means of providing library service to a county's rural inhabitants, less common than either of the two just described, is through a city-county library established and administered jointly by the two governmental units.

Whichever of the three plans of county library service is followed, use is frequently made, for distributing purposes, of branch libraries or deposit stations, or both. Branches, like the main library, are manned by trained personnel and extend various forms of assistance to readers. Deposit stations, on the other hand, have neither trained personnel nor reading-room facilities. They consist merely of book collections, changed at regular intervals and located in convenient places, such as schoolhouses, post offices, stores, gasoline stations, or even private homes, with some responsible person agreeing to keep a record of books borrowed and returned. Of growing importance as a distributing agency, especially in making books available to the inhabitants of isolated regions, is the bookmobile.[65] This is a closed motor truck specially equipped with bookshelves, which visits rural homes on regular schedules and from which books may be borrowed to be returned on subsequent visits.[66] According to 1950 estimates more than 400 bookmobiles were in use in the United States, with each of several states having more than 25 in operation.[67] Though some bookmobiles are used in urban communities, the large majority are employed in providing rural library service.

The earliest county libraries were established about the turn of the present century, and during the first quarter of the century the county library was the most widely used device in extending library service to rural areas. More recently, however, growing use has been made of the multicounty or regional library.[68] Under this plan, two or more neighboring counties, through contractual agreement or the establishment of a library district, co-operate in providing library service for their respective inhabitants. The plan is especially well adapted to use by relatively poor, sparsely settled counties which might find it impracticable to operate individual county libraries. Combining the populations of two or more such counties for library purposes may provide sufficient demand to justify the establishment of a modern library, at the same time that the pooling of financial resources makes practicable the support of such an institution. Most states have now enacted legislation authorizing counties to co-operate with each other in providing library service, and regional libraries

[65] Problems of bookmobile service are discussed in Schenk, *op. cit.*, chap. 8.

[66] Morgan, *loc. cit.*

[67] Margie S. Malmberg, "Books at Your Doorstep," *The County Officer,* Vol. XV, No. 2, pp. 10-13, 23-24 (May, 1950).

[68] Morgan, *loc. cit.;* Helen M. Harris, "The Regional Library," in Joeckel, *Library Extension: Problems and Solutions,* pp. 87-97.

have actually been established in substantial number, the movement having been most active in some of the southern states. Thus, during the decade from 1937 to 1947, 13 regional libraries, serving from 2 to 13 counties each, were organized in Kentucky, Tennessee, Alabama, Georgia, North Carolina, and Virginia. These libraries are variously financed by contributions from a number of sources, including county governments, school districts, state library extension funds, and the Tennessee Valley Authority.[69] By 1950 Georgia alone was reported as having 14 regional libraries serving 29 counties.[70]

STATE LIBRARY EXTENSION

Town, county, and regional libraries are not the only agencies concerned with providing library facilities for rural residents. Every state now maintains some sort of library extension agency charged with the promotion of local library service. In some states library extension is merely a secondary activity of a state library designed primarily to serve the reference needs of state officers and as a repository for historical documents; in others, an independent library commission has been established for the primary purpose of promoting library extension; and, in still others, the library extension agency is a division of the state department of education. Whatever its form, the extension agency is usually charged with encouraging the establishment of local libraries and the improvement of library personnel, sometimes sharing with local governing bodies in the appointment of local librarians. It provides various forms of advice and assistance to local libraries, and in general it promotes the expansion of local library coverage. In addition, the state agency ordinarily offers a book service of its own, through extension loans and traveling libraries, to small local libraries, schools, clubs, and individual citizens. The lending of books by mail to individuals, though in practice reaching a relatively small number of persons, is of particular significance in isolated rural areas not served by any local library. Where states provide financial aid to local governments for library purposes, as about half of the states now do, the state grants ordinarily are channeled through the library extension agency.[71]

In New England, where the town rather than the county is the principal

[69] M. H. Satterfield, "Intergovernmental Coöperation in the Tennessee Valley," *Journal of Politics*, Vol. IX, pp. 31-58 (February, 1947).

[70] Helen A. Ridgway, "Library Legislation and Planning," *The Book of the States: 1950-51* (Chicago, Council of State Governments, 1950), pp. 299-303.

[71] Julia Wright Merrill, comp., *The State Library Agency: Its Functions and Organization*, 5th ed. (Chicago, American Library Association, 1945); Leigh, *op. cit.*, pp. 69-70; Ridgway, *loc. cit.;* Paul A. T. Noon, "The Rôle of the State Agency in Library Extension," in Joeckel, *Library Extension: Problems and Solutions*, pp. 160-170; Fred F. Beach, Ralph M. Dunbar, and Robert F. Will, *The State and Publicly Supported Libraries* (Washington, U. S. Office of Education, 1956), chap. 4.

unit of local government in rural areas and where most towns have long maintained libraries, though many of them are small and poorly supported, a pattern of state library activity has developed somewhat different from that in other states. Instead of promoting the organization of county or multicounty libraries, the tendency in New England is for the state government to provide facilities for co-ordinating and supplementing town library services through state-operated regional library centers. In Vermont, where the plan has been made most fully effective, the entire state was divided in 1937 into library regions, each with a regional library managed by a trained librarian and equipped with a bookmobile. These regional libraries are supported primarily from state funds, but to a minor extent from private gifts. Books lent from the regional libraries supplement the local town services, and the regional librarians in their co-ordinating capacity encourage local libraries to lend books for use outside their respective towns. Thus Vermont's regional organization seeks both to increase the stock of books available to local residents and to marshal local resources for maximum use. Massachusetts and New Hampshire are also reported to have established state-operated regional library centers serving portions of those states.[72]

Through town, county, and regional libraries, supplemented by state library extension, substantial progress has been made during recent decades in providing library facilities for the inhabitants of rural areas. That much remains to be done is quite apparent, however, when it is borne in mind that only about one fourth of all American counties even today have complete local library coverage, and that some 30,000,000 farm and village residents, constituting half of the entire rural population, are without local library service of any kind.

REFERENCES

Books, Reports, and Special Studies

Alves, Henry F., Anderson, Archibald W., and Fowlkes, John Guy, *Local School Unit Organization in Ten States* (Washington, U. S. Office of Education, 1938).

American Library Association, *Rural Public Library Service* (Chicago, 1945).

Bostwick, Arthur E., *The American Public Library*, 4th ed. (New York, Appleton, 1929).

Briscoe, Alonzo O., *The Size of the Local Unit for Administration and Supervision of Public Schools* (New York, Teachers College Bureau of Publications, 1935).

Burris, Benjamin J., *The County School System: How Organized and Administered* (Indianapolis, Indiana State Department of Public Instruction, 1924).

[72] Leon Carnovsky, "Library Service to Rural Communities," in Floyd W. Reeves, ed., *Education for Rural America* (Chicago, University of Chicago Press, 1945), pp. 143-159; Julia Wright Merrill, comp., *Regional and District Libraries,* rev. ed. (Chicago, American Library Association, 1942), pp. 11-13.

BUTTERWORTH, Julian E., *The County Superintendent in the United States* (Washington, U. S. Office of Education, 1932).

COCKING, Walter D., and GILMORE, Charles H., *Organization and Administration of Public Education,* Staff Study No. 2 for the Advisory Committee on Education (Washington, Government Printing Office, 1938).

Council of State Governments, *The Forty-eight State School Systems* (Chicago, 1949).

DEFFENBAUGH, Walter S., and COVERT, Timon, *School Administrative Units, with Special Reference to the County Unit* (Washington, U. S. Office of Education, 1933).

DEYOUNG, Chris A., *Introduction to American Public Education,* 2d ed. (New York, McGraw-Hill, 1950).

FOGHT, H. W., *Rural Education,* U. S. Bureau of Education Bulletin (Washington, 1919), No. 7.

FREUDENTHAL, Daniei K., *State Aid to Local School Systems* (Berkeley, University of California Bureau of Public Administration, 1949).

HIGHSAW, Robert B., and THAMES, Harold S., *A Guidebook of the County Superintendent of Education* (University, University of Mississippi Bureau of Public Administration, 1951).

HOWARD, George C., Jr., and HOWARD, Edith Foster, *City-county Educational Relationships in Tennessee* (Knoxville, University of Tennessee Bureau of Public Administration, 1950).

HUMBLE, Marion, *Rural America Reads: A Study of Rural Library Service* (New York, American Association for Adult Education, 1938).

JOECKEL, Carleton B., *The Government of the American Public Library* (Chicago, University of Chicago Press, 1935).

———, *Library Service,* Staff Study No. 11 for the Advisory Committee on Education (Washington, Government Printing Office, 1938).

———, ed., *Library Extension: Problems and Solutions* (Chicago, University of Chicago Press, 1946).

———, and WINSLOW, Amy, *A National Plan for Public Library Service* (Chicago, American Library Association, 1948).

JOHNSEN, Julia E., comp., *County Libraries* (New York, Wilson, 1930).

Kentucky Legislative Research Commission, *Kentucky's Schools: Past, Present, and Future* (Frankfort, Ky., 1953).

LEIGH, Robert D., *The Public Library in the United States* (New York, Columbia University Press, 1950).

MCDIARMID, E. W., and MCDIARMID, John, *The Administration of the American Public Library* (Urbana, University of Illinois Press, 1943); published in co-operation with the American Library Association.

MERRILL, Julia Wright, comp., *Regional and District Libraries,* rev. ed. (Chicago, American Library Association, 1942).

———, comp., *State Grants to Public Libraries,* rev. ed. (Chicago, American Library Association, 1942).

Minnesota Legislative Research Committee, *The Office of County Superintendent of Schools* (St. Paul, Minn., 1952).

MORT, Paul R., and REUSSER, Walter C., *Public School Finance,* 2d ed. (New York, McGraw-Hill, 1951).

National Commission on School District Reorganization, *Your School District* (Washington, National Education Association, 1948).

National Education Association, *Rural Teachers in 1951-52,* Research Bulletin (Washington, 1953), Vol. XXXI, No. 1.

NEWSOM, N. William, *The Legal Status of the County Superintendent* (Washington, U. S. Office of Education, 1932).

PITTENGER, Benjamin Floyd, *Local Public School Administration* (New York, McGraw-Hill, 1951).

REEDER, Ward G., *The Fundamentals of Public School Administration,* 3d ed. (New York, Macmillan, 1951).

REEVES, Floyd W., ed., *Education for Rural America* (Chicago, University of Chicago Press, 1945).

REMMLEIN, Madaline Kintner, *The Law of Local Public School Administration* (New York, McGraw-Hill, 1953).

SANDOE, Mildred W., *County Library Primer* (New York, Wilson, 1942).

SCHENK, Gretchen Knief, *County and Regional Library Development* (Chicago, American Library Association, 1954).

SCHLOSS, Samuel, and HOBSON, Carol J., "Statistics of State School Systems: 1951-52," *Biennial Survey of Education in the United States: 1950-52* (Washington, U. S. Office of Education, 1955), chap. 2.

SMITH, Payson, WRIGHT, Frank W., and others, *Education in the Forty-eight States,* Staff Study No. 1 for the Advisory Committee on Education (Washington, Government Printing Office, 1939).

SMITH, Rose Marie, *Education in Rural and City School Systems: Some Statistical Indices for 1947-48* (Washington, U. S. Office of Education, 1951).

———, "Statistical Summary of Education: 1951-52," *Biennial Survey of Education in the United States: 1950-52* (Washington, U. S. Office of Education, 1955), chap. 1.

Tax Foundation, *Public School Financing: 1930-1954* (New York, 1954).

United States Department of Agriculture, *Rural Library Service* (Washington, 1940).

University of Mississippi Bureau of Public Administration, *People Without Books: An Analysis of Library Service in Mississippi* (University, Miss., 1950).

WILSON, Louis R., and WIGHT, Edward A., *County Library Service in the South* (Chicago, University of Chicago Press, 1935).

WORKS, George A., and LESSER, Simon O., *Rural America Today: Its Schools and Community Life* (Chicago, University of Chicago Press, 1942).

Articles

BINGHAM, Mary, "Bookmobiles Are Coming—in Kentucky!" *State Government,* Vol. XXVII, pp. 116-118, 125 (June, 1954).

BUTTERWORTH, Julian E., "Types of County Educational Control in the United States," *Journal of Educational Research,* Vol. XV, pp. 349-356 (May, 1927).

FREEMAN, Roger A., "State Aid and the Support of Our Public Schools," *State Government,* Vol. XXVI, pp. 237-240, 252-253 (October, 1953).

LAMBERT, Sam M., "Today's Rural Teacher," *The County Officer,* Vol. XVIII, pp. 156-158 (June, 1953).

MALMBERG, Margie S., "Books at Your Doorstep," *The County Officer,* Vol. XV, No. 2, pp. 10-13, 23-24 (May, 1950).

PRICE, Paxton Pate, "Bookmobiles on the Missouri Landscape," *State Government,* Vol. XXVII, pp. 20-23 (January, 1954).

RANDOLPH, Dorothy, "Bookwagons in Vermont," *Vermont Life,* Vol. VII, No. 2, pp. 2-5 (Winter, 1952-53).

CHAPTER 18

Agriculture and Conservation

LOCAL GOVERNMENTS IN rural areas are concerned, and increasingly so, with various services relating to agriculture and the conservation of natural resources. Many of these services are administered at the county level through the offices of the county farm agent and his feminine counterpart, the home-demonstration agent. In order to understand the position and activities of these officials, it will be helpful first to give brief consideration to the federal-state-local program of agricultural extension, of which their work constitutes a basic part.

AGRICULTURAL EXTENSION

The agricultural extension program has as its legal basis the Smith-Lever Act passed by the United States Congress in 1914, together with certain complementary federal statutes of later date and implementing state legislation. In the 1914 law, Congress inaugurated a program of annual appropriations to the states for the support of extension education in agriculture and home economics to be carried on by the various land-grant agricultural colleges in co-operation with the United States Department of Agriculture; and subsequent federal statutes have provided for additional appropriations.[1] Apart from modest flat-sum grants in

[1] The land-grant colleges are the institutions receiving federal aid under the Morrill Act of 1862 and subsequent legislation providing grants of land and money to state colleges specializing in agriculture and the mechanic arts. Every state maintains one or more institutions of this nature, with the southern states having traditionally maintained separate institutions for Negroes. In about half of the states, the principal land-grant college is organized as a unit of the state university, but elsewhere it is a separate institution. See George A. Works and Barton Morgan, *The Land-grant Colleges*, Staff Study No. 10 for the Advisory Committee on Education (Washington, Government Printing Office, 1939).

which the states share equally, the federal funds are apportioned among the states on the basis of rural population, or in some instances strictly farm population, and some of the grants carry the requirement that federal moneys be matched dollar for dollar from state and local funds.[2]

In the words of the Smith-Lever Act, the purpose of the extension program is "to aid in diffusing among the people of the United States useful and practical information on subjects relating to agriculture and home economics, and to encourage the application of the same." Extension work is to "consist of the giving of instruction and practical demonstrations in agriculture and home economics to persons not attending or resident in said colleges in the several communities, and imparting to such persons information on said subjects through field demonstrations, publications, and otherwise." [3] Essentially, agricultural extension is a program of off-campus education for farm people. It is designed, writes Clarence B. Smith, former assistant director of extension work for the federal government, "to carry to rural people the studies, the teaching, and the results of research by the State agricultural colleges, State experiment stations, and the United States Department of Agriculture and to help them apply these teachings and research findings in the improvement of the farm, the home, the rural community, rural institutions, and rural life." [4] Some concrete objectives of the program, according to Smith, are: [5]

1. To bring the farmer the knowledge and help that will enable him to farm still more efficiently and to increase his income.
2. To encourage the farmer to grow his own food, set a good table, and live well.
3. To help the members of the farm family to a larger appreciation of the opportunities, the beauties, and the privileges of country life, and to know something about the world in which they live.
4. To promote the social, the cultural, the recreational, the intellectual, and the spiritual life of rural people.
5. To place opportunity before rural people whereby they may develop all their native talents through work, recreation, social life, leadership.
6. To build a rural citizenry, proud of its occupation, independent in its thinking, constructive in its outlook, capable, efficient, self-reliant, with a love of home and country, in its heart.

[2] *Ibid.*, chap. 4. For comprehensive discussions of the extension program, see Clarence B. Smith and Meredith C. Wilson, *The Agricultural Extension System of the United States* (New York, Wiley, 1930); Edmund deS. Brunner and E. Hsin Pao Yang, *Rural America and the Extension Service* (New York, Teachers College Bureau of Publications, 1949); Lincoln D. Kelsey and Cannon C. Hearne, *Coöperative Extension Work*, 2d ed. (Ithaca, N. Y., Comstock Publishing Associates, 1955); Carleton R. Ball, *Federal, State, and Local Administrative Relationships in Agriculture* (Berkeley, University of California Press, 1938), 2 vols.

[3] 38 *U. S. Stat. at L.* 372, secs. 1, 2.

[4] C. B. Smith, *What Agricultural Extension Is* (Washington, U. S. Department of Agriculture, 1944), pp. 1-2.

[5] *Ibid.*, p. 5.

Frequently referred to in the statutes and elsewhere as "co-operative extension," the agricultural extension program is operated and financed jointly by the national government, the states, and the local communities. The co-operating agency at the national level is the Federal Extension Service of the United States Department of Agriculture, and at the state level it is the extension service of the state agricultural college. Local participation most commonly is through the county government. In some instances, however, voluntary organizations of farmers serve, either alone or jointly with the county authorities, as sponsoring agencies. Under farm-organization sponsorship it is usual for county (occasionally town) funds to be appropriated to the sponsoring organization for extension purposes. At one time these tax-derived funds were rather commonly supplemented by funds from organization dues, and, indeed, in some instances the local share of costs was borne in its entirety by the sponsoring agency from its private funds. Today, however, principal reliance for local financial support is upon county appropriations.

Whatever the plan of local sponsorship and financing, actual administration of the extension program, in conformity to federal standards and under the supervision of state leaders, is vested in county extension offices. In charge of each office is a county agricultural agent, commonly called simply the county agent. Most offices include also a home-demonstration agent, who normally functions with a large degree of autonomy, and some have a 4-H Club agent as well.[6] Assistant agents in the various categories and, at times, one or more clerical employees are to be found in some of the wealthier and more populous counties. On the other hand, two or more small counties occasionally combine to employ a single agent. Provisions for housing the county extension office are varied, but most commonly it is assigned quarters in the county courthouse.[7] All but a very few American counties now have agricultural agents, some 80 per cent have home-demonstration agents, and several hundred have 4-H Club agents. Where there is no special 4-H Club agent, boys' and girls' club work ordinarily is carried on by the agricultural and home-demonstration agents. Thus, it will be seen that the agricultural extension program virtually blankets rural America, reaching farmers through the county agricultural agents, farm women through the home-demonstration agents, and the young people of farm communities through 4-H Clubs and rural youth programs.[8]

[6] The official title of the county extension agents is not entirely uniform. In Illinois, for example, they are known respectively as farm advisers and home advisers.

[7] In southern states operating separate agricultural colleges for Negroes, a separate organization of Negro extension agents for assisting Negro farmers has usually paralleled at least in some measure that for the service of white farmers. Concerning Negro county agents, see Gladys Baker, *The County Agent* (Chicago, University of Chicago Press, 1939), chap. 8.

[8] Cf. Charles M. Hardin, *The Politics of Agriculture* (Glencoe, Ill., The Free Press, 1952), p. 30.

The relationship of the county government to the extension program varies from state to state, and sometimes even from county to county within a particular state, being dependent upon state laws and administrative agreements between the state extension services and local sponsoring agencies.[9] County extension agents—agricultural, home-demonstration, and 4-H Club—are appointed at the local level subject to approval by the state and federal extension services. Authority for making the local appointment most commonly rests with the county governing body or some other county government agency. However, where there is farm-organization sponsorship, the sponsoring organization may appoint and supervise the extension agents or share in their appointment and supervision.[10] In most Illinois counties farm organizations for many years constituted the sole sponsoring agencies at the local level, with the governing boards of those organizations serving as local participants in the appointment of extension agents and the county government having no part, financial or otherwise, in the extension program.[11] This plan, however, failed to gain widespread acceptance elsewhere and is now in the process of modification in Illinois.[12] Throughout the country at large, governmental sponsorship of extension work at the county level is far more widespread than nongovernmental and is continuing to gain ground. As data in the following paragraph will indicate, all but a very small percentage of the funds currently expended on the program are derived from governmental sources.

As of 1952 the co-operative extension service had in its employ a total of 12,657 professional workers. Of this number, 64 were in the federal service, 2,994 were employed in the state extension services, and 9,599 manned the county extension offices. During fiscal 1952 total expenditures for the extension program amounted to approximately $78,800,000. A breakdown for the preceding year indicates that 42.2 per cent of all extension funds was provided by the United States government, 31.9 per cent by the states, 22.9 per cent by the counties, and 3 per cent by farmers' organizations. Of the funds thus provided, 1.6 per cent was spent *by* the Federal Extension Service for its own operation, 31.9 per cent by the state services, and 66.5 per cent by the county extension offices. Thus, it appears that although local agencies provided only one fourth of all exten-

[9] Cf. Baker, *op. cit.*, p. 127.

[10] No minimum qualifications for county agents have been fixed as a condition for granting federal aid, but the Federal Extension Service has consistently encouraged the state services to maintain high personnel standards. Cf. *ibid.*, pp. 163-164.

[11] Illinois farm advisers were sponsored by county farm bureaus and home advisers by county home bureaus, with both farm and home advisers handling 4-H Club work either directly or through special youth assistants.

[12] See below, "Extension and the Farm Bureau."

sion funds, two thirds of the total funds were expended in direct support of activities at the county level.[13]

THE COUNTY AGENT [14]

The county agent is the representative in his county of the state agricultural college and the United States Department of Agriculture. Usually he is a native of the state, but not of the county, in which he serves; a graduate of the state agricultural college; the type of person who likes people and enjoys working with them; and active in community affairs, both rural and urban.[15] The primary duty of the county agent consists in advising and assisting the farmers of his county with respect to farm methods and problems. To this end he conducts farm demonstrations and, in his office, at meetings, and on the farms, answers innumerable questions. As a liaison man between the farmers and the federal and state extension services, it is the duty of the agent to make available to farmers knowledge obtained from agricultural research, and to bring farm problems to the attention of the agricultural college. When questions are presented to which the agent does not have answers immediately at hand, the answers frequently can be obtained, and are obtained, from state extension specialists, from the agricultural experiment station operated in connection with the college of agriculture, or from some other state or federal agency.[16]

In the day-by-day performance of their duties, county agents carry on a wide variety of activities. Though their over-all programs have much in common throughout the nation, the points of emphasis naturally vary from state to state and from county to county, depending upon the type of farming that predominates therein. County agents seek, by every practicable means, to assist farmers in increasing their production of livestock, poultry and eggs, field crops, vegetables, and fruits, and in improving the

[13] United States Department of Agriculture, *Report of Coöperative Extension Work in Agriculture and Home Economics: 1952* (Washington, Government Printing Office, 1953), pp. 58-60. By 1955 the total amount of funds allotted for extension work had risen to a point where it exceeded $100,000,000. Cf. C. M. Ferguson, "Coöperative Extension Work under Recent Legislation," *The Book of the States: 1956-57* (Chicago, Council of State Governments, 1956), pp. 383-388.

[14] A comprehensive account of the county agent, his work, and the relation of his office to the different levels of government is provided in Baker, *op. cit.* For briefer treatment of various aspects of the subject, see W. A. Lloyd, "County Agent," in Edward Mowbray Tuttle, ed., *The Book of Rural Life* (Chicago, Bellows-Durham Co., 1925), Vol. III, pp. 1396-1403; Neil M. Clark, "Grassroots Bureaucrat," *Saturday Evening Post,* Vol. CCXVI, No. 17, pp. 26, 69-70, 72 (October 23, 1943); R. W. Trullinger, "Where County Agents Get Their Facts," *The County Officer,* Vol. XV, No. 6, pp. 18-24 (September, 1950); R. E. Carter, "Your County Agent," *ibid.,* No. 8, pp. 4-7, 28 (November, 1950); Frank L. Ballard, "County Agents: A Record of Achievement," *ibid.,* Vol. XVI, pp. 47-52 (February, 1951).

[15] Cf. Baker, *op. cit.,* p. 159.

[16] Cf. Trullinger, *loc. cit.*

quality of their products. They encourage the introduction of new and improved types of seeds developed by agricultural experiment stations and seedsmen. They are constantly on the lookout for the outbreak of plant or livestock diseases or insect infestations, and aid in the suppression of such outbreaks when they occur. They give instruction and demonstrations in farming methods, soil treatment, weed control, soil conservation techniques, fertilizer practices, pasture improvement, and livestock feeding. They spearhead programs to increase milk production, to safeguard the safety of the milk supply through immunization of dairy herds from brucellosis (Bang's disease) and tuberculosis, and to improve beef and dairy herds through artificial insemination.[17] In the matter of marketing, one of the most important services of county agents has been their assistance in the development of co-operative marketing programs through which "groups of local farmers producing the same commodity are encouraged to work together to improve their marketing facilities." These "range from sheep and wool growers' associations and small dairy coöperatives to large coöperative marketing organizations including big dairy coöperatives, tobacco auctions, grain elevators, fruit and vegetable growers' marketing associations and many others."[18] Since the 1930's county agents have been called upon to play an important role in the local administration of various production-control and soil-conservation programs of the federal government; and they participated actively in the program of land-use planning conducted during the late 1930's and early 1940's under the sponsorship of the United States Department of Agriculture and the state agricultural colleges.[19]

But activities of the county agent are by no means confined to matters of agricultural production and marketing. Professor Wallace Ogg has suggested that co-operative extension is concerned with three areas of education: (1) education for making a living, (2) education for living in the home, and (3) education for living as citizens in a democratic society.[20] County extension agents—agricultural, home-demonstration, and 4-H Club—are faced therefore, in addition to their duties of providing education in

[17] Cf. Carter, *loc. cit.*

[18] *Ibid.*, pp. 6, 7.

[19] With respect to the latter program, see United States Bureau of Agricultural Economics, *County Land Use Planning* (Washington, Government Printing Office, 1940), prepared in co-operation with other agencies of the Department of Agriculture; United States Department of Agriculture, *Land Use Planning under Way* (Washington, 1940); Ellery A. Foster and Harold A. Vogel, "Coöperative Land Use Planning: A New Development in Democracy," in *Yearbook of Agriculture: Farmers in a Changing World* (Washington, U. S. Department of Agriculture, 1940), pp. 1138-1156; Leon Wolcott, "National Land-use Programs and the Local Governments," *National Municipal Review,* Vol. XXVIII, pp. 111-119 (February, 1939); John D. Lewis, "Democratic Planning in Agriculture," *American Political Science Review,* Vol. XXXV, pp. 232-249, 454-469 (April, June, 1941).

[20] Wallace E. Ogg, "The Coöperative Extension Service in Today's World," *State Government,* Vol. XXV, pp. 211-215 (September, 1952).

the first and second of these categories, with responsibility for civic training. Thus, we find county agents assisting in the development in rural communities of social and recreational activities, community beautification, and various other programs.[21] In a world wherein our relations with other nations are becoming of ever increasing importance, some state extension services have organized programs of adult education in international affairs.[22] Health-education programs have been inaugurated in some rural communities to disseminate information concerning cancer, heart disease, tuberculosis, and other major diseases, and means of combating them. And other programs of civic and community education, in wide variety, are conducted by the extension service in various states and counties.

Teaching techniques employed by present-day county agents are as varied as the subject matter of their educational programs. Individual farmers are counseled through visits to their farms and through answers to inquiries brought to the county extension office or transmitted by telephone. Group instruction is given at public meetings, frequently with the aid of filmstrips or motion pictures and through practical demonstrations. Printed materials, such as bulletins and circulars published by the Department of Agriculture and the state experiment stations and extension services, are distributed. And newspaper stories, radio, and television may be used in an effort to "put across" the extension program to the rural population.[23]

THE HOME-DEMONSTRATION AGENT

The work of the home-demonstration agent is similar to that of the county agricultural agent, save for the fact that its primary concern is not with the problems of farmers and farm boys but with those of farm wives and girls. The home-demonstration agent ordinarily is a college graduate with a bachelor of science degree in home economics. In addition to home economics, her academic training has often included courses in other subjects selected particularly with a view to fitting her for home-demonstration work, for example, dairying, landscaping, poultry management, gardening, and extension methods. Like the agricultural agent she usually has grown up on a farm or has had experience working with rural people prior to becoming an agent. Frequently she has had teaching experience in rural schools.[24]

Home-demonstration agents seek to assist farm women in improving

[21] Carter, *loc. cit.*

[22] Ogg, *loc. cit.*

[23] The various teaching methods and their relative values are discussed in Brunner and Yang, *op. cit.*, chap. 8.

[24] United States Department of Agriculture, *The Home Demonstration Agent* (Washington, Government Printing Office, 1946), p. 5.

their homes and home living. They provide advice and instruction concerning food selection and preparation; canning and preservation of fruits and vegetables; the nutritional value of different foods and the balancing of diets; textiles, sewing, and the operation and care of sewing machines; the care, repair, and remodeling of clothing; household sanitation; child care; home and community recreation; improved methods of gardening and poultry raising; and a wide variety of related subjects. In addition, they assist in the organization and work of home-demonstration clubs composed of farm women; are responsible for girls' club work where there is no special 4-H Club agent; and work with the agricultural agents on numerous projects of civic and health education. On the more strictly cultural side they encourage good reading, often through special reading courses conducted by home-demonstration clubs, and sometimes organize study courses in music and art appreciation.[25]

In carrying on her educational activities the home-demonstration agent, like the agricultural agent, employs many different methods of reaching farm people, both individually and in groups. She has numerous callers at her office, gives information over the telephone, answers inquiries by mail, visits farm homes, conducts public meetings and demonstrations, works with women's and girls' clubs, and sends out published materials. In 1949, according to Madge J. Reese of the Federal Extension Service, the average home-demonstration agent worked with 17 adult home-demonstration groups and with 312 girls in 4-H Clubs; made 267 farm or home visits; conferred with 521 office visitors; answered 641 telephone calls; prepared 95 news articles and stories for the press; broadcast or prepared 12 radio programs; distributed 2,876 bulletins; conducted 147 demonstration meetings; participated in 67 other extension meetings; and engaged in various other activities, many of them not readily measurable on a numerical basis. Through such widely varied activities in rural communities, home-demonstration agents and their assistants make a genuine contribution to improving the economic, social, and spiritual well-being of farm families.[26]

4-H CLUB WORK

A major aspect of county extension programs is the educational work with rural youth conducted through 4-H Clubs.[27] As previously indicated,

[25] *Ibid.*, pp. 6-27; Ball, *op. cit.*, Vol. II, p. 786; Florence E. Ward, "Home Demonstration Work," in Tuttle, *op. cit.*, Vol. V, pp. 2607-2615; Madge J. Reese, "Home Demonstration Work: Education for Living," *The County Officer,* Vol. XV, No. 3, pp. 12-17, 27, 29 (July, 1950).

[26] Reese, *loc. cit.*

[27] The following account draws heavily upon Gertrude L. Warren, *Organization of 4-H Club Work: A Guide for Local Leaders,* rev. ed. (Washington, U. S. Department of Agriculture, 1948). See also, Gertrude L. Warren, "4-H Clubs Build the Citizens of Tomorrow," *The County Officer,* Vol. XV, No. 2, pp. 16-20, 25-28 (May, 1950); Fern Shipley, "In 4-H You Build Citizenship," *ibid.*, Vol. XVIII, pp. 236-239

these clubs are supervised in their organization and operation by county extension agents—by special 4-H Club agents where such are provided but in the great majority of the counties by the agricultural and home-demonstration agents. For each club there is a local "leader"—usually a public-spirited man or woman of the community who is interested in young people and is willing to give generously of time and energy in attending club meetings, supplying advice and instruction to members, and guiding the club's activities in general. Ordinarily there is also organized within each county a 4-H Club council or sponsoring committee which studies needs on a county-wide basis and aids in the over-all planning of club activities.

Any rural boy or girl within the age limits set by his state extension service, who is able to equip himself to carry on a demonstration of some better farming or homemaking practice, is eligible for membership in a 4-H Club. The usual age limits are ten and twenty years. A few clubs, with the unanimous consent of their members, have established nominal dues; but ordinarily the only price of membership is the effort to produce a piece of work that will demonstrate an improved method in agriculture or homemaking. Some clubs are composed of boys and girls doing one particular kind of work; but in other instances the club is a community organization to which all eligible boys and girls may belong, with each selecting the line of work that he or she wishes to pursue. Each club chooses its own officers, such as president, vice-president, secretary, treasurer, and news reporter, and establishes whatever committees are deemed appropriate.

The educational objectives of 4-H Club work have been summarized as follows: [28]

1. To help rural boys and girls to develop desirable ideals and standards for farming, homemaking, community life, and citizenship, and a sense of responsibility for their attainment.
2. To afford rural boys and girls technical instruction in farming and homemaking, that they may acquire skill and understanding in these fields and a clearer vision of agriculture as a basic industry, and of homemaking as a worthy occupation.
3. To provide rural boys and girls an opportunity to "learn by doing" through conducting certain farm and home enterprises, and demonstrating to others what they have learned.
4. To teach rural boys and girls the value of research, and to develop in them a scientific attitude toward the problems of the farm and the home.

(October, 1953); and United States Department of Agriculture, *The Home Demonstration Agent,* pp. 16-19. The clubs take their names from the four "H words" contained in the pledge required of members: "I pledge my Head to clearer thinking, my Heart to greater loyalty, my Hands to larger service, and my Health to better living for my club, my community, and my country."

[28] Warren, *Organization of 4-H Club Work,* p. 2.

5. To train rural boys and girls in coöperative action to the end that they may increase their accomplishments and, through associated efforts, better assist in solving rural problems.
6. To develop in rural boys and girls habits of healthful living, to provide them with information and direction in the intelligent use of leisure, and to arouse in them worthy ambitions and a desire to continue to learn, in order that they may live fuller and richer lives.
7. To teach and to demonstrate to rural boys and girls methods designed to improve practices in agriculture and homemaking, to the end that farm incomes may be increased, standards of living improved, and the satisfactions of farm life enhanced.

Club activities take a variety of forms. Regular meetings are held at stated intervals, in many instances monthly. At these meetings members plan their programs, discuss the projects of individual members, receive from local leaders and extension agents advice and instruction on farming and homemaking problems, and enjoy a social good time. Recreational activities, in addition to those in connection with club meetings, often include tours, hikes, and picnics, and perhaps a week or two at a summer camp. A central feature in 4-H Club work is the special project selected and carried on by each club member. These projects are extremely varied in nature. For a boy a project may consist, for example, of growing a plot of corn, cotton, or some other crop; raising a pig, a calf, or a flock of poultry; growing a garden; or operating and repairing farm machinery. Girls' projects include such activities as the planning and preparation of meals; making of clothing; keeping personal accounts; poultry care; and vegetable and landscape gardening. Projects are carried on under the direction of the club leader and the general supervision of the extension agent. Each club member, insofar as practicable, keeps a record of costs and labor in connection with his project, explains his work to other members at club meetings, prepares an exhibit as part of an annual exhibition of club work, and writes a final report.

Four-H Clubs are widely recognized as educational and character-building agencies of major importance among rural youth. Indeed, so outstanding has been the success of 4-H Club work in rural and semirural areas that clubs have now been organized in a number of strictly urban communities with projects in handicrafts, electricity, and the like replacing those that can be conducted only on farms. At present, more than 80,000 4-H Clubs are in existence in the United States, with a total membership of more than 2,000,000 boys and girls, and the demand for club work is growing each year.[29]

[29] United States Department of Agriculture, *Report of Coöperative Extension Work in Agriculture and Home Economics: 1952*, p. 51; Shipley, *loc. cit.*

EXTENSION AND THE FARM BUREAU[30]

As observed at earlier points in this discussion, sponsorship of agricultural extension at the local level in some instances is provided by farm organizations which are essentially private, or at most only quasi-public, in character. Though these organizations have long included some "county agricultural committees," "county extension associations," and the like, by far the most common form of farm-organization sponsorship in the past has been that provided through county farm bureaus.[31] Farm-bureau sponsorship has been the target of considerable criticism from the early years of the extension program. It seems appropriate, therefore, in concluding our consideration of agricultural extension, to comment briefly upon the farm-bureau movement, the problems arising from farm-bureau participation in extension work, and the present status of the extension-farm-bureau relationship.

Farm bureaus or equivalent organizations under other names, having as their purpose the advancement of sound farm management, were established in a few counties prior to enactment of the Smith-Lever Law. After passage of the federal legislation the establishment of such organizations, with promotion of extension education as their objective, was encouraged by the Department of Agriculture on the ground that the extension program could be administered more effectively through organized farm groups than by seeking to reach 2,000 or more farmers in the average county through individual farm visits and poorly attended meetings.[32] The number of county organizations multiplied rapidly as a result of this encouragement, and the name *farm bureau* came to be widely adopted. Many states, in their legislation implementing the federal law, specifically designated the local farm bureau as the sponsoring agency for extension at the county level; and in others bureau sponsorship was established without specific statutory authorization.

Soon, however, the farm bureaus, originally strictly local organizations, began to associate themselves in federations, both state and national. In every state some or all of the county bureaus eventually were organized into a state farm-bureau federation; and in 1920 there was established at

[30] In the preparation of this section the author benefited from the counsel and assistance of Professor William J. Block of The Citadel, whose doctoral dissertation was concerned with the extension-farm-bureau relationship—William J. Block, "The Separation of the Farm Bureau and the Extension Service as a Political Issue" (Unpublished Ph.D. thesis, University of Illinois, 1956). Gratitude for the supplying of helpful data is extended also to Professor William G. Kammlade, associate director of Extension Service in Agriculture and Home Economics at the University of Illinois.

[31] In 1948 extension work in Missouri's 114 counties was sponsored by 58 county farm bureaus, 31 county extension associations, 23 Missouri Farmers' Associations, one Grange, and one soil-improvement association. See H. W. Gilbertson, *Extension-Farm Bureau Relationships, 1948* (Washington, U. S. Department of Agriculture, 1949), p. 11, mimeo.

[32] Cf. Brunner and Yang, *op. cit.*, pp. 65-67.

the national level the American Farm Bureau Federation, with which all 48 state federations are now affiliated.[33] At the same time that the county bureaus were thus joining in the formation of a central organization which was to become nationwide in extent, many of them began to engage in various commercial and legislative activities.[34] Some undertook the operation of purchasing or marketing co-operatives through which member farmers might buy supplies or sell their products; and the farm-bureau federations soon came to be recognized generally, both in state capitals and in Washington, as exerting a powerful influence in the shaping of farm legislation.

This assumption of functions markedly different from their original activities of an educational nature brought down upon the farm bureaus sharp criticism of their fitness to serve as sponsors for agricultural extension—criticism that has continued to the present time.[35] Censure of the extension-farm-bureau relationship has centered in some measure in rival farm organizations, such as the National Grange and the Farmers' Union, but finds proponents also among individual farmers, businessmen, extension officials, and students of government.[36] Critics allege that, under farm-bureau sponsorship, county agents are inclined to give priority to the serving of bureau members and to neglect nonmember farmers of the county. Furthermore, it is argued by merchants and others that allocation of public funds to county farm bureaus engaged in commercial activities amounts to governmental subsidization of a nongovernmental organization operating in competition with private enterprise.

In view of these criticisms, an agreement was entered into in 1921 between the United States Department of Agriculture and the American Farm Bureau Federation defining the relationships between agricultural extension and its farm-bureau sponsors and the proper field of activity of county extension agents. Known as the True-Howard agreement and constituting, in a sense, a code of ethics, this instrument stipulated that

[33] The last of the state federations to be established was that of Rhode Island, which was organized in 1952 and affiliated with the American Farm Bureau Federation in 1953. Some of the state organizations have official titles deviating somewhat from the usual terminology of "state farm-bureau federation," the Illinois federation, for example, being known as the Illinois Agricultural Association, and that of Rhode Island as the Rhode Island Association of Farmers.

[34] More than two thirds of the nation's counties were reported in the mid-1940's as having farm bureaus. See R. B. Corbett, "Know Your Farm Bureau," *Nation's Agriculture,* Vol. XXII, No. 7, pp. 7-8 (July-August, 1947). Total farm bureau membership for 1953 exceeded 1,500,000 families—*Annual Report of the Secretary of the American Farm Bureau Federation* (Chicago, 1953).

[35] The extent of bureau participation in noneducational activities varies widely. In a few states county bureaus apparently carry on no commercial or legislative activities, confining themselves to educational work. See Gilbertson, *op. cit.,* p. 10.

[36] Cf. Hardin, *op. cit.,* chap. 3; Brunner and Yang, *op. cit.,* pp. 69-71; Baker, *op. cit.,* pp. 210-212; Grant McConnell, *The Decline of Agrarian Democracy* (Berkeley, University of California Press, 1953), *passim.*

county agents must perform service for all farm people of the county, whether members of the farm bureau or not, and that they must not solicit bureau memberships, engage in commercial activities of the bureau, or take part in any other bureau activities outside their duties as extension agents.[37] The substance of this agreement was embodied in a regulation issued by the Secretary of Agriculture in 1922.

Notwithstanding the True-Howard agreement and the implementing departmental order, criticism of the extension-farm-bureau tie continued; and some states amended their statutes to eliminate provision for farm-bureau sponsorship of the extension program. In 1948 a joint committee of the Department of Agriculture and the Association of Land-Grant Colleges and Universities recommended discontinuance of all legal connections between the extension service and the farm bureau or other farm organizations. This committee recognized the public service that had been rendered by farm bureaus in fostering extension work and invited their continued interest, along with that of other organized groups of farmers, in the extension program. Furthermore, the committee noted that where the True-Howard agreement had been strictly observed, no specific relationship difficulties between farm bureau and extension service had arisen. Emphasis was placed, however, on the belief of other farm organizations that co-operative arrangements between county extension units and the farm bureau give, or at least appear to give, an advantage to this one farm organization. The official report of the group declared: [38]

> This committee expresses its conviction that it is not sound public policy for extension to give preferred service to any farm organization or to be in a position of being charged with such actions. The committee is further convinced that it would be in the public interest for any formal operating relationships between the Extension Service and any general farm organization such as the Farm Bureau to be discontinued at the earliest possible moment.

[37] The prohibition concerning participation in commercial activities does not preclude county agents from giving educational assistance in the organization of co-operatives, as distinguished from participating in their actual management and operation.

[38] Joint Committee of the United States Department of Agriculture and the Association of Land-Grant Colleges and Universities, *Report on Extension Programs, Policies, and Goals* (Washington, Government Printing Office, 1948), pp. 19-20. To this conclusion of the joint committee vigorous dissent was registered by one member, the late H. P. Rusk, then dean of the College of Agriculture of the University of Illinois. Agricultural extension in Illinois had long been conducted under farm-bureau sponsorship, both financial and administrative. Dean Rusk believed that strict adherence to the True-Howard agreement should be required, but he saw "no sound reason for prohibiting formal agreements clearly defining the joint and several responsibilities of the coöperating parties, their rights and limitations." Noting the substantial contributions of money made by Illinois county farm and home bureaus for the support of extension work, he expressed the conviction "that extension work cannot be of maximum effectiveness and influence without some type of coöperating organization at the local level" and "that the local organization that contributes to the financial support of this program is much more effective than the merely advisory organizations." For Dean Rusk's dissenting statement, see *ibid.*, pp. 23-24.

This report was subsequently given formal approval by the Association of Land-Grant Colleges and Universities, and several additional states amended their statutes to dissolve or weaken the tie between extension and the farm bureau. In some instances local organizations known as county agricultural extension councils were established to be supported from county appropriations and to supplant the county farm bureaus as extension sponsors. Continued concern over the problem was evidenced in 1950 by the introduction in Congress of proposed legislation which, had it been enacted, would have withheld federal aid for extension work from states where, by either law or informal agreement, the farm bureau or any other association of farmers is established as the official sponsoring agency.[39]

Finally, in 1954, a directive was issued by the Secretary of Agriculture prohibiting employees of the Department of Agriculture from accepting "the use of free office space or contributions for salary or traveling expense from any general or specialized organization of farmers."[40] Since county agricultural agents, in their federal capacity, are employees of the department, and since some farm bureaus were still furnishing agents with office space in bureau buildings or paying a portion of their salaries, the secretary's directive was a signal for further steps in the direction of severing the extension-farm-bureau relationship. For example, Iowa, long a major-relationship state, enacted a separation law establishing elective county agricultural extension councils to take over from farm bureaus the sponsorship of the extension programs.[41] These extension councils operate as public corporate bodies on funds provided by the county boards of supervisors; and, whereas the farm bureaus used both county tax funds and membership dues in providing local financial support for extension work, such support will now be derived entirely from tax sources. Even in Illinois, where the extension-farm-bureau tie has perhaps been strongest, measures have been taken in the direction of modification. In 1955 the governing boards of Illinois county farm bureaus were officially designated as county extension councils, and arrangements were made for farm-bureau contributions to the salaries of county farm advisers (county agents) and other extension personnel to be channeled through the state extension service rather than paid directly to the employees concerned. And in 1956 the farm-bureau boards were supplanted as official sponsors of the extension program by county

[39] See Hardin, *op. cit.*, p. 43.

[40] U. S. Department of Agriculture, Office of the Secretary, *Memorandum No. 1368: Activities of Department Employees with Relation to General and Specialized Organizations of Farmers* (November 24, 1954).

[41] *Acts and Joint Resolutions of Iowa* (1955), chap. 107. Each county of the state is constituted a county agricultural extension district (except that Pottawattamie County is divided into two districts), and one council member is elected from each township of the district.

agricultural extension councils appointed by the state extension director, but with the farm bureaus continuing their financial participation in the program through contributions to the state extension service.

Whatever the advantages and disadvantages of farm-bureau sponsorship of agricultural extension, the plan has been losing ground for some time, and increasingly so during recent years. As bureau sponsorship declines, the role of the counties in the program, played directly through the county governing bodies or indirectly through specially organized extension councils, becomes correspondingly of greater importance. Some states probably will continue such extension-farm-bureau relationships as are permissible under the 1954 directive. Furthermore, since habits of long standing ordinarily do not change abruptly, the co-operation built up through the years between extension agents and farm-bureau officers is likely, in many instances, to continue at least temporarily on an informal basis. It seems clear, however, that major, formal relationships of the kinds once existing in Illinois, Iowa, Kansas, New York, and a few other states will soon be, if indeed it cannot fairly be said that they already are, a thing of the past.[42]

WEED-CONTROL PROGRAMS

Although county extension work is one of the most widespread, and perhaps the best known, of the local government functions in the agricultural field, it is not the only local service directed toward protecting and promoting the agricultural economy and conserving our natural resources. Among other functions of particular value to farmers are the weed-control activities of local governments. "Weeds steal water, light, and minerals needed by crop plants. They increase the farmer's labor and equipment costs, and lower the quality of his products."[43] The loss to American agriculture from weeds is enormous, probably exceeding the combined losses from insect pests and crop diseases.[44]

Farmers now make considerable use of chemical weed killers, but the older technique of merely cutting weeds before they seed continues to occupy an important place in control activities. Many states have laws requiring landowners to cut noxious weeds on their premises. It is commonly provided that where owners fail to comply with such requirements,

[42] The county farm bureaus that sponsor agricultural extension in Rhode Island confine their activities to extension education and are not federated in a state association. They are to be distinguished from the county organizations comprising the Rhode Island Association of Farmers, which is the state affiliate of the American Farm Bureau Federation.

[43] United States Department of Agriculture, *Report of Coöperative Extension Work in Agriculture and Home Economics: 1950* (Washington, Government Printing Office, 1951), p. 31.

[44] Cf. "Weed Control in Iowa," *Iowa Law Review*, Vol. XXXIV, pp. 348-353 (January, 1949).

the work shall be performed by a designated local official and the cost thereof assessed against the land. Illinois, for example, makes eradication in the event of owner delinquency the duty of a township commissioner of noxious weeds or, in counties which have established weed-control departments, of a county weed-control commissioner.[45] In some states special weed-eradication districts are organized for carrying on control work. The weeds declared to be noxious and made the subject of active eradication campaigns vary from state to state. Commonly included within the list are such hard-to-control weeds as Canadian thistle, Russian knapweed, perennial peppergrass, bindweed, puncture vine, hoary cress, leafy spurge, and barberry.

CONTROL OF PREDATORS

A serious problem of livestock and poultry raising, especially in the more sparsely settled western states, is the danger to flocks and herds from predatory animals.[46] A predatory animal is one which lives by preying upon various species of animals or birds that are beneficial to man's interests.[47] Included among the more common predators are wolves, coyotes, mountain lions, bobcats, and foxes. Every year American farmers and ranchmen incur millions of dollars in losses as a result of the depredations of such animals. Indeed, the value of meat, wool, and fowl destroyed by coyotes alone in the single year of 1943 has been estimated at from $10,000,000 to $15,000,000.[48]

As a means of reducing the hazard from predators, most states have established control programs, and in some of these programs the local governments play a part. Two principal systems of predator control are now in common use: (1) the system of government-paid professional hunters, and (2) the bounty system. The first of these systems involves a governmental program of direct extermination, and the second seeks to encourage private individuals to hunt down and kill predators. According to a recent survey, 8 states employ the professional hunter system exclusively, 22 states the bounty system, and 10 states a combination of the two methods, with only 8 states having no organized program of predator control. In general, most western and southwestern states use state hunters or a combination of the hunter and bounty systems; and the straight

[45] In nontownship counties of the state having no county department, weed commissioners may be appointed by the county governing board to serve within the various road districts.

[46] See Michael Norman, "The War against the Predators," *Outdoor Life,* Vol. CIII, No. 3, pp. 37-39, 125-127 (March, 1949).

[47] Cf. Minnesota Legislative Research Committee, *The Control of Predatory Animals* (St. Paul, Minn., 1952), p. i.

[48] See O. A. Fitzgerald, "Every Hand against Him," *Country Gentleman,* Vol. CXIV, No. 2, pp. 17, 58-59 (February, 1944).

bounty system is most commonly employed in New England and the Midwest. The states without predator control are for the most part in the southeastern group. Professional hunters usually are employed on a straight salary basis. In some instances the salary is paid entirely by the state, but in others, where the control program is operated co-operatively with the United States Fish and Widlife Service, the cost is shared by the federal government. Some bounty states make the entire cost of bounties a charge upon the state treasury; others, however, provide that a part of all of the cost shall be borne by local governmental units. The payment of bounties by local governments in some instances is compulsory under state law, and in others it is optional with the units concerned.[49] The units of local government most commonly involved in bounty payments are the counties and townships, though some states have organized special predatory-animal districts to administer the control programs. In Wyoming, for example, each organized county constitutes a "predatory animal district" under the management of a board of directors elected by the sheep owners of the district.

Local bounty payments in some instances are made from the general funds of the units concerned, and in others they are financed by special taxes upon the livestock and poultry to be protected. Thus, for bounty purposes, South Dakota counties levy a head tax on sheep and cattle; Utah counties an ad valorem tax on sheep and turkeys; and Wyoming counties, for the support of their respective predatory-animal districts, an ad valorem tax on sheep. Of special interest because of their unusual nature are control programs in Michigan and Missouri, patterned somewhat after the system of county agricultural agents, whereby extension trappers and hunters employed by the state instruct farmers and others in the most effective methods of eliminating predators.[50]

THE PROBLEM OF SOIL EROSION

Rural America's most valuable asset, aside from its human resources, is its soil; and conservation of soil productivity is essential not only to the farm population but to the national economy in general. Soil is rendered nonproductive in two principal ways: by depletion of fertility through continued cropping and by actual loss of topsoil through erosion.[51] Of these, erosion is the more spectacular and, ultimately, the more serious. Land that is merely "crop poor" can be restored to productivity, and fairly quickly, by use of commercial fertilizers, the planting of leguminous

[49] *The Control of Predatory Animals*, pp. 1, 26-39.

[50] For a brief description of the Michigan and Missouri programs, see *ibid.*, pp. 5, 40.

[51] Cf. Stuart Chase, *Rich Land, Poor Land* (New York, Whittlesey House, 1936), p. 37.

and other soil-building crops, crop rotation, and other soil-building practices. But so slow is the natural process by which soil is formed from its parent materials—it is believed to require anywhere from 300 to 1,000 years or more to produce a single inch of topsoil—that land from which all the topsoil has been eroded may, for practical purposes, be regarded as permanently ruined.[52] When the country was first opened for settlement, forests, grass, and other natural cover provided adequate protection against erosion; but with the removal of much of this protective cover and the placing of vast areas in cultivation, the soil, in the absence of proper conservation practices, became a ready prey to the two principal eroding forces—water and wind.

The extent to which erosion has already taken place in the United States and the rate at which it is now progressing are nothing short of appalling. A survey of the 1930's indicated that approximately 282,000,000 acres of the country's crop and grazing land had been ruined or badly damaged by erosion; and that another 775,000,000 acres of crop, grazing, forest, and other land had eroded to some extent.[53] Of the 460,000,000 acres of first-class crop land still remaining in the United States, all but about 100,000,000 acres is susceptible to damage by erosion, waterlogging, and floods. Each year we are losing around half a million acres of land through needless erosion and waterlogging, with an even larger acreage being damaged in lesser degree.[54] Available measurements indicate that 3,000,000,000 tons or more of solid matter is washed annually from American fields and pastures—some 730,000,000 tons being deposited each year in the Gulf of Mexico by the Mississippi River alone.[55] Wind erosion has been especially devastating at times in the so-called Dust Bowl area centering in western Oklahoma and Kansas and eastern Colorado. In that comparatively dry region soaring grain prices, occasioned by wartime demand or otherwise, recurrently have served as a signal for plowing and planting to wheat thousands of acres of grassland—acres which thereby have become a ready prey to wind erosion. On a single day during a 1934 dust storm, according to one estimate, 300,000,000 tons of rich topsoil was lifted from the Great Plains to be deposited in places where it would cause damage and discomfort.[56] The early 1950's witnessed a series of widespread dust storms affecting portions of Missouri, Nebraska, Wyoming, and Arizona, but working particularly serious havoc in western Texas

[52] Hugh H. Bennett, *Soil Conservation* (New York, McGraw-Hill, 1939), p. 8.

[53] Hugh H. Bennett, *Our American Land: The Story of Its Abuse and Its Conservation*, rev. ed. (Washington, U. S. Department of Agriculture, 1950), p. 4.

[54] H. H. Bennett, *Progress in Soil Conservation* (Washington, U. S. Department of Agriculture, 1950), pp. 1, 2.

[55] Bennett, *Soil Conservation*, p. 9.

[56] Stuart Chase, "When the Crop Lands Go," *Harper's Magazine*, Vol. CLXXIII, pp. 225-233 (August, 1936).

and Oklahoma and parts of Kansas, Colorado, and New Mexico. One such storm in the spring of 1954 deposited an estimated 185,000 tons of dust on Oklahoma City alone.[57] The cost of erosion in diminished soil productivity in the United States amounts annually to hundreds of millions of dollars.[58]

SOIL-CONSERVATION DISTRICTS

Soil conservation has long constituted one of the recognized objectives of extension education. However, the most comprehensive program for erosion prevention and soil conservation yet undertaken in this country is that carried on by local soil-conservation districts in co-operation with the Soil Conservation Service of the United States Department of Agriculture.[59] This program had its inception when, shortly after the creation of the Soil Conservation Service in 1935, the Department of Agriculture drafted and recommended to the states a model enabling act for the establishment of soil-conservation districts. In 1937, 22 states enacted laws following rather closely the provisions of this model, and thereafter the enactment of enabling legislation and the organization of districts proceeded apace. By 1946 every state had enacted a soil-conservation law. In 46 states these statutes provide for the establishment of local soil-conservation districts. New Hampshire's law establishes a single district coterminous with the state, but the state's area has been divided into subdistricts. The Connecticut statute authorizes assistance to individual farmers and voluntary associations, and in practice the program is carried on through work areas, commonly called districts. By 1955 some 2,600 soil-conservation districts had been organized in the various states, embracing approximately 1,400,000,000 acres of land and 4,800,000 farms—90 per cent of all the farms in the country.[60] Most of the districts had qualified for assistance from the Soil Conservation Service; and 1,500,000 farmers and ranchers operating 450,000,000 acres were reported to be

[57] *Time*, Vol. LXIII, No. 13, p. 21 (March 29, 1954).

[58] Cf. Bennett, *Soil Conservation*, p. 11.

[59] An excellent treatise covering all aspects of the program is W. Robert Parks, *Soil Conservation Districts in Action* (Ames, Iowa State College Press, 1952). See also, Hardin, *op. cit.*, chap. 5; Soil Conservation Service, *Soil Conservation Districts for Erosion Control* (Washington, U. S. Department of Agriculture, 1937); Glenn K. Rule, *Soil Conservation Districts in Action on the Land* (Washington, U. S. Department of Agriculture, 1941); Herman Walker, Jr., and W. Robert Parks, "Soil Conservation Districts: Local Democracy in a National Program," *Journal of Politics*, Vol. VIII, pp. 538-549 (November, 1946).

[60] Soil Conservation Service, *Soil Conservation Districts: Status of Organization, by States, Approximate Acreage, and Farms in Organized Districts* (Washington, U. S. Department of Agriculture, 1955), mimeo. Some of the soil-conservation districts reported by the Soil Conservation Service do not meet the requirements of the Census Bureau for classification as separate governmental units, and the bureau's count of districts is therefore somewhat smaller. The data used in the present discussion are those of the Soil Conservation Service.

co-operating actively in district programs.[61] The geographic location of districts in the various states as of 1955 is indicated on the map in Fig. XII.[62] At that time 16 states were completely covered by soil-conservation districts.[63]

Though the organization and powers of soil-conservation districts vary in detail as among the different states, most of the enabling statutes follow at least in some measure the model act of the Department of Agriculture, and the general pattern is everywhere much the same. Local districts usually are established, under the supervision of a state soil-conservation committee,[64] by vote of the owners or occupiers of land within the area concerned.[65] In most instances district boundaries follow county lines, each district embracing one or more counties. In some cases, however, county lines are disregarded and an effort is made to include within a particular district land confronted with a common erosion problem. A district may consist, for example, of a watershed, a type-of-farming area, or an extent-of-erosion area, and thus embrace less than an entire county, or all or parts of several counties. The governing body of each local district is a board of supervisors or directors which in most states consists of five members, three being elected by the farmers of the district and two appointed by the state committee.

The powers of soil-conservation districts ordinarily are of two kinds, districts being authorized (1) to formulate and administer voluntary erosion-control projects and (2) to adopt compulsory land-use regulations. In practice, most districts have confined themselves to exercising powers of the first type, under which erosion-control programs are put into effect through co-operative agreements between the district and its farmers. Each district, through its board of supervisors, enters into a "memorandum of understanding" with the United States Department of Agriculture concerning the district's program and work plan as a whole and the receiving of federal assistance. Agreements are then made between the district and individual landowners and occupiers with regard to erosion-control work and soil-conservation practices on their respective farms.[66] Practices

[61] Donald A. Williams, "Soil Conservation Service," *The Book of the States: 1956-57* (Chicago, Council of State Governments, 1956), pp. 378-382.

[62] Shown on the map, in addition to soil-conservation districts, are some 20 other conservation districts—principally Montana grass-conservation districts—being assisted by the Soil Conservation Service.

[63] Alabama, Arkansas, Connecticut, Delaware, Iowa, Kansas, Kentucky, Massachusetts, Mississippi, Nebraska, New Hampshire, New Jersey, North Carolina, Rhode Island, South Carolina, and Vermont.

[64] This committee often includes in its membership the principal state agricultural officer and the director of the state's agricultural experiment station.

[65] Some states restrict voting on district matters to land*owners,* while others extend the voting privilege to all occupiers of land, whether owners or tenants.

[66] H. H. Bennett, "The Soil Conservation Service: Organization and Operations," *The Book of the States: 1948-49* (Chicago, Council of State Governments, 1948), pp. 289-300.

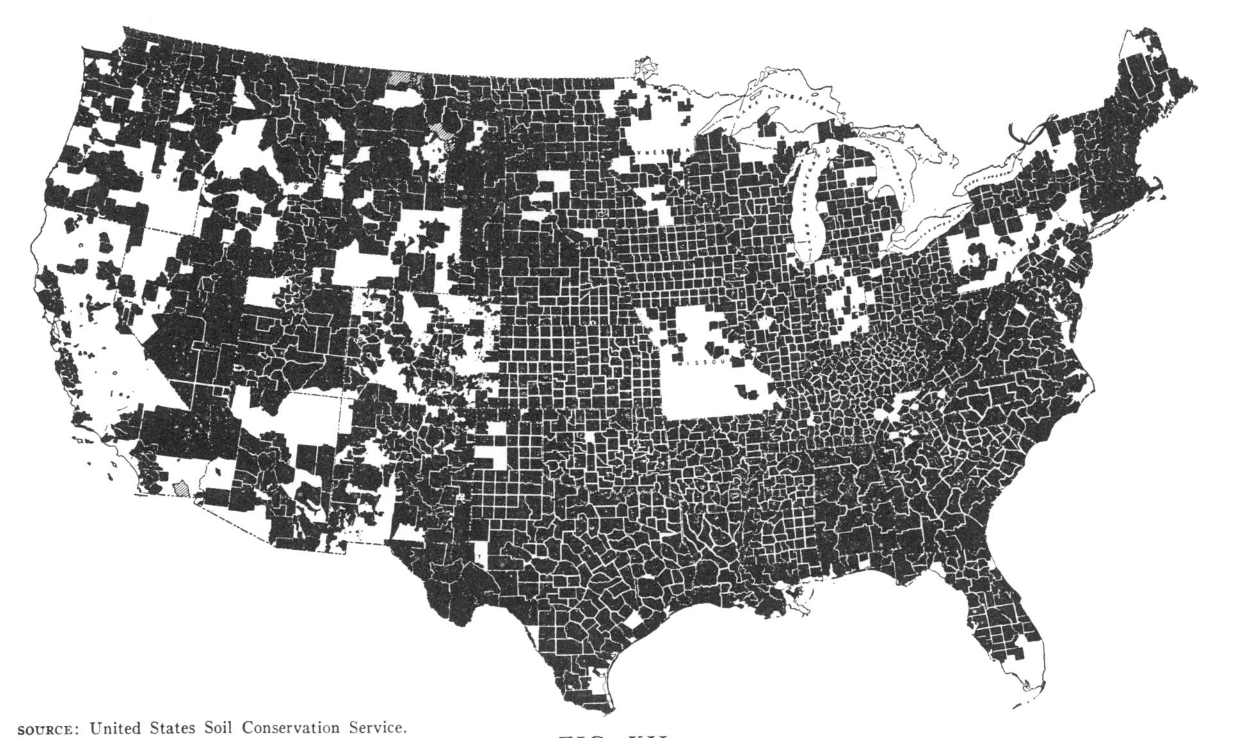

SOURCE: United States Soil Conservation Service.

FIG. XII

Soil-Conservation Districts (black) Established as of July 1, 1955 and Other Conservation Districts (shaded) Being Assisted by the Soil Conservation Service

provided for under these agreements include such measures as terracing, contour farming, strip cropping, stubble mulching, tree planting, cover cropping, and pasture and range seeding.[67]

The more drastic power of enacting land-use ordinances can be exercised by the district supervisors only with approval of the landowners or occupiers in a referendum election; but such ordinances, when thus approved, have the effect of law and are enforceable by judicial process.[68] Enacted under police-power authority delegated by state statute, a local land-use regulation may be either positive or negative in nature; "that is, it may command the landowner or occupier to carry out a certain practice on his land or it may command him to refrain from using his land in some specified way."[69] Regulatory ordinances enacted have been of three principal types: (1) sod-land ordinances, (2) blow-land ordinances, and (3) grazing regulations. Sod-land ordinances prohibit the plowing up of sod land unless special permission is granted by the district supervisors. The typical blow-land ordinance provides that if soil is blowing from the land of one owner to that of another, the district board may order the first owner to take appropriate measures, vegetative or mechanical, to check or prevent the blowing; and, in the event that such an order is not complied with, the board may itself perform the necessary work and assess the cost against the offending land. Grazing ordinances limit the number of livestock to be grazed on pasture or range land.[70] Although a large majority of the states empower their soil-conservation districts to impose land-use regulations, in practice little use has been made of this authority.

[67] *Terracing* is the ridging of land on the contour to check water runoff. *Contour farming* involves plowing, planting, cultivating, and harvesting sloping fields on the contour, around hillsides instead of up- and downhill. *Strip cropping* involves planting strips of close-growing plants, such as grass or clover, between alternate strips of cultivated row crops. *Field stripping* is stripping at right angles to the main slope of the land, so that the grass strips will hold water and prevent it from eroding the cultivated crops. *Wind stripping* is stripping at right angles to the prevailing wind. *Stubble mulching* is the practice of leaving grain stubble and straw on the ground to conserve moisture and check erosion, instead of burning such crop residues or plowing them under. Also called subsurface tillage, stubble mulching requires the use of cultivating implements that do not turn the soil upside down. *Cover crops* are legumes or other dense crops grown on cultivated areas at times when there are few other plants to afford protection from wind and water erosion. Explanations of these and other conservation practices are to be found in Bennett, *Our American Land,* pp. 21-27.

[68] Concerning the nature and use of such ordinances, see Parks, *op. cit.,* pp. 147-159; Philip M. O'Brien, Thomas L. Gaston, and Tom Dale, *Land Use Regulation in Soil Conservation Districts* (Washington, U. S. Department of Agriculture, 1947); Stanley W. Voelker, *Land-use Ordinances of Soil Conservation Districts in Colorado* (Fort Collins, Colorado Agricultural and Mechanical College Agricultural Experiment Station, 1952); "Legal Techniques for Promoting Soil Conservation," *Yale Law Journal,* Vol. L, pp. 1056-1070 (April, 1941); Edwin E. Ferguson, "Nation-wide Erosion Control: Soil Conservation Districts and the Power of Land-use Regulation," *Iowa Law Review,* Vol. XXXIV, pp. 166-187 (January, 1949).

[69] Voelker, *op. cit.,* p. 6.

[70] Parks, *op. cit.,* pp. 151-154; Voelker, *op. cit.,* p. 7.

Actually, employment of the power has been confined almost entirely to Colorado, where, at the end of 1951, 13 districts had enacted ordinances, though only half a dozen were still in effect.[71] Outside Colorado, apparently, only two or three districts have adopted land-use regulations.

In its administration and financing the soil-conservation-district program is a co-operative enterprise that involves government at all levels—national, state, and local—and farmers both as individuals and in groups. Soil-conservation districts, though in the nature of public corporate entities, have in most states neither taxing nor borrowing power. Ordinarily, therefore, although district work is carried on under the immediate direction of the district supervisors or managers responsible to them, the necessary labor, materials, and equipment, or the funds for their purchase and hire, must be contributed by local farmers or by federal, state, county, or township agencies. The respective roles of the several agencies involved in the program vary somewhat from state to state and from district to district, but the over-all picture is reasonably uniform.[72] Most important among the federal contributions is the provision of technical assistance in the planning and applying of conservation practices. "The planning and application of measures and practices for conserving the soil of a farm demands knowledge in agronomy, engineering, biology, forestry, hydrology, and other specialized fields." [73] This knowledge is supplied by the United States Soil Conservation Service through its conservationists, farm planners, soil surveyors, and other staff specialists, who advise and assist the local districts. In the early years of the district program the Soil Conservation Service also loaned substantial amounts of equipment to districts and, in some instances, provided them with planting stock, such as trees and shrubs. These forms of federal assistance, however, have, for the most part, now been discontinued.[74]

State contributions to the soil-conservation-district program are principally in the form of appropriations to the state soil-conservation committee for committee expenses and direct assistance to local districts. Funds allotted to the districts are used for such purposes as travel and other expenses of district supervisors; office expense; acquisition, maintenance,

[71] The Colorado experience to 1952 is covered fully in Voelker, *op. cit.* District blow-land ordinances were rendered unnecessary in Colorado by a general statute of 1951 imposing this type of land-use regulation on a state-wide basis and making boards of county commissioners responsible for its local administration (*ibid.*, p. 52). Concerning subsequent developments, legislative and otherwise, see Paul W. Swisher, "The Wind Erosion Program in Colorado," *State Government,* Vol. XXVII, pp. 180-182 (September, 1954).

[72] The following description of federal, state, and local government roles is based on Parks, *Soil Conservation Districts in Action.*

[73] *Ibid.*, p. 17.

[74] *Ibid.*, pp. 15-19. An indirect form of federal subsidization of district activities consists of agricultural conservation payments to farmers by the Production and Marketing Administration for conservation practices carried on under district auspices (*ibid.*, pp. 19-24).

and operation of equipment; services of contractors; planting materials; and the hiring of laborers to assist landowners and occupiers with conservation work. In addition to direct appropriations of money for district support, some state contribution to the program is made in the form of services and assistance rendered to districts by various state administrative agencies—especially by the state extension services but frequently also by other agencies, such as state highway departments, forestry departments, and wildlife commissions. County and township contributions take a variety of forms. Some local governments make direct appropriations of funds for district operations. Services of certain county officials, such as the highway engineer and the county attorney, are sometimes made available to districts; and a number of counties provide free office space for district headquarters and for local Soil Conservation Service technicians. State and local financial assistance to soil-conservation districts, though not unimportant, is small in comparison with federal contributions. A few districts perform erosion-control work with highway machinery rented from state or county agencies or loaned by such agencies to the district authorities; but such arrangements are not common, in part because public highway machinery is often sorely needed for road work at the very times of year when conservation work is to be done. Some machinery is district-owned, but taking the country as a whole, all but a very small part of the mechanical work of soil-conservation districts is performed under contract with equipment owned by private operators.[75]

The soil-conservation-district movement has been one of the most significant developments in recent agricultural history. Through the district program governments at all levels have co-operated with each other and with lay citizens in an organized attack on a peril of nation-wide importance—erosion of America's soil. Although the program is still too young to permit final appraisal of its value, its achievements already have been substantial, and it has demonstrated promising potentialities for future worth.[76]

PUBLIC-LAND MANAGEMENT

Counties, townships, and other local governments sometimes own or administer public lands acquired by purchase or through tax forfeiture and held for forestry or other purposes. Land management as a function of state and local government has come to be of particular importance in the Lake states of Michigan, Minnesota, and Wisconsin, where, during the past quarter century, a vast new public domain has developed as the result of tax delinquency. In these states, during the late 1920's and the

[75] *Ibid.*, pp. 77-87, 167-170.
[76] Cf. *ibid.*, pp. 223-224.

1930's, more than 18,000,000 acres of land, principally in the northern cutover regions, reverted to the states and counties for nonpayment of taxes; and, of this area, some 14,000,000 acres remained in public ownership in the early 1950's.[77]

In Michigan, tax-reverted lands are owned and administered primarily by the state. However, the state department of conservation is empowered by law to convey such lands for a nominal consideration to local governmental units to be used for public purposes, such as forests, parks, and playgrounds; and some conveyances have been made under this authority to counties, townships, and school districts. Forfeited lands in Minnesota are owned by the state, but extensive acreage has been turned over to the counties for management or sale, with a number of counties having appointed county land commissioners to handle sales work. In Wisconsin title to tax-forfeited lands vests in the counties; and the counties of that state today own some 3,000,000 acres of land thus acquired, most of it being administered as county forest.[78] Many Wisconsin counties have established special committees of their governing boards to deal with forestry management, and several have appointed full- or part-time agents to work under the county boards or board committees in county land administration.

PARKS AND FORESTS

Public parks and forests combine in varying degree recreational facilities and conservation objectives. Although the nomenclature employed is not uniform, the term *park* ordinarily denotes an area designed primarily for recreation, and a *forest*, notwithstanding that it may serve recreational purposes, is administered primarily with a view to conservation of natural resources. In general, though there are numerous exceptions, a forest is likely to include more extensive acreage than a park.

In a survey conducted by the National Park Service in co-operation with the American Institute of Park Executives and the National Recreation Association, reports on county parks, as of 1940, were received from 152 counties, which together administered 779 park properties with an aggregate area of almost 200,000 acres. Some additional counties undoubtedly were operating parks at the time of the survey, and the total acreage in county parks is known to have increased since that date. California, Michigan, and Wisconsin are among the states having county parks

[77] These data and the discussion in the following paragraph are based on the admirable study made by Raleigh Barlowe, *Administration of Tax-reverted Lands in the Lake States* (East Lansing, Michigan State College Agricultural Experiment Station, 1951).

[78] See below, "Parks and Forests."

in largest numbers. Though some county parks are located within municipalities, it is probable that more than two thirds of the total number are outside city limits. Many county parks are equipped with one or more types of recreational facilities, such as picnic areas, camping grounds, tennis courts, softball diamonds, baseball diamonds, horseshoe courts, and shuffleboard courts. County park management in some instances is directly in the hands of the county governing body, and in others it is a responsibility of a special park board or other agency.[79] Some parks in rural areas, including a number of those usually classed in the county category, are administered and financed by special park or forest-preserve districts; and rural parks are occasionally maintained by townships.

Many states now authorize the establishment of county forests, in some instances by land purchase, in others by setting aside tax-reverted lands, and in still others by either of these means. Though county forests frequently have picnic and camping grounds, and some are the sites of 4-H camps and other recreational facilities, their chief objective ordinarily is management of the land in accordance with forestry principles. Those principles are commonly understood to include, for example, the thinning of young stands of timber, the limiting of harvest cutting to approximately the growth being produced, the making of cuttings in a manner to facilitate natural re-establishment of forest on cutover areas, and the planting of areas not reforested by nature.[80]

Indiana, Kentucky, Michigan, New York, and the Carolinas are among the states having one or more county forests.[81] Several Minnesota counties administer as "county memorial forests" tracts of state-owned forest land acquired through tax forfeiture.[82] It is in Wisconsin, however, that county forestry has been most extensively developed, some 2,000,000 acres of tax-reverted lands in that state having been set aside as forests in 27 counties.[83] An important factor in promoting development of the Wisconsin program has been the element of state financial assistance. County forest lands are exempt from property taxes but nonetheless are entitled

[79] National Recreation Association, *Municipal and County Parks in the United States: 1940* (New York, 1942), p. 47; National Recreation Association, *Recreation and Park Yearbook: A Review of Local and County Recreation and Park Developments, 1900-1950*, Midcentury Edition (New York, 1951), pp. 13, 20.

[80] Cf. J. H. Allison, "County Forestry in Minnesota and Wisconsin," *The Conservation Volunteer*, publication of the Minnesota Department of Conservation, Vol. XII, No. 70, pp. 32-38 (May-June, 1949).

[81] See Lawrence L. Durisch and Hershal L. Macon, *Upon Its Own Resources: Conservation and State Administration* (University, University of Alabama Press, 1951), pp. 47-48; Barlowe, *op. cit.*, p. 23; M. H. Satterfield, "The Growth of County Functions since 1930," *Journal of Politics*, Vol. III, pp. 76-88 (February, 1941); Kenneth L. Schellie, "County Forest Program in Indiana," *State Government*, Vol. XX, pp. 115, 132 (April, 1947).

[82] Allison, *loc. cit.*

[83] Cf. F. G. Wilson, "County Forests of Wisconsin," *State Government*, Vol. XX, pp. 116-117 (April, 1947); Barlowe, *op. cit.*, p. 43.

to entry under the state's Forest Crop Law. Privately owned land entered under this statute pays on standing timber an annual tax of only 10 cents per acre—an amount considerably less than the usual property levy—and on timber, when harvested, a severance tax of 10 per cent of the stumpage value. To replace property-tax losses, the state makes annual payments to local governments of 10 cents per acre for all forest land, both private and county, entered under the law, the counties receiving 20 per cent of these payments and the townships and school districts 40 per cent each. In addition to sharing in these tax-replacement payments, Wisconsin counties, under the state's County Forest Reserve Law, receive an annual grant from the state of 10 cents per acre for their own lands entered under the forest-crop statute for use in forest management and improvement. In return for this grant, counties are required to pay to the state, as a severance tax, 50 per cent of the stumpage value of all timber harvested from their forest reserves.[84]

The major part of the acreage in Wisconsin's county forests has now been entered under the Forest Crop Law; and the inducements offered by that statute and the County Forest Reserve Law have effectively encouraged counties to extend their forest holdings and to practice scientific forestry management. Most of the counties with forests have purchased special equipment for their forestry crews, and several have engaged in forest road and dam-building projects. Under authority to purchase forest land and exchange other county-owned land to consolidate forest holdings, some have carried on land-purchase programs and sponsored the removal of isolated settlers. To improve timber stands, all of the counties have engaged in planting programs, and two have established county nurseries. In several instances substantial profit already has been enjoyed from timber sales. Most of the counties, in fact, now harvest some stumpage almost every year; and all the county forests promise eventually to provide a valuable source of local revenue.[85]

Though counties lead other units of local government in public forest acreage, numerous public forests in rural areas are owned or administered by towns, townships, and school districts. Many Massachusetts towns, for instance, have town forests variously acquired by gift, purchase, tax forfeiture, and other means.[86] And in Michigan and Minnesota several hundred school districts own or administer forest lands.[87]

[84] Barlowe, *op. cit.*, pp. 43-44. See also, "Forestry Aid Payments Challenged in Supreme Court Test," *Wisconsin Counties*, Vol. XVI, No. 4, p. 21 (October, 1953), and "Forest Crop Aid Financing Sustained by Supreme Court," *ibid.*, No. 6, p. 10 (December, 1953).

[85] Barlowe, *op. cit.*, pp. 48-49.

[86] Harris A. Reynolds, "The Town Forest in Massachusetts," in Charles J. Rohr, Alfred A. Brown, and Vernon P. Helming, eds., *Local Government in Massachusetts* (Amherst, Massachusetts State College Bureau of Public Administration, 1941), pp. 48-56.

[87] Barlowe, *op. cit.*, pp. 22, 35.

RURAL ZONING

Zoning, as practiced by local governments, involves the establishment of districts of various types and the regulation therein of the kinds of buildings that may be erected and the uses that may be made of buildings and land. Authority to impose zoning regulations has long been one of the powers usually delegated to municipalities for exercise within their corporate limits; and during recent decades there has been a tendency to confer the power upon counties and townships with respect to unincorporated areas. Today, approximately three fourths of the states have enabling laws authorizing zoning by counties, townships, or both.[88] About half of these enabling acts exempt agricultural lands and buildings from their provisions, thereby limiting zoning activity for the most part to the regulation of suburban building. In more than a dozen states, however, the zoning power extends to open-country as well as suburban lands, thus permitting zoning of a more strictly rural nature—the kind which is particularly relevant to the subject matter of this chapter. County and township zoning regulations are made effective through the adoption of appropriate ordinances by the governmental units concerned. Though in some instances requiring approval by the local voters, rural zoning ordinances ordinarily are adopted and amended by county or township governing bodies.[89]

Zoning in strictly rural areas is concerned almost entirely with the regulation of land use. Its basic purpose is twofold: (1) to conserve natural resource and encourage their more effective use; and (2) to reduce the cost of local government by preventing the wasteful scattering of rural population. Rural zoning regulations vary with respect to the number and nature of the types of districts provided. Many ordinances, however, establish districts of three types: forestry, recreational, and agricultural or unrestricted. Land within forestry districts is restricted to a list of enumerated uses. Among the uses commonly permitted are grow-

[88] Some of these laws apply to all counties or townships of the state concerned; others, however, apply only to counties, towns, or townships of designated classes. In a few instances zoning authority for unincorporated areas has been vested in certain special-purpose districts rather than in the regular county or township governments.

[89] A survey of the law and practice of zoning in rural areas is provided in Erling D. Solberg, *Rural Zoning in the United States* (Washington, U. S. Department of Agriculture, 1952). See also United States Bureau of Agricultural Economics, *Rural Zoning and Land Use Planning* (Washington, Government Printing Office, 1940), prepared in co-operation with other agencies of the Department of Agriculture; United States Department of Agriculture, *State Legislation for Better Land Use* (Washington, Government Printing Office, 1941), chap. 1; Walter Rowlands, Fred Trenk, and Raymond Penn, *Rural Zoning in Wisconsin* (Madison, University of Wisconsin Agricultural Experiment Station, 1948); Louis A. Wolfanger, *Your Community and Township Zoning* (East Lansing, Michigan State College Agricultural Experiment Station, 1945).

ing of forest products; forest industries; public and private parks, playgrounds, and camp grounds; recreational camps and resorts; private summer cottages; hunting and fishing cabins; trappers' cabins; mines and quarries; hydroelectric dams and power plants; and the harvesting of wild crops, such as marsh hay, tree fruits, and berries. In recreational districts the same uses are permitted as in forestry districts, with family dwellings added so that owners may protect their properties during the entire year; but, as in forestry districts, farming is prohibited.[90] Land within agricultural or unrestricted districts may be used for any lawful purpose, including farming. The prohibition of farming in forestry and recreation districts is designed to prevent soil erosion as well as the spoliation of timber and recreational values on land unsuited to cultivation. It serves also to restrain the settlement of farmers in isolated regions where schools, roads, health protection, and other governmental services could be supplied only in inferior quality and at high unit costs. Thus, it will be seen that rural zoning, by regulating the use of privately owned lands, seeks to achieve much the same basic objectives as those sought through public land ownership under the forestry programs considered in the preceding section.

By 1949, 173 counties in 23 states were known to have adopted zoning ordinances, rural or otherwise; [91] and similar action had been taken by a number of towns and townships. Since that date, some additional counties and townships have zoned. Zoning of the rural variety is particularly advantageous in such areas as the cutover regions of northern Michigan, Wisconsin, and Minnesota; and in each of these states it is now being practiced to some extent. Wisconsin, in fact, leads all the states in the zoning of rural areas, with 27 of her counties reported in 1952 as having adopted rural zoning ordinances. Under the Wisconsin law the provisions of a county zoning ordinance become effective within a particular township of the county only when approved by the township governing board, but township approval has been extensive.[92]

Zoning regulations, in rural areas as elsewhere, are prospective rather than retrospective in nature. The police power, which serves as the legal

[90] Solberg, *op. cit.*, pp. 34-35.

[91] The Solberg survey (see n. 89 above) reports this number of *rural* ordinances, but the term *rural* is there used in a broad sense to include suburban as well as open-country zoning.

[92] Fred A. Clarenbach, "The Planning Function in Rural Government," *American Journal of Economics and Sociology*, Vol. XI, pp. 261-279 (April, 1952). In addition to the 27 counties with rural zoning ordinances, 12 Wisconsin counties by 1952 had adopted ordinances providing for other types of zoning regulations, such as those applicable to suburban buildings. In all, therefore, 39 of the state's 71 counties had enacted zoning ordinances of some sort. Of the 738 townships in those 39 counties, 347 had approved the regulations. In four Wisconsin counties without county ordinances, township zoning ordinances had been adopted in one or more townships (*ibid*).

basis of zoning, supports reasonable restrictions upon future uses of privately owned land but generally does not permit the compulsory elimination of existing uses otherwise lawful. Therefore, although the establishment of new farms in forestry and recreation districts may be prohibited by zoning ordinance, farms in operation prior to enactment of the zoning regulation must ordinarily be permitted to continue as "nonconforming uses." For this reason, rural zoning ordinances, to be of maximum effectiveness, should be enacted in advance of the establishment of farms in areas to be zoned for forestry or recreation. Since rural zoning is a relatively new development, dating only from the 1920's, it is not unusual to find in forestry and recreation districts some farms which were in operation before enactment of the zoning regulations. Some communities, after the enactment of a zoning ordinance, have experienced a considerable degree of success in encouraging the elimination of such nonconforming uses through the voluntary relocation of isolated farmers. In Wisconsin, for example, it was reported in 1949 that approximately 800 isolated settlers and their families had been voluntarily relocated, largely as the result of inducements offered by the county governments.[93] In some instances the counties purchased outright the farms of these settlers, and in others county-owned land in unrestricted areas was exchanged for settlers' property in restricted districts. At times the county authorities assisted, with county trucks, in moving household goods and other personal property to the new location. Such endeavors by counties to eliminate nonconforming uses appear in general to have been well rewarded, with relocation costs frequently being returned to the local taxpayers within two or three years through savings in public expenditures, such as those for roads and school transportation.[94] On the basis of Wisconsin's experience, voluntary relocation under public auspices seems clearly to provide an effective supplement to rural zoning ordinances as a means of conserving natural resources and reducing local government costs.

REFERENCES

Books, Reports, and Special Studies

BAKER, Gladys, *The County Agent* (Chicago, University of Chicago Press, 1939).

BALL, Carleton R., *Federal, State, and Local Administrative Relationships in Agriculture* (Berkeley, University of California Press, 1938), 2 vols.

BARLOWE, Raleigh, *Administration of Tax-reverted Lands in the Lake States* (East Lansing, Michigan State College Agricultural Experiment Station, 1951).

[93] W. A. Rowlands, "Zoning Is Shaping the Destiny of Wisconsin's Undeveloped Areas," *Better Roads*, Vol. XIX, No. 11, pp. 23-26 (November, 1949).

[94] *Ibid.;* Rowlands, Trenk, and Penn, *op. cit.*, pp. 28-29.

BENNETT, Hugh H., *Our American Land: The Story of Its Abuse and Its Conservation*, rev. ed. (Washington, U. S. Department of Agriculture, 1950).

———, *Progress in Soil Conservation* (Washington, U. S. Department of Agriculture, 1950).

———, *Soil Conservation* (New York, McGraw-Hill, 1939).

BLACK, John D., *Federal-state-local Relations in Agriculture* (Washington, National Planning Association, 1950).

BRUNNER, Edmund deS., and YANG, E. Hsin Pao, *Rural America and the Extension Service* (New York, Teachers College Bureau of Publications, 1949).

CHASE, Stuart, *Rich Land, Poor Land* (New York, Whittlesey House, 1936).

EMMONS, Lloyd C., "The Contribution of the Land-grant College to Rural Education," in Floyd W. Reeves, ed., *Education for Rural America* (Chicago, University of Chicago Press, 1945), pp. 73-85.

FOSTER, Ellery A., and VOGEL, Harold A., "Coöperative Land Use Planning: A New Development in Democracy," in *Yearbook of Agriculture: Farmers in a Changing World* (Washington, U. S. Department of Agriculture, 1940), pp. 1138-1156.

GILBERTSON, H. W., *Extension-Farm Bureau Relationships: 1948* (Washington, U. S. Department of Agriculture, 1949), mimeo.

KELSEY, Lincoln D., and HEARNE, Cannon C., *Coöperative Extension Work*, 2d ed. (Ithaca, N. Y., Comstock Publishing Associates, 1955).

KILE, Orville M., *The Farm Bureau through Three Decades* (Baltimore, Waverly Press, 1948).

LLOYD, W. A., "County Agent," in Edward Mowbray Tuttle, ed., *The Book of Rural Life* (Chicago, Bellows-Durham Co., 1925), Vol. III, pp. 1396-1403.

MCMAHON, John A., *Coöperative Agricultural Extension Work in North Carolina* (Chapel Hill, University of North Carolina Institute of Government, 1955).

Minnesota Legislative Research Committee, *The Control of Predatory Animals* (St. Paul, Minn., 1952).

National Recreation Association, *Municipal and County Parks in the United States: 1940* (New York, 1942).

———, *Recreation and Park Yearbook: A Review of Local and County Recreation and Park Developments, 1900-1950*, Midcentury Edition (New York, 1951).

NIEDERFRANK, E. J., *Main Types of County Extension Organization and Related Social Factors* (Washington, U. S. Department of Agriculture, 1948).

O'BRIEN, Philip M., GASTON, Thomas L., and DALE, Tom, *Land Use Regulation in Soil Conservation Districts* (Washington, U. S. Department of Agriculture, 1947).

PARKS, W. Robert, *Soil Conservation Districts in Action* (Ames, Iowa State College Press, 1952).

REYNOLDS, Harris A., "The Town Forest in Massachusetts," in Charles J. Rohr, Alfred A. Brown, and Vernon P. Helming, eds., *Local Government in Massachusetts* (Amherst, Massachusetts State College Bureau of Public Administration, 1941), pp. 48-56.

ROWLANDS, W. A., and TRENK, F. B., *Rural Zoning Ordinances in Wisconsin* (Madison, University of Wisconsin Agricultural Extension Service, 1936).

ROWLANDS, Walter, TRENK, Fred, and PENN, Raymond, *Rural Zoning in Wisconsin* (Madison, University of Wisconsin Agricultural Experiment Station, 1948).

RULE, Glenn K., *Soil Conservation Districts in Action on the Land* (Washington, U. S. Department of Agriculture, 1941).

SMITH, C. B., *What Agricultural Extension Is* (Washington, U. S. Department of Agriculture, 1944).

———, and WILSON, Meredith C., *The Agricultural Extension System of the United States* (New York, Wiley, 1930).

Soil Conservation Service, *Soil Conservation Districts for Erosion Control* (Washington, U. S. Department of Agriculture, 1937).

SOLBERG, Erling D., *Rural Zoning in the United States* (Washington, U. S. Department of Agriculture, 1952).

———, *Rural Zoning Tools and Objectives* (Washington, U. S. Department of Agriculture, 1953).

United States Bureau of Agricultural Economics, *County Land Use Planning* (Washington, Government Printing Office, 1940), prepared in co-operation with other agencies of Department of Agriculture.

———, *Rural Zoning and Land Use Planning* (Washington, Government Printing Office, 1940), prepared in co-operation with other agencies of the Department of Agriculture.

United States Department of Agriculture, *The Home Demonstration Agent* (Washington, Government Printing Office, 1946).

———, *Land Use Planning under Way* (Washington, 1940).

———, *Report of Coöperative Extension Work in Agriculture and Home Economics* (Washington, Government Printing Office, annually).

———, *State Legislation for Better Land Use* (Washington, Government Printing Office, 1941).

VOELKER, Stanley W., *Land-use Ordinances of Soil Conservation Districts in Colorado* (Fort Collins, Colorado Agricultural and Mechanical College Agricultural Experiment Station, 1952).

WARD, Florence E., "Home Demonstration Work," in Edward Mowbray Tuttle, ed., *The Book of Rural Life* (Chicago, Bellows-Durham Co., 1925), Vol. V, pp. 2607-2615.

WARREN, Gertrude L., *Organization of 4-H Club Work: A Guide for Local Leaders,* rev. ed. (Washington, U. S. Department of Agriculture, 1948).

WOLFANGER, Louis A., *Your Community and Township Zoning* (East Lansing, Michigan State College Agricultural Experiment Station, 1945).

Articles

ALLISON, J. H., "County Forestry in Minnesota and Wisconsin," *The Conservation Volunteer,* publication of the Minnesota Department of Conservation, Vol. XII, No. 70, pp. 32-38 (May-June, 1949).

ARMS, Florence C., "County Agent," *Vermont Life,* Vol. VIII, No. 3, pp. 53-57 (Spring, 1954).

BALLARD, Frank L., "County Agents: A Record of Achievement," *The County Officer,* Vol. XVI, pp. 47-52 (February, 1951).

CARTER, R. E., "Your County Agent," *The County Officer,* Vol. XV, No. 8, pp. 4-7, 28 (November, 1950).

CHASE, Stuart, "When the Crop Lands Go," *Harper's Magazine,* Vol. CLXXIII, pp. 225-233 (August, 1936).

CLARENBACH, Fred A., "The Planning Function in Rural Government," *American Journal of Economics and Sociology,* Vol. XI, pp. 261-279 (April, 1952).

EDSALL, James V., "County Zoning," *Local Government Notes,* publication of the University of Illinois Extension Service in Agriculture and Home Economics, No. 46 (May 24, 1954).
FERGUSON, Edwin E., "Nation-wide Erosion Control: Soil Conservation Districts and the Power of Land-use Regulation," *Iowa Law Review,* Vol. XXXIV, pp. 166-187 (January, 1949).
GREENE, Lee S., "Rural Zoning in Wisconsin," *National County Magazine,* Vol. I, No. 3, pp. 18-19 (June, 1935).
———, "Rural Zoning in the American States," *Town Planning Review,* Vol. XVIII, pp. 79-98 (December, 1938).
HERBERT, P. A., "Michigan Enacts a Rural Zoning Law," *Journal of Land and Public Utility Economics,* Vol. XI, pp. 309-310 (August, 1935).
HERROLD, George H., "Zoning for Counties," *National County Magazine,* Vol. I, No. 2, pp. 12, 24, 28 (May, 1935).
KING, Seth S., "'Point IV' Man on *Our* Farms [the County Agent]," *New York Times Magazine,* pp. 17, 44, 47, 49 (May 8, 1955).
"Legal Techniques for Promoting Soil Conservation," *Yale Law Journal,* Vol. L, pp. 1056-1070 (April, 1941).
LEWIS, John D., "Democratic Planning in Agriculture," *American Political Science Review,* Vol. XXXV, pp. 232-249, 454-469 (April, June, 1941).
MARSHALL, James H., "Rural Zoning Legislation in Tennessee," *Journal of Land and Public Utilities Economics,* Vol. XIII, pp. 418-420 (November, 1937).
MUSBACH, William F., and WILLIAMS, Melville C., "Rural Zoning in Minnesota," *Journal of Land and Public Utilities Economics,* Vol. XVI, pp. 105-109 (February, 1940).
OGG, Wallace E., "The Coöperative Extension Service in Today's World," *State Government,* Vol. XXV, pp. 211-215 (September, 1952).
REESE, Madge J., "Home Demonstration Work: Education for Living," *The County Officer,* Vol. XV, No. 3, pp. 12-17, 27, 29 (July, 1950).
ROWLANDS, W. A., "County Zoning for Agriculture, Forestry, and Recreation in Wisconsin," *Journal of Land and Public Utilities Economics,* Vol. IX, pp. 272-282 (August, 1933).
———, "Zoning Is Shaping the Destiny of Wisconsin's Undeveloped Areas," *Better Roads,* Vol. XIX, No. 11, pp. 23-26 (November, 1949).
SCHELLIE, Kenneth L., "County Forest Program in Indiana," *State Government,* Vol. XX, pp. 115, 132 (April, 1947).
SHIPLEY, Fern, "In 4-H You Build Citizenship," *The County Officer,* Vol. XVIII, pp. 236-239 (October, 1953).
SMITH, Herbert H., "Making Zoning Work in Rural Communities," *New Jersey Municipalities,* Vol. XXXII, No. 5, pp. 22-26 (May, 1955).
STOLTENBERG, Carl H., "Rural Zoning in Minnesota: An Appraisal," *Land Economics,* Vol. XXX, pp. 153-163 (May, 1954).
SWISHER, Paul W., "The Wind Erosion Program in Colorado," *State Government,* Vol. XXVII, pp. 180-182 (September, 1954).
TRENK, F. B., "Community Forests Established by Counties," *Wisconsin Counties,* Vol. XIV, No. 12, pp. 5, 22 (June, 1952).
TRULLINGER, R. W., "Where County Agents Get Their Facts," *The County Officer,* Vol. XV, No. 6, pp. 18-24 (September, 1950).
WALKER, Herman, Jr., and PARKS, W. Robert, "Soil Conservation Districts: Local Democracy in a National Program," *Journal of Politics,* Vol. VIII, pp. 538-549 (November, 1946).

WARREN, Gertrude L., "4-H Clubs Build the Citizens of Tomorrow," *The County Officer*, Vol. XV, No. 2, pp. 16-20, 25-28 (May, 1950).

"Weed Control in Iowa," *Iowa Law Review*, Vol. XXXIV, pp. 348-353 (January, 1949).

WILSON, F. G., "County Forests of Wisconsin," *State Government*, Vol. XX, pp. 116-117 (April, 1947).

WOLCOTT, Leon, "National Land-use Programs and the Local Governments," *National Municipal Review*, Vol. XXVIII, pp. 111-119 (February, 1939).

ZENOR, Dean, "County Zoning in Iowa," *The County Officer*, Vol. XVI, pp. 18-20 (January, 1951).

PART FIVE

Fiscal Policy and Administration

CHAPTER 19

Taxation and Finance

THE RISING COST OF LOCAL GOVERNMENT

LOCAL GOVERNMENT COSTS in recent years have risen sharply. During the ten-year period from 1944 to 1954 county expenditures almost trebled, increasing from $1,600,000,000 to $4,600,000,000; [1] and there have been marked increases also in the expenditures of townships, school districts, and other local units. These higher governmental costs have been attributable in part to the fact that the rise in the general price level, with the corresponding decline in the purchasing power of the dollar, has necessitated the expenditure of larger sums to obtain the same level of services. Another major factor has been the constant demand for expansion and improvement of the services provided by local governments. Public demand has been strong for more and better roads, welfare services, and educational facilities, and local budgets have been increased to meet that demand. Still another factor has been the increased amounts of state aid, and to a lesser extent federal aid, that have been made available for the financing of certain local services, with the state and federal grants stimulating the broadening and improvement of local programs. In some instances rising costs have been the result in part of population increases.[2]

If the price level remains constant or rises, it seems safe to predict that increases in local government expenditures will continue. State and federal aids are likely to increase rather than decrease, and some communities will continue to gain in population. But it is in increasing demand for services that the key to rising costs is most clearly to be found. This is particularly true in the case of the local highway function, where the

[1] United States Bureau of the Census, *County Finances: 1944 Compendium* (Washington, Government Printing Office, 1947), p. 8; United States Bureau of the Census, *Summary of Governmental Finances in 1954* (Washington, 1955), p. 25.

[2] Cf. Harry O. Lawson, *Recent Trends in County Finance: 1947-1951* (Lawrence, University of Kansas Governmental Research Center, 1953), p. 23.

increasing number of automobiles brings with it a demand for road improvement, and in that of education, where elementary and secondary school facilities are already being taxed beyond normal capacity and enrollments continue to mount from year to year. All in all, the providing of funds to meet the growing costs of public services is today, and promises to remain in the future, one of the foremost problems of our local governments.

SOURCES OF LOCAL REVENUE

In the financing of their operations local governments in rural America rely upon two principal sources of revenue: property taxation and state aid. At one time property taxes constituted almost the sole source of local revenue. Today, such levies, though still producing for the country as a whole more local revenue than any other single source, must share with state aid their position of major importance. The relative importance of property taxes and state aid in the local government picture varies considerably from state to state as well as among the different classes of governmental units. There is some variation also among individual units of a given class within a single state. The property tax is estimated to have produced approximately 90 per cent of the total income of West Virginia counties for 1952, and 72 per cent of the 1950 revenue of New Jersey counties.[3] In Arkansas counties, on the other hand, the property tax provided only 31 per cent of the total general revenue for 1950, while state aid provided 41 per cent. In 27 of that state's 75 counties, state aid accounted for half or more of the 1950 general revenue, and in one county 74 per cent of the general revenue came from state sources.[4] Seventy-five of Mississippi's 82 counties obtained more than half of their 1950 revenue from state and other outside sources, as distinguished from the local property tax and other internal sources.[5] And most Michigan townships levy no property tax but finance their governments exclusively from their apportionment of state sales-tax revenues.[6]

Minor sources of local revenue include, for various units and at various times, certain local nonproperty taxes, small amounts of federal aid, and miscellaneous nontax sources. The nature of these minor revenue sources is indicated more fully at subsequent points in this chapter. There are

[3] Harold J. Shamberger, *County Government and Administration in West Virginia* (Morgantown, West Virginia University Bureau for Government Research, 1952), p. 32; James M. Collier, *County Government in New Jersey* (New Brunswick, N. J., Rutgers University Press, 1952), p. 53.

[4] Edward W. Reed and Henry M. Alexander, *The Government and Finance of Counties in Arkansas* (Fayetteville, University of Arkansas Bureau of Business and Economic Research, 1953), pp. 52, 62.

[5] Gordon K. Bryan, *County Revenues and Expenditures in Mississippi: 1950* (State College, Mississippi State College Social Science Research Center, 1952), p. 1.

[6] Howard D. Hamilton, "Why State Cost Has Gone Up," *National Municipal Review,* Vol. XLII, pp. 123-128, 141 (March, 1953).

also occasional instances of a local government unit receiving aid from one or more other local units.

In 1954, according to Census Bureau reports, local government units in the United States, other than municipalities, received total revenues in the following amounts: [7]

Type of unit	*Amount in millions*
Counties	$4,517
Towns and townships	940
School districts	6,483
Other special districts	1,158

For units of each type the respective percentages of total revenue derived from property taxation, state aid, and other sources were as follows: [8]

Source	*Counties*	*Towns and townships*	*School districts*	*Other special districts*
Property tax	46%	60%	49%	19%
State aid	36	23	40	3
Other sources	18	17	11	78 [9]

THE LOCAL TAXING POWER

A tax may be defined as a compulsory contribution for the support of government, exacted without regard to individual benefits.[10] In the field of taxation, as in other fields, local governments possess only such authority as has been conferred upon them by the states. Some local units in home-rule states, principally municipalities, are granted certain taxing authority by state constitutional provision, and authority so conferred is not subject to legislative abridgment. For the most part, however, the local taxing power is granted by the state legislatures through statutory enactments. Where this is the case, local governments are subject not only to all limitations imposed upon the taxing power of the state itself by the federal and state constitutions but also to any additional restrictions which the state legislature may see fit to impose by statute.

Under the doctrine of "intergovernmental tax immunity," which the courts have found implicit in the United States Constitution, neither the states nor their subdivisions may tax instrumentalities of the national government. Other limitations imposed by the federal constitution upon state and local taxing power flow from the due-process and equal-protection clauses of the Fourteenth Amendment. To comply with the due-process requirement, tax measures must meet certain procedural standards—for example, in the matter of notice and hearing—and must

[7] *Summary of Governmental Finances in 1954,* p. 20.

[8] Computed from *ibid.*

[9] Largely earnings and charges.

[10] Cf. Merlin H. Hunter and Harry K. Allen, *Principles of Public Finance* (New York, Harper, 1940), p. 169.

not be confiscatory; and the equal-protection clause operates to prohibit arbitrary or discriminatory classification for tax purposes.

Limitations imposed upon the taxing power by state constitutions are of varied character. Constitutional provisions ordinarily exempt certain classes of property from taxation or specify what classes may be exempted by statute. Most commonly exempted is publicly owned property and property used for educational, religious, or charitable purposes. In some states the property of veterans, up to a specified value, is exempt. Several states have "homestead" exemptions, under which owner-occupied homes are wholly or partially nontaxable; and some exempt certain industrial and agricultural properties. For the country at large, it has been estimated that about one sixth of all real estate falls within the various exemption categories.[11] As a result, property-tax revenues suffer serious curtailment unless the rates on nonexempt property are correspondingly increased. Though some classes of exempt property tend to be concentrated in urban areas, certain exemptions, such as those accorded homesteads and the property of veterans, substantially narrow the tax base in rural communities. A number of constitutions still retain the requirement, once widely prevalent, that all nonexempt property be taxed at uniform and equal rates; and rate limitations of one kind or another are common.[12] With respect to nonproperty taxes, the requirement is sometimes made that levies apply uniformly to the classes of occupations, privileges, or transactions upon which they are imposed.

PROPERTY TAXATION

Property taxes, as previously indicated, constitute the most important single source of local government revenue in the United States; and practically every local unit, with the exception of some special districts, is empowered to impose property levies. For purposes of taxation and otherwise, two classes of property are commonly distinguished—real and personal. Real estate consists principally of land, buildings, and other improvements of a permanent nature. Personalty includes all property other than real estate and may be further divided into two categories—tangible and intangible. Among the more common forms of tangible personalty are household furnishings, automobiles, livestock, and farm and industrial machinery. Intangible personalty consists of such incorporeal forms of wealth as stocks and bonds, promissory notes, and bank accounts.

General Property Tax. In its earliest form in this country the property tax was a land tax of a fixed sum per acre or per hundred acres, with lands commonly divided into two or more classes or grades and the better grades

[11] K. P. Sanow, "Property Tax Exemption," *State Government,* Vol. XIX, pp. 108-114 (April, 1946).

[12] See below, "Tax-rate Limits."

taxed at higher rates. Supplementary to the land tax, levies were soon imposed upon specific kinds of personal property, such as horses, cattle, and slaves. After about 1815, however, taxes on land and selected types of personalty were gradually expanded into the *general* property tax—an ad valorem levy upon all property not specifically exempted— and by the time of the Civil War the general property tax had been definitely established as the basic form of state and local taxation.[13] Implicit in the general property tax is the theory that every property owner should contribute to the support of government in direct proportion to the value of his property of whatever kind, the rate of levy being the same on property of all classes—real estate, tangible personal property, and intangible personalty.

Criticisms of the General Property Tax. Though providing a lucrative and relatively elastic source of revenue, the general property tax has various faults. Some of these are inherent in the very nature of the tax itself, but others are largely administrative shortcomings. In its basic theory, the tax errs in assuming that all property has the same taxpaying ability. Unless the tax base is to be impaired, taxes on property must be paid out of income therefrom; therefore, in the final analysis, the taxpaying ability of property depends upon its ability to produce income. Actually, property varies widely in income-producing capacity. Some properties produce no income at all, whereas others are highly productive; and between these extremes are all intermediate degrees of productivity. Yet the rate of taxation within a given jurisdiction is the same on all property, whether it produces much income or little or none at all.

Another weakness of the general property tax lies in the fact that much nonexempt property actually escapes taxation. When this form of taxation first developed, America possessed a simple agricultural economy, and most property was in the form of real estate and tangible personalty which could readily be found and listed by assessors. Today, on the contrary, a large percentage of taxable property consists of intangibles which it is virtually impossible for the assessor to discover unless they are voluntarily listed by the owner. In practice, nonlisting of intangibles is widespread, and the same is true to a lesser degree of certain forms of tangible personalty, such as jewelry, which can easily be concealed. So generally prevalent is the nonlisting of these types of property in some jurisdictions that practically all intangible property and much tangible personalty escapes taxation altogether. Under these circumstances, the so-called general property tax ceases to be general except in theory and becomes actually a tax on real estate and such tangible personalty as cannot readily be concealed. Thus, persons whose property is largely in the form of intangibles escape their just share of the tax burden, and that

[13] Cf. William J. Shultz and C. Lowell Harriss, *American Public Finance*, 5th ed. (New York, Prentice-Hall, 1949), pp. 323-324.

burden becomes correspondingly heavier upon other property owners. Since the intangible forms of wealth which most commonly escape taxation are more heavily concentrated in urban areas than in rural, it is the rural people who suffer most from the resulting inequity. Further difficulties in property-tax administration arise from the widespread use of small assessment districts and popularly elected assessors.[14]

Classified Property Taxes. In an effort to overcome some of the weaknesses of the general property tax, many states now classify property in some manner for taxation purposes. The classified property tax has been defined by Simeon Leland as "the *ad valorem* taxation of property by its segregation into groups or types and the application to these various classes of different effective rates."[15] Though a few states permitted classification at an earlier date, the movement for classified property taxation has been, for the most part, a product of the twentieth century, with one state after another amending its constitution to eliminate uniformity requirements. At present, approximately three fourths of the states have constitutional authority for classification, and more than half have actually adopted classified property taxes in some form.[16]

A few states, with Minnesota as an outstanding example, have adopted fairly comprehensive systems of classification. In most instances, however, classification has gone no further than placing intangibles in a class apart from real estate and tangible personalty for taxation at a special low rate. Proponents of classification seek its justification in part on the ground that it permits account to be taken of the varying taxpaying ability of different types of property. It is also contended that a low-rate tax on intangibles will draw that form of property out of hiding and secure its listing for taxation. Experience in this respect, however, has been somewhat disappointing. Although low rates, where applied, have resulted in the assessment of more intangibles than before, evasion has continued to be widespread. In some instances, indeed, receipts from intangibles under classification appear actually to have been less than under the general property tax.[17]

PROPERTY-TAX ADMINISTRATION

Administrative agencies and procedures in the field of property taxation vary in detail from state to state, and sometimes within a single state, but

[14] See below, pp. 499-500.

[15] Simeon E. Leland, *The Classified Property Tax in the United States* (Boston, Houghton Mifflin, 1928), p. 41. As Leland points out (*ibid.*, p. 42), differentiation in effective rates may be secured either by uniform assessments and differential rates or by uniform rates and differential assessments.

[16] Hunter and Allen, *op. cit.*, p. 338; National Association of Assessing Officers, *Assessors' News Letter*, Vol. XX, p. 21 (March, 1954).

[17] Harold M. Groves, *Financing Government*, 4th ed. (New York, Holt, 1954), pp. 82-84. Several states now exempt intangibles altogether from taxation as property.

the general picture is much the same throughout the country. Though at one time property taxes constituted a major source of state and local revenue, tax assessment and collection have always been left for the most part to local government officials. During recent years the states have tended to rely less and less upon property levies for their own purposes, thus relinquishing the tax more fully to local use. Today, the property tax is a distinctly minor source of revenue as far as the states themselves are concerned, a number of states having completely abandoned the property levy for state revenue purposes. Nevertheless, the states continue to exercise a degree of supervision over local tax administration, and the present tendency appears to be toward a gradual increase in this supervision.

Assessment. The first step in administering the property tax is that of assessment, that is, the listing and valuation of the taxable property of each owner. Personal property is assessed annually. Assessment of real estate is made annually in some states, but in others it occurs at less frequent intervals, such as every two or four years. Though certain classes of property, such as public utilities, intangibles, and mineral and forest lands, are frequently assessed by state agencies, assessment is for the most part in the hands of locally elected county, township, or city assessors. Some cities make their own separate assessments and impose their municipal levies thereon. The more common practice, however, is for a single assessment, made by a township or county assessor, to serve as the tax base for all levying units.

As suggested at a preceding point, effective administration of the property tax is hindered by the smallness of assessment districts and the methods by which assessors are chosen. In part or all of some 19 states the town or township is the primary assessment district, and most local assessors, both in these states and elsewhere, are popularly elected.[18] The small districts make it necessary that the assessors serve on a part-time basis, and popular election is not conducive to the selection of properly qualified persons. All too often the assessor is a local politician with few qualifications for the difficult and technical task of assigning valuations to real and personal properties of every conceivable kind. Small assessment districts, moreover, encourage competitive undervaluation. Where, for example, township assessments constitute the basis upon which county levies are imposed, there is an incentive for each assessor to attempt to keep his valuations below those of neighboring townships, since success in doing so will correspondingly reduce the contribution which his constituents are required to make for the support of the county government. If, in addition, a state levy is imposed upon the township assessment, the ad-

[18] Cf. National Association of Assessing Officers, *Assessment Organization and Personnel* (Chicago, 1941), pp. 35-43, 157-161; William G. Murray, "State Action for Better Assessments," *State Government*, Vol. XXVIII, pp. 90-94 (April, 1955).

vantage flowing from undervaluation will be further increased. Such inequalities among townships may, of course, be adjusted in some measure by equalization agencies, but their complete elimination can scarcely be expected.

Satisfactory assessment administration would seem to require assessment districts of sufficient area to justify full-time assessors and selection of those assessors under a system of examinations designed to secure qualified personnel. Such a plan would suggest selection by appointment, yet Kentucky applies an examination system to elective assessors.[19] Though progress toward larger assessment districts and qualified assessing personnel has been slow, the headway being made is gratifying. Iowa, in 1947, for example, abolished the office of township assessor and made the county auditor ex officio county assessor. Although the auditor is an elective official, full-time deputy assessors were selected on the basis of examinations given by the state tax commission.[20] In 1949 the Iowa law was amended to separate the office of county assessor from that of auditor and to provide for the appointment of the assessor, as well as of full-time deputies, on an examination basis.[21] South Dakota, in 1955, established a county assessment officer and provided for use of the county, rather than townships and municipalities, as the principal assessment area.[22] Several other states have recently taken action along somewhat similar lines; and still others, without going so far as to adopt the county-unit plan, have provided county assessment supervisors with varying degrees of authority over township assessors. A majority of the states now employ the county as the basic unit for assessment purposes, but even in these most assessors continue to be elected.[23]

Review and Equalization. Assessment rolls prepared by local assessors commonly pass through the hands of one or more local administrative boards for review and equalization, and in some instances there are state agencies of review and equalization as well. The review process involves the correction of clerical errors, the addition of omitted property, the hearing of complaints by aggrieved property owners, and the raising or lowering of individual assessments found to be out of line. Equalization involves the ordering of horizontal increases or decreases in the assessments of entire assessment districts or taxing jurisdictions so that similar properties will be treated substantially alike for valuation purposes, regardless of where they are situated. The importance of equalization is

[19] *Assessment Organization and Personnel*, p. 180.

[20] *Acts and Joint Resolutions of Iowa* (1947), chap. 240.

[21] *Ibid.* (1949), chap. 198. For a description and evaluation of the Iowa system, see Howard L. Mefferd, "A Merit System for County Assessors," *The County Officer*, Vol. XVI, pp. 250-253 (October, 1951).

[22] *Laws of South Dakota* (1955), chap. 422.

[23] See Murray, *loc. cit.*

enhanced by the relationship now commonly existing between assessed valuation and formulas used for the distribution of state aid. Many state-aid programs require that a local government, in order to qualify for state assistance, impose a local property levy at a prescribed minimum rate for support of the service concerned. Illinois townships, for example, are required to impose a public-assistance (poor-relief) levy of 10 cents on each $100 of assessed valuation in order to be eligible for state aid in this field. Thus, if property is assessed in one township at 80 per cent of its actual value and in another at 40 per cent, the taxpayers of the former must make a contribution relatively double that required of taxpayers of the latter before the state will step in with its subsidy. The equalization process seeks, among other things, to minimize inequalities of this nature by assuring, insofar as possible, that the ratio of assessed value to the actual value of taxable property is substantially the same in the various local jurisdictions.

Collection. The final step in the tax-administration process is that of collection. Though occasionally individual local units collect their own taxes, the more usual plan is for a single collecting officer, frequently at the county level, to collect all property taxes and subsequently make remittance to the various levying units, including the state if a state property levy is imposed. The office of county collector at times is a separate and distinct office, but more commonly the county treasurer, or in some instances the sheriff, serves ex officio as collector. Some states permit the payment of some or all property taxes in two installments, with an interval of several months between.[24]

State Supervision. Practically every state has a state tax commission or equivalent administrative agency vested with some degree of supervisory authority over local tax administration. Among the powers conferred upon the tax commission in various states are those of conducting tax research, advising and assisting local assessors, prescribing assessment forms, issuing rules and regulations concerning assessment procedures, removing local assessors from office, hearing and deciding appeals from local boards of review, acting as a state equalization agency, ordering reassessments where the original rolls are found to be faulty, and assessing in the first instance certain classes of property.[25] A most helpful service that is being undertaken by more and more tax commissions is the holding of periodic meetings at which local assessors are instructed concerning assessment procedures and problems. Some commissions also prepare manuals for the guidance of assessors in their work.

[24] Cf. Jens P. Jensen, *Property Taxation in the United States* (Chicago, University of Chicago Press, 1931), p. 313.

[25] *Assessment Organization and Personnel,* pp. 328-347; Jens P. Jensen, *Government Finance* (New York, Crowell, 1937), pp. 260-261.

TAX-RATE LIMITS

The power of local governments to levy property taxes is commonly subject to percentage or millage limitations upon the rates that may be levied for various purposes. These limitations are imposed occasionally by constitutional provision, but more often by statute. Counties in a given state, for example, may be empowered to levy up to two mills on each dollar of assessed valuation for road purposes, two mills for public assistance, and one mill for health service. Townships frequently are subject to limitations of the same character, and the taxing authority of special districts ordinarily is carefully circumscribed. Sometimes it is provided that the maximum rates specified by constitution or statute, though binding upon local governing bodies, may be exceeded by action of the local voters in referendum elections.

In a special category in the property-tax field is the *over-all* type of limitation occasionally adopted by constitutional or statutory provision. These provisions fix maximum *total* rates which may not be exceeded by the *combined* levies, local and state, upon a single piece of property.[26] The total local rate permitted under an over-all limitation may be apportioned among the taxing units concerned by statutory provision, or, as is the more common practice, a designated administrative agency, say at the county level, may be empowered to make the apportionment.[27] In practice, over-all limitations have proved to be of doubtful wisdom. Faced with such drastic restrictions, local governmental units have sought in various ways to circumvent their effectiveness. In some instances assessed valuations have been raised to offset rate reductions, and in others resort has been had to borrowing for current expenses. Where efforts at evasion have failed, reductions in revenue resulting from the rate limitations have frequently necessitated curtailments in essential local services, such as law enforcement and education.

LOCAL NONPROPERTY TAXES

Nonproperty taxes, which now supply the major portion of state revenue, are used also in some measure by local governments.[28] At the local

[26] Glen Leet and Robert M. Paige, eds., *Property Tax Limitation Laws* (Chicago, Public Administration Service, 1934); A. Miller Hillhouse and Ronald B. Welch, *Tax Limits Appraised* (Chicago, Public Administration Service, 1937). It was reported in 1955 that nine states currently imposed over-all rate limitations. Roger A. Freeman, "What Ails Property Tax?" *National Municipal Review*, Vol. XLIV, pp. 506-511 (November, 1955).

[27] See Clyde F. Snider, "Fiscal Control at the County Level," *National Municipal Review*, Vol. XXX, pp. 579-586 (October, 1941).

[28] On the subject generally, see Randall S. Stout and Eugene A. Myers, "The Development of Permissive Local Taxation since 1945," *Current Economic Comment*, publication of the University of Illinois Bureau of Economic and Business Research, Vol. XIII, No. 3, pp. 20-35 (August, 1951).

level, however, it is principally the municipalities that make use of these levies. Counties, townships, and special districts are less commonly empowered to impose nonproperty taxes than are cities and villages, and where the power exists on the part of such units, it has as yet been used rather sparingly. In those instances in which local governments other than municipalities impose nonproperty levies, they are likely to be units largely urban or semiurban in character. Nevertheless, some more strictly rural units do employ such taxes; and it seems safe to predict that their use in rural areas will increase somewhat in the future, even though slowly.

It has long been common for counties or townships to impose license taxes upon retail liquor establishments and commercial amusements operating in unincorporated areas. As of 1951, seven counties—four in Alabama, two in New York, and one in Virginia—and one Louisiana parish were known to have sales or gross-receipts taxes.[29] The local sales-tax rate, county or otherwise, has usually been 1 per cent or one half of 1 per cent. At the county level, as elsewhere, the sales tax is rather commonly accompanied by a compensating use levy imposed upon articles on which the sales tax has not been paid because they were purchased outside the taxing jurisdiction. California, a state which has had broad experience with municipal sales and use taxes, in 1955 authorized the imposition of such levies by counties at the rate of 1 per cent. Under the California law, the county taxes are to be administered by the state board of equalization, which is to be reimbursed by the counties concerned for administrative costs. Retailers are entitled to credit against their county taxes for amounts paid to cities under similar levies.[30]

Some 20 states permit or require the collection of a poll tax by counties or school districts.[31] In 1952, gasoline taxes were imposed by nine counties in Alabama and three in Mississippi, and cigarette taxes by two Florida counties.[32] Nassau and Saratoga counties in New York tax parimutuel pools.[33] In Pennsylvania hundreds of school districts and a considerable number of townships have imposed a variety of nonproperty levies under broad enabling legislation originally enacted in 1947.[34] This legislation,

[29] Eugene C. Lee, "The County Sales Tax and Local Revenues," *The County Officer*, Vol. XVI, pp. 165-169, 186 (July, 1951). The Alabama levies were state imposed. See also, Eugene C. Lee, *The County Sales Tax and Other Local Revenues* (Berkeley, University of California Bureau of Public Administration, 1951); W. R. MacDougall, "The County Sales Tax: A Logical Revenue Source," *The County Officer*, Vol. XVII, pp. 141-144 (May, 1952).

[30] *Statutes of California* (1955), chap. 1311.

[31] Lee, "The County Sales Tax and Local Revenues," *loc. cit.*

[32] United States Treasury Department, *Federal-state-local Tax Coördination* (Washington, 1952), pp. 54, 64-65.

[33] Stout and Myers, *loc. cit.*

[34] *Laws of Pennsylvania* (1947), No. 481. Cf. H. F. Alderfer, "Pennsylvania's New Local Taxes," *State Government*, Vol. XXI, pp. 144-145, 154 (July, 1948).

applicable to various types of local government units though not to counties, permits the levy, with certain specified exceptions and within prescribed rate limitations, of virtually any tax which falls within the state's own taxing power but which the state does not itself impose. Greatest in number of the local taxes imposed under this authorization are the per capita or poll levies. Numerous also are taxes on admissions to amusements, local income taxes, deed-transfer taxes, and taxes on mechanical devices. In addition, there are business and privilege taxes of various kinds, trailer taxes, and sundry levies of miscellaneous nature.[35]

STATE AID

Growth of State Aid. State aid to local governments, rural and urban, increased from less than $2,000,000,000 in 1945 to $5,600,000,000 in 1954, and, in the latter year, constituted approximately 30 per cent of all state expenditures. Of the total 1954 aid, $2,600,000,000 went to school districts, $1,600,000,000 to counties, $217,000,000 to towns and townships, and $36,000,000 to nonschool special districts.[36] Together, these items constituted 79 per cent of the total aid for the year, the remaining 21 per cent going to municipalities (see Fig. XIII).

Reasons for Growth. Reasons for the growth of state aid have been several. For one thing, the state governments have come to recognize a general state-wide interest in many of the services provided by the local units and to acknowledge a corresponding responsibility to see to it that these services are adequately financed. As a result, the states not only contribute generously to the support of such local functions as roads and schools but do so in many instances in such a manner as to subsidize the poorer local units more heavily than those which are better able to finance their own activities. Secondly, state financial assistance is sometimes used to stimulate local government units to undertake certain service programs which appear to state legislatures to be desirable but which the local authorities might not be willing to undertake if it were necessary to finance the entire cost from locally raised funds. In the third place, the extending of state monetary assistance with conditions attached is frequently employed as a means of controlling local action and securing local compliance with state standards. Though the states are legally compe-

[35] See Pennsylvania Department of Internal Affairs, *Taxes Levied under Act 481* (April 1, 1952). The enabling legislation carries an over-all limitation to the effect that local units may not raise from taxes imposed thereunder amounts of money in excess of those which could be raised by imposition of specified rates upon real estate.

[36] United States Bureau of the Census, *Historical Review of State and Local Government Finances* (Washington, 1948), p. 21; United States Bureau of the Census, *Compendium of State Government Finances in 1954* (Washington, Government Printing Office, 1955), p. 7; and *Summary of Governmental Finances in 1954*, p. 20.

tent to require local compliance with their mandates irrespective of the financial factor, it is often felt to be good policy to offer financial assistance in return for that compliance.[37] In practice, therefore, in state-local as in federal-state relationships, intergovernmental aid becomes a device through which the "aiding" government exercises varying degrees of control over the "aided." Finally, as suggested at an earlier point, the states have been reluctant to confer upon their local governments authority to levy the more productive nonproperty taxes, such as those on sales and

FIG. XIII

State Aid to Local Governments: 1954 (Percentage of State Aid Allotted to Local Units of Various Classes)

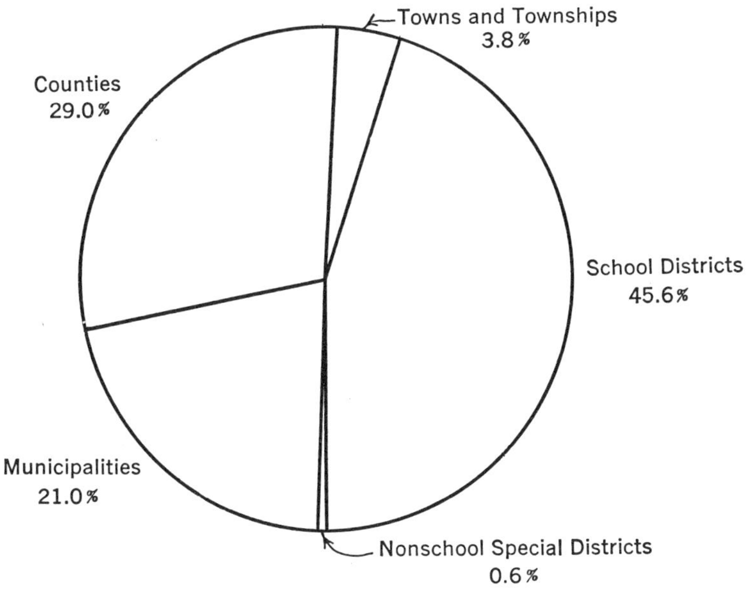

SOURCE: Computed from United States Bureau of the Census, *Summary of Governmental Finances in 1954* (Washington, 1955), p. 20.

income.[38] As long as the states reserve these lucrative revenue sources to themselves, denying to the local governments the power to impose levies in these categories, it has seemed no more than reasonable that the states should turn back to the local units, through state aid, a portion of the proceeds from the state-collected taxes. Only in this manner will it be possible, in many instances, for the local governments to maintain satisfactory service standards without undue increases in local property levies.

[37] See above, chap. 4, "Grants-in-aid and Tax Sharing."
[38] See above, "Local Nonproperty Taxes."

Forms of State Aid. State aid to local governments is extended in two principal forms: the grant-in-aid and the shared tax. The grant-in-aid ordinarily consists of an appropriation from general state funds for allocation to local governments on some predetermined basis. Under the tax-sharing plan, part or all of the proceeds from a specified tax levied and collected by the state are distributed to local governmental units. Among the taxes thus shared by various states with their local governments are motor-fuel taxes, motor-vehicle license taxes, liquor taxes, income taxes, and sales taxes.[39]

Every state now provides financial aid to local governments through grants-in-aid, shared taxes, or both. Though each of the two plans is widely used, the grant-in-aid in some respects appears preferable to the shared tax. One of the principal objections to the shared tax lies in the fact that the amount of funds available for distribution to local units depends upon the productivity of the tax rather than upon local needs. In practice, local needs for state assistance may be greatest at the very time when, perhaps because of an economic depression, revenues from the tax concerned are at their lowest point. Another shortcoming of the shared tax is its instability as a local revenue source. Tax yields always vary somewhat from year to year and may vary widely with changing economic conditions. Therefore, where the amount of revenue to be received by local governments from the state depends upon the productivity of one or more specific taxes, there is inevitably present an element of uncertainty which makes it difficult for local governments to engage in proper financial planning. Grants-in-aid, consisting as they usually do of appropriations from the general state treasury, are not dependent in amount upon the productivity of any one or more designated taxes and thus can be maintained at a relatively stable point. These reasons appear to account, at least in part, for the action of New York State in inaugurating, in the 1940's, a system of per capita grants to towns (townships) and municipalities to replace, in large measure, a pre-existing program of shared taxes.[40]

State-aid Programs. State-aid programs are most extensive in the fields of education, welfare, and highways. Of the $5,600,000,000 in state aid in 1954, $2,900,000,000 was allocated to education, $1,000,000,000 to welfare services, and $871,000,000 to roads.[41] Thus, school aid constituted slightly more than half of the total, and the three functions together accounted for nearly 85 per cent. Other local services coming in for smaller amounts of aid include hospitals, health administration, public safety,

[39] Cf. American Municipal Association, *State-collected Municipally Shared Taxes* (Chicago, 1946) and its *1948 Supplement*.

[40] *Laws of New York* (1946), chap. 301.

[41] *Compendium of State Government Finances in 1954*, p. 28. The term *intergovernmental expenditure*, employed by the Census Bureau, includes certain minor items in addition to grants-in-aid and shared taxes, but these are so small in amount as to be negligible for present purposes.

housing, and conservation of natural resources.[42] Though state aid is most commonly extended in support of designated functions of local government, some assistance, in both grant-in-aid and tax-sharing categories, is given for the general support of the receiving units. In these instances, the state contributions ordinarily are placed in the general funds of the local governments concerned to be used for any lawful purpose at the discretion of the local governing bodies. Aid of this *general* character, given without explicit restriction on the purposes for which the money may be used, tends to be popular with local governing authorities because it permits a relatively high degree of flexibility in the determination of local fiscal policy. In 1954, slightly more than 10 per cent of all state aid was extended for general local purposes rather than support of specified services.

State-aid Formulas. Having determined to extend assistance to a particular class of local governments, either in support of a designated function or for local purposes generally, a state legislature is confronted with two problems: (1) it must determine the total amount of aid to be given per year or biennium; and (2) it must prescribe a plan or formula for apportioning this total among the individual participating units.

In some instances the total amount is set by the terms of the appropriation act at a fixed and definite sum which is not to be modified or diminished. In contrast to this fixed-sum plan are various types of indeterminate provision. One of these is the so-called open-end authorization, providing for expenditure of whatever amount of state funds is necessary to meet the requirements of a prescribed distributive formula. Also indeterminate in character is the provision for distributing a specified share of a designated state tax, with the actual amount of aid dependent upon tax yield. As observed in a recent publication of the Census Bureau:[43]

> Between the absolutely fixed and the completely indeterminate types of aid provisions are numerous gradations and combinations of methods. Thus, a specified share of some revenue source may be authorized for aid, but with the total sum for the current period limited also by a specific-amount appropriation. Again, a definite amount may be appropriated as a maximum, subject to reduction by the operation of a distributive formula or by administrative action.

Formulas employed for apportioning aid to individual units also vary widely. Occasionally, it is provided that all units concerned shall share equally in aid payments, each unit receiving the same amount as every

[42] A state-by-state analysis of state-aid programs as of 1952 will be found in United States Bureau of the Census, *State Payments to Local Governments in 1952* (Washington, Government Printing Office, 1954). With respect to programs in the highway field, see also, John R. Kerstetter, *Local Government's Share of State-collected Highway Funds and Revenues: A 1955 Resurvey* (Washington and Chicago, American Municipal Association, 1955).

[43] *State Payments to Local Governments in 1952*, p. 5.

other. Sometimes apportionment is on the basis of population. In the case of tax sharing it is sometimes provided that each unit shall receive aid in proportion to the amount of the "shared" tax collected therein. School aid is sometimes apportioned on the basis of number of pupils, and highway aid on the basis of road mileage.[44] Many aid programs, particularly those involving grants as distinguished from shared taxes, provide for apportionment according to some sort of equalization formula designed to enable local units having little taxable property to maintain local services of prescribed minimum standards. A plan commonly applied to local schools, for example, requires that a school district, in order to qualify for state aid, levy a property tax at a specified minimum rate and provides that if the proceeds from that levy are insufficient to maintain "standard" school facilities, the state will supply whatever additional funds are necessary.

Pros and Cons of State Aid. Proponents of state aid contend that the device operates as a wholesome stimulus to local governments to provide socially desirable services which they would not otherwise undertake and to maintain more satisfactory service standards than would be possible if they were compelled to rely entirely upon their own financial resources. It is further argued that since many local services are of state-wide as well as local interest, it is the duty of the state not only to participate in their financial support but to do so in a way that will equalize the local tax burden between units with much taxable property and those with little. And one of the strongest arguments for state aid finds its basis in an alleged moral obligation on the part of the states to share in some measure with their local units revenues derived from the lucrative nonproperty taxes which the local governments are denied authority to levy for their own use.

In opposition to state aid it is argued that since acceptance of state control is usually a part of the price exacted for state assistance, the system endangers local self-government. In warning against undue extension of state-aid programs, it is pointed out that excessive reliance upon state financial assistance is not conducive to economy and a proper feeling of responsibility at the local level. Furthermore, it is claimed that state aid, by subsidizing small and wasteful governmental units, perpetuates the existence of many units which should be eliminated in the interest of efficiency and economy. Offsetting this contention, however, it may be pointed out that state aid *may be* used, and at times *is* used, as a means of encouraging, or virtually compelling, the elimination of unduly small units. School consolidation, for example, has been effectively encouraged in some instances by denying state aid to districts operating schools for fewer than a specified number of pupils.

[44] *Ibid.*, pp. 5-6.

Whatever its relative advantages and dangers, state aid has now become firmly established as a major feature of local government financing. Today's problem, therefore, is not that of deciding whether state aid is to be continued—that it will be continued there can be little doubt—but that of devising means of improving existing programs and determining the extent to which present programs should be expanded and new programs inaugurated.[45]

FEDERAL AID

Federal aid to the states constitutes a substantial factor in state revenues, and a portion of the federal moneys received by the states is redistributed to their local units as an element in state aid. On the other hand, *direct* federal aid to local governments has not developed extensively. As creatures of the state which are fully subject to state control, local governmental units can enter into direct dealings with the federal government only as authorized by state law; and to a considerable extent the states have preferred that federal funds destined for local use be channeled through state agencies. Nevertheless, there are several federal-aid programs under which, in some or all states, depending upon state statutes, federal payments are made directly to the local units concerned. In 1954 direct federal aid to local governments, rural and urban, amounted to $299,000,000. Of this sum, $258,000,000 was in the form of grants-in-aid, the remainder being comprised of shared revenues, payments in lieu of taxes on federally owned property, payments for services, such as tuition payments for veterans' education, and miscellaneous other payments. Almost two thirds of the total amount of direct aid was extended in support of various educational programs, with highways, welfare, public health, and other functions coming in for assistance in smaller amounts.[46]

NONTAX REVENUES

State and federal aid to local governments constitutes nontax revenue from the standpoint of the receiving units; but, ordinarily, it consists of funds secured by the paying governments through taxation. On the other hand, several minor sources of local revenue are of a nontax nature in the strict sense of providing funds raised originally by means other than taxation. Fines imposed for violation of state statutes and local ordinances fall within this category. Another source consists of fees charged for local licenses and for various services performed by local officers. Fees for local liquor licenses, for court costs, and for the recording of deeds would be examples of such charges.[47]

[45] See below, "The Central Revenue Problem."

[46] *Summary of Governmental Finances in 1954*, pp. 8, 26.

[47] In some instances part or all of the fee money collected for services is retained by the collecting officer as compensation. See above, chap. 6, "The Fee System."

Of substantial importance to some local governments is revenue from special assessments. A special assessment is a charge levied upon real estate to defray all or part of the cost of a public improvement which, over and above its benefits to the community at large, confers an additional special benefit upon the property concerned. The special assessment differs from a tax principally in being imposed for, and in proportion to, special benefits conferred. Municipalities employ special assessments more extensively than do other local units, using this method of financing quite commonly for such public improvements as streets, sewers, and parks. However, assessment financing is occasionally used by counties and townships, particularly in connection with highway improvements; and special districts created for such purposes as irrigation, drainage, water supply, and levee construction often finance their work entirely through special assessments.[48] Though a special assessment ordinarily is imposed as a single charge, payment is commonly permitted to be made in installments, with interest, over a designated number of years. In order to raise funds to meet construction costs at the time the improvement is made, it is usual to issue and sell special-assessment bonds which constitute a lien upon the property assessed. Retirement of these obligations then takes place as assessment installments are paid from year to year.

Still another source of nontax revenue in the case of some local governments consists of income from publicly owned business enterprises. Although business enterprises owned by counties and townships are small in number as compared with those owned by municipalities (municipal ownership of utilities being fairly widespread), they are not unimportant. Some 30 North Carolina counties and several counties in Maryland operate liquor dispensaries.[49] County-owned airports, water-supply systems, electric light and power systems, toll bridges, and miscellaneous other enterprises are to be found in a few instances.[50] Water systems, electric utilities, and other business enterprises are operated by occasional towns and townships.[51] A few counties, towns, townships, and school districts derive some revenue from the ownership and management of forests or other public lands.[52]

Nontax revenues of the kinds mentioned are of major importance to some individual units of government, such as counties operating liquor dispensaries and special districts which rely heavily upon special assess-

[48] United States Bureau of the Census, *Property Taxation: 1941* (Washington, 1942), chap. 2. Cf. William O. Winter, *The Special Assessment Today with Emphasis on the Michigan Experience* (Ann Arbor, University of Michigan Press, 1952).

[49] Twiley W. Barker, Jr., "State Liquor Monopolies in the United States" (Unpublished Ph.D. thesis, University of Illinois, 1955), pp. 64-67.

[50] United States Bureau of the Census, *County Finances: 1945* Compendium (Washington, Government Printing Office, 1947), pp. 2, 12, 82-86.

[51] United States Bureau of the Census, *Finances of Townships and New England Towns: 1942* (Washington, Government Printing Office, 1944), p. 10.

[52] See above, chap. 18, "Public-land Management," "Parks and Forests."

ments for financing their activities. For the country as a whole, however, such revenue sources play a distinctly minor role in local government financing.

THE CENTRAL REVENUE PROBLEM

If local government costs continue to increase, as they give every promise of doing, the provision of adequate local revenues seems virtually certain to constitute, throughout the foreseeable future, a major problem of the local governments themselves and of the states in their capacity as regulators of local affairs.[53] Property taxes might, of course, be made to produce more revenue; and, indeed, it appears probable that as far as absolute amounts are concerned, income from property levies will continue to rise. But there is today a widespread conviction that property already is bearing a disproportionate share of the total tax burden; and it is scarcely conceivable that this source alone will be expanded to the point necessary to meet revenue needs. Aside from increased property taxes, two principal possibilities present themselves in the search for more local revenue: increased state aid and increased use of local nonproperty taxes. Whether one or the other of these courses is adopted, the ultimate source of the additional revenue will be largely the same, that is, nonproperty levies, such as those on sales, income, and motor fuel. The choice lies between having these taxes imposed and collected by the state, with a portion of the proceeds distributed to the local units through grants-in-aid or tax sharing, and having the levies imposed, and perhaps also collected, by the individual local governments. The fact that most of the taxes concerned can probably be administered more effectively and economically at the state level than at the local might seem to suggest a preference for state aid. On the other hand, the dangers apparently inherent in excessive reliance upon state aid argue for meeting new revenue needs at least in part through locally imposed taxes.[54] Each local government could then, on its own responsibility, impose the local levies or not in accordance with its individual needs and circumstances. The consciousness of paying local taxes has a wholesome effect, likely to be missing as regards state-aid funds, on the individual's attitude toward his local government and his expectation of services from it.[55] All factors considered, it appears that a sensible program might meet growing revenue needs through a combination of state-aid increases and new local levies, with emphasis upon one or the other as circumstances may suggest in the

53 See above, "The Rising Cost of Local Government."

54 See above, "Pros and Cons of State Aid."

55 Cf. Clyde F. Snider, "Potential New Sources of Municipal Revenue," *Report of the Revenue Laws Commission of the State of Illinois* (Springfield, Ill., 1949), pp. 349-388, 383.

respective states. Where the local taxes used are those already imposed at the state level, consideration should be given to the possibility of having the new local levies collected by the state, along with its own levy, and the proceeds therefrom, less collection costs, remitted to the levying units. Such a plan preserves local autonomy in matters of tax policy, secures the advantages of state-wide administration, and avoids duplication of administrative machinery. State collection of local taxes already is provided for in some instances, as in the case of California's county sales tax, and deserves more widespread use as local nonproperty levies become more common.

PURPOSES OF EXPENDITURES

As of 1954, local governments other than municipalities were spending in the neighborhood of $14,000,000,000 annually.[56] Of this total amount, approximately half was spent by school districts, a third by counties, and the remainder by towns, townships, and nonschool special districts. The purposes for which a government incurs expenditures reflect the activities it administers and the services it provides for its inhabitants. With schools, highways, and welfare activities taking the spotlight as the major functions of local government, it is not surprising that the items for these services account for the bulk of local spending. Of 1954 county expenditures, nearly a quarter went to highways and welfare, respectively, and more than a tenth to education. In the case of townships, education and highways each accounted for more than a quarter of the total, and welfare for almost a tenth. Together, these three major services accounted for more than 58 per cent of all county and township expenditures.[57] Aside from these services, a substantial item, particularly in the case of counties, is that for law enforcement and support of the judicial function. Lesser budgetary items are assigned to health protection, agricultural improvement, conservation of natural resources, and the miscellaneous other activities in which counties and townships engage. School and other special districts spend for the purposes indicated by their respective titles. In addition to the vast amounts spent by school districts for educational purposes, special-district expenditures include lesser sums for drainage, irrigation, water supply, housing, sanitation, fire protection, soil conservation, and a variety of other functions.

For local government generally, as in the case of government at the higher levels, only a relatively small percentage of total expenditures is devoted to those activities and services sometimes classified under the heading of *general government* or *general control*. Included within this category are expenditures for the per diem or salaries of members of the local governing body; compensation of other general administrative offi-

[56] Municipal expenditures, at the same time, were at a rate of some $10,000,000,000.

[57] See *Summary of Governmental Finances in 1954*, pp. 25, 27.

cers;[58] maintenance of local public buildings; and various activities of a generalized character, such as personnel administration and the conduct of elections. Since items of this nature comprise so small a portion of total public expenditures, realistic attempts to effect drastic economy or retrenchment in government must ordinarily take into account reductions in the larger "service" items and not confine themselves to expenditures for general control. However, in the case of small and sparsely populated local units, such as many townships, general control expenditures tend to be higher than elsewhere in relation to other governmental costs, and under these circumstances the formation of larger units through consolidation might result in substantial savings.[59]

BUDGET PRACTICES

Local government expenditures are authorized through appropriation ordinances or resolutions adopted by local governing bodies or, where such are provided, by voters' meetings. Appropriation measures, if they are to serve most satisfactorily in the financing of public services, must be based upon careful advance planning. Planning of this nature is known as budgeting. A public budget has been defined as "a complete financial plan for a definite period, which is based upon careful estimates both of the expenditure needs and of the probable income of the government."[60] In the case of the local governments the standard budget period is one year. The budget year, however, is the official *fiscal* year of the unit concerned, and this may or may not coincide with the calendar year. In some instances, the fiscal year of local governments is fixed by statute, and where this is the case the period is likely to be uniform for all local units throughout the state or at least for those of a particular class. In other instances state law permits individual units to determine their own fiscal year, a plan which frequently results in variation within a single state, even among units of the same type.

Scientific budgeting has made more headway at the national and state levels of government, and among municipalities at the local level, than among rural local units. However, many rural units now operate under formal budget plans of one kind or another. Many states have enacted so-called local budget laws applicable to all local units or to those of one or more classes, and some of these are reasonably adequate in their provisions. Too often, however, the statutes do nothing or little more than require the formulation of a single annual appropriation ordinance. To be

[58] See above, chap. 6, "Officers of General Administration."

[59] See above, chap. 9, "Declining Importance of the Township."

[60] A. E. Buck, *Budget Making* (New York, Appleton, 1921), p. 2. On the subject generally, see A. E. Buck, *Public Budgeting* (New York, Harper, 1929); John A. Perkins, "Preparation of the Local Budget," *American Political Science Review*, Vol. XL, pp. 949-958 (October, 1946).

sure, the requirement of a comprehensive ordinance represents a step in advance of the haphazard practices of earlier periods, when several appropriation ordinances were frequently considered and enacted independently of each other with only a vague hope that revenue measures would produce the funds necessary to meet authorized expenditures. But such a requirement falls far short of provision for a comprehensive fiscal plan (budget) based upon past experience, the present situation, and expected future needs. And even the requirement of a single appropriation ordinance, it appears, is often ignored in actual practice.

Students of government are in substantial agreement that, where the legislative and executive organs are separated, the budget is most appropriately prepared by the chief executive and submitted to the legislature for consideration and action. In local government, however, and particularly among rural units, legislative and executive powers so often are vested in the same officials that the principle of the executive budget is not readily applicable. Relatively few counties, for example, have a chief executive officer, though in the counties having such an officer budget preparation is ordinarily one of his duties.[61] A number of other counties have been provided with budget boards or officers of one kind or another, and in some states the finance committee of the county board is designated as the budget-making authority. In townships having a principal administrative officer that official frequently is charged with the budget-making function.[62] Elsewhere, the township budget may be prepared by the township governing board, a special budget board, or a citizens' budget committee. In Illinois, for example, the township budget ordinarily is prepared by the board of town auditors for submission to the annual meeting. However, any township may, by action of the township meeting, make other provision for budget preparation; and, under this authority, some townships at various times have established citizens' committees to replace the board of auditors as the budget agency.

Attention has been called in an earlier chapter to the growing use in New England towns of citizens' finance committees for budget-making purposes.[63] Where finance committees are not used, budget preparation ordinarily devolves upon the board of town selectmen or, where a town manager is provided, upon that official. Special-district budgets are prepared in various instances by the regular governing board of the district or a committee thereof, by the principal administrative officer of the district, where such a functionary exists, or by a special budget board.

Local budgets in some states, as noted in a previous chapter, are subject to approval by a state administrative agency with respect to their

[61] See above, chap. 7.
[62] See above, chap. 9, "Chief Township Officer."
[63] See above, chap. 8, "Finance Committees."

form and, sometimes also, with respect to their substance.[64] In general, state administrative supervision seems to have had a wholesome effect on local budgeting. State legislatures, furthermore, are gradually establishing budget systems for additional local units and strengthening existing systems. Nevertheless, many local governments still are without anything that can justifiably be considered a budget system. Better budgeting remains, therefore, one of the serious needs of local government in rural areas and elsewhere.

ACCOUNTING AND AUDITING

Accurate accounting and competent auditing are essentials of efficient fiscal administration. Only by these means can reasonable assurance be had that moneys appropriated for public services will be expended honestly and in accordance with the intent of the appropriating body. Early in the present century the benefits of improved and uniform methods of county accounting were aptly summarized as follows: [65]

1. Each county will have an accurate and complete record of all its financial affairs—one which will disclose at all times its financial condition and the condition of each of its funds and accounts.
2. The accounts of revenues and expenses being standard and the classification uniform of administration, it will be possible to make intelligent comparisons of expenses and revenues for different years.
3. Because the system will be uniform and employed in all counties of the state, it will become possible to make significant comparison between the different counties of the state.
4. By reason of all this, the officers of the county will be in a position to plan more intelligently the financial program for the future.

This statement is as valid today as it was when originally written, and it could be applied to local governments generally as appropriately as to counties.[66]

Notwithstanding the desirability of accurate and intelligible accounting, methods of local bookkeeping in practice have left much to be desired. Not only have accounts been poorly kept in many instances, but there has frequently been little uniformity among the various local units. Local officials at times have devised their own accounting "systems," largely unintelligible to other persons, including successors in office. Under such circumstances it has not only been difficult to determine the legality of expenditures but has been virtually impossible to make comparisons

[64] See above, chap. 4, "Approval and Review."

[65] Mark Graves, "Simplification of County and Local Municipal Finances," *Proceedings of the Second Conference for Better County Government in New York State* (White Plains, N. Y., 1916), pp. 74-81, 80.

[66] Some specific obstacles to modernization of county bookkeeping are discussed by Arthur J. Peel, "Some Problems of County Government Accounting," *American City*, Vol. XXX, pp. 605-607 (June, 1924).

among different units. During recent decades there has been a marked extension of state supervision over local accounting, and this has resulted in substantial improvement. Practically every state now provides some degree of supervision over accounts of all local governments or those of particular classes. In many instances state administrative agencies prescribe the forms for local accounts. Although state-prescribed forms at times are ignored by local officials, state prescription, especially when accompanied by state inspection or audit, goes far toward raising accounting standards.

If they are to serve their purpose fully, local accounts must not only be kept in an accurate and intelligible manner but must be thoroughly audited at appropriate intervals.[67] In general, the annual audit seems advisable, and it is widely used. However, there are many instances in which provision is made for auditing only biennially or even less frequently; and, indeed, there are still some local governments which do not provide for regular auditing of any kind. Since the purpose of the audit is to check on the accuracy of administrative bookkeeping and the legality of the expenditures of administrative agencies, it cannot properly be performed by an agency which is subject to control by the local administrative authorities; rather, it should be of an external and independent character. It may appropriately be conducted (1) by a local public auditor who is popularly elected; (2) by a public auditor chosen by the local governing body, where that body is limited to policy determination and there is a principal executive officer charged with administrative oversight; (3) by qualified private accountants hired for the purpose; or (4) by state examiners.

Although some local governments, particularly counties from among those in the more populous group, have their own auditors, the greater part of the auditing of local accounts is performed by private accountants or state examiners. Auditing by private accountants is quite satisfactory where the accountants chosen are competent and are paid a sufficient sum to enable them to perform their task in a thoroughgoing manner. Unfortunately, as the result of a penny-wise policy on the part of some local authorities, the amount appropriated for auditing purposes is frequently inadequate to pay for more than a very superficial examination. Furthermore, some units employ competitive bidding in the letting of auditing

[67] The audit here referred to is known in accounting terminology as the *postaudit,* for the reason that it occurs *after* the disbursement of the funds involved. Concerning the distinction between this and the *preaudit,* occurring *before* disbursement, see above, chap. 6, "Officers of General Administration," pp. 154-155. The following comments on local auditing are based in part on a memorandum prepared by the author in 1950 for the Illinois Commission to Study State Government; see Illinois Commission to Study State Government, *Organization and Functioning of the State Government: Staff Studies* (Springfield, Ill., 1950), Vol. IV, No. 79, "State-Local Relations," pp. 7-10.

contracts—a practice of doubtful wisdom in view of the extreme difficulty of providing accurate specifications concerning the scope and quality of an audit.[68]

Experience with state auditing of local accounts seems in general to have been gratifying.[69] Examiners specializing in governmental work and responsible to the state rather than the local units are in a position to perform unbiased audits of local accounts and to assist untrained and inexperienced local officials in becoming familiar with proper accounting practices. Especially in its application to the smaller and less populous local units, state auditing, coupled with state prescription of accounting forms, appears to offer a feasible approach to the problem of safeguarding public funds and assuring that they will be expended in accordance with legislative intent. An incidental but significant effect of uniform accounts and state auditing is to facilitate the collection and publication on a statewide basis of comprehensive financial data concerning local government.[70]

PURCHASING

Closely related to budgeting and accounting is the matter of purchasing procedures.[71] Expenditures for supplies, materials, and equipment consume, in the average government, from 20 to 30 per cent of the total operating budget,[72] being second in amount only to expenditures for personal services. At one time purchasing procedures were quite generally informal and decentralized, with each officer being permitted to do his own official buying in his own way. During the past half century, however, many governments have introduced centralized purchasing systems as a means of fostering economy and efficient administration.

Centralized purchasing has been defined as "the delegation to one office of the authority to purchase supplies, materials, and equipment needed for use by all the several operating branches of the organization." [73] Where purchasing is decentralized, each department or agency is likely to fill its needs at retail prices. With centralization, on the other hand, the pooling of departmental requirements results in larger orders,

[68] Cf. H. K. Allen, *Control of Expenditures in the Local Governmental Units of Illinois* (Urbana, University of Illinois Bureau of Business Research, 1940), p. 31.

[69] See above, chap. 4, "Inspection."

[70] As examples of helpful compilations of local finance data, see Indiana State Board of Accounts, *Statistical Report, State of Indiana* (Indianapolis, Ind., annually); Maryland State Fiscal Research Bureau, *Local Government Finances in Maryland* (Baltimore, Md., annually); Ohio Bureau of Inspection and Supervision of Public Offices, *Comparative Statistics: Counties of Ohio* (Columbus, Ohio State Auditor, annually).

[71] A standard treatise on the subject generally is Russell Forbes, *Governmental Purchasing* (New York, Harper, 1929).

[72] Russell Forbes, *Centralized Purchasing: A Sentry at the Tax Exit Gate*, rev. ed. (New York, National Association of Purchasing Agents, 1941), p. 5.

[73] *Ibid.*

which may frequently be filled at wholesale and which facilitate the use of standard specifications and competitive bidding. Furthermore, centralization often permits the employment of professional buyers skilled in the prediction of market trends and purchasing techniques. As a result of these various factors, unit costs are often substantially reduced. Indeed, centralized purchasing, when free from political interference and efficiently administered, appears to effect an average saving of from 10 to 15 per cent.[74]

At the beginning of the 1940's, some 75 American counties were reported to be practicing centralized purchasing; [75] and it is estimated that about 100 counties are currently (1956) operating under the centralized plan.[76] Although the counties employing the plan are, for the most part, the more populous ones, the list includes some of smaller population. In the most populous counties the purchasing organization tends to be elaborate and its staff large. Thus, the purchasing and stores department of Los Angeles County, Cal., was reported in 1941 to have a staff of about 130 persons.[77] In several counties, including that of Los Angeles, the personnel of the purchasing department, including the purchasing agent, is selected under a merit system.

County purchasing, like other aspects of county administration, is under the general supervision and control of the county governing board. Where centralized purchasing prevails the purchasing agent is usually appointed by the board, except that under the manager plan he is normally an appointee of the manager; and in any event it is the board that prescribes purchasing procedures. Among counties not having a regular purchasing department, and this, of course, includes the vast majority of all counties, purchasing practices vary widely. In some instances the county boards themselves do the purchasing. A fairly common practice among smaller counties is for the board to authorize the heads of the respective departments and institutions to do their own purchasing, subject sometimes to board approval. Under still another plan the county board designates one of its members or some other county official, such as the auditor, clerk, or judge, to do the county's buying.[78]

[74] *Ibid.*, pp. 37-38. Concerning other advantages of centralized purchasing procedures, see *ibid.*, pp. 6 ff.; Forbes, *Governmental Purchasing*, pp. 4-10.

[75] Joseph W. Nicholson, *County Purchasing* (New York, National Association of Purchasing Agents, 1940), p. 15; Robert A. Martino, "County Purchasing Methods Reviewed," *National Municipal Review*, Vol. XXIX, pp. 388-395 (June, 1940). Eighteen of these counties, or nearly one fourth of the total number, were in California. Martino, *loc. cit.*

[76] This estimate was made by Albert H. Hall, executive vice president of the National Institute of Governmental Purchasing, in a letter to the author dated March 15, 1956.

[77] Paul Beckett, "Public Purchasing Methods: Los Angeles County and City," *The Tax Digest*, Vol. XIX, pp. 196-197, 211-214 (June, 1941).

[78] Martino, *loc. cit.*

A somewhat different approach to the purchasing problem is provided by various arrangements under which two or more governmental units make their purchases jointly, or one or more units use the purchasing facilities of another. An outstanding example of joint purchasing is afforded by the Cincinnati region in Ohio where, for a quarter century, joint purchasing procedures have been used for various items by Hamilton County, the city of Cincinnati, the University of Cincinnati, the public-school district, and the public library.[79] Milwaukee County, Wis., co-operates with the city of Milwaukee and various other local government agencies in the purchase of certain supplies.[80] Some examples of joint purchasing by two or more school districts have been reported.[81] The purchasing department of Los Angeles County, Cal., serves as the central buying agency for more than 200 school districts, improvement districts, and other local jurisdictions within the county.[82] Several states now authorize local governmental units to make purchases through the state purchasing department, and a few counties and school districts have availed themselves of this privilege.[83]

Arrangements of the types considered in the preceding paragraph are especially well adapted to meeting the needs of those small governmental units that would find it too costly to provide their own purchasing agencies. It is to be hoped that the future will see considerable expansion in the authorization and use of such arrangements. Though some progress has been made during recent years, much remains to be done in the improvement of local government purchasing procedures, particularly in rural areas.

THE LOCAL BORROWING POWER[84]

In the financing of their activities and services local governments frequently find it necessary, or at any rate desirable, to resort to borrowing. As agencies of delegated powers, the local units have only such debt-incurring authority as has been conferred upon them by the states, and the powers so conferred are hedged about by many limitations. Most state constitutions impose limitations upon local borrowing, and, whether or

[79] Nicholson, *op. cit.*, pp. 10-12; James D. Kitchen, *Coöperative Governmental Purchasing* (Los Angeles, University of California Bureau of Governmental Research, 1953), pp. 3-6.

[80] Kitchen, *op. cit.*, pp. 6-7.

[81] Charlton F. Chute, "Coöperative Purchasing in the United States and Canada," *National Municipal Review*, Vol. XXVII, pp. 499-504 (October, 1938).

[82] Kitchen, *op. cit.*, p. 8.

[83] *Ibid.*, pp. 13-15; Weldon Cooper, "Alabama Counties Use State Purchasing Facilities," *National Municipal Review*, Vol. XXIX, p. 333 (May, 1940).

[84] On problems of local borrowing generally, see Paul Studensky, *Public Borrowing* (New York, National Municipal League, 1930); Carl H. Chatters and Albert M. Hillhouse, *Local Government Debt Administration* (New York, Prentice-Hall, 1939).

not there are constitutional restrictions, an abundance of statutory limitations usually will be found.

Restrictions on local borrowing, as would be expected, vary in character from state to state.[85] Usually, there will be a limitation on the amount of indebtedness that may be incurred, expressed as a percentage of the assessed valuation of taxable property. Most states impose restrictions on the purposes of borrowing, including a prohibition of lending credit to private persons or corporations. The length of the term for which local government bonds may run is commonly limited, as is also the rate of interest that may be paid. A majority of the states now require that the bonds of some or all local units be issued in serial form.[86] In a few states local borrowing is subject to some degree of state administrative control.[87] Finally, it is to be noted that though the borrowing power is vested occasionally in the local governing body, this is distinctly the exception. In the great majority of local units, debt may be incurred only with the approval of the voters in a referendum election. In a few states only taxpayers are eligible to vote in such elections.

This superabundance of limitations upon the power of local governments to incur indebtedness doubtless has operated in some measure as a deterrent to overborrowing and defaults. On the other hand, limitations in terms of amount are at times virtually nullified by the establishment of special districts that are coterminous with, or overlap, the general government units and have their own borrowing power, or by the use of public authorities for borrowing purposes.[88] Furthermore, since special-assessment bonds and revenue bonds ordinarily are exempt from the regular debt limits, special-assessment or revenue-bond financing is sometimes resorted to by a local unit to enable it to incur additional indebtedness after its general constitutional or statutory borrowing power has been exhausted.[89] In the final analysis, provisions of a purely negative nature cannot assure wise borrowing policy. Within constitutional and statutory limits, it is still possible to borrow for unnecessary improvements or for other imprudent purposes. Aside from state administrative supervision, which is not extensive, unwise use of the local debt-incurring power *within* legal limits can be prevented only through discreet and vigilant action of local legislative bodies and the voters in approving or disapproving borrowing proposals.

[85] A summary and tabular analysis of constitutional and statutory provisions in the respective states will be found in Lane W. Lancaster, "State Limitations on Local Indebtedness," *The Municipal Year Book* (Chicago, International City Managers' Association, 1936), pp. 313-327.

[86] See below, "Debt Retirement."

[87] Examples are mentioned above, chap. 4, "Approval and Review."

[88] See above, chap. 10.

[89] The nature of revenue bonds is explained below, "Borrowing Practices."

BORROWING PRACTICES

The purposes for which local governments most commonly borrow are (1) in anticipation of revenues, (2) for expenditures arising from emergencies, and (3) for construction of public improvements. In many governmental units the fiscal year and tax calendar are so poorly synchronized that tax revenues are not due and payable until the fiscal year is several months advanced. When this is the case, it is ordinarily necessary for the government to borrow funds to meet its payroll and other expenditures until tax moneys begin to reach the treasury. During the 1930's many local units, along with the state and national governments, borrowed to meet relief costs and other expenditures flowing from the depression emergency. Fire, tornado, flood, and earthquake are among the other causes of occasional disaster which may call for emergency borrowing by local governments.

From the standpoint of amounts involved, public improvements account for the bulk of local government borrowing. Units of all major classes have occasion to brorrow for such purposes. School buildings, county courthouses and town halls, major highway improvements, and irrigation and reclamation projects are among the undertakings calling for construction expenditures in such amounts that it is usually not feasible to attempt to meet them from current revenues. In such cases, funds ordinarily are borrowed to meet construction costs, and the loan then is repaid from tax revenues over a period of several years. When borrowing for a public improvement, bond maturities should normally be so arranged that the loan will be repaid in its entirety within the useful life of the improvement concerned; and in practice it may frequently be wise policy, in times of prosperity, to liquidate public-improvement indebtedness well in advance of the end of this period of usefulness.

Public borrowings are commonly said to be of two classes: short-term and long-term. Short-term borrowings, or temporary borrowings, as they are sometimes called, are usually in anticipation of taxes or the proceeds from bond issues or to meet emergency expenditures unforeseen when the budget was adopted.[90] Borrowings of this nature are represented by bank loans, tax-anticipation warrants, and other short-term instruments; and ordinarily they are repaid during the current fiscal year or, at the latest, early in the following year. Short-term borrowings constitute only a very small portion of all local indebtedness. In 1954, for example, short-term debt constituted only about 7 per cent of the total outstanding indebtedness of local governments other than municipalities.[91] Along with unpaid bills and any other demand or short-term obligations, short-term borrow-

[90] Studensky, *op. cit.*, p. 1; Chatters and Hillhouse, *op. cit.*, p. 165.
[91] Computed from *Summary of Governmental Finances in 1954*, p. 33.

ings make up the *floating* debt of the governmental unit concerned, in contrast to its more permanent *funded* or *bonded* debt.[92]

Long-term borrowing is usually effected through the issuance of bonds to be redeemed from revenues of future years. Government bonds are of two principal types: general-obligation bonds and revenue bonds. General-obligation bonds are secured by a pledge of the full faith and credit of the issuing government and are sometimes referred to as full-faith-and-credit bonds. Ordinarily, the holder of general-obligation bonds is entitled, if necessary, to compel by judicial process the levy of a local tax to pay the principal amount of the bonds and interest thereon, as these become due. In contrast, revenue bonds, which are most commonly issued for the financing of a public utility, a toll bridge, or some other income-producing enterprise, are secured only by a pledge of the revenues accruing from the project concerned, supplemented in some instances by a lien upon the enterprise property. Because of the limited nature of their security, revenue bonds are commonly considered less desirable investments than general-obligation bonds and therefore must ordinarily bear a higher rate of interest. This being the case, it is somewhat more costly to finance an enterprise through revenue bonds than through general-obligation borrowing, though the cost of revenue-bond financing is borne by customers of the enterprise concerned rather than by the taxpayers as such. The use of revenue bonds in local government financing is growing somewhat though such obligations continue to constitute but a small part of all local indebtedness. Among the different local government units, revenue-bond financing is used most by municipalities and certain varieties of special districts, since these units engage more extensively than do counties and townships in enterprises of a business or semibusiness nature.[93]

DEBT RETIREMENT

Until comparatively recently, local government bonds were ordinarily of the term, or sinking-fund, type. Under this plan, all bonds of a particular issue mature at the same time—say 10, 15, or 20 years after the date of issue. To provide for their retirement when due, a sinking fund is established, into which a fixed sum is to be paid each year and the moneys in which are invested in approved interest-bearing securities. The amount to be placed in the sinking fund annually is so calculated that together with the interest earned by moneys in the fund, it should equal the face amount of the bond issue on the date of maturity. Bond interest, meanwhile, is paid from current revenues.

[92] Floating debt may be contrasted also with *fixed debt,* a term that is broader than funded debt, including not only bonds but various other long-term obligations, such as judgments and long-term notes. Chatters and Hillhouse, *op. cit.,* p. 494.

[93] On the nature and uses of revenue-bond financing, see "Revenue Bonds," *Municipal Finance,* Vol. XXI, No. 4 (May, 1949).

Term bonds proved generally unsatisfactory because of various weaknesses in the sinking-fund plan of retirement. In the first place, county boards and other fiscal agencies sometimes failed to levy the necessary tax for sinking-fund purposes or to make the required appropriation to the fund. Again, since sinking-fund moneys might not be needed for debt redemption for a number of years, there was constant temptation to borrow therefrom for seemingly more urgent purposes, and such borrowings were not always repaid. Finally, if interest rates declined, securities purchased for the sinking fund were likely to produce less income than anticipated. For any or all of these reasons, when an issue of term bonds matured, the moneys in the sinking fund might be inadequate for bond redemption. Because of difficulties such as these, sinking-fund bonds during recent decades have steadily declined in popularity, and bonds of the serial type have gained in favor.

Serial bonds are retired from current revenues, maturities being staggered so that only a designated portion of an issue becomes due in any one year. Where it is desired, for example, to repay a particular loan over a period of 20 years, maturities may be arranged so that one twentieth of the principal amount becomes due each year. In such a case, the bonds are known as *straight serials.* Since interest as well as payments on principal must be met from current revenues, the straight-serial plan places a heavier total burden upon the taxpayers during the earlier years of the repayment period than during later years, when payments on principal have resulted in corresponding reductions in the interest item. In order to overcome this disadvantage and equalize the tax burden throughout the repayment period, maturities may be so arranged that principal payments are smaller during the early years, when interest payments are heavy, and larger during later years, when interest payments are lighter. Bonds issued under this arrangement, which seeks to make total annual payments for principal *and* interest approximately equal throughout the repayment period, are known as *annuity serials.* Because serial bonds eliminate the necessity of a sinking fund, with all of its shortcomings, most bonds now issued by local governments are in serial form of one variety or another.

A special feature which may be included in either term or serial bonds is a provision permitting the issuing government, after a designated number of years but before the maturity date, to call and pay the bonds at par or, sometimes, at a specified small premium. Such a call privilege injects an additional element of flexibility into financial adminstration. If interest rates decline, substantial savings may sometimes be made by calling outstanding indebtedness and issuing new securities at lower interest rates. The call feature has long been quite common in bonds of private corporations and deserves more extensive use in local government borrowing than it has yet been accorded.

TRENDS IN LOCAL INDEBTEDNESS

The amount of local government indebtedness varies considerably from time to time. The following analysis shows the total debt (in millions) of the various local units other than municipalities for selected years from 1913 to 1954: [94]

Year	*Counties*	*Towns and townships*	*School districts*	*Other special districts*
1913	$ 393	$ 80	$ 119	$ 36
1922	1,387	130	1,127	639
1932	2,775	433	2,170	1,393
1942	1,846	273	1,701	2,853
1946	1,417	166	1,283	2,597
1952	2,018	619	3,806	4,125
1953	2,454	656	4,712	4,577
1954	2,710	801	5,923	5,310

Prior to the World War I, public indebtedness in the United States, including that of the rural local units, was relatively low. In 1913, the total debt of the local units here under consideration was well under $1,000,000-000. During that war and the postwar years local indebtedness increased steadily; and the economic depression of the 1930's was the occasion for widespread borrowing by governments at all levels to meet vast expenditure programs for work and direct relief. Following the depression, the local governments of most types reduced their indebtedness somewhat; the reduction being especially marked during the years of World War II, when substantial payments were made on outstanding obligations and, with labor and materials generally unavailable for ordinary civil construction, there was little new borrowing for capital outlays. The end of hostilities brought a general resumption of construction programs which had been interrupted by wartime restrictions and, with it, a reversal in local debt trends. Recent years have witnessed a steady increase in local government indebtedness, and further increases in the future seem likely. Although some increase may be expected in the indebtedness of local governments of all classes, the rise will probably be greatest in the case of school districts, as building programs are pushed to care for growing enrollments, and in that of nonschool special districts, as they build and expand public-improvement facilities, such as sewerage systems and waterworks. Individual local units will continue, of course, to vary from the general trends, some units being vested with broader borrowing power than others and some using more freely than others the debt-incurring authority they possess.

The total indebtedness of the local government units here considered—

[94] *Historical Review of State and Local Government Finances,* p. 18; *Summary of Governmental Finances in 1954,* p. 33.

counties, towns and townships, and special districts—amounted in 1954 to approximately $15,000,000,000. This may seem, in itself, a very modest amount to be owed in a nation of some 160,000,000 inhabitants having an annual national income in excess of $300,000,000,000. It must be remembered, however, that the borrowings of local units in the categories mentioned constitute but a small portion of our total governmental debt. To the $15,000,000,000 owed by these units must be added, if we are to have the complete picture, another $15,000,000,000 owed by municipalities, $10,000,000,000 owed by the states, and an enormous federal debt of $270,000,000,000. This makes a total public debt as of 1954 of $310,000,000,000, a sum approaching $2,000 per capita. To be sure, approximately 90 per cent of the total is indebtedness of the federal government. But the entire amount, save for certain relatively small sums in revenue bonds, is an obligation of the American taxpaying public—a fact which must be borne in mind if a true perspective is to be maintained. All this would seem to suggest that until the federal debt is materially reduced, proposals for increased local borrowing should be considered with more than ordinary care.

REFERENCES

Books, Reports, and Special Studies

ALLEN, H. K., *Control of Expenditures in the Local Governmental Units of Illinois* (Urbana, University of Illinois Bureau of Business Research, 1940).

Assessment of Real Property in Kentucky Counties (Frankfort, Commonwealth of Kentucky Department of Revenue, 1939).

BITTERMANN, Henry J., *State and Federal Grants-in-aid* (Chicago, Mentzer, Bush & Co., 1938).

BRYAN, Gordon K., *County Finances in Mississippi* (State College, Mississippi State College Social Science Research Center, 1950).

———, *County Revenues and Expenditures in Mississippi: 1950* (State College, Mississippi State College Social Science Research Center, 1952).

CATHERWOOD, M. P., *Receipts and Expenditures of 876 New York Towns in 1934* (Ithaca, N. Y., Cornell University Agricultural Experiment Station, 1936).

CHATTERS, Carl H., and HILLHOUSE, Albert M., *Local Government Debt Administration* (New York, Prentice-Hall, 1939).

COMPTON, Ralph T., *Fiscal Problems of Rural Decline: A Study of the Methods of Financing the Costs of Government in Economically Decadent Rural Areas of New York State,* Special Report of the New York State Tax Commission (Albany, 1929).

Council of State Governments, *Federal Grants-in-aid* (Chicago, 1949).

———, *Grants-in-aid and other Federal Expenditures within the States,* rev. ed. (Chicago, 1947).

ENGLAND, Eric, "Rural Taxation," in *Yearbook of Agriculture: Farmers in a Changing World* (Washington, U. S. Department of Agriculture, 1940), pp. 771-789.

Federal, State, and Local Government Fiscal Relations, Sen. Doc. 69, 78th Cong., 1st sess. (Washington, Government Printing Office, 1943).

GALBRAITH, J. K., *California County Expenditures* (Berkeley, University of California Agricultural Experiment Station, 1934).

GRAVES, Mark, "Simplification of County and Local Municipal Finances," *Proceedings of the Second Conference for Better County Government in New York State* (White Plains, N. Y., 1916), pp. 74-81.

HALCROW, Harold G., *Fiscal Policies of Montana Counties* (Bozeman, Montana State College Agricultural Experiment Station, 1949).

HARRIS, Joseph P., *County Finances in the State of Washington* (Seattle, University of Washington Press, 1935).

HILLHOUSE, A. Miller, and WELCH, Ronald B., *Tax Limits Appraised* (Chicago, Public Administration Service, 1937).

HINCKLEY, Russell J., *State Grants-in-aid*, Special Report of the New York State Tax Commission (Albany, 1935).

HULSE, F. E., and WALKER, W. P., *Property Tax Problems in Rural-urban Fringe Areas* (College Park, University of Maryland Agricultural Experiment Station, 1952).

JENSEN, Jens P., *Property Taxation in the United States* (Chicago, University of Chicago Press, 1931).

KIMMEL, Lewis H., *Governmental Costs and Tax Levels* (Washington, Brookings Institution, 1948).

LAWSON, Harry O., *Recent Trends in County Finance: 1947-1951* (Lawrence, University of Kansas Governmental Research Center, 1953).

LEE, Eugene C., *The County Sales Tax and Other Local Revenues* (Berkeley, University of California Bureau of Public Administration, 1951).

LEET, Glen, and PAIGE, Robert M., eds., *Property Tax Limitation Laws* (Chicago, Public Administration Service, 1934).

MCDONALD, James T., *County Finance in Kansas: 1952-1954* (Lawrence, University of Kansas Governmental Research Center, 1956).

MCKINLEY, John R., *Local Revenue Problems and Trends* (Berkeley, University of California Bureau of Public Administration, 1949).

MCMAHON, John A., *Sources of County Revenue* [*in North Carolina*], 2d ed. (Chapel Hill, University of North Carolina Institute of Government, 1954).

MILLER, Loren B., *Local Finance and Procedure* (Detroit, Michigan Commission of Inquiry into County, Township, and School District Government, 1933).

Municipal Finance Officers' Association of the United States and Canada, *County Finance and Accounting Standards* (Chicago, 1937).

National Association of Assessing Officers, *Assessment Organization and Personnel* (Chicago, 1941).

National Industrial Conference Board, *State and Local Taxation of Property* (New York, 1930).

NICHOLSON, Joseph W., *County Purchasing* (New York, National Association of Purchasing Agents, 1940).

PEAK, George, and REEVES, J. E., *Kentucky County Debts: June 30, 1938* (Lexington, University of Kentucky Bureau of Business Research, 1940).

PELLETIER, Lawrence L., *Financing Local Government* (Brunswick, Me., Bowdoin College, 1948).

PRESCOTT, Frank W., *County Finance in the South* (Dallas, Southern Methodist University, Arnold Foundation, 1937).

SHAMBERGER, Harold J., *A Report on West Virginia Municipal and County Budgets: 1953* (Morgantown, West Virginia University Bureau for Government Research, 1953).

STUDENSKY, Paul, *Public Borrowing* (New York, National Municipal League, 1930).

Tax Foundation, *Facts and Figures on Government Finance* (New York, biennially).

———, *Recent Trends in Local Taxes: 1942-1947* (New York, 1948).

Tax Institute, *More State Aid or More Local Taxes?* (New York, 1948).

United States Bureau of the Census, *Compendium of State Government Finances in 1954* (Washington, Government Printing Office, 1955).

———, *County Finances: 1945 Compendium* (Washington, Government Printing Office, 1947).

———, *Finances of School Districts: 1942* (Washington, Government Printing Office, 1944).

———, *Finances of Townships and New England Towns: 1942* (Washington, Government Printing Office, 1944).

———, *Historical Review of State and Local Government Finances* (Washington, 1948).

———, *Historical Statistics on State and Local Government Finances: 1902-1953* (Washington, Government Printing Office, 1955).

———, *Property Taxation: 1941* (Washington, 1942).

———, *State Aid to Local Governments* (Washington, 1948).

———, *State Payments to Local Governments in 1952* (Washington, Government Printing Office, 1954).

———, *Summary of County Government Finances in 1946* (Washington, 1948).

University of Oregon Bureau of Municipal Research and Service, *Revenue Sources of Oregon Counties: 1953-54* (Eugene, Ore., 1956).

VANLANDINGHAM, Kenneth E., *Financial Management in Kentucky Counties* (Lexington, University of Kentucky Bureau of Government Research, 1951).

WALKER, William Paul, and NYSTROM, Paul E., *State Revenue Distributions to Local Units in Maryland with Special Reference to Tax Burdens of Farmers* (College Park, University of Maryland Agricultural Experiment Station, 1954).

WATKINS, Kermit, *Economic Implications of State Grants-in-aid* (Lawrence, University of Kansas Bureau of Business Research, 1956).

WILLIAMS, Sheldon W., *Governmental Costs and Taxes in 150 Vermont Towns* (Burlington, University of Vermont Agricultural Experiment Station, 1948).

WINTER, William O., *The Special Assessment Today with Emphasis on the Michigan Experience* (Ann Arbor, University of Michigan Press, 1952).

See also the standard textbooks in the field of public finance.

Articles

BRYAN, Gordon K., "The County Revenue System in Mississippi," *The County Officer,* Vol. XVII, pp. 135-140, 151 (May, 1952).

BUEHLER, Alfred G., "The Income Tax as a Local Revenue," *Bulletin of the National Tax Association,* Vol. XXXIII, pp. 34-40 (November, 1947).

"California Counties Levy Sales Tax," *National Municipal Review,* Vol. XLV, pp. 454-455 (October, 1956).

CLINE, Denzel C., and COMBS, William H., "Fiscal Pattern of Michigan Townships," *Bulletin of the National Tax Association,* Vol. XXXI, pp. 82-88, 98-109 (December, 1945, January, 1946).

HAMMAR, Conrad H., "Expenditures of Local Governments," *Journal of Farm Economics,* Vol. XIX, pp. 727-740 (August, 1937).

HEER, Clarence, "Comparative Costs of County Government in the South," *Social Forces,* Vol. XI, pp. 263-268 (December, 1932).

———, "The Rural Tax Problem," *Social Forces,* Vol. VIII, pp. 109-118 (September, 1929).

LEE, Eugene C., "The County Sales Tax and Local Revenues," *The County Officer,* Vol. XVI, pp. 165-169, 186 (July, 1951).

MACDOUGALL, William R., "The County Sales Tax: A Logical Revenue Source," *The County Officer,* Vol. XVII, pp. 141-144 (May, 1952).

MANVEL, Allen D., "County Government Finances—Recent Levels and Trends," *The County Officer,* Vol. XIX, pp. 76-79 (April, 1954).

MARTINO, Robert A., "County Purchasing Methods Reviewed," *National Municipal Review,* Vol. XXIX, pp. 388-395 (June, 1940).

MEFFERD, Howard L., "A Merit System for County Assessors," *The County Officer,* Vol. XVI, pp. 250-253 (October, 1951).

"Mississippi State Financial Aid to Counties," *Public Administration Survey,* publication of the University of Mississippi Bureau of Public Administration, Vol. I, No. 4 (March, 1954).

PEEL, Arthur J., "Some Problems of County Government Accounting," *American City,* Vol. XXX, pp. 605-607 (June, 1924).

PERKINS, John A., "Preparation of the Local Budget," *American Political Science Review,* Vol. XL, pp. 949-958 (October, 1946).

PORTER, Kirk H., "Property Taxes—The Doom of the County," *National Municipal Review,* Vol. XXIV, pp. 144-146 (March, 1935).

SNIDER, Clyde F., "Fiscal Control at the County Level," *National Municipal Review,* Vol. XXX, pp. 579-586 (October, 1941).

STOUT, Randall S., and MYERS, Eugene A., "The Development of Permissive Local Taxation since 1945," *Current Economic Comment,* publication of the University of Illinois Bureau of Economic and Business Research, Vol. XIII, No. 3, pp. 20-35 (August, 1951).

VANLANDINGHAM, Kenneth E., "Financial Management in Kentucky Counties," *The County Officer,* Vol. XVII, pp. 70-73 (March, 1952).

———, "State Aid for Kentucky Units of Local Government: Some Constitutional Problems," *Kentucky Law Journal,* Vol. XLI, pp. 271-301 (March, 1953).

PART SIX

Reorganization

CHAPTER 20

Problems and Prospects

HAVING EXAMINED THE organization and functioning of local governments of the types found in rural areas, and having noted at various points some of the shortcomings of the existing system, we turn in this final chapter to a consideration of certain measures which have been proposed, and to some extent are being adopted, in an effort to improve and modernize our local institutions. Problems of local reorganization fall into several categories, each related in some measure to the others. Without attempting an all-inclusive enumeration, there are problems of (1) area, (2) internal organization, (3) allocation of functions, (4) finance, and (5) state-local relations.

The discussion here will deal in large part with problems relating primarily to the need for areal readjustments—problems which have been accorded only incidental attention at previous points. Problems in the remaining categories have been dealt with at some length in preceding chapters, but it seems appropriate in this concluding survey to call attention again to some of their salient features for purposes of summary and emphasis.[1]

AREAL PROBLEMS

The number and variety of local governmental units in the United States were described earlier.[2] The existence of approximately 100,000 such units inevitably gives rise to many units of small area and to much overlapping. These small, overlapping areas, in turn, have resulted in widespread confusion, waste, and inefficiency.

[1] Problems of internal organization are considered in chaps. 5-10; functions and their allocation in chaps. 12-18; financial problems in chap. 19; and state-local relations in chaps. 2-4.

[2] See above, chap. 2.

In the first place, our complicated system of local areas is confusing to the citizen and voter. The typical citizen lives under several layers of local government. Even in the most strictly rural areas it is not uncommon to find at least three local governments—county, township, and school district—superimposed one upon another; and in many communities governmental layers are considerably more numerous. Under such circumstances, the maze of overlapping units frequently becomes so complicated that it is virtually impossible for the average citizen to obtain a clear mental picture of his local government and to take an intelligent interest in local public affairs. In the second place, the multiplicity of local governments is uneconomical. With few exceptions, each unit of government has its own set of officials and, although the pay of many individual officers may be small, their compensation in the aggregate constitutes a considerable burden upon the taxpayer.

Finally, many small units are today administering functions which could be handled more efficiently by larger areas. As units for the construction and maintenance of roads, for example, most townships and many counties find it financially impossible, or at least unduly burdensome, to employ qualified engineering personnel and provide modern mechanical equipment. In suppressing disease and carrying on health-promotion activities, fairly large units are necessary in order to provide trained, full-time personnel and modern equipment; yet the township continues in some states to be the unit charged with primary responsibility for public-health work in rural areas. Provision of relief or public assistance cannot satisfactorily be made the responsibility of small local units, since communities containing relatively large numbers of dependents are often the very ones which do not have the taxable property necessary to support them. And, in the field of education, it is becoming increasingly clear that the small district must give way to larger administrative and financial units if educational opportunity is to be equalized and effective instruction provided.

GEOGRAPHIC CONSOLIDATION

If, as seems apparent, the smallness of existing areas is in part responsible for present-day governmental ills, a possible remedy which immediately suggests itself is that of geographic consolidation. Should it not be possible, by establishing fewer and larger units through a program of consolidation, to make our system of local government more understandable, economical, and efficient? The principle of consolidation is applicable to local units generally, but it has been most frequently urged with respect to counties and school districts.

COUNTY CONSOLIDATION

County consolidation has been widely advocated by political scientists and others as a desirable step in the direction of local reorganization. County-consolidation studies of various kinds have been made in at least two thirds of the states,[3] and in several instances specific plans for consolidation have been suggested.[4] Present-day counties were laid out in "horse and buggy" days, seemingly on the assumption that it was desirable to have counties of such size that the county seat would be reasonably accessible to all citizens. This assumption was probably valid at that time and appears to be equally so today; but, with the automobile and improved roads, the county seat of a much larger county is now even more accessible to citizens than was that of the small county a few decades ago.

Many states have constitutional or statutory provisions authorizing contiguous counties to consolidate voluntarily; yet since the beginning of the present century the more than 3,000 counties in the country have been reduced in number by only three through voluntary consolidation.[5] In 1919, rural James County in Tennessee consolidated with neighboring Hamilton County, which contains the city of Chattanooga; and in 1932 the two rural Georgia counties of Campbell and Milton were merged with Fulton County, containing the city of Atlanta.[6] Throughout this entire period there has not been a single instance of consolidation involving rural counties only.

The extremely slow progress of county consolidation by voluntary means is not difficult to understand. A proposal to consolidate one county with another is likely to meet with bitter opposition from various elements in the county that would lose its legal identity by the merger. Officials and politicians will usually be found in opposition, and many ordinary

[3] Arthur C. Millspaugh, *Local Democracy and Crime Control* (Washington, Brookings Institution, 1936), p. 104.

[4] For illustrative proposals for individual states, see Scoville R. Heckart and G. S. Klemmedson, *County Consolidation in Colorado* (Fort Collins, Colorado Agricultural College, Colorado Experiment Station, 1933); Vernon G. Sorrell and J. Raymond Stuart, *County Consolidation in New Mexico* (Albuquerque, University of New Mexico, 1934); Selden C. Menefee, *A Plan for Regional Administrative Districts in the State of Washington* (Seattle, University of Washington, 1935); C. E. Allred and B. H. Luebke, *Areal and Functional Consolidation of Tennessee Counties* (Knoxville, University of Tennessee, 1943); Nevada Legislative Counsel Bureau, *County Consolidation and Reorganization in Nevada* (Carson City, Nev., 1948); Melvin Clyde Hughes, *County Government in Georgia* (Athens, University of Georgia Press, 1944), chap. 11. On county consolidation in general, see Millspaugh, *op. cit.*, pp. 104-122; J. W. Manning, "The Progress of County Consolidation," *National Municipal Review*, Vol. XXI, pp. 510-514 (August, 1932); Richard L. Neuberger, "Economy Begins at Home," *ibid.*, Vol. XLI, pp. 501-503, 530 (November, 1952).

[5] In addition, two of South Dakota's "unorganized" counties have been eliminated—one by consolidation with another unorganized county, and a second by annexation to an organized county. See below, n. 37.

[6] Both of these consolidations were effected under special legislative enabling acts.

citizens will, from a sense of local pride or patriotism, oppose the abolition of their county. Tradesmen and residents of the municipality which would lose its status as a county seat are usually prepared to fight consolidation—a disposition that is quite understandable inasmuch as the very economic life of many county-seat cities is largely dependent upon the location there of the county offices.[7] Moreover, opposition may be encountered also in the county with which it is proposed to consolidate one or more other counties, even though the loss on its part of legal identity or the county seat is not involved. This is especially true if the county or counties to be merged with the continuing county are relatively "poor" from the standpoint of taxable property, since merger may then result in an increased tax rate in the continuing county in order to provide proper services in the areas consolidated therewith. Fear of effective opposition from the residents of urban Hamilton County may well be the reason why the Tennessee legislature, in authorizing the James-Hamilton merger, provided for popular referendum in rural James County only, making consolidation compulsory upon Hamilton when approved by James.

Some combination of various elements of opposition will usually be strong enough to defeat proposals for the voluntary merger of counties; and state legislatures, even where they have the power, are reluctant to force consolidation in the face of widespread popular opposition. Barring the remote possibility of a program of compulsory consolidation, the only method of securing county mergers would seem to be through a program of popular education which would convince the average voter that it is good business to place economy and efficiency in local government above local pride and politics. Such a program, even if feasible, would require much time, and it therefore seems fairly clear that no substantial reduction in the number of governmental units may be expected in the near future through the physical consolidation of counties.

The costs of county government which would most likely be reduced substantially by consolidation are those of an overhead nature, especially expenditures for officers' salaries, office expenses, and courthouse maintenance. A study of the probable results of consolidation in selected Nebraska counties indicates that other costs, constituting from two thirds to three fourths of total expenditures, would not be influenced appreciably by merger.[8] Moreover, as the Nebraska study suggests, a distinction should be made between reducing county governmental costs and merely redistributing those costs. When, for example, a rural county merges with an urban county, the tax rate in the former is almost certain to decrease. But, if

[7] A human-interest account of early struggles over county-seat locations is to be found in Homer Croy, "How Come Your County Seat?" *Successful Farming*, Vol. XLVI, No. 11, pp. 44, 110-112 (November, 1948).

[8] Edward B. Schmidt, *County Consolidation: Relation of Size of Counties to the Cost of County Government in Nebraska* (Lincoln, University of Nebraska, 1934), p. 4.

high standards of service are inaugurated within the rural area, the tax rate in the urban territory may remain the same or actually increase. This results from the fact that there is shifted to the urban taxpayers a part of the cost of supplying services to the rural area—a shift which may be desirable in the interest of better government but which should be recognized as a transfer of, rather than a reduction in, governmental costs. With regard to the two consolidations actually effected—the one in Tennessee and the other in Georgia—it appears that the taxpayers of the rural areas have benefited both through lower taxes and through better roads, schools, and other local services, but that much of this benefit has been at the expense of the urban taxpayers.[9] Indeed, during the five years following the Georgia merger, expenditures within the area embraced by the former rural counties exceeded tax revenues therefrom by about $100,000 annually.[10]

SCHOOL CONSOLIDATION

Consolidation of school districts for many years proceeded slowly. The earlier laws providing for consolidation were almost entirely optional in nature, with the result that local pride and politics operated, as in the case of county-consolidation statutes, though not so effectively, to retard action. Furthermore, districts with too few pupils to justify operating schools of their own frequently found it to their economic advantage to transport their pupils to neighboring districts and pay tuition charges for them rather than to merge with operating districts and pay the higher tax rate required for maintaining and staffing school plants. In view of this situation, the taxpayers of many sparsely populated districts, though having closed their own schools, successfully resisted merger in order to retain their district organization for "tax-protective" purposes. The slow pace of consolidation prior to the 1940's is vividly illustrated by the experience of Illinois where, notwithstanding the existence of more than 12,000 districts and the availability of permissive legislation, only 227 districts were eliminated by consolidation during the 32 years from 1905 to 1937.[11]

More recently, the inauguration of new consolidation programs in a number of states has given the movement added impetus.[12] Though some

[9] *Ibid.*, pp. 51-52; Arthur W. Bromage and Thomas H. Reed, *Organization and Cost of County and Township Government* (Detroit, Michigan Commission of Inquiry into County, Township, and School District Government, 1933), pp. 73-74.

[10] E. H. Bradley, "An Appraisal of County Consolidation in Georgia," *National Municipal Review*, Vol. XXVI, pp. 366-367 (July, 1937).

[11] Illinois Legislative Council, *Some Aspects of School Administration in Illinois* (Springfield, Ill., 1938), pp. 22-23.

[12] See Dorothy C. Tompkins, *Reorganization of School Districts* (Berkeley, University of California Bureau of Public Administration, 1951); Kentucky Legislative Research Commission, *School District Mergers* (Frankfort, Ky., 1954); California Commission on School Districts, *A Report on School District Reorganization in California: 1946-1948* (Sacramento, Cal., 1949); Kansas Legislative Council, *School*

mergers have continued to take place through local action of a strictly voluntary character, the most extensive consolidations have generally been achieved in states, such as Illinois, which have allocated state aid in a manner that penalizes small districts, or where, as in Kansas, outright compulsion has been employed. During the ten-year period from 1942 to 1952 the total number of school districts in the United States was reduced by more than one third; and the consolidation movement is still actively under way.[13] That the task is still far from completed is evidenced by the fact that in 1954 nearly 60,000 districts were still in existence.[14] The need for consolidating school districts is even more urgent than that for county consolidation, and it is therefore gratifying that the school-reorganization movement is making substantial progress. Experience indicates that no consolidation program purely voluntary in nature is likely to effect the desired degree of merger within any reasonable period of time and, therefore, that some element of compulsion, direct or indirect, is necessary if satisfactory results are to be expected. Present trends suggest that the future will probably find more and more states turning to compulsory programs of school consolidation or "encouraging" consolidation effectively by providing special forms of state aid to consolidated districts or by denying aid to districts with low attendance which refuse to consolidate.[15]

CITY-COUNTY CONSOLIDATION

A special type of consolidation which has been effected in some instances is the merger, within a given area, of city and county governments. Though primarily a concern of urban communities, this form of consolidation bears an important relationship to the problems of surrounding rural areas, particularly with respect to their financial needs. The purpose of city-county consolidation is to lessen duplication and over-

District Reorganization: Kansas Experience, 1945-1947 (Topeka, Kan., 1947); Minnesota Legislative Research Committee, *School District Reorganization in Minnesota* (St. Paul, Minn., 1952); Nebraska Legislative Council, *Report of Committee on the Reorganization of School Districts* (Lincoln, Neb., 1950); Kenneth E. McIntyre, "Progress in School District Reorganization," *American School Board Journal,* Vol. CXXIV, No. 5, pp. 47-49, 80 (May, 1952); E. Maxwell Benton, "Better Schooling, Less Cost," *National Municipal Review,* Vol. XXXVIII, pp. 494-497 (November, 1949); Eugene Davis, "Reorganization of Iowa School Districts," *Iowa Law Review,* Vol. XXXIX, pp. 570-607 (Summer, 1954); Harlan Beem, "School District Reorganization in Illinois," *State Government,* Vol. XXIV, pp. 178-181, 198 (July, 1951); Leslie L. Chisholm, "School District Reorganization Today," *ibid.,* Vol. XXV, pp. 197-199, 216 (September, 1952).

[13] See above, chap. 17, "The Consolidation Movement."

[14] United States Bureau of the Census, *School Districts in the United States in 1954* (Washington, 1955).

[15] An excellent analysis of the school-consolidation movement and of various approaches to the problem followed in different states will be found in John C. Bollens, *Special District Governments in the United States* (Berkeley, University of California Press, 1957), pp. 197-227.

lapping by having a single set of officials perform functions that otherwise would be performed by two governments. Consolidation of city and county governments has been preceded in several instances by a separation of the city concerned, at times after extension of its boundaries to take in additional territory, from the county in which it has been located.[16] Metropolitan cities which have been thus separated from their counties and provided with governments for the performance of both city and county functions are San Francisco, Denver, Baltimore, and St. Louis.[17] Virginia cities (though not the state's less populous municipalities, known as towns) are also separated from their respective counties, their governments performing both city and county services.[18]

A form of city-county merger somewhat different from the separation plan just noted, is that in which the city's boundaries are extended to embrace the entire county in which it is situated.[19] The best example of this type of consolidation is to be found in Philadelphia. There the city's boundaries have been made coterminous with those of Philadelphia County; though the merger of city and county offices has never been complete, and efforts to make it more so were reported in 1955 to have been blocked at least temporarily by adverse court decision.[20] Partial consolidation of city and county governments exists also in the areas of Boston, New Orleans (city-parish), and New York City; and in the late 1940's the government of the city of Baton Rouge, La., was partially consolidated with that of East Baton Rouge Parish.

Though having serious limitations as a general approach to the problem of overlapping governments,[21] city-county consolidation appears, in practice, to have been beneficial in some measure to the urban communities concerned. At times, however, consolidation raises grave financial problems for neighboring rural areas. When the separation plan is followed, territory included within a new city-county, or subsequently annexed thereto, ceases to be under the jurisdiction, for tax purposes or otherwise, of the county or counties of which it was formerly a part. Thus the organization and growth of consolidated city-counties reduce the area and the tax base of other counties in the vicinity. When it is remembered that

[16] Cf. Victor Jones, *Metropolitan Government* (Chicago, University of Chicago Press, 1942), p. 130.

[17] The first two of these are legally designated, respectively, as the city and county of San Francisco and the city and county of Denver. Baltimore and St. Louis are designated merely as cities, though their governments perform county as well as city functions.

[18] See Raymond B. Pinchbeck, "City-county Separation in Virginia," *National Municipal Review,* Vol. XXIX, pp. 467-472 (July, 1940).

[19] Cf. Thomas H. Reed, "City-county Consolidation," *National Municipal Review,* Vol. XXIII, pp. 523-525 (October, 1934).

[20] "Court Decision Delays Philadelphia Merger," *ibid.,* Vol. XLIV, p. 210 (April, 1955).

[21] Cf. Council of State Governments, *The States and the Metropolitan Problem: A Report to the Governors' Conference* (Chicago, 1956), pp. 74-75, 84-85.

the territory included within city-counties is ordinarily urban or semi-urban in character, and therefore relatively high in assessed valuation, it is readily understandable that the counties losing such territory may, as a result, find it difficult to raise the necessary funds for financing their local services. This situation has been encountered in varying degrees, for example, in Henrico and other Virginia counties, as a result of the annexation of portions of their territory by neighboring "independent" cities.[22] If, instead of following the separation plan, city boundaries are made county-wide, except in the case of a small urbanized county, such as Philadelphia, there is likely to be a considerable amount of rural territory which will be required to pay taxes for providing urban services to urban residents.[23] All in all, city-county consolidation, though offering some advantages to large urban communities, should be used with caution in areas of smaller population, lest the fiscal capacity of rural counties be unreasonably impaired or rural residents of city-counties be required to support urban services.

Similar in purpose to city-county consolidation is the consolidation, in Connecticut, of the governments of several cities and boroughs with those of the respective towns in which they are located. In most of these mergers, however, provision is made for a system of separate taxing districts whereby the taxpayers of the entire area pay for governmental services of general benefit, and only the taxpayers of the urban area pay for special urban services.[24]

TOWNSHIP ABOLITION

One possible means of simplifying American local government would be the complete abolition of governmental units of a particular class or type and the transfer of their functions to other units. In New England, where the town is the primary local unit and counties are of distinctly minor importance, there have been some proposals for the abolition of county government.[25] But the unit the elimination of which has been most widely advocated is the township as it exists in 16 states, principally in the northeastern and north central regions.[26] Townships in these states usually have an area of some 36 square miles—too small for the economical financing or efficient administration of governmental activities. The

[22] See *Adjustment of the Boundaries of Virginia Municipalities and Adjacent Counties,* Report of the Commission to Study Urban Growth to the Governor and the General Assembly of Virginia (Richmond, Va., Division of Purchases and Printing, 1951).

[23] Cf. Reed, *loc. cit.;* L. R. Chubb, "The Financial Aspects of City-county Consolidation," *National Municipal Review,* Vol. XXVIII, pp. 101-104 (February, 1939).

[24] See Max R. White, "Town and City Consolidation in Connecticut," *American Political Science Review,* Vol. XXXVI, pp. 492-502 (June, 1942).

[25] See above, chap. 2, "Relative Importance of Various Classes of Units."

[26] See above, chap. 2, "Towns and Townships."

principal functions ordinarily performed fall in the fields of law enforcement, property assessment, public assistance, and highway maintenance, and in each of these the county usually will be found carrying on similar or related work. Thus, the township constable is the counterpart in miniature of the county sheriff; township assessment officers commonly are supervised in some measure by county tax agencies; where townships administer outdoor assistance, the almshouse is usually a county institution; and, though the least-traveled roads may be maintained by the township, those more generally traveled are likely to be under county jurisdiction.

Not only do township activities tend to duplicate and overlap county functions, but there seems to be a considerable degree of consensus that the midwestern township is more artificial in character than either the town in New England or the county elsewhere. More than in the case of units of the latter types, residents of a particular township must frequently look beyond the borders of their local political unit for satisfaction of their social, religious, trade, and other nonpolitical interests.[27] Thus, a village may grow up in one corner of a township and become the trade and church center for the inhabitants of one or more neighboring townships, though distant residents of its own township trade and attend church in villages of other townships. School districts often cut across township lines. Under these circumstances the township clearly does not accord with social and economic centers of activity; and it is not surprising that so highly artificial a unit has become a principal target of those who would eliminate some local governmental units in the interest of economy and efficiency.

The declining importance of the township as a local governmental unit was considered at some length in an earlier chapter.[28] Studies in various states have strongly indicated that township government is unnecessarily wasteful and costly and that the taxpayers could obtain the same or better services for less money if townships were abolished and their functions transferred to the county.[29] In considering the necessity for township government, it should be borne in mind that in more than half of the states townships as governmental units have never existed. Moreover, in one state—Oklahoma—townships were actually abolished, for all practical purposes, by a constitutional amendment of 1933 depriving them of the

[27] T. B. Manny, *Attitudes toward Rural Government* (Washington, U. S. Bureau of Agricultural Economics, 1929), pp. 4-6.

[28] See above, chap. 9.

[29] See, for example, M. H. Hunter, *Costs of Township and County Government in Illinois* (Urbana, University of Illinois Bureau of Business Research, 1933); H. K. Allen, *Costs and Services of Local Government in Selected Illinois Counties* (Urbana, Universtiy of Illinois Bureau of Business Research, 1936); Bromage and Reed, *op. cit.;* William L. Bradshaw and Milton Garrison, *Township Organization in Missouri* (Columbia, University of Missouri, 1936).

power to levy taxes. The Oklahoma legislature then transferred to the county those functions which had been performed by the township, the most important being that of highway construction and maintenance. Experience under the new setup seems to have demonstrated that the counties have provided as good services as had the townships, and at considerably less cost.[30] In another state—Iowa—township government has degenerated to such an extent that the Census Bureau has omitted the state's townships from its most recent counts of governmental units.[31]

The principal argument for retention of the township is that it keeps government "close to the people" and provides a "training school of democracy." This argument, however, loses much of its effectiveness when one considers the widespread lack of interest in township government and elections and the small attendance at township meetings in the states whose laws provide for such assemblies.[32] On the basis of experience, and in view of modernized methods of travel and communication, the conclusion seems inescapable that the functions of present-day townships could be more efficiently and economically performed by counties and that townships should therefore be abolished.[33] A committee on county government of the National Municipal League, after careful study, has recommended that townships gradually be eliminated by transferring township functions to the county, city, or state; permitting individual townships to deorganize or consolidate; and providing that townships may be abolished by county option.[34] Township abolition, of course, would require considerable time. Tradition is strong, and the township is a traditional institution. Its elimination would be opposed by well-organized township officials in the name of democracy. Moreover, in some states constitutional changes would be required. Notwithstanding these difficulties, however, there is strong evidence that abolition of the township would promote efficiency and economy in government at the local level.[35]

[30] L. D. Melton, "The Elimination of Township Government in Oklahoma," *National Municipal Review*, Vol. XXVII, pp. 405-407 (August, 1938).

[31] Cf. Richard C. Spencer, "Iowa Townships Still Here?" *ibid.*, Vol. XLI, pp. 397-399 (September, 1952).

[32] See above, chap. 9, "Township Meetings."

[33] For a statement of the contrary view, see William B. Guitteau, *Ohio's Townships: The Grassroots of Democracy* (Toledo, Toledo Printing Co., 1949).

[34] Arthur W. Bromage, "Recommendations on Township Government," Committee on County Government of the National Municipal League Report No. 3, *National Municipal Review*, suppl., Vol. XXIII, pp. 139-145 (February, 1934).

[35] Cf. Frank G. Bates, "The Indiana Township—An Anachronism," *National Municipal Review*, Vol. XXI, pp. 502-504 (August, 1932); Arthur W. Bromage, "Shall We Save the Township?" *ibid.*, XXV, pp. 585-588 (October, 1936); Clyde F. Snider, "The Twilight of the Township," *ibid.*, Vol. XLI, pp. 390-396 (September, 1952). For a proposal of a new type of "rural municipality" to replace the traditional township, see Theodore B. Manny, *Rural Municipalities: A Sociological Study of Local Government in the United States* (New York, Century, 1930). The boundaries of the rural municipality, according to its proponents, would be so drawn that the unit would consist not of "standardized 'blocks' of the earth's surface such as town-

LOCAL DEORGANIZATION

An alternative to state-wide abolition of local units of a particular class is the provision for deorganization, on either a voluntary or a compulsory basis, of individual units. Under this plan the particular unit concerned may or may not retain its identity as a geographic and taxing area, but in any event its governmental organization is dissolved and local governmental services are provided within its borders by some neighboring or overlying unit.[36]

Three of South Dakota's counties are "unorganized," [37] each being attached to an adjacent organized county for judicial purposes and the performance of essential governmental services; and both of the Dakotas have enacted legislation authorizing the voluntary deorganization of counties.[38] The North Dakota law applies only to counties of less than 4,000 population, but that of South Dakota is applicable to any organized county. Deorganization under either law is to be accomplished by petition and popular vote within the county to be deorganized.[39] In South Dakota, the state legislature is to designate by joint resolution the organized county to which a deorganizing county is to be attached for judicial and other governmental purposes. North Dakota provides that a deorganizing county may make an agreement with an adjoining county for attachment thereto, and that if this is not done, the governor shall designate by proclamation the county to which the deorganized county is to be attached. Both states provide that taxes shall be levied upon the property within a deorganized county to pay any outstanding indebtedness incurred prior to deorganization. Apparently no county has thus far been deorganized under either of these laws, though at least one North Dakota county

---

ships," but of "real groups of living human beings as nearly homogeneous in their common interests as it is possible to obtain"—*ibid.*, p. 221.

36 For a more extensive discussion of deorganization, see William S. Carpenter, *Problems in Service Levels: The Readjustment of Services and Areas in Local Government* (Princeton, N. J., Princeton University Press, 1940), chap. 4. According to Professor Carpenter, at least 36 states have provided by general law for the deorganization of counties, townships, municipalities, or special districts; and in some other states, especially those of New England, local governmental units may be deorganized by special legislative act. Relatively little use, however, has thus far been made of deorganization statutes—*ibid.*, pp. 96-97.

37 There were five such counties in the state prior to 1943, when the legislature, by special act, consolidated the unorganized county of Washington with that of Shannon. Subsequently, the unorganized county of Armstrong was annexed to the organized county of Dewey under enabling legislation of 1951; see *Laws of South Dakota* (1943), chap. 23; *ibid.* (1951), chap. 37.

38 *Laws of North Dakota* (1939), chap. 122; *Laws of South Dakota* (1943), chap. 45. See also, Kenneth Wernimont, "County Disorganization for North Dakota," *National Municipal Review*, Vol. XXVIII, pp. 769-772 (November, 1939).

39 In North Dakota, if the petition is signed by more than 50 per cent of the voters of the county, no election is held, further action upon the petition being by judicial proceedings in the district court.

—that of Billings, in 1940—has voted upon and defeated a proposal for deorganization.

Of the township states, Minnesota seems to have accomplished most in the way of township deorganization. Under the laws of that state, county governing boards may by resolution dissolve any township within their respective borders (1) when the township has failed to exercise its powers for a period of ten years; (2) when the assessed valuation of the township falls below $40,000; (3) when the tax delinquency of the township, exclusive of taxes delinquent by reason of being legally contested, amounts to 50 per cent of the assessed valuation; or (4) when the state or federal government has acquired title to 50 per cent of the real estate of the township.[40] A few townships have been dissolved by county boards under this permissive authority. Dissolutions in greater number, however, were effected between 1933 and 1937, during which period the statutes made it mandatory upon county boards to dissolve any township where township government had failed to function for ten years or where there existed certain specified conditions of low assessed valuation, high tax delinquency, or widespread government ownership of real estate.[41] In all, some 130 Minnesota townships appear to have been deorganized since the early 1930's. Though this number is not insignificant, it represents a reduction of less than 7 per cent in the total number of townships in the state.[42] Most or all of the deorganizations have occurred in the northern cutover region of the state. When Minnesota townships are deorganized their functions—chief among which are road construction and maintenance, assessment of property, and supervision of elections—are transferred to their respective counties.[43] Another state which has had a number of township deorganizations under permissive legislation, with functions transferred to the counties, is North Dakota.[44] Under North Dakota law, deorganization is effected by voter petition therefor, followed by favorable vote at the annual township meeting.[45]

In Maine, approximately 40 per cent of the state's area, principally in the northwestern portion, has never been organized into towns but is

[40] *Minnesota Statutes* (1953), sec. 368.47. In certain counties the question of dissolution is subject to popular referendum upon petition therefor.

[41] Cf. *Session Laws of Minnesota* (1933), chap. 377; *ibid.* (1935), chap. 342; Carpenter, *Problems in Service Levels*, pp. 100-102, 116. Apparently, however, this statutory mandate was not obeyed by the county boards in all cases. See William Anderson, "Minnesota—Dissolution of Townships," *National Municipal Review*, Vol. XXIV, p. 229 (April, 1935).

[42] There were 1,844 townships in Minnesota in 1952 as compared with 1,973 in the early 1930's. William Anderson, *The Units of Government in the United States* (Chicago, Public Administration Service, 1934), p. 11; United States Bureau of the Census, *Governments in the United States in 1952* (Washington, Government Printing Office, 1953), p. 11.

[43] Cf. Carpenter, *Problems in Service Levels*, pp. 116-120.

[44] *Ibid.*, pp. 104-105.

[45] *North Dakota Revised Code* (1943), secs. 58-0225 to 58-0229.

administered directly by the state; and, during recent years, additions have been made to this "unorganized" territory through the deorganization of individual towns by special legislative acts.[46] Towns thus deorganized usually have been so sparsely settled and had assessed valuations so low that they have found the maintenance of organized local government unduly burdensome. They have therefore sought and received from the state legislature permission to surrender their corporate charters and revert to unorganized status. Essential governmental services in the areas thus deorganized are provided by state and county officials and, in a few instances, by officers of adjacent towns. Poor relief and education become state charges, except that in deorganized towns having more than 200 inhabitants the schools are supported by local taxation. In providing school facilities, the state commissioner of education may maintain schools within the deorganized areas, transport pupils to neighboring towns, or board pupils near some school. Local roads are under jurisdiction of the county commissioners. Assessment of property for taxation falls to the state tax assessor. Residents of deorganized areas vote in neighboring towns for national, state, and county officers. It will be noted that when deorganization occurs in Maine, most town functions are transferred to the state rather than to the counties. This is not surprising in view of the relative insignificance of the New England county as a unit of local government.[47]

Deorganization furnishes a means whereby the inhabitants of sparsely settled areas may be provided with essential governmental services without being subjected to the exorbitant taxation which would be necessary to support local governmental organization therein. Where, as in the county-deorganization laws of the Dakotas, it is provided that governmental services shall be performed and taxes levied in deorganized units by the governments of adjacent units at the same level, the criticism may arise that the inhabitants of deorganized areas are left without a voice in their local government. Criticism of this nature is less valid where provision is made for government of the deorganized area by a larger overlying unit. This, as has been noted, is the plan followed in the case of deorganized townships in Minnesota and North Dakota, where government is provided by the county, and in that of deorganized Maine towns, which are governed by the state.

[46] There also have been some instances of deorganization of Maine plantations. Concerning the plantation as a governmental unit, see above, chap. 8, "Maine Plantations."

[47] O. J. Scoville, "Liquidating Town Government in Decadent Rural Areas of Maine," *Journal of Land and Public Utilities Economics,* Vol. XIII, pp. 285-291 (August, 1937); William S. Carpenter, "Deorganization in Maine," *American Political Science Review,* Vol. XXXII, pp. 1139-1142 (December, 1938); John W. Fleming, "Maine's Unorganized Territory Creates Few Problems," *National Municipal Review,* Vol. XXVIII, pp. 228-233, 237 (March, 1939). Two Vermont towns were deorganized in 1937; see *Acts and Resolves of Vermont* (1937), Nos. 269, 292.

TRANSFER OF FUNCTIONS

Yet another means of reducing the waste and inefficiency flowing from unduly small governmental areas is the transfer of specific functions from smaller to larger units. The function thus far most frequently transferred is that of road construction and maintenance. Within the past 30 years, for example, county highways have been transferred to the state in North Carolina, Delaware, West Virginia, and most Virginia counties. Indiana, Iowa, and Michigan have transferred township roads to the county; and in Arkansas the county has supplanted subdivisional road districts for highway purposes. Various counties in Kansas, Washington, and Texas have adopted the county-unit plan of highway administration under optional statutes, thereby transferring to county jurisdiction local roads previously maintained by townships or road districts.[48] Assessment of property for taxation is another function that has been transferred in several states from township to county jurisdiction.[49]

Generally speaking, transfer of highway and assessment administration to larger governmental units appears to have produced results sufficiently gratifying to recommend more widespread use of larger units in these and other fields. Proposals for transfer of functions are likely to encounter opposition from officials of the units from which the transfer is to be made and, also, from other persons who believe they see in any degree of centralization a danger to local self-government. This opposition, however, is rarely as vocal or effective as it is where complete abolition or deorganization of the smaller units is sought.

FUNCTIONAL CONSOLIDATION

One of the most promising developments in the field of local government during recent years has been the growing use of what is coming to be known as *functional consolidation*. Functional consolidation, as distinguished from physical or geographic consolidation, involves the co-operation of two or more local governmental units in the performance of particular functions. This co-operation may be effected either by establishing a special district or through contractual agreement. Where the first of these methods is used, there is ordinarily established a district including within its boundaries two or more general government units of a given type—that is, counties, townships, or municipalities. This district then performs for the inhabitants within its limits, through its own agencies, a specific governmental function previously performed by the

[48] See Clyde F. Snider, "State-rural Relations," *The Book of the States: 1945-46* (Chicago, Council of State Governments, 1945), pp. 54-60; see also above, chap. 14, "Trend toward Centralization."

[49] See above, chap. 19, "Property-tax Administration," p. 500.

various general government units individually. Districts created for such purposes may be full-fledged governmental units, with their separate corporate identity and their own taxing power,[50] or they may be mere administrative areas financed by the component general government units. Under the contract method, two or more local units of the same or different types agree either to establish a joint department or agency to perform the service concerned for all units that are parties to the agreement or to have one of the units involved provide the service for one or more others in return for a money payment.[51] Functional consolidation is sometimes the result of a mandatory law, but more often takes place voluntarily under permissive authority conferred upon the local units by constitutional or statutory provision. It is to be found both in urban and in rural areas. In metropolitan areas, an important element in bringing about functional consolidation is the fact that certain governmental services, such as health protection, water supply, and sewerage, can be supplied most effectively by a single governmental organization operating throughout the region. In rural areas, though a similar motive may be influential in many cases, a special reason for functional consolidation lies in the need for a unit large enough to make economically feasible the employment of qualified technical personnel and the provision of modern equipment in the field concerned.

The contract variety of functional consolidation, though newer than the special-district type, is spreading more rapidly.[52] Many states have enacted legislation enabling local governmental units to enter into contracts for the co-operative performance of specifically named functions. Thus, several states authorize the establishment by this means of multi-county welfare departments and health departments. Other services that may be provided through intergovernmental contract in various states include libraries, recreational facilities, airports, fire protection, water supply, and sewage disposal. Of even more significance has been the adoption by approximately a dozen states, since 1930, of constitutional or statutory provisions conferring broad authority upon local governmental units to enter into contracts for the performance of a wide range of local functions. Indeed, some states have now gone so far as to authorize the contractual performance of any governmental function common to the contracting units. Some of these constitutional provisions and statutes apply only to intercounty co-operation, whereas others authorize counties to contract also with any governmental units within their borders, and still

[50] See above, chap. 10.

[51] The *district* and *contract* methods of functional consolidation are not mutually exclusive, since special administrative districts are sometimes established by general government units through contractual agreement.

[52] A discussion of functional consolidation of this type will be found in Carpenter, *Problems in Service Levels*, chap. 2. Professor Carpenter designates contracts effecting functional consolidation by the term *interjurisdictional agreements*.

others permit contracts between or among units of the same or different types in almost any combination. In most instances a local unit is empowered to enter into a contract by action of its governing board, though in some cases there must be popular approval of the agreement in a referendum election.

Two of the broadest enabling statutes are those of Louisiana and Minnesota, enacted in 1942 and 1943, respectively. The Louisiana law empowers parishes to act jointly with each other, or with municipalities or special districts, in any undertaking within the power of the co-operating units. Such joint arrangements may include, but are not limited to, activities concerning:

1. Police, fire, and health protection.
2. Public utility services.
3. Collection and disposal of garbage and other refuse.
4. Construction and maintenance of public improvements.
5. Recreational and educational facilities.
6. Flood-control, drainage, and reclamation projects.
7. The purchase of materials, supplies, and equipment.

Agreements for joint undertakings must be in writing; must be approved by ordinance or resolution of the governing bodies of the units concerned; and may provide for a joint committee or other administrative agency to administer their terms.[53] The Minnesota statute provides that two or more governmental units (defined as including all cities, villages, boroughs, counties, towns, and school districts) may, by agreement entered into through action of their governing bodies, jointly exercise any power common to the contracting parties.[54]

Especially noteworthy is the fact that two state constitutions of recent adoption—those of Missouri and Georgia, both ratified in 1945—expressly authorize functional consolidation in broad terms. Missouri provides that contiguous counties, not exceeding ten in number, may, by popular vote in each county concerned, join in performing any common function or service or in the employment of any county officer or employee common to the counties. Furthermore, any municipality or political subdivision of the state may, in the manner provided by law, contract with other municipalities or subdivisions, or with other states or their municipalities or subdivisions, or with the United States, for the construction or operation of any public improvement, or for a common service.[55] The Georgia provision is as follows: [56]

[53] *Acts of Louisiana* (1942), reg. sess., No. 246. Cf. Clyde F. Snider, "County and Township Government in 1942," *American Political Science Review*, Vol. XXXVII, pp. 1041-1051 (December, 1943).

[54] *Session Laws of Minnesota* (1943), chap. 557.

[55] *Constitution of Missouri* (1945), Art. VI, secs. 14, 16.

[56] *Constitution of Georgia* (1945), Art. VII, sec. 6.

The State, state institutions, any city, town, municipality or county of this State may contract for any period not exceeding fifty years, with each other or with any public agency, public corporation or authority now or hereafter created for the use by such subdivisions or the residents thereof of any facilities or services of the State, state institutions, any city, town, municipality, county, public agency, public corporation or authority, provided such contracts shall deal with such activities and transactions as such subdivisions are by law authorized to undertake.

Other states with constitutional or statutory provisions conferring broad authority for functional consolidation of the contractual type include California, Nevada, Ohio, Pennsylvania, and Wisconsin.

It is scarcely surprising that functional consolidation thus far has been employed most extensively in some of the metropolitan areas, where governmental units tend to be most numerous and problems of overlapping most serious. In the 1940's some 200 intergovernmental contracts were reported as currently in effect in the Los Angeles area of California, many of these being agreements under which the government of Los Angeles County performed property-assessment, health-protection, and other services for various cities within its borders.[57] More than 700 interjurisdictional agreements, dealing with road construction and maintenance, education, and a variety of other matters, were recently reported as existing in the Philadelphia metropolitan region—an area embracing five counties in Pennsylvania and three in New Jersey.[58] But rural units also are making ever wider use of functional consolidation in both district and contractual forms. Multicounty health districts or departments, for example, are to be found in varying number in New Mexico, Indiana, Illinois, Virginia, and several other states; and there are many instances of city-county health departments. Virginia has four district homes (almshouses), serving 27 counties and cities, and a number of jails each of which is operated jointly by two or more counties or cities and counties.[59] Multicounty and city-county libraries are steadily becoming more numerous. All told, functional consolidation offers a practicable means whereby counties of small population and meager resources may join with each other, or with municipalities or other units within their borders, to provide co-operatively various

[57] Frank M. Stewart and Ronald M. Ketcham, "Intergovernmental Contracts in California," *Public Administration Review*, Vol. I, pp. 242-248 (Spring, 1941); Judith Norvell Jamison, "Neighboring Areas Join Hands," *National Municipal Review*, Vol. XXXV, pp. 111-114 (March, 1946).

[58] Jeptha J. Carrell, "Learning to Work Together," *National Municipal Review*, Vol. XLIII, pp. 526-533 (November, 1954).

[59] For other examples of functional consolidation in Virginia, see Virginia State Chamber of Commerce, *Opportunities for Economy in County Government in Virginia* (Richmond, Va., 1947), pp. 22-32; Robert H. Tucker, "Progress in Virginia County Government," *The Commonwealth*, publication of the Virginia State Chamber of Commerce, Vol. XVI, pp. 7-9, 26-27 (January, 1949).

local services which the respective units find it difficult to provide on an individual basis.

PROBLEMS OF INTERNAL ORGANIZATION

Determination of the most desirable area, or combination of areas, for carrying on the functions of local government is but one aspect of the general problem of local reconstruction. Having determined, insofar as it is possible to do so, what areas should exist for governmental purposes, there still remain other equally important problems, one of which is the task of providing those areas with efficient internal organization for carrying on their work.

The need for internal reorganization in local government is perhaps most obvious in the case of the county. The county is the most nearly universal of all local government units in the United States, performs a large variety of functions, and spends a great deal of tax money. Moreover, it is with respect to the county that tradition has operated most effectively to prevent the abandonment of ancient and outmoded forms. Probably the most pressing need of county government today is for a single chief executive, elective or appointed, to exercise over-all supervision of county administrative agencies. Another need in many instances is for reorganization of the county governing board. That body should be large enough to serve satisfactorily as the policy-determining body of the county, yet not so large as to be unwieldy; and its members should ordinarily be elected from the county at large. If a county executive is established, the board should be relieved of its administrative duties and its function should be limited to the determination of county policy. The archaic office of coroner should be replaced by the medical-examiner system; and the county clerk should be chosen by the county board instead of by popular election.

A form of county reorganization which might well be more widely adopted is that of office consolidation. It has long been recognized that many counties, especially those in sparsely populated areas, have excessive numbers of offices and that in numerous instances a single officer might well perform the duties now devolved upon two or more. Office consolidation would shorten the ballot, should reduce overhead costs, and might also result in the attraction of better-qualified personnel to the more important consolidated offices. A number of states have constitutional or statutory provisions authorizing consolidation of county offices, and some consolidations have actually taken place. Michigan's constitution, for example, provides that the offices of county clerk and register of deeds may be consolidated at the discretion of the board of supervisors, and several of the state's rural counties have made such consolidations.[60] The county

[60] *Constitution of Michigan* (1908), Art. VIII, sec. 3.

clerk is ex officio register of deeds in some three fourths of the counties of Nebraska, and in more than a third of the state's counties he serves also as clerk of the district court.[61] In the less populous counties of Illinois the clerk of the circuit court is ex officio recorder of deeds.[62] Montana's legislature, pursuant to a constitutional amendment of 1934, has authorized the consolidation of any two or more of eight constitutional offices in any county by order of the board of county commissioners.[63] Several counties have consolidated some of their offices under this legislation, though in some instances the consolidation orders have subsequently been rescinded.[64] Each of three optional forms of government made available to North Dakota counties by legislation of 1941 provides for a substantial degree of office consolidation in any county adopting the new plan.[65] In California counties operating under general state law,[66] county offices may be consolidated into various combinations by ordinance of the board of supervisors.[67] As of 1950, according to Professor John Bollens, 96 consolidations were in effect in 47 of the state's 48 general-law counties. For example, 34 counties had consolidated the offices of coroner and public administrator; 11 the offices of treasurer and tax collector; 8 the offices of sheriff and coroner; and 6 the offices of auditor, clerk, and recorder. Most of the consolidations had been effected in rural counties and apparently were designed to combine two or three part-time elective offices into a single full-time position.[68]

In New England town government, recent innovations are serving to improve town organization and to adapt traditional forms to present-day conditions. These developments include the representative or limited town meeting, finance committees, and town managers. At an earlier point in this chapter it was suggested that the midwestern township should be

[61] Nebraska Legislative Council, *Report of the Committee on Reorganization of County Government* (Lincoln, Neb., 1950), p. 17.

[62] *Constitution of Illinois* (1870), Art. X, sec. 8; *Illinois Revised Statutes* (1955), chap. 115, sec. 1.

[63] *Constitution of Montana* (1889), Art. XVI, sec. 5 (as amended): *Revised Codes of Montana* (1947), secs. 16-2501 to 16-2507. The offices concerned are those of clerk, sheriff, treasurer, superintendent of schools, surveyor, assessor, coroner, and public administrator.

[64] Roland R. Renne, "County Office Consolidations in Montana," *National Municipal Review*, Vol. XXVIII, pp. 143-148 (February, 1939).

[65] *Laws of North Dakota* (1941), chaps. 130, 131, 132. See also, Ernest Engelbert, "A Decade of County Government Reorganization in North Dakota," *American Political Science Review*, Vol. XXXVI, pp. 508-515 (June, 1942).

[66] As distinguished from those under home-rule charters.

[67] *Deering's California Government Code Annotated*, 1951 ed. with 1955 suppl., sec. 24300.

[68] John C. Bollens, "Administrative Integration in California Counties," *Public Administration Review*, Vol. XI, pp. 26-34 (Winter, 1951). See also, Frederic L. Alexander, "Consolidation of County Offices," *The Tax Digest*, Vol. XX, pp. 305-306, 315 (September, 1942); H. F. Scoville, "Thrift via County Consolidation," *National Municipal Review*, Vol. XXVIII, pp. 708-711 (October, 1939).

abolished. If the township is retained, its governmental organization should be overhauled. Desirable steps in this direction would be elimination of the township meeting where it exists by law but fails to function properly; establishment, where such does not now exist, of a principal township administrative officer; and abandonment of township justices of the peace in favor of a system of salaried trial justices with county-wide jurisdiction. In the township, as in the county, tradition has been a strong force in preventing the modernization of governmental machinery. This fact, however, has been relatively less serious in the case of the township, which performs fewer functions and exists in only a third of the states.

A need in rural local units of all types is for extension of the merit system of personnel administration. In the case of the smaller units, personnel services can probably best be provided through a state personnel agency.

ALLOCATION OF FUNCTIONS

Where, as under our system, government is organized on different levels and into various types of units on the same level, a perennial problem is that of devising a satisfactory allocation of functions among the respective levels and units. What functions are to be assigned to the federal government, what to the states, and what to governments at the local level? With respect to local functions, what distribution is to be made among counties, towns and townships, and special districts? Questions such as these continually confront those seeking to operate our governmental institutions and to improve their functioning.

Under our federal system, the distribution of powers between the national and state governments, and therefore their respective capacities to perform functions in various fields, are determined by provision of the United States Constitution. Of the powers thus reserved to the states, those to be passed on to, or shared with, the local governmental units, are determined by state action, in some measure by home-rule provisions of state constitutions but more generally by state legislative action. The assignment of functions to the various local governments, therefore, becomes largely a problem of state legislative policy.

In deciding what government should perform a particular function, a traditional approach centered about an attempt to have local performance of functions of local interest and state performance of those of state-wide interest. Today, however, the standard of state versus local interest is unsatisfactory as a measuring stick, since some degree of state-wide interest attaches to practically every function. To be sure, insofar as varying degrees of interest can be distinguished, a limited application may still be made of the "interest" formula, but it can scarcely be employed as a controlling factor. Rather than attempt to distinguish between local and state-wide interest, it would appear more sensible to seek the assignment of each function to that unit of government which can perform it most efficiently and economically. Under a democratic system, good government, of course, involves more than efficiency and economy—it requires also an appropriate degree of popular control, direct or indirect, over governmental operations. At one time it was widely believed that popular control could be made properly effective only within areas small enough so that the voters could know their public officials personally and meet them face to face. With present-day facilities for information and communication, voters may have more thorough knowledge of county officers and candidates than of those of smaller units, such as townships or special districts; and it not infrequently happens that the voter is better informed concerning state and national officers than he is concerning local officers generally. This being the case, it cannot be assumed that intelligent popular control is necessarily less prevalent in larger than in smaller units. Today, the choice of a governmental unit to be charged with a particular function is sometimes determined by present tax and debt limits, the function being assigned to that unit which, under existing limitations, can most readily raise the funds required for financing the service. It would be better in such cases to assign the function to the unit which appears best suited for its performance and then to see to it that that unit is provided with the necessary financial resources.

There is a current trend, as noted at many points in preceding chapters, to transfer the performance of governmental functions from smaller to larger political units; and this trend, as long as popular control is duly preserved, seems to be generally commendable as promoting economy and efficient administration. Also worthy of note is the fact that modern government does not involve the assignment of every public function exclusively to a single unit or to units of a single class, but that many services are provided on a co-operative basis by two or more units at the same level or at different levels. Many local functions, through grant-in-aid programs or otherwise, are performed co-operatively with the state or national government, or with both; and, to an ever increasing extent, pairs or groups of local units, through a variety of interlocal arrangements, are providing for the co-operative performance of common functions. Finally, it may be suggested that no distribution of governmental functions among the states and their various subdivisions should be considered as permanent and unchangeable. Any arrangement that exists at a given time must be looked upon as sufficiently flexible to permit shifts and reassignments as conditions change and as experience indicates that transfers would be in the public interest.[69]

[69] On the subject generally, see Professor William Anderson's thought-provoking chapter, "Dividing up the Functions of Government," *The Nation and the States, Rivals or Partners?* (Minneapolis, University of Minnesota Press, 1955), chap. 9.

PROBLEMS OF FINANCE

The problem of financing local government has many facets. How much money should be expended in support of the various local services? What proportion of the total amount should be contributed by the state? Should the state's contribution take the form of grants-in-aid or tax sharing, or some combination of the two? What state taxes should be employed to raise state-aid funds? Should state aid be given in support of designated services only or in support of local government generally? Should locally raised funds come entirely from property taxes, or should other local revenue sources be tapped? What nonproperty taxes should the local units be empowered to levy, and at what rates? Should local nonproperty taxes be administered by the local levying units, or should provision be made for state administration? What can be done to improve the administration of the local property tax? Under what circumstances should local governments borrow? Over what period of time should local indebtedness be retired, and should local bonds be of the sinking-fund or the serial form? What procedures should be provided for local budgeting, accounting, and auditing? These are typical of the financial questions which continually face state legislatures, local governing bodies, and the local voters.

Some local expenditures are made mandatory by the state, and over these the local authorities may have little control. The determination of discretionary expenditures, however, remains a major responsibility of local governing bodies. With growing demands for local services, local expenditures during recent years have increased sharply. The additional funds required to meet these higher expenditures have been provided for the most part, in rural units, through increases in local property taxes and state aid. In some instances, however, the imposition of local nonproperty taxes has been authorized, and doubtless there will be other such authorizations in the future. Where the same form of tax is imposed at both state and local levels, substantial advantages may sometimes be secured by providing for state collection of the local levy. In the property-tax field, some improvement is being made in assessment personnel and procedures, but much remains to be done. Some local governments need additional borrowing power, while others need to use more prudently the power they already possess. An enlargement of the borrowing power of general-purpose units should operate in many instances to deter the organization of overlying special-purpose districts. Much improvement continues to be called for in local budgeting, accounting, and auditing practices. As progress occurs in this field it is to be hoped that more and more states will provide, as some but all too few have done already, for the compilation and publication of comparative fiscal data concerning their various local governments.

PROBLEMS OF STATE-LOCAL RELATIONS

So fully do the states control and regulate their local governments that in the final analysis virtually every local problem becomes, directly or indirectly, a problem in state-local relations. When the state-local relationship is viewed in broad perspective, however, two basic problems emerge: (1) What degree of freedom should be accorded local units in determining the form of their organization, the nature and extent of their activities, and the means of financing those activities? (2) By what method or methods can the state best exercise the control and supervision over local government which it chooses to retain?

The powers and duties of local governmental units are prescribed in some measure by state constitutional provision but more generally by state statute. A few states have constitutional home-rule provisions permitting counties to frame and adopt their own charters and, in doing so, to exercise a substantial degree of freedom in determining their organizational machinery. For populous urban counties the home-rule privilege appears advantageous. In the case of rural counties, however, the need for diversity in organization can probably be met satisfactorily through carefully drawn optional legislation offering several alternative plans from which individual counties may choose and perhaps permitting some further adaptation by local governing bodies. By whatever means provided, it seems clear that local units, by and large, deserve broader discretion than they now possess in determining their organization and functioning. State constitutional provisions tending to cast all counties in a common mold and vest them with uniform powers, regardless of differences in individual needs and wishes, and even in some instances establishing township offices, should be eliminated or modified. Only in this manner can state legislatures be enabled to deal effectively with local government needs and problems and to confer suitable discretion upon the local units. Clothed with ample authority in organizational and financial matters, local governments might reasonably be expected to assume a higher degree of responsibility than is now theirs in the financing of local activities, and thus a deterrent might be provided to the current tendency toward ever higher subsidies from the states.

Whether or not the discretionary powers of local governments are broadened, the states may be expected to continue control programs designed to assure that local powers will be exercised within state-prescribed limitations and, in some instances, to assure that they will be exercised wisely. Two forms of state control over local government are commonly distinguished: judicial and administrative. Under the first, enforcement of constitutional and statutory provisions relating to local government is left to the courts, to be carried out in cases duly instituted before them. Under the administrative form, control and supervisory duties are delegated to state administrative officers or agencies. Administrative control offers certain advantages over judicial. Problems can be handled promptly without waiting on clogged court dockets; each problem can be decided on its individual merits without the necessity of following judicial precedent; and professional supervisory personnel, trained or experienced in the field of activity involved, can be provided by the control agency. Devices employed in administrative supervision range all the way from outright compulsion of various sorts to the mere offering of advice or assistance which the local units are free to accept or not as they see fit. In actual practice the milder devices, partly because they are less objectionable to local officials and citizens, frequently seem to be equally effective with, or more effective than, those of a coercive nature. Supplementing the usual provisions for judicial control, a balanced program of state administrative supervision appears to be a desirable feature of state-local relations. Wisely contrived and competently administered, such a program should tend to preserve and strengthen local self-government rather than to destroy or supplant it.

THE ROAD AHEAD

Any attempt to prophesy in detail the course which local government reorganization will take in the years to come would be extremely hazardous. However, on the basis of experience and present trends, general predictions may be ventured with some degree of confidence.

It seems reasonable to expect that efforts to improve the internal organization of local government along lines similar to those discussed at various points in this book will continue and that, over the years, many of these will meet with success. Tradition, constitutional obstacles,[70] and the reluctance of state legislators to impose changes of a compulsory nature will combine to make the process of modernizing local government machinery a slow one, but that progress will take place there can be little doubt. It also seems reasonably certain that there will be gradual improvement in matters of finance, functional allocation, and state-local relations.

With respect to areal readjustments the prospect is less clear. Changes of this nature are even more difficult to effect than changes in other categories. Yet some progress can confidently be expected, especially in the direction of reducing the number of local governmental units of certain types. County consolidation, however desirable, encounters practical obstacles that thus far have proved virtually insurmountable. In this situa-

[70] Cf. Howard P. Jones, "Constitutional Barriers to Improvement in County Government," Committee on County Government of the National Municipal League Report No. 1, *National Municipal Review*, suppl., Vol. XXI, pp. 525-542 (August, 1932); M. H. Satterfield, "Counties in a Straitjacket," *ibid.*, Vol. XXXVII, pp. 81-85, 124 (February, 1948).

tion it is improbable that the number of counties will be substantially reduced through consolidation in the foreseeable future. On the other hand, consolidation of school districts is already far advanced in a number of states and is likely to be given further impetus by additional laws making consolidation of small schools compulsory or providing for the administration of state aid in a manner to encourage mergers. Though consolidation of county and city governments has as yet been effected in relatively few instances, it is quite possible that the future may see its adoption in some other urban communities. If this occurs, care should be taken to provide neighboring rural areas with adequate safeguards against tax inequities. Deorganization of individual counties, towns, and townships is not likely to proceed rapidly; but, where the necessary enabling legislation exists, some units in sparsely settled areas will doubtless deorganize their governments to lessen their tax burden. Voluntary deorganization seems to offer greatest possibilities in states, such as Maine and South Dakota, which have traditionally had some unorganized territory.[71] Statewide abolition of townships is fraught with practical difficulties. Nevertheless, elimination of township government has been accomplished in Oklahoma, and virtually so in Iowa, and it is not improbable that similar developments eventually will come in other states. Though many special-purpose districts should be abolished and their functions transferred to appropriate general government units, dissolutions of special districts during recent years have been more than offset by the creation of new units of the same category.

Gradual transfer of specific functions from smaller to larger units seems certain to continue, and progressively more use will be made of functional consolidation, particularly of the contract variety. Functional consolidation is in a sense an alternative to geographic merger, offering the advantages of the larger unit in the provision of certain services in instances where complete consolidation is for various reasons impracticable. Though the district form of functional consolidation is advantageous in some instances and tends to be more durable than the intergovernmental contract,[72] it is subject to the objection that it further increases the number of local units. The contractual form, on the other hand, obviates this disadvantage and provides a flexible and practicable means of co-operation between any number of local units of the same or different types.

In summary, it would seem that the following deserve consideration in any program for readjustment of local government areas in rural America:

1. Geographic consolidation of units within a particular class, such as counties or school districts.
2. Elimination of the midwestern township as a governmental area, with transfer of its functions to the county.

[71] Cf. Carpenter, *Problems in Service Levels*, p. 123.
[72] Cf. Bollens, *Special District Governments in the United States*, p. 8.

3. Deorganization of individual counties, towns, or townships, with transfer of their functions to neighboring or overlying governments.
4. Elimination of some nonschool special districts, with the powers now exercised by such districts being conferred instead upon appropriate general government units.
5. Transfer of individual functions from smaller to larger units without disturbing existing political boundaries.
6. Co-operative performance of selected functions by pairs or groups of governmental units under various forms of functional consolidation.

Some of these devices, such as school-district consolidation and the co-operative performance of functions, have already been employed successfully on a wide scale; others, though less used as yet, offer substantial potentialities for the future. Any practicable plan for reorganizing local areas should have among its primary objectives a reduction in both the total number of governmental units and the number of layers of government under which the individual citizen lives.[73] We must abandon the idea that the degree of popular control over local government is directly proportional to the number of local units. Quite to the contrary, a simplification of local government, including the elimination of overlapping areas as far as reasonably possible, should actually foster democratic control and stimulate vigorous participation in local affairs.

REFERENCES

Books, Reports, and Special Studies

Adjustment of the Boundaries of Virginia Municipalities and Adjacent Counties, Report of the Commission to Study Urban Growth to the Governor and the General Assembly of Virginia (Richmond, Va., Division of Purchases and Printing, 1951).

Allred, C. E., and Luebke, B. H., *Areal and Functional Consolidation of Tennessee Counties* (Knoxville, University of Tennessee, 1943).

Anderson, William, *The Reorganization of Local Government in Minnesota* (Minneapolis, League of Minnesota Municipalities, 1933).

California Commission on School Districts, *A Report on School District Reorganization in California: 1946-1948* (Sacramento, Cal., 1949).

Carpenter, William S., *Problems in Service Levels: The Readjustment of Services and Areas in Local Government* (Princeton, N. J., Princeton University Press, 1940).

Cook, Katherine M., ed., *Reorganization of School Units* (Washington, U. S. Office of Education, 1936).

County Consolidation (Frankfort, Kentucky Legislative Council, 1937), published in co-operation with the Governor's Cabinet.

Covert, Timon, *Rural School Consolidation* (Washington, U. S. Office of Education, 1930).

[73] An interesting suggestion of "a rationalized scheme of local government units for the United States" may be found in William Anderson, *The Units of Government in the United States,* new ed. (Chicago, Public Administration Service, 1942), pp. 44-47.

DOVELL, J. E., *City-county Consolidation: Its Possibilities in Florida* (Gainsville, University of Florida Public Administration Clearing Service, 1956).

EULER, Harrison L., *County Unification in Kansas* (New York, Teachers College Bureau of Publications, 1935).

FESLER, James W., *Area and Administration* (University, University of Alabama Press, 1949).

FORD, Robert S., and THARP, Claude R., *Reorganization of Michigan's County Government* (Ann Arbor, University of Michigan Bureau of Government, 1946).

HECKART, Scoville R., and KLEMMEDSON, G. S., *County Consolidation in Colorado* (Fort Collins, Colorado Agricultural College, Colorado Experiment Station, 1933).

JAY, C. A., *County Reorganization in Texas* (Dallas, Southern Methodist University, Arnold Foundation, 1934).

Kansas Legislative Council, *Reorganization of School Districts in Kansas: 1945-46* (Topeka, Kan., 1946).

———, *School District Reorganization; Kansas Experience: 1945-1947* (Topeka, Kan., 1947).

Kentucky Legislative Research Commission, *School District Mergers* (Frankfort, Ky., 1954).

KETCHAM, Ronald M., *Intergovernmental Coöperation in the Los Angeles Area* (Los Angeles, University of California Bureau of Governmental Research, 1940).

MAUCK, Elwyn A., *Improving the Government of Wicomico County [Maryland]* (College Park, University of Maryland Bureau of Public Administration, 1948).

MENEFEE, Selden C., *A Plan for Regional Administrative Districts in the State of Washington* (Seattle, University of Washington, 1935).

Minnesota Legislative Research Committee, *School District Reorganization in Minnesota* (St. Paul, Minn., 1952).

National Commission on School District Reorganization, *Your School District* (Washington, National Education Association, 1948).

Nebraska Legislative Council, *Report of the Committee on Reorganization of County Government* (Lincoln, Neb., 1950).

———, *Report of Committee on the Reorganization of School Districts* (Lincoln, Neb., 1954).

Nevada Legislative Counsel Bureau, *County Consolidation and Reorganization in Nevada* (Carson City, Nev., 1948).

Ohio Governor's Commission on County Government, *The Reorganization of County Government in Ohio,* Report to the Governor (Columbus, Ohio, 1934).

REEVES, J. E., and BACH, Hager W., *County Reorganization and the State Constitution* (Lexington, University of Kentucky Bureau of Government Research, 1951).

Reorganization of Local Government in New York State, Sixth Report of the New York State Commission for the Revision of the Tax Laws (Albany, N. Y., 1935).

SCHMIDT, Edward B., *County Consolidation: Relation of Size of Counties to the Cost of County Government in Nebraska* (Lincoln, University of Nebraska, 1934).

SORRELL, Vernon G., and STUART, J. Raymond, *County Consolidation in New Mexico* (Albuquerque, University of New Mexico, 1934).

TOMPKINS, Dorothy C., *Reorganization of School Districts* (Berkeley, University of California Bureau of Public Administration, 1951).

Vermont State Planning Board, *Report on Survey of Unorganized Towns and Gores* (Montpelier, Vt., 1943).

Articles

ASKEW, J. Thomas, "Will Counties Merge?" *National Municipal Review,* Vol. XXIII, pp. 520-522 (October, 1934).

ATKINS, Richard A., "The First Hundred Years [of Consolidation in Boston and Suffolk County]," *National Municipal Review,* Vol. XXX, pp. 90-95 (February, 1941).

ATKINSON, R. C., "County Reorganization in Ohio," *American Political Science Review,* Vol. XXX, pp. 104-110 (February, 1936).

BEEM, Harlan, "School District Reorganization in Illinois," *State Government,* Vol. XXIV, pp. 178-181, 198 (July, 1951).

BENTON, E. Maxwell, "Better Schooling, Less Cost," *National Municipal Review,* Vol. XXXVIII, pp. 494-497 (November, 1949).

BETTERS, Paul V., "North Carolina Centralizes," *National Municipal Review,* Vol. XXI, pp. 493-498 (August, 1932).

BLAIS, Merlin, "County Consolidation: Is It Practical?" *Commonwealth Review,* Vol. XVII, pp. 181-191 (July–November, 1935).

BRADLEY, E. H., "An Appraisal of County Consolidation in Georgia," *National Municipal Review,* Vol. XXVI, pp. 366-367 (July, 1937).

BRADSHAW, H. C., "Reorganization of Counties," *Journal of Farm Economics,* Vol. XIX, pp. 741-749 (August, 1937).

BRADSHAW, William L., "The County Consolidation Movement," *Southwestern Social Science Quarterly,* Vol. XII, pp. 321-327 (March, 1932).

BROMAGE, Arthur W., "Shall We Save the Township?" *National Municipal Review,* Vol. XXV, pp. 585-588 (October, 1936).

BROWN, Roy E., and ROACH, Lester T. "Consolidation of Counties in North Dakota," *Quarterly Journal of the University of North Dakota,* Vol. XXIII, pp. 202-210 (1932-1933).

BRYAN, Gordon K., "County Reorganization in Mississippi," *The County Officer,* Vol. XVIII, pp. 106-109, 130 (May, 1953).

CARPENTER, William S., "Deorganization in Maine," *American Political Science Review,* Vol. XXXII, pp. 1139-1142 (December, 1938).

CHISHOLM, Leslie L., "School District Reorganization Today," *State Government,* Vol. XXV, pp. 197-199, 216 (September, 1952).

———, "School District Reorganization Today," *State Government,* Vol. XXIX, pp. 86-88, 97 (May, 1956).

CHUBB, L. R., "County Government Progress in New York State," *American Political Science Review,* Vol. XXX, pp. 90-96 (February, 1936).

———, "The Financial Aspects of City-county Consolidation," *National Municipal Review,* Vol. XXVIII, pp. 101-104 (February, 1939).

COMBS, William H., "City-county Separation and Consolidation in Tennessee," *Tennessee Law Review,* Vol. XVI, pp. 217-228 (February, 1940).

COTTRELL, Edwin A., "Local Government Progress in California," *American Political Science Review,* Vol. XXVIII, pp. 1084-1087 (December, 1934).

DAVIS, Eugene, "Reorganization of Iowa School Districts," *Iowa Law Review,* Vol. XXXIX, pp. 570-607 (Summer, 1954).

DOVELL, J. E., "County Reorganization and the Florida Constitution," *The County Officer,* Vol. XVIII, pp. 204-208 (September, 1953).

DURHAM, G. Homer, "Consolidation in Utah Local Government," *The County Officer,* Vol. XVIII, pp. 243-245, 256 (October, 1953).

ENGELBERT, Ernest, "A Decade of County Government Reorganization in North Dakota, *American Political Science Review,* Vol. XXXVI, pp. 508-515 (June, 1942).

FAIRLIE, John A., "Reorganization in Counties and Townships," *Annals of the American Academy of Political and Social Science,* Vol. CXIII, pp. 187-194 (May, 1924).

GREENE, Lee S., "The Progress of County Government Reform in Wisconsin," *American Political Science Review,* Vol. XXX, pp. 96-102 (February, 1936).

GRUENBERG, Frederick P., "Philadelphia's City-county Dilemma," *National Municipal Review,* Vol. XXIX, pp. 385-387, 395 (June, 1940).

HAMMAR, Conrad H., "Functional Realignment vs. County Consolidation," *National Municipal Review,* Vol. XXI, pp. 515-518 (August, 1932).

HOLLAND, Lynwood M., "Reorganization of Government in DeKalb County, Georgia," *The County Officer,* Vol. XXI, pp. 223-224, 226-228 (October, 1956).

JAMISON, Judith Norvell, "Neighboring Areas Join Hands," *National Municipal Review,* Vol. XXXV, pp. 111-114 (March, 1946).

KEY, V. O., Jr., and GETTYS, Luella, "The County Reorganization Movement," *Social Studies,* Vol. XXVII, pp. 382-386 (October, 1936).

LACY, Arthur J., "Townships Must Go," *National Real Estate Journal,* Vol. XXXII, No. 3, pp. 13-14 (February 2, 1931).

McCOMBS, Carl E., "Reorganizing of Local Government in New York State," *National Municipal Review,* Vol. XXII, pp. 129-132 (March, 1933).

McINTYRE, Kenneth E., "School Redistricting in the Forty-eight States," *American School Board Journal,* Vol. CXX, No. 4, pp. 25-27 (April, 1950).

———, "Progress in School District Reorganization," *American School Board Journal,* Vol. CXXIV, No. 5, pp. 47-49, 80 (May, 1952).

———, "The Progress and Problems of Redistricting," *American School Board Journal,* Vol. CXXVIII, No. 3, pp. 38-40 (March, 1954).

MANNING, J. W., "County Consolidation in Tennessee," *American Political Science Review,* Vol. XXII, pp. 733-735 (August, 1928).

———, "County Consolidation in Tennessee," *National Municipal Review,* Vol. XVII, pp. 511-514 (September, 1928).

———, "County Consolidation as a Means of Tax Reduction," *South Atlantic Quarterly,* Vol. XXXI, pp. 150-155 (April, 1932).

———, "The Progress of County Consolidation," *National Municipal Review,* Vol. XXI, pp. 510-514 (August, 1932).

———, "County Consolidation: Is It Desirable?" *National County Magazine,* Vol. I, No. 2, pp. 7-8, 25 (May, 1935).

MELTON, L. D., "The Elimination of Township Government in Oklahoma," *National Municipal Review,* Vol. XXVII, pp. 405-407 (August, 1938).

NEUBERGER, Richard L., "Economy Begins at Home," *National Municipal Review,* Vol. XLI, pp. 501-503, 530 (November, 1952).

PATE, James E., "Virginia's Experience with New Forms of County Government," *National Municipal Review,* Vol. XXIV, pp. 265-266 (May, 1935).

PINCHBECK, Raymond B., "City-county Separation in Virginia," *National Municipal Review,* Vol. XXIX, pp. 467-472 (July, 1940).

PUTNEY, Bryant, "Reorganization of County Government," *Editorial Research Reports,* Vol. I, pp. 129-148 (February 24, 1939).

REED, Thomas H., "City-county Consolidation," *National Municipal Review*, Vol. XXIII, pp. 523-525 (October, 1934).

———, "County Government Reorganization," *Legal Notes on Local Government*, Vol. 1, No. 2, pp. 1-5 (May, 1936).

RENNE, Roland R., "County Office Consolidations in Montana," *National Municipal Review*, Vol. XXVIII, pp. 143-148 (February, 1939).

SCHMIDT, Edward B., "County Consolidation: Would It Pay?" *National County Magazine*, Vol. I, No. 4, pp. 10-12 (July, 1935).

SCOVILLE, H. F., "Thrift via County Consolidation," *National Municipal Review*, Vol. XXVIII, pp. 708-711 (October, 1939).

SCOVILLE, O. J., "Liquidating Town Government in Decadent Rural Areas of Maine," *Journal of Land and Public Utilities Economics*, Vol. XIII, pp. 285-291 (August, 1937).

SHANNON, J. B., "County Consolidation," *Annals of the American Academy of Political and Social Science*, Vol. CCVII, pp. 168-175 (January, 1940).

SMITH, Alfred F., "San Francisco: A Pioneer in the Consolidation Movement," *National Municipal Review*, Vol. XXX, pp. 152-156 (March, 1941).

SNIDER, Clyde F., "The Twilight of the Township," *National Municipal Review*, Vol. XLI, pp. 390-396 (September, 1952).

SPARLIN, Estal E., "Missouri Counties Streamlined," *National Municipal Review*, Vol. XXXV, pp. 337-343 (July, 1946).

SPENCER, Richard C., "Iowa Townships Still Here?" *National Municipal Review*, Vol. XLI, pp. 397-399 (September, 1952).

SPICER, George W., "Virginia's Progress in County Government," *American Political Science Review*, Vol. XXVIII, pp. 1074-1078 (December, 1934).

STEWART, Frank M., "City-county Contractual Relationships," *Public Management*, Vol. XIX, pp. 14-17 (January, 1937).

———, and KETCHAM, Ronald M., "Intergovernmental Contracts in California," *Public Administration Review*, Vol. I, pp. 242-248 (Spring, 1941).

TUCKER, Robert H., "Progress in Virginia County Government," *The Commonwealth*, publication of the Virginia State Chamber of Commerce, Vol. XVI, pp. 7-9, 26-27 (January, 1949).

UHL, Raymond, "Functional Consolidation in the Counties of Virginia," *National Municipal Review*, Vol. XXV, pp. 601-603 (October, 1936).

WAGER, Paul W., "State Operation Saves Money in North Carolina," *American Political Science Review*, Vol. XXVIII, pp. 1078-1081 (December, 1934).

———, "Effects of North Carolina's Centralization," *National Municipal Review*, Vol. XXVI, pp. 572-577 (December, 1937).

———, "County Consolidation by Indirection," *National Municipal Review*, Vol. XXVIII, pp. 96-100 (February, 1939).

WEIL, Elmer R., "What about County Compacts?" *The County Officer*, Vol. XX, pp. 131-132 (June, 1955).

WERNIMONT, Kenneth, "County Disorganization for North Dakota," *National Municipal Review*, Vol. XXVIII, pp. 769-772 (November, 1939).

WHITE, Max R., "Town and City Consolidation in Connecticut," *American Political Science Review*, Vol. XXXVI, pp. 492-502 (June, 1942).

WHITWELL, Charles G., "The New Parish-city Government of Baton Rouge," *Southwestern Social Science Quarterly*, Vol. XXIX, pp. 227-231 (December, 1948).

"Your Old-fashioned County Government," *Changing Times: The Kiplinger Magazine*, Vol. III, No. 10, pp. 40-41 (October, 1949).

General Bibliography

BIBLIOGRAPHICAL AIDS

BADEN, Anne L., comp., *County Government and Its Reorganization in the United States: A Bibliographical List of Recent Writings* (Washington, Library of Congress, Division of Bibliography, 1934).

Bibliographic Index: A Bibliography of Bibliographies (New York, Wilson, 1937–).

Boston University Bureau of Public Administration, *Bibliography on State and Local Government in New England* (Boston, Mass., 1952).

BOUNDS, Roger J., comp., *A Bibliography on the Reorganization and Consolidation of Local Government* (Washington, U. S. Chamber of Commerce, 1932).

BURCHFIELD, Laverne, *Our Rural Communities: A Guidebook to Published Materials on Rural Problems* (Chicago, Public Administration Service, 1947).

CLEMENT, Ina, "A Bibliography on County Government: A Selected List of the Leading Articles and Publications Relating to County Government Which Have Appeared since 1920," *National Municipal Review,* Vol. XXI, pp. 521-524 (August, 1932).

CONOVER, Helen F., comp., *County Government and Its Reorganization in the United States: A List of Recent References* (Washington, Library of Congress, Division of Bibliography, 1937).

FAIRLIE, John A., "Reports on State, Local, and Metropolitan Government," *American Political Science Review,* Vol. XXVII, pp. 317-329 (April, 1933).

———, and KNEIER, Charles M., *County Government and Administration* (New York, Century, 1930), bibliography pp. 533-559.

GREER, Sarah, *A Bibliography of Public Administration* (New York, Columbia University Institute of Public Administration, 1933), pp. 52-61.

HELLMAN, Florence S., comp., *A List of Recent References on County Government in the United States* (Washington, Library of Congress, Division of Bibliography, 1940).

HODGSON, James G., *The Official Publications of American Counties: A Union List with an Introduction on the Collecting of County Publications* (Fort Collins, Colo., 1937).

KEHL, M. Margaret, comp., *County Government: An Annotated List of References, June 1, 1915, to December 31, 1931.* Reprinted from *Municipal Reference Library Notes* (New York, New York Public Library, 1932).

POWELL, F. W., "Bibliography of the Office of Coroner," *National Municipal Review*, Vol. IV, pp. 531-537 (July, 1915).

Public Affairs Information Service Bulletin (New York, Public Affairs Information Service, 1915–), a current bibliography of selected material in English relating to economics and public affairs.

SAWYER, Rollin A., Jr., comp., *A List of Works on County Government Including County Publications: References to Material in the New York Public Library*. Reprinted from *Bulletin of the New York Public Library* (New York, 1915).

"Selected Bibliography on County Government," *National Municipal Review*, Vol. XXVIII, pp. 180-182 (February, 1939).

STATE CONSTITUTIONS

An excellent and well-indexed compilation of the constitutions of the 48 states, as of the date of publication, is New York State Constitutional Convention Committee, *Constitutions of the States and United States*, Report of the Committee (Albany, 1938), Vol. III. Recent editions of the constitutions, including amendments, are printed in the revised or compiled statutes of the respective states and usually may be obtained also in pamphlet form from the secretaries of state.

STATE STATUTES

The statutes of the respective states are generally available in two forms:

(1) *Session Laws*. Published under varying titles after each regular session of the legislature, the session laws comprise all laws enacted in the particular session concerned. Laws enacted at special sessions are sometimes published separately, and in other instances they are included in the regular-session volumes. The session laws are official state publications.

(2) *Revised Statutes, Compiled Statutes,* or *Codes*. Published at various intervals in the different states, in some instances officially and in others by commercial publishers, these volumes are designed to set forth, under topical arrangement, all laws of general application in effect as of the date of publication. In this form, the statutes frequently are supplemented in at least some measure by annotations referring to pertinent court cases. When annotations are extensive the publication may be entitled *Annotated Statutes*.

STATE JUDICIAL DECISIONS

Decisions and opinions of the highest state court are published in most states in official court *Reports* and are available for all states in the *National Reporter System*, issued by the West Publishing Company. Where there is an appellate court between the supreme court and the courts of general trial jurisdiction, appellate court decisions and opinions are usually published in the same manner as those of the highest tribunal.

LOCAL GOVERNMENT PUBLICATIONS

Official publications of counties, townships, and special districts are generally meager, especially with regard to the units serving rural areas. Copies of county home-rule *charters*, in pamphlet form, may ordinarily be secured from the clerks of the counties concerned. The governing bodies of some counties, scattered among several states, publish their official *proceedings* in book or pamphlet form. Many New England towns publish annual *reports* of their activities and finances; and elsewhere occasional counties, townships, and special districts issue such reports. All told, however, only a small proportion of the local units publish official reports other than the bare itemizations of receipts and disbursements commonly inserted in local newspapers in compliance with statutory requirement. In those instances where more comprehensive reports are issued, annually or otherwise, copies may ordinarily be obtained from the clerk of the unit concerned or from whatever officer serves as clerk to the governing body. In the case of counties and towns having manager government, available reports may usually be secured from the manager's office.

BOOKS, REPORTS, AND SPECIAL STUDIES

ALDERFER, Harold F., *American Local Government and Administration* (New York, Macmillan, 1956).

———, and others, *Report of the Pennsylvania Local Government Survey,* Transactions of the American Philosophical Society, N. S. (Philadelphia, 1935), Vol. XXV.

ALLEN, H. K., *Costs and Services of Local Government in Selected Illinois Counties* (Urbana, University of Illinois Bureau of Business Research, 1936).

ANDERSON, William, *Local Government and Finance in Minnesota* (Minneapolis, University of Minnesota Press, 1935).

———, and LEHMAN, Bryce E., *An Outline of County Government in Minnesota with Special Reference to Hennepin, Ramsey, and St. Louis Counties* (Minneapolis, University of Minnesota Press, 1927).

ANDREWS, Columbus, *Administrative County Government in South Carolina* (Chapel Hill, University of North Carolina Press, 1933).

Arlington County, Va., *Handbook on County Government Organization,* 2d ed. (Arlington, Office of the County Manager, 1954).

BAKER, Ruth E., *This Is Cook County* (Chicago, Cook County Council, League of Women Voters, 1951).

BEMIS, George W., and BASCHÉ, Nancy, *Los Angeles County as an Agency of Municipal Government* (Los Angeles, Haynes Foundation, 1946).

Blue Earth County Council on Intergovernmental Relations, *Democracy Trains Its Microscope on Government in Blue Earth County, Minnesota* (Mankato, Minn., 1945).

BOLLENS, John C., LANGDELL, Patricia W., and BINKLEY, Robert W., Jr., *County Government Organization in California,* rev. ed. (Berkeley, University of California Bureau of Public Administration, 1947).

———, and SCOTT, Stanley, *Local Government in California* (Berkeley, University of California Press, 1951).

BOSWORTH, Karl A., *Black Belt County: Rural Government in the Cotton Country of Alabama* (University, University of Alabama Bureau of Public Administration, 1941).

———, *Tennessee Valley County: Rural Government in the Hill Country of Alabama* (University, University of Alabama Bureau of Public Administration, 1941).

BOWEN, Don L., and FRIEDMAN, Robert S., *Local Government in Maryland* (College Park, University of Maryland Bureau of Governmental Research, 1955).

BRADSHAW, William L., *County Government Manual for the Missouri Constitutional Convention of 1943* (Columbia, Statewide Committee for the Revision of the Missouri Constitution, 1943).

BRANNON, Victor D., *State Auditor and Fiscal Control in Missouri Counties* (Columbia, University of Missouri, 1939).

BROMAGE, Arthur W., *American County Government* (New York, Sears Publishing Co., 1933).

———, and REED, Thomas H., *Organization and Cost of County and Township Government* (Detroit, Michigan Commission of Inquiry into County, Township and School District Government, 1933).

California Commission on County Home Rule, *County Government in California,* Final Report of the Commission (Sacramento, 1931).

CAMPBELL, Ernest H., and LEGG, Herbert H., Jr., *County Government in the State of Washington: Effect of Adoption of Proposed County Home Rule Constitutional Amendment* (Seattle, University of Washington Bureau of Governmental Research and Services, 1948).

CAPE, William H., and FELT, Franklin O., *Handbook for South Dakota County Officials* (Vermillion, University of South Dakota Governmental Research Bureau, 1954).

CARLETON, R. L., *Local Government and Administration in Louisiana* (Baton Rouge, Louisiana State University Press, 1935).

CARTER, Edward Weamer, *Mandatory Expenditures of Local Governments in Pennsylvania* (Privately printed, 1934).

CATHERWOOD, M. P., *Rural Government in New York* (Ithaca, New York State College of Agriculture, 1935), rev. ed. (1936).

CLAUNCH, John M., *The Government of Dallas County, Texas* (Dallas, Southern Methodist University Press, 1954).

COLE, William E., and CROWE, Hugh P., *Recent Trends in Rural Planning* (New York, Prentice-Hall, 1937).

COLLIER, James M., *County Government in New Jersey* (New Brunswick, N. J., Rutgers University Press, 1952).

Colquitt County Council on Intergovernmental Relations, *Colquitt County, Georgia: A Field Laboratory for Study and Experiment in Intergovernmental Relations* (Moultrie, Ga., 1947).

County Government, Annals of the American Academy of Political and Social Science (Philadelphia, 1913), Vol. XLVII, a symposium.

County Government in Virginia: A Symposium (University, Va., Bureau of Public Administration, Division of Publications, 1942).

County Government in Wisconsin (Madison, Wisconsin Historical Records Survey, 1942), 3 vols., mimeo.

CROUCH, Winston W., MCHENRY, Dean E., BOLLENS, John C., and SCOTT, Stanley, *State and Local Government in California* (Berkeley, University California Press, 1952).

DOVELL, J. E., *Florida's County Government* (Gainesville, University of Florida Public Administration Clearing Service, 1952).

DUNCAN, John Paul, *County Government: An Analysis* (Oklahoma City, Oklahoma State Legislative Council, 1948).

———, *County Government: Constitutional Data* (Oklahoma City, Oklahoma State Legislative Council, 1948).

———, *County Government: Forms* (Oklahoma City, Oklahoma State Legislative Council, 1948).

Everstine, Carl N., *Local Government: A Comparative Study* (Baltimore, Maryland Legislative Council, 1944).

Faeth, Henry J., *The Connecticut County: A Description of Its Organization, Function and Relationship with Other Governmental Units,* rev. Patricia Stuart (Storrs, University of Connecticut Institute of Public Service, 1954).

Fairlie, John A., *Local Government in Counties, Towns, and Villages* (New York, Century, 1906).

———, *Town and County Government in Illinois,* Report of the Joint Legislative Committee, 47th General Assembly of Illinois (Springfield, Ill., 1913), Vol. II.

———, and Kneier, Charles M., *County Government and Administration* (New York, Century, 1930).

Gilbertson, H. S., *The County: The "Dark Continent" of American Politics* (New York, National Short Ballot Organization, 1917).

———, *The System of County Government in Kentucky* (Evanston, Ill., privately printed, 1924).

The Government of Nassau County [New York], A Report Made to the Board of Supervisors by the Municipal Consultant Service of the National Municipal League (Mineola, N. Y., 1934).

Governor's Advisory Commission, *County Government and Taxation in Delaware,* Report to the Governor (Dover, Del., 1932).

Gray, Walter S., comp., *County Government in Essex, N. J.,* (Newark, N. J., Essex County Board of Chosen Freeholders, 1953).

Griffenhagen and Associates, *Proposals for the Reorganization of Local Government in Illinois,* Report to the Illinois Commission on Taxation and Expenditures (Chicago, 1932).

Henry County Council on Intergovernmental Relations, *Adventure in Governmental Gearing: A Progress Report of the Henry County [Indiana] Demonstration* (New Castle, Ind., 1946).

Hughes, Melvin Clyde, *County Government in Georgia* (Athens, University of Georgia Press, 1944).

Hunter, M. H., *Costs of Township and County Government in Illinois* (Urbana, University of Illinois Bureau of Business Research, 1933).

Hurd, T. N., *Local Government in Tompkins County, New York* (Ithaca, N. Y., Cornell University Agricultural Experiment Station, 1936).

Illinois Tax Commission, *Receipts and Disbursements of Townships and Road Districts, 1925-1936,* Survey of Local Finance in Illinois (Springfield and Chicago, 1939), Vol. IV; published in co-operation with the Work Projects Administration.

Institute for Government Research of the Brookings Institution, *County Government in Alabama,* Report on a Survey Submitted to Governor B. M. Miller (Washington, 1932), Vol. V, Pt. 4.

———, *The Government of Montgomery County, Maryland* (Washington, 1941).

———, *Report on a Survey of the Organization and Administration of County Government in North Carolina* (Washington, 1930).

———, *Report on a Survey of the Organization and Administration of State and County Government in Mississippi* (Jackson, Mississippi Research Commission, 1932).

———, *Report on a Survey of the Organization and Administration of the State, County, and Town Governments of New Hampshire* (Washington, 1932).

Institute for Government Research of the Brookings Institution, *Report on a Survey of Organization and Administration of Oklahoma* (Oklahoma City, Okla., Harlow Publishing Corp., 1935), esp. chaps. 3, 5, 6, 9, 14, 17, 21.

JAMES, Herman G., *Local Government in the United States* (New York, Appleton, 1921).

———, *County Government in Texas,* rev. Irvin Stewart (Austin, University of Texas, 1925).

KERWIN, Jerome G., "The American Pattern of Local Government," in Carleton B. Joeckel, ed., *Library Extension: Problems and Solutions* (Chicago, University of Chicago Press, 1946), pp. 25-31.

KILPATRICK, Wylie, *County Management: A Review of Developing Plans of County Administration in Virginia and North Carolina* (University, Va., *ca.* 1929).

———, *Problems in Contemporary County Government: An Examination of the Process of County Administration in Virginia* (University, University of Virginia Institute for Research in the Social Sciences, 1930).

KLEMMEDSON, G. S., *The Cost of Local Government in Larimer County, Colorado,* (Fort Collins, Colorado Agricultural College, Colorado Experiment Station, 1930).

LANCASTER, Lane W., *Government in Rural America,* 2d ed. (New York, Van Nostrand, 1952).

LANGLEY, James M., *The End of an Era: County Government Has Become Obsolete in New Hampshire* (Concord, N. H., Concord Monitor, 1947).

Local Government and the War (Washington, War Production Board, 1942).

Los Angeles County Board of Supervisors, *Los Angeles County: A Handbook of Its Government and Services* (Los Angeles, Cal., 1950); published in co-operation with the Office of the County Superintendent of Schools.

Los Angeles County Bureau of Efficiency, *Growth of County Functions, Los Angeles County, California: 1852 to 1934* (Los Angeles, Cal., 1936).

MANNING, John W., *Government in Kentucky Counties* (Lexington, University of Kentucky Bureau of Government Research, 1937).

MANNY, T. B., *Attitudes toward Rural Government* (Washington, U. S. Department of Agriculture, 1929).

———, *Rural Municipalities: A Sociological Study of Local Government in the United States* (New York, Century, 1930).

MAXEY, Chester C., *County Administration: A Study Based upon a Survey of County Government in the State of Delaware* (New York, Macmillan, 1919).

Mississippi Economic Council, *Is This Your County? A Study of Mississippi County Government with Recommendations* (Jackson, Miss., 1953).

MOORE, H. R., *Local Government in Two Rural Ohio Counties* (Wooster, Ohio Agricultural Experiment Station, 1938).

MURPHY, Wallace C., *County Government and Administration in Texas* (Austin, University of Texas, 1933).

National Municipal League, *Model County Charter* (New York, National Municipal League, 1956).

New York Bureau of Municipal Research, *County Government in Virginia,* Report on a Survey Made to the Governor and His Committee on Consolidation and Simplification (Richmond, Va., 1928).

Ohio Institute, *County Organization and Government in Ohio* (Columbus, Ohio, 1932).

Oneïda County Survey Committee, *A Study of the Government of Oneida County* [*New York*], Report to the Board of Supervisors (Utica, N. Y., 1951).

The Organization, Functions and Expenditures of Local Government in New Jersey, Commission to Investigate County and Municipal Taxation and Expenditures Report No. 1 (Trenton, N. J., 1931).

PARKS, Robert, "Trends in Rural Local Government," in Jasper B. Shannon, ed., *The Study of Comparative Government,* Essays Written in Honor of Frederic Austin Ogg (New York, Appleton-Century-Crofts, 1949), pp. 195-213.

PEPPER, Henry C., *County Government in Colorado* (Fort Collins, Colorado Agricultural College, Colorado Experiment Station, 1934).

PORTER, Kirk H., *County and Township Government in the United States* (New York, Macmillan, 1922).

Public Administration Service, *Montgomery County Survey: Report on Local Governmental Services in Dayton and Montgomery County, Ohio* (Chicago, 1940).

REED, Edward W., and ALEXANDER, Henry M., *The Government and Finance of Counties in Arkansas* (Fayetteville, University of Arkansas Bureau of Business and Economic Research, 1953).

RENNE, Roland R., *Montana County Organization, Services, and Costs* (Bozeman, Montana State College Agricultural Experiment Station, 1935).

ROHR, Charles J., BROWN, Alfred A., and HELMING, Vernon P., eds., *Local Government in Massachusetts* (Amherst, Massachusetts State College Bureau of Public Administration, 1941).

Santa Clara County Council on Intergovernmental Relations, *A Practical Basis for Developing Better Intergovernmental Relations: An Experiment Conducted in Santa Clara County* [*California*] (San Jose, Cal., 1947).

SHAMBAUGH, Benjamin F., ed., *County Government and Administration in Iowa* (Iowa City, Iowa State Historical Society, 1925).

SHAMBERGER, Harold J., *County Government and Administration in West Virginia* (Morgantown, West Virginia University Bureau for Government Research, 1952).

SHUMATE, Roger B., *Local Government in Nebraska* (Lincoln, Nebraska Legislative Council, 1939).

SIMS, Carlton C., *County Government in Tennessee* (Chicago, privately printed, 1932); distributed by the University of Chicago Libraries.

SMITH, Herbert C., *Rural Local Government in Ohio* (Columbus, Ohio, School and College Service, 1940).

SNIDER, Clyde F., *County Government in Illinois* (Springfield, Illinois Tax Commission, 1943).

———, and SAPPENFIELD, Max M., "County and Township Government in Indiana," in *Report of the Indiana State Committee on Governmental Economy* (Indianapolis, Ind., 1935), pp. 99-185.

Tennessee Valley Authority, *County Government and Administration in the Tennessee Valley States* (Washington, Government Printing Office, 1940).

Texas Legislative Council, *Local Government* (Austin, Tex., 1952), Pt. 1, *Setting and Primary Income Sources;* Pt. 2, *Revenues and Expenditures, State-local Relations.*

THARP, Claude R., *A Manual of County Administrative Organization in Michigan* (Ann Arbor, University of Michigan Press, 1944).

United States Bureau of the Census, *County and City Data Book: 1952* (Washington, Government Printing Office, 1933).

University of California (Los Angeles) Bureau of Governmental Research, *County Government in California* (Sacramento, County Supervisors Association of California, 1951).

University of Oklahoma Bureau of Government Research, *Duties and Powers of County Officers in Oklahoma* (Norman, Okla., 1952).

Virginia Commission on County Government, *Report of the Commission on County Government to the General Assembly of Virginia* (Richmond, Va., 1931).

———, *Report on Progress in County Government, County Consolidation and the Fee System in Virginia and Other States* (Richmond, Va., 1934).

———, *A Further Report on Progress in County Government and County Consolidation* (Richmond, Va., 1936).

———, *Report of the Virginia Commission on County Government to the Governor and the General Assembly* (Richmond, Va., 1940).

Virginia State Chamber of Commerce, *Opportunities for Economy in County Government in Virginia* (Richmond, Va., 1947).

WAGER, Paul W., *County Government and Administration in North Carolina* (Chapel Hill, University of North Carolina Press, 1928).

———, ed., *County Government across the Nation* (Chapel Hill, University of North Carolina Press, 1950).

Wayne County Board of Auditors, *Manual, County of Wayne, Michigan* (Detroit, Mich., 1930).

WELLS, Roger H., *American Local Government* (New York, McGraw-Hill, 1939).

ARTICLES

The *American Political Science Review,* from 1937 to 1949, carried annual articles summarizing developments in the field of county and township government. These articles appear variously in the October, December, and February issues.

ATKINSON, R. C., "Principles of a Model County Government," *National Municipal Review,* suppl., Vol. XXII, pp. 469-486 (September, 1933).

AUSTENSEN, Phillip J., and ZATMAN, J. B., "Montgomery County [Maryland] at the Crossroads," *The County Officer,* Vol. XIX, pp. 116-120 (May, 1954).

BLAIR, George S., "Some Current Comments on County Government in Pennsylvania," *The County Officer,* Vol. XIX, pp. 158-160 (August, 1954).

———, "A New Look at the 'Dark Continent' of American Politics," *The County Officer,* Vol. XIX, pp. 182-186, 194 (September, 1954).

BOZEMAN, C. Howard, "County Government in Tennessee as I See It," *The County Officer,* Vol. XVI, pp. 206-208 (August, 1951).

BRECKENRIDGE, A. C., "Nebraska County Government: 100 Years," *The County Officer,* Vol. XIX, pp. 80-88 (April, 1954).

BROMAGE, Arthur W., "County Government in Michigan," *Papers of the Michigan Academy of Science, Arts and Letters,* Vol. XVI, pp. 439-451 (1931).

———, "Investigating County and Township Government in Michigan," *American Political Science Review,* Vol. XXVII, pp. 80-84 (February, 1933).

———, "Recent Trends in Local Government in Michigan," *American Political Science Review,* Vol. XXX, pp. 102-104 (February, 1936).

———, "Bringing County and Township up to Date in Michigan," *National Municipal Review,* Vol. XXVIII, pp. 134-142 (February, 1939).

CATHERWOOD, M. P., "Some Problems of County Government," *Journal of Farm Economics,* Vol. XVIII, pp. 711-723 (November, 1936).

"County Government Structure in Mississippi," *Public Administration Survey,* publication of the University of Mississippi Bureau of Public Administration, Vol. II, No. 6 (July, 1955).

DALAND, Robert T., "A Bright Prospect for Alabama Counties?" *The County Officer,* Vol. XVIII, pp. 191-194 (July-August, 1953).

DONOVAN, Francis J., "A Rebirth of County Government," *The County Officer,* Vol. XVII, pp. 194-197, 209 (July, 1952).

———, "The Substance of County Government," *The County Officer,* Vol. XX, pp. 174-176 (September, 1955).

DOVELL, J. E., "Florida's County Government," *The County Officer,* Vol. XVIII, pp. 70-75, 80 (March, 1953).

"Ever-normal County [DeWitt County, Ill.]", *Fortune,* Vol. XXI, No. 6, pp. 83-89, 108, 110, 113 (June, 1940).

FAIRLIE, John A., "County and Town Government in Illinois," *Annals of the American Academy of Political and Social Science,* Vol. XLVII, pp. 62-78 (May, 1913).

FERGUSON, Homer, "Effective County Administration," *The County Officer,* Vol. XVII, pp. 241-245 (August, 1952).

FRIEDLAND, L. L., "The County as a Unit of Government," *The County Officer,* Vol. XXI, pp. 95-96 (May, 1956).

GOSNELL, Cullen B., "DeKalb County [Georgia] Reorganizes," *National Municipal Review,* Vol. XLV, pp. 349-350 (July, 1956).

HEIN, C. J., "Kansas Counties Basic Administrative Areas for Many Governmental Services," *The County Officer,* Vol. XX, pp. 214-216 (October, 1955).

JOHNSON, A. Rex, "Planning for New County Horizons," *The County Officer,* Vol. XX, pp. 6-10 (January, 1955).

KNEIER, Charles M., "Development of Newer County Functions," *American Political Science Review,* Vol. XXIV, pp. 134-140 (February, 1930).

KYLE, Lyle C., "County Problems in Woodbury County, Iowa: A Case Study," *The County Officer,* Vol. XXI, pp. 67-69, 75-76 (April, 1956).

LOEB, Isidor, "County Government in Missouri," *Annals of the American Academy of Political and Social Science,* Vol. XLVII, pp. 48-61 (May, 1913).

MCBRIDE, Conrad L., "Local Self-government: A County Challenge," *The County Officer,* Vol. XX, pp. 122-124 (June, 1955).

MCMANUS, Jack, "Expanding Powers of Counties in Wisconsin," *Wisconsin Counties,* Vol. XVII, No. 10, pp. 5, 8, 14, 18 (April, 1955).

MANNING, J. W., "Governance in Tennessee Counties," *Southwestern Political and Social Science Quarterly,* Vol. XI, pp. 173-181 (September, 1930).

———, "The County in the United States," *Southwest Review,* Vol. XX, pp. 303-318 (Spring, 1935).

MANVEL, Allen D., "Post-war Trends in County Finances and Employment," *The County Officer,* Vol. XV, No. 1, pp. 15-16, 29 (April, 1950).

MARS, David, "The Government of the Connecticut County," *The County Officer,* Vol. XXI, pp. 121-122, 133-135 (June, 1956).

MITCHELL, Nicholas P., "Southern Counties: Diagnosis and Prognosis," *National Municipal Review,* Vol. XXVIII, pp. 534-539 (July, 1939).

The *National Municipal Review* carries a regular department entitled "County and Township," in which various current developments are reported. The issues of the journal for August, 1932, October, 1934, and February, 1939, are symposia on county government.

OVERMAN, Edward S., "New Forms of County Government in Virginia," *The County Officer,* Vol. XVII, pp. 357-359 (December, 1952).

PARKS, Wade R., "County Government in Montana," *National Municipal Review,* Vol. VIII, pp. 153-157 (March, 1919).

PATE, James E., "The Principle of Local Self-government in Virginia," *American Political Science, Review,* Vol. XXVII, pp. 84-90 (February, 1933).

———, "Virginia Counties Turn Cities," *National Municipal Review,* Vol. XLI, pp. 387-389 (September, 1952).

PINCHBECK, Raymond B., "The State Commission of Local Government," *National Municipal Review,* Vol. XXVIII, pp. 80-88, 155 (February, 1939).

Public Administration Service, "The Changing County," *National Municipal Review,* Vol. XLV, pp. 433-437 (October, 1956).

REED, Henry E., "County Government in Oregon—a Growing Problem," *National Municipal Review,* Vol. X, pp. 95-103 (February, 1921).

RENNE, Roland R., "Measuring the Efficiency of County Government [in Montana]," *National Municipal Review,* Vol. XXIV, pp. 162-169 (March, 1935).

———, "County Officials and Efficiency in Government [in Montana]," *National Municipal Review,* Vol. XXIV, pp. 444-447 (August, 1935).

ROSS, Russell M., "Twentieth Century Functions: The Ultimate Salvation of the County," *The County Officer,* Vol. XXI, pp. 64-65 (April, 1956).

SATTERFIELD, M. H., "The Growth of County Functions since 1930," *Journal of Politics,* Vol. III, pp. 76-88 (February, 1941).

———, "Trends in Rural Local Government in the South," *Journal of Politics,* Vol. X, pp. 510-535 (August, 1948).

SCROGGS, William O., "Parish Government in Louisiana," *Annals of the American Academy of Political and Social Science,* Vol. XLVII, pp. 39-47 (May, 1913).

SHULL, Frank L., "County Government: Its Function in Governmental Affairs," *Commonwealth Review,* Vol. XVIII, pp. 57-63 (March, 1936).

SMITH, Alfred E., "New York County Government Archaic," *National Municipal Review,* Vol. XV, pp. 399-402 (July, 1926).

SNIDER, Clyde F., "American County Government: A Mid-century Review," *American Political Science Review,* Vol. XLVI, pp. 66-80 (March, 1952).

SPARLING, Samuel E., "Responsibility in County Government," *Political Science Quarterly,* Vol. XVI, pp. 437-449 (September, 1901).

THOMAS, James D., "County Government in Alabama," *The County Officer,* Vol. XVII, pp. 114-115, 117 (April, 1952).

UPDYKE, Frank A., "County Government in New England," *Annals of the American Academy of Political and Social Science,* Vol. XLVII, pp. 26-38 (May, 1913).

WAGER, Paul W., "State Centralization in the South," *Annals of the American Academy of Political and Social Science,* Vol. CCVII, pp. 144-150 (January, 1940).

WALKER, Herman, Jr., and HANSEN, Peter L., "Local Government and Rainfall: The Problem of Local Government in the Northern Great Plains," *American Political Science Review,* Vol. XL, pp. 1113-1123 (December, 1946).

WEIDNER, Edward W., "The Confused County Picture," *National Municipal Review,* Vol. XXXV, pp. 166-171, 228-232, 239, 288-294 (April, May, June, 1946).

Index